The American People
Creating a Nation and a Society

Volume Two   Since 1865

General Editors
Gary B. Nash
University of California, Los Angeles

Julie Roy Jeffrey
Goucher College

John R. Howe
University of Minnesota

Allan M. Winkler
Miami University of Ohio

Peter J. Frederick
Heritage University

Charlene Mires
Villanova University

Allen F. Davis
Temple University

Carla Gardina Pestana
Miami University of Ohio

vango books Read it. Get it.

New York   San Francisco   Boston   Upper Saddle River
London   Toronto   Sydney   Tokyo   Singapore   Madrid
Mexico City   Munich   Paris   Cape Town   Hong Kong   Montreal

Library of Congress Cataloging-in-Publication Data

The American people: creating a nation and a society / Gary B. Nash . . . [et al.].
   p. cm.
Includes index.
ISBN 978-0-205-64279-3 (combined)—ISBN 978-0-205-64282-3 (v. 1)—ISBN 978-0-205-64283-0 (v. 2),
1. United States—History.   I. Nash, Gary B.
E178.1.A49355 2009
973—dc22   2008026904

Editor-in-Chief: Priscilla McGeehon
Executive Editor: Michael Boezi
Executive Marketing Manager: Sue Westmoreland
Editorial Assistant: Vanessa Gennarelli
Operations Supervisor: Mary Ann Gloriande
Operations Specialist: Maura Zaldivar
Director of Media and Assessment: Brian Hyland
VangoBooks Process Coordinator: Xiaohong Zhu
Cover Preparation: Ron Walko
AV Project Manager: Mirella Signoretto
Senior Managing Editor: Ann Marie McCarthy
Project Manager: Denise Brown
Full-Service Production and Composition: Eric Arima/Elm Street Publishing Services
Manager, Rights and Permissions: Zina Arabia
Manager, Visual Research: Beth Brenzel
Manager, Cover Visual Research and Permissions: Karen Sanatar
Image Permission Coordinator: Cynthia Vincenti
Printer/Binder: Webcrafters, Inc.
Cover Printer: Phoenix Color/Hagerstown

Credits and acknowledgments borrowed from other sources and reproduced, with permission, in this textbook appear on p. C-1.

Cover Photo: Stan Shoneman; Omni-Photo Communications, Inc. New York, Southampton. Large American flag being unfurled by group of people.

VangoBooks™ is an imprint of Pearson Education
Pearson® is a registered trademark of Pearson plc

Pearson Education Ltd., London
Pearson Education Singapore, Pte. Ltd
Pearson Education, Canada, Ltd
Pearson Education–Japan
Pearson Education Australia PTY, Limited

Pearson Education North Asia, Ltd
Pearson Educación de Mexico, S.A. de C.V.
Pearson Education Malaysia, Pte. Ltd
Pearson Education Upper Saddle River, New Jersey

10 9 8 7 6 5 4 3 2 1

ISBN 13: 978-0-205-64283-0
ISBN 10:   0-205-64283-7

CONTENTS

The Yoruba people of West Africa have an old saying: "However far the stream flows, it never forgets its source." Why, we wonder, do such ancient societies as the Yoruba find history so important, whereas today's American students question its relevance? This book aims to help students appreciate the usefulness of history.

History cannot make good citizens, but without history we cannot understand the choices before us and think wisely about them. Lacking a collective memory of the past, we are unaware of the human condition and the long struggles of men and women everywhere to deal with the problems of their day and to create a better society. Without historical knowledge, we deprive ourselves of knowing about the full range of approaches people have taken to political, economic, social, and cultural life; the efforts Americans have adopted to resolve human problems; and the measures they have taken to confront the obstacles in their way. With knowledge of how events beyond our national boundaries have affected our own history and how our actions have influenced other nations, we are better able to understand and deal with the challenges of contemporary globalism. In a twenty-first century marked by the increasing ethnic and racial diversity of American society, history is of central importance in preparing us to exercise our rights and responsibilities as free people in an increasingly interdependent global world.

History has a deeper, even more fundamental importance: the cultivation of the private person whose self-knowledge and self-respect provide the foundation for a life of dignity and fulfillment. Historical memory is the key to self-identity, to seeing one's place in the long stream of time, in the story of humankind.

When we study our own history, that of the American people, we see a rich and extremely complex human story that stretches back to the last ice age when nomadic hunters arrived in the Americas from Siberia. This country, whose written history began thousands of years later with a convergence of Native Americans, Europeans, and Africans, has always been a nation of diverse peoples—a magnificent mosaic of cultures, religions, and skin shades. This book explores how American society assumed its present shape and developed its present forms of government; how as a nation we have conducted our foreign affairs and managed our economy; how as individuals and in groups we have lived, worked, loved, married, raised families, voted, argued, protested, and struggled to fulfill our dreams and the noble ideals of the American experiment.

While this book covers significant public events such as presidential elections, wars and diplomatic treaties, and economic legislation, we have integrated this familiar national narrative with the smaller stories that describe and give meaning to our shared past. When, for example, national political events are discussed, we analyze their impact on social and economic life at the state and local levels. Wars are described not only as they unfolded on the battlefield and in the salons of diplomats but also on the home front, where they are history's greatest motor of social change. The interaction of ordinary Americans with extraordinary events runs as a theme throughout this book.

Above all, we have tried to show the "humanness" of our history as it is revealed in people's everyday lives. This textbook is marked by the words of ordinary Americans, the authentic human voices of those who participated in, responded to, and helped shape epic events such as war, slavery, industrialization, and reform movements.

Four Recurring Themes

Our primary goal is to provide students with a rich, balanced, and thought-provoking treatment of the American past. By this, we mean a history that treats the lives and experiences of Americans of all national origins and cultural backgrounds, at all class levels of society, and in all regions of the country. It also means a history that seeks connections among the many factors—political, economic, technological, social, religious, intellectual, and biological—that have molded and remolded American society over four centuries. And, finally, it means a history that encourages students to think about how they share an inherited and complex past filled with both notable achievements and thorny problems.

The only history befitting a democratic nation is one that inspires students to initiate a frank and informed dialogue with their past. Historians continually revise their understanding of what happened in the past. Historians reinterpret history because they find new evidence on old topics, add new voices, and are inspired by new sensibilities to ask questions about the past that did not interest earlier historians. Therefore, we hope to promote class discussions and inquiry organized around four recurring themes we see as basic to the American historical experience:

- The peopling of America: What diverse peoples have come together to form this nation? How have their experiences shaped our larger national history? What tensions did they face in America? What contributions have they made?
- Democratic dreams: How has our political system—and how have the principles that sustain it—developed over time? What changes and continuities have helped shape American values? How has the nation coped with the needs and demands of diverse groups in the quest for a better society?
- Economic, religious, and cultural change: In what ways have economic, technological, and environmental developments affected the American people? How have religious shifts affected the nation? How have reform movements shaped the character of American life?
- America and the world: How have global events and trends shaped the United States? How has America's relationship with other nations and people evolved? What impact has America had on the rest of the world?

In writing a history that revolves around these themes, we have tried to convey two dynamics that operate in all societies. First, as we observe people continuously adjusting to new developments, such as industrialization, urbanization, and internationalism, over which they seemingly have little control, we realize that people are not paralyzed by history but are the fundamental creators of it. People retain the ability, individually and collectively, to shape the world in which they live and thus in considerable degree to control their own lives.

Second, we emphasize the connections that always exist among social, political, economic, and cultural events. Just as our individual lives are never neatly parceled into separate spheres of activity, the life of a society is made up of a complicated and often messy mixture of forces, events, and accidental occurrences. In this text, political, economic, technological, and cultural factors are intertwined like strands in a rope as ordinary and extraordinary American people seek to fulfill their dreams.

Structure of the Book

The chapters of this book are grouped into six parts that relate to major periods in American history. The title of each part suggests a major theme that helps characterize how the American people changed over time: from a colonizing to revolutionary to expanding to industrializing people, and in the last hundred years a modernizing and, most recently, a "resilient" people, adapting to challenging new forces in the world.

The authors of this book are committed to writing a text that helps student learning. They have therefore adopted a structure to enhance students' comprehension of the material covered by each chapter. Each chapter begins with an *outline* that provides an overview of the chapter's organization. Next, a personal story, called "American Stories," recalls the experience of an ordinary or lesser-known American. The story puts a human face on history, suggesting that our past was shaped by ordinary as well as extraordinary people. Chapter 3, for example, is introduced with an account of the life of Anthony Johnson, who came to Virginia as a slave but who managed to gain his freedom along with his wife, Mary, and in the face of racial prejudice lost his hard-earned land. This brief anecdote introduces the overarching themes and major concepts of the chapter and its organizing structure.

Following the personal American story, a *brief chapter overview* links the story to the text. Each overview includes three recurring ways we seek to help students better understand, remember, and more permanently learn the significant history in the chapter; for example, in Chapter 3:

1. The overview connects Anthony and Mary Johnson's story to the *overarching themes and major concepts* of the chapter, in this case the multiracial peopling and character of American society, how enslaved Africans, Native Americans, and European immigrants interacted and coped with diversity and change, and the violent instability of late-seventeenth-century colonial economic, social, and political life.
2. These themes recall the *four recurring themes* from the Preface, in this case the multiethnic peopling of America, how diverse Americans responded to the stresses of daily life in an effort to achieve their dreams, and how the American people sought to turn their religious and political ideals into reality amidst conflicting pressures and forces.
3. Third, the overview lays out the *organizational structure* of the chapter, in this case the comparisons among six regional areas of early colonization and how each developed a different pattern of life in an effort to implement ideal goals.

We aim to facilitate the learning process for students in other ways as well. Every chapter ends with pedagogical features to reinforce and expand the narrative. A *Timeline* reviews the major events and developments covered in the chapter. A *Conclusion* briefly summarizes the main concepts and developments elaborated in the chapter, emphasizes the larger themes explored in that chapter, and serves as a bridge to the following chapter. *Questions for Review and Reflection* are intended to help students review and reflect on the major themes of the chapter and to connect them to the four major recurring themes and questions.

Features and Changes to This Edition

The new VangoBooks format is a departure from other editions of *The American People.* VangoBooks are innovative course materials designed to better meet the needs of today's students. VangoBooks are portable, present the need-to-know information, at about half the cost of a traditional textbook.

- **The prose has been streamlined to strengthen the narrative.** Though not as short as the Concise Edition of *The American People,* the text in this comprehensive version has been cut by 10 to 15%, eliminating detail which distracted from the main narrative.
- **To improve focus, graphs and maps that did not directly support the narrative have been dropped.** While the number of images has been pared down, the most important maps—with captions that encourage students to think about the significance of the material being presented—have all been retained.
- **The number of major themes explored in the book has been reduced,** so that each chapter can more effectively clarify and develop pertinent themes.
- **The distinctive and popular feature, "Recovering the Past," remains.** These RTPs, as the authors affectionately call them, introduce students to the fascinating variety of evidence—ranging from household inventories, folk tales, and diaries to tombstones, advertising, and popular music—that historians have learned to employ in reconstructing the past. Each RTP gives basic information about the source and its use by historians and then raises questions, under the heading "Reflecting on the Past," for students to consider as they study the example reproduced for their inspection.
- **A strong international context for American history also remains.** Believing that in today's global society it is particularly important for students to think across national boundaries and to understand the ways in which our history intersects

with the world, we have provided an international framework. Rather than developing a separate discussion of global events, we have woven an international narrative into our analysis of the American past. We have shown the ways in which the United States has been influenced by events in other parts of the world and the connection between the history of other nations and our own. We have also drawn attention to the aspects of our history that appear to set the nation apart. Tables, charts, and maps with a global focus provide an additional dimension for this international context.

In short, this Vango edition is aimed to make the study of history more meaningful for today's students. We hope students will also appreciate the more convenient size and shape of the Vango edition and its reasonable cost.

Acknowledgments

This Vango edition of *The American People* has benefited from the helpful comments of scholars as well as the experience of instructors and students who have used previous editions of the textbook. Their comments have informed the major changes implemented here. Those whose reviews helped in the preparation of this edition include: Elizabeth Alexander, Texas Wesleyan University; Neal A. Brooks, Community College of Baltimore County; Jean Choate, Coastal Georgia Community College; Dolores Davison, Foothill College; Anthony Heideman, Front Range Community College; Mary Hoogterp, Mesa College; Michael Howe, Morgan Community College; Don Knox, Vernon College; Michael Lawson, Northland Pioneer College; Marianne McKnight, Salt Lake Community College; Jim Piecuch, Kennesaw State University; Esther Robinson, Cy-Fair College; Scott Walker, Arizona State University; Michael White, Temple College.

Our aim has been to write a balanced and vivid history of the development of the American nation and its society. We also provide a variety of support materials to help make teaching and learning enjoyable and rewarding. The reader will be the judge of our success. We welcome your comments.

Gary B. Nash
Julie Roy Jeffrey

Instructor Supplements for Qualified College Adopters

All supplements specific to *The American People* will be offered online at Pearson's *Instructor Resource Center* (www.pearsonhighered.com/irc). As part of Pearson Education's commitment to helping you maximize your time at every stage of course preparation, we offer access to our Instructor Resource Center (IRC). Once you have registered for this instructor-only resource, you can log in to premium online products, browse and download book-specific instructor resources, and receive immediate access and instructions to installing course management content to your campus server, all from your book's Web page in our online catalog. If you already have access to CourseCompass or Supplements Central, you can log in to the IRC immediately using your existing login and password. Otherwise, visit the Instructor Resource Center welcome page at www.pearsonhighered.com/irc to register for access today.

VangoBooks.com VangoBooks.com/nash is an open-access Web site that offers educational tools and content specific to *The American People* to help your students more fully understand the course. Sample tests and quizzes with True/False, Multiple Choice, and Fill-in-the-Blank questions are correlated to chapters of the book. Students can even submit their answers for immediate online grading!

Instructor's Manual and Test Bank This guide is based on ideas generated in active learning workshops and is tied closely to the text. In addition to suggestions on how to generate lively class discussion and involve students in active learning, this supplement also offers lists of resources, including films, slides, photo collections, records, and audio. The *Test Bank* contains approximately 2,000 Multiple Choice, True/False, Short Answer, and Essay questions. All questions are keyed to specific pages in the text.

TestGen-EQ Computerized Testing System This flexible, easy-to-master computerized test bank includes all of the items in the printed test bank and allows instructors to select specific questions, edit existing questions, and add their own items to create exams. Tests can be printed in several different formats and can include figures, such as graphs and tables.

Text-specific Transparency Set A set of color transparency acetates showing maps from the text can be used in lectures.

Other supplements offered by Pearson include:

Discovering American History Through Maps and Views Transparency Set Created by Gerald Danzer of the University of Illinois at Chicago, the recipient of the AHA's James Harvey Robinson Prize for his work in the development of map transparencies, this set of 140 full-color slides—now available online—is a unique instructional tool. It contains an introduction to teaching history through maps and a detailed commentary on each transparency. The collection includes cartographic pictorial maps, views, photos, urban plans, building diagrams, and works of art. Available online at www.pearsonhighered.com/irc.

Visual Archives of American History, Updated Edition Available on two CD-ROMs and with added content, this encyclopedic collection of instructor resources contains dozens of narrated vignettes and videos as well as hundreds of photos and illustrations ready for use in PowerPoint presentations, course Web sites, or online courses.

Student Supplements for Qualified College Adopters

VangoBooks.com Visit VangoBooks.com/nash to take your understanding of the material to the next level. The site breaks down the information in the text by topic and by chapter, and features Multiple Choice, True/False, and Short Answer questions to test your knowledge. You can email your quiz results to your instructor or tutor for grading—set up a handy profile to expedite this process, so you don't have to enter the information every time. Still need more help? The site also includes access to other resources such as printable flash cards and supplemental websites.

VangoCard for American History Colorful, affordable, and packed with useful information, VangoCards make studying easier, more efficient, and more enjoyable. Course information is distilled down to the basics, helping students quickly master the fundamentals, review a subject for understanding, or prepare for an exam. Because it's laminated for durability, you can keep the VangoCard for years to come and pull it out for a quick review.

Research Navigator Guide This guidebook includes exercises and tips on how to use the Internet in your study of U.S. history. It also includes an access code for Research Navigator—the easiest way for students to start a research assignment or research paper. Research Navigator is composed of three exclusive databases of credible and reliable source material, including EBSCO's ContentSelect Academic Journal Database, the *New York Times* Search by Subject Archive, and the "Best of the Web" Link Library. This comprehensive site also includes a detailed help section.

Longman American History Atlas A full-color reference tool and visual guide to American history that includes almost 100 maps and covers the full scope of history. Atlas overhead transparencies are also available to adopters. The Longman American History Atlas is available at no extra charge when bundled with the textbook.

Mapping America: A Guide to Historical Geography, **Third Edition** Written by Ken Weatherbie of Del Mar College, this two-volume workbook contains 35 exercises correlated to the text that review basic American historical geography and ask students to interpret the role geography has played in American history. *Mapping America: A Guide to Historical Geography* is available at no additional charge to qualified college adopters when bundled with the text.

American History Firsthand Created by editors Julie Roy Jeffrey and Peter Frederick, this unique looseleaf anthology is designed to give students an up-close-and-personal view of history. The collection includes loose facsimiles of written documents, visual materials and artifacts, songs and sheet music, portraits, cartoons, film posters, and more, so that students can learn firsthand what history is and what historians do. "Placing the Sources in Context" and "Questions to Consider" accompanying each set of materials in the collection help guide students through the practice of historical analysis.

Voices of **The American People** This collection of primary documents reflects the rich and varied tapestry of American life and is correlated directly to the content and organization of *The American People*. It is available to qualified college adopters at no additional charge when bundled with a new book.

Sources of the African American Past, **Second Edition** Edited by Roy Finkenbine of the University of Detroit at Mercy, this collection of primary sources covers key themes in the African American experience from the West African background to the present. Balanced between political and social history, it offers a vivid snapshot of the lives of African Americans in different historical periods and includes documents representing women and different regions of the United States. Available at a minimum cost to qualified college adopters when bundled with the text.

Women and the National Experience, **Second Edition** Edited by Ellen Skinner of Pace University, this primary source reader contains both classic and unusual documents describing the history of women in the United States. The documents provide dramatic evidence that outspoken women attained a public voice and participated in the development of national events and policies long before they could vote. Chronologically organized and balanced between social and political history, this reader offers a striking picture of the lives of women across American history. Available at a minimum cost to qualified college adopters when bundled with the text.

Reading the American West, Edited by Mitchell Roth of Sam Houston State University, this primary source reader uses letters, diary excerpts, speeches, interviews, and newspaper articles to let students experience how historians do research and how history is written. Every document is accompanied by a contextual headnote and study questions. The book is divided into chapters with extensive introductions. Available at a minimum cost to qualified college adopters when bundled with the text.

A Short Guide to Writing About History, **Sixth Edition** by Richard Marius and Melvin E. Page, this practical text teaches students how to incorporate their own ideas into their papers and to tell a story about history that interests them and their peers. Focusing on more than just the conventions of good writing, this text shows students how first to think about history, and then how to organize their thoughts into coherent essays. The *Short Guide* covers both brief essays and the document resource paper as it explores the writing and researching processes; examines different modes of historical writing, including argument; and concludes with guidelines for improving style.

Library of American Biography Series Each concise biography in this distinguished series focuses on an individual whose actions and ideas significantly influenced American history and relates the life of the subject to the issues and events of the time period. Now featuring the guiding hand of series editor Mark C. Carnes, the series is being revised and updated with today's students in mind. Each volume is offered at a lower price, and study and discussion questions have been added at the end of each new volume to encourage students to reflect on the role of the subject in the shaping of American history. Classic books in the series include Edmund S. Morgan, *The Puritan Dilemma: The Story of John Winthrop;* Harold C. Livesay, *Andrew Carnegie and the Rise of Big Business;* William T. Youngs, *Eleanor Roosevelt: A Personal and Public Life.* Many new titles have been added in recent years, including several figures from the second half of the 20th Century.

Penguin Books The partnership between Penguin Putnam USA and Longman Publishers offers your students a discount on many titles when bundled with any Longman survey. Available titles include *Narrative of the Life of Frederick Douglass* by Frederick Douglass, *Why We Can't Wait* by Martin Luther King, Jr., *Beloved* by Toni Morrison, and *Uncle Tom's Cabin* by Harriet Beecher Stowe. For a complete listing of titles, go to www.pearsonhighered /penguin.

GARY B. NASH received his Ph.D. from Princeton University. He is currently Director of the National Center for History in the Schools at the University of California, Los Angeles, where he teaches colonial and revolutionary American history. Among the books Nash has authored are *Quakers and Politics: Pennsylvania, 1681–1726* (1968); *Red, White, and Black: The Peoples of Early America* (1974, 1982, 1992, 2000); *The Urban Crucible: Social Change, Political Consciousness, and the Origins of the American Revolution* (1979); *Forging Freedom: The Formation of Philadelphia's Black Community, 1720–1840* (1988); *First City: Philadelphia and the Forging of Historical Memory* (2002); and *The Unknown American Revolution: The Unruly Birth of Democracy and the Struggle to Create America* (2005). A former president of the Organization of American Historians, his scholarship is especially concerned with the role of common people in the making of history. He wrote Part 1 and served as a general editor of this book.

JULIE ROY JEFFREY earned her Ph.D. in history from Rice University. Since then she has taught at Goucher College. Honored as an outstanding teacher, Jeffrey has been involved in faculty development activities and curriculum evaluation. She was Fulbright Chair in American Studies at the University of Southern Denmark, 1999–2000. Jeffrey's major publications include *Education for Children of the Poor* (1978); *Frontier Women: The Trans-Mississippi West, 1840–1880* (1979, 1997); *Converting the West: A Biography of Narcissa Whitman* (1991); and *The Great Silent Army of Abolitionism: Ordinary Women in the Antislavery Movement* (1998). She collaborated with Peter Frederick on *American History in a Box*, two volumes (2002). She is the author of many articles on the lives and perceptions of nineteenth-century women. Her research continues to focus on abolitionism as well as on history and film. She wrote Parts 3 and 4 in collaboration with Peter Frederick and acted as a general editor of this book.

JOHN R. HOWE received his Ph.D. from Yale University. At the University of Minnesota, he has taught the U.S. history survey and courses on the American revolutionary era and the early republic. His major publications include *The Changing Political Thought of John Adams* (1966), *From the Revolution Through the Age of Jackson* (1973), *The Role of Ideology in the American Revolution* (1977), and *Language and Political Meaning in Revolutionary America* (2003). His present research deals with the social politics of verbal discourse in late eighteenth- and early nineteenth-century Boston. He has received a Woodrow Wilson Graduate Fellowship, a John Simon Guggenheim Fellowship, and a Research Fellowship from the Charles Warren Center for Studies in American History. Howe wrote Part 2 of this book.

PETER J. FREDERICK received his Ph.D. in history from the University of California, Berkeley. Currently a Distinguished Professor of American History and Culture at Heritage University on the Yakima Nation reservation in Washington, his career of innovative teaching began at California State University, Hayward, in the 1960s and continued at Wabash College (1970–2004) and Carleton College (1992–1994). Recognized nationally as a distinguished teacher and for his many articles and workshops on teaching and learning, Frederick was awarded the Eugene Asher Award for Excellence in Teaching by the AHA in 2000. He has also written several articles on life-writing and a book, *Knights of the Golden Rule: The Intellectual as Christian Social Reformer in the 1890s*. With Julie Jeffrey, he recently published *American History in a Box*. He coordinated and edited all the "Recovering the Past" sections and coauthored Parts 3 and 4.

ALLEN F. DAVIS earned his Ph.D. from the University of Wisconsin. A former president of the American Studies Association, he is a professor of history at Temple University and editor of *Conflict and Consensus in American History* (9th ed, 1997). He is the author of *Spearheads for Reform: The Social Settlements and the Progressive Movement* (1967); *American Heroine: The Life and Legend of Jane Addams* (1973); and *Postcards from Vermont: A Social History* (2002). He is coauthor of *Still Philadelphia* (1983); *Philadelphia Stories* (1987); and *One Hundred Years at Hull-House* (1990). Davis wrote Part 5 of this book.

ALLAN M. WINKLER received his Ph.D. from Yale University. He has taught at Yale and the University of Oregon, and he is now Distinguished Professor of History at Miami University of Ohio. An award-winning teacher, he has also published extensively about the recent past. His books include *The Politics of Propaganda: The Office of War Information, 1942–1945* (1978); *Home Front U.S.A.: America During World War II* (1986, 2000); *Life Under a Cloud: American Anxiety About the Atom* (1993, 1999); and *The Cold War: A History in Documents* (2000), and *Franklin D. Roosevelt* *and the Making of Modern America* (2006). His research centers on the connections between public policy and popular mood in modern American history. Winkler wrote Part 6 of this book.

CARLA GARDINA PESTANA received her Ph.D. from the University of California at Los Angeles. She taught at Ohio State University, where she served as a Lilly Teaching Fellow and launched an innovative on-demand publishing project. Currently she holds the W. E. Smith Professorship in History at Miami University. Her publications include *Liberty of Conscience and the Growth of Religious Diversity in Early America* (1986), *Quakers and Baptists in Colonial Massachusetts* (1991), and *The English Atlantic in an Age of Revolution, 1640–1661* (2004). She is also the co-editor, with Sharon V. Salinger, of

Inequality in Early America (1999). At present, she is completing a book on religion in the British Atlantic world to 1830 for classroom use. She contributed to Part 1 of this edition of *The American People*.

CHARLENE MIRES earned her Ph.D. in history at Temple University. At Villanova University, she teaches courses in nineteenth- and twentieth-century U.S. history, public history, and material culture. She is the author of *Independence Hall in American Memory* (2002) and serves as editor of the Pennsylvania History Studies Series for the Pennsylvania Historical Association. A former journalist, she was a co-recipient of the Pulitzer Prize for general local news reporting with other staff members of the Fort Wayne (Indiana) *News-Sentinel*. She contributed to Part 5 of this edition of *The American People*.

CHAPTER 16

The Union Reconstructed

In a scene like the one depicted in this Winslow Homer painting titled *A Visit from the Old Mistress*, imagine Adele Allston returning to her plantation to reunite with former slaves. What sort of new relationships might they form in a world that had been profoundly changed by the wrenching Civil War?

(Winslow Homer, A Visit from the Old Mistress, 1876, National Museum of American Art/Art Resource, NY)

American Stories

Blacks and Whites Redefine Their Dreams and Relationships

In April 1864, a year before Lincoln's assassination, Robert Allston died, leaving his wife, Adele, and his daughter, Elizabeth, to manage their many rice plantations. Elizabeth felt a "sense of terrible desolation and sorrow" as the Civil War raged around her. With Union troops moving through coastal South Carolina in the winter of 1864–1865, Elizabeth's sorrow turned to "terror" as Union soldiers arrived and searched for liquor, firearms, and valuables. The women fled. Later, Yankee troops encouraged the Allston slaves to take furniture, food, and other goods from the Big House. Before they left, the liberating Union soldiers gave the keys to the crop barns to the semifree slaves.

After the war, Adele Allston swore allegiance to the United States and secured a written order for the newly freed African Americans to relinquish those keys. She and Elizabeth returned in the summer of 1865 to reclaim the plantations and reassert white authority. She was assured that although the blacks had guns, "no outrage has been committed against the whites except in the matter of property." But property was the issue. Possession of the keys to the barns, Elizabeth wrote, would be the "test case" of whether former masters or former slaves would control land, labor, and its fruits, as well as the subtle aspects of interpersonal relations.

Nervously, Adele and Elizabeth confronted ex-slaves at their old home. To their surprise, a pleasant reunion took place as the Allston women greeted the blacks by name, inquired after their children, and caught up on their lives. A trusted black foreman handed over the keys to the barns. This harmonious scene was repeated elsewhere.

But at one plantation, the Allstons met defiant and armed African Americans, who ominously lined both sides of the road as the carriage arrived. An old black driver, Uncle Jacob, was unsure whether to yield the keys to the barns full of rice and corn, put there by slave labor. Mrs. Allston insisted. As Uncle Jacob hesitated, an angry young man shouted out: "If you give up the key, blood'll flow." Uncle Jacob slowly slipped the keys back into his pocket.

The African Americans sang freedom songs and brandished hoes, pitchforks, and guns to discourage anyone from going to town for help. Two blacks, however, slipped away to find some Union officers. The

Allston women spent the night safely, if restlessly, in their house. Early the next morning, they were awakened by a knock at the unlocked front door. There stood Uncle Jacob. Silently, he gave back the keys.

The story of the keys reveals most of the essential human ingredients of the Reconstruction era. Defeated southern whites were determined to resume control of both land and labor. The law and federal enforcement generally supported the property owners. The Allston women were friendly to the blacks in a maternal way and insisted on restoring prewar deference in black–white relations. Adele and Elizabeth, in short, both feared and cared about their former slaves.

The African American freedpeople likewise revealed mixed feelings toward their former owners: anger, loyalty, love, resentment, and pride. They paid respect to the Allstons but not to their property and crops. They wanted not revenge but rather economic independence and freedom.

Northern officials played a most revealing role. Union soldiers, literally and symbolically, gave the keys of freedom to the freed men and women, but did not stay around long enough to guarantee that freedom. Despite initially encouraging blacks to plunder the master's house and seize the crops, in the crucial encounter after the war, northern officials had disappeared. Understanding the limits of northern help, Uncle Jacob handed the keys to land and liberty back to his former owner. The blacks realized that if they wanted to ensure their freedom, they had to do it themselves.

This chapter describes what happened to the conflicting goals and dreams of three groups as they sought to redefine new social, economic, and political relationships during the postwar Reconstruction era. It also shows how America sought to reestablish stable democratic governments. Amid vast devastation and bitter race and class divisions, Civil War survivors sought to put their lives back together. Victorious but variously motivated northern officials, defeated but defiant southern planters, and impoverished but hopeful African Americans could not all fulfill their conflicting goals and dreams, yet each had to try. Reconstruction would be divisive, leaving a mixed legacy of human gains and losses.

The Bittersweet Aftermath of War

"There are sad changes in store for both races," the daughter of a Georgia planter wrote in the summer of 1865. To understand the bittersweet nature of Reconstruction, we must look at the state of the nation after the assassination of President Lincoln.

The United States in 1865

Constitutionally, the "Union" faced a crisis in April 1865. What was the status of the 11 former Confederate states? The North had denied the South's constitutional right to secede but needed four years of civil war and over 600,000 deaths to win the point. Lincoln's official position had been that the southern states had never left the Union and were only "out of their proper relation" with the United States. The president, therefore, as commander in chief, had the authority to decide how to set relations right again. Lincoln's congressional opponents retorted that the rebellious states had broken their constitutional ties, were now like "conquered provinces," and that Congress should resolve the constitutional issues and direct Reconstruction.

Politically, differences between Congress and the White House mirrored a wider struggle between the two branches of the national government. During war, as has usually been the case, the executive branch assumed broad powers to mobilize resources and ensure domestic security. Many believed that Lincoln had far exceeded his constitutional authority and that his successor, Andrew Johnson, was worse. Would Congress reassert its authority?

In April 1865, the Republican party ruled nearly unchecked. Republicans claimed huge achievements in winning the war, preserving the Union, and freeing the slaves. They had enacted sweeping economic programs on behalf of free labor, economic growth, and the creation of land-grant colleges to teach agricultural and mechanical skills. But the still-young party remained an uneasy grouping of former Whigs, Unionist Democrats, and antislavery idealists.

The Democrats were in shambles. Republicans depicted southern Democrats as traitorous rebels and northern Democrats as weak-willed, disloyal, and opposed to economic progress. Nevertheless, in the election of 1864, needing to show that the war was a bipartisan effort, the Republicans had named a Tennessee Unionist Democrat, Andrew Johnson, as Lincoln's vice president. Now the tactless Johnson headed the government.

Economically, the United States in the spring of 1865 presented stark contrasts. Northern cities and railroads hummed with productive activity; southern cities and railroads lay in ruins. Northern banks flourished; southern financial institutions were bankrupt. Mechanized northern farms were more productive than ever; southern farms and plantations, especially those along Sherman's march, resembled a "howling waste."

Socially, the widespread devastation in the South affected southern attitudes. A later southern writer, Wilbur Cash, explained, "If this war had smashed the Southern world, it had left the essential Southern mind and will . . . entirely unshaken." Many white southerners were determined to resist Reconstruction and restore their former life and institutions; others, the minority who had remained quietly loyal to the Union, sought reconciliation.

In this context, nearly 4 million newly freed blacks faced the challenges of freedom. After initial joy and celebration in jubilee songs, freedmen and freedwomen

---

The United States in 1865: Crises at the End of the Civil War

Given the enormous casualties, costs, and crises of the immediate aftermath of the Civil War, what attitudes, goals, dreams, and behaviors would you predict for the three major groups?

Military Casualties

360,000 Union soldiers dead
260,000 Confederate soldiers dead
620,000 Total dead
375,000 Seriously wounded and maimed
995,000 Casualties nationwide in a total male population of 15 million (nearly 1 in 15)

Physical and Economic Crises

The South devastated; its railroads, industry, and some major cities in ruins; its fields and livestock wasted

Constitutional Crisis

Eleven former Confederate states not a part of the Union, their status unclear and future status uncertain

Political Crisis

Republican party (entirely of the North) dominant in Congress; a former Democratic slaveholder from Tennessee, Andrew Johnson, in the presidency

Social Crisis

Nearly 4 million black freedpeople throughout the South facing challenges of survival and freedom, along with thousands of hungry, demobilized Confederate soldiers and displaced white families

Psychological Crisis

Incalculable stores of resentment, bitterness, anger, and despair, North and South, white and black

Conflicting Goals During Reconstruction

Examine these conflicting goals, which, at a human level, were the challenge of Reconstruction. How could each group possibly fulfill its goals when so many of them conflict with those of other groups? You may find yourself referring back to this chart throughout the chapter. How can each group fulfill its goals?

Victorious Northern ("Radical") Republicans

- Justify the war by remaking southern society in the image of the North
- Inflict political but not physical or economic punishment on Confederate leaders
- Continue programs of economic progress begun during the war: high tariffs, railroad subsidies, national banking
- Maintain the Republican party in power
- Help the freedpeople make the transition to full freedom by providing them with the tools of citizenship (suffrage) and equal economic opportunity

Northern Moderates (Republicans and Democrats)

- Quickly establish peace and order, reconciliation between North and South
- Bestow on the southern states leniency, amnesty, and merciful readmission to the Union
- Perpetuate land ownership, free labor, market competition, and other capitalist ventures
- Promote local self-determination of economic and social issues; limit interference by the national government
- Provide limited support for black suffrage

Old Southern Planter Aristocracy (Former Confederates)

- Ensure protection from black uprising and prevent excessive freedom for former slaves
- Secure amnesty, pardon, and restoration of confiscated lands
- Restore traditional plantation-based, market-crop economy with blacks as cheap labor force
- Restore traditional political leaders in the states
- Restore traditional paternalistic race relations as basis of social order

New "Other South": Yeoman Farmers and Former Whigs (Unionists)

- Quickly establish peace and order, reconciliation between North and South
- Achieve recognition of loyalty and economic value of yeoman farmers
- Create greater diversity in southern economy: capital investments in railroads, factories, and the diversification of agriculture
- Displace the planter aristocracy with new leaders drawn from new economic interests
- Limit the rights and powers of freedpeople; extend suffrage only to the educated few

Black Freedpeople

- Secure physical protection from abuse and terror by local whites
- Achieve economic independence through land ownership (40 acres and a mule) and equal access to trades
- Receive educational opportunity and foster the development of family and cultural bonds
- Obtain equal civil rights and protection under the law
- Commence political participation through the right to vote

---

quickly realized their continuing dependence on former owners. A Mississippian woman said:

> I used to think if I could be free I should be the happiest of anybody in the world. But when my master come to me, and says—Lizzie, you is free! it seems like I was in a kind of daze. And when I would wake up in the morning I would think to myself, Is I free? Hasn't I got to get up before day light and go into the field of work?

For Lizzie, and 4 million other blacks, everything—and nothing—had changed.

Hopes Among the Freedpeople

Throughout the South in the summer of 1865, optimism surged through the old slave quarters as Richmond blacks chanted: "Slavery chain done broke at last! Gonna praise God till I die!" But the slavery chain broke slowly, link by link. After Union troops swept through an area, "we'd begin celebratin'," one man said, but Confederate soldiers would follow, or master and overseer would return, and "tell us to go back to work." The freedmen and freedwomen learned, therefore, not to rejoice too quickly or openly.

This 1867 engraving shows two southern women and their children soon after the Civil War. In what ways are they similar and in what ways different? Is there a basis for bonds of sisterhood? What separates them, if anything? From *Frank Leslie's Illustrated Newspaper,* February 23, 1867.

(The Granger Collection, New York)

established the legitimacy of children and meant access to land titles and other economic opportunities. Marriage brought special burdens for black women who assumed the double role of housekeeper and breadwinner. Their determination to create a traditional family life and care for their children resulted in the withdrawal of many women from plantation field labor.

Freedpeople also demonstrated their new status by choosing surnames. Names connoting independence, such as Washington, were common. Revealing mixed feelings toward their former masters, some would adopt their master's name, while others would pick "any big name 'ceptin' their master's." Emancipation changed black manners around whites as well. Masks fell, and expressions of deference—tipping a hat, stepping aside, calling whites "master" or "ma'am"—diminished. For blacks, these changes were necessary expressions of selfhood, proving that race relations had changed; whites, however, saw such behaviors as "insolence" and "insubordination."

Education and land were priorities. A Mississippi farmer vowed to "give my children a chance to go to school, for I consider education next best ting to liberty." A traveler through the South counted "at least five hundred" schools "taught by colored people." Other than the passion for education, the primary goal for most freedpeople was land. "All I want is to git to own fo' or five acres ob land, dat I can build me a little house on and call my home," a Mississippi black said. Through educational and economic independence, freedpeople like Lizzie would make sure that emancipation was real.

During the war, some Union generals had put liberated slaves in charge of confiscated and abandoned lands. In the Sea Islands of South Carolina and Georgia, African Americans had been working 40-acre plots of land and harvesting their own crops for several years, and some even held title to these lands. Northern philanthropists had organized others to grow cotton for the Treasury Department to prove the superiority of free labor. In Mississippi, thousands of former slaves worked 40-acre tracts on leased lands ironically once owned by Jefferson Davis. In this highly successful experiment, they made profits sufficient to repay the government for initial costs, then lost the land to Davis's brother.

Gradually, though, African Americans began to test the reality of freedom. Typically, their first step was to leave the plantation, if only for a few hours or days. "If I stay here I'll never know I am free," said a South Carolina woman, who went to work as a cook in a nearby town. Some freedpeople cut their ties entirely—returning to an earlier master, or, more often, going into towns and cities to find jobs, schools, churches, and association with other blacks, safe from whippings and retaliation.

Many blacks left the plantation in search of a spouse, parent, or child sold away years before. Advertisements detailing these sorrowful searches filled African American newspapers. For those who found a spouse and for those who had been living together in slave marriages, freedom meant getting married legally in mass ceremonies in the first months of emancipation. In addition to its moral importance, legal marriage

Many freedpeople expected a new economic order as fair payment for their years of involuntary work. "Gib us our own land," said one, "and we take care ourselves; but widout land, de ole massas can hire us or starve us, as dey please." Freedmen expected the "forty acres and a mule" that had been promised (although one man was willing to settle for less, desiring only one acre—"Ef you make it de acre dat Marsa's house sets on"). Once they obtained land, education, and family unification, some looked forward to equal civil rights and the vote—along with protection from vengeful defeated Confederates.

The White South's Fearful Response

White southerners had equally strong dreams and expectations. Middle-class (yeoman) farmers and poor whites stood beside rich planters in bread lines, all hoping to regain land and livelihood. Suffering from "extreme want and destitution," as a Cherokee County, Georgia, resident put it, southern whites responded to the immediate postwar crises with feelings of outrage, loss, and injustice. "My pa paid his own money for our niggers," one man said, "and

Describe what you see in these two scenes from 1865, one an early photograph of a group of newly freed former slaves leaving the cotton fields after a day of labor, the other a painting titled *The Armed Slave.* What has changed and not changed from slavery times? What is the meaning of the painting? Note the position of gun and bayonet. Could you create a story about these two images?

(Top: © Collection of The New-York Historical Society; Bottom: William Spang, *The Armed Slave.* The Civil War Library and Museum, Philadelphia)

The Promise of Land: 40 Acres

Note the progression in various documents in this chapter from promised lands (this page), to lands restored to whites (p. 392), to work contracts (p. 397), to semiautonomous tenant farms (p. 398). Freedom came by degrees to freedpeople. To what extent was this progress?

To All Whom It May Concern
Edisto Island, August 15th, 1865
George Owens, having selected for settlement forty acres of Land, on Theodore Belab's Place, pursuant to Special Field Orders, No. 15, Headquarters Military Division of the Mississippi, Savannah, Ga., Jan. 16, 1865; he has permission to hold and occupy the said Tract, subject to such regulations as may be established by proper authority; and all persons are prohibited from interfering with him in his possession of the same.

By command of   R. SAXTON
                       Brev't Maj. Gen.,
                       Ass't Comm.
                       S.C., Ga., and Fla.

The Black Codes, widespread violence against freedpeople, and President Johnson's veto of the civil rights bill gave rise to the sardonic title "(?)Slavery Is Dead(?)" in this Thomas Nast cartoon. Describe the two scenes and the two images of justice. What is Nast saying?

(Courtesy of The Newberry Library, Chicago)

that's not all they've robbed us of. They have taken our horses and cattle and sheep and everything." Others mourned the loss of former faithful slaves: "My dear black mammy has left us," a Florida woman wrote, "I feel lost.... Whatever will I do without my Mammy?"

A dominant emotion was fear. The entire structure of southern society was shaken, and the semblance of racial peace and order that slavery had provided was shattered. Having lost control of all that was familiar, whites feared everything—from losing their cheap labor to having blacks sit next to them on trains to having to do housework. Eliza Andrews complained that it seemed to her a "waste of time for people who are capable of doing something better to spend their time sweeping and dusting while scores of lazy negroes that are fit for nothing else are lying around idle."

Ironically, given the rape of black women during slavery, southern whites' worst fears were of rape and revenge. African American "impudence," some thought, would lead to legal intermarriage and "Africanization," the destruction of the purity

of the white race. Black Union soldiers seemed especially ominous. But these fears were exaggerated, as demobilization of black soldiers came quickly, and rape and violence against whites was extremely rare.

Believing their world turned upside down, the former planter aristocracy sought to set it right again. To reestablish white dominance, southern legislatures passed "Black Codes" in the first year after the war. Many of the codes granted freedpeople rights that were highly qualified. Complicated passages explained under exactly what circumstances blacks could testify against whites or own property (mostly they could not). Forbidden were racial intermarriage, bearing arms, possessing alcoholic beverages, sitting on trains (except in baggage compartments), being on city streets at night, and congregating in large groups.

Many of the qualified rights guaranteed by the Black Codes were only passed to induce the federal government to withdraw its remaining troops from the South. This was a crucial issue, for in many places marauding groups of whites were terrorizing defenseless blacks. In one small district in Kentucky, for example, a government agent reported in 1865:

> Twenty-three cases of severe and inhuman beating and whipping of men; four of beating and shooting; two of robbing and shooting; three of robbing; five men shot and killed; two shot and wounded; four beaten to death; one beaten and roasted; three women assaulted and ravished; four women beaten; two women tied up and whipped until insensible....

Freedpeople clearly needed protection and the right to testify in court against whites.

Key provisions of the Black Codes regulated freedpeople's economic status. "Vagrancy" laws provided that any blacks not "lawfully employed" (by a white employer) could be arrested, jailed, fined, or hired out to a man who would assume responsibility for their debts and behavior. The codes regulated black laborers' work contracts with white landowners, including severe penalties for leaving before the yearly contract was fulfilled and rules for proper behavior, attitude, and manners. A Kentucky newspaper was blunt: "The tune...will not be 'forty acres and a mule,' but... 'work nigger or starve.'"

National Reconstruction Politics

The Black Codes directly challenged the national government in 1865. Would it use its power to uphold the codes, white property rights, and racial intimidation, or to defend the liberties of freedpeople? Although the primary drama of Reconstruction pitted white landowners against black freedmen over land, labor, and liberties in the South, these local struggles were affected by Reconstruction and race relations policy set by politicians in Washington. That drama extends to today.

Presidential Reconstruction by Proclamation

After initially demanding that the defeated Confederates be punished for "treason," President Johnson soon adopted a more lenient policy. On May 29, 1865, he issued two proclamations setting forth his Reconstruction program. Like Lincoln's, it rested on the claim that the southern states had never left the Union.

Johnson's first proclamation continued Lincoln's policies by offering "amnesty and pardon, with restoration of all rights of property" to most former Confederates who would swear allegiance to the Constitution and the Union. Johnson revealed his Jacksonian hostility to "aristocratic" planters by

Promised Land Restored to Whites

Richard H. Jenkins, an applicant for the restoration of his plantation on Wadmalaw Island, S.C., called "Rackett Hall," the same having been unoccupied during the past year and up to the 1st of Jan. 1866, except by one freedman who planted no crop, and being held by the Bureau of Refugees, Freedmen and Abandoned Lands, having conformed to the requirements of Circular No. 15 of said Bureau, dated Washington, D.C., Sept. 12, 1865, the aforesaid property is hereby restored to his possession.

... The Undersigned, Richard H. Jenkins, does hereby solemnly promise and engage, that he will secure to the Refugees and Freedmen now resident on his Wadmalaw Island Estate, the crops of the past year, harvested or unharvested; also, that the said Refugees and Freedmen shall be allowed to remain at their present houses or other homes on the island, so long as the responsible Refugees and Freedmen (embracing parents, guardians, and other natural protectors) shall enter into contracts, by leases or for wages, in terms satisfactory to the Supervising Board.

Also, that the undersigned will take the proper steps to enter into contracts with the above described responsible Refugees and Freedmen, the latter being required on their part to enter into said contracts on or before the 15th day of February, 1866, or surrender their right to remain on the said estate, it being understood that if they are unwilling to contract after the expiration of said period, the Supervising Board is to aid in getting them homes and employment elsewhere.

exempting ex-Confederate government leaders and rebels with taxable property valued over $20,000. They could, however, apply for individual pardons, which Johnson granted to nearly all applicants.

In his second proclamation, Johnson accepted the reconstructed government of North Carolina and prescribed the steps by which other southern states could reestablish state governments. First, the president would appoint a provisional governor, who would call a state convention representing those "who are loyal to the United States," including persons who took the oath of allegiance or were otherwise pardoned. The convention must ratify the Thirteenth Amendment, which abolished slavery; void secession; repudiate Confederate debts; and elect new state officials and members of Congress.

Under Johnson's plan, all southern states completed Reconstruction and sent representatives to Congress, which convened in December 1865. Defiant southern voters elected dozens of former officers and legislators of the Confederacy, including a few not yet pardoned. Some state conventions hedged on ratifying the Thirteenth Amendment, and some asserted former owners' right to compensation for lost slave property. No state convention provided for black suffrage, and most did nothing to guarantee civil rights, schooling, or economic protection for the freedmen. Eight months after Appomattox, the southern states were back in the Union, freedpeople were working for former masters, and the new president was firmly in charge. Reconstruction seemed to be over.

Congressional Reconstruction by Amendment

Late in 1865, northern leaders painfully saw that almost none of their postwar goals were being fulfilled and that the Republicans were likely to lose their political power. Would Democrats and the South gain by postwar elections what they had lost by civil war?

A song popular in the North in 1866 posed the question, "Who shall rule this American Nation?"—those who would betray their country and "murder the innocent freedmen" or those "loyal millions" who had shed their "blood in battle"? The answer was obvious. Congressional Republicans, led by

Congressman Thaddeus Stevens of Pennsylvania and Senator Charles Sumner of Massachusetts, decided to set their own policies for Reconstruction. Although labeled "radicals," the vast majority of Republicans were moderates on the economic and political rights of African Americans.

Rejecting Johnson's position that the South had already been reconstructed, Congress exercised its constitutional authority to decide on its own membership. It refused to seat the new senators and representatives from the old Confederate states. It also established the Joint Committee on Reconstruction to investigate conditions in the South, which reported widespread white resistance, disorder, and the appalling treatment of freedpeople.

Congress passed a civil rights bill in 1866 to protect the fragile rights of African Americans and extended for two more years the Freedmen's Bureau, an agency providing emergency assistance at the end of the war. Johnson vetoed both bills and called his congressional opponents "traitors." His actions drove moderates into the radical camp, and Congress passed both bills over his veto—both, however, watered down by weakening the power of enforcement. Southern courts regularly disallowed black testimony against

---

RECONSTRUCTION AMENDMENTS

Constitutional Seeds of Dreams Deferred for 100 Years (or More)

What three fundamental rights were guaranteed by these three amendments? What patterns do you see? How well were the dreams of the freedmen and women fulfilled?

Substance	Outcome of Ratification Process	Final Implementation and Enforcement
Thirteenth Amendment—Passed by Congress January 1865		
Prohibited slavery in the United States	Ratified by 27 states, including 8 southern states, by December 1865	Immediate, although economic freedom came by degrees
Fourteenth Amendment—Passed by Congress June 1866		
(1) Defined equal national citizenship; (2) reduced state representation in Congress proportional to number of disfranchised voters; (3) denied former Confederates the right to hold office; (4) Confederate debts and lost property claims voided and illegal	Rejected by 12 southern and border states by February 1867; Congress made readmission depend on ratification; ratified in July 1868	Civil Rights Act of 1964
Fifteenth Amendment—Passed by Congress February 1869		
Prohibited denial of vote because of race, color, or previous servitude (but not sex)	Ratification by Virginia, Texas, Mississippi, and Georgia required for readmission; ratified in March 1870	Voting Rights Act of 1965

Note: See exact wording in U.S. Constitution in the Appendix.

whites, acquitted whites of violence, and sentenced blacks to compulsory labor.

In such a climate, southern racial violence erupted. In a typical outbreak, in May 1866, white mobs in Memphis, encouraged by local police and a newspaper that urged the mob to "go ahead and kill the last damned one of the nigger race," rampaged for over 40 hours, killing, beating, robbing, and raping virtually helpless black residents and burning houses, schools, and churches. Forty-eight people, all but two of them black, died. The local Union army commander took his time restoring order, arguing that his troops "hated Negroes too." A congressional inquiry concluded that Memphis blacks had "no protection from the law whatever."

A month later, Congress sent to the states for ratification the Fourteenth Amendment, the single most significant act of the Reconstruction era. The first section of the amendment promised permanent constitutional protection of the civil rights of blacks by defining them as citizens. States were prohibited from depriving "any person of life, liberty, or property, without due process of law," and citizens were guaranteed the "equal protection of the laws." Section 2 granted black male suffrage in the South, inserting the word "male" into the Constitution for the first time, and said states denying the black vote would have their representation reduced. Other sections of the amendment barred leaders of the Confederacy from national or state offices (except by act of Congress), repudiated the Confederate debt, and denied claims of compensation to former slave owners. Johnson urged the southern states to reject the Fourteenth Amendment, and 10 immediately did so.

The Fourteenth Amendment was the central issue of the 1866 midterm election. Johnson barnstormed the country asking voters to throw out the "radical" Republicans and trading insults with hecklers. Democrats north and south appealed openly to racial prejudice in charging that the Fourteenth Amendment would "Africanize" America, threatening both the marketplace and the bedroom. Republicans responded by attacking Johnson personally, waving the "bloody shirt" to remind voters of Democrats' treason during the civil war. Self-interest and local issues moved voters more than fiery speeches, and Republicans won an overwhelming victory. The mandate was clear: presidential Reconstruction had not worked, and Congress could present its own.

Early in 1867, Congress passed three Reconstruction acts. The southern states were divided into five military districts, whose commanders had broad powers to maintain order and protect civil and property rights. Congress also defined a new process for readmitting a state. Qualified voters—including blacks and excluding unreconstructed rebels—would elect delegates to state constitutional conventions that would write new constitutions guaranteeing black suffrage. After the new voters of the states had ratified these constitutions, elections would be held to choose governors and state legislatures. When a state ratified the Fourteenth Amendment, its representatives to Congress would be accepted, completing readmission to the Union.

The President Impeached

Congress also restricted presidential powers and established legislative dominance over the executive branch. The Tenure of Office Act, designed to prevent Johnson from firing the outspoken Secretary of War Edwin Stanton, limited the president's appointment powers. Other measures trimmed his powers as commander in chief.

Johnson responded exactly as congressional Republicans had anticipated. He vetoed the Reconstruction acts, hindered the work of Freedmen's Bureau agents, limited the activities of military commanders in the South, and removed cabinet officers and other officials sympathetic to Congress. The House Judiciary Committee charged the president with "usurpations of power" and of acting in the "interests of the great criminals" who had led the rebellion. But moderate House Republicans defeated the impeachment resolutions.

In August 1867, Johnson dismissed Stanton and asked for Senate consent. When the Senate refused, the president ordered Stanton to surrender his office, which he refused, barricading himself inside. The House quickly approved impeachment resolutions, charging the president with "high crimes and misdemeanors." The three-month trial in the Senate early in 1868 was similar to the trial of President Bill Clinton 130 years later in that evidence was skimpy that Johnson, like Clinton, had committed any constitutional crime justifying his removal. With seven moderate Republicans joining Democrats against conviction, the effort to find the president guilty fell one vote short of the required two-thirds majority. Not until the late twentieth century (Nixon and Clinton) would an American president face removal from office through impeachment.

Moderate Republicans were fearful that by removing Johnson, they might get Ohio senator Benjamin Wade, a leading radical Republican, as president. Wade had endorsed woman suffrage, rights for labor unions, and civil rights for African Americans. As moderate Republicans gained strength in 1868 through their support of the eventual presidential election winner, Ulysses S. Grant, radicalism lost most of its power within Republican ranks.

What Congressional Moderation Meant for Rebels, Blacks, and Women

Congress's political battle against the president was not matched by a principled resolve on behalf of the freedpeople. State and local elections of 1867 showed that voters preferred moderate Reconstruction policies. It is important to look not only at what Congress did during Reconstruction but also at what it did not do.

With the exception of Jefferson Davis, Congress did not imprison rebel Confederate leaders, and only one person, the commander of the infamous Andersonville prison camp, was executed. Congress did not insist on a long probation before southern states could be readmitted to the Union. It did not reorganize southern local governments. It did not mandate a national program of education for freedpeople. It did not confiscate and redistribute land to the freedmen. It did not, except indirectly and with great reluctance, provide economic help to black citizens.

Congress did, however, grant citizenship and suffrage to freedmen, but not to freedwomen. But Northerners were no more prepared than southerners to make all African Americans fully equal citizens. Between 1865 and 1869, voters in seven northern states turned down referendums proposing black (male) suffrage. Such proposals gained support in the North only after the election of 1868, when General Grant, the supposedly invincible military hero, barely won the popular vote in several states. Republicans needed black votes, so in 1870, Congressional Republicans, who had twice rejected a constitutional suffrage amendment, finally passed the Fifteenth Amendment, forbidding all states to deny the vote "on account of race, color, or previous condition of servitude." A Pittsburgh black preacher observed, "the Republican party had done the Negro good, but they were doing themselves good at the same time."

One casualty of the Fourteenth and Fifteenth Amendments was the goodwill of women who had worked for their suffrage for two decades. They had hoped that male legislators would recognize their wartime service in support of the Union and were shocked that black males got the vote but not loyal white (or black) women. Elizabeth Cady Stanton and Susan B. Anthony, veteran suffragists and opponents of slavery, opposed the Amendments, breaking with abolitionist allies such as Frederick Douglass, who had long supported woman suffrage yet declared that this was "the Negro's hour." Anthony vowed to "cut off this right arm of mine before I will ever work for or demand the ballot for the Negro and not the woman."

Disappointment over the suffrage issue helped split the women's movement in 1869. Anthony and Stanton continued their fight for a national amendment for woman suffrage and a long list of property, educational, and sexual rights, while other women focused on securing the vote state by state. Abandoned by radical and moderate men alike, women had few champions in Congress and their efforts were put off for half a century.

Congress compromised the rights of African Americans as well as women. It gave blacks the vote but not land, the opposite of what they preferred. Almost alone, Thaddeus Stevens argued that "forty acres...and a hut would be more valuable...than the...right to vote." But Congress never seriously considered his plan to divide the land of the "chief rebels" into 40-acre plots for freedmen. Congress did pass the Southern Homestead Act of 1866, making public lands available to blacks and loyal whites in five southern states. But the land was poor and inaccessible; no tools or seed were provided; and most blacks were bound by contracts that prevented them from making claims before the deadline. Only about 4,000 African American families even applied for the Homestead Act lands, and fewer than 20 percent of them saw their claims completed. White claimants did little better.

The Lives of Freedpeople

Union army major George Reynolds boasted late in 1865 that in the area of Mississippi under his command, he had "kept the negroes at work, and in a good state of discipline." Clinton Fisk, a well-meaning white who helped found a black college in Tennessee, told freedmen in 1866 that they could be "as free and as happy" working again for their "old master...as any where else in the world." Such pronouncements reminded blacks of white preachers' exhortations during slavery to work hard and obey their masters. Ironically, Fisk and Reynolds were agents of the Freedmen's Bureau, the agency intended to aid the black transition from slavery to freedom.

The Freedmen's Bureau

Never in American history has one small agency—underfinanced, understaffed, and undersupported—been given a harder task than the Bureau of Freedmen, Refugees and Abandoned Lands. Controlling less than 1 percent of southern lands, the Bureau's name is telling; its fate epitomizes Reconstruction.

The Freedmen's Bureau performed many essential services. It issued emergency food rations, clothed and sheltered homeless victims of the war, and established medical and hospital facilities. It provided funds to relocate thousands of freedpeople. It helped blacks search for relatives and get legally married. It represented African Americans in local civil courts to ensure that they got fair trials. Working with northern missionary aid societies and southern black churches, the

Bureau became responsible for an extensive education program, and by 1870 there were almost 250,000 pupils in 4,329 agency schools.

The Bureau's largest task was to promote African Americans' economic well-being. This included settling blacks on abandoned lands and getting them started with tools, seed, and draft animals, as well as arranging work contracts with white landowners. But the Freedmen's Bureau, determined not to instill a new dependency, more often than not supported the needs of white landowners to find cheap labor than of blacks to become independent farmers.

Although a few agents were idealistic northerners eager to help freedpeople adjust to freedom, most were Union army officers more concerned with social order than social transformation. Working in a postwar climate of resentment and violence, Freedmen's Bureau agents were overworked, underpaid, spread too thin (at its peak only 900 agents were scattered across 11 states), and constantly harassed by local whites. Even the best-intentioned agents would have agreed with General Howard's belief in the nineteenth-century American values of self-help, minimal government interference in the marketplace, the sanctity of private property, contractual obligations, and white superiority.

On a typical day, overburdened agents would visit local courts and schools, file reports, supervise the signing of work contracts, and handle numerous complaints, most involving contract violations between whites and blacks or property and domestic disputes among blacks. A Georgia agent wrote that he was *"tired out* and *broke down....* Every day for 6 months, day after day, I have had from 5 to 20 complaints, *generally trivial* and of no moment." To find work for freedmen, agents often sided with white landowners by telling blacks to obey orders, trust employers, and accept disadvantageous contracts. One agent sent a man who had complained of a severe beating back to work with the advice, "Don't be sassy [and] don't be lazy when you've got work to do."

Despite numerous constraints, the agents accomplished much. In little more than two years, the Freedmen's Bureau issued 20 million rations (nearly one-third to poor whites); reunited families and resettled some 30,000 displaced war refugees; treated some 450,000 people for illness and injury; built 40 hospitals and more than 4,000 schools; provided books, tools, and even some land, to the freedmen; and occasionally protected their civil rights. The great African American historian and leading black intellectual W. E. B. Du Bois wrote, "In a time of perfect calm, amid willing neighbors and streaming wealth," it "would have been a herculean task" for the Bureau to fulfill its many purposes. But in the midst of hunger, hate, sorrow, suspicion, and cruelty, "the work of...social regeneration was in large part foredoomed to failure."

But Du Bois also recognized that in laying the foundation for black labor, future land ownership, a public school system, and recognition before courts of law, the Freedmen's Bureau was "successful beyond the dreams of thoughtful men."

Economic Freedom by Degrees

Despite the best efforts of the Freedmen's Bureau, the failure of Congress to provide the promised 40 acres and a mule forced freedpeople into a new economic dependency on former masters. Blacks made some progress, however, in degrees of economic autonomy and were partly responsible, along with international economic developments, in forcing the white planter class into making major changes in southern agriculture.

First, a land-intensive system replaced the labor intensity of slavery. Land ownership was concentrated into fewer and even larger holdings than before the war. From South Carolina to Louisiana, the wealthiest tenth of the population owned about 60 percent of the real estate in the 1870s. Second, these large planters increasingly concentrated on one crop, usually cotton, and were tied into the international market. This resulted in a steady drop in food production. Third, one-crop farming created a new credit—and dependency—system whereby most farmers, black and white, rented land, seed, farm implements, provisions, and housing from local merchants.

This new system took a few years to develop after emancipation. At first, most African Americans signed contracts with white landowners and worked fields in gangs very much as during slavery. Supervised by superintendents who still used the lash, all members of the family had to toil from sunrise to sunset for meager wages and a monthly allotment of bacon and meal. Many freedpeople resented this new semiservitude, refused to sign the contracts, and sought independence working the land themselves. A South Carolina freedman said, "If I can't own de land, I'll hire or lease land, but I won't contract."

Many blacks, therefore, broke contracts, ran away, haggled over wages, engaged in work slowdowns, burned barns, and sought other means of negotiation to get away from the contract system. In the Sea Islands and rice-growing regions of coastal South Carolina and Georgia, resistance was especially strong. The freedmen "refuse work at any price," a bureau agent reported, and the women "wish to stay in the house or the garden all the time." Insisting on "no more outdoor work," they also wanted to send their children to school rather than to the fields and apprenticeships.

Blacks' insistence on autonomy and land of their own forced a change from the contract system to tenancy and sharecropping. Families would hitch mules to

A Freedman's Work Contract

As you read this rather typical work contract defining the first economic relationship between whites and blacks in the early months of the postwar period, note the regulation of social behavior and deportment, as well as work and "pay" arrangements. How different is this from slavery? As a freedman or freedwoman, would you have signed such an agreement? Why or why not? What options would you have had?

State of South Carolina
Darlington District
Articles of Agreement
This Agreement entered into between Mrs. Adele Allston Exect of the one part, and the Freedmen and Women of The Upper Quarters plantation of the other part Witnesseth:

That the latter agree, for the remainder of the present year, to reside upon and devote their labor to the cultivation of the Plantation of the former. And they further agree, that they will in all respects, conform to such reasonable and necessary plantation rules and regulations as Mrs.Allston's Agent may prescribe; that they will not keep any gun, pistol, or other offensive weapon, or leave the plantation without permission from their employer; that in all things connected with their duties as laborers on said plantation, they will yield prompt obedience to all orders from Mrs.Allston or his [sic] agent; that they will be orderly and quiet in their conduct, avoiding drunkeness and other gross vices; that they will not misuse any of the Plantation Tools, or Agricultural Implements, or any Animals entrusted to their care, or any Boats, Flats, Carts or Wagons; that they will give up at the expiration of this Contract, all Tools & c., belonging to the Plantation, and in case any property, of any description belonging to the Plantation shall be willfully or through negligence destroyed or injured, the value of the Articles so destroyed, shall be deducted from the portion of the Crops which the person or persons, so offending, shall be entitled to receive under this Contract.

Any deviations from the condition of the foregoing Contract may, upon sufficient proof, be punished with dismissal from the Plantation, or in such other manner as may be determined by the Provost Court; and the person or persons so dismissed, shall forfeit the whole, or a part of his, her or their portion of the crop, as the Court may decide.

In consideration of the foregoing Services duly performed, Mrs.Allston agrees, after deducting Seventy five bushels of Corn for each work Animal, exclusively used in cultivating the Crops for the present year; to turn over to the said Freedmen and Women, one half of the remaining Corn, Peas, Potatoes, made this season. He [sic] further agrees to furnish the usual rations until the Contract is performed.

All Cotton Seed Produced on the Plantation is to be reserved for the use of the Plantation. The Freedmen, Women and Children are to be treated in a manner consistent with their freedom. Necessary medical attention will be furnished as heretofore.

Any deviation from the conditions of this Contract upon the part of the said Mrs.Allston or her Agent or Agents shall be punished in such manner as may be determined by a Provost Court, or a Military Commission. This agreement to continue till the first day of January 1866.

Witness our hand at The Upper Quarters this 28th day of July 1865.

their old slave cabin and drag it to their plot, as far from the Big House as possible. Sharecroppers received seed, fertilizer, implements, food, and clothing. In return, the landlord (or a local merchant) told them what and how much to grow, and he took a share—usually half—of the harvest. The croppers' half usually went to pay for goods bought on credit from the landlord. Thus, sharecroppers remained tied to the land.

Tenant farmers had only slightly more independence. Before a harvest, they promised to sell their crop to a local merchant in return for renting land, tools, and other necessities. From the merchant's store they also had to buy goods on credit (at higher prices than whites paid) against the harvest. At "settling up" time, income from sale of the crop was compared to accumulated debts. It was possible, especially after an unusually bountiful season, to come out ahead and

eventually to own one's own land. But tenants rarely did; in debt at the end of each year, they had to pledge the next year's crop. With world cotton prices low, big landowners generated profits through large-scale operations, and their tenants rarely made much money. If tenants were able to pay their debts, landowners frequently altered loan agreements. Thus, debt peonage replaced slavery, ensuring a continuing cheap labor supply to grow cotton and other staples.

Despite this bleak picture, painstaking, industrious work by African Americans helped many to accumulate a measure of income, personal property, and autonomy, especially in the household economy of producing eggs, butter, meat, food crops, and other staples. Debt did not necessarily mean a lack of subsistence living. In Virginia the declining tobacco crop forced white planters to sell off small parcels of land to blacks. Throughout the

Sharecroppers and tenant farmers, though more autonomous than contract gang laborers, remained dependent on the landlord for their survival. Yet how different is this from the photograph at the top of p. 390? What are the differences, and how do you explain the change?

(Brown Brothers)

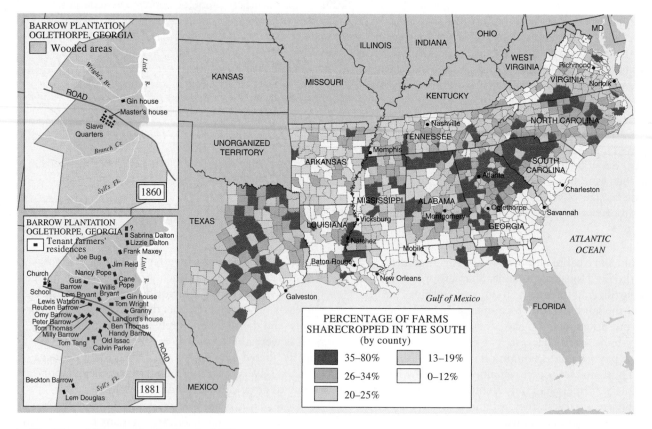

The Rise of Tenancy in the South, 1880

Although no longer slaves and after resisting labor contracts and the gang system of field labor, the freedpeople (as well as many poor whites) became tenant farmers, working on shares in the New South. The former slaves on the Barrow plantation in Georgia, for example, moved their households to individual 25-to 30-acre tenant farms, which they rented from the Barrow family in annual contracts requiring payment in cotton and other cash crops. Where was the highest percentage of tenant farms, and how do you explain it? How would you explain the low-percentage areas? What do you notice about how circumstances have changed—and not changed—on the Barrow plantation?

South, a few African Americans became independent landowners—about 3–4 percent by 1880, but closer to 25 percent by 1900.

White Farmers

Changes in southern agriculture affected yeoman and poor white farmers as well, and planters worried about a coalition between poor black and white farmers. As a white Georgia farmer said in 1865, "We should tuk the land, as we did the niggers, and split it, and giv part to the niggers and part to me and t'other Union fellers." But confiscation and redistribution of land was no more likely for white farmers than for blacks. Whites, too, had to concentrate on growing staples, pledging their crops against high-interest credit, and facing perpetual indebtedness. In the upcountry piedmont area of Georgia, for example, the number of whites working their own land dropped from nine in ten before the Civil War to seven in ten by 1880, while cotton production doubled.

Reliance on cotton meant fewer food crops and therefore greater dependence on merchants for provisions. In 1884, Jephta Dickson of Jackson County, Georgia, purchased more than $50 worth of flour, meal, meat, syrup, peas, and corn from a local store; 25 years earlier he had been almost completely self-sufficient. Fencing laws seriously curtailed the livelihood of poor whites raising pigs and hogs, and restrictions on hunting and fishing reduced the ability of poor whites and blacks alike to supplement incomes and diets.

In the worn-out flatlands and barren mountainous regions of the South, poor whites' antebellum poverty, health, and isolation worsened after the war. A Freedmen's Bureau agent in South Carolina described the poor whites in his area as "gaunt and ragged, ungainly, stooping and clumsy in build." They lived a marginal existence, hunting, fishing, and growing corn and potato crops that, as a North Carolinian put it, "come up puny, grow puny, and mature puny." Many poor white farmers, in fact, were even less productive than black sharecroppers. Some became farmhands at $6 a month (with board). Others fled to low-paying jobs in cotton mills, where they would not have to compete against blacks.

The cultural life of poor southern whites reflected both their lowly position and their pride. Their emotional religion centered on camp meeting religious revivals where, in backwoods clearings, men and women praised God, told tall tales of superhuman feats, and exchanged folk remedies for poor health. Their ballads and folklore told of debt, chain gangs, and deeds of drinking prowess. Their quilt making and house construction reflected a marginal culture in which everything was saved and reused.

In part because their lives were so hard, poor whites clung to their belief in white superiority. Many joined the Ku Klux Klan (founded by six Confederate veterans) and other southern white terrorist groups that emerged between 1866 and 1868. A federal officer reported, "The poorer classes of white people...have a most intense hatred of the Negro." Actually populated by a cross-section of southern white classes, the Klan expressed its hatred in midnight raids on teachers in black schools, laborers who disputed their landlords' discipline, Republican voters, and any black whose "impudence" caused him not to "bow and scrape to a white man, as was done formerly."

Black Self-Help Institutions

Victimized by Klan intimidation and violence, African Americans found their hopes and dreams thwarted. A Texan, Felix Haywood, recalled: "We thought we was goin' to be richer than white folks, 'cause we was stronger and knowed how to work.... But it didn't turn out that way. We soon found out that freedom could make folks proud but it didn't make 'em rich." It was clear to many black leaders, therefore, that because white institutions could not fulfill the promises of emancipation, blacks would have to do it themselves.

Traditions of black community self-help survived in the organized churches and schools of the antebellum free Negro communities and in the "invisible" cultural institutions of the slave quarters. After the Civil War, the membership in African American churches exploded. The Negro Baptist Church grew from 150,000 members in 1850 to 500,000 in 1870, while the membership of the African Methodist Episcopal Church increased fourfold in the postwar decade, from 100,000 to more than 400,000 members. Similar growth occurred in the Reformed Zion Union Apostolic and other churches.

African American ministers continued to exert community leadership. Many led efforts to oppose discrimination, some by entering politics: more than one-fifth of the black officeholders in South Carolina were ministers. As preachers, however, they focused on sin, salvation, and revivalist enthusiasm. An English visitor in 1867–1868 noted the intensity of black "devoutness." As one woman explained: "We make noise 'bout ebery ting.... I want ter go ter Heaben in de good ole way."

The freedpeople's desire for education was as strong as for religion. A school official in Virginia said that the freedmen were "down right crazy to learn"; another said that blacks were "determined to be self-taught." At first, most teachers were northern "schoolmarms." One Yankee teacher, Esther Douglass, found "120 dirty, half naked, perfectly wild black children" in her schoolroom near Savannah. After eight months she reported, "their progress was wonderful"; they

Along with land of their own and equal civil rights, what freedpeople wanted most was education. What do you see in the faces (and dress) of these school children? Why was education so important? What obstacles were in the way?

(Valentine Museum, Richmond, Virginia)

could read, sing hymns, and repeat Bible verses. Such glowing reports waned as white (and black) teachers grew frustrated with crowded facilities, limited resources, white opposition, and high absenteeism caused by fieldwork. In Georgia, for example, only 5 percent of black children went to school for part of any one year between 1865 and 1870, as opposed to 20 percent of white children.

Blacks increasingly preferred their own teachers, and assumed more responsibility for the costs of schooling. By 1868, 43 percent of Freedmen's Bureau teachers were black, and in Louisiana and Kentucky blacks contributed more to education than the Bureau itself. Moreover, black teachers were consistently positive. Charlotte Forten, who taught in the Sea Islands, noted that even after a half day's "hard toil" in the fields, her older pupils were "as bright and as anxious to learn as ever." Despite the taunting insults of "the haughty Anglo-Saxon race," she said, blacks showed "a desire for knowledge, and a capability for attaining it." To train teachers such as Forten, northern philanthropists founded Fisk, Howard, Atlanta, and other black universities in the South between 1865 and 1867.

By 1870 there was a 20 percent gain in black adult literacy, a figure that, against difficult odds, would continue to grow for all ages to the end of the century, when more than 1.5 million black children attended schools with 28,560 black teachers. African American schools, like churches, became community centers. They published newspapers, provided training in trades and farming, and promoted political participation and land ownership with increasingly scientific methods of farming. These efforts made black schools objects of local white hostility. A Virginia freedman told a congressional committee that in his county, anyone starting a school would be killed. In 1869, in Tennessee alone, 37 black schools were burned to the ground.

White opposition to black education and land ownership stimulated African American nationalism and separatism. In the late 1860s, Benjamin "Pap" Singleton, a former Tennessee slave, urged freedpeople to abandon politics and migrate westward. He organized a land company, purchased public property in Kansas, and in the early 1870s took several groups from Tennessee and Kentucky to establish separate black towns in the prairie state. In following years, thousands of "exodusters" from the Lower South bought some 10,000 infertile acres in Kansas. But natural and human obstacles to self-sufficiency often proved insurmountable. By the 1880s, despairing of ever finding economic independence in the United States, Singleton and other nationalists advocated emigration to Canada and Liberia. Other black leaders such as Frederick Douglass continued to press for full citizenship rights within the United States.

Reconstruction in the Southern States

Douglass's confidence in the power of the ballot seemed warranted in the enthusiastic early months under the Reconstruction Acts of 1867. With President Johnson neutralized, the Republican congressional program finally prevailed. Local Republicans, taking advantage of the inability or refusal of many southern whites to vote, overwhelmingly elected their delegates to state constitutional conventions in the fall of 1867. Guardedly optimistic and sensing the "sacred importance" of their work, black and white Republicans began creating new state governments.

Republican Rule

Contrary to early twentieth-century pro-southern historians, the southern state governments under Republican rule were not dominated by illiterate black majorities intent on "Africanizing" the South. Nor were these governments unusually corrupt or extravagant, nor did they use massive numbers of federal troops to enforce their will. By 1869, only 1,100 federal soldiers remained in Virginia, and most federal troops in Texas were guarding the frontier against Mexico and hostile Native Americans. Lacking strong military backing, the new state governments would face increasingly violent harassment.

Diverse coalitions made up the new governments elected under congressional Reconstruction. These "black and tan" governments (as opponents called them) were actually predominantly white, except for the lower house of the South Carolina legislature. Many of the new leaders were local people interested more in economic growth and sectional reconciliation than in radical social reforms. A second group consisted of northern Republican capitalists who headed south to invest in land, railroads, and new industries. Others included Union veterans, missionaries, and teachers inspired to work in Freedmen's Bureau schools. Such people were unfairly labeled "carpetbaggers."

Moderate African Americans made up a third group in the Republican state governments. A large percentage of black officeholders were well-educated preachers, teachers, and soldiers from the North. Others were self-educated southern black tradesmen and landowners. In South Carolina, of some 255 black state and federal officials elected between 1868 and 1876, only 15 percent owned no property. This class composition meant that black leaders often supported policies that largely ignored the land redistribution needs of the black masses. African American leaders reminded whites that they too were southerners, seeking only, as an 1865 petition put it, that "the same laws which govern white men shall govern black men…in equity and justice."

The primary accomplishment of Republican rule in the South was to eliminate undemocratic features from prewar state constitutions. All returning states provided universal male suffrage and loosened requirements for holding office. Laws were enacted ending imprisonment for debt, shortening the list of crimes punishable by death, relieving poverty, and caring for

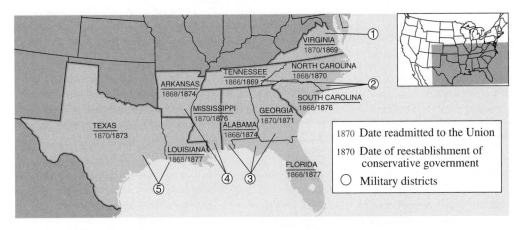

The Return of Conservative Democratic Control in Southern States During Reconstruction

Note that the duration of Republican governments in power to implement even moderate Reconstruction programs varied from state to state. In North Carolina and Georgia, for example, Republican rule was very brief, while in Virginia it never took place at all. "Redemption," the return of conservative control, took longest in three Deep South states. How would you explain these variations among the southern states?

the disabled. Many southern states passed laws granting property rights to married women.

Republican governments also reconstructed the South financially by overhauling tax systems and approving generous railroad and other capital investment bonds. Harbors, roads, and bridges were rebuilt; hospitals and asylums were established; and the South's first public school system was created. Although these schools were largely segregated, for the first time, rich and poor, black and white alike had access to education. By the 1880s, school attendance increased from 5 percent to more than 40 percent for blacks and from 20 percent to more than 60 percent for whites.

These modernizing achievements came in the face of strong opposition. A convention of Louisiana planters labeled the Republican leaders the "lowest and most corrupt body of men ever assembled in the South." There was some corruption, mostly in land sales, railway bonds, and construction contracts. But this was similar to corruption in postwar northern politics.

Despite—or perhaps because of—the modest black role in southern state governments, which Du Bois described as "negro honesty, knowledge, and efficiency," Republican rule was short-lived. It lasted longest in the Deep South, where the black population was equal to or greater than the white. In Virginia, Republicans ruled hardly at all. In South Carolina, African American leaders' unwillingness to use their power to help black laborers contributed to their loss of political control. In Alabama a flood of northern capital created a new industrial and merchant class to rival the old planter aristocracy. And in Louisiana, class divisions among blacks and white paramilitary violence, which led to the killing of 60 blacks at Colfax in 1873, without judicial consequences, seriously weakened the Republican regime.

Violence and "Redemption"

The primary reason for the return of Democrats to power in southern states was the widespread use of violence. A Mississippi paper said, "We must render this either a white man's government, or convert the land into a Negro man's cemetery." The Ku Klux Klan was only one of several secret terrorist organizations that forcibly drove black and white Republicans from office. Although violence was pervasive throughout the South, North Carolina and Mississippi typified the pattern.

After losing a close election in North Carolina in 1868, conservatives waged a concentrated campaign of terror in several areas of strong Unionist support. If the Democrats could win these counties in 1870, they would most likely win statewide. Before the election, several prominent Republicans were killed, including a white state senator, whose throat was cut, and a leading

black Union League organizer, who was hanged in the courthouse square with a sign pinned to his breast: "Bewar, ye guilty, both white and black." Scores of citizens were flogged, fired from their jobs, or driven in the middle of the night from burning homes and barns. Courts consistently refused to prosecute anyone for these crimes, which local papers blamed on "disgusting negroes and white Radicals." The violence worked. In the election of 1870, some 12,000 fewer Republicans voted in the two crucial counties than had voted two years earlier, and the Democrats swept back into power.

In Mississippi's state election in 1875, Democrats used similar tactics, including death threats, in what became known as the "Mississippi Plan." Local Democratic clubs formed armed militias, marching defiantly through black areas, breaking up Republican meetings, and provoking riots to justify killing hundreds. Armed men posted during voter registration intimidated Republicans. At the election itself, voters were either "helped" by gun-toting whites to cast a Democratic ballot, or chased away by clubs. Counties that had given Republican majorities in the thousands managed a total of less than a dozen votes in 1875.

Congress and President Grant did not totally ignore southern violence. Three Force Acts, passed in 1870 and 1871, had given the president strong powers to protect voters from force or fraud, but were rarely used. A Ku Klux Klan Act had declared secret organizations using disguise and coercion to deprive others of equal protection of the laws illegal, and Congress created a joint committee to investigate Klan violence. Its 1872 report had filled 13 huge volumes with horrifying testimony. Grant sent messages to Congress proclaiming the right to vote, and dispatched troops to South Carolina, but not to Mississippi, to stop violence against black Republicans.

Calling their victory "redemption," conservative Democrats resumed control of each state government. Reconstruction ended by a combination of persistent white southern resistance, violence and coercion, and a failure of northern will. As Albion Tourgée wrote, in his Reconstruction-era novel, "The spirit of the dead Confederacy was stronger than the mandate of the nation to which it had succumbed in battle."

Northern Republicans lost interest in defending African Americans, and realized that they could keep political power without black votes. In 1875, Grant's advisers told him that Republicans might lose an important Ohio election unless he rejected appeals by Mississippi blacks for troops to guarantee free elections. He did so, saying that he and the nation "had tired of these annual autumnal outbreaks." The success of the Democrats' Mississippi Plan in 1875, repeated a year later in South Carolina and Louisiana, indicated that congressional reports and acts and presidential proclamations did little to stop the reign of

Recovering the Past

NOVELS

We read novels and other forms of fiction for pleasure, that is, for the enjoyment of plot, character development, style, symbolism, and timeless themes. "Classic" novels such as *Moby Dick, Huckleberry Finn, The Great Gatsby, The Invisible Man,* and *Beloved* explore enduring questions of good and evil, of innocence and knowledge, of noble dreams fulfilled and shattered. We enjoy novels because we often find ourselves identifying with one of the major characters. Through that person's struggles, triumphs, relationships, and search for identity, we gain insights about our own.

Even though they may be historically untrue, we can also read novels as social history, for they reveal much about the attitudes, dreams, fears, and ordinary, everyday experiences of human beings in a particular period. They show how people responded to the major events of that era. The novelist, like the historian, is a product of time and place and has an interpretive point of view. Consider the two novels about Reconstruction quoted here. Neither is reputed for great literary merit, yet both reveal much about the impassioned attitudes of the post–Civil War era. *A Fool's Errand* was written by Albion Tourgée, a northerner, while *The Clansman* was written by Thomas Dixon, Jr., a southerner.

Tourgée was a young northern teacher and lawyer who fought with the Union army and moved to North Carolina after the war to begin a legal career. He became a judge and was an active Republican, supporting black suffrage and helping to shape the new state constitution. Because he boldly criticized the Ku Klux Klan for its campaign of terror against blacks, his life was threatened many times. When he left North Carolina in 1879, he published an autobiographical novel about his experiences as a judge challenging Klan violence against the freedpeople.

The "fool's errand" in the novel is that of the northern veteran Comfort Servosse, who, like Tourgée, seeks to fulfill humane goals on behalf of both blacks and whites in post–Civil War North Carolina. His efforts are thwarted, however, by threats, intimidation, a campaign of violent "outrages" against Republican leaders in the county, and a lack of support from Congress. Historians have verified the accuracy of many of the events in Tourgée's novel. While exposing the brutality of the Klan, Tourgée features loyal southern Unionists, respectable planters ashamed of Klan violence, and even guilt-ridden, poor white Klansmen who try to protect or warn intended victims.

In the year of Tourgée's death, 1905, another North Carolinian published a novel with a very different account of Reconstruction. Thomas Dixon, Jr., was a lawyer, North Carolina state legislator, Baptist minister, pro-Klan lecturer, and novelist. *The Clansman,* subtitled *A Historical Romance of the Ku Klux Klan,* reflects turn-of-the-century attitudes most white southerners still had about Republican rule during Reconstruction. According to Dixon, once the "Great Heart" Lincoln was gone, a power-crazed, vindictive, radical Congress, led by scheming Austin Stoneman (Thaddeus Stevens), sought to impose corrupt carpetbagger and brutal black rule on a helpless South. Only through the inspired leadership and redemptive role of the Ku Klux Klan was the South saved from the horrors of rape and revenge.

Dixon dedicated *The Clansman* to his uncle, who was a Grand Titan of the Klan in North Carolina during the time when two crucial counties were being transformed from Republican to Democratic through intimidation and terror. No such violence shows up in Dixon's novel. When the novel was made the basis of D. W. Griffith's film classic *Birth of a Nation* in 1915, the novel's attitudes were firmly imprinted on the twentieth-century American mind.

Both novels convey Reconstruction attitudes toward the freedpeople. Both create clearly defined heroes and villains. Both include exciting chase scenes, narrow escapes, daring rescues, and tragic deaths. Both include romantic subplots. Yet the two novels are strikingly different.

Reflecting on the Past Even in these brief excerpts, what differences of style and attitude do you see in the descriptions of Uncle Jerry and Old Aleck? What emotional responses do you have to these passages? How do you think turn-of-the-twentieth-century Americans might have responded?

A FOOL'S ERRAND   ALBION TOURGÉE (1879)

When the second Christmas came, Metta wrote again to her sister:

"The feeling is terribly bitter against Comfort on account of his course towards the colored people. There is quite a village of them on the lower end of the plantation. They have a church, a sabbath school, and are to have next year a school. You can not imagine how kind they have been to us, and how much they are attached to Comfort. . . . I got Comfort to go with me to one of their prayer-meetings a few nights ago. I had heard a great deal about them, but had never attended one before. It was strangely weird. There were, perhaps, fifty present, mostly middle-aged men and women. They were singing in a soft, low monotone, interspersed with prolonged exclamatory notes, a sort of rude hymn, which I was surprised to know was one of their old songs in slave times. How the chorus came to be endured in those days I can not imagine. It was

'Free! free! free, my Lord, free!
An' we walks de hebben-ly way!'

"A few looked around as we came in and seated ourselves; and Uncle Jerry, the saint of the settlement, came forward on his staves, and said, in his soft voice,

"'Ev'nin', Kunnel! Sarvant, Missus! Will you walk up, an' hev seats in front?'

"We told him we had just looked in, and might go in a short time; so we would stay in the back part of the audience.

"Uncle Jerry can not read nor write; but he is a man of strange intelligence and power. Unable to do work of any account, he is the faithful friend, monitor, and director of others. He has a house and piece of land, all paid for, a good horse and cow, and, with the aid of his wife and two boys, made a fine crop this season. He is one of the most promising colored men in the settlement: so Comfort says, at least. Everybody seems to have great respect for his character. I don't know how many people I have heard speak of his religion. Mr. Savage used to say he had rather hear him pray than any other man on earth. He was much prized by his master, even after he was disabled, on account of his faithfulness and character."

THE CLANSMAN

THOMAS DIXON, JR. (1905)

At noon Ben and Phil strolled to the polling-place to watch the progress of the first election under Negro rule. The Square was jammed with shouting, jostling, perspiring negroes, men, women, and children. The day was warm, and the African odour was supreme even in the open air....

The negroes, under the drill of the League and the Freedmen's Bureau, protected by the bayonet, were voting to enfranchise themselves, disfranchise their former masters, ratify a new constitution, and elect a legislature to do their will. Old Aleck was a candidate for the House, chief poll-holder, and seemed to be in charge of the movements of the voters outside the booth as well as inside. He appeared to be omnipresent, and his self-importance was a sight Phil had never dreamed. He could not keep his eyes off him....

[Aleck] was a born African orator, undoubtedly descended from a long line of savage spell-binders, whose eloquence in the palaver houses of the jungle had made them native leaders. His thin spindle-shanks supported an oblong, protruding stomach, resembling an elderly monkey's, which seemed so heavy it swayed his back to carry it.

The animal vivacity of his small eyes and the flexibility of his eyebrows, which he worked up and down rapidly with every change of countenance, expressed his eager desires....

He was already mellow with liquor, and was dressed in an old army uniform and cap, with two horse-pistols buckled around his waist. On a strap hanging from his shoulder were strung a half-dozen tin canteens filled with whiskey.

terror against black and white Republicans throughout the South. Despite hundreds of arrests, all-white juries refused to find whites guilty of crimes against blacks. The U.S. Supreme Court backed them in two 1874 decisions throwing out cases against whites convicted of preventing blacks from voting and declaring key parts of the Force Acts unconstitutional. Officially the Klan's power ended, but the attitudes (and tactics) of Klansmen would continue long into the next century.

Shifting National Priorities

The American people in the North, like their leaders, were tired of battles over freedpeople. Frustrated with the difficulties of trying to transform an unwilling South, the easiest course was to give citizenship and the vote to African Americans, leaving them to fend for themselves. Americans of increasing ethnic diversity were primarily interested in starting families, finding work, and making money. Slovakian immigrants fired furnaces in Pittsburgh; Chinese men pounded in railroad ties for the Central Pacific over the Sierra Nevada mountains and across the Nevada desert; Yankee women taught in one-room schoolhouses in Vermont for $23 a month; Mexican *vaqueros* drove Texas cattle herds to Kansas; and Scandinavian families battled heat, locusts, and exorbitant railroad rates on Dakota farmsteads.

American priorities had shifted at both the individual and national levels. Failing to effect a smooth transition from slavery to freedom for freedpeople, northern leaders focused their efforts on accelerating and solidifying their programs of economic growth and industrial and territorial expansion.

As North Carolina Klansmen convened in dark forests in North Carolina in 1869, the Central Pacific and Union Pacific railroads met in Utah, linking the Atlantic and Pacific. As southern cotton production revived, northern iron and steel manufacturing and western settlement of the mining, cattle, and agricultural

How "free" is this voter? In this cartoon, titled "Of course he wants to vote the Democratic Ticket," one of the two pistol-wielding men is saying: "You're as free as air, ain't you? Say you are, or I'll blow your black head off!" Note that another freedman is being led down the street to the polling place. Do you think he will also vote Democratic or for the party of Lincoln?

(CORBIS)

frontiers surged. As black farmers haggled over work contracts with landowners in Georgia, white workers organized the National Labor Union in Baltimore. As Elizabeth and Adele Allston demanded the keys to their crop barns in the summer of 1865, the Boston Labor Reform Association demanded that "our…education, morals, dwellings, and the whole Social System" needed to be "reconstructed." If the South would not be reconstructed, labor relations might be.

The years between 1865 and 1875 featured not only the rise (and fall) of Republican governments in the South but also a spectacular surge of working-class organizations. Stimulated by the Civil War to improve working conditions in northern factories, trade unions and labor reform associations flourished, culminating in the founding of the National Labor Union in 1866. By 1873, an estimated 300,000 to 500,000 American workers enrolled in some 1,500 trade unions, the largest such increase in the nineteenth century. This growth inevitably stirred class tensions. In 1876, hundreds of freedmen in the rice region along the Combahee River in South Carolina went on strike to protest a 40-cent-per-day wage cut, clashing with local sheriffs and white Democratic rifle clubs. A year later, also fighting wage cuts, thousands of northern railroad workers went out in a nationwide wave of strikes, clashing with police and the National Guard.

As economic relations in America changed, so did the Republican party, changing from a party of moral reform to material interest. In the ongoing struggle in American political values between "virtue and commerce," self-interest was again winning. Abandoning

the Freedmen's Bureau as an inappropriate federal expense, Republican politicians had no difficulty handing out huge grants of money and land to the railroads. As freedpeople were told to fend for themselves, the Union Pacific was given subsidies of between $16,000 and $48,000 for each mile of track it laid. As Susan B. Anthony and other suffragists tramped through the snows of upstate New York petitioning for the right to vote, Boss Tweed and other urban bosses defrauded New York taxpayers of millions of dollars. As Native Americans in the Great Plains struggled to preserve the sacred Black Hills from gold prospectors protected by U.S. soldiers, government officials in the East "mined" public treasuries.

By 1869, the year financier Jay Gould almost cornered the gold market, the nation was increasingly defined by its sordid, materialistic "go-getters." Henry Adams, descendant of two presidents, was living in Washington, D.C., at the time. As he explained in his 1907 autobiography *The Education of Henry Adams,* he had had high expectations in 1869 that Grant, like George Washington, would restore moral order and peace. But when Grant announced his cabinet, a group of army cronies and rich friends to whom he owed favors, Adams felt betrayed, charging that Grant's administration "outraged every rule of decency."

Honest himself, Grant showed poor judgment of others. The scandals of his administration touched his relatives, his cabinet, and two vice presidents. Outright graft, loose prosecution, and generally negligent administration flourished in a half dozen

Under a caption quoting a Democratic party newspaper, "This is a white man's government," this Thomas Nast cartoon from 1868 shows three white groups (stereotyped as apelike northern Irish workers, unrepentant former Confederates, and rich northern capitalist Democrats) joining hands to bring Republican Reconstruction to an end almost before it began. They stand on the back of a black Union soldier still clutching the flag and reaching in vain for a ballot box. What is each standing figure holding in his hands? What else do you see here? What's in the background? No single image better captures the story of the end of Reconstruction.

(*Harper's Weekly,* September 5, 1868/The Granger Collection, New York)

departments. The Whiskey Ring affair, for example, cost the public millions of dollars in lost tax revenues siphoned off to government officials. Gould's gold scam received the unwitting aid of Grant's Treasury Department and the knowing help of the president's brother-in-law.

Nor was Congress pure. Crédit Mobilier, a dummy corporation supposedly building the transcontinental railroad, received generous bonds and contracts in exchange for giving congressmen gifts of money, stocks, and railroad lands. An Ohio congressman described the House of Representatives in 1873 as an "auction room where more valuable considerations were disposed of under the speaker's hammer than any place on earth."

The election of 1872 showed that the public was uninterested in reform. "Liberal" Republicans, disgusted with Grant, formed a third party calling for lower tariffs and fewer grants to railroads, civil service reform, and the removal of federal troops from the South. Their candidate, Horace Greeley, editor of the New York *Tribune,* was also nominated by the Democrats, whom he had spent much of his earlier career condemning. Despite his wretched record, Grant easily won a second term.

The End of Reconstruction

Soon after Grant's second inauguration, a financial panic, caused by railroad mismanagement and the collapse of some eastern banks, started a terrible depression that lasted throughout the mid-1870s. In these hard times, economic issues dominated politics, further diverting attention from southern blacks. As Democrats took control of the House of Representatives in 1874 and looked toward winning the White House in 1876, politicians talked about the latest Grant scandals, the currency, and tariffs, but no one said much about freedpeople. In 1875, Congress passed a civil rights bill but it was not enforced, and in 1883 the Supreme Court declared it unconstitutional. Congressional Reconstruction, long dormant, was over.

The election of 1876, closest in American history until 2000, sealed the end. Republicans nominated a former governor of Ohio, Rutherford B. Hayes, partly because of his reputation for honesty, partly because he had been a Union officer (a necessity for post–Civil War candidates), and partly because, as Henry Adams put it, he was "obnoxious to no one." The Democrats chose Governor Samuel J. Tilden of New York, a civil service reformer who had broken the corrupt Tweed ring.

Like Al Gore in 2000, Tilden won a popular-vote majority and appeared to have enough electoral votes (184 to 165) for victory—except for 20 disputed votes, all but one in three Deep South states (one of them Florida) where Republicans still controlled the voting apparatus despite Democratic intimidation. To settle the dispute, Congress created a commission of eight Republicans and seven Democrats who voted along party lines to give Hayes all 20 votes and a narrow electoral-college victory, 185 to 184.

Outraged Democrats protested the outcome and threatened to prevent Hayes's inauguration. There was talk of a new civil war. But unlike the 1850s, a North–South compromise emerged. Northern investors wanted the government to subsidize a New Orleans-to-California railroad. Southerners wanted northern dollars but not northern political influence—no social agencies, no federal enforcement of the Fourteenth and Fifteenth Amendments, and no military occupation, not even the symbolic presence left in 1876.

Timeline

1865	Civil War ends
	Lincoln assassinated; Andrew Johnson becomes president
	Johnson proposes general amnesty and Reconstruction plan
	Racial confusion, widespread hunger, and demobilization
	Thirteenth Amendment ratified
	Freedmen's Bureau established
1865–1866	Black Codes
	Repossession of land by whites; freedpeople work contracts
1866	Freedmen's Bureau renewed and Civil Rights Act passed over Johnson's veto
	Ku Klux Klan formed
1867	Reconstruction Acts passed over Johnson's veto
	Impeachment controversy
	Freedmen's Bureau ends
1868	Fourteenth Amendment ratified
	Ulysses Grant elected president
1868–1870	Ten states readmitted under congressional plan
1869	Georgia and Virginia reestablish Democratic party control
1870	Fifteenth Amendment ratified
1870s–1880s	Black "exodusters" migrate to Kansas
1870–1871	North Carolina and Georgia reestablish Democratic control
1872	Grant reelected president; scandals follow
1874	Alabama and Arkansas reestablish Democratic control
1875	Civil Rights Act passed
	"Mississippi Plan" reestablishes Democratic control
1876	Hayes–Tilden election
1876–1877	South Carolina, Louisiana, and Florida reestablish Democratic control
1877	Compromise of 1877; Rutherford B. Hayes assumes presidency and ends Reconstruction
1880s	Tenancy and sharecropping prevail in the South
	Disfranchisement and segregation of southern blacks begins

As the inauguration approached, these forces of mutual self-interest concluded the "compromise of 1877" in which Hayes was declared president. After his inauguration, he ordered the last federal troops out of the South, sending them west to fight Native Americans; appointed a former Confederate general to his cabinet; supported federal aid for economic and railroad development in the South; and most significantly, promised to let southerners handle race relations themselves. On a goodwill trip to the South, he told blacks that "your rights and interests would be safer if . . . let alone by the general government." The message was clear: Hayes would not enforce the Fourteenth and Fifteenth Amendments, initiating a pattern of governmental inaction and abandonment of African Americans that lasted to the 1960s. But the immediate crisis was averted, officially ending Reconstruction.

Conclusion
A MIXED LEGACY

In the 12 years between Appomattox and Hayes's inauguration, victorious northern Republicans, defeated white southerners, and hopeful black freedpeople each dreamed of goals the others mostly refused to give. Yet each got something. The compromise of 1877 cemented the reunion of South and North, providing new opportunities for economic development in both regions. The Republican party achieved its economic goals and generally held the White House, though not always Congress, until 1932. As ex-Confederate states came back into the Union, southerners retained their grip on southern lands and black labor, though not without struggle and significant changes. The Allstons' freedmen, for example, refused to sign work contracts, even when offered various favors, and in 1869 Adele Allston had to sell much of her lands—to whites.

In 1880, Frederick Douglass wrote: "Our Reconstruction measures were radically defective.... To the freedmen was given the machinery of liberty, but there was denied to them the steam to put it in motion....The old master class...retained the power to starve them to death, and wherever this power is held there is the power of slavery." The wonder, Douglass said, was "not that freedmen have made so little progress, but, rather, that they have made so much; not that they have been standing still, but that they have been able to stand at all."

Freedpeople had made strong gains in education and in economic and family survival. Despite sharecropping and tenancy, black laborers organized themselves to achieve a measure of autonomy and opportunity in their lives. Finally, the three Reconstruction amendments, despite flagrant violation over the next 100 years, held out the promise that the dreams of equal citizenship and democratic political participation would yet be realized.

QUESTIONS FOR REVIEW AND REFLECTION

1. At the end of the Civil War, what were the goals and dreams of defeated southern whites, victorious northerners, and emancipated freedpeople? Can you name three for each group?
2. How did each group pursue its goals and dreams, what resources did each have, and how did they conflict with each other between 1865 and 1877?
3. What differences existed *within* each of the three major groups?
4. What was the relationship between northern presidential and congressional politics and southern daily life and race relations during Reconstruction?
5. What is your assessment of how well American democratic politics and values served the dreams of diverse American peoples in the postwar era?

CHAPTER 17

Rural America: The West and the New South

Ranching in the West
Here a lone cowboy herds cattle. Although novels and movies often romanticize cowboys, their job was far from glamorous or financially rewarding. How would you describe the landscape in this photograph? How does it suggest some of the realities of herding cattle?

(Brown Brothers)

American Stories

Realizing Dreams: Life on the Great Plains

In 1873, Milton Leeper, his wife, Hattie, and their baby, Anna, climbed into a wagon piled high with their possessions and set out to homestead in Boone County, Nebraska. Once on the claim, the Leepers dreamed confidently of their future. Hattie wrote to her sister in Iowa, "I like our place the best of any around here. When we get a fine house and 100 acres under cultivation," she added, "I wouldn't trade with any one." But Milton had broken only 13 acres when disaster struck. Hordes of grasshoppers appeared, and the Leepers fled their claim and took refuge in the nearby town of Fremont.

There they stayed for two years. Milton first worked at a store and then hired out to other farmers. Hattie sewed, kept a boarder, and cared for chickens and a milk cow. The family lived on the brink of poverty but never gave up hope. "Times are hard and we have had bad luck," Hattie acknowledged, but "I am going to hold that claim . . . there will [be] one gal that won't be out of a home." In 1876, the Leepers triumphantly returned to their claim with the modest sum of $27 to help them start over.

The grasshoppers were gone, there was enough rain, and preaching was only half a mile away. The Leepers, like others, began to prosper. Two more daughters were born and cared for in the comfortable sod house—"homely" on the outside but plastered and cozy within. As Hattie explained, the homesteaders lived "just as civilized as they would in Chicago."

Their luck did not last. Hattie, pregnant again, fell ill and died in childbirth along with her infant son. Heartbroken, Milton buried his wife and child and left the claim. The last frontier had momentarily defeated him, although he would try farming in at least four other locations before his death in 1905.

The same year that the Leepers established their Boone County homestead, another family tried their luck in a Danish settlement about 200 miles west of Omaha. Rasmus and Ane Ebbesen and their eight-year-old son, Peter, had arrived in the United States from Denmark in 1868, lured by the promise of an "abundance" of free land "for all willing to cultivate it." By 1870, they had made it as far west as Council Bluffs, Iowa. There they stopped to earn the capital that would be necessary to begin farming. Rasmus dug ditches for the railroad, Ane worked as a cleaning woman in a local boarding-house, and young Peter brought drinking water to thirsty laborers who were digging ditches for the town gas works.

Like the Leepers, the Ebbesens eagerly settled on their homestead and began to cultivate the soil. Peter later recalled that the problems that the family had

anticipated never materialized. Even the rumors that the Sioux, "flying demons" in the eyes of settlers, were on the rampage proved false. The real problems the family faced were unexpected: rattlesnakes, prairie fires, and an invasion of grasshoppers. The grasshoppers were just as devastating to the Ebbesen farm as they had been to the Leeper homestead. But unlike the Leepers, the Ebbesens stayed on the claim. Although the family "barely had enough" to eat, they survived the three years of grasshopper infestation.

In the following years, the Ebbesens thrived. Rasmus had almost all the original 80 acres under cultivation and purchased an additional 80 acres from the railroad. A succession of sod houses rose on the land and finally even a two-story frame house, paid for with money Peter earned teaching school. By the time they were in their 50s, they could look with pride at their "luxurient and promising crop." But once more natural disaster struck: a "violent hailstorm . . . which completely devastated the whole lot."

The Ebbesens were lucky, however. A banker offered to buy them out, although the amount was $1,000 less than what the family calculated as the farm's "real worth." But it was enough for the purchase of a "modest" house in town. Later, there was even a "dwelling of two stories and nine rooms . . . with adjacent park."

The stories of the Leepers and the Ebbesens, though different in their details and endings, hint at some of the problems confronting rural Americans in the last quarter of the nineteenth century. As a mature industrial economy transformed agriculture and shifted the balance of economic power permanently away from America's farmlands to the country's cities and factories, many farmers found it impossible to realize the traditional dream of rural independence and prosperity. Even bountiful harvests no longer guaranteed success. "We were told two years ago to go to work and raise a big crop; that was all we needed," said one farmer. "We went to work and plowed and planted; the rains fell, the sun shone, nature smiled, and we raised the big crop they told us to; and what came of it? Eight cent corn, ten cent oats, two cent beef and no price at all for butter and eggs—that's what came of it." Native Americans also discovered that changes in rural life threatened their values and dreams. As the Sioux leader Red Cloud told railroad surveyors in Wyoming, "We do not want you here. You are scaring away the buffalo."

This chapter explores several of this book's basic themes as it analyzes the agricultural transformation of the late nineteenth century. Highlighting the ways in which rural Americans—red, white, yellow, and black—joined the industrial world, it asks how diverse groups responded to new economic and social conditions. The rise of large-scale agriculture in the West, the exploitation of its natural resources, and the development of the Great Plains form a backdrop for discussing the impact of white settlement on western tribes and assessing how well native peoples were able to preserve their culture and traditions. In an analysis of the South, the efforts of whites to create a "New South" contrast with the underlying realities of race and cotton. Although the chapter shows that most black southerners faced discrimination and economic peonage during this period, it also describes new black protest tactics and ideologies. Finally, the chapter highlights the ways in which agricultural problems of the late nineteenth century, which would persist during the twentieth century, led American farmers to become reformers.

Modernizing Agriculture

Between 1865 and 1900, the nation's farms more than doubled in number as Americans flocked west of the Mississippi. Farmers raised specialized crops with modern machinery and sped them to market over an expanding railroad system. And they became capitalists, and, as one farmer observed, had to "understand farming as a business."

While small family farms still typified American agriculture, vast mechanized operations devoted to one crop appeared, especially west of the Mississippi River. The bonanza farms, established in the late 1870s on the northern plains, symbolized the trend to large-scale agriculture. Thousands of acres in size, these wheat farms required large capital investments; corporations owned many of them. Like factories, they depended on machinery, hired hundreds of workers, and relied on efficient managers. Although bonanza farms were not typical, they dramatized the agricultural changes that were occurring everywhere on a smaller scale.

Despite their success in adapting farming to modern conditions, farmers were slipping from their dominant position in the workforce. In 1860, they represented almost 60 percent of the labor force; by 1900, less than 37 percent of employed Americans farmed. At the same time, farmers' contribution to the nation's wealth declined from one-third to one-quarter.

American Agriculture and the World

The expansion of American agriculture was tied to changing global patterns and demands. During the nineteenth century, the population of Europe exploded. While some Europeans still cultivated the land, increasing numbers abandoned farming for industrial work. In Britain, farmers, only 10 percent of the total workforce, could not produce enough to feed the nation. Like other European countries, Great Britain imported substantial food supplies for its citizens. The growing demand prompted American farmers along with their counterparts in Eastern Europe, Australia, and New Zealand to expand their operations for the European market.

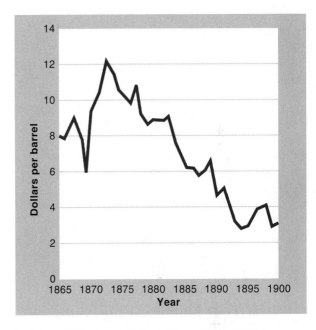

Price of Wholesale Wheat Flour, 1865–1900

The plummeting price of wheat flour was just one indication of the difficulties farmers faced in the late nineteenth century. How much lower was the price of wheat flour in 1900 than in 1865?

Source: U.S. Bureau of the Census.

In efforts to improve crop yields and livestock, American farmers both benefited from and contributed to trends in agriculture elsewhere in the world. German scientists facilitated agricultural expansion after 1850 by developing better seeds, livestock, and chemical fertilizers. The American land-grant university system, established during the Civil War, provided farmers with access to research into and development of better strains of crops and animals and more effective farming methods. For their part, American farmers led the way in using farm machinery such as the horse-drawn harvester, showing agriculturalists in other parts of the world how to raise bigger harvests.

The move toward global integration depended on improved transportation at home and abroad. Reliable, cheap transportation in the United States allowed farmers to specialize: wheat on the Great Plains, corn in the Midwest. Eastern farmers turned to vegetable, fruit, and dairy farming—or sold out. Cotton, tobacco, wheat, and rice dominated in the South, and grain, fruits, and vegetables prevailed in the Far West. The development of steamships and an ever-expanding European network of railroads ensured that American goods and products could move swiftly, efficiently, and cheaply across land and sea to distant markets.

As farmers specialized for national and international markets, their success depended increasingly on outside forces and demands. Bankers and investors, many of them European, provided the capital to improve transportation and expand operations; intermediaries stored and sometimes sold produce; and railroads and steamships carried it to market. A prosperous economy at home and abroad put money into laborers' pockets for food purchases. But when several European countries banned American pork imports between 1879 and 1883, fearing trichinosis, American stock raisers suffered. As Russian, Argentinean, and Canadian farmers turned to wheat cultivation, increased competition in the world market affected the United States' chief cash crop. Moreover, the worldwide deflation of prices for crops such as wheat and corn affected all who raised these crops for the international market, including American farmers.

The Character of American Agriculture

Technological innovation played a major role in facilitating American agricultural expansion. Harvesters, binders, and other new machines, pulled by work animals, diminished much of the drudgery of farming life, making the production of crops easier, more efficient, and cheaper. Moreover, they allowed a farmer to cultivate far more land than was possible with hand tools. But machinery was expensive, and many American farmers borrowed to buy it. In the decade of the 1880s, mortgage indebtedness grew two and a half times as fast as agricultural wealth.

Only gradually did farmers realize the perils of their new situation in the world. Productivity rose 40 percent between 1869 and 1899. But the harvests for crops such as wheat were so large that the domestic market could not absorb them. Foreign competition and deflation further affected steadily declining prices. In 1867, corn sold for 78 cents a bushel; by 1889, it had tumbled to 23 cents. Wheat similarly plummeted from about $2 a bushel in 1867 to only 70 cents a bushel in 1889. Cotton profits also spiraled downward.

Falling prices did not automatically hurt all farmers. Because the supply of money rose more slowly than productivity, all prices declined—by more than half

between the end of the Civil War and 1900 (for a discussion of the money issue, see Chapter 19). Farmers were receiving less for their crops but also paying less for their purchases. But deflation may have encouraged overproduction. To make the same amount of money, many farmers believed they had to raise larger and larger crops. As they did, prices fell even lower. Furthermore, deflation increased the real value of debts. In 1888, it took 174 bushels of wheat to pay the interest on a $2,000 mortgage at 8 percent. By 1895, it took 320 bushels. Falling prices thus affected most negatively farmers in newly settled areas who borrowed heavily to finance their new operations.

The West

In 1893, the young American historian Frederick Jackson Turner addressed historians gathered at Chicago's World's Fair, and his remarks must have startled some of his listeners. The age of the American frontier had ended, Turner declared, pointing to recent census data that suggested the disappearance of vacant land in the West. Although Turner overstated his case (for even in the twentieth century much of the West remained uninhabited), his analysis reflected rapid expansion into the trans-Mississippi West after the Civil War. Between 1870 and 1900, acreage devoted to farming tripled west of the Mississippi, while from 1880 to 1900, the western population grew at a faster rate than that of the nation as a whole.

The Frontier Thesis in National and Global Context

Turner considered the end of the frontier a milestone in the nation's history. The frontier had played a central role, he argued, in shaping the American character and American institutions. Over the course of American history, the struggle to tame the wilderness had changed settlers from Europeans into Americans and created a rugged individualism that "promoted democracy." Turner's thesis, emphasizing the unique nature of the American experience and linking it to the frontier, won many supporters. His interpretation complemented long-held ideas about the exceptional nature of American society and character. It accorded with what many saw as a long struggle to conquer what Turner called the "wilderness."

But the American westward movement was less unusual than Turner suggested. The settlement of the trans-Mississippi West was part of a global pattern that redistributed European populations into new areas of the world. Paralleling their American counterparts, farmers, miners, and ranchers were claiming land in Argentina, Brazil, New Zealand, Australia, Canada, and South Africa. Like Americans, they argued that native occupants had failed to make the land productive, and they used their technological superiority to wrest the land from those they considered backward and inferior. Around the world, many native peoples were facing domination by settler societies or retreating as far away from "civilization" as they could.

Turner's frontier scheme gave the place of honor to the frontier farmer who transformed and civilized the wilderness. Before the Civil War, however, real farmers avoided settling many parts of the West, especially the Great Plains, an area from 200 to 700 miles wide, extending from Canada to Texas. Much of this region, especially beyond the ninety-eighth meridian, had little rain. The absence of trees seemed to symbolize the plains' unsuitability for agriculture.

The Cattleman's West, 1860–1890

While the region of the Great Plains initially discouraged farmers, its grasses provided the foundation for the cattle kingdom. Cattle raising dated back to Spanish mission days, but the commercial cattle frontier was the unanticipated result of the Union's success in separating Texas from Confederate cattle markets. By war's end, millions of longhorns roamed the Texas range. The postwar burst of railroad construction provided the means of turning cattle into dollars. In the late 1860s and 1870s, cowboys herded thousands of longhorns north to towns such as Abilene, Kansas, where they were loaded on trains for Chicago and Kansas City packinghouses.

Ranchers on the Great Plains bought some of the cattle and bred them with Hereford and Angus cows to create cattle acclimatized to severe winters. In the late 1870s and early 1880s, huge ranches arose from eastern Colorado to the Dakotas. Such ventures, many owned by outside investors, paid handsomely. Cattle on the public domain cost owners little but commanded good prices. The cowboys (one-third of them Mexican and black) who herded the steers made meager wages, just enough for a fling at the trail's end.

By the mid-1880s, the first phase of the cattle frontier was ending as farmers moved onto the plains, buying and fencing public lands once used for grazing. But the arrival of farmers was only one factor in the changing cattle frontier. Ranchers overstocked their herds in the mid-1880s. Hungry cattle ate everything in sight, then weakened as grass became scarce. Memorable blizzards followed the very hot summer of 1886. By spring, 90 percent of the cattle were dead. Frantic owners dumped their surviving cattle on the market, getting $8 or less per animal.

Ranchers who survived the disaster adopted new techniques. Experimenting with new breeds, they began to fence in their herds and to feed them grain during the winter. Since consumers were hungering for tender beef, these new methods suited the market. Ranching, like farming, was becoming a modern business.

Farmers on the Great Plains, 1865–1890s

Views of the agricultural possibilities of the Great Plains brightened after the Civil War, with railroads playing a key role in publicizing the region's potential. Now that rail lines crossed the continent, they needed customers, settlers, and freight to make a profit. Along with town boosters and land speculators, also hoping to capitalize on their investments, railroads joined in extravagant promotional campaigns. "This is the sole remaining section of paradise in the western world," promised one newspaper. "All the wild romances of the gorgeous orient dwindle into nothing when compared to the everyday realities of Dakota's progress." Propaganda reached beyond the United States to Scandinavia, Germany, and elsewhere. Dismissing the fear that the plains lacked adequate rainfall, promotional material assured readers that "All that is needed is to plow, plant, and attend to the crops properly; the rains are abundant." Above-average rainfall in the 1880s strengthened the case.

During the first boom period of settlement, from 1879 to the early 1890s, tens of thousands of eager families began farming on the Great Plains. The majority came from Illinois, Iowa, and Missouri. Like the Ebbesens, many others were immigrants, making the Great Plains the second most important destination for foreign immigration. The largest numbers came from Germany, the British Isles, and Canada, but Scandinavians, Czechs, and Poles also arrived. Unlike many migrating to American cities for work, they came with their families and intended to stay.

Some claimed land under the Homestead Act, which granted 160 acres to any family head or adult who lived on the claim for five years or paid $1.25 an acre after six months of residence. Because homestead land was frequently less desirable, however, most settlers bought land from railroads or land companies. Starting up costs were thus higher than the Homestead Act would suggest. Although western land was cheap compared with eastern farmland, a farmer was lucky to buy a good quarter section for under $500. Machinery added another $700. Although some farmers thought leasing rather than buying land made economic sense, many rented only because they lacked capital. In 1880, some 20 percent of the Plains farmers were tenants, and this percentage rose over time.

Late-nineteenth-century industrial innovations helped settlers overcome some the natural obstacles.

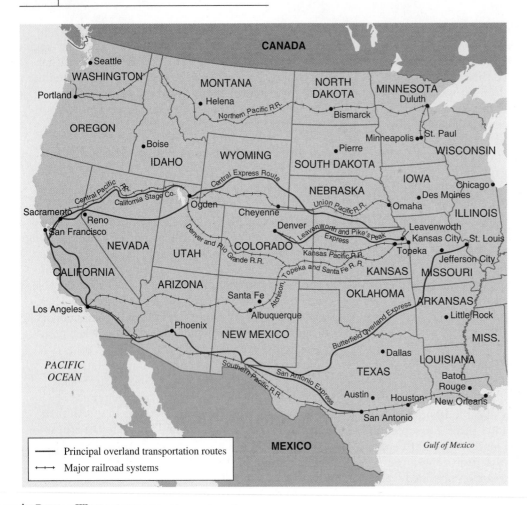

Routes West

On this map, you can trace the various overland routes to the West. How many railroad lines ran across the West? Notice how the railroads contributed to urban growth as trains made their way west. The transcontinental railroads also provided the basis for the economic and demographic expansion and helped to tie East and West together.

The shortage of timber for fencing and housing had encouraged early emigrants to go elsewhere. But in the 1870s, Joseph Glidden developed barbed wire as a cheap alternative to timber fencing. Other innovations met other challenges. Twine binders, which speeded up grain harvesting, reduced the threat of losing crops to the unpredictable weather. And mail-order steel windmills for pumping water from deep underground wells relieved some of the water shortages by the 1890s.

Industrial innovations, however, could not resolve all of the problems confronting Great Plains settlers. Miriam Peckham, a Kansas homesteader, wrote:

> I tell you Auntie no one can depend on farming for a living in this country. Henry is very industrious and this year had in over thirty acres of small grain, 8 acres of corn and about an acre of potatoes. We have sold our small grain...and it come to $100; now deduct $27.00 for cutting, $16.00 for threshing, $19.00 for hired help, say nothing of boarding our help, none of the trouble of drawing

> 25 miles to market and 25 cts on each head for ferriage over the river and where is your profit. I sometimes think this a God forsaken country, the [grass]hopper hurt our corn and we have 1/2 a crop and utterly destroyed our garden. If one wants trials, let them come to Kansas.

This letter highlights the uncertainties of frontier life: high costs, market fluctuations, pests, and natural disasters. Since many plains pioneers took up their homesteads with only a few dollars in their pockets, survival often depended on how well families managed to do during the crucial first years.

The first boom on the Great Plains halted abruptly in the late 1880s and early1890s. Falling prices cut profits. Then, the unusual rainfall that had lured farmers into the semiarid region near the 100th meridian vanished. A devastating drought followed. One farmer reported in 1890 that he had earned $41.48 from his wheat crop, yet his expenses for seed and threshing amounted to $56.00. The destitute survived on boiled

The Wheat Harvest

This 1880 photo highlights the role of machine and animal power rather than human power during the wheat harvest. With more land under cultivation, there was a strong impetus to develop larger and/or more efficient harvesting machines.

(CORBIS)

weeds, a few potatoes, and a little bread and butter. Many lost their farms to creditors. Some stayed on as tenants. Homesteaders like the Leepers gave up. By 1900, two-thirds of homesteaded farms had failed. In western Kansas, the population declined by half between 1888 and 1892 and eastward-bound wagons bore a sad epitaph: "In God We Trusted: In Kansas We Busted."

Both ranching and agriculture had a long-term impact on the region's environment. Ranchers disrupted a complex natural balance when they killed off antelope, elk, wolves, and wildlife. As cattle on overstocked ranges devoured perennial grasses, less nutritious grasses sprang up and, in turn, sometimes disappeared altogether. Lands once a lush home for large herds of cattle turned into deserts of sagebrush, weeds, and dust. Farmers who bought steel windmills to pump water from deep underground depleted the water table level. When they removed sod to build their houses and plowed, they removed the earth's protective covering. Heavy winds, common on the prairies, could lift exposed topsoil and carry it miles away. Deep plowing, essential for dry farming techniques introduced after the drought of the 1880s, worsened the situation. The dust bowl of the 1930s was the eventual outcome of such human interventions.

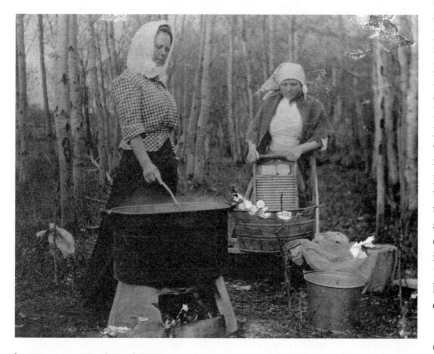

Domestic Work in the West

This photograph shows some of the hard physical labor involved in homesteading. How many steps were involved in doing the family laundry? The clothing of these women, probably settlers in North Dakota, identifies them as immigrants. Their presence reminds us that the West was the home of diverse peoples including Asians, European newcomers, Native Americans, black migrants, and Hispanics whose families had lived in the West for generations.

(The Fred Hulstrand History in Pictures Collection, NDSU, Fargo, ND)

Cornucopia on the Pacific

When gold was discovered in California, Americans rushed west to find it. But as one father told his son, "Plant your lands; these be your best gold fields." He was right; with the completion of a national railroad system, farming became California's greatest asset. But California

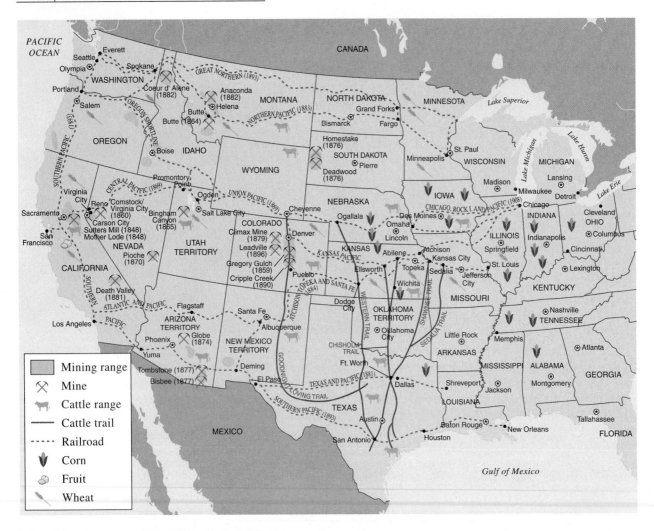

The New Economy of the West, 1850–1893

Describe the areas where corn was an important crop. What states were important wheat producers? Where were the most important mining centers? What areas of the West were involved in ranching?

farming resembled neither the traditional picture of rural life nor the dreams of homesteaders; instead it depended upon railroads, and vast farms using machinery and irrigation to cultivate the land.

Little of California's land was homesteaded or developed as modest family farms. When California entered the Union, speculators acquired much of the property held by Mexican ranchers and sold it at prices beyond the reach of many small farmers. Those small farmers and ranchers who managed to acquire holdings found it hard to compete with large, mechanized operators using cheap migrant laborers, usually Mexican or Chinese. One wheat farm in the San Joaquin Valley was so vast that workers started plowing in the morning at one end of the 17-mile field, ate lunch at its halfway point, and camped at its end that night.

The value of much of California's agricultural land, especially the southern half of the Central Valley, depended on water. By the 1870s, water, land, and

railroad companies, using the labor and expertise of Chinese workers, were taking on the huge costs of building dams, headgates, and canals. They passed on the costs of construction to settlers now eager to acquire hitherto barren lands along with water rights. By 1890, over a quarter of California's farms were irrigated. The irrigation ditches symbolized the importance of technology and a managerial attitude toward the land that characterized late-nineteenth-century agriculture, particularly in California.

Although grain was initially California's most valuable crop, it faced stiff competition from farmers on the plains and in other parts of the world. Some argued that land capable of raising luscious fruits "in a climate surpassing that of Italy, is too valuable for the cultivation of simple cereals." But high railroad rates and lack of refrigeration limited the volume of fresh fruit and vegetables sent to market. As railroad managers in the 1880s realized the potential profit of California

AGRICULTURAL PRODUCTIVITY, 1800–1900

The astonishing gains in the productivity of wheat farmers point to the use of reapers that cut and bound the wheat and thrashers that knocked the grain off the stalks. The combine integrated both operations and also cleared and bagged the grain.

Crop and Productivity Indicator	1800	1840	1880	1900
Wheat				
Worker-hours/acre	56	35	30	15
Yield/acre (bushels)	15	15	13	14
Worker-hours/100 bushels	373	233	152	108
Corn				
Worker-hours/acre	86	69	46	38
Yield/acre (bushels)	25	25	26	26
Worker-hours/100 bushels	344	276	180	147
Cotton				
Worker-hours/acre	185	135	119	112
Yield/acre (bushels)	147	147	179	191
Worker-hours/bale	601	439	318	280

Source: U.S. Bureau of the Census.

produce, they cut rates and introduced refrigerated railroad cars. In June 1888, fresh apricots and cherries successfully survived the trip from California to New York. Fruit and vegetable production rose, benefiting from the agricultural expertise of Chinese laborers, tenant farmers, and Chinese entrepreneurs. So important were their contributions that some have argued that Chinese know-how was mainly responsible for the shift to produce farming. Before long, California fruit was sold as far away as London.

The Mining West

Mining hastened rapid western growth and development. The first and best-known mining rush occurred in 1848 when gold was discovered in California, but others followed as precious metals—silver, iron, copper, coal, lead, zinc, and tin—lured thousands west to Colorado, Montana, Idaho, and Nevada as well as to states such as Minnesota. Mining discoveries were transformative events, for they attracted people and businesses west, often to places far away from agricultural settlements. Hastily built mining communities might be eyesores, but they had bustling urban characters. If and when the strike was over, however, residents abandoned the mining camps and towns as fast as they had rushed into them. The pattern of boom and bust characterized much of mining life.

Cripple Creek, Colorado

This photograph shows the houses and mining buildings at "The Summit," a mining camp at Cripple Creek, Colorado, in the 1880s. How does this picture suggest the impact of mining on the environment? What would it be like to live and work at The Summit?

(Photo by W. E. Hook, Denver Public Library, Western History Collection)

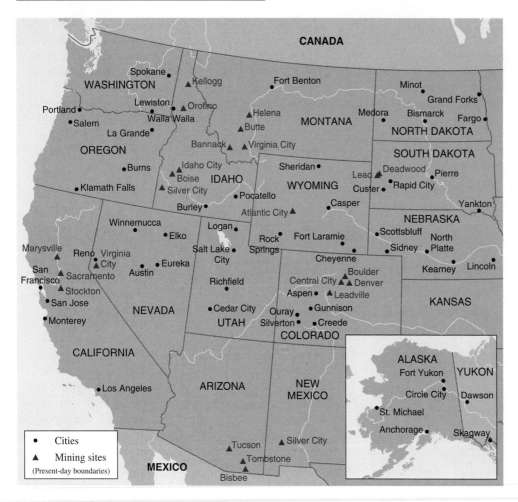

Mining in the West

The map depicts the major areas for mining between 1848 and 1900 as well as some of the important western cities and towns. In what ways did mining stimulate urban growth in the West? What relationships between mining and regional development do you see suggested here?

The reality of late-nineteenth-century mining was nothing like the popular stereotype of the independent miner panning for gold. Retrieving minerals from rock was difficult, expensive, and dangerous, and required a large workforce, industrial tools, and railroad links. Miners worked far below the earth's surface in poorly ventilated tunnels, with no means for removing human or animal waste. Temperatures could reach as high as 120 degrees. Accidents were part of a job that depended on blasting equipment and industrial machinery. In 1884, a Montana miner drilled into an unexploded dynamite charge and lost his eyes and ear. He received no compensation, for the court decided that the accident "was the result of an unforeseen and unavoidable accident incident to the risk of mining." As the next chapter will show, in time, western miners became one of the most radical groups of industrial workers.

Exploiting Natural Resources

Mining was a big business with high costs and a basic dynamic that encouraged rapid and thorough exploitation of the earth's resources. The decimation of the nation's forests went hand in hand with large-scale mining and the railroads' construction. Both railroads and mining depended on wood—railroads for wooden ties, mines for shaft timber and ore reduction. In California, the California State Board of Agriculture estimated in the late 1860s that one-third of the state's forests had already disappeared.

When lumber companies cut down timber, they affected the flow of streams and destroyed the habitat supporting birds and animals. Like the activities of farmers and ranchers, companies that stripped the earth of its forest cover were also contributing to soil erosion. The idea that the public lands belonging to the federal government ought to be rapidly developed supported such exploitation of the nation's natural resources. Often, in return for royalties, the government leased parts of the public domain to companies that hoped to extract valuable minerals, not to own the land permanently. In other cases, companies bought land, but not always legally. In 1878, Congress passed the Timber and Stone Act, which initially applied to Nevada, Oregon, Washington, and California. This legislation allowed the sale of 160-acre parcels of the public domain considered "unfit for cultivation" and "valuable chiefly for timber." Timber companies quickly took advantage of the new law by hiring men willing to register for claims and then to turn them over to timber interests. By the century's end, over 3.5 million acres of the public domain had been acquired under the legislation, and most of it was in corporate hands.

The rapacious and rapid exploitation of resources combined with the increasing pace of industrialization made some Americans uneasy. Many believed that forests stimulated rainfall and that their destruction would adversely affect the climate. Others, like John Muir, lamented the destruction of the country's great natural beauty.

In 1868, Muir came upon the Great Valley of California, "all one sheet of plant gold, hazy and vanishing in the distance…one smooth, continuous bed of honey-bloom." He soon realized, however, that a "wild, restless agriculture" and "flocks of hoofed locusts, sweeping over the ground like a fire" would destroy such loveliness. Muir became a preservation champion. He played a part in the creation of Yosemite National Park in 1890, participated in a successful effort to allow President Benjamin Harrison to classify certain parts of the public domain as forest reserves (the Forest Reserve Act of 1891), and in 1892 established the Sierra Club. At the same time, conservation ideas were also emerging. Gifford Pinchot, who became a leading advocate of these ideas, was less interested in the preservation of the nation's wilderness areas than in careful management of its natural resources. "Conservation," he explained, "means the wise use of the earth and its resources for the lasting good of man." Both perspectives, however, were more popular in the East than in the West, where the seeming abundance of natural resources and the profit motive diminished support.

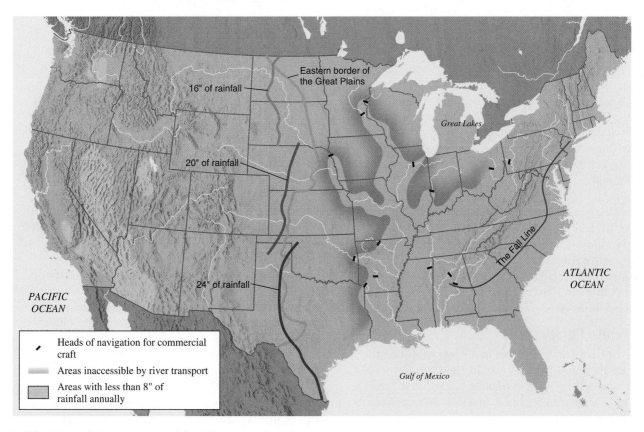

The Natural Environment of the West

Study the patterns of rainfall and the natural features of the West, including rivers and mountain ranges. What do these patterns suggest about native vegetation and the prospects for farming? What is revealed about the role of water and irrigation in the West? What difficulties facing the settlers are revealed?

Resolving the Native American Question

Black Elk, an Oglala Sioux, listened to a story his grandfather had told his father:

> A long time ago…there was once a Lakota [Sioux] holy man, called Drinks Water, who dreamed what was to be…long before the coming of the Wasichus [white men]. He dreamed…that a strange race had woven a spider's web all around the Lakotas. And he said: "When this happens, you shall live in square gray houses, in a barren land, and beside those square gray houses you shall starve."

Black Elk saw this strange dream come true.

As farmers settled the West and became entangled in a national economy, they clashed with the Native American tribes who lived on the land. In California, disease and violence killed 90 percent of the Native American population within 30 years of the gold rush. Elsewhere, the struggle among Native Americans, white settlers, the U.S. Army, and government officials and reformers was prolonged and bitter. Some tribes moved onto government reservations with little protest. But most—including the Nez Percé in the Northwest, the Apache in the Southwest, and the Plains Indians—resisted stubbornly.

Background to the Plains Wars

The lives of most Plains Indians revolved around the buffalo. Increased emigration to California and Oregon in the 1840s and 1850s disrupted tribal pursuits and animal migration patterns. Initially, the federal government tried to persuade the Plains tribes to stay away from white wagon trains and white settlers. The effort did not meet with much success.

During the Civil War, some of the eastern tribes forced to relocate in Oklahoma supported the Confederacy. Others sided with the Union. But after the war, all were branded as "traitors." The federal government callously nullified earlier pledges and treaties, leaving Native Americans defenseless against further incursions on their lands. As settlers pushed into Kansas, the tribes living in Kansas were shunted into Oklahoma.

The White Perspective

When the Civil War ended, red and white people on the Great Plains were already at war. In 1864, the Colorado militia massacred a band of friendly Cheyenne at Sand Creek. Cheyenne, Sioux, and Arapaho soon responded in kind. The Great Plains wars had begun.

Although not all whites condoned this butchery, the congressional commission authorized to make peace viewed Native Americans' future narrowly. The commissioners, including the commander of the army in the West, Civil War hero William T. Sherman, believed that the West belonged to an "industrious, thrifty, and enlightened population" of whites. Native Americans must relocate to western South Dakota or Oklahoma to learn white ways with annuities, food, and clothes to ease their transition to "civilized" life.

At two major conferences in 1867 and 1868, chiefs listened to these drastic proposals to end traditional native life. Some agreed; others, like one Kiowa chief, insisted, "I don't want to settle. I love to roam over the prairies." In any case, the agreements were not binding because no chief had authority to speak for his tribe. For its part, the U.S. Senate delayed approving the treaties. Supplies promised to Indians who settled in the arid reserved areas never materialized, and wildlife proved too sparse to support them. These Indians soon drifted back to their former hunting grounds.

Sherman warned, "All who cling to their old hunting ground are hostile and will remain so till killed off." When persuasion failed, the U.S. Army went to war. "The more we can kill this year," Sherman remarked, "the less will have to be killed the next war." In 1867, he ordered General Philip Sheridan to deal with the tribes. Sheridan introduced winter campaigning, aimed at seeking out Indians who divided into small groups during the winter and exterminating them.

Completion of the transcontinental railroad in 1869 added yet another pressure for "solving" the Indian question. Transcontinental railroads wanted rights-of-way through tribal lands and needed white settlers to make their operations profitable. Few whites considered Native Americans to have any right to lands they wanted.

In his 1872 annual report, the commissioner for Indian affairs, Francis Amasa Walker, addressed two fundamental questions: how to prevent Indians from blocking white migration to the Great Plains, and what to do with them over the long run. Walker suggested buying off the "savages" with promises of food and gifts, luring them onto reservations, and there imposing a "rigid reformatory discipline," necessary because Indians were "unused to manual labor." Though Walker wanted to save the Indians from destruction, he offered only one grim choice: "yield or perish."

The Tribal View

Native Americans defied such attacks on their ancient way of life and protested the wholesale violation of treaties. Black Elk remembered that, in 1863, when he was only three, his father had his leg broken in a fierce battle against the white men. "When I was older," he recalled,

Recovering the Past

MAGAZINES

Weekly and monthly magazines constitute a rich primary source for the historian, offering a vivid picture of the issues of the day and useful insights into popular tastes and values. With advances in the publishing industry and an increasingly literate population, the number of these journals soared in the years following the Civil War. In 1865, only 700 periodicals were published. Twenty years later, there were 3,300. As the

National Magazine grumbled, "Magazines, magazines, magazines! The newsstands are already groaning under the heavy load, and there are still more coming."

Some of these magazines were aimed at the mass market. *Frank Leslie's Illustrated Newspaper,* established in 1855, was one of the most successful. At its height, circulation reached 100,000. Making skillful use of pictures (sometimes as large as

Harper's Weekly delivered powerful messages about the Native Americans in its choice of illustrations.

INDIAN SCOUTS CELEBRATING THE VICTORY OVER BLACK KETTLE. [SKETCHED BY THOS. R. DAVIS]

THE SCALPED HUNTER.—[PHOTOGRAPHED BY WM. S. SOULE.]

two by three feet and folded into the magazine), the weekly covered important news of the day as well as music, drama, sports, and books. Although Leslie relied more heavily on graphics and sensationalism than do modern news weeklies, his publication was a forerunner of *Newsweek* and *Time*.

Another kind of magazine was aimed primarily at middle- and upper-class readers. Editors such as the oft-quoted Edwin Lawrence Godkin of *The Nation,* with a circulation of about 30,000, hoped to influence those in positions of authority and power by providing a forum for the discussion of reform issues. In contrast, *Scribner's* revealed a more conservative, middle-of-the-road point of view. Both magazines, however, exuded a confident, progressive tone that was characteristic of middle-class Americans.

Harper's Weekly was one of the most important magazines designed primarily for middle- and upper-class readers. Established in 1857, this publication continued in print until 1916. The success of *Harper's Weekly,* which called itself a "family newspaper," rested on a combination of its moderate point of view and an exciting use of illustrations and cartoons touching on contemporary events. The popular cartoons of Thomas Nast appeared in this magazine. In large part because of the use of graphics, the circulation of *Harper's Weekly* reached a peak of 160,000 in 1872.

Illustrated here is a page from the January 16, 1869, issue of *Harper's Weekly.* The layout immediately suggests the importance of graphics. Most of the page is taken up with the three pictures. The top and bottom pictures are wood engravings based on drawings by Theodore R. Davis, one of *Harper's* best-known illustrator-reporters. The center picture was derived from a photograph.

The story featured on this page concerns a victory of General George Custer in the war against the Cheyenne tribe that the U.S. Army was waging that winter. Davis had been a correspondent in the West covering Custer's actions in 1867. But when news of Custer's victory arrived, Davis was back in New York. He thus drew on his imagination for the two scenes reproduced on the next page. What kind of characterization of Native Americans does Davis give in the picture at the top of the page? What view of American soldiers does he suggest? At the bottom of the page, you can see soldiers slaughtering "worthless" horses while Cheyenne teepees burn in the background. Would the average viewer have any sympathy for the plight of the Cheyenne after looking at this picture? This "victory," in fact, involved the slaughter not only of horses but also of all males over age 8.

The editors' decision to insert a picture that had nothing to do with the incident being reported was obviously significant. As you can see, the subject in the center illustration is a white hunter who had been killed and scalped by Indians. By considering the choice of graphics and text, you can begin to discover how magazines provide insight, not only into the events of the day but also into the ways magazines shaped the values and perspectives of nineteenth-century men and women.

Reflecting on the Past What kind of special relationship were the editors suggesting by placing the picture of one dead white hunter in the center of a page that primarily covered a specific conflict between the Indians and the U.S. Army? How might the reader respond to the group of pictures as a whole? How do you? How does the text contribute to the overall view of the Indian–white relationship that the pictures suggest? ▪

I learned what the fighting was about....Up on the Madison Fork the Wasichus had found much of the yellow metal that they worship and that makes them crazy, and they wanted to have a road up through our country to the place where the yellow metal was; but my people did not want the road. It would scare the bison and make them go away, and also it would let the other Wasichus come in like a river. They told us that they wanted only to use a little land, as much as a wagon would take between the wheels; but our people knew better.

Black Elk's father and many others soon realized that fighting was the only "way to keep our country." But "wherever we went, the soldiers came to kill us."

Broken promises fired Indian resistance. In 1875, the federal government allowed gold prospectors into the Black Hills, part of the Sioux reservation and one of their sacred places. Chiefs Sitting Bull, Crazy Horse,

and Rain-in-the-Face led the angry Sioux on the warpath. At the Battle of Little Big Horn in 1876, they vanquished General George Custer. But their bravery and skill could not permanently withstand the power of the well-supplied, well-armed, and determined U.S. Army. Elsewhere, the pattern of resistance and ultimate defeat was repeated. In Texas, General Sherman vanquished Native American tribes, and in the Pacific Northwest, Nez Percé Chief Joseph surrendered in 1877.

The wholesale destruction of the buffalo that were central to Indian life was an important element in white victory. Plains Indians could be wasteful of buffalo in areas where the animals were abundant, but white miners and hunters wiped out the herds. Sportsmen shot the beasts from train windows. Railroad crews ate the meat. Ranchers' cattle competed for grass. And demand for buffalo bones for fertilizer and hides for robes and shoes encouraged the decimation.

An Indian School

These girls, attending an Indian school, are neatly dressed in identical dresses and aprons, with hair pulled into buns rather than braided. What does this picture reveal about the objective of this education for young Indian girls?

(Bettmann/CORBIS)

The slaughter of 13 million animals by 1883 appears disgraceful today. Certainly, Indians considered white men demented. "They just killed and killed because they like to do that," said one, whereas when "we hunted the bison...[we] killed only what we needed." But the destruction of the herds pleased whites who were determined to curb the movements of Native Americans.

The 1887 Dawes Act

Changing federal policy was aimed at ending Native American power and culture. In 1871, Congress abandoned the practice, in effect since the 1790s, of treating the tribes as sovereign nations. Other measures supported the effort to attempt to undermine tribal integrity and leaders. Federal authorities extended government jurisdiction to the reservations and warned tribes not to gather for religious ceremonies.

The Dawes Severalty Act of 1887 pulled together the strands of federal Indian policy and set its course for the rest of the century. Believing that tribal bonds kept Indians in savagery, reformers intended to destroy them. Rather than allotting reservation lands to tribal groups, the act allowed the president to distribute these lands to individuals. The lure of private property, the framers of the bill reasoned, would undermine communal norms and tribal identity and encourage the adoption of settled agricultural life. Those who accepted an allotment would become citizens and presumably abandon their tribal identity. But another force was at work as speculators' support for the legislation suggested. Even if each Indian family head claimed a typical share of 160 acres, millions of "surplus" acres would remain for white settlers to purchase. Within 20 years of the Dawes Act, 60 percent of Indian lands had been sold, with the federal government holding the profits "in trust" for its "civilizing" mission.

The Ghost Dance: An Indian Renewal Ritual

By the 1890s, this grim reality prepared many Native Americans for the message of the Paiute prophet, Wovoka. Predicting the destruction of the white race through natural disasters, Wovoka promised that Indians who performed the Ghost Dance would survive and gain new strength as their ancestors and wild game returned to life. Wovoka's prophecies spread rapidly. Believers expressed their hope for change through new rituals of ghost or spirit dancing, hypnosis, and meditation.

American settlers were uneasy even though the prophet did not encourage harming whites. Indian agents tried to prevent the ghost dances and filed hysterical reports. One agent determined that the Sioux medicine man Sitting Bull, a strenuous opponent of American expansion, was a leading

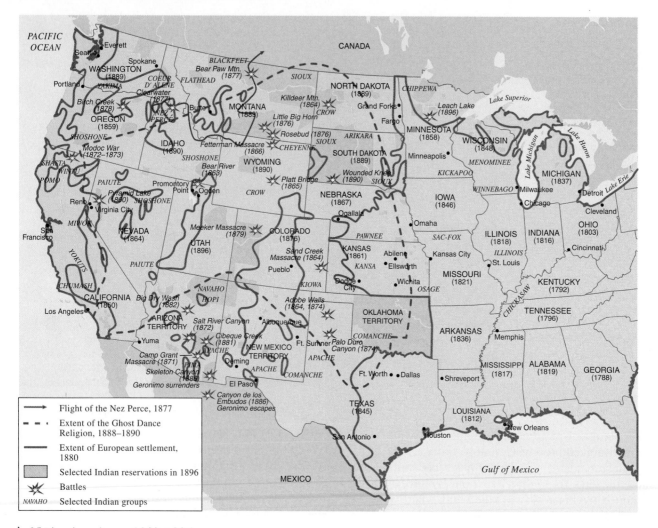

Native Americans, 1850–1896

What does this map reveal about the character of white settlement in 1880? Can you see any relationship between that pattern and the location of reservations? How widespread was the Ghost Dance movement?

troublemaker and decided to arrest him. In the confusion, Indian police killed Sitting Bull. Bands of Sioux fled the reservation with the army in swift pursuit. In late December 1890, the army caught up with them at Wounded Knee Creek. Although the Sioux had raised a flag of truce and started turning over weapons, a scuffle led to a bloody massacre. Using the most up-to-date machine guns and Hotchkiss cannons, the army killed more than 200 men, women, and children. An eyewitness described the desolate scene a few days later. "Among the fragments of burned tents...we saw the frozen bodies lying close together or piled one upon another."

With such measures, white Americans defeated the western tribes. Once independent, proud, and strong, Native Americans suffered dependency, poverty, and social and cultural disorganization on the reservations, in grim Indian schools, and in city slums. The country's original inhabitants had no place in the American nation.

The New South

The trans-Mississippi West was transformed as native peoples were subdued, the Great Plains were settled, and commercial agriculture helped knit the region into the larger world. Mining camps turned into industrial centers. Western cities grew at a fast pace; by 1900, nearly 40 percent of westerners lived in cities. The large number of itinerant workers who worked in mines, forests, and fields provided a flexible workforce that supported economic growth.

In contrast to this pattern, the southern economy sputtered. Of all the nation's agricultural regions, the

South was the poorest. In 1880, southerners' yearly earnings were only half the national average. The agricultural labor force was neither efficient, nor mobile, nor prosperous enough to invest in needed improvements. The dream some southerners harbored of creating an agricultural South to rival the industrial North never came true. The region remained dependent on the North, its industrial workers poorly paid, caught in dead-end jobs with little hope of advancement.

Postwar Southerners Face the Future

After the painful war and Reconstruction, compelling arguments for regional self-sufficiency rang out. Advocates for a "New South" argued that southern backwardness did not stem from the war itself as so many southerners wished to believe but from southern conditions, especially a cotton-based economy. Defeat only made clearer the reality that power and wealth came from factories, machines, and cities.

In hundreds of speeches, editorials, pamphlets, articles, and books, spokesmen for the New South tried to persuade fellow southerners to replace genteel prewar ideals with the ethic of hard work. Because the South was short of capital, New South advocates also held attractive investment opportunities to northern bankers and manufacturers. Several southern state governments offered tax exemptions and the cheap labor of leased convicts. Texas and Florida awarded the railroads land grants, and cities including Atlanta and Louisville mounted huge industrial exhibitions. Middle-class southerners increasingly accepted new entrepreneurial values.

During the late nineteenth century, northern money flowed south as dollars replaced the moral fervor and political involvement of the Civil War and Reconstruction. In the 1880s, northerners increased their investment in the cotton industry sevenfold and financed the expansion of the southern railroad system. Northern capital fueled southern urban expansion. By 1900, some 15 percent of all southerners lived in cities, compared to 7 percent in 1860. (The national averages for these years were 40 and 20 percent, respectively.)

Birmingham, Alabama, symbolized the New South. In 1870, the site was a cornfield. The next year, two northern real estate speculators arrived, attracted by the area's rich iron deposits. Despite cholera and the depression of the 1870s, Birmingham rapidly became the center of the southern iron and steel industry. By 1890, a total of 38,414 people lived in the city. Coke ovens, blast furnaces, rolling mills, iron foundries, and machine shops belched. Mills and factories poured out millions of dollars' worth of finished goods, and eight railroad lines carried them away.

Other southern cities also flourished. Memphis prospered from its lumber industry and the manufacturing of cottonseed products while Richmond became the country's tobacco capital even as its flour mills and iron and steel foundries continued to produce wealth. Augusta, Georgia, led the emerging textile industry that blossomed in Georgia, the Carolinas, and Alabama.

The Other Side of Progress

New South leaders—a small group of merchants, industrialists, and planters—bragged about their iron and textile industries and paraded statistics to prove the success of modernization. The South, one writer boasted, was "throbbing with industrial and railroad activity." But progress was slow, and older values persisted. Even New South spokesmen romanticized the recent past, impeding full acceptance of a new economic order. While southern industry grew in absolute terms, it declined in relative terms. Whereas in 1860 the South had 17 percent of the country's manufacturing concerns, by 1904, it had only 15 percent.

Moreover, the South failed to reap many of industrialization's possible benefits. The South remained an economic vassal of the North. Southern businessmen grew in number, but with the exception of the American Tobacco Company, no great southern corporations arose. Instead, southerners worked for northern companies and corporations, which absorbed southern businesses or dominated them financially. Profits and critical decision-making power flowed north. In many cases southern mills and factories were allowed to handle only the early stages of processing; Northern factories finished the goods.

Individual workers in the new industries may have preferred factory life to sharecropping, but their rewards were meager. The presence of thousands of women and children in factories highlighted husbands' and fathers' inability to earn a "family wage." As usual, women and children were paid less than men. Justifying these policies, one Augusta factory president claimed that the employment of children was "a matter of charity with us; some of them would starve if they were not given employment.... Ours are not overworked. The work we give children is very light." Actually, many children at his factory were doing the same work as adults, but for children's pay.

In general, workers earned less and toiled longer in the South than elsewhere. Per capita income was the same in 1900 as it had been in 1860—half the national average. In North Carolina in the 1890s, workers were paid an average of 50 cents a day with a 70-hour week.

Black workers, 6 percent of the southern manufacturing force by 1890 (with the exception of textile mills that excluded them), usually had the worst jobs and the lowest pay.

Cotton Still King

Although New South advocates envisioned the South's transformation from a rural to an industrial society, they always recognized the need for agricultural change. "It's time for an agricultural revolution," proclaimed Henry Grady, the New South's most vocal spokesman. Overdependence on "King Cotton" hobbled southern agriculture by making farmers the victims of faraway market forces and an oppressive credit system. Subdivide old cotton plantations into small diversified farms, Grady urged, that would raise choice produce for urban markets and yield "simply wonderful profits."

A new agricultural South with new class and economic arrangements did emerge, but not the one Grady envisioned. Despite the breakup of some plantations, large landowners were resourceful in keeping their property and dealing with postwar

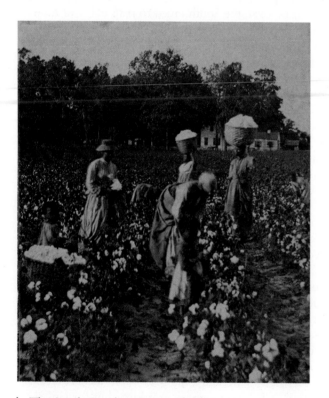

The South Carolina Cotton Fields

What evidence does this photograph, taken in the 1870s, provide for understanding the character of black life after the Civil War and the limitations of the New South's effort to transform southern life?

(Photography Collection, Robert N. Dennis Collection of Stereoscopic Views, The New York Public Library/Art Resource, NY)

conditions, as Chapter 16 showed. As they adopted new agricultural arrangements, former slaves sank into peonage.

White farmers on small and medium-size holdings fared only slightly better than black tenants and sharecroppers. Immediately after the war, high cotton prices tempted them to raise as much cotton as they could. Then prices began a disastrous decline, from 11 cents a pound in 1875 to less than 5 cents in 1894. Yeoman farmers became entangled in debt. Each year, farmers bought supplies on credit from merchants so they could plant the next year's crop and support their families until harvest. In return, merchants demanded their exclusive business and acquired a lien (claim) on their crops. But when farmers sold their crops at declining prices, they usually discovered that they had not earned enough to settle with the merchant, who had charged dearly for store goods and whose annual interest rates might exceed 100 percent. Each year, thousands of farmers fell further behind. By 1900, more than half of the South's white farmers and three-quarters of its black farmers were tenants. Tenancy increased all over rural America, but nowhere faster than in the Deep South.

These patterns had baneful results for individual southerners and for the South as a whole. Caught in a cycle of debt and poverty, few farmers could think of improving techniques or diversifying crops. Desperate to pay debts, they concentrated on cotton despite falling prices. Landowners pressured tenants to raise a market crop. Far from diversifying, farmers increasingly limited their crops. By 1880, the South was not growing enough food to feed its people adequately.

The Nadir of Black Life

Grady and other New South advocates visualized a strong, prosperous, and industrialized South, a region that could deal with the troublesome race issue without interference. Grady had few regrets over the end of slavery, which he thought had contributed to southern economic backwardness. Realizing that black labor would be crucial to the transformation he sought, he advocated racial cooperation. But racial cooperation did not mean equality. Grady assumed that blacks were racially inferior and supported an informal system of segregation. "The negro is entitled to his freedom, his franchise, to full and equal legal rights," Grady wrote in 1883. But "social equality he can never have."

By the time of Grady's death in 1889, a much harsher perspective on southern race relations had emerged. In 1891, at a national assembly of women's clubs in Washington, D.C., Frances Watkins Harper, a black speaker, writer, and former abolitionist, appealed to the white women at the meeting not to abandon black suffrage. "I deem it a privilege to present the negro," she said, "not as a mere dependent asking for Northern sympathy or Southern compassion, but as a member of the body politic who has a claim upon the nation for justice, simple justice." Women, of all people, should not seek to achieve their own right to vote at the expense of the vote for black men, she explained. "Instead of taking the ballot from his hands, teach him how to use it, and add his quota to the progress, strength, and durability of the nation."

The decision by congressional leaders in 1890 to shelve a proposed act for protecting black civil rights and the defeat of the Blair bill providing federal assistance for educational institutions left black Americans vulnerable, as Harper realized. The traditional sponsor of the rights of freedpeople, the Republican party, left blacks to fend for themselves as a minority in the white South. The courts also abandoned blacks. In 1878, the Supreme Court declared unconstitutional a Louisiana statute banning discrimination in transportation. In 1882, the Court voided the Ku Klux Klan Act of 1871, which had been passed to break the power of the Klan. In 1883, the provisions of the Civil Rights Act of 1875, which assured blacks of equal rights in public places, were declared unconstitutional on the grounds that the federal government did not have the right to involve itself in racial relations between individuals.

Northern leaders did not oppose these actions. In fact, northerners increasingly promulgated negative stereotypes in magazines, newspapers, cartoons, advertisements, "coon songs," serious art and theater, and the minstrel shows that dominated northern entertainment. The *Atlantic Monthly* in 1890 anticipated a strong current in magazine literature when it expressed doubts that this "lowly variety of man" could ever be brought up to the intellectual and moral standards of whites. Other magazines openly opposed suffrage as wasted on people too "ignorant, weak, lazy and incompetent" to make good use of it. *Forum* magazine suggested that "American Negroes" had "too much liberty." When this freedom was combined with natural "race traits" of stealing and hankering after white women, the *Forum* advised in 1893, black crime increased. Only lynching and burning would deter the "barbarous" rapist and other "sadly degenerated" Negroes corrupted since the Civil War by independence and too much education.

Encouraged by northern public opinion, and with the blessing of Congress and the Supreme Court, southern citizens and legislatures sought to make blacks permanently second-class members of southern society. In the political sphere, white southerners amended state constitutions to disfranchise black voters. By various legal devices—the poll tax, literacy tests, "good character" and "understanding" clauses administered by white

voter registrars, and all-white primary elections—blacks lost the right to vote. The most ingenious method was the "grandfather clause," which specified that only citizens whose grandfathers were registered to vote on January 1, 1867, could cast their ballots. This virtually excluded blacks. Although the Supreme Court outlawed blatantly discriminatory laws such as grandfather clauses, a series of other constitutional changes such as those just mentioned, beginning in Mississippi in 1890 and spreading to all 11 former Confederate states by 1910, effectively excluded the black vote. The results were dramatic. Louisiana, for example, contained 130,334 registered black voters in 1896. Eight years later, there were only 1,342.

In a second tactic in the 1890s, state and local laws legalized informal segregation in public facilities. Beginning with railroads and schools, "Jim Crow" laws were extended to libraries, restaurants, hospitals, prisons, parks and playgrounds, cemeteries, toilets, drinking fountains, and nearly every other place where blacks and whites might mingle. The Supreme Court upheld these laws in 1896 in *Plessy* v. *Ferguson* by declaring that "separate but equal" facilities did not violate the equal protection clause of the Fourteenth Amendment because separation did not necessarily mean the inferiority of a group. The Court's decision opened the way for as many forms of legal segregation as southern lawmakers could devise.

Political and social discrimination made it ever more possible to keep blacks permanently confined to agricultural and unskilled labor. In 1900, nearly 84 percent of black workers nationwide engaged in some form of agricultural labor as farmhands, overseers, sharecroppers, or tenant or independent farmers or in service jobs, primarily domestic service and laundry work. These had been the primary slave occupations. The remaining 16 percent worked in forests, sawmills, mines, and, with northward migration, northern cities. As whites systematically excluded blacks from trades, the percentage of blacks laboring in these jobs dropped to under 10 percent, although at the end of the Civil War, at least half the skilled craftsmen in the South had been black. The factory work that blacks had been doing was also reduced, largely to separate poor blacks and whites and to undercut unionization. The exclusion of blacks from industry prevented them from acquiring the skills and habits that would enable them to rise into the middle class as would many European immigrants and their children by the mid-twentieth century.

Blacks did not accept their declining position passively. In the mid-1880s, they enthusiastically joined the mass worker organization the Knights of Labor (discussed in Chapter 18), first in cities such as Richmond and Atlanta and then in rural areas. But southern whites feared that the Knights' policies of racial and economic cooperation might lead to social equality. The Charleston *News and Courier* warned darkly about "mongrels and hybrids." As blacks continued to join it, whites fled the organization. White violence finished it off.

Lynching and other forms of violence against blacks increased. Lynching was a way to show both black men and white women the dire consequences of stepping out of line. On February 21, 1891, the *New York Times* reported that in Texarkana, Arkansas, a mob apprehended Ed Coy, a 32-year-old black man who was charged with the rape of a white woman. He was tied to a stake and then burned alive. As Coy proclaimed his innocence to a large crowd, his alleged victim somewhat hesitatingly put the torch to his oil-soaked body. The *Times* report concluded that only by the "terrible death such as fire…can inflict" could other blacks "be deterred from the commission of like crimes." Ed Coy was one of more than 1,400 black men lynched or burned alive during the 1890s. About one-third were charged with sex crimes. The rest were accused of a variety of "crimes" related to not knowing their place; this included marrying or insulting a white woman, testifying in court against whites, or having a "bad reputation."

Diverging Black Responses

White discrimination and exploitation nourished new protest tactics and ideologies among blacks. For years, Frederick Douglass had been proclaiming that blacks should remain loyal Americans and trust the Republican party. But on his deathbed in 1895, his last words were allegedly, "Agitate! Agitate! Agitate!"

Agitation had its costs. In Memphis, Tennessee, Ida B. Wells, the first female editor of an important newspaper, launched an antilynching campaign in 1892. So hostile was the response from the white community that Wells carried a gun to protect herself. When white citizens finally destroyed the press and threatened her partner, Wells left Memphis to pursue her activism elsewhere.

Calls for black separatism within white America rang out. Insisting that blacks must join together to fight the rising tide of discrimination, T. Thomas Fortune in 1891 organized the Afro-American League. The League, a precursor of the NAACP, encouraged independent black voting, opposed segregation and lynching, and urged the establishment of black institutions such as banks to support black businesses. As a sympathetic journalist explained, "The solution of the problem is in our own hands.…The Negro must preserve his identity." In the 1890s, black leaders lobbied to make the Oklahoma Territory, recently opened to white settlement, an all-black state. Blacks founded 25 towns there as well as many towns in other states and even in Mexico. But these attempts, like earlier ones, were short-lived, for they were crippled by limited funds and by the hostility of white neighbors.

There were more radical voices, too. Bishop Henry McNeal Turner, a former Union soldier and prominent black leader, despaired of ever securing equal rights for American blacks. He described the Constitution as "a dirty rag, a cheat, a libel" and said that it ought to be "spit upon by every Negro in the land." In 1894, he organized the International Migration Society to return blacks to Africa, arguing that "this country owes us forty billions of dollars" to help. He succeeded in sending two boatloads of emigrants to Liberia, but this colonization effort worked no more successfully than those earlier in the century.

As Frederick Douglass had long argued, no matter how important African roots might be, blacks had been in the Americas for generations and would have to win justice and equal rights here. W. E. B. Du Bois, the first black to receive a Ph.D. from Harvard, agreed. Yet in 1900, he attended the first Pan-African Conference in London, where he argued that blacks must lead the struggle for liberation both in Africa and in the United States. It was at this conference that Du Bois first made his prophetic comment that "the problem of the Twentieth Century" would be "the problem of the color line."

Despite these vigorous voices of militant anger and nationalistic fervor, most black Americans continued to follow the slow, moderate, self-help program of Booker T. Washington, the best-known black leader in America. Born a slave, Washington had risen through hard and faithful work to become the founder (in 1881) and principal of Tuskegee Institute in Alabama, which he personally and dramatically built into the nation's largest and best-known industrial training school. At Tuskegee, young blacks received a highly disciplined education in scientific agricultural techniques and vocational skilled trades. Washington believed that economic self-help and the familiar Puritan virtues of hard work, frugality, cleanliness, and moderation would lead to success for African Americans despite the realities of racism. He spent much of his time traveling through the North to secure philanthropic gifts to support Tuskegee. In time, he became a favorite of the American entrepreneurial elite whose capitalist assumptions he shared.

In 1895, Washington was asked to deliver a speech at the Cotton States and International Exposition in Atlanta, celebrating three decades of industrial and agricultural progress since the Civil War. He took advantage of that invitation, a rare honor for a former slave, to make a significant statement about the position of blacks in the South. Without a hint of protest, Washington decided "to say something that would cement the friendship of the races." He therefore proclaimed black loyalty to the economic development of the South while accepting the lowly status of southern blacks. "It is at the bottom of life we must begin, and not at the top," he declared. "In all things that are purely social we can be as separate as the fingers, yet one as the hand in all things essential to mutual progress." Although Washington worked actively behind the scenes for black civil rights, in Atlanta, he publicly renounced black interest in either the vote or civil rights as well as social equality with whites. Whites throughout the country enthusiastically acclaimed Washington's address, but many blacks called his "Atlanta Compromise" a serious setback in the struggle for black rights.

Washington has often been charged with conceding too quickly that political rights should follow rather than precede economic well-being. In 1903, Du Bois confronted Washington directly in *The Souls of Black Folk*, arguing instead for the "manly assertion" of a program of equal civil rights, suffrage, and higher education in the ideals of liberal learning. A trip through the Black Belt of Dougherty County, Georgia, showed Du Bois the "forlorn and forsaken" condition of southern blacks. The young sociologist saw that most blacks were confined to dependent agricultural labor, "fighting a hard battle with debt" year after year. Although "here and there a man has raised his head above these murky waters…a pall of debt hangs over the beautiful land." Beneath all others was the cotton picker, who, with his wife and children, would have to work from sunup to sundown to pick 100 pounds of cotton to make 50 cents. The lives of most blacks were still tied to the land of the South. If they were to improve their lives, rural blacks would have to organize.

Farm Protest

During the post–Civil War period, many farmers, black and white, began to realize that only through collective action could they improve rural life. Not all were dissatisfied; midwestern farmers and those near city markets adjusted to changing economic conditions. Southern and western farmers, however, faced new problems that led to the first mass organization of farmers in American history.

The Grange in the 1860s and 1870s

The earliest effort to organize white farmers came in 1867 when Oliver Kelley founded the Order of the Patrons of Husbandry. Originally a social and cultural organization, it soon was protesting the powerlessness of the "immense helpless mob" of farmers, victims of "human vampires." The depression of the 1870s (discussed in Chapter 18)

sharpened discontent. By 1875, an estimated 800,000 had joined Kelley's organization, now known as the National Grange.

The Grangers recognized some, but not all, of the complex changes that had created rural problems. Some of their "reforms" attempted to bypass intermediaries by establishing buying and selling cooperatives. Although many cooperatives failed, they indicated that farmers realized the need for unified action. Midwestern farmers also accused grain elevator operators of cheating them, and they pointed to the railroads, America's first big business, as the worst offenders. As Chapter 18 will show, cutthroat competition among railroad companies generally brought lower rates. But even though charges dropped nationwide, railroads often set high rates in rural areas, and their rebates to large shippers discriminated against small operators.

Farmers recognized that confronting the mighty railroads demanded cooperation with others, like western businessmen whose interests railroads also hurt, and political action. Between 1869 and 1874, businessmen and farmers successfully pressed Illinois, Iowa, Wisconsin, and Minnesota to pass so-called Granger laws (an inaccurate name, for the Grangers did not deserve complete credit for them) establishing maximum rates that railroads and grain elevators could charge. Other states set up railroad commissions to regulate railroad rates, or outlawed railroad pools, rebates, passes, and other practices that seemed to represent "unjust discrimination and distortion."

Railroad companies and grain elevators quickly challenged the new laws. In 1877, the Supreme Court upheld them in *Munn* v. *Illinois*. Even so, it soon became apparent that state commissions might regulate local rates but not long-haul rates. While Granger laws did not control the railroads and raised questions difficult to resolve on the local level, they established an important principle. The Supreme Court had made it clear that state legislatures could regulate businesses of a public nature such as the railroads. When the Court reversed its ruling in *Wabash* v. *Illinois* in 1886, pressure increased on Congress to continue the struggle.

The Interstate Commerce Act of 1887

In 1887, Congress responded to farmers, railroad managers who wished to curb the fierce competition that threatened to bankrupt their companies, and shippers who objected to transportation rates by passing the Interstate Commerce Act. That legislation required that railroad rates be "reasonable and just," that rate schedules be made public, and that practices such as rebates be discontinued. The act also set up the first federal regulatory agency, the Interstate Commerce Commission (ICC) with power to investigate and prosecute lawbreakers but with only limited authority to control commerce conducted between states.

Like state railroad commissions, the ICC found it difficult to define a reasonable rate. Moreover, thousands of cases overwhelmed the tiny staff in the early months of operation. In the long run, the lack of enforcement power was most serious. The ICC's only recourse was to bring offenders into the federal courts for lengthy legal proceedings. Few railroads worried about defying it. When they appeared in court four or five years later, they often won their cases from judges suspicious of new federal authority. Between 1887 and 1906, a total of 16 cases made their way to the Supreme Court, which decided 15 of them in the railroads' favor.

The Southern Farmers' Alliance in the 1880s and 1890s

The Grange declined in the late 1870s as the nation recovered from depression. But farm protest did not die. Depression struck farmers once again in the late 1880s and worsened in the early 1890s. Official statistics told the familiar, dismal story of falling grain prices on the plains and prairies. The national currency shortage, which usually reached critical proportions at harvest time, helped drive agricultural prices ever lower. Debt and shipping costs, however, climbed. It sometimes cost a farmer as much as one bushel of corn to send another bushel to market. Distraught farmers again tried organization, education, and cooperation.

The Southern Farmers' Alliance became one of the most important reform organizations of the 1880s. Its ambitious organizational drive sent lecturers across the South and onto the Plains where they proposed programs that would meet their objective of "Equal rights to all, special privileges to none." Among the Alliance's efforts were experiments with cooperatives to free farmers from the clutches of supply merchants, banks, and other credit agencies. While cooperatives often failed, the Alliance also supported legislative efforts to regulate powerful monopolies and corporations that, they believed, gouged farmers. Many Alliance members believed that increasing the money supply was critical to improving the position of farmers and supported a national banking system empowered to issue paper money. Finally, the Alliance called for a variety of measures to improve the quality of rural life. Better rural public schools, state agricultural colleges, and improvements in the status of women were all on its agenda.

By 1890, rural discontent swept more than a million farmers into the Alliance. Included in this burst of organization growth were black as well as white farmers. Organized in 1888, the Colored Farmers' Alliance recognized that farmers of both races shared common economic problems and therefore must cooperate. But many southern cotton farmers, depending on black labor, disagreed. In 1891, black cotton pickers on plantations near Memphis went on strike. Revealing the racial tensions simmering just below the surface, white posses chased the strikers and lynched 15 of them.

The Ocala Platform, 1890

In December 1890, the National Alliance gathered in Ocala, Florida, to develop a platform. Most delegates believed that the federal government had failed to address the farmers' problems. They attacked both parties as too subservient to the "will of corporation and money power."

Much of the Alliance's program was radical in the context of late-nineteenth-century political life. It called for the direct election of U.S. senators and supported lowering the tariff (a topic much debated in Congress) with the dangerous-sounding justification that prices must be reduced for the sake of the "poor of our land." The money plank boldly envisioned a new banking system controlled by the federal government. The platform also called for the government to take an active economic role by increasing the amount of money in circulation in the form of treasury notes and silver. More money would cause inflation and help debtors pay off loans.

The platform also called for subtreasuries (federal warehouses) in agricultural regions where farmers could store their produce at low interest rates until market prices favored selling. To tide farmers over, the federal government would lend farmers up to 80 percent of the current local price for their produce. Other demands included a graduated income tax and the regulation of transportation and communication networks—or, if regulation failed, their nationalization.

Even though a minority of farmers belonged to the Alliance, many Americans feared it. The New York Sun reported that the Alliance had caused a "panic" in the two major parties.

Although the Alliance was not formally in politics, it supported sympathetic candidates in the fall elections of 1890. A surprising number of them won. Alliance victories in the West hurt the Republican party enough to cause President Harrison to refer to "our election disaster." Before long, many Alliance members were pressing for an independent political party. Legislators elected with Alliance support did not necessarily bring action on issues of interest to farmers, or even respect. On the national level, no one had much interest in the Ocala platform. But among rural spokesmen, the first to realize the necessity of forming an independent third party was Georgia's Tom Watson, who also knew that success in the South would depend on unity between white and black farmers.

Timeline

1860s	Cattle drives from Texas begin
1865–1867	Sioux wars on the Great Plains
1867	National Grange founded
1869	Transcontinental railroad completed
1869–1874	Granger laws
1873	Financial panic triggers economic depression
1874	Barbed wire patented
1875	Black Hills gold rush incites Sioux war
1876	Custer's last stand at Little Big Horn
1877	*Munn* v. *Illinois*
	Bonanza farms in the Great Plains
1878	Timber and Stone Act
1880s	Attempts to create a "New South"
1881	Tuskegee Institute founded
1883–1885	Depression
1884	Southern Farmers' Alliance founded
1886	Severe winter ends cattle boom
	Wabash v. *Illinois*
1887	Dawes Severalty Act
	Interstate Commerce Act
	Farm prices plummet
1888	Colored Farmers' Alliance founded
1890	Afro-American League founded
	Sioux ghost dance movement
	Massacre at Wounded Knee
	Ocala platform
	Yosemite National Park established
1890s	Black disfranchisement in the South
	Jim Crow laws passed in the South
	Declining farm prices
1891	Forest Reserve Act
1892	Sierra Club founded
1895	Booker T. Washington's "Atlanta Compromise" address
1896	*Plessy* v. *Ferguson*

Conclusion

FARMING IN THE INDUSTRIAL AGE

The late nineteenth century brought turbulence to rural America. The "Indian problem," which had plagued Americans for 200 years, was tragically solved for a while, but not without resistance and bloodshed. Few whites found these events troubling. Most were caught up in the challenge of responding to a fast-changing world. Believing themselves to be the backbone of the nation, white farmers brought Native American lands into cultivation, modernized their farms, and raised bumper crops. But success and a comfortable competency eluded many of them. Some, like Milton Leeper, never gave up hope or farming. Many were caught in a cycle of poverty and debt. Others fled to towns and cities as did the Ebbesen family. Once there, many joined the industrial workforce, described in the next chapter. Some turned to collective action and politics. Their actions demonstrate that they did not merely react to events but attempted to shape them.

QUESTIONS FOR REVIEW AND REFLECTION

1. Compare and contrast farming on the Great Plains with farming in California.
2. How did technology affect agriculture and mining in the West?
3. Describe the differing viewpoints of Native Americans and whites and the differing cultural values lying behind these viewpoints.
4. What were the reasons that the New South did not achieve its goals?
5. Compare and contrast the treatment of Native Americans and African Americans in this period. Are there any similarities?
6. In what ways did agricultural life in the West and South create conditions that did not mesh with the ideals of American life?

CHAPTER 18

The Rise of Smokestack America

This anxious scene of a strike hints at the tensions between workers and owners during the industrial era.

(Robert Koehler (1850–1917), *The Strike*, 1886. Oil on canvas. Deutsches Historisches Museum, Berlin, Germany/Bridgeman Art Library)

American Stories

Telling His Story: O'Donnell and the Senators

By 1883, Thomas O'Donnell, an Irish immigrant, had lived in the United States for more than a decade. He was 30 years old, married, with two young children. His third child had died in 1882, and O'Donnell was still in debt for the funeral. Money was scarce, for O'Donnell was a textile worker in Fall River, Massachusetts, and not well educated. "I went to work when I was young," he explained, "and have been working ever since." However, O'Donnell worked only sporadically at the mill. New machines needed "a good deal of small help," and the mill owners preferred to hire man-and-boy teams. Because O'Donnell's children were very young, he often saw others preferred for day work. Once, when he was passed over, he asked the boss "what am I to do; I have got two little boys at home . . . how am I to get something for them to eat; I can't get a turn when I come here. . . . I says, 'Have I got to starve; ain't I to have any work?'"

O'Donnell and his family were barely getting by, even though he worked with pick and shovel when he could. He estimated that he had earned only $133 the previous year. Rent came to $72. The family spent $2 for a little coal but depended for heat on driftwood that O'Donnell picked up on the beach. Clams were a major part of the family diet, but on some days there was nothing to eat at all.

The children "got along very nicely all summer," but by November they were beginning to "feel quite sickly." It was hardly surprising. "One has one shoe on, a very poor one, and a slipper, that was picked up somewhere. The other has two odd shoes on, with the heel out." His wife was healthy, but not ready for winter. She had two dresses, one saved for church, and an "undershirt that she got given to her, and . . . an old wrapper, which is about a mile too big for her; somebody gave it to her."

O'Donnell was describing his family's marginal existence to a Senate committee gathering testimony in Boston in 1883 on the relations between labor and capital. As the senators heard the tale, they asked him why he did not go west. "It would not cost you over $1,500," said one senator. The gap between the worlds of the senator and the worker could not have been more dramatic. O'Donnell replied, "Well, I never saw over a $20 bill . . . if some one would give me $1,500 I will go." Asked by the senator if he had friends who could provide him with the funds, O'Donnell sadly replied no.

The senators, of course, were far better acquainted with the world of comfort and leisure than with the poverty of families like the O'Donnells. From their vantage point, the fruits of industrial progress were clear. As the United States became a world industrial leader in the years after the Civil War, its factories poured forth an abundance of ever-cheaper goods ranging from steel rails and farm reapers to mass-produced parlor sets. These were years of tremendous growth and broad economic and social change. Manufacturing replaced agriculture as the leading source of economic growth between 1860 and 1900. By 1890, a majority of the American workforce held nonagricultural jobs; more than a third lived in cities. A rural nation of farmers was becoming a nation of industrial workers and city dwellers.

As O'Donnell's appearance before the Senate committee illustrates, industrial and technological advances profoundly changed the nature of American life. For O'Donnell and others like him, the benefits of this transformation were hard to see. Although no nationwide studies of poverty existed, estimates suggest that perhaps half of the American population was too poor to take advantage of the new goods of the age. Eventually, the disparity between the reality of life for humble families like the O'Donnells and American ideals would give rise to attempts to improve conditions for working-class Americans, but it is unlikely that O'Donnell ever profited from such efforts.

This chapter examines the maturing of the American industrial economy, a phenomenon that affected all facets of American life, from the rhythms of daily life and work to the allocation of wealth. Focusing on the years between 1865 and 1900, it describes the rise of heavy industry and the factors that contributed to it, including the mass production of machine-made goods, a new organization of the workplace, and the emergence of big business. It then examines the cities housing the diverse peoples that provided the workers and consumers driving American industry. The chapter's central theme grows out of O'Donnell's story: As the United States built up its railroads, cities, and factories, its production and profit orientation resulted in unequal distribution of wealth and power. New inequalities did not go unquestioned, however, as workers used strikes and other forms of resistance to assert their dignity and power and to demand more generous compensation for the labor they performed. The ineffectiveness of these efforts highlights the obstacles confronting those protesting the status quo.

The Character of Industrial Progress

When Americans went to war in 1861, agriculture was the country's leading source of economic growth. Forty years later, manufacturing had taken its place. Big business became the characteristic form of economic organization. Able to raise the capital to build huge factories, acquire expensive, modern, and efficient machinery, and hire hundreds of workers, big industrial firms poured out a bounty of goods. Indeed, the production of manufactured goods outpaced population growth.

Dramatically rising industrial productivity was linked to the changing character of the industrial sector. Pre–Civil War manufacturers concentrated either on producing textiles, clothing, and leather products for consumers or on processing agricultural and natural resources such as grain, logs, and lumber. The rapid growth of heavy industry after the war was based on manufacturing steel, iron, and machinery that fueled further industrial development rather than solely furnishing consumers.

Industrialization helped to shape and transform regional character. From New England to the Midwest stretched the country's industrial heartland. New England remained a center of light industry, while the Midwest still processed natural resources.

Now, however, the production of iron, steel, and transportation equipment joined older manufacturing operations there. In the Far West, manufacturers concentrated on processing the region's natural resources, but heavy industry made strides as well. In the South, the textile industry put down roots by the 1890s.

The Contribution of Technology

As the following example of the steel industry suggests, an accelerating pace of technological change also contributed to the industrial transformation of the late nineteenth century by allowing more efficient production that, in turn, generated new needs and further innovation. Before the Civil War, skilled workers used a slow, expensive process to produce an iron so soft that train rails wore out within a few years. The need for a harder metal stimulated the development of the Bessemer converter that transformed iron into steel by forcing air through the liquid iron, thus reducing the carbon. The new process facilitated the rapid expansion of the steel industry and had the added advantage of reducing the need for highly paid skilled workers.

The Homestead Steel Works

The Homestead Steel Works, pictured here in about 1890, was located near Pittsburgh, Pennsylvania. The vast scale of the enterprise suggests the ways in which technological innovation stimulated the expansion of the steel industry in the late nineteenth century. Although the two small figures in the foreground humanize the picture, what does this picture suggest about the character of work in the steel mills?

(Courtesy of Rivers of Steel Archives)

While neither an inventor nor an engineer, entrepreneur Andrew Carnegie grasped both the importance of technological innovations and the benefits of new ways of organizing the industry. Carnegie's company and others as well acquired access to raw materials and markets and brought all stages of steel manufacturing, from smelting to rolling, into one mill. Output soared, and prices fell. When Andrew Carnegie introduced the Bessemer process in his plant in the mid-1870s, the price of steel dropped from $100 a ton to $12 a ton by 1900.

In turn, the production of a cheaper, stronger, more durable material than iron created new goods, new demands, and new markets, and stimulated further technological change. Bessemer furnaces were geared toward making steel rails. Experimentation with the open-hearth process, using very high temperatures, yielded steel usable by bridge and ship builders, engineers, architects, and even designers of subways. Steel use increased dramatically.

New power sources also facilitated American industry's shift to mass production. In 1869, about half of the nation's industrial power came from water. Then the opening of new anthracite deposits made coal cheaper, and American industry rapidly converted to steam. By 1900, steam engines generated 80 percent of the nation's industrial energy supply. But soon electricity began to replace steam as a power source. Its development owed much to Thomas Edison, who had decided in 1878 to solve the problem of electric lighting. Rather than relying on individual creativity, Edison believed that professional collaboration fostered successful innovation. His research lab had a range of specialists and facilities that included an advanced library, a chemical lab, and eventually a glassblowing lab. From these beginnings came the electric light, the generator, and eventually the electric machine.

Railroads: Pioneers of Big Business

As this discussion makes clear, no one cause triggered the transformation of the American economy; rather a range of factors contributed to it. Among them was the completion of an effective and speedy national transportation and communications network. The network owed much to the largess of both federal and state governments that granted railroads lands from the public domain. The first transcontinental railroad was finished in 1869. Four additional transcontinental lines and miles of feeder and branch roads were laid down in the 1870s and 1880s with telegraph lines running alongside them. Transportation and communications worked together to create a national market that supported mass production and mass marketing.

Railroads also pioneered new management techniques that helped their own operations and those of other big businesses to be more productive and efficient. Railroads were large and complicated organizations that could not be run in the same way as smaller businesses. In 1854, the Erie Railroad hired engineer and inventor Daniel McCallum to discover how to make managers and the many employees more accountable. The system he worked out divided responsibilities, separated management from operations, and ensured a regular flow of information. His organizational model transformed railroads and proved useful for other businesses as they grew in scale.

Despite the generosity of government, railroads required unprecedented amounts of capital to finance construction. These high costs and heavy indebtedness encouraged aggressive business practices that led to instability in the industry. Slashing wages as a way of economizing often resulted in powerful worker unrest. Fierce competition led some companies to offer customers lower rates or secret rebates (cheaper fares in exchange for all of a company's traffic) to secure their business. Such practices instigated rate wars. Customers might benefit from declining freight rates, but they could end in bankruptcy for the railroad. In an attempt to bring some order to the railroad business in the 1870s, railroad leaders set up "pools"—informal agreements that set uniform rates or divided up the traffic. Yet these deals never completely succeeded. Too often, companies broke them, especially during business downturns.

Growth in Other Industries

By the last quarter of the century, the textile, metal, and machinery industries equaled the railroads in size. By 1900, more than 1,000 American factories had giant labor forces ranging between 500 and 1,000 workers. The huge size of such "workforce," as elsewhere combined with the subdivision of work contributed to the pattern of increasing production.

Business expansion was accomplished in one of two ways (or a combination of both). Some owners, like steel magnate Andrew Carnegie, integrated their businesses vertically—adding operations either before or after the production process. Even though he had introduced the most up-to-date innovations in his steel mills, Carnegie acquired his own sources of pig iron, coal, and coke—"backward" integration—to avoid dependence on suppliers. When Carnegie gained control of steamships and railroads to transport his finished products, he was integrating "forward." Companies that integrated vertically frequently achieved economies of scale through more efficient management techniques.

Other companies copied the railroads and integrated horizontally by combining similar businesses. They did not intend to control the various stages of production but rather to gain a monopoly of the market to eliminate competition and to stabilize prices. John D. Rockefeller used horizontal integration to control the oil market. Rockefeller bought or drove out competitors of his Standard Oil of New Jersey. Although the company never achieved a complete monopoly, by 1898 it was refining 84 percent of the nation's oil. While horizontal integration sometimes brought economies and greater profits, monopolistic control over prices did boost earnings.

In the oil business, Rockefeller observed, "the day of individual competition . . . is past and gone." As giant businesses competed intensely, often cutting wages and prices, they absorbed or eliminated smaller and weaker producers. Business ownership became increasingly concentrated. In 1870, some 808 American iron and steel firms competed in the marketplace. By 1900, fewer than 70 were left.

As businesses grew, like the railroads, they recognized the many advantages of legal incorporation. A corporation could raise money to finance large-scale operations by selling stock. Its legal identity meant that it survived the death of original and subsequent shareholders while the principle of limited liability protected the personal assets of both shareholders and investors. Such characteristics made investing in corporations more attractive.

Financing Postwar Growth

The economic transformation sketched here demanded huge amounts of capital along with the willingness to accept financial risks. The creation of the railroad system alone cost more than $1 billion by 1859; after the war another $10 billion went to complete the national railroad network. Foreign investors contributed a third of it. Americans too began to devote an increasing percentage of the national income to investment.

Although savings and commercial banks continued to invest depositors' capital, investment banking houses such as Morgan & Co. played a new and vital role in transferring resources to economic enterprises. These banks acquired blocks of corporate bonds (which offered set interest rates and eventually the repayment of principal) at a discount for interested investors and also sold stocks (which paid dividends only if the company made a profit). Because stocks were riskier investments than bonds, buyers were cautious at first. But when John Pierpont Morgan, a respected investment banker, began to market stocks, they became more popular. The market for industrial securities expanded rapidly in the 1880s and 1890s.

Although some Americans distrusted the financial markets, they were integral to the economic expansion of the late nineteenth century.

American Industry and the World

The industrialization of the late nineteenth century represented the second stage of the great transformation that began in Great Britain in the eighteenth century. By reorganizing production, often through the use of machinery, early manufacturers were able to turn out more and cheaper goods than at any time in human history. Innovation created the textile, mining, and metal industries and stimulated changes in transportation and communications. From Britain, industrialization spread to other countries in Europe as well as to the United States.

The second stage of the Industrial Revolution was marked by the application of science and technology to manufacturing and by the creation of new ways to mass-produce goods. The United States was the leader in developing techniques of mass production, while Germany excelled in using science and technology to reshape production. Technological innovations transformed German industry. As in the United States, giant firms turned out goods (especially heavy machinery and chemicals) for ever-lower prices. Along

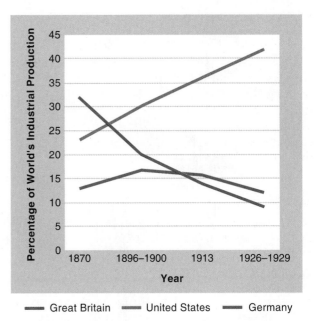

World's Industrial Output

This graph shows the changing pattern of industrial production among the world's most significant manufacturing nations. In which period did American industry make its greatest gains? What lies behind these rapid gains? What economic impact does the graph suggest that World War I (1914–1918) had on the three countries? How might the patterns of the 1920s shape the three countries' experiences during the 1930s?

with Great Britain, Germany and the United States produced two-thirds of the world's manufactured products between 1870 and 1930.

Great Britain, the world's most powerful nation during the nineteenth century, had long been its economic leader. But now the balance of power began to shift as German and American businesses developed large new enterprises, introduced new ways of organizing and efficiently managing them, invested heavily in equipment, and promoted research. Great Britain lost ground, preferring traditional ways of organizing businesses rather than the new corporate structure. British manufacturing continued to be centered in older industries such as textiles, while British investors channeled their capital away from domestic industries toward investment opportunities abroad. American railroads and subways were constructed partly with the assistance of British investors.

The full impact of the changed position of the United States in the world triggered by its industrial might became fully apparent only in the twentieth century. But the importance of connections with other nations was obvious. Standard Oil sent two-thirds of the kerosene it refined to overseas markets. Firms manufacturing sewing machines, office machines such as typewriters, and farm machinery dominated the world market. Singer Sewing Machine had a factory in Scotland in the 1880s and two decades later manufactured more than 400,000 machines in Moscow, employing 2,500 workers and 300 managers. American locomotives were exported to South America, parts of Africa and Europe, the Middle East, and Asia. The Baldwin Locomotive Works of Philadelphia produced as many engines as any other locomotive company in the world.

These connections between American business and other nations meant that events elsewhere in the world could affect the American economy. Furthermore, they suggested the intricate ties binding American business to other parts of the world. American industrial production contributed to the economic development of other countries around the globe, while American business also competed with foreign producers. John D. Rockefeller told a congressional committee that Standard Oil "spared no expense in forcing its products into the markets of the world among people civilized and uncivilized," and that the company was "holding its market against the competition of Russia and all the many countries which are producers of oil and competitors against American oil."

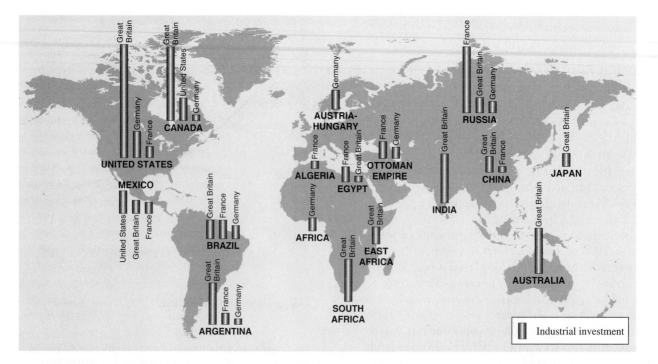

European and American Industrial Investment, 1900

Here we can see the broad impact that industrialized countries had on the rest of the world. Although industrialization was initially centered in western Europe and the United States, its influence was global. Industrial countries sought new markets, new sources of raw material, and new places for investment and development. In what places was the United States most interested? Where did individual European countries invest heavily? How would you compare the global impact of the United States to that of major European countries?

An Erratic Global Economy

Affected by national and worldwide economic trends, the transformation of the American economy was neither smooth nor steady. Two depressions, from 1873 to 1879 and from 1893 to 1897, surpassed the severity of economic downturns before the Civil War. Collapsing land values, unsound banking practices, and changes in the supply of money had caused antebellum depressions. The depressions of the late nineteenth century, when the economy was larger and more interdependent, were industrial, intense, and accompanied by widespread unemployment, a phenomenon new to American life. They were also related to economic declines in European industrial nations.

The business cycle had a recurring rhythm. The global pattern of falling prices encouraged fierce business competition that led to overproduction and the flooding of the market with goods. When the market was saturated, sales and profits declined, and the economy spiraled downward. Owners laid off workers (who lived solely on their wages for their livelihood). As workers economized and bought less food, farm prices plummeted. Farmers, like wage workers, cut purchases. Business stagnated. Finally, the railroads were hurt. Eventually, the cycle bottomed out, but millions of workers lost employment, thousands of businesses went bankrupt, and many Americans suffered.

Urban Expansion in the Industrial Age

As postwar manufacturers shifted from water to steam power, industries located in urban locations offered workers, specialized services, local markets, and railroad links to raw materials and distant markets. Industry, rather than commerce or finance, fueled urban expansion between 1870 and 1900, and cities of all sizes grew. New York and Philadelphia doubled and tripled their populations. Smaller cities, especially those in the industrial Midwest and the South, shared the growth; far western cities grew most rapidly of all. In 1870, some 25 percent of Americans lived in cities; by 1900, fully 40 percent of them did.

A Growing Population

The American population grew about 2 percent a year, but cities expanded more rapidly. Births contributed only modestly to urban explosion. Urban families tended to have fewer children than rural ones, and the host of urban health hazards meant that the death rate for infants was twice as high in cities as in the countryside. In the 1880s, half the children born in Chicago did not live to celebrate their fifth birthdays.

The real cause of rapid urban growth was the spectacular ability of the cities to attract newcomers from the nation's small towns and farms and abroad. In America's farmlands, machines were replacing human hands and freeing young people from agricultural life. The appeal of the city lay in the promise of employment. Although urban jobs were often dirty, dangerous, and exhausting, so was farm work. Furthermore, by 1890 industrial workers were earning hundreds of dollars more a year than farm laborers even though living costs were higher in urban areas. Additionally, the "gilded metropolis" offered a host of "marvels" absent from rural life. Shops, theaters, restaurants, department stores, baseball games, and the crowds amazed and amused young people coming from towns and farms.

Southern blacks, often single and young, also joined the migratory stream into the cities. In the West and North, blacks formed only a tiny part of the population, but in southern cities they were more numerous. About 44 percent of late-nineteenth-century Atlanta's residents were black, and so were 38 percent of Nashville's.

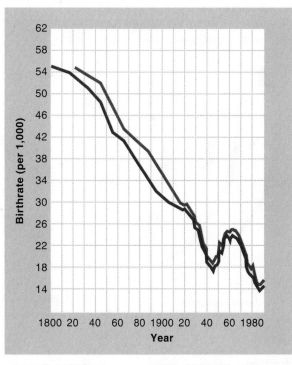

— Total Birthrate — White Birthrate

Falling Birthrates

This chart shows the falling birthrate over the course of almost 200 years. By 1860, the average size of an American family was 5.3 members as compared to 5.8 in 1800. In what 20-year period during the nineteenth century did the largest decline in birthrates occur?

While the American birthrate was falling, it was higher than in Europe. By 1860, natural increase and immigration combined to make the American population as a whole larger than the British population. It was not long before the United States was also larger than Germany and France.

The New Immigration, 1880–1900

Sadie Frowne was born in a small village in Poland, where her mother ran a small grocery store and her father farmed. After her father died, times were hard, and mother and daughter came by steerage to New York, where they had relatives. Although she was only 13 years old, Sadie went to work, first as a domestic servant and then in a sweatshop. Her mother found a job in an underwear factory. Mother and daughter were part of a mass migration from Europe that sent 40 million people to the United States between 1815 and 1915 and another 20 million to Canada and Latin America. Like the Frownes, three-quarters of the newcomers arriving in the United States in the last quarter century stayed in the Northeast. Many of the rest settled in cities across the nation, where they soon outnumbered native-born whites.

Until 1880, three-quarters of the immigrants, so-called "old immigrants," hailed from the British Isles, Germany, and Scandinavia. Irish and Germans were the largest groups. Then the pattern slowly changed.

By 1890, "old immigrants" composed only 60 percent of the total number of newcomers. "New immigrants" such as the Frownes from southern and eastern Europe made up most of the rest. Italian Catholics and eastern European Jews (many of them Orthodox) were most numerous, followed by Slavs (Russians and Poles).

A variety of forces prompted the tide of migration. Better and cheaper transportation made the trip possible. Trains reached far into eastern and southern Europe. Even steerage passengers on transatlantic vessels could now expect a bed and communal washroom. The modernization of European economies also stimulated immigration. New agricultural techniques led landlords to consolidate their land, evicting longtime tenants. Some moved to European cities, others to Canada or South America. The largest group went to the United States. Artisans, their skills made obsolete by machinery, also pulled up stakes. But dissatisfaction with life at home also played a part. Especially in Russia, government persecutions and the expansion of military drafts drove millions of Jews and other minorities to emigrate.

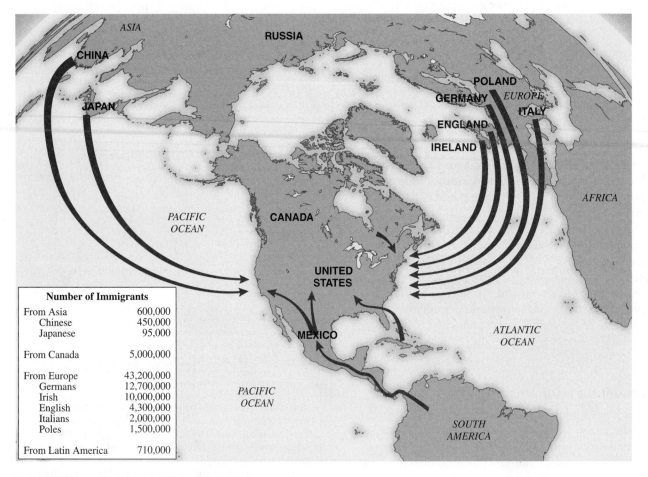

Number of Immigrants	
From Asia	600,000
Chinese	450,000
Japanese	95,000
From Canada	5,000,000
From Europe	43,200,000
Germans	12,700,000
Irish	10,000,000
English	4,300,000
Italians	2,000,000
Poles	1,500,000
From Latin America	710,000

Migration to the United States, 1860–1910

This map makes clear the many parts of the world that sent population to the United States. Many of those who came were dislodged by economic changes in their home countries. What were the most important short-term consequences of these migratory streams? What have been the most important long-term consequences?

Opportunity in "golden" America was the lure. State commissioners of immigration and American railroad and steamship companies wooed potential immigrants. Friends and relatives wrote optimistic letters promising help in finding work. American industrial cities were great places for "blast frnises and Rolen milles," explained one unskilled worker. Often letters included money for the passage or pictures of friends in alluringly fashionable clothes.

Like rural and small-town Americans, Europeans came primarily to work. Most were young, single men with few skills. Jews, however, came most often in family groups, and women predominated among the Irish. When times were good and American industry needed unskilled laborers, migration was heavy. In bad times, numbers fell off. Many immigrants hoped to earn enough money in America to realize their ambitions at home, and as many as a third eventually went back.

Although the greatest influx of Mexicans would come in the twentieth century, Mexican laborers also migrated to the United States. Like Europe, Mexico was in the throes of modernization. Overpopulation and new land policies uprooted many inhabitants, while the construction of a railroad from the Texas border 900 miles into Mexico in 1895 facilitated migration. Many Mexicans ended up in the Southwest and West, often working on railroads and in mines.

RECIPIENTS OF EUROPEAN MIGRATION, 1846–1932

While most migration from Europe was headed toward the United States, immigrants flocked to South America, Canada, and Australia and New Zealand as well. In Argentina, Italian immigrants made up a larger percentage of the population than they did in the United States and thus influenced Argentinean culture more profoundly than they affected American culture. What does this table suggest about the push–pull factors in the process of migration?

(Estimates in millions)

United States	34.2
Argentina and Uruguay	7.1
Canada	5.2
Brazil	4.4
Australia and New Zealand	3.5
Cuba	.9

Overpopulation, turmoil, unemployment, and crop failures brought Asians, mostly from south China, to the "Land of the Golden Mountains." Although only 264,000 Chinese came to the United

Life in the Old Country

Here we see a village street in Russia in the late nineteenth century. What is the condition of the street? What signs of utilities are there? How are the children clothed? What might immigrants who came from this village think about the urban conditions they encountered in the United States?

(Keystone-Mast Collection, URL/California Museum of Photography, University of California, Riverside)

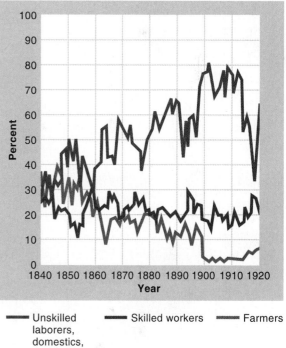

Working-Class Immigration, 1840–1920

The large numbers of unskilled workers coming to the United States were responding to the need for unskilled labor during the second Industrial Revolution.

Source: U.S. Bureau of the Census.

States between 1860 and 1900, they constituted a significant minority on the West Coast. Most were unskilled male contract laborers, away from wives and families for years. They held some of the worst jobs in the West. They worked in mining and agriculture and on railroad and levee construction, and labored in factory and laundry work. To serve them, contractors brought in Chinese women to serve as prostitutes. Virtually enslaved, few of these women could pay off the costs of their passage or escape from brothel life.

The importance of migration from Europe, Mexico, and Asia can hardly be overestimated. Immigrants contributed to the country's rapid urbanization and provided much of the labor needed to accomplish the economic transformation of the late nineteenth century. Their presence also helped transform American society. The American population became far more heterogeneous in terms of ethnicity and religion than any other industrial nation. Since most immigrants were workers, they altered the character of the laboring class. Differences between immigrant groups and between immigrants and American workers weakened immigrants' ability to respond to employers with one voice. The presence of those who spoke little or no English and

had values and experiences very different from those of native-born Americans challenged American ideals, beliefs, and practices.

The Industrial City, 1880–1900

The late-nineteenth-century industrial city had new physical and social arrangements. Slums, nothing new, grew disturbingly, but grand mansions, handsome business and industrial buildings, grandiose civic monuments, parks, and acres of substantial middle-class homes also characterized urban life.

By the last quarter of the nineteenth century, the jumbled arrangements of the antebellum city based upon the necessity of walking to work disappeared. First the slow, horse-drawn "omnibus," then faster and bigger horse railways, and finally cable cars, trolleys, and subways extended city boundaries and allowed people who could afford to pay the fares to live far from their work. Distinctive central districts became places for professional employment and shopping. Surrounding the business center were areas of light manufacturing and wholesale activity with housing for workers. Beyond these working-class neighborhoods stretched middle-class residential areas and then the suburbs, with "pure air, peacefulness," and "natural scenery."

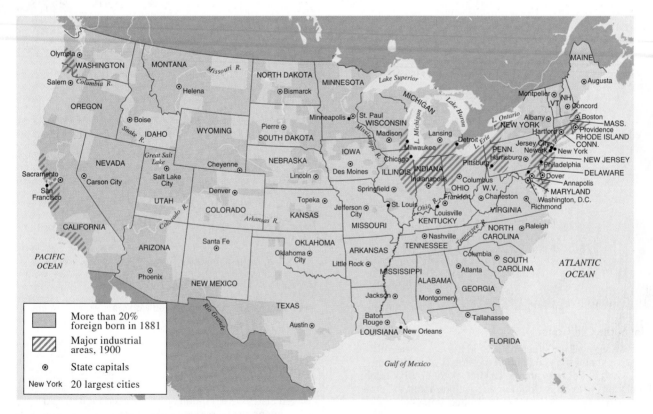

Foreign Immigration, 1880–1920

What areas does this map show that immigrants favored? Which did they avoid and why?

Scattered throughout the city were pockets of industrial activity surrounded by crowded working-class housing.

This new pattern, still characteristic of American cities today, reversed the early nineteenth-century urban form, in which the most desirable housing was in the heart of the city. Now it was on the perimeter. New living arrangements were also more segregated by race and class than those in the preindustrial walking city.

Lower East Side, New York

Here is a picture of life on Hester Street on New York's Lower East Side. Study the photograph to see what it reveals about living conditions in New York City. What indications are there of commercial activity? Why are there so many women on the street and so few men? What is suggested about children? What does the picture suggest about city services to this poor neighborhood? What are the major contrasts between this part of New York and the downtown scene shown on p. 444?

(New York City Views, Milstein Division of U.S. History, Local History & Genealogy, The New York Public Library/Art Resource, NY)

Neighborhoods and Neighborhood Life

Working-class neighborhoods clustered near the center of most industrial cities. Here lived newcomers from the American countryside and, because most immigrants settled in cities, crowds of foreigners as well. Although such districts often had an ethnic flavor, they were not ghettos. Immigrants and native-born Americans often lived in the same neighborhoods, on the same streets, and even in the same houses.

Working-class districts were often what would be called slums today, and it was not until the turn of the century that the public health movement began to improve living conditions there. Neighborhoods were crowded and unsanitary with inadequate public services. Many workers lived in houses once occupied by middle- and upper-class residents, now divided and subdivided to accommodate more people than originally intended. Others squeezed into tenements, built to accommodate as many families as possible. Outdoor privies, shared by several families, were the rule. Water came from outdoor hydrants, and women had to carry it inside. Such indoor fixtures as existed frequently emptied waste directly into unpaved alleys. Refuse piles stank in the summer and froze in the winter. Even when people kept their own living quarters clean, their outside environment was unsanitary. It was no surprise that urban death rates were so high.

Working-class housing, however, was far from uniform. Skilled workers might rent comfortable quarters, and a few even owned their own homes. Unskilled and semiskilled workers were not so fortunate. Yet despite the often drab circumstances, families succeeded in creating a sense of community. A wide range of institutions and associations came to life. Religious and ethnic associations helped immigrants feel at home. Jews gathered in their synagogues, Hebrew schools, and Hebrew- and Yiddish-speaking literary groups. Germans had their family saloons and educational and singing societies. Such organizations provided companionship, a social network, spiritual consolation, and a bridge between life in the "old country" and life in America. Yet they also separated those involved in them from native-born Americans and other ethnic groups.

African Americans faced the worst living conditions in the city, confined to segregated black neighborhoods in the North and back alleys and small streets in the South. But they too were sustained by a rich religious and associational life. Rapidly growing black churches like the African Methodist Episcopal Church retained the emotional exuberance of slave

New York City

Downtown New York City in 1890 hosted a mixture of horse-drawn vehicles and the new "horseless carriages." The nonresidential nature of the central business district gave a special character to the late-nineteenth-century city. What sorts of people appear in the picture? What signs of their social class does the picture provide?

(Brown Brothers)

religion. Black members of mainline Protestant denominations established separate branches that provided fellowship and support. The emergence of a small black middle class of ministers, businessmen, doctors, and lawyers furnished leaders for urban black communities.

Beyond working-class neighborhoods and pockets of black housing lay streets of middle-class houses. Here lived the urban lower middle class: clerks, shop-keepers, bookkeepers, salespeople, and small tradespeople. Their salaries allowed them to buy or rent houses with some privacy and comfort. Separate spaces for cooking and laundry work kept hot and often odorous housekeeping tasks away from other living areas. Many houses boasted up-to-date gas lighting and bathrooms. Outside, the neighborhoods were cleaner and more attractive than in the inner city. Residents could pay for garbage collection, gaslights, and other improvements.

On the fringes of the city were the districts peopled by the substantial middle class and the rich, who made their money in business, commerce, and the professions or inherited family fortunes. Public transportation sped them to and from their offices. Their houses were comfortable and inviting. Robert Work, a modestly successful cap and hat merchant, lived with his family in West Philadelphia and commuted more than four miles to work. The 1880 census revealed that the household contained two servants, two boarders, Robert's wife, and their son, who was in school. The Works' house had running hot and cold water, indoor bathrooms, central heating, and other modern conveniences. Elaborately carved furniture, rugs, draperies, and lace curtains probably graced the downstairs, where the family entertained and gathered for meals. Upstairs, comfortable bedrooms provided a maximum of privacy for family members. The live-in servants, who did most of the housework, shared little of this space or privacy, and were probably restricted to the kitchen, the pantry, and bedrooms in the attic.

The Social Geography of the Cities

In industrial cities of this era, people were sorted by class, income, occupation, and race. Physical distances between upper- and middle-class neighborhoods and working-class neighborhoods eliminated or distorted firsthand knowledge of each other and bred social disapproval. While middle-class newspapers criticized "crowds of idlers, who, day and night, infect Main Street," often the "idlers" were men who could not find employment. A working-class woman's response to visitors who were attacking the use of alcohol captures the critical view from the bottom of society. "When the rich stopped drinking, it would be time to speak to the poor about it."

The Life of the Middle Class

The sharp comments made by different classes of Americans suggest the economic and social polarization that late-nineteenth-century industrialization spawned. For middle-class Americans, there was much to value in the new age. Between 1865 and 1890, average middle-class income rose about 30 percent. By 1900, fully 36 percent of urban families owned their homes.

More leisure time and greater access to consumer goods signaled industrialism's power to transform the lives of middle-class Americans. Plentiful immigrant servant girls relieved urban middle-class wives of many housekeeping chores, and smaller families lightened the burdens of motherhood. New department stores began to appear in the central business districts

Middle-Class Comfort

This photograph of a middle-class house in River Forest, Illinois, suggests the comfort available to those who could afford it and the ways suburban life shielded the middle class from the squalor and ugliness of industrial life. What does the exterior of the house suggest about what the inside might be like? How are the porch and garden treated? Why was the porch so large?

(Culver Pictures)

in the 1870s, feeding the desire for material possessions and revolutionizing retailing. Shopping for home furnishings and clothes became integral to many middle-class women's lives.

New Freedoms for Middle-Class Women

As many middle-class women acquired leisure time and enhanced purchasing power, they also won new freedoms. Several states granted women more property rights in marriage, adding to their growing sense of independence. Casting off confining crinolines, they now wore a shirtwaist blouse and ankle-length skirt that was more comfortable for working, school, and sports.

Using their new freedom, women joined organizations of all kinds—literary societies, charity groups, reform clubs. There they gained organizational experience, awareness of their talents, and contact with people and problems outside their traditional family roles. The depression of 1893 stimulated many women to investigate slum and factory conditions, and some began even earlier. Jane Addams, who told her college classmates in 1881 to lead lives "filled with good works and honest toil," went on to found Hull House, a famous social settlement.

After the Civil War, educational opportunities for women expanded. New women's colleges offered programs similar to those at competitive men's colleges, while midwestern and western state schools dropped prohibitions against women. In 1890, some 13 percent of all college graduates were women; by 1900, nearly 20 percent were. Higher education prepared middle-class women for conventional female roles as well as for work and public service. A few courageous graduates overcame many barriers to enter the professions. By the early twentieth century, the number of women professionals (including teachers) was increasing at three times the rate for men.

Job opportunities for educated middle-class women, however, were generally limited to the social services and teaching, a highly demanding but poorly paying field that grew as urban schools expanded under the pressure of a burgeoning population. By the 1890s, the willingness of middle-class women to work for low pay opened up new forms of employment in office work, nursing, and department stores. But moving up to high-status jobs proved difficult, even for middle-class women.

One reason for the greater independence of American women was that they were having fewer babies. This was especially true of educated women. In 1900, nearly one married woman in five was childless. Advances in birth control technology (the modern diaphragm was developed in 1880) helped make new patterns possible. Decreasing family size and an increase in the divorce rate (1 out of 12 marriages in 1905) fueled male fears. Arguments against the new woman intensified as many men reaffirmed Victorian stereotypes of "woman's sphere." One male orator in 1896 inveighed against the new woman's public role because "a woman's brain involves emotions rather than intellect." Male campaigns against prostitution and for sex hygiene, as well as efforts to reinforce traditional sex roles, reflected deep fears that female passions might weaken male vigor.

Male Mobility and the Success Ethic

As middle-class women's lives were changing, so were men's. Expansion of the postwar economy and changes in the structure of American business opened up many new job opportunities for middle-class men. The growing complexity of census classifications reveals some of these new jobs. Where the census taker had once noted only the occupation of "clerk," now were listed "accountant," "salesman," and "shipping clerk." As the lower ranks of the white-collar world became more specialized, the number of middle-class jobs increased.

Because these new careers required more education, the educational system expanded. Public high schools increased from 160 in 1870 to 6,000 in 1900. By that year, most states and territories had compulsory school attendance laws. Enrollment in colleges and universities nearly doubled, from 53,000 in 1870 to 101,000 in 1900. Universities gained a new stature in American life. Land-grant state universities (made possible by the Morrill Act of 1862) expanded, and philanthropists established research universities such as Stanford, Johns Hopkins, and the University of Chicago.

These developments led to greater specialization and professionalism. Before the Civil War, a Swedish pioneer in Wisconsin described a young mason who "laid aside the trowel, got himself some medical books, and assumed the title of doctor." But by the 1890s, with government licensing and the rise of professional schools, the word *career* began to take on its modern meaning. No longer were tradespeople likely to read up on medicine and become doctors. Organizations such as the American Medical Association and the American Bar Association were regulating and professionalizing membership.

The need for lawyers, bankers, architects, and insurance agents to serve business and industry expanded career opportunities. As large companies formed and became bureaucratized, business required many more managerial positions. As the public sector expanded, new careers in social services and government opened up as well. Young professional experts with graduate training in the social sciences filled many of them. The professional disciplines of history, economics, sociology, psychology, and political science all date from the last 20 years of the nineteenth century.

The social ethic of the age stressed that economic rewards were available to anyone who fervently sought them. Many people argued that, unlike in Europe, where family background and social class determined social rank, in America, few barriers held back those of good character and diligent work habits. It was endlessly pointed out that while John D. Rockefeller had raised turkeys as a boy and Andrew Carnegie's mother had been a washerwoman, both men had risen spectacularly through their own efforts. Horatio Alger's rags-to-riches novels, read by millions, reinforced the message. In his popular novel, *Ragged Dick,* the hero begins as a ragged shoeshine boy living on the streets. An unexpected gift of a new suit of clothes helps to raise Dick's aspirations to "learn the business and grow up 'spectable." As he begins the process of becoming respectable, good fortune intervenes again. Dick rescues a child who tumbles into the icy waters of the harbor. Her father completes the hero's transformation from Ragged Dick to Richard Hunter, Esq., by offering him a job as a clerk in his counting house. Although moralists pointed to virtuous habits as crucial in Alger's heroes, success often depended as much on luck as on pluck.

Unlimited and equal opportunity for upward advancement in America has never been as easy as the "bootstraps" ethic maintains. But the persistence of the success myth owes something to the fact that many Americans, particularly those who began well, did rise rapidly. Native-born, middle-class whites tended to have the skills, resources, and connections that opened up the most desirable jobs. The typical big businessman was a white, Anglo-Saxon Protestant from a middle- or upper-class family whose father was most likely in business, banking, or commerce.

Industrial Work and the Laboring Class

David Lawlor, an Irish immigrant who came to the United States in 1872, might have agreed with the message of the Alger stories. As a child, he worked in the Fall River textile mills and read Horatio Alger in his free time. Like Alger's heroes, he went to night school and rose in the business world, eventually becoming an advertising executive.

But Lawlor's success was exceptional. Most working-class Americans labored long hours on dangerous factory floors, in cramped sweatshops, or in steamy basement kitchens for meager wages. As industrialization transformed the nature of work and the composition of the workforce, traditional opportunities for mobility and even for a secure livelihood slipped from the grasp of many working-class Americans.

The Impact of Ethnic Diversity

Immigrants made up a sizable portion of the urban working class in the late nineteenth century. They formed 20 percent of the labor force and more than 40 percent of laborers in the manufacturing and extractive industries. In cities, where they tended to settle, they accounted for more than half the working-class population.

Industrial work, urban life, labor protest, and local politics were influenced by the fact that more than half the urban industrial class was foreign, unskilled, perhaps illiterate, and often possessed only a limited command of the English language. Eager for the unskilled positions rapidly being created as mechanization and mass production took hold, immigrants often shared little with native-born workers or even with one another. Because of immigration, American working-class society was a mosaic of nationalities, cultures, religions, and interests.

The ethnic diversity of the industrial workforce helps explain its occupational patterns. Generally occupation was related to ethnic background and experience. At the top of the working-class hierarchy, native-born Protestant whites held a disproportionate share of well-paying skilled jobs. They were the aristocrats of the working class. Their jobs demanded expertise and training, as had been true of skilled industrial workers in the pre–Civil War period. But their occupations bore the mark of late-nineteenth-century industrialism. They were machinists, iron puddlers and rollers, engineers, foremen, mechanics, and printers.

Skilled northern European immigrants filled most of the middle-rank positions. Often they had held similar jobs in their homeland. The Germans found work as tailors, bakers, brewers, and shoemakers, while Cornish and Irish miners secured skilled jobs in midwestern and western mines. The Jews, who had tailoring experience in their homelands, became the backbone of the garment industry (where they faced little competition from American male workers, who considered it unmanly to work on women's clothes).

But most of the "new immigrants" from southern and central Europe had no urban industrial experience. They labored in the unskilled, dirty jobs near the bottom of the occupational ladder. They relined blast furnaces in steel mills, carried raw materials or finished products from place to place, or cleaned up after skilled workers. Often, they were carmen or day laborers on the docks, ditchdiggers, or construction workers. Hiring was often on a daily basis, arranged through intermediaries such as the Italian padrone. Unskilled work provided little in the way of either job stability or income.

At the bottom, blacks occupied the most marginal positions as janitors, servants, porters, and laborers. Racial discrimination generally excluded them from industrial jobs, even though their occupational background differed little from that of rural white immigrants. There were always plenty of whites eager to work, so it was not necessary to hire blacks except occasionally as scabs during a labor strike. "It is an exceptional case where you find any colored labor in the factories, except as porters," observed one white. "Neither colored female…nor male laborer is engaged in the mechanical arts."

The Changing Nature of Work

The rise of big business, characterized by mechanization and mass production, changed the size and shape of the workforce and the nature of work itself. More and more Americans became wage earners. The number of manufacturing workers doubled between 1880 and 1900, with the fastest expansion in the unskilled and semiskilled ranks.

But the need for skilled workers remained. New positions, as in steam fitting and structural ironwork, appeared as industries expanded and changed. Increasingly, older skills became obsolete, however. And all skilled workers faced the possibility that technical advances would eliminate their favored jobs or that employers would hire unskilled helpers to take over parts of their jobs. In industries as different as shoemaking, cigar making, and iron puddling, new methods of production and organization undermined the position of skilled workers.

INCREASE IN SIZE OF INDUSTRIES, 1860–1900

This table highlights the dramatic changes in the workplace over a 40-year period. Think about what the figures suggest about the experience of work. What industries typically had the largest workforces in 1900? What industries had the most dramatic increases in the size of their workforces between 1860 and 1900?

Industry	Average Number of Workers per Establishment	
	1860	1900
Cotton goods	112	287
Glass	81	149
Iron and steel	65	333
Hosiery and knit goods	46	91
Silk and silk goods	39	135
Woollen goods	33	67
Carpets and rugs	31	213
Tobacco	30	67
Slaughtering and meatpacking	20	61
Paper and wood pulp	15	65
Shipbuilding	15	42
Agricultural implements	8	65
Leather	5	40
Malt liquors	5	26

Source: U.S. Bureau of the Census.

Work Settings and Experiences

The workplace could be a dock or cluttered factory yard, a multistoried textile mill, a huge, barnlike steel mill with all the latest machinery, or a mine tunnel hundreds of feet underground. A majority of American manufacturing workers now labored in factories, and the numbers of those working in large plants dominated by the unceasing rhythms of machinery increased steadily.

Some Americans, however, still toiled in small shops and sweatshops tucked away in basements, lofts, or immigrant apartments. Even in these smaller settings, the pressure to produce was relentless, for volume, not hours, determined pay. When contractors cut wages, workers had to speed up to earn the same pay.

The organization of work divided workers. Those paid by the piece competed against the speed, agility, and output of other workers. In large factories, workers separated into small work groups and mingled only rarely with the rest of the workforce. The clustering of ethnic groups in certain types of work also undermined working-class solidarity.

A Garment Factory

Many young Jewish women worked in the garment industry. You see an example of their working conditions here. How would you describe these women's workplace? How safe is it? How comfortable is it? What might it be like to work here in the summer? Who are the men in the background?

(Brown Brothers)

All workers had a very long working day in common. Although the factory day had fallen from the 12 hours expected before the Civil War, people still spent more than half their waking hours on the job—usually 10 hours a day, six days a week. Different occupations had specific demands. Bakers worked 65 hours a week; canners worked 77. Sweatshop workers might labor far into the night, long after factory workers had gone home.

Work was usually unhealthy, dangerous, and comfortless. Although a few states passed laws to regulate work conditions, enforcement was spotty. Few owners observed regulations about toilets, drinking facilities, or washing areas. Nor did they concern themselves with the health or safety of their employees. Women, bent over sewing machines, developed digestive illnesses and curved spines. Poorly ventilated mines stank of human waste and spoiled garbage, with temperatures sometimes rising above 120 degrees. Miners worked with dynamite and all too often died in cave-ins caused by inadequate timber supports in the mine shafts. When new drilling machinery was introduced into western mines, it produced tiny stone particles that caused lung disease.

Accident rates in the United States far exceeded those of Europe's industrial nations. Each year, 35,000 workers died from industrial mishaps. Iron and steel mills were the big killers, although the railroads alone accounted for 6,000 fatalities a year during the 1890s. Nationwide, nearly one-quarter of the men reaching age 20 in 1880 would not live to see 44 (compared with 7 percent today). American business owners had

little legal responsibility—and some felt none—for employees' safety or health. The law placed the burden of avoiding accidents on the workers, who were expected to quit if they thought conditions were unsafe.

Industrial workers labored at jobs that were also increasingly specialized and monotonous. The size of many firms allowed a kind of specialization that was impossible in a small enterprise. Even skilled workers did not produce a complete product, and the range of their skills was narrowing. "A man never learns the machinist's trade now," one New Yorker grumbled. "The different branches of the trade are divided and subdivided so that one man may make just a particular part of a machine and may not know anything whatever about another part of the same machine." Cabinetmakers found themselves not crafting cabinets but putting together and finishing pieces made by others. In such circumstances, many skilled workers complained that they were being reduced to drudges and wage slaves. This discontent with the nature of work contributed to working-class unrest.

Still, industrial work provided some personal benefits. New arrangements helped humanize the workplace. Workers who obtained jobs through family and friends labored alongside them. In most industries, the foreman controlled day-to-day activities. He chose workers from the crowds at the gate, fired those who proved unsatisfactory, selected appropriate materials and equipment, and determined the order and pace of production. Because the foreman was himself a member of the working class who had climbed his way up, he might sympathize with subordinates. Yet the foreman could also be authoritarian and harsh, especially if the workers he supervised were unskilled or belonged to another ethnic group.

The Worker's Share in Industrial Progress

The huge fortunes accumulated by famous industrialists such as Andrew Carnegie and John D. Rockefeller during the late nineteenth century dramatized the pattern of wealth concentration that had begun in the early period of industrialization. In 1890, the top 1 percent of American families possessed more than a quarter of the wealth, whereas the share held by the top 10 percent was about 73 percent. Economic growth still benefited people who influenced its path, and they claimed the lion's share of the rewards.

But what of the workers who tended the machines that lay at the base of industrial wealth? Working-class Americans made up the largest segment of the labor force (more than 50 percent), so their experience reveals important facets of the American social and economic systems and American values.

Statistics of increasing production, of ever more goods, tell part of the story. Figures on real wages also reveal something important. Industry still needed skilled workers and paid them well. Average real wages rose more than 50 percent between 1860 and 1900. Skilled manufacturing workers, about one-tenth of the nonagricultural working class in the late nineteenth century, saw their wages rise by about 74 percent. But wages for the unskilled increased by only 31 percent. The differential was substantial and widened as the century drew to a close.

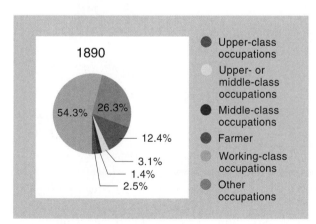

Labor Force Distribution, 1890

Whereas a majority of Americans in the twentieth century defined themselves as middle class, in the nineteenth century, most Americans held working-class jobs. Approximately what percentage of workers held middle- or upper-class jobs?

Source: U.S. Bureau of the Census.

Taken as a whole, the working class accrued substantial benefits in the late nineteenth century, even if its share of the total wealth did not increase. American workers had more material comforts than their European counterparts. But the general picture conceals the realities of working-class economic life. A U.S. Bureau of Labor study of working-class families in 1889 revealed great disparities of income: a young girl in a silk mill made $130 a year; a laborer earned $384 a year; a carpenter took home $686. The carpenter's family lived in a four-room house. Their breakfast usually included meat or eggs, hotcakes, butter, cake, and coffee. The silk worker and the laborer, by contrast, ate bread and butter as the main portion of two of their three daily meals. Their yearly income fell far short of the $600 to $800 that was necessary for a family to survive in any comfort.

For workers without steady employment, rising real wages were meaningless. Workers, especially those who were unskilled, often found work only sporadically. When times were slow or conditions depressed, as they were between 1873 and 1879 and 1893 and 1897, employers, especially in small firms, laid off both skilled and unskilled workers and reduced wages. Even in a good year like 1890, one out of every five men outside agriculture had been unemployed at least a month. One-quarter lost four months or more.

Unemployment insurance did not exist, so workers had no cushion against losing their jobs. One woman grimly recalled, "If the factory shuts down without warning, as it did last year for six weeks, we have a growing expense with nothing to counterbalance." Older workers who had no social security or those who had accidents on the job but no disability insurance had severely reduced incomes. Occasionally, kindhearted employers offered assistance in hard times, but it was rarely enough. The Lawrence Manufacturing Company compensated one of its workers $50 for the loss of a hand and awarded another $66.71 for a severed arm.

Although nineteenth-century ideology pictured men as breadwinners, many working-class married men could not earn enough to support their families. A working-class family's standard of living thus often depended on its number of workers. Today, two-income families are common. But in the nineteenth century, married women did not usually take outside employment, although they contributed to family income by taking in sewing, laundry, and boarders. In 1890, only 3.3 percent of married women worked in the paid labor force.

The Family Economy

If married women did not work for pay outside their homes, their children did. The laborer whose annual earnings amounted to only $384 depended on his

TWO NINETEENTH-CENTURY BUDGETS

What do these two monthly family budgets reveal about different standards of living and different consumption choices? What do you consider the most significant differences between the lives of these two families? In 2001 dollars, the laborer took home $448 a month while the accountant earned about $1,259 a month. The laborer spent about $530 on his monthly expenses while the accountant's budgeted expenses came to about $817.

	Monthly budget of a laborer, his wife, and one child in 1891; his income is $23.67	Monthly budget of a married bank accountant with no children in 1892; his income is about $66.50
Food	$6.51	$13.22
Rent	9.02	9.88
Furniture	3.61	0.30
Taxes and insurance	3.32	7.11
Utilities	2.94	4.99
Sundries	1.09	2.10
Liquor and tobacco	0.66	0.42
Medicine	0.29	0.27
Clothes	0.21	0.19
Dry goods	0.16	2.45
Postage	0.10	—
Transportation	0.08	1.71
Reading material	—	0.53
	$27.99	$43.17

Source: Chart from *The Changing Face of Inequality* by Oliver Zunz © University of Chicago Press. Reprinted with permission.

NUMBER OF WOMEN EMPLOYED IN SELECTED INDUSTRIES, 1870–1910

This chart shows the growth of women workers in several key industries. Although far fewer women had paid jobs than men, they were never absent from the workplace.

	Industry					
Year	Chemical	Electrical	Paper	Printing	Food	Metal
1870	403	—	6,242	4,397	2,460	5,217
1880	862	—	14,126	9,322	4,503	7,668
1890	2,140	—	22,444	24,640	10,169	15,232
1900	3,427	—	27,261	32,938	19,713	21,335
1910	15,198	12,093	33,419	47,640	48,099	56,208

Source: U.S. Department of Labor, Women's Bureau, *Women's Occupations Through Seven Decades*, Bulletin no. 218 (Washington, D.C.: Government Printing Office, 1947), 95, 120, 121, 123, 130, 133.

13-year-old son, not his wife, to go out and earn an extra $196, critical to the family's welfare. Sending children into the labor market was an essential survival strategy for many working-class Americans. In 1880, one-fifth of the nation's children between ages 10 and 14 held jobs.

Child labor was closely linked to a father's income, which in turn depended on skill, ethnic background, and occupation. Immigrant families more frequently sent their young children out to work (and also had more children) than native-born families. Middle-class reformers who sentimentalized childhood disapproved of parents who put their children to work. As one investigator of working-class life reported, "Father never attended school, and thinks his children will have sufficient schooling before they reach their tenth year, thinks no advantage will be gained from longer attendance at school, so children will be put to work as soon as able." Reformers believed that such fathers condemned their children to future destitution by denying them education. Actually, sending children to work was a means of coping with the immediate threat of poverty, financing the education of one of the children, or paying off the mortgage.

Many more young people over age 14 were working for wages than was the case for children. Half of all Philadelphia's students had quit school by that age. Daughters as well as sons were expected to take positions, although young women from immigrant families were more likely to work than young American women. As *Arthur's Home Magazine* for women pointed out, a girl's earnings would help "to relieve her hard-working father of the burden of her support, to supply home with comforts and refinements, to educate a younger brother." By 1900, nearly 20 percent of American women were in the labor force.

Employed women earned far less than men. An experienced female factory worker might be paid between $5 and $6 a week, whereas an unskilled male laborer could make about $8. Discrimination, present from women's earliest days in the workforce, persisted. Still, factory jobs were desirable because they often paid better than other kinds of work open to women.

By the 1890s, new forms of employment in office work, nursing, and clerking in department stores offered some young women attractive opportunities. In San Francisco, the number of clerical jobs doubled between 1852 and 1880. But most women faced limited employment options, and ethnic taboos and cultural traditions helped shape choices. About a quarter of working women secured factory jobs. Italian and Jewish women (whose cultural backgrounds virtually forbade their going into domestic service) clustered in the garment industry, and Poles and Slavs went into textiles, food processing, and meatpacking. In some industries, such as textiles and tobacco, women composed an important segment of the workforce. But about 40 percent of them, especially those from Irish, Scandinavian, and black families, took jobs as maids, cooks, laundresses, and nurses.

Domestic service was arduous, with few machines to lighten the labor. A Minneapolis housemaid described an exhausting routine. "I used to get up at four o'clock every morning and work till ten P.M. every day of the week. Mondays and Tuesdays, when the washing and ironing was to be done,

I used to get up at two o'clock and wash or iron until breakfast time." Nor could domestics count on much sympathy from their employers. "Do not think it necessary to give a hired girl as good a room as that used by members of the family," said one lady of the house. "She should sleep near the kitchen and not go up the front stairs or through the front hall to reach her room." Live-in servants received room and board plus $2 to $5 a week. The fact that so many women took domestic work despite the job's disadvantages speaks clearly of their limited opportunities.

The dismal situation facing working women drove some, such as Rose Haggerty, into prostitution. Burdened with a widowed and sickly mother and four young brothers and sisters, Rose was only 14 years old when she started work at a New York paper-bag factory. Her fortunes improved when a friend helped her buy a sewing machine. Rose then sewed shirts at home, often working as long as 14 hours a day, to support her family. Suddenly, the piecework rate for shirts was slashed, and, desperate, Rose contemplated suicide. But when a sailor offered her money for spending the night with him, she realized she had an alternative. Prostitution meant food, rent, and heat for her family. "Let God Almighty judge who's to blame most," the 20-year-old Rose reflected, "I that was driven, or them that drove me to the pass I'm in."

Prostitution appears to have increased in the late nineteenth century, although there is no way of knowing the actual numbers of women involved. Probably most single women accepted the respectable jobs open to them. They tolerated discrimination and low wages because their families depended on their contributions. They also knew that when they married, they would probably leave the paid workforce forever.

Marriage hardly ended women's work, however. Like colonial families, late-nineteenth-century working-class families operated as cooperative economic units. The unpaid domestic labor of working-class wives was critical to family survival. With husbands away for 10 to 11 hours a day, women bore the burden of child care and the domestic chores. Because working-class families could not afford labor-saving conveniences, housework was time-consuming and arduous. Without an icebox, a working-class woman spent part of each day shopping for food (more expensive in small quantities). Doing laundry entailed carrying water from outside pumps, heating it on the stove, washing the clothes, rinsing them with fresh water, and hanging them up to dry. Ironing was a hot and unpleasant job in small and stuffy quarters. Keeping an apartment or house clean when the atmosphere was grimy and unpaved roads were littered with refuse and horse dung was a challenge.

CONGRESSIONAL HEARINGS

Students of history can discover fascinating materials on nineteenth-century life by exploring the published records of the American political system. Privately published from 1833 to 1873, the *Congressional Globe* details the proceedings of the Senate and the House, revealing the nature of congressional deliberations in an era when debate, such as that over the Compromise of 1850 in the Senate, was the focus of the national political process. After 1873, the government published these proceedings in the *Congressional Record*. The *Record* is not a literal transcription of debate, for members can edit their remarks, insert speeches, and add supporting materials. Still, it gives a good sense of the proceedings of both the Senate and the House.

Much of the serious work of government, past and present, takes place in congressional committees. One foreign observer called Congress "not so much a legislative assembly as a huge panel from which committees are selected." The committee system is almost as old as the constitutional system itself and is rooted in the Constitution's granting of lawmaking power to Congress. From the start, Congress divided into assorted committees to gather information, enabling members to evaluate legislative proposals intelligently.

Two kinds of committees existed in the House and Senate. Standing committees had permanent responsibility for reviewing legislative proposals on a host of financial, judicial, foreign, and other affairs. By 1892, the Senate had 44 standing committees and the House had 50. Select committees were temporary, often charged with investigating specific problems. In the late nineteenth century, congressional committees investigated such problems as Ku Klux Klan terrorism, the sweatshop system, tenement house conditions, and relations between labor and capital. In each case, extensive hearings were held.

Congressional hearings have become increasingly important sources of historical evidence in recent years. They show the Senate and the House of Representatives in action as they seek to translate popular sentiment into law.

But they also reveal public attitudes as they record the voices of Americans testifying in committee halls. Because one function of legislative hearings is to enable diverse groups to express their frustrations and desires, they often contain the testimony of witnesses drawn from many different social and economic backgrounds. Included here is the partial testimony of a Massachusetts laborer who appeared before the Senate Committee on Education and Labor in 1883. Because working-class witnesses like this man usually left no other record of their experiences or thoughts, committee reports and hearings provide valuable insight into the lives and attitudes of ordinary people.

Hearings also reveal the attitudes and social values of committee members. Hence, caution is needed in the use of hearings. Witnesses often have vested interests and are frequently coached and cautious in what they communicate on the stand. Rather than seeking to illuminate issues, committee members often speak and explore questions for other—usually political—reasons.

Despite these limitations, committee hearings are rich sources of information. In this excerpt, what can you learn about the life of the witness testifying before the committee? In what way do the values of the committee members conflict with those of the witness? Why is the chairman so harsh toward the witness? Is he entirely unsympathetic? Why do you think the questioner overemphasizes the relationship between moral beliefs and economic realities? What kind of social tensions does the passage reveal?

Reflecting on the Past Have you observed any recent hearings of congressional investigating committees on television? Are moral behavior and hunger still topics of concern for Americans? How is the interaction between modern "haves" and "have-nots" similar to and different from the interaction between this laborer and the committee members in 1883? Do ethical beliefs and economic realities still separate social classes?

Hearings on the Relations Between Labor and Capital

Q. You get a dollar a day, wages?—A. That is the average pay that men receive. The rents, especially in Somerville, are so high that it is almost impossible for the working men to live in a house.

Q. What rent do you pay?—A. For the last year I have been paying $10 a month, and most of the men out there have to pay about that amount for a house—$10 a month for rooms.

Q. For a full house, or for rooms only?—A. For rooms in a house.

Q. How many rooms?—A. Four or five.

Q. How much of your time have you been out of work, or idle, for the last full year, say?—A. I have not been out of work more than three weeks altogether, because I have been making a dollar or two peddling or doing something, when I was out of work, in the currying line.

Q. Making about the same that you made at your trade?—A. Well, I have made at my trade a little more than that, but that is the average.

Q. Are you a common drunkard?—A. No, sir.

Q. Do you smoke a great deal?—A. Well, yes, sir; I smoke as much as any man.

The CHAIRMAN. I want to know how much you have got together in the course of a year, and what you have spent your money for, so that folks can see whether you have had pay enough to get rich on.

The WITNESS. A good idea.

The CHAIRMAN. That is precisely the sort of idea that people ought to know. How much money do you think you have earned during this last year; has it averaged a dollar a day for three hundred days?

The WITNESS. I have averaged more than that; I have averaged $350 or $400. I will say, for the year.

Q. You pay $10 a month rent; that makes $120 a year?—A. Yes, sir.

The CHAIRMAN. I have asked you these questions in this abrupt way because I want to find out whether you have spent much for practices that might have been dispensed with. You say you smoke?

The WITNESS. Yes, sir.

Q. How much a week do you spend for that?—A. I get 20 cents worth of tobacco a week.

Q. That is $10.40 a year?—A. Yes, sir.

Q. And you say you are not a common drunkard?—A. No, sir.

Q. Do you imagine that you have spent as much more for any form of beer, or ale, or anything of that kind, that you could have got along without?—A. No, sir.

Q. How much do you think has gone in that way?—A. About $1 or $2.

Q. During the whole year?—A. Yes, sir.

Q. That would make $11.40 or $12.40—we will call it $12—gone for wickedness. Now, what else, besides your living, besides the support of your wife and children?—A. Well, I don't know as there is anything else.

Q. Can you not think of anything else that was wrong?—A. No, sir.

Q. Twelve dollars have gone for sin and iniquity; and $120 for rent; that makes $132?—A. Yes.

Q. How many children have you?—A. Two.

Q. Your family consists of yourself, your wife, and two children?—A. Yes.

Q. One hundred and thirty-two dollars from $400 leaves you $268, does it not?—A. Yes, sir.

Q. And with that amount you have furnished your family?—A. Yes, sir.

Q. You have been as economical as you could, I suppose?—A. Yes.

Q. How much money have you left?—A. Sixty dollars in debt.

Q. How did you do that?—A. I don't know, sir.

Q. Can you not think of something more that you have wasted?—A. No, sir.

Q. Have you been as careful as you could?—A. Yes, sir.

Q. And you have come out at the end of the year $60 in debt?—A. Yes, sir.

Q. Have you been extravagant in your family expenses?—A. No, sir; a man can't be very extravagant on that much money. . . .

Q. And there are four of you in the family?—A. Yes, sir.

Q. How many pounds of beefsteak have you had in your family, that you bought for your own home consumption within this year that we have been speaking of?—A. I don't think there has been five pounds of beefsteak.

Q. You have had a little pork steak?—A. We had a half a pound of pork steak yesterday; I don't know when we had any before.

Q. What other kinds of meat have you had within a year?—A. Well, we have had corn beef twice I think that I can remember this year—on Sunday, for dinner.

Q. Twice is all that you can remember within a year?—A. Yes—and some cabbage.

Q. What have you eaten?—A. Well, bread mostly, when we could get it; we sometimes couldn't make out to get that, and have had to go without a meal.

Q. Has there been any day in the year that you have had to go without anything to eat?—A. Yes, sir, several days.

Q. More than one day at a time?—A. No.

Q. How about the children and your wife—did they go without anything to eat too?—A. My wife went out this morning and went to a neighbor's and got a loaf of bread and fetched it home, and when she got home the children were crying for something to eat.

Q. Have the children had anything to eat to-day except that, do you think?—A. They had that loaf of bread—I don't know what they have had since then, if they have had anything.

Q. Did you leave any money at home?—A. No, sir.

Q. If that loaf is gone, is there anything in the house?—A. No, sir; unless my wife goes out and gets something; and I don't know who would mind the children while she goes out.

As managers of family resources, married women bore important responsibilities. What American families had once produced for themselves now had to be bought. It was up to the working-class wife to scour secondhand shops to find cheap clothes for her family. Domestic economies were vital to survival. Women also supplemented family income by taking in work. Jewish and Italian women frequently did piecework and sewing at home. Other families kept boarders. Immigrant families in particular often made ends meet by taking single, young countrymen into their homes. Having boarders meant providing meals and clean laundry, juggling different work schedules, and sacrificing privacy. But the advantages of extra income far outweighed the disadvantages for many working-class families.

Black women's working lives reflected the obstacles African Americans faced in late-nineteenth-century cities. Although only about 7 percent of married white women worked outside the home, African American women did so both before and after marriage. In southern cities in 1880, about three-quarters of single black women and one-third of married black women worked outside the home. Because industrial employers would not hire African American women, most of them were domestics or laundresses. The high percentage of married black women in the labor force reflected the marginal wages their husbands earned. But it may also be explained in part by the lesson learned during slavery that children could thrive without the constant attention of their mothers.

Capital Versus Labor

Class conflict characterized late-nineteenth-century industrial life. Although workers welcomed the progress that factories made possible, many rejected their employers' values, which emphasized individual gain at the expense of collective good. While owners reaped most of the profits, workers believed they were turning into wage slaves and that the process threatened to undermine the republic itself.

On-the-Job Protests

Workers and employers struggled over control of the workplace. Many workers staunchly resisted unsatisfactory working conditions and the tendency of bosses to treat them "like any other piece of machinery, to be made to do the maximum amount of work with the minimum expenditure of fuel." Skilled workers, such as iron puddlers and glassblowers, had indispensable knowledge about the production process as well as practical experience and were in a key position to direct on-the-job actions. Sometimes they attempted to make critical work decisions. Detroit printers, for example, tried to retain the right to distribute headlines and white space (the "fat") rather than letting their bosses hand out the fat as a special reward and means of increasing competition among workers. Others hoped to humanize work. Cigar makers clung to their custom of having one worker read to others as they performed their tedious chores.

Workers sought to regulate the pace of production. Too many goods meant an inhuman pace of work and even overproduction, layoffs, and lowered prices paid for piecework. So an experienced worker might whisper to a new hand, "See here, young fellow, you're working too fast. You'll spoil our job for us if you don't go slower."

A newspaper account of a glassblowers' strike in 1884 illustrates the clash between capital and labor. With an eye toward bigger profits, the boss tried to increase output. "He knew if the limit was taken off, the men could work ten or twelve hours every day in the week; that in their thirst for the mighty dollar they would kill themselves with labor; they would 'black sheep' their fellows by doing the labor of two men." But his employees resisted his proposal, refusing to drive themselves to exhaustion for a few dollars more. "They thundered out no. They even offered to take a reduction that would average ten percent all around, but they said, 'We will keep the forty-eight box limit.' Threats and curses would not move them." For these workers, a decent pace of work and a respectable wage were more important than promises of extra money.

In attempting to protect themselves and the dignity of their labor, workers devised ways of combating employer attempts to speed up the production process. Denouncing fellow workers who refused to honor production codes as "hogs," "runners," "chasers," and "job wreckers," they ostracized and even injured them. As the banner of the Detroit Coopers' Union proudly proclaimed at a parade in 1880: "Each for himself is the bosses' plea / [but] Union for all will make you free."

Absenteeism, drunkenness at work, and general inefficiency were other widespread worker practices that contained elements of protest. In three industrial firms in the late nineteenth century, one-quarter of the workers stayed home at least one day a week. Some of these lost days were due to layoffs, but not all. The efforts of employers to impose stiff fines on absent workers suggested their frustration with uncooperative workers.

To a surprising extent, workers made the final protest by quitting their jobs altogether. Most employers responded by penalizing workers who left without giving sufficient notice—but to little avail. A Massachusetts labor study in 1878 found that although two-thirds of the workers surveyed had been in the same occupation for more than 10 years, only 15 percent of them were in the same job. A similar rate of turnover occurred in the industrial workforce in the early twentieth century. Workers unmistakably and clearly voted with their feet.

Strike Activity After 1876

The most direct and strenuous attempts to change conditions in the workplace came in the form of thousands of strikes punctuating the late nineteenth century. In 1877, railroad workers staged the first and most violent nationwide industrial strike of the nineteenth century. The immediate cause of the disturbance was the railroad owners' decision to reduce wages. But the rapid spread of the strike from Baltimore to Pittsburgh and then to cities as distant as San Francisco, Chicago, and Omaha, as well as the violence of the strikers, who destroyed railroad property and kept trains idle, indicated more fundamental discontent.

An erratic economy, high unemployment rates, and the lack of job security all contributed to the conflagration. More than 100 people died before federal troops ended the strike. The frenzied response of the propertied class, which saw the strike as the beginning of revolution and favored the intervention of the military, forecast the pattern of later conflicts. Time and time again, middle- and upper-class Americans would turn to the power of the state to crush labor activism.

A wave of confrontations followed the strike of 1877. Between 1881 and 1905, a total of 36,757 strikes erupted, involving more than 6 million workers—three times the strike activity in France.

These numbers indicate the involvement of more than the "poorest part" of the working class. Many investigations of this era found evidence of widespread working-class discontent. When Samuel M. Hotchkiss, commissioner of the Connecticut Bureau of Labor Statistics, informally surveyed the state's workers in 1887, he was shocked by the "feeling of bitterness," the "distrust of employers," and the "discontent and unrest." These sentiments exploded into strikes, sabotage, and violence, most often linked to demands for higher wages and shorter hours.

Nineteenth-century strike activity underwent important changes, however, as the consciousness of American workers expanded. In the period of early industrialization, discontented laborers rioted in their neighborhoods rather than at their workplaces. Between 1845 and the Civil War, however, strikes at the workplace began to replace neighborhood riots. Although workers showed their anger against their employers by turning out and often calling for higher wages, they had only a murky sense that the strike could be a weapon to force employers to improve working conditions.

As industrialization transformed work and an increasing percentage of the workforce entered factories, collective actions at the workplace spread. Local and national unions played a more important role in organizing protest, conducting 60 percent of the strikes between 1881 and 1905. As working-class leaders realized more clearly the importance of collective action and perceived that transportation had knit the nation together, they worked to coordinate local and national efforts. By 1891, more than one-tenth of the strikes called by

Labor Unrest

This depiction of working-class unrest appeared in *Harper's Weekly* in 1894. Why does the artist give a prominent place to the National Guardsmen and the destruction wrought during the trouble? Contrast the individualized guardsmen with the faceless mob in the background and draw some general conclusions about the artist's choices and intent.

(The Granger Collection, New York)

unionized workers were sympathy strikes. Coordination among strikers employed by different companies improved as workers made similar wage demands. Finally, pay among the most highly unionized workers became less of an issue. Workers sought more humane conditions. Some attempted to end subcontracting and the degradation of skills. Others, such as the glassblowers, struggled to enforce work rules. Indeed, by the early 1890s, more than one-fifth of strikes involved the rules governing the workplace.

Labor Organizing, 1865–1900

Civil War experience colored postwar labor organizing. As one working-class song pointed out, workers had borne the brunt of that struggle. "You gave your son to the war / The rich man loaned his gold / And the rich man's son is happy to-day, / And yours is under the mold." Workers who had fought to save the Union argued that wartime sacrifices justified efforts for justice and equality in the workplace.

Labor leaders quickly realized the need for national as well as local organizations to protect the laboring class against "despotic employers." In 1866, several craft unions and reform groups formed the National Labor Union (NLU). Claiming 300,000 members by the early 1870s, the organization supported a range of causes including temperance, women's rights, and the establishment of cooperatives to bring the "wealth of the land" into "the hands of those who produce it."

The call for an eight-hour day reveals some of the basic assumptions of the organized labor movement. Few workers saw employers as a hostile class or wanted to destroy the economic system. But they did believe bosses were often dangerous tyrants whose demands for their time threatened to turn citizens into slaves. The eight-hour day would curb the power of owners and allow workers the time to cultivate the qualities necessary for republican citizenship.

Many of the NLU's specific goals survived, although the organization did not. An unsuccessful attempt to create a political party and the depression of 1873 decimated the NLU. Survival and job searches took precedence over union causes.

The Knights of Labor and the AFL

As the depression wound down, a new mass organization, the Noble and Holy Order of the Knights of Labor, rose to prominence. Founded as a secret society in 1869, the order became public and national when Terence V. Powderly was elected Grand Master Workman in 1879. The Knights of Labor insisted that workers deserved "the full enjoyment of the wealth they create." Convinced that the industrial system denied workers their fair share as producers of wealth,

the Knights of Labor proposed a cooperative system of production paralleling the existing system. Cooperative efforts would provide workers with the economic independence necessary for citizenship, and an eight-hour day would allow them time for moral, intellectual, and political pursuits.

The Knights of Labor was open to all American "producers," defined as all contributing members of society—skilled and unskilled, black and white, men and women, even merchants and manufacturers. Only the idle and the corrupt (gamblers, saloonkeepers, speculators, bankers, lawyers) were excluded. Many shopkeepers joined, advertising themselves as a "friend of the workingman." This inclusive membership policy provided the organization with the potential power of great numbers. The organization grew in spurts, attracting miners between 1874 and 1879, skilled urban tradespeople between 1879 and 1885, and unskilled workers thereafter.

Although Powderly frowned on strikes, the organization reaped the benefit of grassroots strike activity. Local struggles proliferated after 1883. In 1884, unorganized workers of the Union Pacific Railroad walked off the job when management announced a wage cut. Within two days, the company caved in, and the men joined the Knights. The next year, a successful strike against the Missouri Pacific Railroad brought in another wave of members. Then, in 1886, the Haymarket Riot in Chicago caused such a growth in labor militancy that in that single year the membership of the Knights of Labor ballooned from 100,000 to 700,000.

The "riot" at Haymarket was, in fact, a peaceful protest meeting connected with a lockout at the McCormick Reaper Works. When the Chicago police arrived to disperse the crowd, a bomb exploded. Seven policemen died. Although no one knows who planted the bomb, eight anarchists were tried and convicted. Three were executed, one committed suicide, and the others served prison terms.

Alarmed by the Haymarket Riot, employers determined to destroy the Knights of Labor, but internal weaknesses also contributed to the organization's decline. A strike against Jay Gould's southwestern railroad system in 1886 collapsed. Consumer and producer cooperatives fizzled; the policy of accepting both black and white workers led to discord in the South. The two major political parties co-opted labor politicians. Furthermore, national leaders of the organization also failed. Powderly could neither unify his diverse following nor control militants opposing him. By 1890, membership plummeted to 100,000, although the Knights continued to play a role well into the 1890s.

The American Federation of Labor (AFL), founded in 1886, became the nation's dominant union in the 1890s. The history of the Knights pointed up the problems of a national union admitting all who worked for wages, but officially rejecting strikes as a tactic. The leader of the AFL, Samuel Gompers, had a different notion of effective worker organization. He was convinced that skilled workers should put their specific occupational interests first, so that they could control the supply of skilled labor and keep wages up.

Gompers organized the AFL as a federation of skilled trades—cigar makers, iron molders, ironworkers, carpenters, and others—each one autonomous, yet linked through an executive council to work together for prolabor national legislation and mutual support during boycott and strike actions. He repudiated dreams of a cooperative commonwealth or of ending the wage system, instead focusing on immediate "bread and butter" issues—higher wages, shorter hours, industrial safety, and the right to organize. Although Gompers rejected direct political action as a means of obtaining labor's goals, he believed in the value of the strike. A shrewd organizer, he knew from bitter experience the importance of dues high enough to sustain a strike fund through a long, tough fight.

Under Gompers's leadership, the AFL grew from 140,000 in 1886 to nearly 1 million by 1900. Although his notion of a labor organization was elitist, he steered his union through a series of crises, fending off challenges from socialists on his left and corporate opposition to strikes on his right. But there was no room in his organization for the unskilled or for blacks. The AFL did make a brief, halfhearted attempt to unionize women in 1892, but men resented women as coworkers and preferred them to stay in the home. The AFL agreed. In 1900, the International Ladies' Garment Workers Union (ILGWU) was established. Although women were its backbone, men dominated the leadership.

Working-Class Setbacks

Despite the growth of working-class organizations, workers lost many battles. Some of the more spectacular clashes reveal why working-class activism often failed and why so many workers lived precariously.

In 1892, silver miners in Coeur d'Alene, Idaho, struck when their employers installed machine drills in the mines, reduced skilled workers to shovelmen, and cut wages. The owners, supported by state militiamen and the federal government, successfully broke the strike by using scabs, but not without fighting. Several hundred union men were eventually tried and found guilty of a wide variety of charges. Out of the defeat emerged the Western Federation of Miners (WFM), whose chief goal was an eight-hour law for miners.

The Coeur d'Alene struggle set the pattern for many subsequent strikes. Mine owners fought strikes by shutting off credit to union men, hiring strikebreakers and armed guards, and infiltrating unions with spies. Violence was frequent, usually ending with the arrival of state militia, arrests or intimidation, legal action, and blacklisting. Despite this, the WFM won as many strikes as it lost.

The Homestead and Pullman Strikes of 1892 and 1894

Labor's worst setback came in 1892 at the Homestead steel mills near Pittsburgh. Carnegie had purchased the Homestead plant and put Henry Clay Frick in charge. Together, they wanted to break the union that threatened to extend its organization of the steel industry. After three months of stalemated negotiations over a new wage contract, Frick issued an ultimatum. Workers must accept wage cuts or be replaced. Frick barricaded the entire plant and hired 300 armed Pinkerton guards. As they arrived on July 6, they and armed steelworkers fought a daylong gun battle. Several men on both sides were killed, and the Pinkertons retreated. Then, at Frick's request, the governor of Pennsylvania sent 8,000 troops to crush the strike and the union. Two and a half weeks later, a New York anarchist tried to assassinate Frick.

The Homestead strike dramatized the lengths to which both labor and capital would go. Eugene Debs, an ardent organizer of railroad workers, wrote, "If the year 1892 taught the workingmen any lesson worthy of heed, it was that the capitalist class, like a devilfish, had grasped them with its tentacles and was dragging them down to fathomless depths of degradation."

Debs saw 1893 as the year in which organized labor would "escape the prehensile clutch of these monsters." Instead, 1893 brought a serious depression and more setbacks for labor. Undaunted, Debs combined several of the separate railroad brotherhoods into a united American Railway Union (ARU). Within a year, more than 150,000 railroadmen joined the ARU, and Debs won a strike against the Great Northern Railroad, which had attempted to slash wages.

Debs faced his toughest crisis at the Pullman Palace Car Company in Chicago. The company maintained a model company town near Chicago—naturally, called Pullman—where management controlled all aspects of workers' lives. Late in 1893, as the depression worsened, the Pullman Company cut wages by one-third and laid off many workers, without reducing rents or prices in its stores. Desperate Pullman workers joined the ARU in the spring of 1894 and struck.

In late June, after Pullman refused to submit the dispute to arbitration, Debs led the ARU into a sympathy strike supporting the striking Pullman workers. Remembering the ill-fated railroad strike of 1877, Debs advised his lieutenants to "use no violence" and "stop no trains." Rather, he sought to boycott trains handling

Pullman cars throughout the West. As the boycott spread, the General Managers Association (GMA), which ran the 24 railroads centered in Chicago, came to Pullman's support. Hiring 2,500 strikebreakers, the GMA appealed to the state and federal governments for military and judicial support in stopping the strike.

Governor Richard Altgeld of Illinois, sympathizing with the workers and believing that local law enforcement was sufficient, opposed using federal troops. But U.S. attorney general Richard Olney, a former railroad lawyer, obtained a court injunction on July 2 to end the strike as a "conspiracy in restraint of trade." Two days later, President Cleveland ordered federal troops to crush the strikers. Violence escalated rapidly. Local and federal officials hired armed guards, and the railroads paid them to help the troops. Within two days, strikers and guards were fighting bitterly. As troops poured into Chicago, the violence worsened, leaving scores of workers dead.

Debs knew he needed wider labor support. "We must all stand together or go down in hopeless defeat," he warned other unions. When Gompers refused support, the strike collapsed. Debs and several other leaders were found guilty of contempt of court. His arrest and the defeat of the Pullman strike killed the American Railway Union. In 1895, in *In re Debs,* the Supreme Court upheld the legality of using an injunction to stop a strike, giving management a powerful weapon against unions. Most unions survived the difficult days of the 1890s, but the labor movement emerged as a distinct underdog in its conflicts with organized capital.

Although in smaller communities strikes against outside owners might win local middle-class support, most labor conflicts encountered the widespread middle- and upper-class conviction that unions were un-American. Many people claimed to accept the idea of worker organizations, but argued unions should not participate in making economic or work decisions. Most employers violently resisted union demands as infringements of their right to manage their business. The sharp competition of the late nineteenth century, combined with a pattern of falling prices, stiffened employers' resistance to workers' demands. State and local governments and the courts frequently supported them.

The severe depressions of the 1870s and 1890s further undermined working-class activism. Workers could not focus on union issues when survival itself was in question. Many unions collapsed during hard times.

A fundamental problem was the reluctance of most workers to organize even in favorable times. In 1870, less than one-tenth of the industrial workforce belonged to unions, about the same as on the eve of the Civil War. Thirty years later, despite the expansion of the workforce, only 8.4 percent (mostly skilled workers) were union members. Why were workers so slow to join unions? Many native-born American workers still clung to the tradition of individualism or dreamed of entering the middle class. In addition, diverse work settings and ethnic and religious differences made it difficult for workers to recognize common bonds. Some Americans blamed immigrants for both low wages and failed worker actions. Those foreigners, planning to return to their homeland, had limited interest in changing conditions in the United States—and because their goal was to work, they took jobs as scabs. Much of the violence that accompanied working-class actions erupted when owners brought in strikebreakers.

Tensions between workers was evident in the anti-Chinese campaign of the 1870s and 1880s. White workers in the West began to blame the Chinese for economic hardships. In 1877, a meeting of San Francisco workers supporting the eight-hour day exploded into a rampage against the Chinese. In following years, angry mobs killed Chinese workers in Tacoma, Seattle, Denver, and Rock Springs, Wyoming. Local hostility was expressed at the national level when, in 1882, Congress passed the Chinese Exclusion Act with the support of the Knights of Labor, prohibiting the immigration of Chinese workers for a 10-year period. It was extended in 1892 and made permanent in 1902.

Yet many immigrants, especially skilled ones, supported unions and cooperated with native-born Americans. Often ethnic bonds tied members to one another and to the community. For example, in the 1860s and 1870s, as the Molders' Union in Troy, New York, battled with manufacturers, its Irish membership won sympathy and support from the Irish-dominated police force, the Roman Catholic Church, fraternal orders, and public officials.

The importance of workers' organizations lay not so much in their success as in the implicit criticism they offered of American society. Workers lashed out at an economic order that robbed them of their dignity and humanity. As producers of wealth, they protested that so little of it was theirs. As members of the working class, they rejected the middle-class belief in individualism and social mobility.

The Balance Sheet

Industrial expansion raised living standards for the increasing numbers of Americans, especially those in the middle and upper class. They were able to purchase dozens of products, manufactured, packaged, and promoted in an explosion of technological inventions and shrewd marketing techniques. They had comfortable living quarters in attractive urban districts. The men of the family had more professional and business opportunities than ever before.

Skilled workers also enjoyed many benefits produced by industrialization. But most laboring people found it impossible to earn much of a share in the new material bounty. Newly arrived immigrants especially suffered from low pay and economic uncertainty. Long hours on the job and the necessity of walking to and from work left workers with little free time. Family budgets could include, at best, only small amounts for recreation. Even a ticket to a baseball game was a luxury.

Although few Americans worried about it, many experienced some of the adverse environmental effects of industrialization. By the late nineteenth century, industrial processes were polluting urban air, eastern lakes and rivers, and creating acid soil. In Birmingham, Alabama, for example, the production of iron and steel befouled the air with smoke, soot, and ashes. Coal tar, a by-product of the process, was dumped, making the soil infertile.

Despite modern disapproval of these consequences of industrialization, the intellectual rationale stressed growth, development, and the rapid exploitation of the country's resources—not conservation. And our view of the harshness of working-class life partly grows out of contemporary standards of what is acceptable today. Because so few working-class men or women recorded their thoughts and reactions, it is hard to know just what they expected or how they viewed their experiences. But culture and background influenced their perspectives. The family tenement, one Polish immigrant remarked, "seemed quite advanced when compared with our home" in Poland. A Lithuanian agreed. "Even though the toilet was in the hall, and the

Timeline

1843–1884	"Old immigration"
1844	Telegraph invented
1850s	Steam power widely used in manufacturing
1859	Value of U.S. industrial production exceeds value of agricultural production
1866	National Labor Union founded
1869	Transcontinental railroad completed
	Knights of Labor organized
1870	Standard Oil of Ohio formed
1870s–1880s	Consolidation of continental railroad network
1873	Bethlehem Steel begins using Bessemer process
1873–1879	Depression
1876	Alexander G. Bell invents telephone
	Thomas Edison establishes his "invention factory" at Menlo Park, New Jersey
1877	Railroad workers hold first nationwide industrial strike
1879	Thomas Edison invents incandescent light
1882	Chinese Exclusion Act
1885–1914	"New immigration"
1886	American Federation of Labor founded
	Haymarket Riot in Chicago
1887	Interstate Commerce Act
1890	Sherman Anti-Trust Act
1892	Standard Oil of New Jersey formed
	Coeur d'Alene strike
	Homestead steelworkers strike
1893	Chicago World's Fair
1893–1897	Depression
1894	Pullman railroad workers strike
1900	International Ladies' Garment Workers Union founded
	Corporations responsible for two-thirds of U.S. manufacturing

whole floor used it, yet it was a toilet. There was no such thing in Lithuania." A 10-hour job in the steel mill might be an improvement over dawn-to-dusk farmwork that brought no wages.

Studies of several cities show that nineteenth-century workers moved up the occupational ladder. One worker in five in Los Angeles and Atlanta during the 1890s, for example, managed to climb into the middle class. While most immigrant workers were stuck in ill-paid, insecure jobs, their children ended up doing better. The son of an unskilled laborer might move on to become a semiskilled or skilled worker as new immigrants took the jobs at the bottom. Second-generation Irish made progress, especially in the West and the Midwest. Even in Boston, 40 percent of the children of Irish immigrants obtained white-collar jobs.

Mobility, like occupation, was related to background. Native-born whites, Jews, and Germans rose more swiftly and fell less often than Irish, Italians, or Poles. Cultural attitudes, family size, education, and group leadership all contributed to different ethnic mobility patterns. Jews, for example, valued education and sacrificed to keep children in school. By 1915, Jews represented 85 percent of the free City College student body in New York City, 20 percent of New York University's student body, and one-sixth of those studying at Columbia University. With an education, they moved upward. The Slavs, however, who valued a steady income over mobility and education, took their children out of school and sent them to work at an early age. They believed that this course of action not only helped the family but gave the child a head start in securing reliable, stable employment. The southern Italian proverb "Do not make your child better than you are" suggests the value Italians placed on family rather than individual success. Differing attitudes and values led to different aspirations and career patterns.

Two groups enjoyed little mobility: African Americans and Hispanic Americans. African Americans were largely excluded from the industrial occupational structure and were restricted to unskilled jobs. Unlike immigrant industrial workers, they did not have the opportunity to move to better jobs as new, unskilled workers took the positions at the bottom. A study in Los Angeles suggests that Hispanic residents made minimal gains. Their experiences elsewhere may have been much the same.

Although immigrants' occupational mobility was limited, other kinds of rewards often compensated for the lack of success at the workplace. Home ownership for groups such as the Irish, who in their homeland had rarely owned their own homes, was an achievement that also could bring in extra income from boarders and provide some cushion against the uncertainties of industrial life and old age. Adept politicians, the Irish came to dominate big-city government in the late nineteenth century,

filling many city jobs, particularly in the police force. The Irish were also successful in the construction industry and dominated the hierarchy of the Catholic church. Likewise, participation in social clubs and fraternal orders compensated in part for lack of advancement at work. Ethnic associations, parades, and holidays provided a sense of identity and security that offset the limitations of the job world.

Moreover, a few rags-to-riches stories always encouraged those who struggled. For example, the family of John Kearney in Poughkeepsie, New York, achieved modest success. After 20 years as a laborer, John started his own business as a junk dealer and even bought a simple house. His sons started off in better jobs than their father. One became a grocery store clerk and then later a baker, a policeman, and, finally, at age 40, an inspector at the waterworks. Another was an iron molder, and the third son was a post office worker and eventually the superintendent of city streets. If this success paled next to that of industrial giants such as Andrew Carnegie and John D. Rockefeller, it was still enough to keep the American dream alive.

Conclusion

THE COMPLEXITY OF INDUSTRIAL CAPITALISM

The rapid growth of the late nineteenth century made the United States one of the world's industrial giants. Many factors contributed to the "wonderful accomplishments" of the age. They ranged from sympathetic government policies to the rise of big business and the emergence of a cheap industrial workforce. But it was also a turbulent period. Many Americans benefited only marginally from the new wealth. Some of them protested by joining unions, walking out on strike, or initiating on-the-job actions. Most lived their lives more quietly and never had the opportunity that Thomas O'Donnell did of telling their story to others. But middle-class Americans began to wonder about the O'Donnells of the country. It is to their concerns, worries, and aspirations that we now turn.

QUESTIONS FOR REVIEW AND REFLECTION

1. What factors explain the United States' rise to industrial and economic prominence in the late nineteenth century?
2. In what ways did American cities change in this period?
3. Explain which groups were able to realize the American dream of success and which were not and why.
4. Compare and contrast the experiences of middle-class and working-class women.
5. What factors undermined the working-class efforts at collective action and which promoted them? In your opinion, which were the most important factors underlying the failures of the working class?

CHAPTER 19

Politics and Reform

Gilded Age Election: 1892 painting by John Klir "The Lost Bet"

Although this 1892 painting by John Klir shows the outcome of a "Lost Bet" in the election that year, note the ethnic, racial, and class diversity of the street crowds, momentarily united in the enjoyment of watching the humiliated loser pulling his victorious opponent (and a wagon full of American flags). What kind of diversity do you see in the painting? Will a more diverse America hold together?

(Library of Congress [LC-USZC4–2113])

American Stories

A Utopian Novelist Warns of Two Americas

At the start of his best-seller *Looking Backward* (1888), Edward Bellamy likened the American society of his day to a huge stagecoach. Dragging the coach along sandy roads and over steep hills were the "masses of humanity." While they strained desperately "under the pitiless lashing of hunger" to pull the coach, at the top sat the favored few, riding in breezy comfort yet fearful that they might fall from their seats and have to pull the coach themselves.

Bellamy's famous coach allegory began a utopian novel in which the class divisions and pitiless competition of the nineteenth century were replaced by a classless, caring, cooperative new society. Economic anxieties and hardships were supplanted by satisfying labor and leisure. In place of the coach, all citizens in the year 2000 walked together and shopped in equal comfort and security under a huge umbrella (not unlike modern malls) over the sidewalks of the city.

The novel opens in 1887. The hero, a wealthy Bostonian, falls asleep worrying about the effect local labor struggles might have on his upcoming wedding. When he wakes up, it is the year 2000. Utopia has been achieved peacefully through the development of one gigantic trust, owned and operated by the national government. All citizens between ages 21 and 45 work in an industrial army with equal pay and work difficulty. Retirement after 45 is devoted to hobbies, reading, culture, and the minimal leadership necessary in a society without crime, corruption, poverty, or war.

Bellamy's book was popular with educated middle-class Americans, who were attracted by his vision of a society in which humans were both morally good and materially well off—and in which core values of the 1880s survived intact, including individual incentive, private property, and rags-to-riches presidents. He filled the novel with futuristic technological wonders, such as television and credit cards, a double-dream surprise ending, and a love story. Women in 2000 married for love and were relieved of housework by labor-saving gadgets. Although they worked in the industrial army (in "lighter occupations"), their primary role was still to supervise domestic affairs, nurture the young, and beautify culture.

Like most middle-class Americans of his day, Bellamy disapproved of European socialism. Although some features of his utopia were socialistic, he called his system "nationalism." This appealed to a new generation of Americans who had put aside Civil War antagonisms to embrace the greatness of a growing, if economically divided, nation. In the early 1890s, with Americans buying nearly 10,000 copies of *Looking Backward* every week, more than 160 Nationalist clubs were formed to crusade for the adoption of Bellamy's ideas.

The inequalities of wealth described in Bellamy's coach scene reflected a political life in which many participated, but only a few benefited. The wealthiest 10 percent, who rode high on the coach, dominated national politics, while untutored bosses held sway in governing cities. Except for token expressions of support, national political leaders ignored the cries of factory workers, immigrants, farmers, African Americans, Native Americans, and other victims of the vast transformation of American industrial, urban, and agrarian life in the late nineteenth century. But as the century closed, middle-class Americans like Bellamy, as well as labor, agrarian, and ethnic leaders, proposed various reforms. Their concern was never more appropriate than during the depression of the mid-1890s, a real-life social upheaval that mirrored the worst features and fears of Bellamy's fictional coach.

In this chapter, we will examine American democratic politics at the national and local level from the end of Reconstruction to the 1890s, a period that bolstered the rich and neglected the corrosive human problems of urban industrial life. Then we will look at the growing social and political involvement of educated middle-class reformers who, despite their distaste for mass politics, were inspired by a religious social gospel to work for social change both locally and nationally. We will conclude with an account of the pivotal importance of the 1890s, and how the Populist revolt, the depression of 1893–1897, and the election of 1896 shook many comfortable citizens out of their apathy and began the reshaping of American politics.

Politics in the Gilded Age

Co-authoring a satirical book in 1873, Mark Twain coined the expression "Gilded Age" to describe Grant's corrupt presidency. The phrase, with its suggestion of shallow glitter, characterized social and political life in the last quarter of the nineteenth century. Politics was marred by corruption, and politicians ignored basic issues for the mass entertainment of pomp, parades, and penny beer. Yet voter participation in national elections between 1876 and 1896 hovered at an all-time high of 73 to 82 percent.

Behind the glitter, two gradual changes occurred that would greatly affect twentieth-century politics. First was the development of a professional bureaucracy of elite specialists in congressional committees and executive offices. These experts emerged as a counterfoil to the perceived dangers of majority rule represented by high voter participation, especially by the millions of new immigrant "newcomers alien to our traditions," as a New Englander put it. Second, after a period of close elections and party stalemate, new issues and concerns fostered a political realignment in the 1890s.

Politics, Parties, Patronage, and Presidents

American government in the 1870s and 1880s clearly supported the interests of riders atop Bellamy's coach. Few nineteenth-century Americans would have agreed that the national government should tackle problems of poverty, unemployment, and trusts. They mistrusted organized power and believed that all would benefit from an expansive economic life free of government interference.

The Gilded Age, Henry Adams observed, was the most "thoroughly ordinary" period ever in American politics. "One might search the whole list of Congress, Judiciary, and Executive during the twenty-five years 1870–95 and find little but damaged reputation." Few eras of American government were so corrupt, and Adams was especially sensitive to the low quality of democratic politics compared to the presidencies of his grandfather John Quincy Adams and great-grandfather John Adams.

During the weak Johnson and Grant presidencies, Congress emerged as the dominant branch of government with power centered in the committee system. Senators James G. Blaine (R-Maine) and Roscoe Conkling (R-New York) typified the moral quality of legislative leadership. Despite lying about having been paid off by favors to railroads, Blaine was probably the most popular Republican politician of the era. Charming, intelligent, witty, and able, he served twice as secretary of state and was a serious contender for the presidency in every election from 1876 to 1892. His intra-party foe, Conkling, dispensed lucrative jobs at the New York customhouse and spent most of his career rewarding the party faithful with government jobs. In more than two decades in Congress, he never drafted a bill.

Legislation was not Congress's primary purpose. In 1879, a disgusted student of legislative politics, Woodrow Wilson, wrote: "No leaders, no principles; no principles, no parties." A British observer, Lord Bryce, concluding that American politics was mainly about the "desire for office and for office as a means of gain," compared the two parties to two bottles of liquor, they bore different labels, yet "each was empty."

Yet these characterizations were not entirely accurate. There were differences, as party professionals solidified their popular base to achieve political ends. Republican votes came from northeastern Yankee industrial interests and Scandinavian Lutherans across the Upper Midwest. Democrats depended on southern whites, northern workers, and urban immigrants. Like today, party affiliation reflected not just economic but also cultural, social, and religious issues. Because the Republican party was willing to mobilize the power of the state to reshape society, people who wanted to regulate moral and economic life were attracted to it. White southerners and various immigrant groups preferred the Democratic party because it opposed government efforts to regulate morals. Said one Chicago Democrat, "A Republican is a man who wants you t' go t' church every Sunday. A Democrat says if a man wants t' have a glass of beer on Sunday he can have it."

In the 1860s, Civil War and Reconstruction issues generated party differences. But after 1876, the two parties were evenly matched, and they avoided controversial stands on national issues. In three of the five presidential elections between 1876 and 1892, a mere 1 percent of the vote separated the two major candidates. In 1880, James Garfield won by only 7,018 votes; in 1884, Grover Cleveland squeaked past Blaine by a popular-vote margin of 48.5 to 48.2 percent. In two elections (1876 and 1888), the electoral-vote winner had fewer popular votes. Only twice, each time for only two years, did one party control the White House and both houses of Congress. Although all the presidents in the era except Cleveland were Republicans, the Democrats controlled the House of Representatives in 8 of 10 sessions of Congress between 1875 and 1895.

Gilded Age presidents were undistinguished and played a minor role in national life. None of them—Hayes (1877–1881), Garfield (1881), Chester A. Arthur (1881–1885), Cleveland (1885–1889 and 1893–1897), and Benjamin Harrison (1889–1893)—served two consecutive terms. None was strongly identified with any particular issue. None has been highly regarded by historians. The only Democrat in the group, Cleveland, differed little from the Republicans. Upon his election in 1884, financier Jay Gould sent him a telegram stating that "the vast business interests of the country will be entirely safe in your hands."

National Issues

Four issues were important at the national level in the Gilded Age: the tariff, currency, civil service, and government regulation of railroads (see Chapter 18). In confronting these issues, legislators tried to serve both their own self-interest and the national interest of an efficient, productive, growing economy.

The federal government depended on tariffs and excise taxes (primarily on tobacco and liquor), along with land sales, for most of its revenue. Republicans stood for a high tariff to protect American business, wage earners, and farmers from foreign competition.

PRESIDENTIAL ELECTIONS, 1872–1892

A British observer of American politics, James Bryce, said in 1888 that "the American usually votes with his party, right or wrong, and the fact that there is little distinction of view between the parties makes it easier to stick to your old friends." To what extent does this chart show that American voters stuck to their party? How close were the elections? What was the usual percent difference? In which two elections did the popular-vote winner, as in 2000, lose the election? Are parties today more like or unlike those from the late nineteenth century?

Year	Candidate	Party	Popular Vote	Electoral Vote
1872	ULYSSES S. GRANT	Republican	3,596,745 (56%)	286
	Horace Greeley*	Democrat	2,843,446 (44%)	0*
1876	Samuel J. Tilden	Democrat	4,284,020 (51%)	184
	RUTHERFORD B. HAYES	Republican	4,036,572 (48%)	185
1880	JAMES A. GARFIELD	Republican	4,449,053 (48.5%)	214
	Winfield S. Hancock	Democrat	4,442,035 (48.1%)	155
	James B. Weaver	Greenback-Labor	308,578	0
1884	GROVER CLEVELAND	Democrat	4,911,017 (48.5%)	219
	James G. Blaine	Republican	4,848,334 (48.2%)	182
	Minor parties		325,739 (03.3%)	0
1888	Grover Cleveland	Democrat	5,540,050 (48.6%)	168
	BENJAMIN HARRISON	Republican	5,444,337 (47.9%)	233
	Minor parties		396,441 (03.5%)	0
1892	GROVER CLEVELAND	Democrat	5,554,414 (46%)	277
	Benjamin Harrison	Republican	5,190,802 (43%)	145
	James B. Weaver	Populist	1,027,329 (9%)	22

*Greeley died before the Electoral College met.

Note: Winners' names are in capital letters.

Democrats demanded a low tariff because "the government is best which governs least." But in passing tariffs politicians accommodated local interests. An Indiana senator explained, "I am a protectionist for every interest which I am sent here by my constituents to protect." Tariff revisions, containing a jumble of mostly higher but some lower rates, were bewilderingly complex as legislators catered to these many special interests.

The currency question was even more complicated. During the Civil War, the federal government had circulated paper money (greenbacks) that could not be exchanged for gold or silver (specie). In the late 1860s and 1870s, politicians debated whether the United States should return to a metallic standard, which would allow paper money to be exchanged for specie. "Hard-money" advocates supported either withdrawing all paper money from circulation or making it convertible to specie. They opposed increasing the volume of money, fearing inflation. "Soft money" Greenbackers argued that there was not enough

currency in circulation for an expanding economy and urged increasing the supply of paper money in order to raise farm prices and cut interest rates.

Hard-money interests had more clout. In 1873, Congress demonetized silver, gradually retiring greenbacks from circulation and putting the nation firmly on the gold standard. But as large supplies of silver were mined in the West, pressure resumed for increasing the money supply by coining silver. Soft-money advocates pushed for the unlimited coinage of silver in addition to gold. In an 1878 compromise, the Treasury was required to buy between $2 million and $4 million of silver each month and to coin it as silver dollars. Despite this increase in the money supply, prices fell, prompting disappointing soft money supporters to push for more silver.

The issue of civil service reform, Henry Adams observed, was a "subject almost as dangerous in political conversation in Washington as slavery itself in the old days before the war." The worst feature of the

Political Advertisements of the 1880s

Although the tariff protectionist Harrison defeated Cleveland in 1888 (the results were reversed in 1892), all Gilded Age presidents were essentially "preservers" rather than innovators. None had approached the greatness of Washington, Lincoln, and the other presidents hovering over Harrison and Morton in this illustration. In a second image from 1888, titled *The Presidential B.B. Club*, politics and business are merged in a tobacco advertisement, which shows Cleveland the fielder tagging out Harrison the batter—true enough for the election of 1892 but not for 1888, which Harrison won. Why baseball? What other images (and people) do you see in these two campaign visuals?

(Left: Library of Congress [LC-USZ62–7177]; right: From the collection of David J. and Janice L. Frent)

spoils system was that parties financed themselves by assessing holders of patronage jobs often as much as 1 percent of their annual salaries. Reformers, mostly middle-class, native-born, white Protestants, demanded competitive examinations to create an honest and professional civil service—but also one that would bar immigrants and their urban political machine bosses from the spoils of office.

Most Americans expected their presidents to reward the faithful with government jobs, but Garfield's assassination by a crazed office seeker created a public backlash. "My God! Chet Arthur in the White House!" a loyal Republican exclaimed, knowing the new president was closely identified with corrupt machine politics. But Arthur surprised doubters by being a capable and dignified president, responsive to growing demands for civil service reform. Congress passed the Pendleton Act of 1883, mandating merit examinations for about one-tenth of federal offices. Gradually, more bureaucrats fell under its coverage, but parties became no more honest. As campaign contributions from government employees dried up, parties turned to huge corporate contributions, which in 1888 helped elect Benjamin Harrison.

The Lure of Local Politics

The fact that the major parties did not disagree substantially on issues such as money and civil service does not mean that nineteenth-century Americans found politics dull. Far more eligible voters turned out in the late nineteenth century than at any time since. The 78.5 percent average turnout to vote for president in the 1880s is a sharp contrast with the near 50 percent of eligible Americans who vote in recent elections.

American men were drawn to the polls in part by the hoopla of party parades, buttons, and banners, but also by local issues. Midwestern farmers turned out to vote for state representatives who favored curbing the power of the railroads. But emotional social issues of race, religion, nationality, alcohol, and education often overrode economic self-interest. Southern whites, stripping the vote away from blacks, supported laws that established segregated railroad cars and other public facilities. Iowa, Illinois, and Ohio farmers voted for temperance and compulsory attendance education laws, while Irish and German Catholics in New York and Milwaukee supported aid to parochial schools and opposed local temperance laws.

Urban immigrants played a large role in stimulating political participation. As traditional native-born elites left local government for more-lucrative and higher-status business careers, urban bosses stepped in. Their control rested on their ability to deliver the immigrant vote, which they secured by operating informal welfare systems. Bosses handed out jobs and money for rent and fuel, and provided personal touches like giving turkeys to poor families at Thanksgiving, bailing drunks out of jail, and attending Jewish weddings, Catholic confirmations, and Italian funerals. As New York Tammany Hall boss, George Washington Plunkitt, explained, "I think that there's got to be in every ward somebody that any bloke can come to—no matter what he's done—and get help."

Party leaders also won votes by making politics exciting. The parades, rallies, buttons, songs, and oratory of late-nineteenth-century campaigns generated excitement as party leaders used hoopla to win votes. In the election of 1884, for example, emotions ran high over the moral lapses of the opposing candidates—Blaine's corruption and Cleveland's illegitimate child. Democrats chanted in election eve rallies: "Blaine! Blaine! James G. Blaine! / Continental liar from the state of Maine!" while Republicans responded: "Ma! Ma! Where's my pa? / Gone to the White House, Ha! Ha! Ha!" Cleveland won in part because a Republican clergyman called the Democrats the party of "rum, Romanism, and rebellion," ensuring Cleveland an outpouring of Catholic support in crucial New York.

Prohibition also provoked spirited local contests. Many Americans considered drinking a serious social problem. Annual consumption of brewery beer had risen from 2.7 gallons per capita in 1850 to 17.9 gallons in 1880. In one city, saloons outnumbered churches 31 to 1. Such statistics shocked those who believed that drinking would destroy character, corrupt politics, and cause poverty, crime, and unrestrained sexuality. Because they were often the targets of violent, drunken men, women especially supported temperance and increasingly sought to ban drinking by making it illegal.

The battle in San Jose, California, where reformers put a referendum to ban the sale of liquor on the ballot, illustrates the strong passions of the temperance issue. Women erected a tent where they held daily temperance meetings heckled by men and even some clergymen. On election eve, large crowds gathered at both the tent and at a pro-liquor rally. The next morning, women roamed the streets urging men to adopt the referendum, while their children marched to saloons, singing, "Father, dear father, come home with me now." By afternoon, the mood grew uglier as women were harassed and threatened by drunken men. The proposal lost by a vote of 1,430 to 918.

Emotional conflicts boiled in the 1880s at the state level over education as well as drinking. In Iowa, Illinois, and Wisconsin, Protestant Republicans sponsored laws mandating that children attend "some public or private day school" where instruction was in English. These laws, not the last move for English-only education, aimed to undermine parochial schools, which taught in the language of the immigrants. In Iowa, where a state prohibition law passed, the Republican slogan was "A schoolhouse on every hill, and no saloon in the valley." Republicans bragged that "Iowa will go Democratic when hell goes Methodist," and indeed they won. But in Wisconsin, a law for compulsory school attendance was so strongly anti-Catholic that it backfired. Many voters, disillusioned with Republican moralism, shifted to the Democrats.

Party leaders sometimes used local and ethnic issues to achieve sordid economic goals. In New Mexico, for example, the Santa Fe ring, a small group of Anglo-Protestant Republican bankers, lawyers, and politicians, had long exploited local anti-Mexican feelings to grab lands. The ring controlled judges and legislators. When desperate Mexican-American tenant farmers turned to sometimes violent protest in the 1880s, the ring used the situation to dispossess Mexican Americans, Native Americans, and poor white squatters from enormous tracts of land.

Middle-Class Reform

Most middle-class white Americans were unmoved by race issues and avoided reformist politics. But urban corruption, poverty, and labor violence frightened many out of their aversion to politics.

Frances Willard and the Women's Christian Temperance Union (WCTU) is an example. As president of the WCTU from 1879 until 1898, Willard headed the largest women's organization in the country. Most WCTU members were churchgoing, white, Protestant women who believed drunkenness caused poverty and family violence. But after 1886, the WCTU reversed its position, attributing drunkenness to unemployment, bad labor conditions, and poverty. Willard joined the Knights of Labor in 1887 and by the 1890s had influenced the WCTU to extend its programs to alleviate the problems of working men, women, and children.

The Gospel of Wealth and Social Darwinism

Willard called herself a Christian socialist because she believed in applying the ethical principles of Jesus to economic life. For her and many other educated, middle-class reformers, Christianity called for a cooperative social order that would reduce inequalities of wealth. But for most Gilded Age Americans, Christianity supported the competitive individualistic ethic. Philadelphia Baptist preacher Russell Conwell's famous sermon "Acres of Diamonds," delivered 6,000 times to an estimated 13 million listeners, praised riches as a sure sign of "godliness" and stressed the power of money to "do good."

Industrialist Andrew Carnegie expressed the ethic most clearly. In an article titled "The Gospel of Wealth" (1889), Carnegie celebrated competition for producing better goods at lower prices. The concentration of wealth in a few hands, he concluded, was "not only beneficial but essential to the future of the race." The fittest would bring order and efficiency out of the chaos of rapid industrialization. Carnegie's defense of the new economic order in his book *Triumphant Democracy* (1886) found many supporters. Partly this was because Carnegie insisted that the rich must spend some of their wealth to benefit their "poorer brethren." Carnegie built hundreds of libraries to help the poor get an uplifting education.

Carnegie's ideas reflected an ideology known as social Darwinism, based on the work of the English naturalist Charles Darwin. In his *Origin of Species,* published in 1859, Darwin concluded that plant and animal species evolved through natural selection. In the struggle for existence, some species managed to adapt to their environment and survived; others failed to adapt and perished. Herbert Spencer, an English social philosopher, applied this "survival of the fittest" notion to human society. Progress, Spencer said, resulted from relentless competition in which the weak were eliminated and the strong climbed to the top, as in Bellamy's coach. Spencer warned against any interference in the economic world by tampering with the natural laws of selection: "The whole effort of nature is to get rid of such as are unfit, to clear the world of them, and make room for better."

Spencer's leading American followers, many of whom like Carnegie and Yale economist William Graham Sumner, gathered in 1882 to celebrate him at a lavish banquet in New York City, insisted that poverty resulted from the struggle for existence. It was "absurd," Sumner wrote, to pass laws permitting society's "worst members" to survive, or to "sit down with a slate and pencil to plan out a new social world."

The scientific vocabulary of social Darwinism injected scientific rationality into what often seemed a baffling economic order. Sumner and Spencer argued that underlying social laws, like those in the natural world, dictated economic affairs. Social Darwinists also believed in the superiority of the Anglo-Saxon race, which they maintained had reached the highest stage of evolution. Their theories were used to justify race supremacy and imperialism (see Chapter 20) as well as the monopolistic efforts of American businessmen.

The Gap Between Rich and Poor

Describe the two living spaces in these two photographs. Note the contrasts between them, one the bedroom in Alexander Stewart's Fifth Avenue mansion, representing society's "fittest" element, the other an immigrant tenement on New York's Lower East Side. How might the inhabitants of these two dwellings differ in their social and political views?

(Left: Brown Brothers; right: International Museum of Photography/George Eastman House)

"The growth of a large business," John D. Rockefeller, Jr., told a YMCA class in Cleveland, happens by "sacrificing" less fit companies. This was, he said, "merely the working out of a law of nature and a law of God."

Reform Darwinism and Pragmatism

Others questioned social Darwinism. Brooks Adams wrote that social philosophers such as Spencer and Sumner were "hired by the comfortable classes to prove that everything was all right." Fading aristocrats such as the Adams family, increasingly displaced by the new rich industrial elite, may have felt a touch of envy. With roots in antebellum abolitionism, women's rights, and other crusades for social justice, men and women intellectual reformers directly challenged the gloomy social Darwinian notion that nothing could be done to alleviate poverty. Franklin Sanborn, for example, an inspector of charities in Massachusetts, founded the American Social Science Association in 1865 to "treat wisely the great social problems of the day." An early advocate of doing social scientific research on society's problems, Sanborn was known as the "leading social worker of his day."

Reformer Henry George, an amateur social scientist, observed that wherever the highest degree of "material progress" had been realized, "we find the deepest poverty." George's book *Progress and Poverty* (1879) dramatically showed the contradictions of American life. With Bellamy's *Looking Backward,* it was the most influential book of the age, selling 2 million copies by 1905. George admitted that economic growth had produced wonders, but he pointed out the social costs and the loss of Christian values. His remedy was to break up land-holding monopolists who profited from the increasing value of their land, which they rented to those who actually did the work. He proposed a "single tax" on the unearned increases in land value.

George's solution may seem simplistic, but his religious tone and optimistic faith in the capacity of humans to effect change appealed to many middle-class intellectuals. Some went further. Sociologist Lester Frank Ward and economist Richard T. Ely both found examples of cooperation in nature and demonstrated that competition and laissez-faire had proved both wasteful and inhumane. Reform Darwinists urged an economic order marked by cooperation and regulation.

Two pragmatists, John Dewey and William James, established a philosophical basis for reform. While Dewey applied principles of democracy to education, James argued the importance of human will in effecting the course of human events. "What is the 'cash value' of a thought, idea, or belief?" James asked. "The ultimate test for us of what a truth means," he suggested, was in the "consequences" of a particular idea and what kind of moral "conduct it dictates."

James and young social scientists including Ward and Ely gathered statistics documenting social wrongs and rejecting social determinism. They argued that the application of intelligence and human agency could change the "survival of the fittest" into the "fitting of as many as possible to survive." Their position encouraged educators, economists, and reformers of every stripe, giving them an intellectual justification to struggle against misery and inequalities of wealth.

Settlements and Social Gospel

Jane Addams saw the gap between progress and poverty in the streets of Chicago in the winter of 1893. "The stream of laboring people goes past you," she wrote, and "your heart sinks with a sudden sense of futility." Born in rural Illinois, Addams founded Hull House in Chicago in 1889 "to aid in the solution of the social and industrial problems...in a great city." Also in 1889, Wellesley literature professor Vida Scudder and six other Smith College graduates formed an organization of college women to work in settlement houses.

Middle-class activists like Addams and Scudder worried in particular about the degradation of life and labor in America's cities, factories, and farms. Most of them drew upon the ethical teachings of Jesus, as well as those of social prophets such as Tolstoy, Hugo, Emerson, and Bellamy for inspiration in solving social problems. They preferred a society marked by cooperation rather than competition—where, as they liked to say, people were guided by the "golden rule rather than the rule of gold." They sought to apply the ethics of Jesus to industrial and urban life in order to bring about the kingdom of heaven on earth. Some preferred to put their reformist goals in more secular terms, and worked within existing institutions. As middle-class intellectuals and professionals, they stressed a practical, educational approach to social problems. They sought change by crusading for tenement-house and factory-conditions legislation, mediating labor disputes, and living among the poor.

The settlement house movement typified 1890s middle-class reformers' blend of idealism and practicality. The primary purpose of settlement houses was to help immigrant families, especially women, adapt Old World rural styles of childbearing, child care, and housekeeping to American urban life. They launched day nurseries, kindergartens, and boarding rooms for immigrant working women; they offered classes in sewing, cooking, nutrition, health care, and English; and they tried to keep young people out of saloons by organizing sports clubs and coffeehouses.

A second purpose of the settlement house movement was to give college-educated women meaningful work at a time when they faced professional barriers and to allow them to preserve the strong feelings of

Lessons and Services of the Settlement House

What is being taught to immigrant women in this typical settlement house poster? The public health clinic is in Vida Scudder's Denison House in Boston. Settlement house work, Scudder wrote, fulfilled "a biting curiosity about the way the Other Half lived, and a strange hunger for fellowship with them." Do you see evidence of cross-cultural, cross-class bonding and fellowship?

(Left: U.S. Government Education Bureau of the National Geographic Image Collection; right: Schlesinger Library, Radcliffe Institute, Harvard University)

sisterhood and service they had experienced at college. A third goal was to gather data exposing social misery in order to spur legislative action—developing city building codes for tenements, abolishing child labor, and improving factory safety. Hull House, Addams said, was intended in part "to investigate and improve the conditions in the industrial districts of Chicago." The settlement house movement, with its dual emphasis on the scientific gathering of facts and spiritual commitment, thus blending academic study and Christian beliefs, nourished the new discipline of sociology, first taught in divinity schools.

By contrast, Dwight Moody preached a traditional evangelical Christianity in American cities, leading hundreds of urban revivals in the 1870s. Mastering the art of the folksy sermon filled with Bible and family stories and an easy path from sin to salvation, the Moody revivals appealed to lower-class, rural folk who were drawn to the city by their hopes and pushed there by economic disappointment. Supported by businessmen who believed that religion would make workers and immigrants more docile, the revivalists battled sin through individual conversion. Moody's revivals helped to nearly double Protestant church membership in the last two decades of the century. Although some urban workers drifted into secular faiths such as socialism, most remained conventionally religious.

Other Protestant ministers embraced the Social Gospel movement of the 1890s, which tied salvation to social betterment. Like the settlement house workers, these religious leaders sought to make Christianity relevant to urban problems. Congregational minister Washington Gladden advocated collective bargaining

and corporate profit sharing. A young Baptist minister in the notorious Hell's Kitchen area of New York City, Walter Rauschenbusch raised an even louder voice. Often called on to conduct funeral services for children killed by the airless, diseased tenements and sweatshops, Rauschenbusch scathingly attacked capitalism and church ignorance of socioeconomic issues. His progressive ideas for social justice and a welfare state were later published in two landmark books: *Christianity and the Social Crisis* (1907) and *Christianizing the Social Order* (1912).

Perhaps the most influential book promoting social Christianity was a best-selling novel *In His Steps*, published in 1897 by Charles Sheldon. The novel portrayed the dramatic changes made possible by a few community leaders who resolved to base all their actions on a single question: "What would Jesus do?" For a minister, this meant seeking to "bridge the chasm between the church and labor." For the idle rich, it meant settlement house work and reforming prostitutes. For landlords and factory owners, it meant improving the living and working conditions of tenants and laborers. Although filled with naive sentimentality characteristic of much of the Social Gospel, *In His Steps* prepared thousands of influential, middle-class Americans for progressive civic leadership.

Reforming the City

No late-nineteenth-century institution needed reforming more than urban government, called by the president of Cornell "the worst in Christendom—the most expensive, the most inefficient, and the most corrupt."

A Philadelphia committee pointed to years of "inefficiency, waste, badly paved and filthy streets, unwholesome and offensive water, and slovenly and costly management." New York and Chicago, where cholera and typhoid epidemics resulted from raw sewage poured into lakes and rivers, were even worse.

Creating a "city beautiful" through environmental remedies was one approach to cleaning up dirty cities. Urban planners put in water mains and sewers and landscape architects built city parks (like Central Park in New York) and planted trees along broadened boulevards lined by elegant homes and public buildings—libraries, museums, theaters, and music halls. But the transformation of urban space rarely reached the squalid sections of the city inhabited by recent immigrants and rural transplants found packed into tenements along filthy streets filled with garbage.

Rapid urban growth swamped city leaders with new demands for service. Flush toilets, thirsty horses pulling street railways, and industrial users of water exhausted the capacity of municipal waterworks built for an earlier age. As city governments struggled, they raised taxes and incurred vast debts, which bred graft and gave rise to the boss. Urban bosses awarded utility franchises and construction contracts to local businesses in return for kickbacks, while new immigrant voters received jobs and welfare in return for their votes. Bosses tipped off friendly real estate agents about projected city improvements and received favors from the owners of saloons, brothels, and gambling clubs in return for help with police protection, bail, and influence with judges. These institutions were vital to the urban economy and played an important role in easing the immigrants' way into American life. For many young women, prostitution meant economic survival. For men, the saloon offered friendship, cheap meals, and job leads.

Bossism deeply offended native-born, ethnocentric urban reformers. Many "goo-goos" (as bosses called advocates of "good government") not only opposed graft and vice but also the different cultural values of immigrants. As one said, immigrants "follow blindly leaders of their own race, are not moved by discussion, and exercise no judgment of their own"—and so were "not fit for the suffrage." Therefore, they advocated the "Americanization" of immigrants in public schools, opposed parochial schooling, and formed clubs and voters' leagues to educate new and old citizens about the failings of municipal government. They delighted in exposing electoral irregularities and large-scale graft, which often led to strident calls for replacing an Irish Catholic mayor with an Anglo-Saxon Protestant.

Ethnic politics colored every reform issue. Anglo-Saxon men favored prohibition partly to remove Irish saloon-owner influence from politics and supported woman suffrage partly to gain a middle-class political advantage against male immigrant voters. Most urban reformers disdained the "city proletariat mob." They proposed replacing bosses with expert city managers,

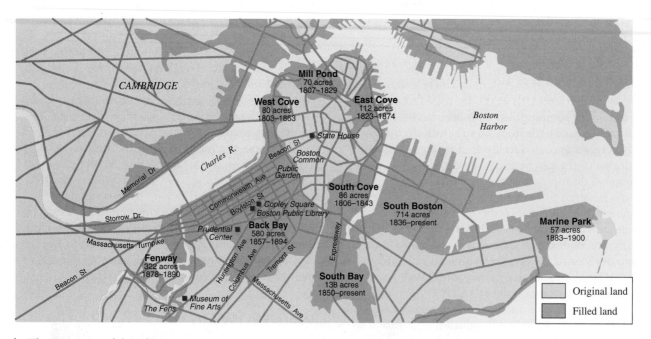

The City Beautiful: Enlarging Boston

As part of the "city beautiful" movement, Boston filled in more than 500 acres of tidal flats and swampy lowlands with gravel, thus adding the fashionable Back Bay along tree-lined Commonwealth Avenue. What is the effect of beautifying cities on different classes and ethnicities? Who benefits? Who uses Central Park in New York City? Who uses the parks in your city or town?

Favors from a Party Boss

Reformers wanted to eliminate the rule of urban party bosses. What in this *Puck* magazine cartoon would they criticize and want to change? What good did bosses do? Did the good outweigh the bad? What is local politics like now in your city?

(Courtesy of The Newberry Library, Chicago)

PUCK

HOW IS IT IN YOUR CITY?

who would bring honest professionalism to city government. They hoped to make government cheaper and thereby lower taxes. One effect of their emphasis on cost efficiency was to cut services to the poor. Another was to disfranchise working-class and ethnic groups, whose political participation depended on the boss system.

Not all urban reformers were so elitist. Samuel Jones, for example, both opposed bossism and passionately advocated political participation by urban immigrants. He himself had begun as a poor Welsh immigrant in the Pennsylvania oil fields but worked his way up to the ownership of several oil fields and a factory in Toledo, Ohio. In 1894, Jones decided to "apply the Golden Rule as a rule of conduct" in his factory, with an eight-hour workday, a $2 minimum daily wage (50 to 75 cents higher than the local average for 10 hours), cooperative insurance, and an annual 5 percent Christmas dividend. Plastering the Golden Rule on factory walls, he hired social outcasts, offered employees cheap hot lunches (for 15 cents) and recreational facilities, and established Golden Rule Hall, where social visionaries could speak.

In 1897, Jones was elected to the first of four terms as mayor of Toledo. A maverick Republican who antagonized prominent citizens, Jones was adored by ordinary people with his advocacy of municipal ownership of utilities; public-works jobs and housing for the unemployed; more civic parks and playgrounds with free pools, skating rinks, and sleigh rides; and free vocational education and kindergartens. A pacifist, he took away policemen's weapons. In police court, Jones regularly dismissed most cases of petty theft and drunkenness on grounds that the accused were victims of social injustice, and he often released prostitutes after fining every man in the room 10 cents—and himself a dollar—for condoning prostitution. Crime in notoriously sinful Toledo fell during his term. When "Golden Rule" Jones died in 1904, nearly 55,000 people, "tears streaming down their faces," filed past his coffin.

The Struggle for Woman Suffrage

Women served, in Jane Addams's phrase, as "urban housekeepers" in the settlement house and good-government movements. Their work reflected the tensions many women felt between their public and private lives, between their obligations to self, family, and society. This tension was seldom expressed openly. A few women, however, began to vent the frustrations of middle-class domestic life. In her novel *The Awakening* (1899), Kate Chopin told the story of a young woman who, in discovering her own sexuality and life's possibilities beyond being a "mother-woman," defied conventional expectations of a woman's role. Her sexual affair and eventual suicide prompted a St. Louis newspaper to label the novel "poison."

Some middle-class women—Addams and Scudder, for example—avoided marriage, preferring the nurturing relationships found in the female settlement house community. "Married life looks to me . . . terribly impoverished for women," a Smith graduate observed, adding, "most of my deeper friendships have been with women." A few women boldly advocated free love or, less openly, formed lesbian relationships. Although most preferred traditional marriages and chose not to work outside the home, the generation of women that came of age in the 1890s married less—and later—than at any other time until today.

Many women reconciled the conflicting pressures between their private and public lives, and deflected male criticism, by seeing their work as maternal. Addams called Hull House the "great mother breast of our common humanity." Frances Willard told Susan B. Anthony in 1898 that "government is only housekeeping on the broadest scale," a job men had botched, requiring women's saving participation. A leading labor organizer was "Mother" Jones, and the fiery feminist anarchist Emma Goldman titled her monthly journal *Mother Earth*. By using nurturant language to describe their work, women furthered the very arguments used against them. Many remained economically dependent on men, and all women still lacked the essential rights of citizenship. How could they be municipal housekeepers if they could not yet even vote?

After the Seneca Falls Convention in 1848, women's civil and political rights advanced very slowly. Although several western states gave women the right to vote in municipal and school board elections, before 1890 only the territory of Wyoming (1869) granted full political equality. Colorado, Utah, and Idaho enfranchised women in the 1890s, but no other states granted suffrage until 1910. This slow pace resulted in part from male opposition led by an odd combination of ministers and saloon interests, as well as men threatened by women voting. "Equal suffrage," said a Texas senator, "is a repudiation of manhood."

In the 1890s, leading suffragists reexamined their situation. The two wings of the women's rights movement, split since 1869, combined in 1890 as the National American Woman Suffrage Association (NAWSA). Although Elizabeth Cady Stanton and Susan B. Anthony continued to head the association, both were in their seventies and leadership passed to younger, more moderate women. At a NAWSA convention in 1896, a resolution critical of Stanton's *Woman's Bible*, a devastating attack on the religious argument against woman suffrage, marked the shift. The new leaders also dropped other issues to focus only on suffrage.

Changing leadership also meant new strategies for getting the vote. Since 1848, suffragists had argued primarily from the principle of "our republican idea, individual citizenship," as Stanton put it in 1892. But younger leaders shifted to three expedient arguments. The first was that women needed the vote to pass self-protection laws to guard against rape and unsafe industrial work. The second argument, Addams's notion of urban housekeeping, pointed out that political enfranchisement would further women's role in cleaning up immoral cities and corrupt politics.

The third expedient argument reflected urban middle-class reformers' prejudice against non-Protestant immigrants. Machine bosses saw to it that immigrant men got to vote, sometimes several times in a day. Suffragists argued that educated, native-born American women should get the vote to counteract the undesirable influence of illiterate male immigrants. In a speech in Iowa in 1894, Carrie Chapman Catt, who would succeed Anthony as president of NAWSA in 1900, argued that the "Government is menaced with great danger...in the votes possessed by the males in the slums of the cities," a danger that could be averted only by giving the vote instead to women. Woman suffrage was finally achieved in 1920. But anti-immigrant attitudes would continue for another century.

Politics in the Pivotal 1890s

Americans mistakenly think of the last decade of the nineteenth century as the "gay nineties," symbolized by mustached baseball players and sporty Gibson girls riding bicycles. The 1890s was indeed a decade of baseball and bicycles but it was also a decade of disturbing gaps between rich and poor. The nineties featured enormous wealth but also dark tenements, grinding work, desperate unemployment, and debilitating poverty. The early 1890s saw Populism and protesting farmers; Wounded Knee and the "second great removal" of Native Americans; segregation, disfranchisement, and lynchings for blacks; and devastating labor defeats at Coeur d'Alene, Homestead, and Pullman.

Anticipated by Bellamy, the 1890s were years of contrasts and crises. Supreme Court justice John Harlan saw a "deep feeling of unrest" everywhere among people worrying that the nation was in "real danger...from aggregations of capital in the hands of a few." Populist "Sockless" Jerry Simpson simply saw a struggle between "the robbers and the robbed."

The pivotal nature of the 1890s hinged on this feeling of polarizing unrest and upheaval as the nation underwent the traumas of change from a rural to an urban society. The new immigration from Europe, the internal migrations of African Americans and white farmers, and the depression of 1893 all widened socioeconomic gaps, accelerating demands for reform. The federal bureaucracy slowly began to adapt to the needs of governing a complex specialized society, and Congress purposefully, if ineffectively, moved to confront national problems.

Republican Legislation in the Early 1890s

As the English and Germans were enacting national health, housing, and social insurance laws, Republicans, who gained control of the American

From the Depths

The conflicts between rich and poor and threat of social upheaval are dramatically illustrated in this turn-of-the-century work titled *From the Depths*. Can you tell a story about what is happening in the picture, and what is likely to happen next?

(Culver Pictures)

Congress in 1888, inched forward with legislation in five areas: trusts, the tariff, the money question, rights for African Americans, and pensions for Civil War veterans. The last was easiest, as a bill providing generous support for Union veterans and their dependents sailed through Congress.

The Sherman Anti-Trust Act in 1890 declared illegal "every contract, combination . . . or conspiracy in restraint of trade or commerce." Although the Act was vague and not really intended to break up big corporations, it was an initial attempt to restrain large business combinations. In *United States* v. *E. C. Knight* (1895), the Supreme Court ruled that the American Sugar Refining Company, which controlled more than 90 percent of the nation's sugar-refining capacity, was not in violation of the Sherman Act.

A tariff bill introduced in 1890 by Ohio Republican William McKinley stirred more controversy. McKinley's bill raised tariffs higher than ever. Despite heated opposition from agrarian interests,

whose products were generally not protected, McKinley's bill passed the House and, after nearly 500 amendments, also the Senate.

Silver was trickier. Recognizing the appeal of free silver to agrarian debtors and organized farmers, Republican leaders feared their party might be hurt by the issue. Senator John Sherman (R-Ohio) proposed a compromise that momentarily satisfied almost everyone. The Sherman Silver Purchase Act ordered the Treasury to buy 4.5 million ounces of silver monthly and to issue treasury notes for it. Silverites were pleased by the proposed increase in the money supply. Opponents felt they had averted the worst—free coinage of silver. The gold standard still stood.

Republicans were also prepared to confront violations of the voting rights of southern blacks in 1890. As usual, political considerations trumped moral ones. Since 1877, the South had become a Democratic stronghold, where party victories could be traced to fraud and intimidation of black Republican voters. Republican legislation, then, was intended to improve party fortunes in the South. A bill proposed by Massachusetts senator Henry Cabot Lodge sought to ensure African American voter registration and fair elections. A storm of Democratic disapproval arose. Former president Cleveland called it a "dark blow at the freedom of the ballot," and the Mobile *Daily Register* claimed that the "Force Bill" "would deluge the South in blood." Senate Democrats delayed action with a filibuster.

To pass the McKinley Tariff, Republican leaders bargained away Lodge's bill, ending major-party efforts to protect African American voting rights in the South until the 1960s. In a second setback for blacks, the Senate, fearful of giving the federal government a role in education, defeated a bill to provide federal aid to black schools in the South that received a disproportionately small share of local and state funds. "The plain truth is," said the New York *Herald*, "the North has got tired of the negro," foreshadowing a similar retreat from civil rights legislation 100 years later.

Labeled the "billion-dollar Congress," the legislative efforts of the summer of 1890, impressive by nineteenth-century standards, fell far short of solving the nation's problems. Trusts grew more rapidly after the Sherman Act than before. Union veterans were pleased with their pensions, but southerners complained that Confederate veterans were left out. Tariff protection was seen as a benefit primarily for eastern manufacturers. Farm prices continued to slide, and gold and silver advocates were only momentarily silenced. African American rights were put off to another time. Polarizing inequalities of wealth remained. Voters abandoned the GOP in droves in the 1890 congressional elections. Two years later, Cleveland won a presidential rematch with Harrison, claiming that government should do more in "support of the people."

Formation of the People's Party, 1892

Farmers knew all too well in 1890 that government did not support them; as Kansas orator Mary E. Lease said, "What you farmers need to do is to raise less corn, and more Hell." In February 1892, the People's, or Populist, party was established with Leonidas Polk as its presidential candidate. "The time has arrived," Polk thundered, "for the great West, the great South, and the great Northwest, to link their hands and hearts together and march to the ballot box and take possession of the government...and run it in the interest of the people." But by July, at the party convention in Omaha, Polk had died and the party nominated James B. Weaver, a Union army veteran from Iowa, for president and a former Confederate soldier for vice president.

The platform preamble, written by Ignatius Donnelly, a Minnesota farmer–politician, blazed with the urgent spirit of the agrarian protest movement, proclaiming that in the midst of political and corporate corruption "the people are demoralized....The fruits of the toil of millions are boldly stolen to build up colossal fortunes...we breed two great classes—paupers and millionaires." To heal that divide and end "oppression, injustice, and poverty," Donnelly advocated restoring government "to the hands of 'the plain people.'"

The Omaha demands expanded the Ocala platform of 1890. They included more direct democracy (popular election of senators, direct primaries, the initiative and referendum, and the secret ballot), and several pro-labor planks (the eight-hour workday, immigration restriction, and condemnation of the use of Pinkerton agents to break strikes). The Populists also endorsed a graduated income tax, free and unlimited coinage of silver at a ratio of 16 to 1, and government ownership of railroads, telephone, and telegraph. "The time has come," the platform said, "when the railroad corporations will either own the people or the people must own the railroads."

Although attempting to widen political debate by promoting a new vision of government activism to resolve farmers' problems, the Populists faced huge obstacles, not least weaning the South from the Democrats and encouraging southern whites to work with blacks. But the new party pressed ahead. Weaver campaigned actively in the South, where he faced egg- and rock-throwing Democrats spreading racial fears. Surprisingly, Weaver won more than 1 million popular votes (the first third-party candidate to do so), and carried four states and parts of two others for a total of 22 electoral votes.

The Populists' support was substantial but regional, coming from western miners and mine owners who favored the demand for silver coinage and from rural Americans from the Great Plains. But the People's party failed to break the Democratic stranglehold on the South. Populists did not appeal to city workers of the Northeast who were suspicious of the party's anti-urban tone and its desire for higher agricultural prices (which meant higher food prices). Perhaps most damaging, the Populists made few inroads among Midwestern farmers, who were relatively more prosperous than farmers elsewhere and saw little value in the Omaha platform. Although the Populists were not yet finished, most discontented farmers in 1892 voted for Cleveland and the Democrats.

The Depression of 1893

Though winning the election, Cleveland soon faced a difficult test. Shortly after taking office, one of the worst depressions ever to grip the American economy began, lasting from 1893 to 1897. Its severity heightened by global economic interdependence, the depression started in Europe and spread to the United States as overseas buyers cut back on their purchases of American products. Shrinking markets abroad soon crippled American manufacturing. Foreign investors, worried about the stability of American currency, dumped some $300 million of their securities in the United States. As gold left the country to pay for these securities, the nation's money supply declined. At the same time, falling prices hurt farmers, who discovered that it cost more to raise their crops and livestock than they could make in the market. Workers fared no better: wages fell faster than the price of food and rent.

The collapse in 1893 was also caused by an overextension of the domestic economy, especially in railroad construction and crops. Farmers, troubled by falling prices, planted more, hoping the market would pick up. But economic confidence gave way to financial panic. When Wall Street crashed early in 1893, investors frantically sold their shares and many people rushed to exchange paper notes for gold, further reducing gold reserves. Banks called in loans, which by the end of the year led to 16,000 business bankruptcies and 500 bank failures. The capital crunch and diminished buying power of Americans forced massive factory closings. Within a year, an estimated 3 million Americans—20 percent of the workforce—lost jobs. People fearfully watched tramps wandering from city to city looking for work, "with thousands of homeless and starving men in the streets" of Chicago.

As in Bellamy's coach image, the misery of the many was not shared by the few, which increased discontent. While unemployed men foraged in garbage dumps for food, the wealthy gave lavish parties, sometimes costing as much as $100,000. While poor families shivered in poorly heated tenements, the very rich built million-dollar summer resorts at Newport, Rhode Island, or grand mansions on New York's Fifth Avenue. While Lithuanian immigrants walked or rode packed

A City of Contrasts in 1893

Describe the contrasts in these two images of boating on the lagoons near the Palace of Electricity at the Chicago World's Columbian Exposition (above) and slum children playing in the streets less than a mile away (left). What is your response?

(Above: Bettman/CORBIS; left, Library of Congress)

streetcars to work, wealthy men luxuriated on huge pleasure yachts.

Nowhere were these inequalities more apparent than in Chicago during the World's Columbian Exposition, which opened on May 1, 1893, five days before a plummeting stock market began the depression. The Chicago World's Fair showcased, as President Cleveland said in an opening-day speech, the "stupendous results of American enterprise." When he pressed an ivory telegraph key, he started electric current that unfurled flags, spouted water through gigantic fountains, lit 10,000 electric lights, and powered huge steam engines. For six months, some 27 million visitors strolled around the White City, admiring its wide lagoons, its neoclassical white plaster buildings, and its exhibit halls filled with inventions. Built at a cost of $31 million, the fair celebrated the marvelous mechanical accomplishments of American enterprise and of the "city beautiful" movement to make cities more livable.

But as fairgoers sipped pink champagne, in immigrant wards less than a mile away people drank contaminated water, crowded into packed tenements, looked in vain for jobs, and frequented saloons and brothels. "If Christ came to Chicago," British journalist W. T. Stead wrote in 1894, this would be "one of the last precincts into which we should care to take Him." Stead's book depicted the "ugly sight" of corruption, poverty, and wasted lives in a city with 200 millionaires and 200,000 unemployed men.

Despite the magnitude of despair during the depression, national politicians and leaders were reluctant to respond. Mass demonstrations forced city authorities to provide soup kitchens and places for the homeless to sleep. When an army of unemployed led by Jacob Coxey marched on Washington in the spring of

1894 to press for public work relief, its leaders were arrested for walking on the Capitol grass. Later that summer, President Cleveland sent federal troops to Chicago to crush the Pullman strike.

The president blamed the depression on the Silver Purchase Act, and convinced Congress to repeal it. But repeal only worsened the financial crisis, highlighted the silver panacea, and hurt conservative Democrats. With workers, farmers, and wealthy silver miners alienated, voters abandoned the Democrats in the midterm elections of 1894, giving both Populists and Republicans high hopes for 1896.

The Crucial Election of 1896

The 1896 presidential campaign, waged during the depression and featuring a battle over the currency, was one of the most critical in American history. Although Cleveland was in disgrace for ignoring depression woes, few leaders in either major party thought the federal government was responsible for alleviating the suffering of the people. But unemployed Polish meatpackers in Chicago, Slavic workers in Pennsylvania blast furnaces, Italian immigrant women in New Haven tenements, and white and black tenant farmers in Georgia all wondered where relief might be found. Would either major party respond to the pressing human needs of the depression? Would the People's party set a new national agenda for politics? These questions were largely resolved in the election of 1896.

As the election approached, Populist leaders, influenced by silver mine owners, became convinced that they must make a single-issue commitment to the free and unlimited coinage of silver at the ratio of 16 to 1. In the throes of the depression, silver took on enormous importance as the symbol of the many grievances of downtrodden Americans. Popular literature captured the rural, moral dimensions of the silver movement. L. Frank Baum's *Wonderful Wizard of Oz* (1900) was a free-silver moral allegory of rural values (Kansas, Auntie Em, the uneducated but wise scarecrow, and the good-hearted tin woodsman) and Populist attitudes and policies (the wicked witch of the East, and the magical silver shoes in harmony with the yellow brick road, in "Oz"—ounces).

The Republicans nominated William McKinley. Twice governor of Ohio, McKinley was identified with the high protective tariff that bore his name. Citing the familiar argument that prosperity depended on the gold standard and protection, Republicans blamed the depression on Cleveland's attempt to lower the tariff.

The excitement of the Democratic convention in July contrasted with the staid, smoothly organized Republican gathering. With Cleveland repudiated, state after state elected delegates pledged to silver. Gold Democrats, however, had enough power to wage a close battle for the platform plank on money. Leading the silver forces was an ardent young silverite, William Jennings Bryan, a 36-year-old former congressman from Nebraska. Few saw him as presidential material, but Bryan arranged to give the closing argument for a silver plank himself. His dramatic speech, one of the most famous in American political history, swept the convention for silver and ensured his nomination. As he concluded his attack on the "goldbugs" and defense of the "holy...cause of liberty," Bryan said:

> Having behind us the producing masses of this nation...and toilers everywhere, we will answer their demand for a gold standard by saying to them: "You shall not press down upon the brow of labor this crown of thorns, you shall not crucify mankind upon a cross of gold."

Bryan stretched out his arms as if on a cross, and the convention exploded in applause.

Populist strategy lay in shambles when the Democrats named a silver candidate. Some party leaders favored fusion with the Democratic ticket but antifusionists were outraged. Unwisely, the Populists also nominated Bryan, with Georgia Populist Tom Watson for vice president. Running on competing silver slates damaged Bryan's chances.

During the campaign, McKinley stayed home in Canton, Ohio, where some 750,000 admirers came to visit him, brought by low excursion rates offered by the railroads. The Republicans made an unprecedented effort to reach voters through an expensive media campaign, heavily financed by major corporations. Party leaders distributed more than 200 million pamphlets in 14 languages to voters advertising McKinley as the "advance agent of prosperity." To unemployed workers, McKinley promised a "full dinner pail." On the money issue he declared that "our currency today is...as good as gold." Free silver, he warned, would cause inflation and more economic disaster. Recovery depended not on money, but on tariff reform to stimulate industry and provide jobs.

Bryan took his case directly to the people. Three million Americans in 27 states heard him speak as he traveled more than 18,000 miles, giving as many as 30 speeches a day. Bryan's message was simple: prosperity required free coinage of silver and government should attend to the needs of the producing classes rather than the vested interests. But the rhetoric favored rural toilers. "The great cities rest upon our broad and fertile prairies," he said in the "Cross of Gold" speech. Urban workers were not inspired by this rhetoric, nor were immigrants by Bryan's prairie moralizing. To influential easterners, the brash young Nebraskan represented a threat. A Brooklyn minister

POLITICAL CAMPAIGN ARTIFACTS: BUTTONS AND POSTERS

Throughout American history, presidential political campaigns have produced, in addition to the streams of speeches, sound bites, and words, mountains of material objects: buttons, badges, banners, bumper stickers, yard signs, posters, and other campaign paraphernalia to persuade voters to support one candidate or another.

The election of 1896 was no exception, producing a plethora of political campaign artifacts on behalf of William McKinley and William Jennings Bryan. The fervor of that pivotal political contest led to the production of thousands of lapel pins, buttons, ribbons, bandanas, shirts, teacups, paper and soap dolls, posters, and other articles intended to influence American voters. Although some of it seems silly, symbolic imagery was important. The examination of just two kinds of material objects —buttons and posters— reveals a great deal about the issues, values, symbolism, and style of the election of 1896.

Reflecting on the Past Examine the buttons pictured here (as well as the "goldbug" and other stickpins). What issues are voters reminded of? How many different ways is the message, reinforced by recurring symbols, repeated on these buttons? Now compare the buttons and pins with the two posters. Do not worry that you cannot read most of the words; focus instead on the visual imagery and such words as you can make out. How do the posters reinforce key symbols, slogans, and substantive issues associated with each candidate? What visual images do the posters add? What audience do you think these campaign artifacts had in mind? What do you conclude about the 1896 campaign on the basis of these material items? Do these artifacts suggest that voters were more or less involved with political issues and party identification than they are today? What artifacts, images, and symbols would best reflect an early twenty-first-century presidential campaign, and what would future historians learn from them? ■

Artifacts from the McKinley and Bryan campaigns

(Left: Courtesy Michael Kelly; right: © David J. and Janice L. Frent Collection/Corbis)

Campaign poster showing William McKinley and his running mate, Garret Hobart.

(Library of Congress [LC-USZC4–3162])

Campaign poster showing William Jennings Bryan, his wife and children, and the text of the "Cross of Gold" speech.

(The Granger Collection, New York)

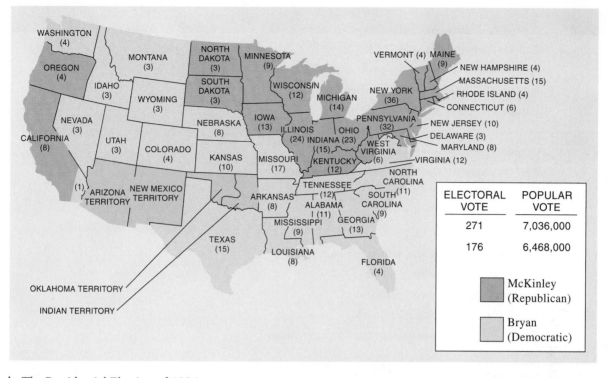

The Presidential Election of 1896

What do you notice about the sectional basis of the voting in McKinley's victory? Why did sections vote the way they did? In his cabled congratulations, Bryan, ever the "democrat," said: "We have submitted the issues to the American people and their will is law." Does the map and the constitutional role of the electoral college validate Bryan's belief that the people's will is law?

declared that the Democratic platform was "made in Hell," and Theodore Roosevelt wrote, "This silver craze surpasses belief. Bryan's election would be a great calamity."

Voters turned out in record numbers. In key states such as Illinois, Indiana, and Ohio, 95 percent of those eligible to vote went to the polls. McKinley won 271 electoral votes to Bryan's 176, the largest margin of victory in a quarter century. Millionaire Mark Hanna jubilantly wired McKinley: "God's in his heaven, all's right with the world."

Although Bryan won more than 6 million votes (47 percent of the total), more than any previous Democratic winner, he failed to carry the Midwest or urban middle and working classes, who had little confidence that free silver would stimulate economic growth. McKinley's promise of a "full dinner pail" was more convincing. Northern laborers feared that inflation would drive up prices and rents faster than wages. Catholic immigrants distrusted Populist Protestantism. In the Great Lakes states, prosperous farmers felt less discontent than farmers elsewhere. Chance also played a part in Bryan's defeat. Bad wheat harvests in India, Australia, and Argentina drove up world grain prices, and many of the complaints of American farmers evaporated.

The New Shape of American Politics

The landslide Republican victory broke the stalemate in post–Civil War American politics. Republicans dropped their identification with the politics of piety and strengthened their image as the party of prosperity and national greatness, which gave them a party dominance that lasted until the 1930s. The Democrats, under Bryan's leadership until 1912, put on the mantle of Populist moralism but were largely reduced to a sectional party, reflecting narrow southern views on money and race. The 1896 election demonstrated that the Northeast and the Great Lakes states had acquired so many immigrants that they now controlled the nation's political destiny. The Populists disappeared, yet within the next 25 years, many Populist issues (direct election of senators, graduated income tax, woman suffrage) were adopted by the two major parties and became law.

Another result of the election of 1896 was a change in the patterns of political participation. Because the Republicans were so dominant in the Northeast and Midwest, and Democrats so powerful in the South, parties had less reason to mobilize large numbers of voters and voters had little motivation to cast a ballot. Many black voters in the South, moreover, were disfranchised, and middle-class

Timeline

1873	Congress demonetizes silver
1875	Specie Resumption Act retires greenback dollars
1877	Rutherford B. Hayes becomes president
1878	Congress permits partial coining of silver
1879	Henry George, *Progress and Poverty*
1880	James A. Garfield elected president
1881	Garfield assassinated; Chester A. Arthur succeeds to presidency
1882	Chinese Exclusion Act
1883	Pendleton Civil Service Act
1884	Grover Cleveland elected president
1887	College Settlement House Association founded
1888	Edward Bellamy, *Looking Backward*
	Benjamin Harrison elected president
1889	Jane Addams establishes Hull House
	Andrew Carnegie promulgates "The Gospel of Wealth"
1890	Sherman Anti-Trust Act
	Sherman Silver Purchase Act
	McKinley Tariff
	Elections bill protecting black voting rights defeated
1890s	Wyoming, Colorado, Utah, and Idaho grant woman suffrage
1892	Cleveland elected president for the second time
	Populist party wins more than 1 million votes
	Homestead steel strike
1893	World's Columbian Exposition, Chicago
1893–1897	Financial panic and depression
1894	Pullman strike
	Coxey's march on Washington
1896	Charles Sheldon, *In His Steps*
	Populist party fuses with Democrats
	William McKinley elected president
1897	"Golden Rule" Jones elected mayor of Toledo, Ohio
	Economic recovery begins

good-government reformers were not as effective as party bosses in turning out urban voters. The tremendous rate of political participation that had characterized the nineteenth century since the Jackson era gradually declined. In the twentieth century, political involvement among poorer Americans declined considerably, a phenomenon unique among western democracies.

McKinley had promised that Republican rule meant prosperity, and as soon as he took office, the economy recovered. Discoveries of gold in the Yukon and the Alaskan Klondike increased the money supply, ending the silver mania. Industrial production returned to full capacity. Touring the Midwest in 1898, McKinley spoke to cheering crowds about the hopeful shift from "industrial depression to industrial activity."

McKinley's election marked not only the return of economic health but also the emergence of the executive as the dominant focus of the American political system. Just as McKinley's campaign saw the extravagant corporate contributions that have marked recent presidential campaigns, his conduct as president foreshadowed the presidency in our time. McKinley rejected traditional views of the president as the passive executor of laws, instead playing an active role in dealing with Congress and the press. His frequent trips away from Washington showed an increasing regard for gathering public opinion in the interests of advancing federal and national power. As we shall see in Chapter 20, McKinley began the transformation of the presidency into a potent force in world affairs as well.

Conclusion
LOOKING FORWARD

This chapter began with Edward Bellamy's imaginary look backward from the year 2000 at the grim economic realities and unresponsive politics of American life in the late nineteenth century. McKinley's triumph in 1896 indicated that in a decade marked by depression, Populist revolt, and cries for action to close the inequalities of wealth—represented by Bellamy's coach—the established order remained intact. Calls for change did not necessarily lead to change. But in the areas of personal action and the philosophical bases for social change, intellectual middle-class reformers such as Edward Bellamy, Frances Willard, Jane Addams, and "Golden Rule" Jones showed the way to progressive reforms in the next century. More Americans were able to look forward to the kind of cooperative, caring, and cleaner world envisioned in Bellamy's utopian novel.

As 1900 approached, people took a predictably intense interest in what the new century would be like. Henry Adams envisioned an ominous future, predicting the explosive and ultimately destructive energy of unrestrained industrial development, symbolized by the "dynamo" and other engines of American and European power. Such forces, he warned, would overwhelm the gentler, moral forces represented by art, woman, and religious symbols. Others were more optimistic, preferring to place their confidence in America's self-image as an exemplary democratic nation. Surely the new century, most thought, would see not only the continued perfection of these values and institutions but also the spread of the American model around the globe. Such confidence resulted in foreign expansion by the American people even before the old century had ended. We turn to that next.

QUESTIONS FOR REVIEW AND REFLECTION

1. How would you characterize the politics of the Gilded Age? How does it compare to present-day politics?
2. What political issues concerned the American people in the late nineteenth century, and do you think they were the appropriate ones?
3. What role did middle-class reformers, especially women, play in dealing with social and political problems in the Gilded Age? How did religion influence reform?
4. Why was the election of 1896 such a crucial and pivotal one in the development of American political parties? How were the policies and areas of support of the two major parties similar to and different from those of the present?
5. Was the American democratic system responsive to the needs of the American people in the Gilded Age? Was it even "democratic"? How well did politics reflect national ideals and values? Does it still?

CHAPTER 20

Becoming a World Power

Dewey at Manila Bay, May 1, 1898 (painting by Rufus Zogbaum): American Expansionism Triumphant. What artistic elements make this a heroic painting?

(CORBIS)

American Stories

Private Grayson Kills a Soldier in the Philippines

In January 1899, the U.S. Senate was locked in a dramatic debate over whether to ratify the Treaty of Paris concluding the recent war with Spain over Cuban independence. At the same time, American soldiers uneasily faced Filipino rebels across a neutral zone around the outskirts of Manila, the capital of the Philippines. Until recent weeks, the Americans and Filipinos had been allies, together defeating the Spanish to liberate the Philippines. The American fleet under Admiral George Dewey had destroyed the Spanish naval squadron in Manila Bay on May 1, 1898. Three weeks later, an American ship brought from exile the native Filipino insurrectionary leader, Emilio Aguinaldo, to lead rebel forces on land, while U.S. gunboats patrolled the seas.

At first, the Filipinos looked on the Americans as liberators. Although the intentions of the United States were never clear, as in a later intervention in Iraq, Aguinaldo believed that, as in Cuba, the Americans had no territorial ambitions. They would simply drive the Spanish out and then leave. In June, therefore, Aguinaldo declared the independence of the Philippines and began setting up a constitutional government. American officials pointedly ignored the independence ceremonies. When the war ended in August, American troops denied Aguinaldo's Filipino soldiers an opportunity to liberate their own capital city and shunted them off to the suburbs. The armistice agreement recognized American rights to the "harbor, city, and bay of Manila," while the proposed Treaty of Paris gave the United States the entire Philippine Islands archipelago.

Tension mounted in the streets of Manila and along 14 miles of trenches separating American and Filipino soldiers. Taunts, obscenities, and racial epithets were shouted across the neutral zone. Barroom skirmishes and knifings filled the nights; American soldiers searched houses without warrants and looted stores. Their behavior was not unlike that of English soldiers in Boston in the 1770s.

On the night of February 4, 1899, Privates William Grayson and David Miller of Company B, 1st Nebraska Volunteers, were on patrol in Santa Mesa, a Manila suburb surrounded on three sides by insurgent trenches. The Americans had orders to shoot any Filipino soldiers in the neutral area. As the two Americans cautiously worked their way to a bridge over the San Juan River, they heard a Filipino signal whistle, answered by another. The two froze as four Filipinos emerged from the darkness on the road ahead. "Halt!" Grayson shouted. The native lieutenant in charge answered, "Halto!"—either mockingly or because he had similar orders. Standing less than 15 feet apart, the two men repeated their commands. After a moment's hesitation, Grayson fired, killing his opponent. The other Filipinos jumped out at them, and Grayson and Miller shot two more. Then they turned and ran back to their own lines shouting warnings of attack. A full-scale battle followed.

The next day, Commodore Dewey cabled Washington that the "insurgents have inaugurated general engagement" and promised a hasty suppression of the insurrection. The outbreak of hostilities ended the Senate debates. On February 6, the Senate ratified the Treaty of Paris, thus formally annexing the Philippines and sparking a war between the United States and Aguinaldo's Filipino nationalist revolutionaries, who represented a small but growing percentage of the population.

In a guerrilla war similar to those that Americans would fight later in Vietnam, Afghanistan, and Iraq, Filipino nationalists tried to undermine the American will by hit-and-run attacks. American soldiers remained in heavily garrisoned cities and undertook search-and-destroy missions to root out rebels and pacify the countryside. The Filipino-American War lasted until July 1902, three years longer than the Spanish-American War that caused it and involving far more troops, casualties, and monetary and moral costs.

How did all this happen? What brought Private Grayson to "shoot my first nigger," as he put it, halfway around the world? For the first time in history, regular American soldiers found themselves fighting outside North America. The "champion of oppressed nations," as Aguinaldo said, had turned into an oppressor nation itself, imposing the American way of life and American institutions on faraway peoples against their will. It would not be the last time.

The war in the Philippines marked a critical transformation of America's role in the world. As the United States sought to exert a wider influence, global events influenced America. Within a few years at the turn of the century, the United States acquired an empire, however small by European standards, and established itself as a world power. In this chapter, we will review the historical dilemmas of America's role in the world. In an increasingly global context, we will examine the U.S. motivations for expansionism in the 1890s and how they were manifested in Cuba, the Philippines, and elsewhere. Finally, we will look at how the fundamental patterns of American foreign policy to this day were established for Latin America, eastern Asia and the Middle East, and Europe. We will see that the tension between idealism and self-interest that has permeated America's domestic history has also guided its foreign policy.

Steps Toward Empire

The circumstances that brought Privates Grayson and Miller from Nebraska to the Philippines originated deep in American history. As early as the seventeenth-century Puritan migration, Americans worried about how to do good in a sinful world. John Winthrop sought to set up a "city on a hill" in the New World, a model community of righteous living for the rest of the world to imitate. "Let the eyes of the world be upon us," Winthrop had said. That wish, reaffirmed during the American Revolution, became a permanent goal of American policy toward the outside world.

America as a Model Society

Nineteenth-century Americans, like the Russians, French, English, and Chinese, continued to believe in their nation's special mission in the world. But only the United States claimed a mission of spreading democratic governments. The Monroe Doctrine in 1823, pointing out the differences between autocratic Europe and America, warned Europe's monarchies to keep out of the New World and not to interfere with emerging Latin American independence movements. In succeeding decades, distinguished European visitors came to observe the "great social revolution" in the United States. They found representative democratic political and legal institutions, a Protestant religious commitment to human perfectibility, unlimited energy, and an ability to apply unregulated economic activity and inventive genius to produce more things for more people.

In an evil world, Americans, then as now, believed that they stood as a transforming force for good. But how could a nation committed to isolationism and to avoiding entanglements with European nations do the transforming? One way was to encourage other countries to observe and imitate the American example. Other nations, however, were often attracted to competing models of modernization, such as socialism, or preferred their own religious traditions, such as Islam. These differences often led to a more aggressive American foreign policy, as seen in the aftermath of 9/11.

Americans have rarely just focused on perfecting the good example at home and waiting for others to copy it, which requires patience and passivity, two traits not characteristic of the American people. Leaders of the United States have therefore actively and sometimes forcefully sought to impose their ideas and institutions on others. These international crusades, as in recent years in the Caribbean, Central America, Afghanistan, and Iraq, have been motivated by a mixture of noble idealism and crass self-interest. Hence, the effort to spread the American model to an imperfect world has been both a blessing and a burden—for others as well as for the American people.

Early Expansionism

Persistent expansionism marked the first century of American independence. Jefferson's purchase of Louisiana in 1803, the taking of Indian lands during the War of 1812, and the midcentury pursuit of "Manifest Destiny" spread the United States across North America. In the 1850s, Americans began to look beyond their own continent as Commodore Perry in 1853 "opened" Japan, and southerners sought more cotton lands in the Caribbean.

After the Civil War, Secretary of State William Seward spoke of an America that would hold a "commanding sway in the world," destined to exert commercial domination in the Pacific. He purchased Alaska from Russia in 1867 for $7.2 million and acquired a coaling station in the Midway Islands near Hawaii, where missionaries and merchants were already active. He advocated annexing Cuba and other Caribbean islands, tried to negotiate a treaty for an American-built canal through Panama, and dreamed of "possession" of the entire North and Central American continent and ultimately "control of the world."

In 1870, foreshadowing the Philippines debates 30 years later, supporters of President Grant, arguing the strategic and economic importance of the Caribbean, tried to persuade the Senate to annex Santo Domingo on the island of Hispaniola. Opponents responded that annexation violated American principles of self-determination and government by consent. They also claimed that brown-skinned Caribbean peoples were unassimilable, and that expansionism would involve foreign entanglements, a large and expensive navy, bigger government, and higher taxes. The Senate rejected annexation.

Although reluctant to add territory outright, Americans eagerly sought commercial dominance in Latin America and Asia. But American talk of building a canal across Nicaragua produced only Nicaraguan suspicions. In 1881, secretary of state James G. Blaine sought to convene a conference of American nations to promote hemispheric peace and trade. Latin Americans may have wondered what Blaine intended, for in 1881 he intervened in three separate border disputes in Central and South America, in each case at the cost of goodwill. After an incident and threat of war with Chile in 1889, Blaine's efforts resulted in the first Pan-American Conference to improve economic ties among the nations of the Americas.

American influence spread to the Pacific. In the mid-1870s, American sugar-growing interests in the Hawaiian Islands put whites in positions of influence over the monarchy. In 1875, they obtained a treaty admitting Hawaiian sugar duty-free to the United

Waging War in the Philippines

When the United States went to war against Spain in 1898, partly to help the Cubans win their independence from harsh Spanish rule, no one could have imagined the ironic outcome. Within a year, Americans would themselves impose imperial rule over the Philippines, marching through and burning villages (as the Twentieth Kansas Volunteers are doing here) and waging war against civilians in a faraway Asian land. How did that happen? Has it happened since?

(Above: Courtesy of The Newberry Library, Chicago; right: Keystone-Mast Collection [24039], URL/California Museum of Photography, University of California at Riverside)

States, and in 1887, the United States won exclusive rights to build a naval base at Pearl Harbor. Native Hawaiians resented the influence of American sugar interests, especially as they brought in Japanese to replace native people in the sugarcane fields, with some 200,000 arriving between 1885 and 1924.

In 1891, the nationalistic queen Liliuokalani assumed the throne and pursued a policy of "Hawaii for the Hawaiians." Two years later, in what one journalist called a revolution "of sugar, by sugar, for sugar," white planters staged a coup with the help of U.S. gunboats and marines, imprisoned the queen, and sought formal

annexation by the U.S. Senate. But when Grover Cleveland, who opposed expansion, returned to the presidency for his second term, he stopped the move. The sugar growers waited patiently for a more desirable time for annexation, which came during the war in 1898.

American Expansionism in Global Context

American forays into the Pacific and Latin America brought the United States increasingly into contact and conflict with European nations. The nineteenth century was marked by European imperial expansionism

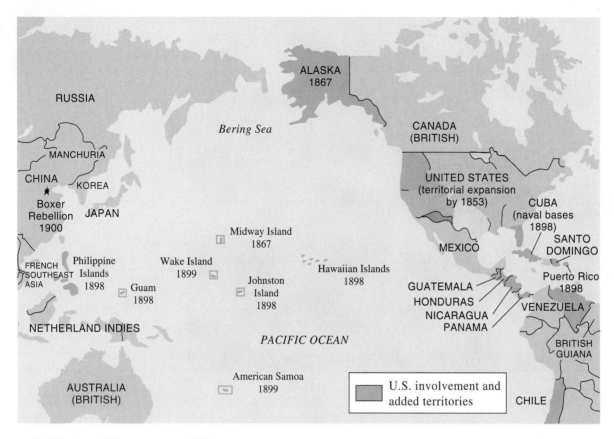

U.S. Territorial Expansion to 1900

U.S. territorial expansion to 1860 is represented in miniature in the U.S. portion of this map. What obvious differences are apparent between earlier expansion and areas of U.S. involvement and acquisitions after 1860 (in green)? How was each new territory acquired? What patterns and problems do you see with this expansion?

throughout much of the world. In southern and south-eastern Asia, the British were in India, Burma, and Malaya; the French in Cambodia, Vietnam, and Laos; the Dutch in Singapore and the East Indies; and the Spanish in the Philippines. These and other colonial powers divided China—its Manchu dynasty weakened by the opium trade, internal conflicts, and European pressure—into spheres of economic influence. A Chinese newspaper editorial complained that other nations "all want to satisfy their ambitions to nibble at China and swallow it." The Russians wrested away Manchuria, and Japan took Korea after intervention in a Korean peasant rebellion in 1894. China was forced to cede Taiwan and southern Manchuria to Japanese influence and control.

In Africa, Europeans scrambled to gain control of both coastal and interior areas, with England, France, Germany, Portugal, and Belgium grabbing the most land and exploiting African peoples. Only two inde-pendent African nations existed in the late nineteenth century: Liberia, founded in 1822 by Americans to resettle free blacks, and the fragmented kingdom of Ethiopia, which thrashed the Italians when they invaded in 1896. With nearly all of Africa colonized,

the only way imperial powers could acquire more land was to fight one another. Thus, in 1899, war broke out in southern Africa between the British and the Boers, descendants of Dutch settlers—a war waged with a savagery Europeans usually reserved for indige-nous peoples. The English destroyed Boer farms and drove civilians into camps where an estimated 20,000 women and children perished from starvation and malnutrition. The British won, but at a horrific cost.

Africa was not then of interest to the United States, but in the Pacific and the Caribbean, it was inevitable that the United States, a late arrival to imperialism, would collide with European rivals. Moving outward from Hawaii closer to the markets of eastern Asia, the United States acquired a naval and coaling station in the Samoan Islands in 1878. American and German naval forces almost fought each other there in 1889—before a typhoon ended the crisis by nearly wiping out both navies. Troubles in the Pacific also occurred in the late 1880s over the American seizure of several Canadian ships in fur seal and fishing disputes in the Bering Sea, settled only by the threat of British naval action and an international arbitration ruling ordering the United States to pay damages.

Closer to home, the United States sought to replace Great Britain as the most influential nation in Central America and northern South America. In 1895, a boundary dispute between Venezuela and British Guyana threatened to bring British intervention against the Venezuelans. President Cleveland, needing a popular political issue during the depression, asked Secretary of State Richard Olney to send a stern message to Great Britain. Invoking the Monroe Doctrine, Olney's note (stronger than Cleveland intended) called the United States "practically sovereign on this continent" and demanded international arbitration to settle the dispute. The British ignored the note, and war loomed. Both sides realized that war would be an "absurdity," and the boundary dispute was settled.

Despite these expansionist blusters, the United States in 1895 had neither the means nor a consistent policy for enlarging its role in the world. The diplomatic service was small and unprofessional. No U.S. embassy official in Beijing spoke Chinese. The U.S. Army, with about 28,000 men, was smaller than Bulgaria's. The navy, dismantled after the Civil War and only partly rebuilt, still had many obsolete ships and ranked no higher than tenth in the world. By 1898, things would change.

Expansionism in the 1890s

In 1893, the historian Frederick Jackson Turner wrote that for three centuries "the dominant fact in American life has been expansion." The "extension of American influence to outlying islands and adjoining countries," he thought, indicated still more expansionism. Turner struck a responsive chord in a country that had always been restless and optimistic. With the western frontier declared closed, Americans would surely look for new frontiers, for mobility and markets as well as for morality and missionary activity. The motivations for the expansionist impulse of the late 1890s resembled those that had prompted Europeans to settle the New World in the first place: greed, glory, and God. We will examine expansionism as a reflection of profits, patriotism, piety, and politics.

Profits: Searching for Overseas Markets

Senator Albert Beveridge of Indiana bragged in 1898 that "American factories are making more than the American people can use; American soil is producing more than they can consume. Fate has written our policy for us; the trade of the world must and shall be ours." Americans such as Beveridge revived older dreams of an American commercial empire in the Caribbean Sea and the Pacific Ocean. American businessmen saw huge profits beckoning in heavily

populated Latin America and Asia, and they wanted to get their share of these markets, as well as access to the sugar, coffee, fruits, oil, and minerals that were abundant in these lands.

Understanding that commercial expansion required a stronger navy and coaling stations and colonies, business interests began to shape diplomatic and military strategy. But not all businessmen in the 1890s liked commercial expansion or a vigorous foreign policy. Some preferred traditional trade with Canada and Europe rather than risky new ventures in Asia and Latin America. Some thought it more important to recover from the depression than annex distant islands.

But the drop in domestic consumption during the depression also encouraged businesses to expand into new markets. The tremendous growth of American production in the post–Civil War years made expansionism more attractive than drowning in overproduction, cutting prices, and firing workers. The National Association of Manufacturers led the way, proclaiming in 1896 that "the trade centers of Central and South America are natural markets for American products."

Despite the 1890s depression, products spewed from American factories at a staggering rate. The

■■■ Exports   ■■■ Imports

American Foreign Trade, 1870–1914

After a rather gradual increase in trade through the boom-and-bust cycles of the 1870s and 1880s and an actual dip during the depression of 1893–1895, American foreign trade saw spectacular increases during the Republican era of Presidents McKinley, Roosevelt, and Taft. What is the relationship between foreign trade and imperial expansion?

Source: U.S. Bureau of the Census.

United States moved from fourth place in the world in manufacturing in 1870 to first place in 1900, doubling the number of factories and tripling the value of farm output. Manufactured goods, led by steel products, agricultural machinery, sewing machines, cash registers, and telephones, grew nearly fivefold between 1895 and 1914. The total value of American exports tripled, from $434 million in 1866 to nearly $1.5 billion in 1900. By 1914, exports had risen to $2.5 billion, a 67 percent increase over 1900. The increased trade continued to go mainly to Europe rather than Asia (less than 5 percent). But interest in Asian markets grew, especially as agricultural output continued to increase and prices stayed low.

Investments followed a similar pattern. American direct investments abroad increased from about $634 million to $2.6 billion between 1897 and 1914. Although the greatest activity was in Britain, Canada, and Mexico, attention increased on actual and potential investment in Latin America and Eastern Asia. Central American investment grew from $21 million in 1897 to $93 million by 1914, mainly in mines, railroads, and banana and coffee plantations. At the turn of the century came the formation and growth of America's largest multinational corporations, including Dupont, Alcoa, American Tobacco, and the United Fruit Company. Although slow to respond to investment and market opportunities abroad, these companies soon supported an aggressive foreign policy.

Patriotism: Asserting National Power

In 1898, a State Department memorandum stated that "we can no longer afford to disregard international rivalries now that we ourselves have become a competitor in the world-wide struggle for trade." The national state, then, should support commercial interests.

More Americans, however, saw expansion in terms of national glory and greatness. In the late 1890s, a group centered around Assistant Secretary of the Navy Theodore Roosevelt and Massachusetts senator Henry Cabot Lodge emerged as highly influential leaders of a changing American foreign policy. These intensely nationalistic young men shifted to what Lodge called the "large policy." Roosevelt agreed that economic interests should take second place to questions of what he called "national honor."

Naval strategist Alfred Thayer Mahan greatly influenced the new foreign policy elite. Mahan's books argued that in a world of Darwinian struggle for survival, national power depended on naval supremacy, control of sea lanes, and vigorous development of domestic resources and foreign markets. He advocated colonies in both the Caribbean and the Pacific, linked by a canal built and controlled by the United States. In

a world of constant "strife" where "everywhere nation is arrayed against nation," he said, it was imperative that Americans "look outward."

Piety: The Missionary Impulse

As Mahan's statements suggest, a strong sense of God-given duty and the missionary ideal of doing good for others also motivated expansionism—and sometimes rationalized the exploitation and oppression of weaker peoples. As a missionary put it in 1885, "The Christian nations are subduing the world in order to make mankind free." Richard Olney agreed, saying in 1898, "the mission of this country is...to forego no fitting opportunity to further the progress of civilization," as defined by American values and geo-political interests.

Josiah Strong, a Congregationalist minister, was perhaps the most ardent advocate of American missionary expansionism. He argued that in the struggle for survival among nations, the United States had emerged as the center of Anglo-Saxonism and was "divinely commissioned" to spread political liberty, Protestant Christianity, and civilized values over the earth. "This powerful race," he wrote, "will move down upon Mexico, down upon Central and South America, out upon the islands of the sea, over upon Africa and beyond." Indiana senator Albert Beveridge agreed, saying in 1899 that God had prepared English-speaking Anglo-Saxons to become "the master organizers of the world to establish and administer governments among savages and senile peoples."

Missionaries carried these ideas to non-Christian lands around the world, especially China. The number of American Protestant missionaries in China increased from 436 in 1874 to 5,462 in 1914, and the estimated number of Christian converts in China jumped from 5,000 in 1870 to nearly 100,000 in 1900. Although this was much less than missionaries hoped, this tiny fraction of the Chinese population included young reformist intellectuals who, absorbing Western ideas, in 1912 helped overthrow the Manchu dynasty. Economic relations between China and the United States increased roughly at the same rate as missionary activity.

Politics: Manipulating Public Opinion

Public opinion and national politics also played a role. The psychological tensions and economic hardships of the depression in the 1890s jarred national self-confidence. Foreign adventures then, as now, provided a distraction from domestic turmoil and promised to restore patriotic pride—and maybe even win votes.

This process was helped by the growth of a highly competitive popular penny press, which brought international issues before a mass readership. When New York City newspapers, notably William Randolph

Hearst's *Journal* and Joseph Pulitzer's *World,* competed in stirring up public support for the Cuban rebels against Spain, politicians dared not ignore the outcry. Daily reports of Spanish atrocities in 1896 and 1897 kept public moral outrage constantly a part of political discourse. When Democrat William Jennings Bryan entered the fray by raising a regiment of Nebraska volunteers for war, the McKinley administration kept him far from battle and therefore far from the headlines.

Politics, then, joined profits, patriotism, and piety in motivating the expansionism of the 1890s. These four impulses interacted to produce the Spanish-American War, the annexation of the Philippine Islands and subsequent war, and the energetic foreign policy of President Theodore Roosevelt.

War in Cuba and the Philippines

Lying 90 miles off Florida, Cuba had been the object of intense American interest for a half century. Spain could not halt the continuing struggle of the Cuban people for a measure of autonomy and relief from exploitive labor in the sugar plantations, even after slavery itself ended. Cuban uprisings and pressure for complete independence raised tensions between Spain and the United States.

The Road to War

When the Cuban revolt flared up anew in 1895, the Madrid government again failed to implement reforms. Instead, it sent General Valeriano Weyler y Nicolau,

dubbed "the butcher" by the American press, with 50,000 troops to quell the disturbance. When Weyler began herding rural Cubans into "reconcentration" camps, Americans were outraged. An outpouring of sympathy swept the nation, especially as sensationalist reports of horrible suffering and the deaths of thousands in the camps ("butchered without mercy") filled American newspapers.

The Cuban struggle appealed to a country convinced of its role as protector of the weak and defender of the right of self-determination. One editorial deplored Spanish "injustice, oppression, extortion, and demoralization," while describing the Cubans as heroic freedom fighters "inspired by our glorious example of beneficent free institutions and successful self-government." Motivated in part by genuine humanitarian concern and a sense of admiration for heroic Cuban freedom fighters, many Americans held rallies to raise money and food for famine relief, and called for land reform and even armed intervention. But neither Cleveland nor McKinley wanted war.

Self-interest also played a role. Since the 1850s, Americans had noted the profitable resources and strategic location of the island. American companies had invested extensively in Cuban sugar plantations. Appeals for reform had much to do with ensuring a stable environment for further investments and trade ($27 million in 1897), as well as for protecting the sugar fields against the ravages of civil war.

The election of 1896 only temporarily diverted attention from Cuba. A new government in Madrid recalled Weyler and made halfhearted concessions.

The *Maine* Blows Up in Havana Harbor

The artist has captured here the horror of the sinking of the *Maine,* with scenes before and after the explosion. What emotions do these images evoke in you? What do you think caused the explosion and how might both diplomats and historians use different explanations?

(Chicago Historical Society [ICHi-08428])

But conditions worsened in the reconcentration camps, and the American press kept harping on the plight of the Cuban people. McKinley, eager not to upset recovery from the depression, skillfully resisted war pressures. But he could not control Spanish misrule or Cuban aspirations for freedom.

Events early in 1898 sparked the outbreak of hostilities. Rioting in Havana intensified both Spanish repression and American outrage. A letter from the Spanish minister to the United States, Dupuy de Lôme, calling McKinley a "weak," hypocritical politician, was intercepted and made public. Americans fumed.

A second event was more serious. When the rioting broke out, the U.S. battleship *Maine* was sent to Havana harbor to protect American citizens. On February 15, a tremendous explosion blew up the *Maine,* killing 262 men. Advocates of American intervention blamed the Spanish. Newspapers trumpeted slogans such as "Remember the *Maine!* To hell with Spain!"

Assistant Secretary of the Navy Theodore Roosevelt had been preparing for war for many years. He said that he believed the *Maine* had been sunk "by an act of dirty treachery on the part of the Spaniards" and would "give anything if President McKinley would order the fleet to Havana tomorrow." When the president did not, Roosevelt privately declared that McKinley had "no more backbone than a chocolate éclair" and continued readying the navy for action. Although a board of inquiry at the time concluded that an external submarine mine caused the disaster, later studies showed that a faulty boiler or some other internal defect set off the explosion, possibilities even Roosevelt later conceded.

After the sinking of the *Maine,* Roosevelt took advantage of the secretary of the navy's absence from the office one day to cable Commodore George Dewey, commander of the U.S. Pacific fleet at Hong Kong. Roosevelt ordered Dewey to fill his ships with coal and, "in the event" of a declaration of war with Spain, to sail to the Philippines and make sure "the Spanish squadron does not leave the Asiatic coast." "The Secretary is away and I am having immense fun running the Navy," Roosevelt wrote in his diary that night.

Roosevelt's act was consistent with policies he had been urging on his more cautious superior for more than a year. As early as 1895, the navy had contingency plans for attacking the Philippines. Influenced by Mahan, Roosevelt wanted to enlarge the navy. He also believed that the United States should construct an interoceanic canal, acquire the Danish West Indies (the Virgin Islands), annex Hawaii, and oust Spain from Cuba. As Roosevelt told McKinley late in 1897, he was putting the navy in "the best possible shape" for the day "when war began."

The public outcry over the *Maine* drowned out McKinley's efforts to avoid war. With the issues politicized, McKinley pressured the Madrid government to make further concessions. Spain did, though refusing to grant full independence to Cuba, and the president finally acted. On April 11, 1898, he sent an ambiguous message to Congress that seemed to call for war. Two weeks later, Congress authorized using troops against Spain and recognized Cuban independence, actions amounting to a declaration of war. In a significant additional resolution, the Teller Amendment, Congress stated that the United States had no intention of annexing Cuba. A Cuban revolutionary general cautiously observed, "I expect nothing from the Americans. We should trust everything to our efforts. It is better to rise or fall without help than to contract debts of gratitude with such a powerful neighbor."

"A Splendid Little War": Various Views

The outbreak of war between Spain and the United States did not go unnoticed in Europe. Kaiser Wilhelm II of Germany sarcastically offered to join with other European monarchs to help Spain resist the efforts of "the American-British Society for International Theft and Warmongering...to snatch Cuba from Spain." But Spain was left to face the United States alone, fully expecting a defeat. When war broke out, a Spanish rear admiral said that the ruptured relations with the United States "would surely be fatal."

Indeed, the war was short and relatively easy for the Americans, and "fatal" for the Spanish, who at the war's conclusion were left with "only two major combat vessels." The Americans won naval battles, at Guam and Puerto Rico for example, virtually without gunfire. At the two major engagements, Manila Bay and Santiago Bay in Cuba, only two Americans died, one from heat prostration while stoking coal. Only 385 men died from Spanish bullets, but more than 5,000 succumbed to tropical diseases. As the four-month war neared its end in August, Secretary of State John Hay wrote Roosevelt that "it has been a splendid little war; begun with the highest motives, carried on with magnificent intelligence and spirit."

The Spanish-American War seemed splendid in other ways, as letters from American soldiers suggest. One young man wrote that his comrades were all "in good spirits" because oranges and coconuts were plentiful and "every trooper has his canteen full of lemonade all the time." Another wrote his brother that he was having "a lot of fun chasing Spaniards."

But the war was not much fun for other soldiers. One said, "Words are inadequate to express the feeling of pain and sickness when one has the fever. For about a week every bone in my body ached and I did not care much whether I lived or not." Another described a man shot in the head as "a mass of blood." Nor was the war splendid for African American soldiers, who

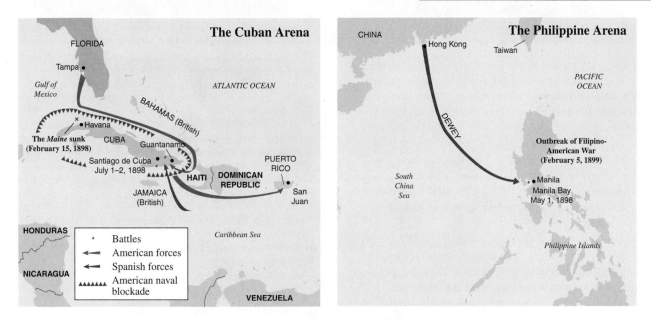

The Spanish-American War
Refer to the map on page 486 to see how far apart these two war zones were. How could the United States more easily manage a widely separated two-ocean empire? What did it need to do? What costs to a two-ocean war? Or any extension of conflict to more than one place?

fought in segregated units and noted stark differences between their rude treatment in the American South yet warm, grateful greetings in Cuba and Puerto Rico.

For Colonel Roosevelt, who resigned from the navy to lead a cavalry unit as soon as war was declared, the war was excitement and political opportunity. After a close brush with death in Cuba, Roosevelt declared with delight that he felt "the wolf rise in the heart" during "the power of joy in battle." But ironically, he needed help from African American soldiers to achieve his goals. His celebrated charge up Kettle Hill near Santiago was made possible by black troops first clearing the hill and then protecting his flank. The "charge" made three-inch headlines and propelled him toward the New York governor's mansion. "I would rather have led that charge," he said later, "than served three terms in the U.S. Senate." More than anyone, Roosevelt used the war to advance not only his political career but also the glory of national expansionism.

The Philippines Debates and War

Roosevelt's ordering Admiral Dewey to Manila initiated a chain of events that led to the annexation of the Philippines. The most crucial battle of the Spanish-American War occurred on May 1, 1898, when Dewey destroyed the Spanish fleet in Manila Bay and cabled McKinley for additional troops. Although the president admitted later that he was uncertain "within two thousand miles" where "those darned islands were," he sent twice as many troops as Dewey had asked for and

immediately began shaping American public opinion to accept the "political, commercial [and] humanitarian" reasons for annexing the Philippines. The Treaty of Paris gave the United States all 7,000 islands in the archipelago in exchange for a $20 million payment to Spain.

The treaty went to the Senate for ratification during the winter of 1898–1899. Senators hurled arguments across the floor of the Senate as American soldiers hurled racial taunts across the neutral zone at Aguinaldo's insurgents near Manila. Private Grayson's encounter, as we have seen, led to the passage of the treaty in a close Senate vote—and began the Filipino-American War and debates over what to do with the Philippines.

The entire nation joined the argument. At stake were two very different views of America's vision of itself in the world. After several months listening to public opinion, McKinley finally recommended annexation. Many Democrats supported the president out of fear of being labeled disloyal. At a time when openly racist thought flourished in the United States, fellow Republicans confirmed McKinley's arguments for annexation, adding even more insulting ones. Filipinos were described as childlike, dirty, and backward, and were compared to blacks and Native Americans. "The country won't be pacified," a Kansas veteran of the Sioux wars told a reporter, "until the niggers are killed off like the Indians." Roosevelt called Aguinaldo a "renegade Pawnee" and said that the Filipinos had no right "to administer the country which they happen to be occupying."

A small but prominent and vocal Anti-Imperialist League vigorously opposed war and annexation. These

Recovering the Past

One of the most enjoyable—and telling—ways of recovering the values and attitudes of the past is through political cartoons. Ralph Waldo Emerson once said, "Caricatures are often the truest history of the times." A deft drawing of a popular or unpopular politician can freeze ideas and events in time, conveying more effectively than columns of print the central issues—and especially the hypocrisies and misbehaviors of an era. Cartoonists are often at their best when they are critical, exaggerating a physical feature of a political figure or capturing public sentiment against the government.

The history of political cartoons in the United States goes back to Benjamin Franklin's "Join or Die" cartoon calling for colonial cooperation against the French in 1754. But political cartoons did not gain notoriety until the advent of Thomas Nast's cartoons in *Harper's Weekly* in the 1870s. Nast drew scathing cartoons exposing the corruption of William "Boss" Tweed's Tammany Hall, depicting Tweed and his men as vultures and smiling deceivers. "Stop them damn pictures," Tweed ordered. "I don't care so much what the papers write about me. My constituents can't read. But, damn it, they can see pictures." Tweed pressured Nast with an offer of $100,000 to "study art" in Europe. The $5,000-a-year artist negotiated up to a half million dollars before refusing the offer. "I made up my mind not long ago to put some of those fellows behind bars," Nast said, "and I'm going to put them there." His cartoons helped drive Tweed out of office.

The emergence of the United States as a world power and the rise of Theodore Roosevelt gave cartoonists plenty to draw about. At the same time, the rise of cheap newspapers such as William Randolph Hearst's *Journal* and Joseph Pulitzer's *World* provided a rich opportunity for cartoonists, whose clever images attracted more readers. When the Spanish-American War broke out, newspapers whipped up public sentiment with lurid fake pictures of fierce Spaniards violating American women and killing helpless Cubans. Hearst used these tactics to increase his paper's daily circulation to 1 million copies.

By the time of the debates over Philippine annexation, many cartoonists took an anti-imperialist stance, pointing out American hypocrisy. Within a year, cartoonists shifted from depicting "The Spanish Brute Adds Mutilation to Murder" (1898) to "Liberty Halts American Butchery in the Philippines" (1899), both included here. Note the similarities and differences. Although Uncle Sam is not nearly as

"The Spanish Brute Adds Mutilation to Murder," by Grant Hamilton in *Judge,* July 9, 1898.

(Culver Pictures)

menacing a killer as the figure of Spain as an ugly gorilla, both cartoons share similarities of an aggressive stance, blood-covered swords, and a trail of bodies behind.

Theodore Roosevelt's rise to the presidency and his broad grin, eyeglasses, and walrus mustache gave cartoonists a perfect target for caricature, as did his energetic style and such distinctive aspects as the "big stick" symbol and his "rough rider" image. The Roosevelt cartoons "Panama or Bust" (1903) and "For President!" (1904), filled with symbols and images, were both printed in American daily newspapers.

Reflecting on the Past What symbols and images do you see in these cartoons? How many can you identify, and how are they used? Who is the female figure, and what does she represent? How would you explain the change of bloodied sword bearer within one year? What is the attitude of the Roosevelt cartoonists toward the president? Can you identify the significance of each symbol? Check some recent newspapers: Who is criticized in political cartoons today, and how do cartoonists reveal their attitudes and political positions? ■

"Liberty Halts American Butchery in the Philippines," from *Life,* 1899.

L. C. Gregg in the Atlanta Constitution.

FOR PRESIDENT!

"Panama or Bust," from the *New York Times,* 1903 (above); "For President!" by L. C. Gregg, in the *Atlanta Constitution,* 1904 (right).

dignitaries included former presidents Harrison and Cleveland, Andrew Carnegie, Jane Addams, and Mark Twain. In arguments heard more recently about Iraq, anti-imperialists argued that taking over other countries contradicted American ideals. First, the annexation of territory without postwar planning (or steps toward statehood) was unwise and unprecedented. Second, to occupy and govern a foreign people without their consent violated American ideals. Third, social reforms needed at home demanded American energies and money. "Before we attempt to teach house-keeping to the world," one writer put it, we needed "to set our own house in order."

Not all anti-imperialist arguments were so noble. They, too, alleged that Filipinos were nonwhite, Catholic, inferior in size and intelligence, and therefore unassimilable. Annexation would lead to miscegenation and contamination of Anglo-Saxon blood, said South Carolina senator Ben Tillman, who opposed "incorporating any more colored men into the body politic." A practical argument suggested that once in possession of the Philippines, the United States would have to defend them and acquire more territories—in turn leading to higher taxes and bigger government, and requiring that American troops fight distant Asian wars.

The last argument became fact when Private Grayson's encounter started the Filipino-American War. Before it ended in 1902, some 126,500 American troops served in the Philippines, 4,234 died there, and

Two Views of War's Results

Compare the photograph with the cartoon from 1898–1899. The photo shows American soldiers standing guard over captured Filipino guerrillas in 1899. The cartoon, by Charles L. (Bart) Batholomew of the *Minneapolis Journal* (July 2, 1898), presents a happier, if stereotyped, view of three new Americans, including one labeled "Philippines" on the skirt to the right. Or are they happier? What is the cartoonist's message? What similarities and differences do you see in these two visual images?

(Photo: Library of Congress)

2,800 more were wounded. The cost was $400 million. Filipino casualties were much higher. In addition to 18,000 killed in combat, an estimated 200,000 Filipinos died of famine and disease as American soldiers burned villages and destroyed crops and livestock. General Jacob H. Smith told his troops that "the more you kill and burn, the better you will please me." Insurgent ineptness, Aguinaldo's inability to extend the fight across ethnic boundaries, and atrocities on both sides increased the frustrations of a lengthening war. The American "water cure" and other tortures were especially brutal.

As U.S. treatment of the Filipinos became more like Spanish treatment of the Cubans, the hypocrisy of American behavior became even more evident. This was especially true for black soldiers. Many identified with the dark-skinned insurgents, whom they saw as tied to the land, burdened by debt, and pressed by poverty like themselves. "I feel sorry for these people," a sergeant in the Twenty-Fourth Infantry wrote. "You have no idea the way these people are treated by the Americans here."

The war starkly exposed the hypocrisies of shouldering "the white man's burden." Aguinaldo wrote that America's "vague verbal offers of friendship and aid" were "drowned . . . out with the boom of cannons and the rattle of Gatling guns." On reading a report that 8,000 Filipinos had been killed in the first year of the war, Carnegie wrote a letter, dripping with sarcasm, congratulating McKinley for "civilizing the Filipinos.... About 8,000 of them have been completely civilized and sent to Heaven. I hope you like it." An anti-imperialist poet and New York legislator, Ernest Howard Crosby, wrote a sarcastic parody of Kipling's poem, which he titled "The Real 'White Man's Burden'":

Take up the White Man's burden.
Send forth your sturdy kin,
And load them down with Bibles
And cannon-balls and gin.
Throw in a few diseases
To spread the tropic climes,
For there the healthy niggers
Are quite behind the times.
They need our labor question too.
And politics and fraud—
We've made a pretty mess at home,
Let's make a mess abroad.

Another writer penned a devastating one-liner: "Dewey took Manila with the loss of one man—and all our institutions."

The anti-imperialists failed either to prevent annexation or to interfere with the war effort. They were out of tune with the period of exuberant expansionist national pride, prosperity, and promise.

Expansionism Triumphant

By 1900, Americans had ample reason to be patriotic. Within a year, the United States had acquired several island territories in the Pacific and Caribbean. But several questions arose over what to do with the new territories. Were they colonies? Would they be granted statehood, or become something else? Did Hawaiians, Puerto Ricans, and Filipinos have the same rights as American citizens on the mainland? Were they protected by the U.S. Constitution?

Although slightly different governing systems were worked out for each new territory, the solution in each case was to define its status as somewhere between a colony and a candidate for statehood. The indigenous people were usually allowed to elect their own legislature, but had governors and other judicial and administrative officials appointed by the American president. The first full governor of the Philippines, McKinley appointee William Howard Taft, effectively moved the Filipinos toward self-government, which came finally in 1946.

The question of constitutional rights was resolved by deciding that Hawaiians and Puerto Ricans, for example, would be treated differently from Texans and Oregonians. In the "insular cases" of 1901, the Supreme Court ruled that these people would achieve citizenship and constitutional rights only when Congress said they were ready. To the question, "Does the Constitution follow the flag?" Secretary of State Elihu Root answered, "Ye-es...the Constitution follows the flag—but doesn't quite catch up with it."

In the election of 1900, Bryan was again the Democratic nominee and tried to make imperialism the "paramount issue" of the campaign. He failed, in part because the country strongly favored annexing the Philippines. In the closing weeks of the campaign, Bryan shied away from imperialism and focused on domestic issues—trusts, the labor question, and free silver.

That did Bryan no good either. Prosperity returned with the discovery of gold in Alaska. The McKinley forces rightly claimed that four years of Republican rule had brought more money, jobs, thriving factories, and manufactured goods, as well as tremendous growth in American prestige abroad. As one politician put it, noting the end of the Populist revolt with the war fervor over Cuba, "The blare of the bugle drowned out the voice of the reformer."

He was more right than he knew. Within one year, expansionist Theodore Roosevelt rose from assistant secretary of the navy to colonel of the Rough Riders to governor of New York. For some Republican politicos, who thought he was too vigorous and independent, this quick rise as McKinley's potential rival came too fast. One way to slow down Roosevelt's progress was to make him vice president, which they did in 1900. But six months into McKinley's second term, an

Republican Campaign Poster

What is the persuasive political point of this 1900 campaign poster to reelect William McKinley? What was life like under the Democrats in 1896 and what has changed? Why would voters want to vote again for McKinley?

(David J. and Janice L. Frent Collection/CORBIS)

anarchist killed him, the third presidential assassination in less than 40 years. "Now look," exclaimed party boss Mark Hanna, who had opposed putting Roosevelt on the ticket, "that damned cowboy is President of the United States!"

Theodore Roosevelt's Energetic Diplomacy

At a White House dinner party in 1905, a guest told a story about visiting the Roosevelt home when "Teedie" was a baby. "You were in your bassinet, making a good deal of fuss and noise," the guest reported, "and your father lifted you out and asked me to hold you." Secretary of State Elihu Root looked up and asked, "Was he hard to hold?" Whether true or not, the story reveals much about President Roosevelt's principles and policies on foreign affairs. As president from 1901 to 1909, and as the most dominating American personality for the 15 years between 1897 and 1912, Roosevelt

made much fuss and noise about the activist role the United States should play in the world, and he often seemed "hard to hold." Yet Roosevelt's energetic foreign policy in Latin America, eastern Asia, and Europe paved the way for the vital role as a world power that the United States would play for the next century.

Foreign Policy as Darwinian Struggle

Roosevelt advocated both individual physical fitness and collective national strength. An undersized boy, he had pursued a rigorous bodybuilding program, and as a young man on his North Dakota ranch, he learned to value the "strenuous life." Reading Darwin taught him that life was a constant struggle for survival. As president, his ideal was a "nation of men, not weaklings." Although he believed in Anglo-Saxon superiority, he admired—and feared—Japanese military prowess. Powerful nations, like individuals, Roosevelt believed, had a duty to cultivate vigor, strength, courage, and moral commitment to civilized values. In practical terms, this meant developing natural resources, building large navies, and being prepared to fight.

Although famous for saying "speak softly and carry a big stick," Roosevelt often not only wielded a large stick but spoke loudly as well. In a speech in 1897, he used the word *war* 62 times, saying, "no triumph of peace is quite so great as the supreme triumphs of war." But despite his bluster, Roosevelt was usually restrained in exercising force. He won the Nobel Peace Prize in 1906 for helping end the Russo-Japanese War. The big stick and the loud talk were meant to preserve order and peace.

Roosevelt divided the world into "civilized" and "uncivilized" nations. Civilized nations had a responsibility to "police" the uncivilized, not only maintaining order but also spreading "superior" values and institutions. Taking on the "white man's burden," civilized nations (usually Anglo-Saxon, English-speaking) sometimes had to wage war on the uncivilized—justly so, he argued, because the victors bestowed the blessings of their culture and racial superiority on the vanquished. But a war between two civilized nations (for example, Germany and Great Britain) would be foolish. Above all, Roosevelt believed in the balance of power. Strong, advanced nations had a duty to use their power to preserve order and peace. With a booming economy and growing population of 75 million, the United States could no longer "avoid responsibilities" to exercise a greater role in world affairs.

Roosevelt developed a highly personal style of diplomacy. Bypassing the State Department, he preferred face-to-face contact and personal exchanges with foreign diplomats and heads of state. He made foreign policy while horseback riding with the German ambassador and while discussing history with a French minister. A British emissary observed that Roosevelt had a "powerful personality" and a commanding knowledge of the world. Ministries from London to Tokyo respected him.

When threats failed to accomplish his goals, Roosevelt used direct personal intervention. "In a crisis the duty of a leader is to lead," he said, noting that Congress was too slow. When he wanted Panama, Roosevelt bragged later, "I took the Canal Zone" rather than submitting a long "dignified State Paper" for congressional debate. And while Congress debated, he gloated, the building of the canal began. Roosevelt's energetic executive activism in foreign affairs, for better or worse, influenced presidents from Woodrow Wilson to George W. Bush.

Taking the Panama Canal

To justify the intervention of 2,600 American troops in Honduras and Nicaragua in 1906, Philander Knox, later a secretary of state, said that "because of the Monroe Doctrine" the United States is "held responsible for the order of Central America." The closeness of the Panama Canal, he said, "makes the preservation of peace in that neighborhood particularly necessary." The canal was not yet finished when Knox spoke, but it had already become a cornerstone of U.S. policy.

After resolving an 1850 treaty with Great Britain to jointly build a canal linking the Atlantic and Pacific, the United States had two problems. The first was where to build it. American engineers rejected a long route through Nicaragua in favor of a shorter, more rugged path across Panama, where a French firm had already begun work. This raised the second problem: Panama was a province of Colombia, which rejected the terms the United States offered. The refusal angered Roosevelt, who called the Colombians "Dagoes" who tried to "hold us up" like highway robbers.

Aware of Roosevelt's fury, encouraged by hints of American support, and eager for the economic benefits that a canal would bring, Panamanian nationalists in 1903 staged a revolution led by several rich families and Philippe Bunau-Varilla of the French canal company. With the help of an American warship to deter Colombian intervention, and the buying off of some Colombian officers, a bloodless revolution occurred on November 3. The next day Panama declared its independence and three days later the United States recognized it. Two weeks later, a treaty established the American right to build and operate a canal through Panama and to exercise "titular sovereignty" over the 10-mile-wide Canal Zone. Panamanians protested in vain. Roosevelt later claimed that the diplomatic and engineering achievement, completed in 1914, would "rank...with the Louisiana Purchase and the acquisition of Texas."

Policing the Caribbean

When Roosevelt took office in 1901, American policy toward Latin America was that although no nation had a right "to get territorial possessions," all nations had equal commercial rights. But as American investments poured into Central America and the Caribbean, the policy changed to one of asserting U.S. dominance in all the Americas, and especially the Caribbean.

This change was demonstrated in 1902 when Germany and Great Britain blockaded Venezuela's ports to force the government to pay defaulted debts. Roosevelt was especially worried that German influence would replace the British. He insisted that the European powers accept arbitration and threatened to "move Dewey's ships" to the Venezuelan coast. The crisis passed, largely for other reasons, but Roosevelt's threat of force made clear the presence and self-interest of the United States in the Caribbean.

The United States kept liberated Cuba under a military governor, Leonard Wood, until 1902, when the Cubans elected a congress and president. The United States honored Cuban independence, as it had promised to do, but in the Platt Amendment, which Cubans reluctantly added to their constitution in 1901, the United States obtained many economic rights in Cuba, a naval base at Guantanamo Bay (and later a prison), and the right to intervene if Cuban sovereignty were ever threatened. Cuban newspapers assailed this violation of their recent independence.

American policy intended to make Cuba a model of how a newly independent nation could achieve orderly self-government with only minimal guidance. Cuban self-government, however, was shaky. When in 1906 a political crisis threatened to spiral into civil war, Roosevelt expressed his fury with "that infernal little Cuban republic." He sent warships to patrol the coastline and special commissioners and troops "to restore order and peace and public confidence." As he left office in 1909, Roosevelt proudly proclaimed, "we have done our best to put Cuba on the road to stable and orderly government." The road was paved with sugar, as U.S. trade with Cuba increased from $27 million to $43 million in the decade following 1898. Along with economic development, which mostly benefited American companies, American involvement in Cuban affairs would continue for over a century.

The pattern was repeated throughout the Caribbean. The Dominican Republic, for example, suffered from unstable governments and great poverty. In 1904, as a revolt erupted, European creditors pressured the Dominican government for payment of $40 million in defaulted bonds. Sending its warships to discourage European intervention, the United States took over the collection of customs in the republic. Two years later, the United States intervened in Guatemala and Nicaragua, where American bankers controlled nearly 50 percent of all trade, the first of several twentieth-century interventions in those countries.

In a policy known as the Roosevelt Corollary to the Monroe Doctrine, the president announced in his annual message to Congress in 1904 that civilized nations should "insist on the proper policing of the world." The goal of the United States, he said, was to have "stable, orderly and prosperous neighbors." A country that paid its debts and kept order "need fear no interference." But "chronic wrong-doing" would require the United States to intervene as an "international police power." Whereas the Monroe Doctrine had warned European nations not to intervene in the Western Hemisphere, the Roosevelt Corollary justified American intervention. Starting with a desire to protect property, loans, and investments, the United States wound up supporting the regimes of despotic elites who owned most of the land, suppressed the poor, and blocked reforms.

After 1904, the Roosevelt Corollary was invoked in several Caribbean countries. Intervention usually meant the landing of U.S. Marines to counter a threat to American property. Occupying capital cities and major seaports, Marines, bankers, and customs

TR as Caribbean Policeman

The "big stick" became a memorable image in American diplomacy as Teddy Roosevelt sought to make the United States a "policeman" not only of the Caribbean basin but also of the whole world. What image does Roosevelt convey, and how are the people of the world responding to him?

(Puck, 1901)

officials remained for several years. Roosevelt's successors, William Howard Taft and Woodrow Wilson, pursued the same interventionist policy. So would more recent presidents: Ronald Reagan (Grenada and Nicaragua), George H. W. Bush (Panama), and Bill Clinton and George W. Bush (Haiti).

Opening Doors to China and Closing Doors to America

Throughout the nineteenth century, American relations with China were restricted to a small but profitable trade. Britain, in competition with France, Germany, and Russia, took advantage of the crumbling Manchu dynasty to force treaties on China, creating "treaty ports" and granting exclusive trading privileges in various parts of the country. After 1898, the United States, with dreams of exploiting the seemingly unlimited markets of China, wanted to join the competition and enlarge its share. Those with moral interests, however, including many missionaries, reminded Americans of their revolutionary tradition against European imperialism. They opposed U.S. commercial exploitation of a weak nation and supported China's political integrity as imperial powers partitioned the country.

Although some admired China's ancient culture, the dominant American attitude viewed the Chinese as heathen, exotic, and backward. Workingmen's riots against the competition of Chinese workers in the 1870s and 1880s and the Chinese Exclusion Act of 1882 barring immigration reflected this negative stereotype. The Chinese, in turn, regarded the

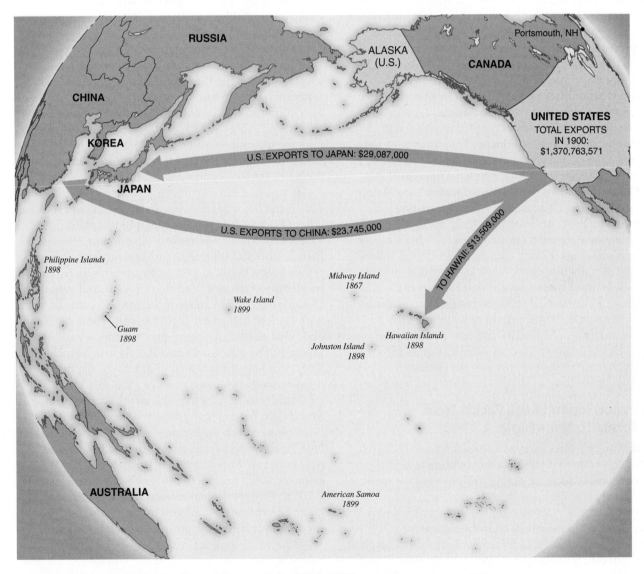

U. S. Involvement in the Pacific and Eastern Asia, 1898–1909

By 1898, the United States expanded far into eastern Asia and the Pacific. Which motivations do you think were most important for U.S. expansionism at the turn of the twentieth century: profits, patriotism, piety, or politics? What major events followed the acquisition of territories in the Pacific and the development of greater trade with eastern Asia? Where in the world is America still a strong presence? Can a nation expand too far?

United States with a mixture of admiration, curiosity, resentment, suspicion, and disdain.

The annexation of Hawaii and the Philippines in 1898 convinced Secretary of State Hay that the United States should announce a China policy. The Open Door notes of 1899–1900 became the cornerstone of U.S. policy in eastern Asia for more than half a century. The first note demanded an open door for American trade by declaring the principle of equal access to commercial rights in China by all nations. The second note, addressing Russian movement into Manchuria, called on all countries to respect the "territorial and administrative integrity" of China. This second principle announced a larger American role in Asia, offering China protection and preserving an East Asian balance of power.

An early test of this new role came during the Boxer Rebellion in 1900. The Boxers were a society of young traditionalist Chinese in revolt against both the Manchu dynasty and the growing Western influence and presence in China. During the summer of 1900, Boxers killed some 242 missionaries and other foreigners and besieged the western quarter of Beijing. An international military force of 19,000 troops, including some 3,000 Americans, ended the siege.

Despite an exclusionist immigration policy and laws inhibiting Chinese in America from becoming naturalized citizens, the idea that the United States had a unique guardian relationship with China persisted into the twentieth century. When Yale-educated Yung Wing had his American citizenship revoked for visiting his homeland in 1898, he bemoaned "how far this Republic has departed from its high ideal." But Chinese students and workers kept coming to the United States, entering illegally through Mexico and British Columbia. In 1905, Chinese nationalists at home boycotted American goods and called for a change in immigration policy. Roosevelt, contemptuous of what he called "backward" Chinese, bristled and sent troops to the Philippines as a threat. He also asked Congress for a modified immigration bill, but nothing came of it.

Balancing Japan in the Pacific from California to Manchuria

Population pressures, war, and a quest for economic opportunities caused Japanese immigration to the United States to increase dramatically around the turn of the century. Some came from Hawaii, where they had "worked like machines" in the sugarcane fields, many dying from overwork and white diseases. Pursuing "huge dreams of fortune…across the ocean," some 200,000 Japanese went directly to the West Coast of the United States to work on railroads and in West Coast canneries, mines, and logging camps.

Others worked on farms in the valleys of California, Oregon, and Washington, many successfully rising to own their own lands and turning marginal farmlands into productive agricultural businesses. Japanese-owned farms increased from 4,698 acres in 1900 to 194,742 by 1910, when they produced 70 percent of the California strawberry crop. Kinji Ushijima, for example, developed 10,000 acres of potato lands worth $500,000 in the fertile deltas between Stockton and Sacramento. By 1912, known then as George Shima, the "Potato King," he was praised by the *San Francisco Chronicle*. But when Shima moved to Berkeley, local newspapers and protesting professors complained of the "Yellow Peril in College Town." Shima refused to move.

Threatened by this competitive success, native white Californians discriminated against Japanese immigrants and limited their ability to own or lease land. They were barred from factory jobs and shunted off to agricultural labor in California fields and orchards. In 1906, the San Francisco school board, claiming that Japanese children were "crowding the whites out of the schools," segregated them into separate schools. Californians passed an anti-Japanese resolution and asked Roosevelt to persuade Japan to stop the emigration. Denouncing anti-Japanese rioting in San Francisco, Roosevelt favored restriction rather than exclusion. In the "Gentlemen's Agreement" notes of 1907–1908, the Japanese agreed to limit the migration of unskilled workers to the United States in return for the repeal of some anti-Japanese laws. But tensions continued.

It was one thing to check Japanese power in California but quite another to stop it in eastern Asia, where Roosevelt was determined to maintain the balance of power. The Boxer Rebellion of 1900 left Russia with 50,000 troops in Manchuria, making it the strongest regional power. Roosevelt's admiration for the Japanese as a "fighting" people and valuable factor in the "civilization of the future" contrasted with his low regard for the Russians, whom he described as "treacherous" and "incompetent." As Japan moved into Korea and Russia into Manchuria, Roosevelt hoped that each would check the other.

Roosevelt welcomed news in 1904 that Japan had successfully mounted a surprise attack on Port Arthur in Manchuria, beginning the Russo-Japanese War. He was "well pleased with the Japanese victory," he told his son, "for Japan is playing our game," but as Japanese victories continued, he worried that Japan might play the game too well, shutting the United States out of Asian markets. Roosevelt tilted toward Russia. When the Japanese expressed an interest in ending the war, the American president was pleased to exert his influence.

Roosevelt's goal was to achieve peace and leave a balanced situation. Nothing better symbolized the new American presence in the world than the 1905 negotiation and signing of a peace treaty in Portsmouth, New Hampshire, ending a war between Russia and Japan halfway around the globe in Manchuria. The Treaty of

Portsmouth left Japan dominant in Manchuria (and Korea) with the United States as the major balance to Japan's power. In the Root-Takahira Agreement of 1908, in return for recognizing these developments, Roosevelt got Japan's promise to honor U.S. control in the Philippines and to make no further encroachments into China.

The agreement barely papered over Japanese-American tensions. Some Japanese blamed Roosevelt for the fact that the Treaty of Portsmouth had not given them indemnities from Russia. American insensitivity on the immigration issue left bad feelings. In Manchuria, the U.S. consul general aggressively pushed an anti-Japanese program of financing capital investment projects in banking and railroads. This policy, known as "dollar diplomacy" under Roosevelt's successor, William Howard Taft, like the pursuit of markets, was larger in prospect than results. Nevertheless, the United States was in Japan's way, and rumors of war circulated.

It was clearly a moment for Roosevelt's "big stick." In 1907, he told Secretary of State Root that he was "more concerned over the Japanese situation than almost any other. Thank Heaven we have the navy in good shape." Although the naval buildup had begun over a decade earlier, under Roosevelt the U.S. Navy developed into a formidable force. In 1907, to make it clear that "the Pacific was as much our home waters as the Atlantic," Roosevelt sent his new, modernized "Great White Fleet" on a goodwill world tour. Pointedly, the first stop was Yokohama, Japan. Although American sailors were greeted warmly, the act may have stimulated a naval buildup in Japan, which came back to haunt the United States at Pearl Harbor in 1941. But for the time being, the balance of power in eastern Asia was preserved.

Preventing War in Europe

The United States had stretched the Monroe Doctrine to justify sending Marines and engineers to Latin America and the navy and dollars to eastern Asia. Treaties, agreements, and the protection of territories and interests entangled the United States with foreign nations from Panama and Nicaragua to the Philippines and Japan. Toward European nations, however, traditional neutrality continued.

Roosevelt believed that the most serious threats to world peace and civilized order lay in the relationships among Germany, Great Britain, and France, especially as these nations collided with one another over colonies in Asia and Africa and engaged in a naval arms race. Roosevelt established two fundamental policies toward Europe that would define the U.S. role throughout the century. The first was to make friendship with Great Britain the cornerstone of U.S. policy. The second was to prevent a general war in Europe. Toward this end, Roosevelt depended on his personal negotiating skills with the leaders of major European nations.

The Venezuelan crisis of 1895 shocked the United States and Britain into an awareness of their mutual interests. Both nations, sharing language and cultural traditions, appreciated the neutrality of the other in their respective colonial wars in the Philippines and South Africa. Roosevelt supported British imperialism because he favored the dominance of the "English-speaking race" and believed that Britain was "fighting the battle of civilization." Both nations, moreover, were worried about growing German power. To protect itself from the German navy, Britain brought its fleet closer to home, concluded a mutual protection treaty with Japan, and trusted the United States to police the Caribbean.

Roosevelt was unashamedly pro-British. He knew, as he wrote to Lodge in 1901, that the United States had "not the least particle of danger to fear" from Britain and that German ambitions and militarism represented the major threat to peace in Europe. As Roosevelt left the presidency in 1909, one of his final acts was to proclaim the special friendship between the United States and Great Britain.

German Kaiser Wilhelm II underestimated the Anglo-American friendship and thought that Roosevelt was really pro-German. Roosevelt cultivated the Kaiser's illusion, flattering him while cleverly rejecting his overtures for diplomatic advantages. During the Moroccan crisis in 1905 and 1906, when Germany and France threatened to go to war over the control of Morocco and the western Mediterranean, Roosevelt arranged a conference in Algeciras, Spain, to head off conflict. The treaty signed in 1906 peacefully settled the Moroccan issue favorably for the French. When the German emperor tried to promote a German-Chinese-American agreement to balance the Anglo-Japanese Treaty in Asia, Roosevelt rebuffed him. Touring Europe in 1910, the former president was warmly entertained by Wilhelm, who continued to misunderstand him. Roosevelt, meanwhile, kept urging his English friends to counter the German naval buildup in order to maintain peace in Europe.

In 1911, Roosevelt wrote that there would be nothing worse than that "Germany should ever overthrow England and establish the supremacy in Europe she aims at." Roosevelt's European policy therefore included cementing friendship with Britain and, while maintaining official neutrality, using diplomacy to prevent European hostilities. The relationship between Great Britain and Germany, however, continued to deteriorate, and by 1914, when World War I broke out, no American was more eager to fight on the British side against the Germans than Colonel Roosevelt of the Rough Riders.

GLOBAL IMPERIAL ACTIVITIES, 1893–1904

Reflecting on the Past Note the growing role of the United States and the global nature of imperialism. Can you locate on a map or globe the many places mentioned in this chart? What implications do you draw about the race and ethnicity of the "where" and the "who"? What larger conclusions do you make about this era of history? Who benefited? Who did not?

Year	Where	Who	What
1893	Hawaii	United States	U.S.-backed annexationists overthrow Hawaiian queen.
1893	Laos	France	Laos becomes a French protectorate.
1893	French Guyana; Ivory Coast	France	France establishes two colonies on two continents.
1894–1895	China	Japan	Japan starts and wins war with China. Japan acquires Taiwan and gets an indemnity for war costs.
1895	South Africa	Britain	British annex Tongaland.
1895	Venezuela	United States; Britain	Tensions over boundary dispute with British Guyana.
1896	Ethiopia	Italy	Italy invades Ethiopia and is defeated by the Ethiopian army.
1896	Rhodesia (Zimbabwe)	Britain	A revolt begins in Rhodesia and is suppressed.
1896–1897	Madagascar	France	French claim Madagascar and depose the queen.
1896–1898	Sudan	Britain	British reconquer Sudan.
1897–1898	Hawaii	United States	United States annexes Hawaii.
1897	China	Germany	Germans occupy Shandong Province.
1898–1899	Philippines	Spain; United States	Annexed by United States after Spanish-American War.
1898–1902	Guam; Puerto Rico; Cuba	Spain; United States	Islands become U.S. territories or protectorates after Spanish-American War.
1899	China	United States	United States establishes Open Door policy.
1899–1902	South Africa; Philippines	Britain; Boers; United States; Philippines	Wars pass control of indigenous peoples to British and Americans.
1899	Ghana	Britain	Ashanti rebellion suppressed.
1900–1901	China	United States; Japan; Britain; Germany; and others	Boxer Rebellion suppressed.
1902	Venezuela	United States; Britain; Germany	Blockade ports and compete with one another over Venezuelan debt crisis.
1903	Colombia/Panama	United States	United States backs Panamanian revolutionaries for independence from Colombia.
1904	Manchuria	Japan; Russia	Japan attacks Port Arthur, starting the Russo-Japanese War.

Timeline

1823	Monroe Doctrine
1853	Trade opens with Japan
1867	Alaska purchased from Russia
1870	Failure to annex Santo Domingo (Hispaniola)
1875	Sugar reciprocity treaty with Hawaii
1882	Chinese Exclusion Act
1887	United States acquires naval base at Pearl Harbor
1889	First Pan-American Conference
1890	Alfred Mahan publishes *Influence of Sea Power upon History*
1893	Hawaiian coup by American sugar growers
1895	Cuban revolt against Spanish
1898	Sinking of the *Maine*
	Dewey takes Manila Bay and Spanish-American War
	Teller Amendment
	Annexation of Hawaiian Islands
	Treaty of Paris; annexation of the Philippines
1899	Senate ratifies Treaty of Paris
1899–1900	Open Door notes and Boxer Rebellion in China
1899–1902	Filipino-American War
1900	William McKinley reelected president
1901	Supreme Court cases on new territories
	McKinley assassinated; Theodore Roosevelt becomes president
1902	U.S. military occupation of Cuba ends
	Platt Amendment
1903	Panamanian revolt and independence
	Hay–Bunau–Varilla Treaty establishes American canal zone
1904	Roosevelt Corollary to the Monroe Doctrine
1904–1905	Russo-Japanese War ended by treaty signed at Portsmouth, New Hampshire
1904–1906	United States intervenes in Nicaragua, Guatemala, and Cuba
1906	Roosevelt receives Nobel Peace Prize
1907–1908	Gentleman's Agreement and Root-Takahira Agreements with Japan
1909	U.S. Navy ("Great White Fleet") sails around the world
1914	Opening of the Panama Canal
	World War I begins

Conclusion

THE RESPONSIBILITIES OF POWER

The realities of power in the 1890s brought increasing international responsibilities. Roosevelt said in 1910 that because of "strength and geographical situation," the United States had itself become "more and more, the balance of power of the whole world." This ominous responsibility was also an opportunity to extend American economic, political, moral, and military influence around the globe even while insulting new and would-be immigrants at home.

As president in the first decade of the twentieth century, Roosevelt (admired by President George W. Bush) established aggressive American policies toward the rest of the world that would last to this day. The United States dominated and policed Central America and the Caribbean Sea to maintain order and protect its investments and other economic interests. In eastern Asia, Americans marched through Hay's Open Door with treaties, troops, navies, missionaries, and dollars to protect the Philippines, develop markets and investments, and try to preserve the balance of power in Eastern Asia (and more recently, the Middle East). In Europe, the United States sought to remain neutral in European affairs and at the same time to cement Anglo-American friendship to prevent "civilized" nations from going to war.

How well these policies worked would unfold in the next 100 years. America's fundamental ambivalence has persisted whether to be an isolationist example to others or an active, interventionist savior. As questionable actions around the world—Private Grayson's and others' in the Filipino-American War, for example—painfully demonstrated, it was increasingly difficult for the United States to be both responsible and good, both powerful and loved. The American people experienced, therefore, both the benefits and burdens of their increasing international role, as they have to this day.

QUESTIONS FOR REVIEW AND REFLECTION

1. What is the fundamental dilemma of American foreign policy inherited from the Puritans, and to what extent do you think it fits historical events?

2. What are the four P's (or the three G's) that explain the motivations for American expansionism in the 1890s, and which do you think is most important?

3. Compare and contrast the causes and consequences of the Spanish-American and Filipino-American wars. What are the major differences between these two conflicts?

4. Give three or four justifications for annexing the Philippine Islands and three or four reasons opposing annexation. Which set of arguments do you think is most compelling?

5. Outline the major principles, with examples, of President Roosevelt's foreign policy in the Caribbean, eastern Asia, and Europe. How well have these policies worked in the 100 years since Roosevelt's time?

6. Do you think that U.S. foreign policy has been primarily as an interventionist savior of other nations or as an interfering expansionist into the affairs of other nations? Or some of both? Give examples.

CHAPTER 21

The Progressives Confront Industrial Capitalism

John Sloan, *Women Drying Their Hair*, 1912

Sloan (1871–1951) was one of the leading members of the "ash can school," a group of artists who experimented with new techniques and painted ordinary scenes of urban life, such as that shown here. His paintings offended many because he flouted genteel codes of propriety and decorum, and he showed working-class women in ways that were just as shocking as progressive-era reports on child labor and prostitution. Why was this painting shocking to Americans in 1912?

(John Sloan (1871–1951) "Sunday, Women Drying Their Hair", 1912, Oil on canvas, 26-1/8 in. × 32-1/8 in (66.36 cm × 81.65 cm). 1938.67, Museum Purchase. Addison Gallery of American Art, Phillips Academy, Andover, Massachusetts. © ARS, NY)

American Stories

A Professional Woman Joins the Progressive Crusade

Frances Kellor, a young woman who grew up in Ohio and Michigan, received her law degree in 1897 from Cornell University and became one of the small but growing group of professionally trained women in the United States. Deciding that she was more interested in solving the nation's social problems than in practicing law, she moved to Chicago, studied sociology, and trained herself as a social reformer. Kellor believed passionately that poverty and inequality could be eliminated in America. She also had the progressive faith that if Americans could only hear the truth about the millions of people living in urban slums, they would rise up and make changes. She was one of the experts who provided the evidence to document what was wrong in industrial America.

Like many progressives, Kellor believed that environment was more important than heredity in determining ability, prosperity, and happiness. Better schools and better housing, she thought, would produce better citizens. While a small group of progressives advocated the sterilization of criminals and the mentally defective, Kellor argued that even criminals were victims of their environment. Kellor demonstrated that poor health and deprived childhoods explained the only differences between criminals and college students. If it were impossible to define a criminal type, then it must be possible to reduce crime by improving the environment.

Kellor was an efficient professional. Like the majority of the professional women of her generation, she never married but devoted her life to social research and social reform. She lived for a time at Hull House in Chicago and at the College Settlement in New York, centers not only of social research and reform but also of lively community. For many young people, the settlement, with its sense of commitment and its exciting conversation around the dinner table, provided an alternative to the nuclear family or the single apartment.

While staying at the College Settlement, Kellor researched and wrote a muckraking study of employment agencies, published in 1904 as *Out of Work*. She revealed how employment agencies exploited immigrants, blacks, and other recent arrivals in the city. Kellor's book, like the writing of most progressives, spilled over with moral outrage. But Kellor went beyond moralism to suggest corrective legislation at the state and national levels. She became one of the leaders of the movement to Americanize the immigrants pouring into the country in unprecedented numbers. Between 1899 and 1920, more than 8 million people came to the United States, most from southern and eastern Europe. Many Americans

feared that this flood of immigrants threatened the very basis of American democracy. Kellor and her coworkers represented the side of progressivism that sought state and federal laws to protect the new arrivals from exploitation and to establish agencies and facilities to educate and Americanize them. Another group of progressives, often allied with organized labor, tried to pass laws to restrict immigration. Kellor did not entirely escape the ethnocentrism that was a part of her generation's worldview, and like most progressives she tried to teach middle-class values to the new arrivals, but she did believe that all immigrants could be made into useful citizens.

Convinced of the need for a national movement to promote reform legislation, Kellor helped found the National Committee for Immigrants in America, which tried to promote a national policy "to make all these people Americans," and a federal bureau to organize the campaign. Eventually, she helped establish the Division of Immigrant Education within the Department of Labor. But a political movement led by Theodore Roosevelt excited her most. More than almost any other individual, Kellor had been responsible for alerting Roosevelt to the problems immigrants faced in American cities. When Roosevelt formed the new Progressive party in 1912, she was one of the many social workers and social researchers who joined him. She campaigned for Roosevelt and directed the Progressive Service Organization, intended to educate voters in all areas of social justice and welfare after the election. After Roosevelt's defeat and the collapse of the Progressive party in 1914, Kellor continued to work for Americanization. She spent the rest of her life promoting justice, order, and efficiency as well as trying to find ways of resolving industrial and international disputes.

While no one person can represent all facets of a complex movement, Frances Kellor's life illustrates two important aspects of progressivism, the first nationwide reform movement of the modern era: first, a commitment to promote social justice, ensure equal opportunity, and preserve democracy; second, a search for order and efficiency in a world complicated by rapid industrialization, immigration, and spectacular urban growth. Like many progressive leaders, Kellor was a part of a global movement to confront these problems, and she was influenced by writers and reformers in England and Germany as well as those in the United States. Progressivism reached its height in the years between 1900 and 1914. Like most American reform movements, the progressive movement did not plot to overthrow the government; rather, it sought to use government to promote American ideals and to ensure survival of the American way of life.

This chapter traces the most important aspects of progressivism. It examines the social justice movement, which sought to promote reform among the poor and to improve life for those who had fallen victim to an urban and industrial civilization. It surveys life among workers, a group the reformers sometimes helped but often misunderstood. Then it traces the reform movements in the cities and states, where officials and experts tried to reduce chaos and promote order and democracy. Finally, it examines progressivism at the national level during the administrations of Theodore Roosevelt and Woodrow Wilson, the first thoroughly modern presidents.

The Social Justice Movement

Historians write of a "progressive movement," but actually there were a number of movements, some of them contradictory, but all focusing on problems created by a rapidly expanding urban and industrial world. Some reformers, often from the middle class, sought to humanize the modern city. They hoped to improve housing and schools and to provide a better life for the poor and recent immigrants. Others were concerned with the conditions of work and the rights of labor. Still others pressed for changes in the political system to make it more responsive to popular interests, including women. Progressivism had roots in the 1890s, when many reformers were shocked by the devastation caused by the depression of 1893, and they were influenced by Henry George's *Progress and Poverty* (1879) and Edward Bellamy's *Looking Backward* (1888). They were appalled by a British pamphlet titled *The Bitter Cry of Outcast London,* which revealed the horrors of the slums of East London. They were also influenced by the British and American Social Gospel movement, which sought to build the kingdom of God on earth by eliminating poverty and promoting equality (see Chapter 19).

The Progressive Movement in Global Context

Most progressives saw their movement in a global context with a particular focus on an Atlantic world. Many had studied at European universities. They attended conferences on urban and industrial problems at the Paris Exposition of 1900, and they belonged to organizations such as the International Association for Labor Legislation, which tried to promote legislation to aid workers. They read the latest sociological studies from Britain, France, and Germany. Many were introduced to the problems of the modern industrial city by walking through the streets of East London or the slums of Berlin. Others were inspired by visiting Toynbee Hall, the pioneer social settlement in London, and by observing the municipal housing and government-owned streetcar lines in Glasgow, Scotland, and Dresden, Germany. At the same time, European reformers visited American cities and took part in American conferences.

The United States lagged behind much of the industrialized world in passing social legislation, perhaps because it lacked the strong labor and socialist movements present in most European countries. Many European countries, along with Australia, New Zealand, and Brazil, passed laws regulating hours and wages and creating pensions for the elderly. Germany enacted sickness, accident, and disability insurance in the 1880s. Great Britain had workers' compensation by the late 1890s, and old age, sickness, and unemployment insurance by 1911, all paid for with public funds. But American cities, unlike those in Europe, were filled with immigrants from a dozen countries who had cultural adjustments and a language barrier to overcome. The American federal system meant that most reform battles had to be fought first at the local and state levels before they could reach the national scene. A unique mix of religion, politics, and moral outrage imparted a particular character to the progressive movement in the United States.

The Progressive Worldview

Intellectually, the progressives were deeply influenced by Darwinism. They believed that the world was in flux, and they rebelled against the fixed and the formal in every field. One of the philosophers of the movement, John Dewey, wrote that ideas could become instruments for change. In his philosophy of pragmatism, William James tried to explain all ideas in terms of their consequences. Most progressives were convinced that environment was much more important than heredity in forming character. Thus, if one could build better schools and houses, one could make better people and a more perfect society. Yet even the more advanced reformers thought in racial and ethnic categories. They believed that some groups could be molded and changed more easily than others. Thus, progressivism did not usually mean progress for blacks.

In many ways, progressivism was the first modern reform movement. It sought to bring order and efficiency to a world that had been transformed by rapid

Recovering the Past

DOCUMENTARY PHOTOGRAPHS

Photographs are a revealing way of recovering the past visually. When looking at a photograph, especially an old one, it is easy to assume that it is an accurate representation of the past. However, much like novelists and historians, photographers have a point of view. They take their pictures for a reason—often to prove a point. As one photographer remarked, "Photographs don't lie, but liars take photographs."

To document the need for reform in the cities, progressives collected statistics, made surveys, described settlement house life, and even wrote novels. But they discovered that the photograph was often more effective than words. Jacob Riis, the Danish-born author of *How the Other Half Lives* (1890), a devastating exposure of conditions in New York City tenement house slums, was also a pioneer in urban photography. Others had taken pictures of dank alleys and street urchins before, but Riis was the first to photograph slum conditions with the express purpose of promoting reform. At first he hired photographers, but then he bought a camera and taught himself how to use it. He even tried a new German flash powder to illuminate dark alleys and tenement rooms to record the horror of slum life.

Riis made many of his photographs into lantern slides and used them to illustrate his lectures on the need for housing reform. Although he was a creative and innovative photographer, his pictures were often far from objective. His equipment was awkward, his film slow. He had to set up and prepare carefully before snapping the shutter. His views of tenement ghetto streets and poor children now seem like clichés, but they were designed to make Americans angry and to arouse them to reform.

Another important progressive photographer was Lewis Hine. Although trained as a sociologist, he taught himself photography. Hine used his camera to illustrate his lectures at the Ethical Culture School in New York. In 1908, he was hired as a full-time investigator by the National Child Labor Committee. His haunting photographs of children in factories helped convince many Americans of the need to abolish child labor. Hine's children were appealing human beings. He showed them eating, running, working, and staring wistfully out factory windows. His photographs avoided the pathos that Riis was so fond of recording, but just as surely they documented the need for reform.

Another technique that the reform photographer used was the before-and-after shot. The two photographs shown on the following page of a one-room apartment in Philadelphia early in the century illustrate how progressive reformers tried to teach immigrants to imitate middle-class manners. The "before" photograph shows a room cluttered with washtubs, laundry, cooking utensils, clothes, tools, even an old Christmas decoration. In the "after" picture,

Lewis Hine, *Carolina Cotton Mill*, 1908.

(Lewis Hine, *Carolina Cotton Mill*, 1908. George Eastman House)

much of the clutter has been cleaned up. A window has been installed to let in light and fresh air. The wallpaper, presumably a haven for hidden bugs and germs, has been torn off. The cooking utensils and laundry have been put away. The woodwork has been stained, and some ceremonial objects have been gathered on a shelf.

What else can you find that has been changed? How well do you think the message of the photographic combinations like this one worked? Would the immigrant family be happy with the new look and condition of their room? Could anyone live in one room and keep it so neat?

Reflecting on the Past As you look at these, or any photographs, ask yourself: What is the photographer's purpose and point of view? Why was this particular angle chosen for the picture? And why center on these particular people or objects? What does the photographer reveal about his or her purpose? What does the photographer reveal unintentionally? How have digital cameras changed photography? On what subjects do reform-minded photographers train their cameras today? ■

The reality of one-room tenement apartments (above) contrasted with the tidiness that reformers saw as the ideal (right).

(Urban Archives, Temple University, Philadelphia, PA)

growth and new technology. Yet elements of nostalgia infected the movement as reformers tried to preserve the handicrafts of a preindustrial age and to promote small-town and farm values in the city. The progressive leaders were almost always middle class, and they consciously tried to teach middle-class values to the immigrants and the working class. Often, the progressives seemed more interested in control than in reform; frequently, their efforts smacked of paternalism.

The progressives were part of a statistics-minded generation. They conducted surveys, gathered facts, wrote reports, and usually believed that their reports would lead to change. The haunting photographs of young workers taken by Lewis Hine, the stark and beautiful city paintings by John Sloan, and the realist novels of Theodore Dreiser and William Dean Howells reflect the progressives' drive to document and record.

The progressives were optimistic about human nature, and they believed that change was possible. In retrospect, they may seem naive or bigoted, but they wrestled with many social questions, some of them old but fraught with new urgency in an industrialized society. What is the proper relation of government to society? In a world of large corporations, huge cities, and massive transportation systems, how much should the government regulate and control? How much responsibility does society have to care for the poor and needy? The progressives could not agree on the answers, but they struggled with the questions.

The Muckrakers

Writers who exposed corruption and other social evils were labeled "muckrakers" by Theodore Roosevelt. Not all muckrakers were reformers—some wrote just for the money—but reformers learned from their techniques of exposé. In part, the muckrakers were a product of a journalistic revolution in the 1890s. Older magazines often had elite audiences and few illustrations. The new magazines had slick formats, more advertising, and wide sales. Competing for readers, editors eagerly published articles telling the public what was wrong in America.

Lincoln Steffens, a young California journalist, wrote articles exposing the connections between respectable businessmen and corrupt politicians. When published as a book in 1904, *The Shame of the Cities* became a battle cry for people determined to clean up city government. Ida Tarbell, a teacher turned journalist, revealed the ruthlessness of John D. Rockefeller's Standard Oil Company. David Graham Phillips uncovered the alliance of politics and business in *The Treason of the Senate* (1906). Robert Hunter, a young settlement worker, shocked Americans in 1904 with his book *Poverty*. In his compelling novel *The Octopus*, Frank Norris dramatized the railroads' stranglehold on farmers, while Upton Sinclair's novel *The Jungle* (1906) described the horrors of the Chicago meatpacking industry.

Child Labor

Nothing disturbed social justice progressives more than the sight of children, sometimes as young as 8 or 10, working long hours in dangerous and depressing factories. The crusade against child labor was a typical social justice reform effort. Its origins lay in the moral indignation of middle-class reformers. But reform went beyond moral outrage as reformers gathered statistics, took photographs documenting abuse of children, and used the evidence to push for local, state, and federal legislation.

Florence Kelley was one of the most important leaders in the crusade against child labor. Kelley had grown up in an upper-class Philadelphia family and graduated from Cornell in 1882. Like Addams and Kellor she was a member of the first generation of college women in the United States. When the University of Pennsylvania refused her admission as a graduate student because she was a woman, she went to the University of Zurich in Switzerland. Her European experience was crucial in transforming her from upperclass dilettante to committed reformer. She married a Polish-Russian scholar and became a socialist. The marriage failed, and some years later, Kelley moved to Chicago with her children, became a Hull House resident, and poured her considerable energies into the campaign against child labor. A friend described her as "explosive, hot-tempered, determined...a smoking volcano that at any moment would burst into flames." When she could find no attorney in Chicago to argue child labor cases against prominent corporations, she went to law school, passed the bar exam, and argued the cases herself.

Kelley and other child labor reformers pressured the Illinois state legislature into passing an anti–child labor law. A few years later, however, the state supreme court ruled it unconstitutional, convincing reformers that national action was necessary. Edgar Gardner Murphy, an Alabama clergyman, suggested the formation of the National Child Labor Committee. Based in New York, this new organization drew up a model state child labor law, encouraged state and city campaigns, and coordinated the movement around the country.

Although two-thirds of the states passed some form of child labor law between 1905 and 1907, many had loopholes that exempted large numbers of children, including newsboys and youngsters who worked in the theater. A national bill was defeated in 1906, but in 1912 the child labor reformers convinced Congress to establish a children's bureau in the Department of Labor. Despite these efforts, compulsory school attendance laws did more to reduce the number of children who worked than federal and state laws, which proved difficult to pass and even more difficult to enforce.

Like other progressive reform efforts, the battle against child labor was only partly successful. Too many businesses, both small and large, were profiting from employing children at low wages. Too many politicians and judges were reluctant to regulate the work of children or adults because work seemed such an individual and personal matter. And some parents, who often desperately needed the money their children earned in the factories, opposed the reformers and even broke the law to allow their children to work.

The reformers also worried over the young people who got into trouble with the law, often for pranks that in rural areas would have seemed harmless. They feared for young people tried by adult courts and thrown into jail with hardened criminals. Reformers organized juvenile courts, in which judges had the authority to put delinquent youths on probation, take them from their families and make them wards of the state, or assign them to an institution. A uniquely American invention, the juvenile court often helped prevent young delinquents from adopting a life of crime. Yet juvenile offenders frequently were deprived of all rights of due process, a fact that the Supreme Court finally recognized in 1967, when it ruled that children were entitled to procedural rights when accused of a crime.

Working Women and Woman Suffrage

Closely connected with the anti–child labor movement was the effort to limit the hours of women's work. Florence Kelley and the National Consumers League led the campaign. The most important court case on women's work came before the U.S. Supreme Court in 1908. Kelley's friend Josephine Goldmark wrote the brief for *Muller* v. *Oregon,* and Goldmark's brother-in-law, Louis Brandeis, argued the case. The Court upheld the Oregon law limiting the workday of women in factories and laundries to 10 hours largely because Goldmark's sociological argument detailed the danger and disease that these women workers faced. Most states fell into line with the Supreme Court decision and passed protective legislation for women, though many companies found ways to circumvent the laws. Even the work permitted by the law seemed too long to some women who had to come home to child care and housekeeping.

By contending that "women are fundamentally weaker than men in all that makes for endurance: in muscular strength, in nervous energy, in the powers of persistent attention and application," reformers won some protection for women workers. But for the next half century, their arguments that women were weaker than men were used to reinforce gender segregation.

In addition to working for protective legislation for working women, the social justice progressives also campaigned for woman suffrage. The early battles for the right of women to vote were fought at the state level, with greatest success in the West. Wyoming (1869), Utah (1870), Colorado (1893), Idaho (1896), Washington (1910), California (1911), Arizona and Oregon (1912), and Montana and Nevada (1914) gave women the right to vote in at least some elections. But this did not mean that western states were more enlightened on gender issues. In the East and Midwest, both with large immigrant populations, suffrage and

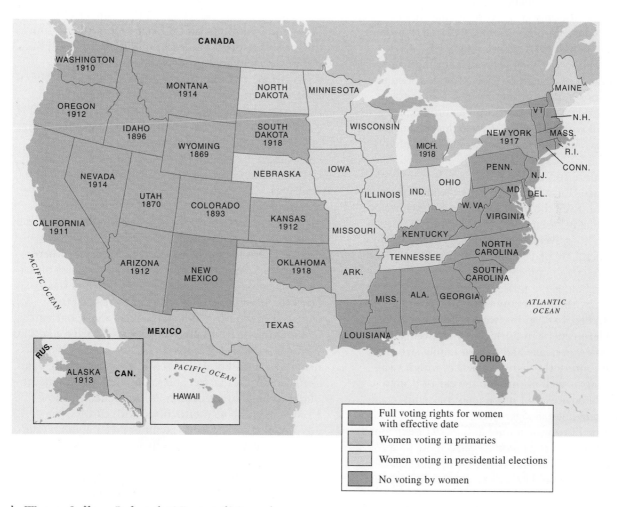

Woman Suffrage Before the Nineteenth Amendment

Western states led the battle for women's right to vote, but key victories in New York (1917) and Michigan (1918), and a carefully organized campaign in all parts of the country, finally led to the ratification of the Nineteenth Amendment. Why was this success considered a triumph of progressive reform?

prohibition were often tied closely together. Many men believed that women, if given the vote, would support prohibition.

The campaign to win the vote for women was a global movement, and suffrage leaders in the United States were in touch with women in other countries. They often met their international counterparts at meetings of the International Woman Suffrage Alliance. The United States lagged behind New Zealand, Finland, Norway, and several other countries in granting female suffrage. Women in Great Britain were allowed to vote in 1918, but not until 1938 could they vote on an equal basis with men.

The political process that eventually led to woman suffrage in the United States was slowed by the difficulty of amending the Constitution and the need to fight the battle one state at a time. But the progressives pressed on. Some suffrage advocates argued that middle-class women would offset the votes of ignorant and corrupt immigrant men, but many progressives supported votes for all women. Jane Addams argued that urban women not only could vote intelligently but also needed the vote to protect, clothe, and feed their families. Women in an urban age, she suggested, needed to be municipal housekeepers. Through suffrage, they would ensure that elected officials provided adequate services—pure water, uncontaminated food, proper sanitation, and police protection. The progressive insistence that all women needed the vote helped ensure the victory for woman suffrage that would come after World War I.

Much more controversial than either votes for women or protective legislation was the movement for birth control. Even the most advanced progressives could not imagine themselves teaching immigrant women how to prevent conception, especially because the Comstock Law of 1873 made it illegal to promote or even write about contraceptive devices.

Margaret Sanger, a nurse who had watched poor women suffer from too many births and even die from dangerous, illegal abortions, was one of the founders of the modern American birth control movement. Middle-class Americans had limited family size in the nineteenth century through abstinence, withdrawal, and abortion, as well as through the use of primitive birth control devices, but much ignorance and misinformation remained. Sanger obtained the latest medical and scientific European studies and in 1914 explained in her magazine, *The Woman Rebel,* and in a pamphlet, *Family Limitation,* that women could separate sex from procreation. She was promptly indicted for violation of the postal code and fled to Europe to avoid arrest.

Birth control remained controversial, and in most states illegal, for many years. Yet Sanger helped bring the topic of sexuality and contraception into the open. When she returned to the United States in 1921, she founded the American Birth Control League, which became the Planned Parenthood Federation in 1942.

Reforming Home and School

Reformers believed that better housing and education could transform the lives of the poor and create a better world. Books such as Jacob Riis's *How the Other Half Lives* (1890) horrified them with its vivid language and haunting photographs of misery in New York's slums.

In the first decade of the twentieth century, the progressives took a new approach toward housing problems. They combined their vision of what needed to be done to improve society with their practical ability to organize public opinion and get laws passed. They collected statistics, conducted surveys, organized committees, and constructed exhibits to demonstrate the effect of urban overcrowding. Then they worked to pass tenement house laws in several cities. These laws created fire codes and regulated the number of windows and bathrooms and the size of apartments, but the laws were often evaded or modified. In 1910, the progressives organized the National Housing Association, and some of them looked ahead to federal laws and even to government-subsidized housing. American housing reformers were inspired by model working-class dwellings in London, municipal housing in Glasgow, and various experiments in government-constructed housing in France, Belgium, and Germany, but they realized that in the United States, they had to start with local regulation.

Ironically, many middle-class women reformers who tried to teach working-class families how to live in their tenement flats had never organized their own homes. Often they lived in settlement houses, where they ate in a dining hall and never had to worry about cleaning, cooking, or doing laundry. Some of them, however, began to realize that the domestic tasks expected of women of all classes kept many of them from taking their full place in society. Charlotte Perkins Gilman, author of *Women and Economics* (1898), dismantled the traditional view of "woman's sphere" and sketched an alternative. Suggesting that entrepreneurs ought to build apartment houses designed to allow women to combine motherhood with careers, she advocated shared kitchen facilities and a common dining room, a laundry run by efficient workers, and a roof-garden day nursery with a professional teacher.

Gilman, who criticized private homes as "bloated buildings, filled with a thousand superfluities," was joined by a few radicals in promoting new living arrangements. However, most continued to view the home as sacred space where the mother ruled supreme and created an atmosphere of domestic tranquility.

Next to better housing, the progressives stressed better schools as a way to produce better citizens. Public school systems were often rigid and corrupt. Far from producing citizens who would help transform society, the schools' emphasis on repetitious rote learning seemed to reinforce conservative habits.

Progressive education, like many other aspects of progressivism, opposed the rigid and the formal in favor of flexibility and change. John Dewey was the key philosopher of progressive education. In his laboratory school at the University of Chicago, he experimented with new methods. He replaced the school desks, which were bolted down and always faced the front, with seats that could be moved into circles and arranged in groups. The movable seat, in fact, became one of the symbols of the progressive education movement.

Dewey insisted that the schools be child-centered, not subject-oriented. Teachers should teach children rather than teach history or mathematics. He did not mean that history and math should not be taught but that those subjects should be related to the students' experience. Students should learn by doing. They should not just learn about democracy; the school itself should operate like a democracy.

Dewey also maintained that schools should become instruments for social reform. But like most progressives, Dewey was never quite clear whether he wanted schools to help students adjust to the existing society or to turn out graduates who would change the world. Although he wavered on that point, the spirit of progressive education, like the spirit of progressivism in general, was optimistic. Dewey's progressive education, which sought to educate all Americans, stood in sharp contrast to European models, in which educating the intellectual and social elite took precedence over schooling the masses.

Crusades Against Saloons, Theaters, and Prostitution

Progressives often displayed moral outrage when it came to the behavior of the working class. American attitudes toward prostitution and prohibition surprised and confused foreign observers, especially many Europeans. Most social justice progressives opposed the sale of alcohol. Some came from Protestant homes in which consumption of liquor was considered a sin, but most advocated prohibition because they saw

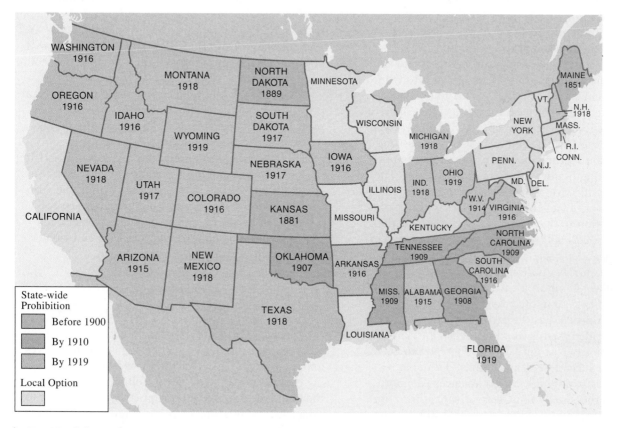

State Prohibition by 1919

Temperance reform had achieved considerable success even before the adoption of the Eighteenth Amendment in 1919. What regional patterns do you observe in the spread of state prohibition laws? What might explain these patterns?

eliminating the sale of alcohol as part of the process of reforming cities and conserving human resources.

Americans did drink great quantities of beer, wine, and hard liquor, and the amount they consumed rose rapidly after 1900, peaking between 1911 and 1915. An earlier temperance movement had achieved some success in the 1840s and 1850s, but only three states still had prohibition laws in force. The modern antiliquor movement was spearheaded in the 1880s and 1890s by the Women's Christian Temperance Union and after 1900 by the Anti-Saloon League and a coalition of religious leaders and social reformers. During the progressive era, temperance forces had considerable success in influencing legislation. Seven states passed temperance laws between 1906 and 1912.

Reformers were appalled to see young children going into saloons to bring home a pail of beer for the family and horrified by tales of alcoholic fathers beating wives and children. But most often progressives focused on the saloon, which they not only viewed as a place for drinking but also linked to drug traffic, prostitution, and political corruption.

Although they never quite understood the role that alcohol played in the social life of many ethnic groups, Jane Addams and other settlement workers appreciated the saloon's importance as a neighborhood social center. Addams started a coffeehouse at Hull House in an attempt to lure people away from saloons. Although the progressives never found an adequate substitute for the saloon, they set to work to pass local and state prohibition laws. Joining forces with diverse groups to push for change, they achieved victory when, on December 22, 1917, Congress sent to the states for ratification a constitutional amendment prohibiting the sale, manufacture, and import of intoxicating liquor within the United States. The spirit of sacrifice for World War I facilitated rapid ratification of the amendment.

In addition to the saloon, progressives saw the urban dance hall and the movie theater as threats to the morals and well-being of young people, especially young women. The motion picture, invented in 1889, developed as an important form of entertainment during the first decade of the twentieth century. At first, the "nickelodeons," as the early movie theaters were called, appealed mainly to a lower-class and largely ethnic audience. Not until World War I, when D. W. Griffith produced long feature films, did the movies begin to attract a middle-class audience. The most popular of these early films was Griffith's *Birth of a Nation* (1915), a blatantly racist and distorted epic of black debauchery during Reconstruction. Many early films were imported from France, Italy, and Germany; because they were silent, it was easy to use subtitles in any language. But one did not need to know the language, or even be able to read, to enjoy the action. That was part of the attraction of the early films. Some films stressed slapstick humor or romance and adventure; others bordered on pornography. The reformers objected not only to the plots and content of the films but also to the location of the theaters (near saloons and burlesque houses) and to their dark interiors. But for young immigrant women, who made up the bulk of the audience at most urban movie theaters, the films provided rare exciting moments in their lives.

Saloons, dance halls, and movie theaters all seemed dangerous to progressives interested in improving life in the city, because all appeared to be somehow connected with the worst evil of all, prostitution. Campaigns against prostitution had been waged since the early nineteenth century, but they were nothing compared with the progressives' crusade to wipe out what they called the "social evil." All major cities and many smaller ones appointed vice commissions and made elaborate studies of prostitution.

The progressive crusade against prostitution attracted many kinds of people, for often contradictory reasons. Racists and immigration restrictionists maintained that inferior people—blacks and recent immigrants, especially those from southern and eastern Europe—became prostitutes and pimps. Most progressives, however, stressed environmental causes. They viewed prostitution, along with child labor and poor housing, as evils that education and reform could eliminate.

Despite their efforts, the progressives failed to end prostitution and did virtually nothing to address its roots in poverty. They wiped out a few red-light districts, closed a number of brothels, and managed to push a bill through Congress (the Mann Act of 1910) that prohibited the interstate transport of women for immoral purposes. Perhaps more important, they persuaded several states to raise the age of consent for women and in 20 states they made the Wassermann test for syphilis mandatory for both men and women before a marriage license could be issued.

The Worker in the Progressive Era

Progressive reformers sympathized with industrial workers who struggled to earn a living for themselves and their families. But often they had little understanding of what it was really like to sell one's strength by the hour. For example, they supported labor's right to organize at a time when labor had few friends, yet they often opposed the strike as a weapon against management. And neither organized labor nor the reformers, individually or in shaky partnership, had power over industry in the years before World War I.

The Changing Nature of Industrial Labor

Many workers—whether from eastern Europe, rural Vermont, or Michigan—confronted a bewildering world based on order and routine. Unlike farm or craft work, factory life was dominated by the clock, the bell tower, and the boss. Workers resisted the mindless routine and relentless pace of factory work, and they subtly sabotaged employers' efforts to control the workplace. They stayed home on holidays when they were supposed to work, took unauthorized breaks, and set their own informal productivity schedules. Often they were fired or quit. In the woollen industry, for example, the annual turnover of workers between 1907 and 1910 was more than 100 percent. In New York needleworker shops in 1912 and 1913, the turnover rate was more than 250 percent. Overall in American industry, one-third of the workers stayed at their jobs less than a year.

The nature of work continued to change in the early twentieth century as industrialists extended late-nineteenth-century efforts to make their factories and workforces more efficient, productive, and profitable. In some industries, new machines revolutionized work and eliminated highly paid, skilled jobs. Power-driven machines, better-organized operations, and finally the moving assembly line, perfected by Henry Ford, transformed the nature of work and turned many laborers into unskilled tenders of machines.

Principles of scientific management, which set new rules for organizing work, were also important. The key figure was Frederick Taylor, the son of a prominent Philadelphia family. After Taylor had a nervous breakdown while at a private school, his physicians prescribed manual labor as a cure, and he went to work as a laborer at the Midvale Steel Company in Philadelphia. Working his way up rapidly while studying engineering at night, he became chief engineer at the factory in the 1880s. Later he used this experience to develop his four principles of scientific management: centralized planning, systematic analysis of each job, detailed instructions to and close supervision of each worker, and an incentive wage system to encourage laborers to work harder and faster.

Taylor studied all kinds of workers and timed the various components of their jobs with a stopwatch in order to determine the fastest way of performing a task. Many owners enthusiastically adopted Taylor's concepts of scientific management, seeing an opportunity to increase their profits and shift control of the workplace from the skilled workers to the managers. Not surprisingly, many workers resented the emphasis on higher productivity and tighter control.

Samuel Gompers, head of the American Federation of Labor (AFL) was quick to recognize that Taylorism would reduce workers to "mere machines." Under Gompers, the AFL prospered during the progressive

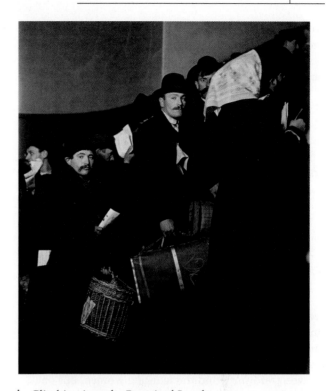

Climbing into the Promised Land

Immigrants from eastern and southern Europe came to the United States in great numbers from 1890 to 1914. Many of them were detained at Ellis Island in New York. There usually was a long wait, embarrassing questions to answer, forms to fill out, a complicated bureaucracy to get past. There was also a medical exam to endure. Some immigrants failed the exam and were rejected and sent back to Europe. Still they came with hope and determination. Lewis Hine titled this photo *Climbing into Ellis Island, 1908.* Did the United States live up to the hopes of most immigrants? What emotions, thoughts, and concerns can you read on the faces of these immigrants?

(Lewis Hine, *Climbing into the Promised Land, Ellis Island, 1908.* © Brooklyn Museum of Art, New York, USA, Gift of Mr. and Mrs. Walter Rosenblum/Bridgeman Art Library.)

era. Between 1897 and 1904, union membership grew from 447,000 to more than 2 million, with three out of every four union members claimed by the AFL. By 1914, the AFL alone had more than 2 million members. Gompers's "pure and simple unionism" was most successful among coal miners, railroad workers, and the building trades. As we saw in Chapter 18, Gompers ignored the growing army of unskilled and immigrant workers and concentrated on raising the wages and improving the working conditions of the skilled artisans who were members of unions affiliated with the AFL.

For a time, Gompers's strategy seemed to work. Several industries negotiated with the AFL as a way of avoiding disruptive strikes. But cooperation was short-lived. Labor unions were defeated in a number of disastrous strikes, and the National Association of Manufacturers (NAM) launched an aggressive counterattack. NAM and other employer associations provided strikebreakers, used industrial spies, and blacklisted union members to prevent them from obtaining other jobs.

The Supreme Court came down squarely on management's side, ruling in the Danbury Hatters case (*Loewe* v. *Lawler,* 1908) that the boycott of an industry by a labor union violated the Sherman Anti-Trust Act. The boycott had been a valuable tool for striking workers, enabling them to picket and pressure companies doing business with their employers during a strike.

Working women and their problems aroused more sympathy among progressive reformers than the plight of working men. The number of women working outside the home increased steadily during the progressive era, from more than 5 million in 1900 to nearly 8.5 million in 1920. But few belonged to unions.

Many upper-class women reformers tried to help working women in a variety of ways. The settlement houses organized day-care centers, clubs, and classes, and many reformers tried to pass protective legislation. Tension and misunderstanding often cropped up between reformers and the working women, but one organization in which there was genuine cooperation was the Women's Trade Union League. Founded in 1903, the league was organized by Mary Kenney and William English Walling, a socialist and reformer, but it also drew local leaders from the working class, such as Rose Schneiderman, a Jewish immigrant cap maker, and Leonora O'Reilly, a collar maker. The league established branches in most large eastern and midwestern cities and served for more than a decade as an important force in organizing women into unions. The league forced the AFL to pay more attention to women, helped during strikes, and publicized the plight of working women.

Garment Workers and the Triangle Fire

Thousands of young women, most of them Jewish and Italian, were employed in the garment industry in New York City. Most were between ages 16 and 25; some lived with their families, and others lived alone or with a roommate. They worked a 56-hour, six-day week and made about $6 a week for their efforts. New York was the center of the garment industry, with more than 600 shirtwaist (blouse) and dress factories employing more than 30,000 workers.

Like other industries, garment manufacturing changed in the first decade of the twentieth century. Once conducted in thousands of dark and dingy tenement rooms, operations became centralized in large loft buildings in lower Manhattan. These buildings were an improvement over the tenements, but many were overcrowded, and they had few fire escapes or safety features. The owners applied scientific management techniques to heighten productivity and thereby increase their profits. But conditions for the workers were miserable. Most of the women had to rent their sewing machines and pay for the electricity they used. They were penalized for making mistakes or talking too loudly. They were usually supervised by a male contractor who badgered and sometimes sexually harassed them.

In 1909, some of the women went on strike to protest working conditions. The International Ladies' Garment Workers Union (ILGWU) and the Women's Trade Union League supported them. But strikers were beaten and sometimes arrested. At a mass meeting in New York on November 22, 1909, Clara Lemlich, a young shirtwaist worker who had been injured on the picket line, rose and in an emotional speech in Yiddish demanded a general strike. The entire audience pledged agreement. The next day, all over the city, the shirtwaist workers went on strike.

"The uprising of the twenty thousand," as the strike was called, startled the nation. One young worker wrote in her diary, "It is a good thing, that strike is. It makes you feel like a grown-up person." The Jews learned a little Italian and the Italians a little Yiddish so that they could communicate. Many social reformers, ministers, priests, and rabbis urged the strikers on. Mary Dreier, an upper-class reformer and president of the New York branch of the Women's Trade Union League, was arrested for marching with the strikers. A young state legislator, Fiorello La Guardia, later a congressman and mayor of New York, was one of many public officials to aid the strikers.

The shirtwaist workers won recognition for their union and some improvements in the factories, but their victory was limited. The young women went back to work amid still oppressive and unsafe conditions. On Saturday, March 25, 1911, a fire broke out on the eighth floor of the 10-story loft building housing the Triangle Shirtwaist Company near Washington Square in New York. There had been several small fires in the factory in previous weeks, so no one thought much about another one. But this fire was different. Within minutes, the top three floors of the factory were ablaze. The owners had locked most of the exit doors. The elevators broke down. There were no fire escapes. Forty-six women jumped to their deaths, some of them in groups of three and four holding hands. More than 100 died in the flames.

Shocked by the Triangle fire, the state legislature appointed a commission to investigate working conditions in the state. One investigator for the commission was a young social worker named Frances Perkins, who in the 1930s would become secretary of labor. She led the politicians through the dark lofts, filthy tenements, and unsafe factories around the state to show them the conditions under which young women worked. The result was state legislation limiting the work of women to 54 hours a week, prohibiting labor by children under age 14, and improving safety regulations in factories. One supporter of the bills in Albany was a young state senator named Franklin Delano Roosevelt.

The investigative commission was a favorite progressive tactic. The federal Industrial Relations Commission, created in 1912 to study the causes of industrial unrest and violence, conducted one of the most important investigations, a study of the labor–management conflict at the Colorado Fuel and Iron Industry near Ludlow, Colorado. In the fall of 1913, miners at the company, which was largely owned by the Rockefeller family, went on strike demanding an eight-hour workday, better safety precautions, and the removal of armed guards. When the company refused to negotiate with the striking workers, the strike turned violent. In the spring of 1914, strikebreakers and national guardsmen armed with machine guns fired on the workers, killing 11 children and 2 women in an incident that became known as the Ludlow Massacre.

The Industrial Relations Commission called John D. Rockefeller, Jr., to testify and implied that he was personally guilty of the murders. The commission decided in its report that violent class conflict could be avoided only by limiting the use of armed guards and detectives, by restricting monopoly, by protecting the right of the workers to organize, and, most dramatically, by redistributing wealth through taxation. The commission's report, not surprisingly, fell on deaf ears. Most progressives, like most Americans, denied the commission's conclusion that class conflict was inevitable.

Radical Labor

Not everyone accepted the progressives' faith in investigations and protective labor legislation. Nor did everyone approve of Samuel Gompers's conservative tactics or his emphasis on getting higher wages for skilled workers. In 1905 in Chicago, about 200 radicals met to organize the Industrial Workers of the World (IWW) as an alternative to the AFL. Like the Knights of Labor in the 1880s, the IWW welcomed all workers regardless of skill, gender, or race.

Eugene Debs attended the organizational meeting. He had become a socialist after the Pullman strike of 1894 and emerged by 1905 as one of the outstanding radical leaders in the country. Also attending were "Big Bill" Haywood of the Western Federation of Miners and the legendary Mary Harris "Mother" Jones, who dressed like a society matron but attacked labor leaders "who sit on velvet chairs in conferences with labor's oppressors." Now in her sixties, "Mother" Jones had been a dressmaker, a Populist, and a member of the

Knights of Labor. During the 1890s, she had marched with miners' wives on the picket line in western Pennsylvania.

The IWW remained a small organization, troubled by internal squabbles and disagreements. Haywood dominated the movement, which played an important role in organizing the militant strikes of textile workers in Lawrence, Massachusetts, in 1912 and the following year in Paterson, New Jersey, and Akron, Ohio. The IWW had its greatest success organizing itinerant lumbermen and migratory workers in the Northwest. But in other places, especially in times of high unemployment, the Wobblies (as they were called) helped unskilled workers vent their anger against their employers.

Most American workers did not feel, as European workers did, that they were involved in a perpetual class struggle with their capitalist employers, but that did not mean that they were docile and passive. Many American workers struggled with their managers over control of the workplace, and workers occasionally went on strike for better wages and working conditions. Immigrants often did not join in these actions. Some immigrant workers, intent on earning enough money to go back home, had no time to join the conflict. Most of those who stayed in the United States held fast to the dream of a better job or moving up into the middle class. They avoided organized labor militancy. They knew that even if they failed, their sons and daughters would profit from the American way. The AFL, not the IWW, became the dominant American labor movement.

Reform in the Cities and States

Reform movements of the progressive era usually started at the local level, then moved to the state, and finally to the nation's capital. Progressivism in the cities and states had roots in the depression and discontent of the 1890s. Reformers called for more democracy, more power for the people, and legislation regulating railroads and other businesses. Yet often the professional and business classes were the movement's leaders. They intended to bring order out of chaos and to modernize the city and the state during a time of rapid growth.

Municipal Reformers

American cities grew rapidly in the last part of the nineteenth and the first part of the twentieth century. New York, which had a population of 1.2 million in 1880, grew to 3.4 million by 1900 and 5.6 million in 1920. Chicago expanded even more dramatically, from 500,000 in 1880 to 1.7 million in 1900 and 2.7 million in 1920. Los Angeles was a town of 11,000 in 1880 but multiplied 10 times by 1900, and then increased another 5 times, to more than a half million, by 1920.

The spectacular and continuing growth of the cities caused problems and created a need for housing, transportation, and municipal services. But many observers worried most about the kinds of people who were moving into the cities. Immigration produced the greatest surge. Fully 40 percent of New York's population and 36 percent of Chicago's was foreign born in 1910; if one included the children of the immigrants, the percentage approached 80 percent in some cities. To many Protestant Americans, the new immigrants seemed to threaten the American way of life and the very tenets of democracy.

The presence of large immigrant populations was the most important difference between American and European cities, and it made attempts to reform the city different in the United States. Twentieth-century reformers, mostly middle-class citizens like those in the nineteenth century, wanted to regulate and control the sprawling metropolis, restore democracy, reduce corruption, and limit the power of the political bosses and their immigrant allies. When these reformers talked of restoring power to the people, they usually meant ensuring control for people like themselves. The chief aim of municipal reform was to make the city more organized and efficient for the business and professional classes.

Municipal reform movements varied from city to city, but everywhere the reformers tried to limit the power of the city political bosses, whom they saw as corrupt and antidemocratic. In Boston, the reformers tried to strengthen the power of the mayor, break the hold of the city council, and eliminate council corruption. They succeeded in removing all party designations from city election ballots, and they extended the term of the mayor from two to four years. But to their chagrin, in the election of 1910, John Fitzgerald, grandfather of John F. Kennedy and foe of reform, defeated their candidate.

The most dramatic innovation in municipal reform was the replacement of both mayor and council with a nonpartisan commission of administrators. This scheme began quite accidentally when a hurricane devastated Galveston, Texas, in September 1900. More than 6,000 people died in the worst natural disaster in the nation's history. The existing government was helpless to deal with the crisis, so the state legislature appointed five commissioners to run the city during the emergency.

The idea spread to Houston, Dallas, and Austin and to cities in other states. It proved most popular in small to medium-sized cities in the Midwest and the Pacific Northwest. By World War I, more than 400 cities had adopted the commission form. Dayton, Ohio, went one step further: after a disastrous flood in 1913, the city hired a manager to run the city and to report to the elected council. Appointed, not elected, the city manager was more a businessman or technician than a politician. Government by experts

A Traffic Jam in Chicago in 1909

Cities grew so rapidly that they often ceased to work. This 1909 photograph shows Dearborn Street looking south from Randolph Street in Chicago. Horse-drawn vehicles, streetcars, pedestrians, and even a few early autos clogged the intersection and created the urban inefficiency that angered municipal reformers. How have urban centers changed today? Have we solved the problem of urban transportation and crowding?

(Chicago Historical Society, [ICHi-04151])

was the perfect symbol of what most municipal reformers had in mind.

The commission and the expert manager did not replace the mayor in most large cities. One of the most flamboyant and successful of the progressive mayors was Tom Johnson of Cleveland. Johnson had made a fortune by investing in utility and railroad franchises before he was 40. But Henry George's *Progress and Poverty* so influenced him that he began a second career as a reformer. Elected mayor of Cleveland in 1901, he reduced transit fares and built parks and municipal bathhouses throughout the city. Johnson also broke the connection between the police and prostitution by promising the madams and brothel owners that he would not bother them if they would be orderly and not steal from their customers or pay off the police.

His most controversial move, however, was advocating city ownership of the street railroads and utilities. Like many American urban reformers, Johnson admired the municipally owned transportation systems in European cities. "Only through municipal ownership," he argued, "can the gulf which divides the community into a small dominant class on one side and the unorganized people on the other be bridged." Johnson was defeated in 1909 in part because he alienated many powerful business interests, but one of his lieutenants, Newton D. Baker, was elected mayor in 1911 and carried on many of his programs. Cleveland was one of many cities that began to regulate municipal utilities or take them over from the private owners.

In Cleveland, both Tom Johnson and Newton Baker promoted the arts, music, and adult education. They also supervised construction of a civic center, library, and museum. In Cleveland and other cities, such "city beautiful" projects were influenced at least in part by the great, classical White City constructed for the Chicago World's Fair of 1893, but even more by grand European boulevards such as the Champs-Élysées in Paris. The city beautiful leaders tried to make their cities more attractive and meaningful for the middle and upper classes. The museums and the libraries were closed on Sundays, the only day the working class could possibly visit them.

Social justice progressives were more concerned with neighborhood parks and playgrounds than with ceremonial boulevards and grand buildings. In Chicago, Hull House established the first public playground. In New York, Jacob Riis, the housing reformer, and Lillian Wald of the Henry Street Settlement campaigned for small parks and for the opening of schoolyards on weekends. Some progressives looked back nostalgically to their rural childhoods and desperately tried to get urban children out of the city in the summertime to attend rural camps. But they also tried to make the city more livable as well as more beautiful.

Most progressives had an ambivalent attitude toward the city. They feared it, and they loved it. Some saw the great urban areas filled with immigrants as a threat to American democracy, but one of Tom Johnson's young assistants, Frederic C. Howe, who had traveled and studied in Europe, wrote a book titled *The City: The Hope of Democracy* (1905). Hope or threat, the progressives realized that the United States had become an urban nation and that the problems of the city had to be faced.

Reform in the States

The progressive movements in the states had many roots and took many forms, but because of the American federal system, the states took on an importance that confused observers from other parts of the world. In some states, especially in the West, progressive attempts to regulate railroads and utilities were simply an extension of Populism. In other states, the reform drive emerged from municipal reform efforts. Most states passed laws during the progressive era designed to extend democracy and give more authority to the people. Initiative and referendum laws allowed citizens to originate legislation and to overturn laws passed by the legislature, and recall laws gave the people a way to remove elected officials.

Much progressive state legislation promoted order and efficiency, but many states passed social justice measures as well. Maryland enacted the first workers' compensation law in 1902, paying employees for days missed because of job-related injuries. By 1917, 37 states (almost all outside the South) had passed workers' compensation laws and 28 states had set maximum hours for women working in industry. Illinois approved a law aiding mothers with dependent children. Several states passed anti–child labor bills, and Oregon's 10-hour law restricting women's labor became a model for other states.

The states with the most successful reform movements elected strong and aggressive governors: Charles Evans Hughes in New York, Hoke Smith in Georgia, Hiram Johnson in California, Woodrow Wilson in New Jersey, and Robert La Follette in Wisconsin. After Wilson, La Follette was the most famous and in many ways the model progressive governor. Of small-town origin and an 1879 graduate of the University of Wisconsin, he began his career as a railroad lawyer and became a reformer only after the depression of 1893. Taking advantage of the general mood of discontent, he won the governorship in 1901. Ironically, he owed his victory to his attack on the railroads. But La Follette was a shrewd politician. He used professors from the University of Wisconsin (in the capital)

LANDMARK SOCIAL LEGISLATION IN THE STATES

1902   Maryland passed the first state worker's compensation law.

1903   Oregon adopted a law limiting women's work to ten hours a day in factories (upheld by the United States Supreme Court in *Muller* v. *Oregon*, 1908).

1911   Illinois enacted the first state law providing public assistance to mothers with dependent children.

1912   Massachusetts passed the first minimum-wage law. A commission fixed wage rates for women and children. This and other similar state laws were overturned by the United States Supreme Court in *Atkins* v. *Children's Hospital*, 1923.

to prepare reports and do statistical studies. Then he worked with the legislature to pass a state primary law and an act regulating the railroads. "Go back to the first principles of democracy; go back to the people" was his battle cry. Journalists helped popularize Wisconsin as the "laboratory of democracy." La Follette won national recognition and was elected to the Senate in 1906.

The progressive movement did improve government and made it more responsible to the people in Wisconsin and other states. For example, the railroads were brought under the control of a railroad commission. But by 1910, the railroads no longer complained about the new taxes and restrictions. They had discovered that it was to their advantage to make their operations more efficient, and often they were able to convince the commission that they should raise rates or abandon the operation of unprofitable lines.

Progressivism in the states, like progressivism everywhere, had mixed results. But the spirit of reform that swept the country was real, and progressive movements on the local level did eventually have

an impact on Washington, especially during the administrations of Theodore Roosevelt and Woodrow Wilson.

Theodore Roosevelt and the Square Deal

President William McKinley was shot in Buffalo, New York, on September 6, 1901, by Leon Czolgosz, an anarchist. McKinley died eight days later, making Theodore Roosevelt, at age 42, the youngest man ever to become president.

No one knew what to expect from Roosevelt. Some politicians thought he was too radical; a few social justice progressives remembered his suggestion that the soldiers should fire on the strikers during the 1894 Pullman strike. Nonetheless, under his leadership, progressivism reshaped the national political agenda. Although early progressive reformers had attacked problems that they saw in their own communities, they gradually understood that some problems could not be

TR's Bully Pulpit

Theodore Roosevelt was a dynamic public speaker who used his position to influence public opinion. Despite his high-pitched voice, he could be heard at the back of the crowd in the days before microphones. Note the row of reporters decked out in their summer straw hats writing their stories as the president speaks. How have presidential speeches and the role of reporters changed since Roosevelt's time?

(Brown Brothers)

solved at the state or local level. The emergence of a national industrial economy had spawned conditions that demanded national solutions.

Progressives at the national level turned their attention to the workings of the economic system. They scrutinized the operation and organization of railroads and other large corporations. They examined threats to the natural environment. They reviewed the quality of the products of American industry. As they fashioned legislation to remedy the flaws in the economic system, they vastly expanded the power of the national government.

A Strong and Controversial President

Roosevelt came to the presidency with considerable experience. He had run unsuccessfully for mayor of New York, served a term in the New York state assembly, spent four years as a U.S. civil service commissioner, and served two years as the police commissioner of New York City. His exploits in the Spanish-American War brought him to the public's attention, but he had also been an effective assistant secretary of the navy and a reform governor of New York. While police commissioner and governor, he had been influenced by a number of progressives. He had supported conservation, an eight-hour workday, and other progressive measures in New York. But no one was sure how he would act as president. He came from an upper-class family, had traveled widely in Europe, and had associated with the important and the powerful all over the world. He had written a number of books and was one of the most intellectual and cosmopolitan presidents since Thomas Jefferson. But there was no guarantee that he would be a progressive in office.

Roosevelt loved being president. He called the office a "bully pulpit," and he enjoyed talking to the people and the press. His appealing personality and sense of humor made him a good subject for the new mass-market newspapers and magazines. The American people called him "Teddy" and named a stuffed bear after him. Sometimes his exuberance got a little out of hand. On one occasion, he took a foreign diplomat on a nude swim in the Potomac River. You have to understand, another observer remarked, that "the president is really only six years old."

Roosevelt was much more than an exuberant six-year-old. He was the strongest president since Lincoln. By revitalizing the executive branch, reorganizing the army command structure, and modernizing the consular service, he made many aspects of the federal government more efficient. He established the Bureau of Corporations, appointed independent commissions staffed with experts, and enlisted talented and well-trained men to work for the government. "TR," as he became known, called a White House conference on the care of dependent children, and in 1905, he even summoned college presidents and football coaches to the White House to discuss ways to limit violence in football. Although he angered many social justice progressives who felt he did not go far enough, he was the first president to listen to the pleas of the progressives and to invite them to the White House. Learning from experts such as Frances Kellor, he gradually became more concerned with social justice. In 1904, running on a platform of a "Square Deal" for the American people, he was reelected by an overwhelming margin.

Dealing with the Trusts

One of Roosevelt's first actions as president was to attempt to control large industrial corporations. He took office in the middle of an unprecedented wave of business consolidation. Between 1897 and 1904, some 4,227 companies combined to form 257 large corporations. U.S. Steel, the first billion-dollar corporation, was formed in 1901 by joining Carnegie Steel with its eight main competitors. The new company controlled two-thirds of the market, and financier J. P. Morgan made $7 million on the deal.

The Sherman Anti-Trust Act of 1890 had been virtually useless in controlling the trusts, and muckrakers and progressives called for new regulation. Some even demanded a return to the age of small business. Roosevelt opposed neither bigness nor the right of businessmen to make money. "We draw the line against misconduct, not against wealth," he said.

To the shock of much of the business community, he directed his attorney general to file suit to dissolve the Northern Securities Company, a giant railroad monopoly put together by James J. Hill and J. P. Morgan. Morgan came to the White House to tell Roosevelt, "If we have done anything wrong, send your man to my man and they can fix it up." A furious Roosevelt let Morgan and other businessmen know that they could not deal with the president of the United States as just another tycoon. The government won its case and proceeded to prosecute some of the largest corporations, including Standard Oil of New Jersey and the American Tobacco Company.

Roosevelt's antitrust policy did not end the power of the giant corporations or even alter their methods of doing business, nor did it force down the price of kerosene, cigars, or railroad tickets. But it did breathe some life into the Sherman Anti-Trust Act and increased the role of the federal government as regulator. It also caused large firms such as U.S. Steel to diversify to avoid antitrust suits.

Roosevelt sought to strengthen the regulatory powers of the federal government in other ways. He steered the Elkins Act through Congress in 1903 and the Hepburn Act in 1906, which together increased the power of the Interstate Commerce Commission (ICC).

The first act eliminated the use of rebates by railroads, a method that many large corporations had used to get favored treatment. The second act broadened the power of the ICC and gave it the right to investigate and enforce rates. Opponents in Congress weakened both bills, however, and the legislation neither ended abuses nor satisfied the farmers and small-business owners who had always been the railroads' chief critics.

Roosevelt firmly believed in corporate capitalism. He detested socialism and felt much more comfortable around business executives than labor leaders. Yet he saw his role as mediator and regulator. His view of the power of the presidency was illustrated in 1902 during the anthracite coal strike. Led by John Mitchell of the United Mine Workers, the coal miners went on strike to protest low wages, long hours, and unsafe working conditions. In 1901, a total of 513 coal miners had died in industrial accidents. The mine owners refused to talk to the miners. They hired strikebreakers and used private security forces to threaten and intimidate the workers.

Roosevelt had no particular sympathy for labor, but in the fall of 1902, schools began closing for lack of coal, and it looked as if many citizens would suffer through the winter. Coal, which usually sold for $5 a ton, rose to $14. Roosevelt called the owners and representatives of the union to the White House, even though the mine owners protested that they would not deal with "outlaws." Finally, the president appointed a commission that included representatives of the union as well as the community. Within weeks, the miners went back to work with a 10 percent raise, back pay, and a nine-hour day. But the agreement failed to recognize the union, and neither side was entirely happy with the agreement.

Meat Inspection and Pure Food and Drugs

Roosevelt's first major legislative reform began almost accidentally in 1904 when Upton Sinclair, a 26-year-old muckraking journalist, started research on the Chicago stockyards. In his 1906 novel about the meat industry, *The Jungle,* Sinclair documented exploitation but his description of contaminated meat drew more attention. He described spoiled hams treated with formaldehyde and sausages made from rotten meat scraps, rats, and other refuse. Hoping to convert his readers to socialism, Sinclair instead turned their stomachs and caused a public outcry for better regulation of the meatpacking industry.

Roosevelt, who read the book, ordered a study of the meatpacking industry and then used the report to pressure Congress and the meatpackers to accept a bill introduced by Albert Beveridge, the progressive senator from Indiana. In the end, the Meat Inspection Act of 1906 was a compromise. It enforced some federal inspection and mandated sanitary conditions in all companies selling meat in interstate commerce. The meatpackers defeated a provision that would have required the dating of all meat. Some of the large companies supported the compromise because it gave them an advantage in their battle with the smaller firms. But the act was a beginning and an example of how muckrakers, social justice progressives, and public outcry eventually led to reform legislation. Passage of the act also shows how Roosevelt used the public mood and manipulated the political process to achieve his goals. Many of the progressive reformers were disappointed with the final result, but Roosevelt was always willing to settle for half a loaf rather than none at all. Ironically, the Meat Inspection Act restored the public's confidence in the meat industry and helped the industry increase its profits.

Taking advantage of the publicity that circulated around *The Jungle,* a group of reformers, writers, and government officials supported legislation to regulate the sale of food and drugs. Americans consumed an enormous quantity of patent medicines, which they purchased through the mail, from traveling salesmen, and from local stores. Many packaged and canned foods contained dangerous chemicals and impurities. One popular remedy, Hosteter's Stomach Bitters, was revealed on analysis to contain 44 percent alcohol. Coca-Cola, a popular soft drink, contained a small amount of cocaine, and many medicines were laced with opium. Many people, including women and children, became alcoholics or drug addicts in their quest to feel better. The Pure Food and Drug Act, which Congress passed on the same day in 1906 as the Meat Inspection Act, was not a perfect bill, but it corrected some of the worst abuses, including eliminating the cocaine from Coca-Cola.

Conservation

Roosevelt, an outdoorsman and amateur naturalist, considered his conservation program his most important domestic achievement. Using his executive authority, he more than tripled the land set aside for national forests, bringing the total to more than 150 million acres.

Because he had traveled widely in the West, Roosevelt understood, as few easterners did, the problems created by limited water in the western states. In 1902, with his enthusiastic support, Congress passed the Newlands Act, named for its chief sponsor, Congressman Francis Newlands of Nevada. The National Reclamation Act (as it was officially called) set aside the proceeds from the sale of public land in 16 western states to pay for the construction of irrigation projects in those states. Although it tended to help big farmers more than small producers, the Newlands Act federalized irrigation for the first time.

More important were Roosevelt's efforts to raise public consciousness about the need to save the nation's natural resources. He appointed a National Conservation Commission charged with making an inventory of the natural resources in the entire country. To chair the commission, Roosevelt appointed Gifford Pinchot, probably the most important conservation advocate in the country.

Pinchot's conservation policies pleased many in the timber and cattle industries; at the same time, they angered those who simply wanted to exploit the land. But his policies were denounced by the followers of John Muir, who believed passionately in preserving the land in a wilderness state. Muir had founded the Sierra Club in 1862 and had led a successful campaign to create Yosemite National Park in California. With his shaggy gray beard, rough blue work clothes, and black slouch hat, Muir seemed like an eccentric to many, but thousands agreed with him when he argued that preserving the American wilderness was a spiritual and psychological necessity for overcivilized and overstimulated urban dwellers. Muir was one of the leaders in a "back to nature" movement at the turn of the century. Many middle-class Americans took up hiking, camping,

and other outdoor activities, and children joined the Boy Scouts (founded in 1910) and the Camp Fire Girls (1912). The "back to nature movement" was not strictly American. The Boy Scouts were patterned after the British Boy Scouts, and hiking and mountain climbing were popular activities in many countries early in the twentieth century.

The conflicting philosophies of conservationist Pinchot and preservationist Muir were most dramatically demonstrated by the controversy over Hetch-Hetchy, a remote valley deep within Yosemite National Park. It was a pristine wilderness area, and Muir and his followers wanted to keep it that way. But in 1901, the mayor of San Francisco decided the valley would make a perfect place for a dam and reservoir to supply his growing city with water for decades to come. Muir argued that wilderness soon would be scarcer than water and more important for the moral strength of the nation. Pinchot, on the other hand, maintained that it was foolish to pander to the aesthetic enjoyment of a tiny group of people when the comfort and welfare of the great majority were at stake.

In the end, the conservationists won out over the preservationists. Roosevelt and Congress sided with

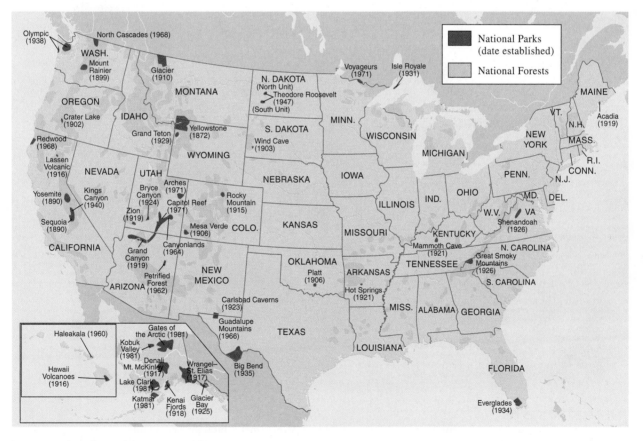

National Parks and Forests

Yellowstone, Yosemite, and a few other national parks were established before Theodore Roosevelt became president, but his passionate interest in conservation led to a movement to set aside and preserve thousands of acres of the public domain. What legacy did this create for future generations?

Pinchot and eventually the dam was built, turning the valley into a lake. But the debate over how to use the nation's land and water would continue throughout the twentieth century.

Progressivism for Whites Only

Like most of his generation, Roosevelt thought in stereotyped racial terms. He called Native Americans "savages" and once remarked that blacks were "wholly unfit for the suffrage." He believed that blacks, Asians, and Native Americans were inferior, and he feared that massive migrations from southern and eastern Europe threatened the United States. This kind of racism was supported by scientific theories accepted by many experts in the universities. Supporters of eugenics, who believed that selective breeding would improve the human race, advocated the forced sterilization of criminals, mental patients, and other undesirable types. Roosevelt was influenced by these theories, but he was first of all a politician, so he made gestures of goodwill

to most groups. He even invited Booker T. Washington to the White House in 1901, though many southerners viciously attacked the president for this breach of etiquette. Roosevelt also appointed several qualified blacks to minor federal posts, notably Dr. William D. Crum to head the Charleston, South Carolina, customs house in 1905.

At other times, however, Roosevelt seemed insensitive to the needs and feelings of black Americans. This was especially true in his handling of the Brownsville, Texas, riot of 1906. Members of a black army unit stationed there, angered by discrimination against them, rioted one hot August night. Exactly what happened no one was sure, but one white man was killed and several were wounded. Waiting until after the midterm elections of 1906, Roosevelt ordered all 167 members of three companies dishonorably discharged. It was an unjust punishment for an unproven crime, and 66 years later, the secretary of the army granted honorable discharges to the men, although most of them were by that time dead.

An American History Class

Tuskegee Institute followed Booker T. Washington's philosophy of black advancement through accommodation to the white status quo. Here students study white American history, but most of their time was spent on more practical subjects. This photo was taken in 1902 by Frances Benjamin Johnson, a pioneer woman photographer. How have classrooms changed in the last hundred years? How have they stayed the same?

(Library of Congress)

The progressive era coincided with the years of greatest segregation in the South, and in southern states, progressivism meant keeping blacks outside the political process. Even the most advanced progressives seldom included blacks in their reform schemes. Like most social settlements, Hull House was segregated, although Jane Addams (more than most progressives) struggled to overcome the racist attitudes of her day. She helped found a settlement that served a black neighborhood in Chicago, and she spoke out repeatedly against lynching. Addams also supported the founding of the National Association for the Advancement of Colored People (NAACP) in 1909, the most important organization of the progressive era aimed at promoting equality and justice for blacks.

The founding of the NAACP is the story of cooperation between a group of white social justice progressives and a number of courageous black leaders. Even in the age of segregation and lynching, blacks in all parts of the country—through churches, clubs, and schools—sought to promote a better life for themselves. The most important black leader who argued for equality and opportunity for his people was W. E. B. Du Bois. He differed dramatically from Booker T. Washington on the proper position of blacks in American life (see Chapter 17). Whereas Washington advocated vocational education, Du Bois argued for the best education possible for the most talented tenth of the black population. Whereas Washington preached compromise and accommodation to the dominant white society, Du Bois increasingly urged aggressive action to ensure equality.

Denouncing Washington for accepting the "alleged inferiority of the Negro," Du Bois called a meeting of young and militant blacks in 1905. They met in Canada, not far from Niagara Falls, and issued an angry statement. "We want to pull down nothing but we don't propose to be pulled down," the platform announced. "We believe in taking what we can get but we don't believe in being satisfied with it and in permitting anybody for a moment to imagine we're satisfied." The Niagara movement, as it came to be called, was small, but it was soon augmented by a group of white liberals concerned with violence against blacks and race riots in Atlanta and even in Springfield, Illinois, the home of Abraham Lincoln. Jane Addams joined the new organization, as did Oswald Garrison Villard, grandson of abolitionist William Lloyd Garrison.

In 1910, the Niagara movement combined with the NAACP, and Du Bois became editor of its journal, *The Crisis*. He toned down his rhetoric, but he tried to promote equality for all blacks. The NAACP was a typical progressive organization, seeking to work within the American system to promote reform. But to Roosevelt and many others who called themselves progressives, the NAACP seemed dangerously radical.

William Howard Taft

After two terms as president, Roosevelt decided to step down. But he soon regretted his decision. Only 50 years old, he was at the peak of his popularity and power. Because the U.S. system of government provides little creative function for former presidents, Roosevelt decided to travel and to go big-game hunting in Africa.

William Howard Taft, Roosevelt's personal choice for the Republican nomination and winner over Democratic candidate William Jennings Bryan in 1908, was a distinguished lawyer, federal judge, and public servant. Born in Cincinnati, Taft had been the first civil governor of the Philippines and Roosevelt's secretary of war. In some ways, he seemed more progressive than Roosevelt. His administration instituted more suits against monopolies in one term than Roosevelt had in two. He supported the eight-hour workday and legislation to make mining safer, and he urged the passage of the Mann–Elkins Act in 1910, which strengthened the ICC by giving it more power to set railroad rates and extending its jurisdiction over telephone and telegraph companies. Taft and Congress also authorized the first tax on corporate profits. He also encouraged the process that eventually led to the passage of the federal income tax, which was authorized under the Sixteenth Amendment, ratified in 1913.

But Taft soon ran into difficulties. His biggest problem was his style. He was a huge man, weighing more than 300 pounds. (Rumors circulated that he had to have a special, oversize bathtub installed in the White House.) Easily ridiculed, the president wrote ponderous prose and spoke uninspiringly. He also lacked Roosevelt's political skills and angered many of the progressives in the Republican party, especially the midwestern insurgents led by Senator Robert La Follette of Wisconsin. Many progressives were annoyed when he signed the Payne–Aldrich Tariff, which midwesterners thought left rates on cotton and wool cloth and other items too high and played into the hands of the eastern industrial interests.

Even Roosevelt was infuriated when his successor reversed many of his conservation policies and fired chief forester Gifford Pinchot. Roosevelt broke with Taft and let it be known that he was willing to run again for president. This set up one of the most exciting and significant elections in American history.

The Election of 1912

Woodrow Wilson won the Democratic nomination for president in 1912. The son and grandson of Presbyterian ministers, Wilson grew up in a comfortable and intellectual southern household and early on seemed more interested in politics than in religion. He graduated from Princeton University in 1879, studied law at the University of Virginia, and practiced law briefly before entering graduate school at the Johns Hopkins University in Baltimore. His book, *Congressional Government* (1885), established his reputation as a shrewd analyst of American politics. Less flamboyant than Roosevelt, he was an excellent public speaker, possessing the power to convince people with his words. In 1902 Wilson was elected president of Princeton University, and during the next few years he established a national reputation as an educational leader. Wilson never lost interest in politics, however, so when offered a chance by the Democratic machine to run for governor of New Jersey, he took it eagerly. In his two years as governor, he showed courage as he quickly alienated some of the conservatives who had helped elect him. Building a coalition of reformers, he worked with them to pass a direct primary law and a workers' compensation law. He also created a commission to regulate transportation and public utility companies. By 1912, Wilson not only was an expert on government and politics but had also acquired the reputation of a progressive.

Roosevelt, who had been speaking out on a variety of issues since 1910, competed with Taft for the Republican nomination, but Taft, as the incumbent president and party leader, was able to win it. Roosevelt then startled the nation by walking out of the convention and forming a new political party, the Progressive party. The new party would not have been formed without Roosevelt, but it was always more than Roosevelt. It appealed to progressives from all over the country who had become frustrated with the conservative leadership in both major parties.

Many social workers and social justice progressives supported the Progressive party because of its platform, which contained provisions they had been advocating for years. The Progressives supported an eight-hour workday, a six-day workweek, the abolition of child labor under age 16, and a federal system of accident, old age, and unemployment insurance. Unlike the Democrats, the Progressives also endorsed woman suffrage.

Most supporters of the Progressives in 1912 did not realistically think they could win, but they were convinced that they could organize a new political movement that would replace the Republican party, just as the Republicans had replaced the Whigs after 1856. To this end, Progressive leaders led by Frances Kellor set up the Progressive Service, designed to apply the principles of social research to educating voters between elections.

The Progressive party convention in Chicago seemed to many observers more like a religious revival meeting or a social work conference than a political gathering. The delegates sang "Onward Christian Soldiers," "The Battle Hymn of the Republic," and "Roosevelt, Oh Roosevelt" (to the tune of "Maryland, My Maryland"). They waved their bandannas, and when Jane Addams rose to second Roosevelt's nomination, a large group of women marched around the auditorium with a banner that read "Votes for Women."

Behind the unified facade lurked many disagreements. Roosevelt had become more progressive on many issues since leaving the presidency. He even attacked the financiers "to whom the acquisition of untold millions is the supreme goal of life, and who are too often utterly indifferent as to how these millions are obtained." But he was not as committed to social reform as some of the delegates. Perhaps the most divisive issue was the controversy over seating black delegates from several southern states. A number of social justice progressives fought hard to include a plank in the platform supporting equality for blacks and for seating the black delegation. Roosevelt, however, thought he had a realistic chance to carry several southern states, and he was not convinced that black equality was an important progressive issue. In the end, no blacks sat with the southern delegates, and the platform made no mention of black equality.

The political campaign in 1912 became a contest primarily between Roosevelt and Wilson; Taft, the Republican candidate and incumbent, was ignored by most reporters who covered the campaign. On one level, the campaign became a debate over political philosophy. What is the proper relationship of government to society in a modern industrial age? Roosevelt spoke of a "New Nationalism." In a modern industrial society, he argued, large corporations were "inevitable and necessary." What was needed was not the breakup of the trusts but a strong president and increased power in the hands of the federal government to regulate business and industry and to ensure the rights of labor, women and children, and other groups. The government should be the "steward of the public welfare." He argued for using Hamiltonian means to ensure Jeffersonian ends, for using strong central government to guarantee the rights of the people.

Wilson responded with a program he called the "New Freedom." Drawing on the ideas of Louis Brandeis, he emphasized the need for the Jeffersonian tradition of limited government with open competition. He spoke of the "curse of bigness" and argued against too much federal power.

The level of debate during the campaign was impressive, making this one of the few elections in American history in which important ideas were actually discussed. It also marked a watershed for political thought for liberals who rejected Jefferson's distrust of a strong central government. It is easy to exaggerate the differences between Roosevelt and Wilson. Certainly, in the end, the things that Roosevelt and Wilson could agree on were more important than the

PRESIDENTIAL ELECTIONS OF THE PROGRESSIVE ERA

Year	Candidate	Party	Popular Vote	Electoral Vote
1900	WILLIAM MCKINLEY	Republican	7,218,039 (51.7%)	292
	William Jennings Bryan	Democratic, Populist	6,358,345 (45.5%)	155
1904	THEODORE ROOSEVELT	Republican	7,628,834 (56.4%)	336
	Alton B. Parker	Democratic	5,084,401 (37.6%)	140
	Eugene V. Debs	Socialist	402,460 (3.0%)	0
1908	WILLIAM H. TAFT	Republican	7,679,006 (51.6%)	321
	William Jennings Bryan	Democratic	6,409,106 (43.1%)	162
	Eugene V. Debs	Socialist	420,820 (2.8%)	0
1912	WOODROW WILSON	Democratic	6,296,547 (41.9%)	435
	Theodore Roosevelt	Progressive	4,118,571 (27.4%)	88
	William H. Taft	Republican	3,486,720 (23.2%)	8
	Eugene V. Debs	Socialist	897,011 (6.0%)	0
1916	WOODROW WILSON	Democratic	9,129,606 (49.4%)	277
	Charles E. Hughes	Republican	8,538,221 (46.2%)	254
	Allan L. Benson	Socialist	585,113 (3.2%)	0

Note: Winners' names appear in capital letters.

issues that divided them. Both Roosevelt and Wilson urged reform within the American system. Both defended corporate capitalism, and both opposed socialism and radical labor organizations such as the IWW. Both wanted to promote more democracy and to strengthen conservative labor unions. And both were very different in style and substance from the fourth candidate, Eugene Debs, who ran on the Socialist party ticket in 1912.

In 1912, Debs was the most important socialist leader in the country. Socialism has always been a minority movement in the United States, but it reached its greatest success in the United States in the first decade of the twentieth century. Thirty-three cities, including Milwaukee, Wisconsin; Reading, Pennsylvania; Butte, Montana; Jackson, Michigan; and Berkeley, California, chose socialist mayors. Socialists Victor Berger from Wisconsin and Meyer London from New York were elected to Congress. The most important socialist periodical, *Appeal to Reason,* published in Girard, Kansas, increased its circulation from about 30,000 in 1900 to nearly 300,000 in 1906. Socialism appealed to a diverse group. In the cities, some who called themselves socialists merely favored municipal ownership of street railways. Some reformers, such as Florence Kelley and William English Walling, joined the party because of their frustration with the slow progress of reform. The party also attracted many recent immigrants, who brought with them a European sense of class and loyalty to socialism.

A tremendously appealing figure and a great orator, Debs had run for president in 1900, 1904, and 1908, but in 1912 he reached much wider audiences in more parts of the country. His message differed radically from that of Wilson or Roosevelt. Unlike the progressives, socialists argued for fundamental change in the American system. Debs polled almost 900,000 votes in 1912 (6 percent of the popular vote), the best showing ever for a socialist in the United States. Wilson received 6.3 million votes; Roosevelt, a little more than 4 million; and Taft, 3.5 million. Wilson garnered 435 electoral votes; Roosevelt, 88; and Taft, only 8.

Woodrow Wilson and the New Freedom

Wilson was elected largely because Roosevelt and the Progressive party split the Republican vote. But once elected, Wilson became a vigorous and aggressive chief executive who set out to translate his ideas about progressive government into legislation. Wilson was the first southerner elected president since the Civil War, but Wilson, like Roosevelt, had to work within his party, and that restricted how progressive he could be. But he was also constrained by his own background and inclinations. Still, like Roosevelt, Wilson became more progressive during his presidency.

Tariff and Banking Reform

Wilson was not as charismatic as Roosevelt. He had a more difficult time relating to people in small groups, but he was an excellent public speaker who dominated through the force of his intellect. He probably had an exaggerated belief in his ability to persuade and a tendency to trust his own intuition too much. His ability to push his legislative program through Congress during his first two years in office was matched only by Franklin Roosevelt during the first months of the New Deal and by Lyndon Johnson in 1965.

Within a month of his inauguration, Wilson went before a joint session of Congress to outline his legislative program. He recommended reducing the tariff to eliminate favoritism, freeing the banking system from Wall Street control, and restoring competition in industry. By appearing in person before Congress, he broke a precedent established by Thomas Jefferson.

The first item on Wilson's agenda was tariff reform. The Underwood Tariff, passed in 1913, was not a free-trade bill, but it did reduce tariff rates on hundreds of items for the first time in many years. Attached to the Underwood bill was a provision for a small and slightly graduated income tax, which had been made possible by the passage of the Sixteenth Amendment. It imposed a modest rate of 1 percent on income over $4,000 (thus exempting a large portion of the population), with a surtax rising to 6 percent on high incomes. The income tax was enacted to replace the money lost from lowering the tariff. Wilson seemed to have no interest in using it to redistribute wealth in America.

The next item on Wilson's agenda was reform of the banking system. A financial panic in 1907 had revealed the need for a central bank, but few people could agree on the exact nature of the reforms. A congressional committee, led by Arsène Pujo of Louisiana, had revealed a massive consolidation of banks and trust companies and a system of interlocking directorates and informal arrangements that concentrated resources and power in the hands of a few firms, such as the J. P. Morgan Company. The progressive faction of the Democratic party, armed with the Pujo Committee's findings, argued for a banking system and a currency controlled by the federal government. But talk of banking reform raised the specter among conservative Democrats and the business community of socialism, populism, and the monetary ideas of William Jennings Bryan.

The bill that passed Congress was a compromise. In creating the Federal Reserve System, it was the first reorganization of the banking system since the Civil War. The bill provided for 12 Federal Reserve banks and a Federal Reserve Board appointed by the president. The bill also created a flexible currency, based on Federal Reserve notes, that could be expanded or contracted as the situation required. The Federal Reserve System was not without its flaws, as later developments would show, and it did not end the power of the large eastern banks; but it was an improvement, and it appealed to the part of the progressive movement that sought order and efficiency.

Despite these reform measures, Wilson was not very progressive in some of his actions during his first two years in office. In the spring of 1914, he failed to support a bill that would have provided long-term rural

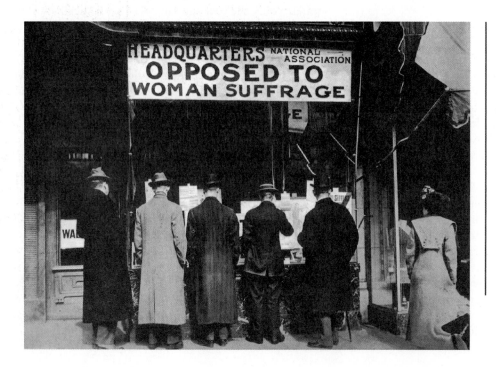

Opposing Woman Suffrage

Many men opposed suffrage for women because they feared the vote would change gender roles and destroy women's feminine ways. They also believed that women with the vote would support prohibition and other dangerous reforms. They often argued that women had no place in the masculine and corrupt world of politics. Many women also opposed suffrage because they believed their husbands and fathers or because they feared change. Would you have supported the vote for women if you had been alive in 1920? How have women's votes changed America?

(Library of Congress [LC-USZ62–25338])

Key Progressive Legislation

National Reclamations Act (Newlands Act), 1902

Used proceeds from sale of public lands in the western states to finance construction and maintenance of irrigation projects.

Elkins Act, 1903

Strengthened the Interstate Commerce Commission Act primarily by eliminating rebates to selected corporations.

Hepburn Act, 1906

Strengthened the Interstate Commerce Commission by giving it power to fix rates and broadening its jurisdiction to include express companies, oil pipelines, terminals, and bridges.

Meat Inspection Act, 1906

Provided for federal inspection of all companies selling meat in interstate commerce.

Pure Food and Drug Act, 1906

Prohibited the manufacture, sale, or transportation of adulterated or fraudulently labeled foods or drugs in interstate commerce.

Mann–Elkins Act, 1910

Put telephone, telegraph, cable, and wireless companies under the jurisdiction of the Interstate Commerce Commission.

Mann Act, 1910

Prohibited interstate transportation of women for immoral purposes.

Sixteenth Amendment to the Constitution, 1913 (proposed in 1909)

Gave Congress the power to impose a federal tax on income from all sources. An inheritance tax was added in 1916.

Federal Child Labor Law (Keatings–Owen Act), 1916

Barred products of child labor from interstate commerce; declared unconstitutional in 1918. Another act passed in 1919 was declared unconstitutional in 1920. In 1924 a child labor amendment to the Constitution was submitted to the states, but was never ratified.

Adamson Act, 1916

Provided for an eight-hour day and time and a half for overtime on interstate railroads.

Federal Farm Loan Act, 1916

Provided farmers with long-term credit.

Eighteenth Amendment to the Constitution, 1919 (proposed in 1917)

Prohibited the manufacture, sale, or transportation of intoxicating beverages; repealed by the Twenty-First Amendment in 1933.

Nineteenth Amendment to the Constitution, 1920 (proposed in 1919)

Provided that the right of citizens of the United States to vote should not be denied or abridged by the United States or any state on account of sex.

credit financed by the federal government. He opposed a woman suffrage amendment, arguing that the states should decide who could vote. He also failed to support an anti–child labor bill after it had passed the House. Most distressing to some progressives, he ordered the segregation of blacks in several federal departments. When southern Democrats, suddenly in control in many departments, began dismissing black federal officeholders, especially those "who boss white girls," Wilson did nothing. When the NAACP complained that the shops, offices, restrooms, and lunchrooms of the post office and treasury departments and the Bureau of Engraving were segregated, Wilson replied, "I sincerely believe it to be in [the blacks'] best interest." When the president endorsed the blatantly racist movie *Birth of a Nation*, others doubted that he believed in justice for the African American people. "Have you a 'new freedom' for white Americans and a new slavery for your African-American fellow citizens?" Boston journalist William Monroe Trotter asked.

Timeline

1901	McKinley assassinated; Theodore Roosevelt becomes president
	Robert La Follette elected governor of Wisconsin
	Tom Johnson elected mayor of Cleveland
	Model tenement house bill passed in New York
	U.S. Steel formed
1902	Anthracite coal strike
1903	Women's Trade Union League founded
	Elkins Act
1904	Roosevelt reelected
	Lincoln Steffens writes *The Shame of the Cities*
1905	Frederic C. Howe writes *The City: The Hope of Democracy*
	Industrial Workers of the World (IWW) formed
1906	Upton Sinclair writes *The Jungle*
	Hepburn Act
	Meat Inspection Act
	Pure Food and Drug Act
1907	Financial panic
1908	*Muller* v. *Oregon*
	Danbury Hatters case (*Loewe* v. *Lawler*)
	William Howard Taft elected president
1909	National Association for the Advancement of Colored People (NAACP) founded
1910	Ballinger–Pinchot controversy
	Mann Act
1911	Frederick Taylor writes *The Principles of Scientific Management*
	Triangle Shirtwaist Company fire
1912	Progressive party founded by Theodore Roosevelt
	Woodrow Wilson elected president
	Children's Bureau established
	Industrial Relations Commission founded
1913	Sixteenth Amendment (income tax) ratified
	Underwood Tariff
	Federal Reserve System established
	Seventeenth Amendment (direct election of senators) passed
1914	Clayton Act
	Federal Trade Commission Act
	AFL has more than 2 million members
	Ludlow Massacre in Colorado

Moving Closer to a New Nationalism

How to control the great corporations in America was a question Wilson and Roosevelt had debated extensively during the 1912 campaign. Wilson's solution was the Clayton Act, submitted to Congress in 1914. The bill prohibited a number of unfair trading practices, outlawed the interlocking directorate, and made it illegal for corporations to purchase stock in other corporations if doing so tended to reduce competition. But the law was vague and hard to enforce, and the courts interpreted it to mean that labor unions remained subject to court injunctions during strikes.

More important than the Clayton Act was the creation of the Federal Trade Commission (FTC). Powerful enough to move directly against corporations accused of restricting competition, the FTC was the idea of Louis Brandeis. Wilson accepted it even though it seemed closer to the philosophy of New Nationalism than to Wilson's New Freedom.

The Federal Trade Commission and the Clayton Act did not end monopoly, and the courts in the next two decades did not increase the government's power to regulate business. The success of Wilson's reform agenda appeared minimal in 1914, but the outbreak of war in Europe and the need to win the election of 1916 would influence him in becoming more progressive in the next years (see Chapter 22).

Neither Wilson nor Roosevelt satisfied the demands of the advanced progressives. These two progressive presidents spent most of their efforts on trying to regulate economic power rather than promoting social justice. Yet the most important legacy of these two powerful politicians was their attempts to strengthen the office of president and the executive branch of the federal government. The nineteenth-century American presidents after Lincoln had been relatively weak, and much of the federal power had resided with Congress. The progressive presidents reasserted presidential authority, modernized the executive branch, and began the creation of the federal bureaucracy, which has had a major impact on the lives of Americans.

Both Wilson and Roosevelt used the presidency as a bully pulpit to make pronouncements, create news, and influence policy. Roosevelt strengthened the Interstate Commerce Commission and Wilson created the Federal Trade Commission, both of which were the forerunners of many other federal regulatory bodies. By breaking precedent and delivering his annual message in person before a joint session of Congress, Wilson symbolized the new power of the presidency.

The nature of politics was changed by more than just the increased power of the executive branch. The new bureaus, committees, and commissions brought to Washington a new kind of expert, trained in the universities, at the state and local level, and in voluntary organizations. Julia Lathrop, a coworker of Jane Addams at Hull House, was one such expert. Appointed by President Taft in 1912 to become chief of the newly created Children's Bureau, she was the first woman ever appointed to such a position. She used her post not only to work for better child labor laws but also to train a new generation of women experts who would take their positions in state, federal, and private agencies in the 1920s and 1930s. Other experts emerged in Washington during the progressive era to influence policy in subtle and important ways. The expert, the commission, the statistical survey, and the increased power of the executive branch were all legacies of the progressive era.

Conclusion
THE LIMITS OF PROGRESSIVISM

The progressive era was a time when many Americans set out to promote reform because they saw poverty, despair, and disorder in a country transformed by immigration, urbanism, and industrialism. But unlike the socialists, the progressives saw nothing fundamentally wrong with the American system. Progressivism, part of a global movement to regulate and control rampaging industrialism, was largely a middle-class effort that sought to help the poor, the immigrants, and the working class. Yet the poor were rarely consulted about policy, and many groups, especially African Americans, were almost entirely left out of reform plans. Progressives had an optimistic view of human nature and an exaggerated faith in statistics, commissions, and committees. They talked of the need for more democracy, but they often succeeded in promoting bureaucracy and a government run by experts. They saw a need to regulate business, promote efficiency, and spread social justice, but these were often contradictory goals. In the end, their regulatory laws tended to aid business and strengthen corporate capitalism, while social justice and equal opportunity remained difficult to achieve. By contrast, most of the industrialized nations of western Europe, especially Germany, Denmark, and Great Britain, passed legislation during this period providing for old-age pensions and health and unemployment insurance.

Progressivism was a broad, diverse, and sometimes contradictory movement that had its roots in the 1890s and reached its height in the early twentieth century. It began with many local movements and voluntary efforts to deal with the problems created by urban industrialism and then moved to the state and finally the national level, where it enlisted government to regulate the private sector and to promote reform. Women played important roles in organizing reform, and many became experts at gathering statistics and writing reports. Eventually, they began to fill positions in the new agencies in the state capitals and in Washington. Frances Kellor was one of those professional women who devoted her life to reform and to helping immigrants. Neither Theodore Roosevelt nor Woodrow Wilson was an advanced progressive, but during both their administrations, progressivism achieved some success. Both presidents strengthened the power of the presidency, and both promoted the idea that the federal government had the responsibility to regulate and control and to promote social justice. Progressivism would be altered by World War I, but it survived, with its strengths and weaknesses, to affect American society through most of the twentieth century.

QUESTIONS FOR REVIEW AND REFLECTION

1. What contributions did women make to the progressive movement?
2. Why did the United States lag behind several European countries, Australia, New Zealand, and Brazil in passing social legislation?
3. Was Prohibition a progressive measure?
4. How did progressivism differ from socialism?
5. What was the long-range legacy of the progressive movement?

CHAPTER 22

The Great War

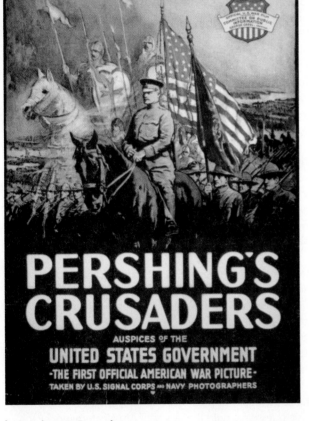

Pershing's Crusaders

This official 1917 U.S. government publication compares American soldiers to medieval knights. It makes explicit the American belief that by entering World War I they were joining not only a war but also a crusade to make the world safe for democracy. They were not just supporting the Allied cause, but they had a special mission to rescue the old world and to spread the American way of life. How do you suppose Europeans reacted to this American sense of mission and superiority?

(Library of Congress, LC-USZC4–1539)

American Stories

A Young Man Enlists in the Great Adventure

On April 7, 1917, the day after the United States officially declared war on Germany, Edmund P. Arpin, Jr., a young man of 22 from Grand Rapids, Wisconsin, decided to enlist in the army. The war seemed to provide a solution for his aimless drifting. It was not patriotism that led him to join the army but his craving for adventure and excitement. A month later, he was at Fort Sheridan, Illinois, along with hundreds of other eager young men, preparing to become an army officer. He felt a certain pride and sense of purpose, and especially a feeling of comradeship with the other men, but the war was a long way off.

Arpin finally arrived with his unit in Liverpool on December 23, 1917, aboard the *Leviathan,* a German luxury liner that the United States had interned when war was declared and then pressed into service as a troop transport. In England, he discovered that American troops were not greeted as saviors. Hostility against the Americans simmered partly because of the previous unit's drunken brawls. Despite the efforts of the U.S. government to protect its soldiers from the sins of Europe, drinking seems to have been a preoccupation of the soldiers in Arpin's outfit. Arpin also learned something about French wine and women, but he spent most of the endless waiting time learning to play contract bridge.

Arpin saw some of the horror of war when he went to the front with a French regiment as an observer, but his own unit did not engage in combat until October 1918, when the war was almost over. He took part in the bloody Meuse-Argonne offensive, which helped end the war. But he discovered that war was not the heroic struggle of carefully planned campaigns that newspapers and books described. War was filled with misfired weapons, mix-ups, and erroneous attacks. Wounded in the leg in an assault on an unnamed hill and awarded a Distinguished Service Cross for his bravery, Arpin later learned that the order to attack had been recalled, but word had not reached him in time.

When the armistice came, Arpin was recovering in a field hospital. He was disappointed that the war had ended so soon, but he was well enough to go to Paris to take part in the victory celebration and to explore some of the famous Paris restaurants and nightclubs. In many ways, the highlight of his war experiences was not a battle or his medal but his adventure after the war was over. With a friend, he went absent without leave and set out to explore Germany. They avoided the military police, traveled on a train illegally, and had many narrow escapes, but they made it back to the hospital without being arrested.

Edmund Arpin was in the army for two years. He was one of 4,791,172 Americans who served in the army, navy, and marines. He was one of the 2 million who went overseas and one of the 230,074 who were wounded. Some of his friends were among the 48,909 who were killed. When he was mustered out of the army in March 1919, he felt lost and confused. Being a civilian was not nearly as exciting as being in the army and visiting new and exotic places.

In time, Arpin settled down. He became a successful businessman, married, and raised a family. A member of the American Legion, he periodically went to conventions and reminisced with men from his division about their escapades in France. Although the war changed their lives in many ways, most would never again feel the same sense of common purpose and adventure. "I don't suppose any of us felt, before or since, so necessary to God and man," one veteran recalled.

For Edmund P. Arpin, Jr., the Great War was the most important event of a lifetime. Just as war changed his life, so, too, did it alter the lives of most Americans. Trends begun during the progressive era accelerated. The power and influence of the federal government increased. Not only did the war promote woman suffrage, prohibition, and public housing, but it also helped create an administrative bureaucracy that blurred the lines between public and private, between government and business—a trend that continued into the twenty-first century.

In this chapter, we examine the complicated circumstances that led the United States into the war and share the wartime experiences of American men and women overseas and at home. We will study not only military actions but also the impact of the war on domestic policies and on the lives of ordinary Americans, including the migration of African Americans into northern cities. The war cut off immigration from Europe and led to a policy of immigrant restriction in the next decade. The war left a legacy of prejudice and hate and raised the basic question, could the tenets of American democracy, such as freedom of speech, survive participation in a major war? The chapter concludes with a look at idealistic efforts to promote peace at the end of the war and the disillusion that followed. Woodrow Wilson's foreign policy, which sought to make the world safe for democracy, marked a watershed in the relationship of the United States to the world. The Great War was global war in every sense, and it thrust the United States into the role of world leadership as an interventionist savior of democratic values. Many Americans were reluctant to accept that role. But whether they liked it or not, the world was a different place in 1919 than it had been in 1914, and that would have a profound influence on American lives.

The Early War Years

Few Americans expected the Great War that erupted in Europe in the summer of 1914 to affect their lives or alter their comfortable world. When a Serbian student terrorist assassinated Archduke Franz Ferdinand of Austria-Hungary in Sarajevo, the capital of the province of Bosnia, a place most Americans had never heard of, the act precipitated a series of events leading to the most destructive war the world had ever known.

The Causes of War

The Great War, as everyone called it at the time, seemed to begin accidentally, but its root causes reached back many years and involved intense rivalry over trade, empire, and military strength. The Great War, which would cost at least 10 million lives and profoundly influence every aspect of culture and society, did not seem inevitable in 1914. There had been wars throughout the nineteenth century, including the Boer War, the Franco-Prussian War, and the American Civil War, but these wars, though bloody, were mostly local. There had not been a major global conflict since the end of the Napoleonic Wars in 1815. In fact, there were many signs of international cooperation, with agreements on telegraphs in 1865, postage in 1875, and copyright in 1880. Most nations had even agreed on international time zones by the 1890s. An international conference at The Hague in the Netherlands in 1899 had set up a World Court to

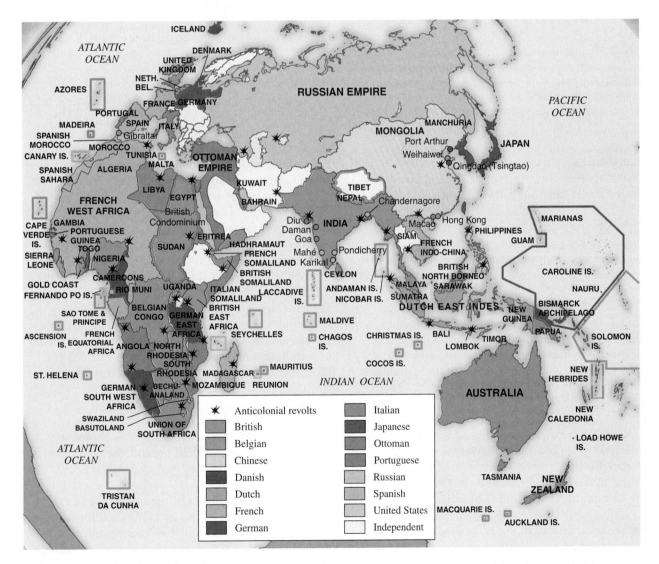

European Empires in 1914

In 1914, European countries had colonies or "spheres of influence" in all parts of the world. Although the United States got into the imperialism game late, it also had an empire and an interest in global trade. European imperialism and competition over trade was very much a factor in the origins of World War I. The war would alter the economic and political map of the world. Which European nations were most powerful in Asia and Africa in 1914? How has this map changed today?

settle disputes before they led to war. Peace advocates and politicians alike promoted disarmament conferences and predicted that better technology and improved communication would lead to permanent peace. "It looks as though we are going to be the age of treaties rather than the age of wars, the century of reason rather than the century of force," a leader of the American peace movement announced.

However, the same forces of improved technology and communication that seemed to bring nations closer together also helped create a rising tide of nationalism—a pride in being French or English or German. In Europe, nations competed over trade, colonies, and spheres of influence in Africa and Asia. Theodore Roosevelt tried to arbitrate differences among Germany, France, and Great Britain over trade at a conference in Morocco in 1905 and 1906, but tension and disagreements remained. At the same time, Austria and Russia clashed over territory and influence in the Balkans, where there was a rising sense of Slavic nationalism. Modern Germany, created from a number of small states in 1871, emerged as a powerful industrial giant. About 1900, Germany began to build a navy large enough to compete with the British fleet, the most powerful in the world. Great Britain, in turn, built even more battleships. As European nations armed, they drew up a complex series of treaties. Austria-Hungary and Germany (the Central Powers) became military allies, and Britain, France, and Russia (the Allied Powers) agreed to assist one another in case of attack. Despite peace conferences and international agreements, many promoted by the United States, the European balance of power rested precariously on layers of treaties that barely obscured years of jealousy and distrust.

The incident in Sarajevo destroyed that balance. The leaders of Austria-Hungary were determined to punish Serbia for the assassination. Russia mobilized to aid Serbia. Germany, supporting Austria-Hungary, declared war on Russia and France. Britain hesitated, but when Germany invaded Belgium to attack France, Britain declared war on Germany. Within a few months, the Ottoman Empire (Turkey) and Bulgaria joined the Central Powers. Italy joined the Allies after being secretly promised additional territory after the war. Japan declared war on Germany not because of an interest in the European struggle but in order to acquire German rights in China's Shantung province and a number of Pacific Islands. Spain, Switzerland, the Netherlands, Denmark, Norway, Sweden, and initially the United States, remained neutral. In August 1914, as Europe rushed toward war, British foreign secretary Sir Edward Grey remarked: "The lamps are going out all over Europe. We shall not see them lit again in our lifetime." His prediction proved to be deadly accurate.

When news of the German invasion of Belgium and reports of the first bloody battles began to reach the United States in late summer, most Americans believed that madness had replaced reason. Europeans "have reverted to the condition of savage tribes roaming the forests and falling upon each other in a fury of blood and carnage," the *New York Times* announced. Woodrow Wilson's official proclamation of neutrality on August 4, 1914, reinforced the belief that the United States had no major stake in the outcome of the war. The president was preoccupied with his own personal tragedy. His wife, Ellen Axson Wilson, died of Bright's disease the day after his proclamation. Two weeks later, still engulfed by grief, he urged all Americans to "be neutral in fact as well as in name,...impartial in thought as well as in action." The United States, he argued, must preserve itself "fit and free" to do what "is honest and disinterested...for the peace of the world." But remaining uninvolved, at least emotionally, was going to be difficult.

American Reactions

Although many Americans worked to promote world peace and a few sought to end the war through mediation, others could hardly wait to take part in the great adventure. Hundreds of young American men, most of them students or recent college graduates, volunteered to join ambulance units in order to take part in the war effort without actually fighting. Among these men were Ernest Hemingway, John Dos Passos, and E. E. Cummings, who later turned their wartime adventures into literary masterpieces. Others volunteered for service with the French Foreign Legion or joined the Lafayette Escadrille, a unit of pilots made up of well-to-do American volunteers attached to the French army. Many of these young men were inspired by an older generation who pictured war as a romantic and manly adventure. One college president talked of the chastening and purifying effect of armed conflict, and Theodore Roosevelt projected an image of war that was something like a football game in which red-blooded American men could test their idealism and manhood.

Many Americans visualized war as a romantic struggle for honor and glory because the only conflict they remembered was the "splendid little war" of 1898. For them, war meant Theodore Roosevelt leading the charge in Cuba and Commodore Dewey destroying the Spanish fleet in Manila harbor with no loss of American life. Many older Americans recalled the Civil War, but the horrors of those years had faded, leaving only the memory of heroic triumphs. As Oliver Wendell Holmes, the Supreme Court justice who had been wounded in the Civil War, remarked, "War, when you are at it, is horrible and dull. It is only when time has passed that you see that its message was divine."

Early reports from the battlefields should have indicated that the message was anything but divine. This would be a modern war in which men died by the thousands, cut down by an improved and efficient technology of killing.

The New Military Technology

Military planners had not anticipated the stalemate that quickly developed. The German Schlieffen plan called for a rapid strike through Belgium to attack Paris and the French army from the rear. However, the French stopped the German advance at the Battle of the Marne in September 1914, and the fighting soon bogged down in a costly and bloody routine. Soldiers on both sides dug miles of trenches and strung out barbed wire. Hundreds of thousands died in battles that gained only a few yards or nothing at all. Rapid-firing rifles, improved explosives, incendiary shells, and tracer bullets all added to the destruction. Most devastating of all, however, was the improved artillery that could fire over the horizon and hit targets many miles behind the lines. Machine guns neutralized frontal assaults, but generals on both sides continued to order their men to charge to almost certain deaths.

The war was both a traditional and a revolutionary struggle. It was the last war in which cavalry was used and the first to employ a new generation of military technologies. By 1918, airplanes, initially used only for observation, were dropping bombs and creating terror below. Tanks first appeared in 1916, but only in the last days of the war did this new offensive weapon begin to neutralize the machine gun. In the spring of 1915, the Germans introduced a terrible new weapon—poison gas. Chlorine gas blinded its victims, caused acid burns on the skin, and consumed the lungs. Gas masks provided some protection but were never entirely effective. Poison gas attacks, used by both sides after 1915, were one of the most terrifying aspects of trench warfare.

For most Americans, the western front, which stretched from Belgium through France, was the most important battleground of the war. But along the eastern front, Russian troops engaged German and Austrian armies in bitter fighting. After Italy joined the conflict in 1915, a third front developed along the northern Italian and Austrian border, while submarines and battleships carried the fight around the world.

The Great War was truly a global struggle. Soldiers from the British Empire, New Zealand, Australia, Canada, and India fought on the western front alongside French-speaking black Africans. The British and the French battled in Africa to capture Germany's African colonies, and the struggle continued until 1918, especially in East Africa. The British, who initially thought they were only going to support the French on the western front, found themselves in the Middle East, in Mesopotamia (Iraq), and fighting Turks in the Dardanelles between the Aegean and the Black Sea. In one of the great disasters of the war, the British attacked Gallipoli, first with battleships and then with hundreds of thousands of men. After losing one-third of their fleet and more than a quarter of a million men, many of them Australians and New Zealanders, the British withdrew. Reports of carnage, on and off the battlefield, poured in. In one of the worst acts of genocide in the world's history, the Turks systematically massacred an estimated 800,000 Armenians. Yet the United States and European countries stood by and did nothing.

Some Americans could hardly wait to join the fighting. Theodore Roosevelt and his friend Leonard Wood, the army chief of staff, led a movement to prepare American men for war. In 1913, Wood established a camp for college men at Plattsburgh, New York, to give them some experience with military life, order, discipline, and command. The young men learned to shoot rifles and to endure long marches and field exercises. Gathered around the campfire at night, they heard veterans tell of winning glory and honor on the battlefield. In their minds at least, they were already leading a bayonet charge against Germany.

Difficulties of Neutrality

Not all Americans were so eager to enter the fray, but many sympathized with one side or the other. Some Americans favored the Central Powers. About 8 million Austrian Americans and German Americans lived in the United States. Some supported their homeland. They viewed Kaiser Wilhelm II's Germany as a progressive parliamentary democracy. The anti-British sentiment of some Irish Americans led them to take sides not so much for Germany as against England. A number of American scholars, physicians, and intellectuals fondly remembered studying in Germany, and they admired its culture and progressive social planning. After all, did not the English-speaking people of the world have special bonds and special responsibilities to promote civilization and ensure justice in the world? American connections with the French were not so close, but they were sentimental. The French, everyone remembered, had supported the American Revolution, and the French people had given the United States the Statue of Liberty, the very symbol of American opportunity and democracy.

Other reasons made real neutrality nearly impossible. U.S. trade with the Allies was much more important than with the Central Powers. Wilson's advisers openly supported the French and the British. Most newspaper owners and editors had close ethnic, cultural, and sometimes economic ties to the British and the French. The newspapers were quick to picture the

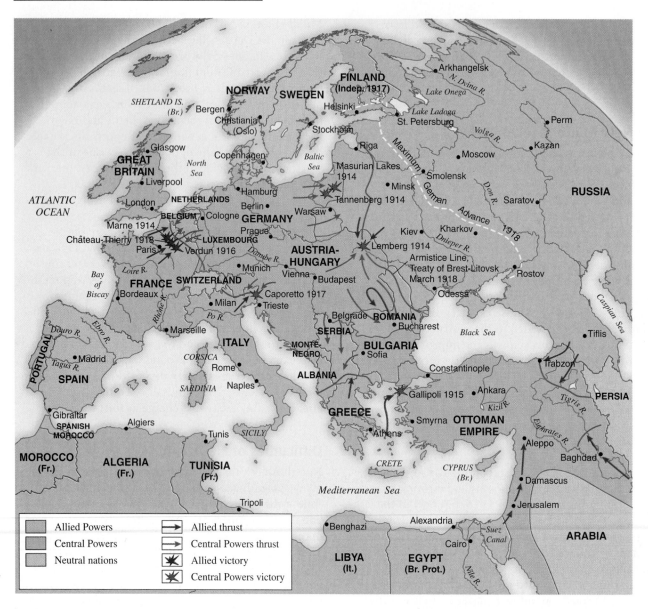

The Great War in Europe and the Middle East

The Great War had an impact not only on Europe but also on North Africa and the Middle East. Even the countries that remained neutral felt the influence of global war. For most Americans, the war was in France on the western front. Where else were major battles fought?

Germans as barbaric Huns and to accept and embellish atrocity stories from the front, some of them planted by British propaganda experts. Gradually for Wilson, and probably for most Americans, the perception that England and France were fighting to preserve civilization from the forces of Prussian evil replaced the idea that all Europeans were barbaric and decadent. But the American people were not yet willing to go to war to save civilization. Let France and England do that.

Woodrow Wilson also sympathized with the Allies for practical and idealistic reasons. He wanted to keep the United States out of the war, but he did not object to using force to promote diplomatic ends. He believed that by keeping the United States out of the war, he

might control the peace. The war, he hoped, would show the futility of imperialism and would usher in a world of free trade in products and ideas. Remaining neutral while maintaining trade with the belligerents became increasingly difficult. Remaining neutral while speaking out about the peace eventually became impossible. The need to trade and the desire to control the peace finally led the United States into the Great War.

World Trade and Neutrality Rights

The United States was part of an international economic community in 1914 and the outbreak of war caused an immediate economic panic. On July 31, 1914, the

Wilson administration closed the stock exchange to prevent the unloading of European securities and panic selling. It also adopted a policy discouraging loans by American banks to belligerent nations. Most difficult was the matter of neutral trade. Wilson insisted on the rights of Americans to trade with both the Allies and the Central Powers, but Great Britain instituted an illegal naval blockade, mined the North Sea, and began seizing American ships, even those carrying food and raw materials to Italy, the Netherlands, and other neutral nations. The first crisis that Wilson faced was whether to accept the illicit British blockade. To do so would be to surrender one of the rights he supported most ardently, the right of free trade.

Wilson eventually accepted British control of the sea. His conviction that the destinies of the United States and Great Britain were intertwined outweighed his idealistic belief in free trade and caused him to react more harshly to German violations of international law than he did to British violators. Consequently, American trade with the Central Powers declined between 1914 and 1916 from $169 million to just over $1 million, whereas trade with the Allies increased during the same period from $825 million to more than $3 billion. At the same time, the U.S. government eased restrictions on private loans to belligerents. With dollars as well as sentiments, the United States gradually ceased to be neutral.

Germany retaliated against British control of the seas with submarine warfare, using its new weapon, the U-boat *(Unterseeboot)*. International law required a belligerent warship to warn a passenger or merchant ship before attacking, but a U-boat rising to the surface to issue a warning would have meant being blown out of the water by an armed merchant ship. On February 4, 1915, Germany announced a submarine blockade of the British Isles. Until Britain gave up its campaign to starve the German population, the Germans would sink even neutral ships. Wilson warned Germany that it would be held to "strict accountability" for illegal destruction of American ships or lives.

In March 1915, a German U-boat sank a British liner en route to Africa, killing 103 people, including one American. How should the United States respond? Wilson's advisers could not agree. Robert Lansing, a legal counsel at the State Department, urged the president to issue a strong protest, charging a breach of international law. William Jennings Bryan, the secretary of state, argued that an American traveling on a British ship was guilty of "contributory negligence" and urged Wilson to prohibit Americans from traveling on belligerent ships in the war zone. Wilson never did settle the dispute, for on May 7, 1915, a greater crisis erupted. A German U-boat torpedoed the British luxury liner *Lusitania* off the Irish coast. The liner, which was not armed but was carrying war supplies, sank in 18 minutes. Nearly 1,200 people, including many women and children, drowned. Among the dead were 128 Americans. Suddenly Americans confronted the horror of total war fought with modern weapons, a war that killed civilians, including women and children, just as easily as it killed soldiers.

Wilson and most Americans had no idea of going to war in the spring of 1915, but the president refused to take Bryan's advice and prevent further loss of American lives by simply prohibiting all Americans from traveling on belligerent ships. Instead, he sent a series of protest notes demanding reparation for the loss of American lives and a pledge from Germany that it would cease attacking ocean liners without warning.

Bryan resigned as secretary of state over the tone of the notes and charged that the United States was not being truly neutral. The president replaced Bryan with Robert Lansing, who was much more eager than Bryan to oppose Germany, even at the risk of war.

The tense situation eased late in 1915. After a German U-boat sank the British steamer *Arabic,* which claimed two American lives, the German ambassador promised that Germany would not attack ocean liners without warning (the *Arabic* pledge). The *Lusitania* crisis caused an outpouring of books and articles urging the nation to prepare for war. However, a group of progressive reformers also formed the American Union Against Militarism. They feared that those urging preparedness were deliberately setting out to destroy social reform at home and to promote imperialism abroad.

Wilson sympathized with the preparedness groups to the extent of asking Congress on November 4, 1915, for an enlarged and reorganized army. The bill met with great opposition, especially from southern and western congressmen, but the Army Reorganization Bill that Wilson signed in June 1916 increased the regular army to just over 200,000 and integrated the National Guard into the defense structure. Few Americans expected those young men to go to war. Even before American soldiers arrived in France, however, Wilson used the army and the marines in Mexico and Central America.

Intervening in Mexico and Central America

Wilson envisioned a world purged of imperialism, a world of free trade, but a world where American ideas and products would find their way. Combining the zeal of a Christian missionary with the conviction of a college professor, he spoke of "releasing the intelligence of America for the service of mankind." Although Wilson denounced the "big stick" and "dollar diplomacy" of the Roosevelt and Taft years, Wilson's administration used force more systematically than did his predecessors. The rhetoric was different, yet just as much as Roosevelt, Wilson tried to maintain stability in countries to the south in order to promote American economic and strategic interests.

At first, Wilson's foreign policy seemed to reverse some of the most callous aspects of dollar diplomacy in Central America. Secretary of State Bryan signed a treaty with Colombia in 1913 in which the United States agreed to pay $5 million for the loss of Panama and virtually apologized for the Roosevelt administration's treatment of Colombia. The Senate, not so willing to admit that the United States had been wrong, refused to ratify the treaty.

The change in spirit proved illusory. After a disastrous civil war in the Dominican Republic, the United States offered in 1915 to take over the country's finances and police force. When the Dominican leaders rejected a treaty making their country virtually a protectorate of the United States, Wilson ordered in the marines. They took control of the government in May 1916. Although Americans built roads, schools, and hospitals, people resented their presence. The United States intervened in Haiti with similar results. In Nicaragua, the Wilson administration kept the marines sent by Taft in 1912 to prop up a pro-American regime and acquired the right, through treaty, to intervene at any time to preserve order and protect American property. Except for a brief period in the mid-1920s, the marines remained until 1933.

Wilson's policy of intervention ran into greatest difficulty in Mexico, a country that had been ruled by dictator Porfirio Díaz, who had long welcomed American investors. By 1910, more than 40,000 American citizens lived in Mexico, and more than $1 billion of American money was invested there. In 1911, however, Francisco Madero, a reformer who wanted to destroy the privileges of the upper classes, overthrew Díaz. Two years later, Madero was deposed and murdered by order of Victoriano Huerta, the head of the army.

Wilson refused to recognize the Huerta government. Everyone admitted that Huerta was a ruthless dictator, but diplomatic recognition, the exchange of ambassadors, and the regulation of trade and communication had never meant approval. In the world of business and diplomacy, it merely meant that a particular government was in power. But Wilson set out to remove what he called a "government of butchers."

At first, Wilson applied diplomatic pressure. Then, using a minor incident as an excuse, he asked Congress for power to involve American troops if necessary. Few Mexicans liked Huerta, but they liked the idea of North American interference even less, and they rallied around the dictator. The United States landed troops at Veracruz, Mexico. Wilson's action outraged many Europeans and Latin Americans as well as Americans.

Wilson's military intervention drove Huerta out of office, but a civil war between forces led by Venustiano Carranza and those led by General Francisco "Pancho" Villa ensued. The United States sent arms to Carranza, who was considered less radical than Villa, and Carranza's soldiers defeated Villa's. When an angry Villa led what was left of his army in a raid on Columbus, New Mexico, in March 1916, Wilson sent an expedition commanded by Brigadier General John Pershing to track down Villa and his men. The strange and comic scene developed of an American army charging 300 miles into Mexico unable to catch the retreating villain. The Mexicans feared that Pershing's army was planning to occupy northern Mexico. Carranza shot off a bitter note to Wilson, accusing him of threatening war, but Wilson refused to withdraw the troops. Tensions rose. An American patrol attacked a Mexican garrison, with loss of life on both sides. In January 1917, just as war seemed inevitable, Wilson agreed to recall the troops and to recognize the Carranza government. Had it not been for the growing crisis in Europe, it is likely that war with Mexico would have resulted.

The United States Enters the War

A significant minority of Americans opposed joining the European war in 1917, and that decision would remain controversial when it was reexamined in the 1930s. But once involved, the government and the American people made the war into a patriotic crusade that influenced all aspects of American life.

The Election of 1916

American political campaigns do not stop even in times of international crisis. As 1915 turned to 1916, Wilson had to think of reelection as well as of preparedness, submarine warfare, and the Mexican campaign. At first glance, the president's chances of reelection seemed poor. If supporters of the Progressives in 1912 returned to the Republican fold, Wilson's chances were slim indeed. Because the Progressive party had done very badly in the 1914 congressional elections, Roosevelt seemed ready to seek the Republican nomination.

Wilson was aware that he had to win over voters who had favored Roosevelt in 1912. In January 1916, he appointed Louis D. Brandeis to the Supreme Court. The first Jew ever to sit on the Court, Brandeis was confirmed over the strong opposition of many legal organizations. His appointment pleased the social justice progressives because he had always championed reform causes. They made it clear to Wilson that the real test for them was whether he supported the anti–child labor and workers' compensation bills pending in Congress.

Within a few months, Wilson reversed his earlier New Freedom doctrines, which called for limited government, and aligned the federal government on the side of reform. In August 1916, Wilson pushed through Congress the Worker's Compensation Bill, which gave some protection to federal employees, and the Keatings–Owen Child Labor Bill, which barred from interstate commerce goods produced by children under age 14 and in some cases under 16. This bill, later declared unconstitutional, was a far-reaching proposal that for the first time used federal control over interstate commerce to dictate the conditions under which businesspeople could manufacture products.

To attract farm support, Wilson pushed for passage of the Federal Farm Loan Act, which created 12 Federal Farm Loan banks to extend long-term credit to farmers. Urged on by organized labor as well as by many progressives, he supported the Adamson Act, which established an eight-hour workday for all interstate railway workers. The flurry of legislation early in 1916 provided one triumph for the progressive movement. The strategy seemed to work, for progressives of all kinds enthusiastically endorsed the president.

The election of 1916, however, turned as much on foreign affairs as on domestic policy. The Republicans ignored Theodore Roosevelt and nominated instead the staid and respectable Charles Evans Hughes, a former governor of New York and future Supreme Court justice. Their platform called for "straight and honest neutrality" and "adequate preparedness." In a bitter campaign, Hughes attacked Wilson for not promoting American rights in Mexico more vigorously and for giving in to the unreasonable demands of labor. Wilson implied that electing Hughes would guarantee war with Mexico and Germany and that his opponents were somehow not "100 percent Americans." As the campaign progressed, the peace issue became more and more important, and the cry "He kept us out of war" echoed through every Democratic rally. The slogan would soon seem strangely ironic.

The election was extremely close. In fact, Wilson went to bed on election night thinking he had lost the presidency. The election was not finally decided until the Democrats carried California (by fewer than 4,000 votes). Wilson won by carrying the West as well as the South.

Deciding for War

Wilson's victory in 1916 seemed to be a mandate for staying out of the European war. Those who supported Wilson as a peace candidate applauded in January 1917 when he went before the Senate to clarify the American position on a negotiated settlement of the war. The German government had earlier indicated that it might be willing to go to the conference table.

Wilson outlined a plan for a negotiated peace without indemnities and annexations. The agreement Wilson outlined contained his idealistic vision of the postwar world as an open marketplace, and it could have worked only if Germany and the Allies were willing to settle for a draw. But neither side was interested in such a conclusion after years of bitter and costly conflict.

The German government refused to accept a peace without victory, probably because early in 1917, the German leaders thought they could win. On January 31, 1917, the Germans announced that they would sink on sight any ship, belligerent or neutral, sailing toward England or France. A few days later, in retaliation, the United States broke diplomatic relations with Germany. An intercepted telegram from the German foreign secretary, Arthur Zimmermann, to the German minister in Mexico increased anti-German feeling. If war broke out, the German minister was to offer Mexico the territory it had lost in Texas, New Mexico, and Arizona in 1848. In return, Mexico would join Germany in a war against the United States. When the Zimmermann note was released to the press on March 1, 1917, many Americans demanded war against Germany. Wilson still hesitated.

As the country waited on the brink of war, news of revolution in Russia reached Washington. That event proved as important as the war itself. The March 1917 revolution in Russia was a spontaneous uprising of workers, housewives, and soldiers against the government of Czar Nicholas II and its conduct of the war. The army had suffered staggering losses at the front. The civilian population was in desperate condition. Food was scarce, and the railroads and industry had nearly collapsed. At first, Wilson and other Americans were enthusiastic about the new republic led by Alexander Kerensky, which promised to continue the struggle against Germany. But on November 6, 1917, the revolution took a more extreme turn. Vladimir Ilyich Ulyanov, known as Lenin, returned from exile in Switzerland and led the radical Bolsheviks to victory over the Kerensky regime. He immediately signed an armistice with Germany that released thousands of German troops, who had been fighting the Russians, to join the battle against the Allies on the western front.

Lenin, a brilliant lawyer and revolutionary tactician, was a follower of Karl Marx (1818–1883). Marx was a German intellectual and radical philosopher who had described the alienation of the working class under capitalism and predicted a growing split between the proletariat (the unpropertied workers) and the capitalists. Lenin extended Marx's ideas and argued that capitalist nations eventually would be forced to go to war over raw materials and markets. Believing that capitalism and imperialism went hand in hand, Lenin argued that the only way to end imperialism was to end capitalism. Communism, Lenin predicted, would eventually dominate the globe, and the new Soviet Union, not the United States, would be the model for the rest of the world to follow. The Russian Revolution threatened Wilson's vision of the world and his plan to bring the United States into the war "to make the world safe for democracy."

More disturbing than the revolution in Russia, however, was the situation in the North Atlantic, where German U-boats sank five American ships between March 12 and March 21, 1917. Wilson no longer hesitated. On April 2, he urged Congress to declare war. His words conveyed a sense of mission about the country's entry into the war, but Wilson's voice was low and somber. "It is a fearful thing," he concluded, "to lead this great, peaceful people into war, into the most terrible and disastrous of all wars." The war resolution swept the Senate 82 to 6 and the House of Representatives 373 to 50.

Once war was declared, most Americans forgot their doubts. Young men rushed to enlist; women volunteered to become nurses or to serve in other ways. Towns were united by patriotism.

A Patriotic Crusade

Not all Americans applauded the declaration of war. Some pacifists and socialists and a few others opposed America's entry into the war. "To whom does war bring prosperity?" Senator George Norris of Nebraska asked on the Senate floor. "Not to the soldier,...not to the broken hearted widow,...not to the mother who weeps at the death of her brave boy....I feel that we are about to put the dollar sign on the American flag."

For most Americans in the spring of 1917, the war seemed remote. A few days after war was declared, a Senate committee listened to a member of the War Department staff list the vast quantities of materials needed to supply an American army in France. One of the senators, jolted awake, exclaimed, "Good Lord! You're not going to send soldiers over there, are you?"

To convince senators and citizens alike that the war was real and that American participation was just, Wilson appointed a Committee on Public Information, headed by George Creel, a muckraking journalist from Denver. The Creel Committee launched a gigantic propaganda campaign to persuade the American public that the United States had gone to war to promote the cause of freedom and democracy and to prevent the barbarous hordes from overrunning Europe and eventually the Western Hemisphere.

The patriotic crusade soon became stridently anti-German and anti-immigrant. Most school districts banned the teaching of German. Sauerkraut

was renamed "liberty cabbage," and German measles became "liberty measles." Many families Americanized their German surnames. Several cities banned music by German composers from symphony concerts. South Dakota prohibited the use of German on the telephone. Occasionally, the patriotic fever led to violence. The most notorious incident occurred in East St. Louis, Illinois, which had a large German population. A mob seized Robert Prager, a young German American, in April 1918, stripped off his clothes, dressed him in an American flag, marched him through the streets, and lynched him. The eventual trial acquitted the ringleaders on the ground that the lynching was a "patriotic murder."

The Wilson administration did not condone domestic violence and murder, but heated patriotism led to irrational hatreds and fears. Suspect were not only German Americans but also radicals, pacifists, and anyone who raised doubts about the American war efforts or the government's policies. The Los Angeles police ignored complaints that Mexicans were being harassed, because after learning of the Zimmermann telegram they believed that all Mexicans were pro-German. In Wisconsin, Senator Robert La Follette, who had voted against the war resolution, was burned in effigy and censured by the faculty of the University of Wisconsin. At a number of universities, professors were dismissed, some for as little as questioning the morality or the necessity of America's participation in the war.

On June 15, 1917, Congress, at Wilson's behest, passed the Espionage Act, which provided imprisonment of up to 20 years or a fine of up to $10,000, or both, for people who aided the enemy or who "willfully cause...insubordination, disloyalty, mutiny or refusal of duty in the military...forces of the United States." The act also authorized the postmaster general to prohibit from the mails any matter he thought advocated treason or forcible resistance to U.S. laws. The act was used to stamp out dissent, even to discipline anyone who questioned the administration's policies.

Congress later added the Trading with the Enemy Act and a Sedition Act. The latter prohibited disloyal, profane, scurrilous, and abusive remarks about the form of government, flag, or uniform of the United States. It even prohibited citizens from opposing the purchase of war bonds. For delivering a speech denouncing capitalism and the war, Socialist party leader Eugene Debs was convicted of violating the Sedition Act and sentenced to 10 years in prison. In 1919, the Supreme Court upheld the conviction, even though Debs had not explicitly urged violation of the draft laws. While still in prison, Debs polled close to 1 million votes in the presidential election of 1920.

"At Last a Perfect Soldier"

This antiwar, antimilitary cartoon appeared in the American radical magazine *The Masses* in July 1916. *The Masses* was an irreverent journal that for a few years published important articles and illustrations by leading artists. It was shut down as subversive during the war by the U.S. government. How does this image contrast to the usual depiction of the soldier as hero? Do you agree with this image of the soldier today?

(*The Masses,* 8, July 1916, [back cover]/The Tamiment Institute Library, New York University)

Ultimately, the government prosecuted 2,168 people under the Espionage and Sedition Acts and convicted about half of them. These figures do not include thousands who were informally persecuted and deprived of their liberties and their right of free speech.

One woman was sentenced to prison for writing, "I am for the people and the government is for the profiteers." Ricardo Flores Magon, a leading Mexican American labor organizer and radical in the Southwest, was sentenced to 20 years in prison for criticizing Wilson's Mexican policy and violating the Neutrality Acts. The attorney general of the United States, speaking of critics, said, "May God have mercy on them for they need expect none from an outraged people and an avenging government."

The Civil Liberties Bureau, an outgrowth of the American Union Against Militarism, protested the blatant abridgment of freedom of speech during the war, but the protests fell on deaf ears at the Justice Department and in the White House. Rights and freedoms have been reduced or suspended during all wars, but the massive disregard for basic rights was greater during World War I than during the Civil War. This was ironic because Wilson had often written and spoken of the need to preserve freedom of speech and civil liberties. During the war, however, he tolerated the vigilante tactics of his own Justice Department, offering no more than feeble protest. Wilson was so convinced his cause was just that he ignored the rights of those who opposed him.

Raising an Army

Debate over a volunteer army versus the draft had been going on for several years before the United States entered the war. People who favored some form of universal military service argued that college graduates, farmers, and young men from the slums of eastern cities could learn from one another as they trained together. Opponents of a draft pointed out that people making such claims were most often the college graduates, who assumed they would command the boys from the slums. The draft was not democratic, they argued, but the tool of an imperialist power bent on ending dissent. Memories of massive draft riots during the Civil War also led some to fear a draft.

Wilson and his secretary of war, Newton Baker, both initially opposed the draft. In the end, both concluded that it was the most efficient way to organize military personnel. Ironically, it was Theodore Roosevelt who tipped Wilson in favor of the draft. Even though his health was failing and he was blind in one eye, the old Rough Rider was determined to recruit a volunteer division and lead it personally against the Germans. The thought of his old enemy Theodore Roosevelt blustering about Europe so frightened Wilson that he supported the Selective Service Act in part, at least, to prevent such volunteer outfits as Roosevelt planned. Congress argued over the bill, the House insisting that the minimum age for draftees should be 21, not 18. On June 5, 1917, some 9.5 million men between ages 21 and 31 registered, with little protest. In August 1918, Congress extended the act to men between ages 18 and 45. In all, more than 24 million men registered and more than 2.8 million were inducted, making up more than 75 percent of soldiers who served in the war.

The draft worked well, but it was not quite the perfect system that Wilson claimed. Draft protests erupted in a few places, the largest in Oklahoma, where a group of tenant farmers planned a march on Washington to take over the government and end the "rich man's war." But the Green Corn Rebellion, as it came to be called, died before it got started. A local posse arrested about 900 rebels and took them off to jail.

Some men escaped the draft. Some were deferred because of war-related jobs, and others resisted by claiming exemption for reasons of conscience. The Selective Service Act did exempt men who belonged to religious groups that forbade members from engaging in war, but religious motivation was often difficult to define, and nonreligious conscientious objection was even more complicated. Thousands of conscientious objectors were inducted. Some served in noncombat positions; others went to prison.

The Military Experience

Family albums in millions of American homes contain photographs of those who were drafted or volunteered: young men in uniform, some of them stiff and formal, some of them candid shots of soldiers on leave in Paris or Washington or Chicago. These photographs testify to the importance of the war to a generation of Americans. For some, the war was a tragic event, as they saw the horrors of the battlefield firsthand. For others, it was a liberating experience and the most exciting period of their lives.

The American Soldier

The typical soldier, according to the U.S. Medical Department, stood 5 feet $7\frac{1}{2}$ inches tall, weighed $141\frac{1}{2}$ pounds, and was 22 years old. He took a physical exam, an intelligence test, and a psychological test, and he probably watched a movie called *Fit to Fight*, which warned him about the dangers of venereal disease. The majority of American soldiers had not attended high school. The median level of education for native whites was 6.9 years, 4.7 years for immigrants, and just 2.6 years for southern blacks. As many as 31 percent of the recruits were declared illiterate, but the intelligence tests were so primitive that they probably tested social class more than anything else. Fully 29 percent of recruits were rejected as physically unfit for service, a finding that shocked health experts.

Most World War I soldiers were ill-educated and unsophisticated young men from farms, small towns, and urban neighborhoods. They came from all social classes and ethnic groups. The military experience changed the lives and often the attitudes of many young men and some women. Women contributed to the war effort as telephone operators and clerk typists in the navy and the marines. Some went overseas as army and navy nurses. Others volunteered with the Red Cross, the Salvation Army, or the YMCA. Yet the military experience in World War I was predominantly male. Even going to training camp was a new and often frightening experience. A leave in Paris or London, or even in New York or New Orleans, was an adventure to remember for a lifetime. Many soldiers saw their first movie in the army or had their first contact with trucks and cars. Military service changed the shaving habits of a generation because the new safety razor was standard issue. The war also led to the growing popularity of cigarettes rather than pipes or cigars because a pack of cigarettes fit into a shirt pocket and a cigarette could be smoked during a short break. The war experience also caused many men to abandon the pocket watch for the more convenient wristwatch, which had been considered effeminate before the war.

The Black Soldier

Blacks had served in all American wars, and many fought valiantly in the Civil War and the Spanish-American War. Yet black soldiers had most often performed menial work and belonged to segregated units. Most black leaders supported American participation in the war. W. E. B. Du Bois, editor of *The Crisis*, predicted that the war experience would cause the "walls of prejudice" to crumble gradually before the "onslaught of common sense." But the walls did not crumble, and the black soldier never received equal or fair treatment during the war.

The Selective Service Act made no mention of race, and African Americans in most cases registered without protest. Many whites, especially in the South, feared having too many blacks trained in the use of arms. In some areas, draft boards exempted single white men but drafted black fathers. Most southern whites found it difficult to imagine a black man in the uniform of the U.S. Army.

White attitudes toward African Americans sometimes led to conflict. In August 1917, violence erupted in Houston, Texas, involving soldiers from the regular army's all-black Twenty-Fourth Infantry Division. Harassed by the Jim Crow laws, which had been tightened for their benefit, a group of soldiers went on a rampage, killing 17 white civilians. More than 100 soldiers were court-martialed; 13 were condemned to death. Those convicted were hanged three days later before any appeals could be filed.

This violence, coming only a month after the race riot in East St. Louis, Illinois, brought on in part by the migration of southern blacks to the area, caused great concern about the handling of African American soldiers. Secretary of War Baker made it clear that the army had no intention of upsetting the status quo. The basic government policy was complete segregation and careful distribution of black units throughout the country.

African Americans were prohibited from joining the marines and restricted to menial jobs in the navy. Some African Americans were trained as junior

GOVERNMENT PROPAGANDA

All governments produce propaganda. Especially in time of war, governments try to convince their citizens that the cause is important and worthwhile even if it means sacrifice. Before the United States entered World War I, both Great Britain and Germany presented their side of the conflict through stories planted in newspapers, photographs, and other devices. Some historians argue that the British propaganda depicting the Germans as barbaric Huns who killed little boys and Catholic nuns played a large role in convincing Americans of the righteousness of the Allied cause.

When the United States entered the war, a special committee under the direction of George Creel did its best to persuade Americans that the war was a crusade against evil. The committee organized a national network of "four-minute men," local citizens with the proper political views who could be used to whip up a crowd into a patriotic frenzy. These local rallies, enlivened by bands and parades, urged people of all ages to support the war effort and buy war bonds. The Creel Committee also produced literature for the schools, much of it prepared by college professors who volunteered their services. One pamphlet, titled *Why America Fights Germany,* described in lurid detail a possible German invasion of the United States. The committee also used the new technology of motion pictures, which proved to be the most effective propaganda device of all.

There is a narrow line between education and propaganda. As early as 1910, Thomas Edison made films instructing the public about the dangers of tuberculosis, and others produced movies that demonstrated how to avoid everything from typhoid to tooth decay. However, during the war, the government quickly realized the power of the new medium and adopted it to train soldiers, instill patriotism, and help the troops avoid the temptations of alcohol and sex.

After the United States entered World War I, the Commission of Training Camp Activities made a film called *Fit to Fight* that was shown to almost all male servicemen. It was an hour-long drama following the careers of five young recruits. Four of them, by associating with the wrong people and through lack of willpower, caught venereal disease. The film interspersed a simplistic plot with grotesque shots of men with various kinds of venereal disease. The film also glorified athletics, especially football and boxing, as a substitute for sex. It emphasized the importance of patriotism and purity for America's fighting force. In one scene, Bill Hale, the only soldier in the film to remain pure, breaks up a peace rally and beats up the speaker. "It serves you right," the pacifist's sister remarks, "I'm glad Billy punched you."

Liberty Bond propaganda

(The Granger Collection, New York)

Fit to Fight was so successful that the government commissioned another film, *The End of the Road,* to be shown to women who lived near military bases. The film is the story of Vera and Mary. Although still reflecting progressive attitudes, the film's message is somewhat different from that of *Fit to Fight.* Vera's strict mother tells her daughter that sex is dirty, leaving Vera to pick up "distorted and obscene" information about sex on the street. She falls victim to the first man who comes along and contracts a venereal disease. Mary, in contrast, has an enlightened mother who explains where babies come from. When Mary grows up, she rejects marriage and becomes a professional woman, a nurse. In the end, she falls in love with a doctor and gets married. *The End of the Road* has a number of subplots and many frightening shots of syphilitic sores. Several illustrations show the dangers of indiscriminate sex. Among other things, the

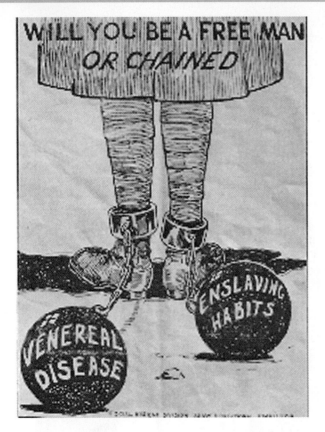

Anti-VD poster issued by the U.S. Commission on Training Camp Activities

(Army Educational Commission)

Scene from *Fit to Fight*

(War Department, Commission on Training Camps)

film preached the importance of science and sex education and the need for self-control.

Reflecting on the Past What do the anti-VD films tell us about the attitudes, ideas, and prejudices of the World War I period? What images do they project about men, women, and gender roles? Would you find the same kind of moralism, patriotism, and fear of VD today? How have attitudes toward sex changed? Were you shown sex education films in school? Were they like these? Who sponsored them? What can historians learn from such films? Does the government produce propaganda today? ▪

officers in the army, but they were assigned to the all-black Ninety-Second Division, where the high-ranking officers were white. Most of the black soldiers, including about 80 percent of those sent to France, worked as stevedores and common laborers under the supervision of white, noncommissioned officers. "Everyone who has handled colored labor knows that the gang bosses must be white if any work is to be done," remarked Lieutenant Colonel U. S. Grant, the grandson of the Civil War general. Other black soldiers acted as servants, drivers, and porters for the white officers. It was a demeaning and ironic policy for a government that advertised itself as standing for justice, honor, and democracy.

Over There

The conflict that Wilson called the war "to make the world safe for democracy" had become a contest of stalemate and slaughter. To this ghastly war, Americans made important contributions. In fact, without their help, the Allies might have lost. But the American contribution was most significant only in the war's final months. When the United States entered the conflict in the spring of 1917, the fighting had dragged on for nearly three years. After a few rapid advances and retreats, the war in western Europe had settled down to a tactical and bloody stalemate. The human costs of trench warfare were horrifying. In one battle in 1916, a total of 60,000 British soldiers were killed or wounded

Entertaining Black Servicemen

Assigned to segregated units, black soldiers were also excluded from white recreation facilities. Here black women from Newark, New Jersey, aided by white social workers, entertain black servicemen. How do you think black men felt about fighting for freedom in a segregated army?

(National Archives)

in a single day, yet the battle lines did not move an inch. By the spring of 1917, the British and French armies were down to their last reserves. Italy's army had nearly collapsed. In the East, the Russians were engaged in a bitter internal struggle, and in November, the Bolshevik Revolution would cause them to sue for a separate peace, freeing the German divisions on the eastern front to join in one final assault in the West. The Allies desperately needed fresh American troops, but those troops had to be trained, equipped, and transported to the front. That took time.

A few token American regiments arrived in France in the summer of 1917 under the command of General John J. "Black Jack" Pershing, a tall, serious, Missouri-born graduate of West Point. He had fought in the Spanish-American War and led the expedition to track down Pancho Villa in Mexico in 1916. When the first troops marched in a parade in Paris on July 4, 1917, the emotional French crowd shouted, *"Vive les Américains"* and showered them with flowers, hugs, and kisses. But the American commanders worried that many of their soldiers were so inexperienced they did not even know how to march, let alone fight. The first Americans saw action near Verdun in October 1917. By March 1918, more than 300,000 American soldiers had reached France, and by November 1918, more than 2 million.

One reason that the U.S. forces were slow to see combat was Pershing's insistence that they be kept separate from the French and British divisions. An exception was made for four regiments of black

soldiers who were assigned to the French army. These soldiers fought so well that the French later awarded three of the regiments the Croix de Guerre, their highest unit citation.

In the spring of 1918, with Russia out of the war and the British blockade becoming more and more effective, the Germans launched an all-out, desperate offensive to win the war before full American military and industrial power became a factor. By late May, the Germans had pushed to within 50 miles of Paris. American troops were thrown into the line and helped stem the German advance at Château-Thierry, Belleau Wood, and Cantigny, place names that proud survivors would later endow with almost sacred significance. Americans also took part in the Allied offensive led by General Ferdinand Foch of France in the summer of 1918.

In September, more than half a million American troops fought near St. Mihiel; this was the first battle in which large numbers of Americans were pressed into action. One enlisted man remembered that he "saw a sight which I shall never forget. It was zero hour and in one instant the entire front as far as the eye could reach in either direction was a sheet of flame, while the heavy artillery made the earth quake." The Americans suffered more than 7,000 casualties, but they captured more than 16,000 German soldiers. The victory, even if it came against exhausted and retreating German troops, seemed to vindicate Pershing's insistence on a separate American army. British and French commanders were critical of

Deadly Weapons of the Great War
New technology made the Great War more horrible in some ways than past wars. British soldiers wearing primitive gas masks operate a Vickers machine gun. The machine gun effectively neutralized the tactic of massive infantry charges, while poison gas attacks increased the number of soldiers with "shell shock" or mental illness. How has war changed since 1918? Is mental illness still a factor among soldiers in time of war?

(Imperial War Museum, London)

what they considered the disorganized, inexperienced, and ill-equipped American forces.

In the fall of 1918, the combined British, French, and American armies drove the Germans back. Faced with low morale among the German soldiers, the mutiny of the German fleet, and the surrender of Austria, Kaiser Wilhelm II abdicated on November 8, and the armistice was signed on November 11. More than 1 million American soldiers took part in the final Allied offensive near the Meuse River and the Argonne forest. Many of the men were inexperienced, and some, who had been rushed through training as "90-day wonders," had never handled a rifle before arriving in France. There were many disastrous mistakes and bungled situations. The most famous blunder was the "lost battalion." An American unit advanced beyond its support and was cut off and surrounded. The battalion suffered 70 percent casualties before being rescued.

The performance of the all-black Ninety-Second Division was also controversial. The Ninety-Second had been deliberately dispersed around the United States and had never trained as a unit. Its higher officers were white, and they repeatedly asked to be transferred. Many of its men were only partly trained and poorly equipped, and they were continually being called away from their military duties to work as stevedores and common laborers. At the last minute during the Meuse-Argonne offensive, the Ninety-Second was assigned to a particularly difficult position on the line. They had no maps and no wire-cutting equipment. Battalion commanders lost contact with their men, and on several occasions, the men broke and ran in the face

of enemy fire. The division was withdrawn in disgrace, and for years politicians and military leaders used this incident to point out that black soldiers would never make good fighting men, ignoring the difficulties under which the Ninety-Second fought and the valor shown by black troops assigned to the French army.

The war produced a few American heroes. Joseph Oklahombie, a Choctaw, overran several German

WORLD WAR I LOSSES

The total cost of the war was estimated at more than $330 billion. The cost in human life was even more horrible. The number of known dead was placed at about 10 million men and the wounded at about 20 million, distributed among chief combatants as follows (round numbers). Which countries bore the brunt of the dead and wounded? How did this influence the peace settlement?

	Dead	Wounded	Prisoner
Great Britain	947,000	2,122,000	192,000
France	1,385,000	3,044,000	446,000
Russia	1,700,000	4,950,000	500,000
Italy	460,000	947,000	530,000
United States	115,000	206,000	4,500
Germany	1,808,000	4,247,000	618,000
Austria-Hungary	1,200,000	3,620,000	200,000
Turkey	325,000	400,000	—

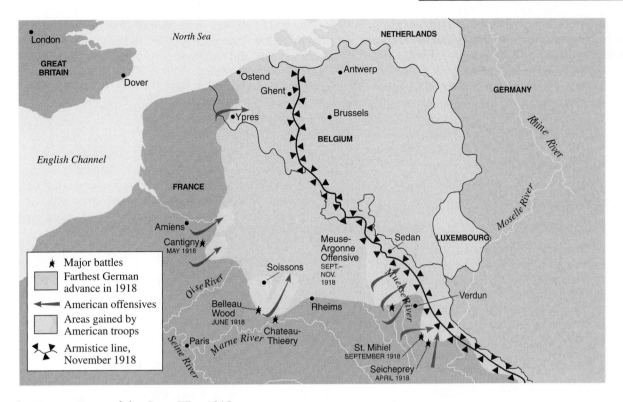

Western Front of the Great War, 1918

For more than three years, the war settled down to a bloody stalemate on the western front. But in 1918, American soldiers played important roles in the Allied offensive that finally ended the war. What can you learn about tactics and strategy during the Great War from studying this map?

machine gun nests and captured more than 100 German soldiers. Sergeant Alvin York, a former conscientious objector from Tennessee, single-handedly killed or captured 160 Germans using only his rifle and pistol. The press made him a celebrity, but his heroics were not typical. Artillery, machine guns, and, near the end, tanks, trucks, and airplanes won the war.

With few exceptions, the Americans fought hard and well. Although the French and British criticized American inexperience and disarray, they admired their exuberance, their "pep," and their ability to move large numbers of men and equipment efficiently. Sometimes Americans simply overwhelmed the enemy with their numbers. They suffered more than 120,000 casualties in the Meuse-Argonne campaign alone. One officer estimated that he lost 10 soldiers for every German his men killed in the final offensive.

The United States entered the war late but still lost more than 48,000 service personnel and had many more wounded. Disease claimed 15 of every 1,000 soldiers each year (compared with 65 per 1,000 in the Civil War). But American losses were tiny compared to those suffered by the European armies. The British lost 900,000 men, the French 1.4 million, and the Russians 1.7 million. Nor was the financial burden as costly for the United States as for its Allies. American units fired French artillery pieces; American soldiers were usually transported in British ships and wore helmets and other equipment modeled after the British. The United States purchased clothing and blankets, even horses, in Europe. American fliers, including heroes such as Eddie Rickenbacker, flew French and British planes. The United States contributed huge amounts of men and supplies in the last months of the war, and that finally tipped the balance. But it had entered late and sacrificed little compared with France and England. That would influence the peace settlement.

A Global Pandemic

The end of the Great War brought relief and joy to many, but in the fall of 1918 an influenza pandemic swept around the world, killing an estimated 50 million people, with 675,000 deaths in the United States in a little more than a year. The Spanish Flu, as it was called (although there is no evidence that it originated in Spain), seems to have started at about the same time in Europe, Asia, America, and even in remote Eskimo villages. Only a small percentage of those who caught the disease died from it, but unlike most epidemics, it hit hardest among young adults. More than 43,000 American servicemen died from the flu (almost as many as died on the battlefield). Early in the epidemic, rumors blamed German germ warfare for the disease, but the

German army was infected as well. No antibiotics or shots could prevent or cure the disease, and the surgical masks required in some cities did no good. Even President Wilson came near death from the disease in the spring of 1919. The flu of 1918–1919 killed more people in a short time than any event in human history, perhaps 20 million worldwide. The speed with which the disease spread around the world was another reminder of how the modern world was interconnected and isolation was impossible.

Domestic Impact of the War

For at least 30 years before the United States entered the Great War, a debate raged over the proper role of the federal government in regulating industry and protecting people who could not protect themselves. Controversy also centered on the question of how much power the federal government should have to tax and control individuals and corporations and the proper relation of the federal government to state and local governments. The war and the problems it raised increased the power of the federal government in a variety of ways. The wartime experience did not end the debate, but the United States emerged from the war a more modern nation, with more power residing in Washington.

Financing the War

The war, by one calculation, cost the United States more than $33 billion. Interest and veterans' benefits bring the total to nearly $112 billion. Early on, when an economist suggested that the war might cost the United States $10 billion, everyone laughed. Yet many in the Wilson administration knew the war was going to be expensive, and they set out to raise the money by borrowing and by increasing taxes.

Secretary of the Treasury William McAdoo was in charge of financing the war. Studying the policies that treasury secretary Salmon Chase had followed during the Civil War, he decided that Chase had made a mistake in not appealing to the emotions of the people. A war must be a "kind of crusade," he remarked. He also learned from the British, French, and German propaganda campaigns. McAdoo's campaign to sell liberty bonds to ordinary American citizens at a very low interest rate appealed to American loyalty. "Lick a Stamp and Lick the Kaiser," one poster urged. Celebrities such as film stars Mary Pickford and Douglas Fairbanks promoted the bonds, and McAdoo employed the Boy Scouts to sell them.

The public responded enthusiastically, but they discovered after the war that their bonds had dropped to about 80 percent of face value. Because the interest on the bonds was tax exempt, well-to-do citizens profited more from buying the bonds than did ordinary men, women, and children. But the wealthy were not as pleased with McAdoo's other plan to finance the war: raising taxes. The War Revenue Act of 1917 boosted the tax rate sharply, levied a tax on excess profits, and increased estate taxes. The next year, another bill raised the tax on the largest incomes to 77 percent. The wealthy protested, but a number of progressives were just as unhappy with the bill, for they wanted to confiscate all income over $100,000 a year. Despite taxes and liberty bonds, however, World War I, like the Civil War, was financed in large part by inflation. Food prices, for example, nearly doubled between 1917 and 1919.

Increasing Federal Power

The major wars of the twentieth century made huge demands on the nations that fought them and helped transform their governments. At first, Wilson tried to work through a variety of state agencies to mobilize the nation's resources. The need for more centralized control and authority soon led Wilson to create a series of federal agencies to deal with the war emergency. The first crisis was food. Poor grain crops for two years and an increasing demand for American food in Europe caused shortages. Wilson appointed Herbert Hoover, a young engineer who had won great prestige as head of the Commission for Relief of Belgium, to direct the Food Administration. Hoover instituted a series of "wheatless" and "meatless" days and urged housewives to cooperate. Women emerged during the war as the most important group of consumers. The government urged them to save, just as later it would urge them to buy.

The Wilson administration used the authority of the federal government to organize resources for the war effort. The War Industries Board, led by Bernard Baruch, a shrewd Wall Street broker, used the power of the government to control scarce materials and, on occasion, to set prices and priorities. Cooperation among government, business, and university scientists to promote research and develop new products was one legacy of the war. The government itself went into the shipbuilding business and ran the railroads. When a severe winter and a lack of coordination brought the rail system near collapse in December 1917, Wilson put all the nation's railroads under the control of the United Railway Administration. The government spent more than $500 million to improve the rails and equipment, and in 1918, the railroads did run more efficiently than they had under private control. Some businessmen complained of "war socialism" and of increased rules and regulations. Like it or not, the war increased the influence of the federal government.

War Workers

The Wilson administration sought to protect and extend the rights of organized labor during the war, while mobilizing the workers necessary to keep the factories running. The National War Labor Board insisted on adequate wages and reduced hours, and it tried to prevent exploitation of women and children working under government contracts. On one occasion, when a munitions plant refused to accept the War Labor Board's decision, the government simply took over the factory. When workers threatened to strike for better wages or hours or for greater control over the workplace, the board often ruled that they either work or be drafted into the army.

The Wilson administration favored the conservative labor movement of Samuel Gompers and the AFL, and the Justice Department put the radical Industrial Workers of the World "out of business." Beginning in September 1917, federal agents conducted massive raids on IWW offices and arrested most of its leaders.

Gompers took advantage of the crisis to strengthen the AFL's position to speak for labor. He supported the administration policies by making it clear that he opposed the IWW as well as socialists and communists. Convincing Wilson that it was important to protect the rights of organized labor during wartime, he announced that "no other policy is compatible with the spirit and methods of democracy." As the AFL won a voice in home-front policy, its membership increased from 2.7 million in 1916 to more than 4 million in 1917. Organized labor's wartime gains, however, would prove only temporary.

The war opened up industrial employment opportunities for black men. With 4 million men in the armed forces and the flow of immigrants interrupted by the war, American manufacturers for the first time hired African Americans in large numbers. In Chicago before the war, only 3,000 black men held factory jobs; in 1920, more than 15,000 did.

Northern labor agents and the railroads actively recruited southern blacks, but the news of jobs in northern cities spread by word of mouth as well. By 1920, more than 300,000 blacks had joined the "great migration" north. This massive movement of people, which continued into the 1920s, had a permanent impact on the South as well as on the northern cities. Like African Americans, thousands of Mexicans

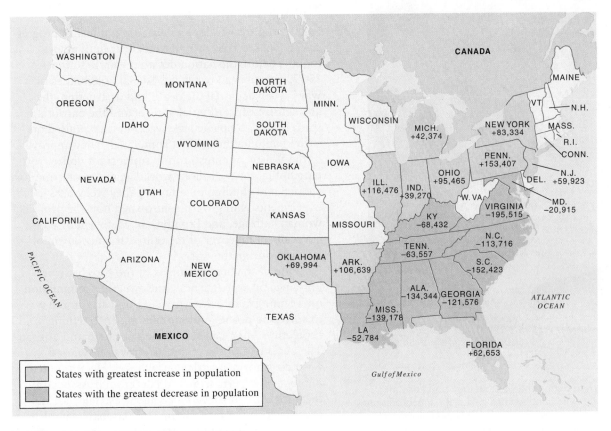

African American Migration, 1910–1920

This map illustrates the massive migration of African Americans from the South to the North during the Great War. Most moved to find better jobs, but in the process they changed the dynamics of race relations in the country. What other changes resulted from this migration?

headed north into the United States, as immigration officials relaxed the regulations because of the need for labor in the farms and factories of the Southwest.

The war also created new employment opportunities for women. Posters and patriotic speeches urged women to do their duty for the war effort. One poster showed a woman at her typewriter, the shadow of a soldier in the background, with the message: "STENOGRAPHERS, WASHINGTON NEEDS YOU." Women responded to these appeals out of patriotism, as well as out of a need to increase their earnings and to make up for inflation, which diminished real wages. Women went into every kind of industry. They labored in brickyards and in heavy industry, became conductors on the railroad, and turned out shells in munitions plants. They even organized the Woman's Land Army to mobilize female labor for the farms. They demonstrated that women could do any kind of job, whatever the physical or intellectual demands. Black women left domestic service for jobs in textile mills, even in the stockyards. However, racial discrimination, even in the North, prevented them from moving too far up the occupational ladder.

Even though women demonstrated that they could take over jobs once thought suitable only for men, their progress during the war proved temporary. Only about 5 percent of the women employed during the war were new to the workforce, and almost all of them were unmarried. For most, it meant a shift of occupations or a move up to a better-paying position. Moreover, the war accelerated trends already underway. It increased the need for telephone operators, sales personnel, secretaries, and other white-collar workers, and in these occupations, women soon became a majority. Telephone operator, for example, became an almost exclusively female job. By 1917, women represented 99 percent of all operators as the telephone network spanned the nation.

The war provided limited opportunities for some women, but it did not change the dominant perception that a woman's place was in the home. After the war was over, the men returned, and the gains made by women almost disappeared. There were 8 million women in the workforce in 1910 but only 8.5 million in 1920.

The Climax of Progressivism

Many progressives, especially the social justice progressives, opposed U.S. entry into the war until a few months before the nation declared war. But after April 1917, many began to see the "social possibilities of war." They deplored the death and destruction, the abridgment of freedom of speech, and the patriotic spirit that accompanied the war. But they praised the social planning the conflict stimulated. They approved of the Wilson administration's support for collective bargaining, the eight-hour workday, and protection for women and children in industry. They welcomed the experiments with government-owned housing projects, woman suffrage, and Prohibition. Many endorsed the government takeover of the railroads and control of business during the war.

One of the best examples of the progressives' influence on wartime activities was the Commission on Training Camp Activities, set up early in the war to solve the problem of mobilizing, entertaining, and protecting American servicemen at home and abroad. The chairman of the commission was Raymond Fosdick, a former settlement worker. He appointed a number of experts from the Playground Association, the YMCA, and social work agencies. They set out to organize community singing and baseball, establish post exchanges and theaters, and even provide university extension lectures to educate the servicemen. The overriding assumption was that the military experience would help produce citizens who would

Icewomen

Women proved during the war that they could do "men's work." These two young women deliver ice, a backbreaking task, but one that was necessary in the days before electric refrigerators. Despite women like these, the war did not change the American ideal that women's proper place was in the home. Has that ideal changed since 1918?

(National Archives)

be ready to vote for social reform once they returned to civilian life.

The Commission on Training Camp Activities also incorporated the progressive crusades against alcohol and prostitution. The Military Draft Act prohibited the sale of liquor to men in uniform and gave the president power to establish zones around military bases where prostitution and alcohol would be prohibited. Some military commanders protested, and at least one city official argued that prostitutes were "God-provided means for the prevention of the violation of innocent girls, by men who are exercising their 'God-given passions.'" Yet the commission, with the full cooperation of the Wilson administration, set out to wipe out sin, or at least to put it out of the reach of servicemen. "Fit to fight" became the motto. It was a typical progressive effort combining moral indignation with the use of the latest scientific prophylaxis. The commissioners prided themselves on having eliminated all the red-light districts near the training camps by 1918. When the boys go to France, the secretary of war remarked, "I want them to have invisible armour to take with them. I want them to have armour made up of a set of social habits replacing those of their homes and communities."

France tested the "invisible armour." The government, despite hundreds of letters of protest from American mothers, decided that it could not prevent the soldiers from drinking wine in France, but it could forbid them to buy or accept as gifts anything but light wine and beer.

Sex was even more difficult to regulate in France than liquor. Both the British and the French armies had tried to solve the problem of venereal disease by licensing and inspecting prostitutes. Georges Clemenceau, the French premier, accused the Americans of spreading disease throughout the French civilian population and offered to provide the Americans with licensed prostitutes. When Clemenceau's letter reached Baker, the secretary of war said, "For God's sake…don't show this to the President or he'll stop the war." The Americans never accepted Clemenceau's offer, and he continued to be baffled by the American progressive mentality.

Suffrage for Women

In the fall of 1918, while American soldiers were mobilizing for the final offensive in France and hundreds of thousands of women were working in factories and serving as Red Cross and Salvation Army volunteers near the army bases, Woodrow Wilson asked the Senate to support extending the vote to women. He argued that woman suffrage was "vital to the winning of the war." Although Wilson had earlier opposed the vote for women and his positive statement at this late date was not necessary, his voice was a welcome addition to a rising chorus of support for an amendment to the Constitution that would permit the female half of the population to vote.

Many still opposed woman suffrage. Some argued that the vote would make women less feminine, more worldly, and less able to perform their primary tasks as wives and mothers. The National Association Opposed to Woman Suffrage protested that only radicals wanted the vote and declared that woman suffrage, socialism, and feminism were "three branches of the same Social Revolution."

Carrie Chapman Catt, an efficient administrator and tireless organizer, devised the strategy that finally secured the vote for women. Catt, who grew up in Iowa, joined the Iowa Woman Suffrage Association at age 28 shortly after her first husband died. Before remarrying, she insisted on a legal agreement giving her four months a year away from her husband to work for the suffrage cause. In 1915, she became president of the National American Woman Suffrage Association (NAWSA), the organization founded in 1890 and based in part on the society organized by Elizabeth Cady Stanton and Susan B. Anthony in 1869.

Catt coordinated the state campaigns with the office in Washington, directing a growing army of dedicated workers. This began to produce results, but a group of more militant reformers, impatient with the slow progress, broke off from NAWSA to form the National Women's Party (NWP) in 1916. This group was led by Alice Paul, a Quaker from New Jersey, who had participated in some of the suffrage battles in England. Paul and her group, using tactics borrowed from the militant British suffragettes, picketed the White House, chained themselves to the fence, and blocked the streets. They carried banners that asked, "MR. PRESIDENT, HOW LONG MUST WOMEN WAIT FOR LIBERTY?" In the summer of 1917, the government arrested more than 200 women and charged them with "obstructing the sidewalk." That was just the kind of publicity the militants sought, and they made the most of it. Wilson, fearing even more embarrassment, began to cooperate with the more moderate reformers.

The careful organizing of NAWSA and the more militant tactics of the NWP both contributed to the final success of the woman suffrage crusade. The war did not cause the passage of the Nineteenth Amendment, but it did accelerate the process. Fourteen state legislatures petitioned Congress in 1917 and 26 in 1919, urging the enactment of the amendment. Early in 1919, the House of Representatives passed the suffrage amendment 304 to 90, and the Senate approved by a vote of 56 to 25. Fourteen months later, the required 36 states had ratified the amendment, and women at last had the vote. "We are no longer petitioners," Catt announced in celebration. "We are not wards of the nation, but free and equal citizens." But the achievement of votes for women would not prove the triumph of feminism, nor the signal for the beginning of a new reform movement that the women leaders expected to occur.

Planning for Peace

Woodrow Wilson turned U.S. participation in the war into a religious crusade to change the nature of international relations. It was a war to make the world safe for democracy—and more. On January 8, 1918, in part to counteract the Bolshevik charge that the war was merely a struggle among imperialist powers, he announced his plan to organize the peace. Called the Fourteen Points, it argued for "open covenants of peace openly arrived at," freedom of the seas, equality of trade, and the self-determination of all peoples. But his most important point, the fourteenth, called for an international organization, a "league of nations," to preserve peace. The victorious Allies, who had suffered grievously in the conflict, had less idealistic goals than did Wilson for peacemaking.

The Versailles Peace Conference

Late in 1918, Wilson announced that he would head the American delegation at Versailles, near Paris, symbolizing his belief that he alone could overcome the forces of greed and imperialism in Europe and bring peace to the world. Wilson and his entourage of college professors, technical experts, and advisers set sail for Paris on the *George Washington* on December 4, 1918. Secretary of State Lansing, Edward House, and a number of other advisers were there; conspicuously missing, however, was Henry Cabot Lodge, chairman of the Senate Foreign Relations Committee and the most powerful man in the Senate, or any other Republican senator.

Lodge's absence would prove a serious blunder, for the Republican-controlled Senate would have to approve any treaty negotiated in Paris. It is difficult to explain Wilson's lack of political insight, except that he disliked Lodge intensely and hated political bargaining and compromise. Preferring to announce great principles, he had supreme confidence in his ability to persuade and to get his way by appealing to the people.

Wilson's self-confidence grew during a triumphant tour through Europe before the conference. The ordinary people greeted him as a savior who had ended the tragic war. But the American president had greater difficulty convincing the political leaders at the peace conference of his genius. In Paris, he faced the reality of European power politics and ambitions

and the personalities of David Lloyd George of Great Britain, Vittorio Orlando of Italy, and Georges Clemenceau of France.

Though Wilson was more naive and idealistic than his European counterparts, he was a clever negotiator who won many concessions at the peace table, sometimes by threatening to go home if his counterparts would not compromise. The European leaders were determined to punish Germany and enlarge their empires. Wilson, however, pressed for a new kind of international relations based on his Fourteen Points. He achieved limited acceptance of the idea of self-determination, his dream that each national group could have its own country and that the people should decide in what country they wanted to live.

From what had been the Austro-Hungarian and Ottoman empires, the peacemakers carved the new countries of Austria, Hungary, Yugoslavia, and Turkey. In addition, they created Poland, Czechoslovakia, Finland, Estonia, Latvia, and Lithuania, in part to help contain the threat of bolshevism in eastern Europe. France was to occupy the industrial Saar region of Germany for 15 years, after which a plebiscite would then determine whether the people wanted to become a part of Germany or France. Italy gained the port city of Trieste, but not the neighboring city of Fiume, with its largely Italian-speaking population. Dividing up the map of Europe was difficult at best, but perhaps the biggest mistake that Wilson and other major leaders made was to give the small nations little power at the negotiating table and to exclude Soviet Russia entirely.

While Wilson won some points at the peace negotiations, he also had to make major concessions. He was forced to give in to the Allied demand that Germany pay reparations (later set at $56 billion), lose much of its oil- and coal-rich territory, and admit to its war guilt. He accepted a mandate system, to be supervised by the League of Nations, that allowed France and Britain to take over portions of the Middle East and Japan to occupy Germany's colonies in the Pacific as well as China's Shantung province. And he acquiesced when the Allies turned Germany's African colonies into "mandate possessions" because they did not want to allow self-determination of blacks in areas they had colonized.

Although Wilson yielded to the Allies on the fate of Germany's former colonies in Africa, he did not envision a reordering of global race relations. He opposed and finally defeated a measure introduced by Japan to include a clause in the league covenant to support racial equality in all parts of the world. W. E. B. Du Bois, who was in Paris as part of the American delegation at the first Pan-African Congress, supported the Japanese resolution for racial equality. He also spoke against colonialism and criticized "white civilization" for

Europe and the Near East After World War I

Led in part by President Wilson's goal to promote the self-determination of people and in part by a desire to block the expansion of Germany and the Soviet Union, the diplomats meeting at Versailles reconfigured the map of Europe and the Near East. Redrawing the map, however, was easier than solving the problems of nationalism and ethnic conflict. How has the map of Europe and the Middle East changed since 1919?

subjugating blacks in various parts of the world. He hoped that the Pan-African movement would become a global effort to unite people of color around the world. But Wilson and the other leaders at Versailles ignored Du Bois.

The Versailles treaty did not represent "peace without victory," as Wilson hoped. The German people felt betrayed. Japan, which had expected to play a larger role in the peace conference, felt slighted. The Italians were angry because they received less territory than they expected. These resentments would later have

grave consequences. Wilson also did not win approval for freedom of the seas or the abolition of trade barriers, but he did gain endorsement for the League of Nations, the organization he hoped would prevent all future wars. The league consisted of a council of the five great powers, elected delegates from the smaller countries, and a World Court to settle disputes. But the key to collective security was contained in Article 10 of the league covenant, which pledged all members "to respect and preserve against external aggression the territorial integrity" of all other members.

Wilson's Failed Dream

While the statesmen met at Versailles to sign the peace treaty hammered out in Paris and to divide up Europe, a group of prominent and successful women met in Zurich, Switzerland. Jane Addams led the American delegation that included Jeannette Rankin, a congresswoman from Montana (one of the few states where women could vote). They formed the Women's International League for Peace and Freedom. Electing Addams president of the new organization, they denounced the harsh peace terms, which called for disarmament of only one side and exacted great economic penalties against the Central Powers.

Hate and intolerance were legacies of the war. They were present at the Versailles peace conference, where Clemenceau especially wanted to humiliate Germany for the destruction of French lives and property. Also hanging over the conference was the

Timeline

1914	Archduke Ferdinand assassinated; World War I begins
	United States declares neutrality
	American troops invade Mexico and occupy Veracruz
1915	Germany announces submarine blockade of Great Britain
	Lusitania sunk
	Arabic pledge
	Marines land in Haiti
1916	Army Reorganization Bill
	Expedition into Mexico
	Wilson reelected
	Workmen's Compensation Bill
	Keatings–Owen Child Labor Bill
	Federal Farm Loan Act
	National Women's Party (NWP) founded
1917	Germany resumes unrestricted submarine warfare
	United States breaks relations with Germany
	Zimmermann telegram
	Russian Revolution
	United States declares war on Germany
	War Revenue Act
	Espionage Act
	Committee on Public Information established
	Trading with the Enemy Act
	Selective Service Act
	War Industries Board formed
1918	Sedition Act
	Flu epidemic sweeps nation
	Wilson's Fourteen Points
	American troops intervene in Russian Revolution
1919	Paris peace conference
	Eighteenth Amendment prohibits alcoholic beverages
	Senate rejects Treaty of Versailles
1920	Nineteenth Amendment grants suffrage for women

Bolshevik success in Russia. The threat of revolution seemed so great that Wilson and the Allies sent American and Japanese troops into Siberia in 1919 to attempt to defeat the Bolsheviks and create a moderate republic. But by 1920, the troops had failed in their mission. They withdrew, but the Soviet Union never forgot the American intervention and the threat of bolshevism remained.

Most Americans supported the concept of the League of Nations in the summer of 1919. A few, such as former senator Albert Beveridge of Indiana, an ardent nationalist, denounced the league as the work of "amiable old male grannies who, over their afternoon tea, are planning to denationalize America and denationalize the nation's manhood." But 33 governors endorsed the plan. In the end, however, the Senate refused to accept American membership in the league. The League of Nations treaty, one commentator has suggested, was killed by its friends and not by its enemies.

First there was Lodge, who had earlier endorsed the idea of some kind of international peacekeeping organization but who objected to Article 10, which obligated all members to come to the defense of the others in case of attack. He claimed that it would force Americans to fight the wars of foreigners. A Republican senator since 1893, he had great faith in the power and prestige of the Senate. He disliked all Democrats, especially Wilson, whose idealism and missionary zeal infuriated him.

Then there was Wilson, whose only hope of passage of the treaty in the Senate was a compromise to bring moderate senators to his side. But Wilson refused to compromise or to modify Article 10 to allow Congress the opportunity to decide whether the United States would support the league in time of crisis. Angry at his opponents, who were exploiting the disagreement for political advantage, he stumped the country to convince the American people of the rightness of his plan. The people did not need to be convinced. They greeted Wilson much the way the people of France had. Traveling by train, he gave 37 speeches in 29 cities in the space of three weeks. When he described the graves of American soldiers in France and announced that American boys would never again die in a foreign war, the people responded with applause.

After one dramatic speech in Pueblo, Colorado, Wilson collapsed. His health had been failing for some months, and the strain of the trip was too much. He was rushed back to Washington, where a few days later he suffered a massive stroke. For the next year and a half, the president was incapable of running the government. Protected by his second wife and his closest advisers, Wilson was partially paralyzed, depressed, and unable to lead a fight for the league.

For a year and a half, the country limped along without a president.

After many votes and much maneuvering, the Senate finally killed the league treaty in March 1920. Had the United States joined the League of Nations, it probably would have made little difference in the international events of the 1920s and 1930s. Nor would American participation in the league have prevented World War II. The United States did not resign from the world of diplomacy or trade, nor did the United States become isolated from the rest of the world by refusing to join the league. But the rejection of the league treaty was symbolic of the refusal of many Americans to admit that the world and America's place in it had changed dramatically since 1914.

Conclusion
THE DIVIDED LEGACY OF THE GREAT WAR

For Edmund Arpin and many of his friends, who left small towns and urban neighborhoods to join the military forces, the war was a great adventure. For the next decades at American Legion conventions and Armistice Day parades, they continued to celebrate their days of glory. For others who served, the war's results were more tragic. Many died. Some came home injured, disabled by poison gas, or unable to cope with the complex world that had opened up to them.

In a larger sense, the war was both a triumph and a tragedy for the American people. The war created opportunities for blacks who migrated to the North, for women who found more rewarding jobs, and for farmers who suddenly discovered a demand for their products. But much of the promise and the hope proved temporary.

The war proved to be a turning point for the progressive movement. The passage of the woman suffrage amendment and the use of federal power in a variety of ways to promote justice and order pleased reformers, who had been working toward these ends for many decades. But the results were often disappointing. Once the war ended, much federal legislation was dismantled or reduced in effectiveness and woman suffrage had little initial impact on social legislation. Yet the power of the federal government did increase during the war in a variety of ways. From taking control of the railroads to building ships and public housing, to regulating the economy, the government took an active role. Much of that role would diminish in the next decade, but a strong, active government during the war would become a model during the 1930s for those who tried to solve the problem of a major depression.

The Great War marked the coming of age of the United States as a world power. At the end of the war, the United States was the world's largest creditor and an important factor in international trade and diplomacy. But the country seemed reluctant to accept the new responsibility. The war and the settlement were at least in part responsible for the global depression of the 1930s, and the problems created by the war led directly to another global war, thus causing the next generation to label the conflict of 1914–1918 World War I. The war stimulated patriotism and pride in the country, but it also increased intolerance, cut off immigration from Europe, and led to disillusionment. With this mixed legacy from the war, the country entered the new era of the 1920s.

QUESTIONS FOR REVIEW AND REFLECTION

1. Why did the United States, so determined to stay out of the Great War in 1914, join the Allied cause enthusiastically in 1917?
2. Why did the war lead to hate, prejudice, and the abridgment of civil liberties?
3. How did the war affect women and minorities in the United States?
4. Why did Wilson's idealistic peace plan fail?
5. What were the long-range consequences of World War I? For the United States? For the world?

CHAPTER 23

Affluence and Anxiety

John Steuart Curry, *Baptism in Kansas*

Curry was one of the 1920s regionalist painters who found inspiration in the American heartland. In this painting, he depicts a religious ritual that underscores the conflict between rural and urban values. Is there still a religious split today between urban and rural America? Or is the cultural divide defined differently today?

(John Steuart Curry, (1897–1946), "Baptism in Kansas". 1928. Oil on canvas. 40" × 50". Collection of the Whitney Museum of American Art, New York.)

American Stories

A Black Sharecropper and His Family Move North

John and Lizzie Parker were black sharecroppers who lived in a "stubborn, ageless hut squatted on a little hill" in central Alabama. They had two daughters—one age 6, the other already married. The whole family worked hard in the cotton fields, but they had little to show for their labor. One day in 1917, Lizzie straightened her shoulders and declared, "I'm through. I've picked my last sack of cotton. I've cleared my last field." Like many southern African Americans, the Parkers sought opportunity and a better life in the North. World War I cut off the flow of immigrants from Europe, and suddenly there was a shortage of workers. Some companies sent special trains into the South to recruit African Americans. John Parker signed up with a mining company in West Virginia. The company offered free transportation for his family. "You will be allowed to get your food at the company store and there are houses awaiting for you," the agent promised.

The sound of the train whistle seemed to promise better days ahead for her family as Lizzie gathered her possessions and headed north. But it turned out that the houses in the company town in West Virginia were little better than those they left in Alabama. After deducting for rent and for supplies from the company store, almost no money was left at the end of the week. John hated the dirty and dangerous work in the mine and realized that he would never get ahead by staying there. But instead of venting his anger on his white boss, he ran away, leaving his family in West Virginia.

John drifted to Detroit, where he got a job with the American Car and Foundry Company. It was 1918, and the pay was good, more than he had ever made before. After a few weeks, he rented an apartment and sent for his family. For the first time, Lizzie had a gas stove and an indoor toilet, and Sally, who was now 7, started school. It seemed as if their dream had come true.

Detroit was not quite the dream, however. It was crowded with all kinds of migrants, many attracted by the wartime jobs at the Ford Motor Company and other factories. The new arrivals increased the racial tension already present in the city. Sally was beaten up by a gang of white youths at school. Even in their neighborhood, which had been solidly Jewish before their arrival, the shopkeepers and the old residents made it clear that they did not like blacks moving into their community. The Ku Klux Klan, which gained many new members in Detroit, also made life uncomfortable for the blacks who had moved north to seek jobs and opportunity.

Suddenly the war ended, and almost immediately John lost his job. Then the landlord raised the rent, and the Parkers were forced to leave their apartment for housing in a section just outside the city near Eight Mile Road. The surrounding suburbs had paved streets, wide lawns, and elegant houses, but this black ghetto had dirt streets and shacks that reminded the Parkers of the company town where they had lived in West Virginia. Lizzie had to get along without her bathroom, for here there was no indoor plumbing and no electricity, only a pump in the yard and an outhouse.

The recession winter of 1921–1922 was particularly difficult. The auto industry and other companies laid off most of their workers. John could find only part-time employment, while Lizzie worked as a domestic servant for white families. Because no bus route connected the black community to surrounding suburbs, she often had to trek miles through the snow. The shack they called home was freezing cold, and it was cramped because their married daughter and her husband had joined them in Detroit.

Lizzie did not give up her dream, however. With strength, determination, and a sense of humor, she kept the family together. In 1924, Sally entered high school. By the end of the decade, Sally had graduated from high school, and the Parkers finally had electricity and indoor plumbing in the house, though the streets were still unpaved. Those unpaved streets stood as a symbol of their unfulfilled dream. The Parkers, like most of the African Americans who moved north in the decade after World War I, had improved their lot, but they still lived outside Detroit—and, in many ways, outside America.

Like most Americans in the 1920s, the Parkers pursued the American dream of success. For them, a comfortable house and a steady job, a new bathroom, and an education for their younger daughter constituted that dream. For others during the decade, the symbol of success might be owning a new automobile or a new suburban house, or perhaps making a killing on the stock market. The Parkers, like all Americans, whether they realized it or not, were influenced by a global market beyond their control. The 1920s, the decade between the end of World War I and the stock market crash, has often been referred to as the "jazz age," a time when the American people had one long party complete with flappers, speakeasies, illegal bathtub gin, and young people dancing the Charleston late into the night. This frivolous interpretation has some basis in fact, but most Americans did not share in the party, for they were too busy struggling to make a living.

In this chapter, we will explore some of the conflicting trends of an exciting decade. First, we will examine the currents of intolerance that influenced almost all the events and social movements of the time. We will also look at some developments in technology, especially the automobile, which changed life for almost everyone and created the illusion of prosperity for all. We will then focus on groups—women, blacks, industrial workers, and farmers—who had their hopes and dreams raised but not always fulfilled during the decade. We will conclude by looking at the way business, politics, and foreign policy were intertwined during the age of Harding, Coolidge, and Hoover.

Postwar Problems

Enthusiasm for social progress evaporated in 1919. Public housing, social insurance, government ownership of railroads, and many other experiments quickly ended. The sense of progress and purpose that the war had fostered withered. The year after the war was marked by strikes and violence and by fear that Bolsheviks, blacks, foreigners, and others were destroying the American way of life. Some of the fear and intolerance resulted from wartime patriotism, while some arose from the postwar economic and political turmoil that forced Americans to deal with new and immensely troubling situations.

The Red Scare

Americans have often feared radicals and other groups that seem to be conspiring to overthrow the American way of life. In the 1840s, in the 1890s, and at other times in the past, Catholics, Mormons, Populists, immigrants, and holders of many political views have all been attacked as dangerous and "un-American." Before 1917, anarchists seemed to pose the worst threat. The Russian Revolution changed that. *Bolshevik* suddenly became the most dangerous and devious radical, while *Communist* was transformed from a member of a utopian community to a dreaded, threatening subversive. For some Americans, *Bolshevik* and *German* became somehow mixed together, especially after the Treaty of Brest–Litovsk in 1918 removed the new Soviet state from the war. In the spring of 1919, with the Russian announcement of a policy of worldwide revolution and with Communist uprisings in Hungary and Bavaria, many Americans feared that Communists planned to take over the United States.

Immediately after the war, there were perhaps 25,000 American Communists, but they never threatened the United States. Some were idealists, such as John Reed, the son of a wealthy businessman, who had been converted to socialism in New York's Greenwich Village. Appalled by the carnage in what he considered a capitalistic war, Reed went to Russia as a journalist, just in time to witness the bloody Bolshevik takeover. His eyewitness account, *Ten Days That Shook the World,* optimistically predicted worldwide revolution. Seeing little hope for that revolution in postwar America, he returned to Moscow, where he died in 1920, disillusioned by the new regime's authoritarian nature.

The "Red Menace" and the Palmer Raids

Reed was one of the romantic American intellectuals who saw great hope for the future in the Russian Revolution. His mentor Lincoln Steffens, the muckraking journalist, remarked after a visit to the Soviet Union a few years later, "I have been over into the future and it works." But relatively few Americans, even among those who had been Socialists, and fewer still among the workers, joined the Communist party. The threat to the American system of government was very slight. But in 1919, the Communists seemed to be a threat, particularly as a series of devastating strikes erupted. Workers in the United States had suffered from wartime inflation, which had almost doubled prices between 1914 and 1919, while most wages remained the same. During 1919, more than 4 million workers took part in 4,000 strikes. Few wanted to overthrow the government; rather, they demanded higher wages, shorter hours, and in some cases more control over the workplace.

On January 21, 1919, some 35,000 shipyard workers went on strike in Seattle, Washington. Within a few days, a general strike paralyzed the city; transportation and business stopped. The mayor called for federal troops. Within five days, using strong-arm tactics, the mayor put down the strike and was hailed as a "red-blooded patriot."

Yet strikes continued elsewhere. In September 1919, all 343,000 employees of U.S. Steel walked out in an attempt to win an eight-hour workday and an "American living wage." The average workweek in the steel industry in 1919 was 68.7 hours; the unskilled worker averaged $1,400 per year, while the minimum subsistence for a family of five was estimated at $1,575. Within days, the strike spread to Bethlehem Steel.

Owners blamed the strikes on the Bolsheviks. They imported strikebreakers, provoked riots, broke up union meetings, and finally used police and soldiers to end the strike. Eighteen strikers were killed. Because most people believed that the Communists had inspired the strike, the issue of long hours and poor pay got lost, and eventually the union surrendered.

To many Americans, strikes were bad enough, but bombs were even worse. On April 28, 1919, a bomb was discovered in a package delivered to the home of the mayor of Seattle. The next day, the maid of a former senator from Georgia opened a package, and a bomb blew her hands off. Other bombings occurred in June, including one that shattered the front of Attorney General A. Mitchell Palmer's home in Washington. The bombings seem to have been the work of misguided radicals who thought they might spark a genuine revolution in America. But their effect was to provide evidence that revolution could be around the corner, even though most American workers wanted only shorter hours, better working conditions, and a chance to realize the American dream.

No one was more convinced than A. Mitchell Palmer. In the summer of 1919, he determined to find and destroy the Red network. He organized a special antiradical division within the Justice Department and put a young man named J. Edgar Hoover in charge of coordinating information on domestic radical activities.

Obsessed with the "Red Menace," Palmer instituted a series of raids, beginning in November 1919. Simultaneously, in several cities, his men rounded up 250 members of the Union of Russian Workers, many of whom were beaten in the process. In December, 249 aliens, including the famous anarchist Emma Goldman, were deported, although very few were Communists and even fewer had any desire to overthrow the government. Palmer's men arrested 500 people in Detroit and 800 in Boston.

The Palmer raids, one of the most massive violations of civil liberties in American history to that time, found few dangerous radicals but did fan the flames of fear and intolerance. In Indiana, a jury quickly acquitted a man who had killed an alien for yelling, "To hell with the United States." Billy Sunday, a Christian evangelist, suggested that the best solution was to shoot aliens rather than to deport them.

Palmer became a national hero, but in the end, only about 600 were deported out of more than 5,000 arrested. The worst of the "Red Scare" was over by the end of 1920, but fear of radicals and emotional patriotism survived to color almost every aspect of politics, daily life, and social legislation.

The Red Scare strengthened many patriotic organizations and societies determined to eliminate Communism from American life. The best known was the American Legion, but there were also the American Defense Society, the Sentinels of the Republic, the United States Flag Association, and the Daughters of the American Revolution. Such groups provided a sense of purpose and a feeling of belonging in a rapidly changing America. But often they were united by obsessive fear of Communists and radicals.

The Ku Klux Klan

Among the superpatriotic organizations claiming to protect the American way of life, the Ku Klux Klan (KKK) was the most extreme. The Klan was organized in Georgia by William J. Simmons, a lay preacher, salesman, and member of many fraternal organizations. He adopted the name and white-sheet uniform of the old antiblack Reconstruction organization that was glorified in 1915 in the immensely popular but racist feature film *Birth of a Nation*. Simmons appointed himself head ("Imperial Wizard") of the new Klan.

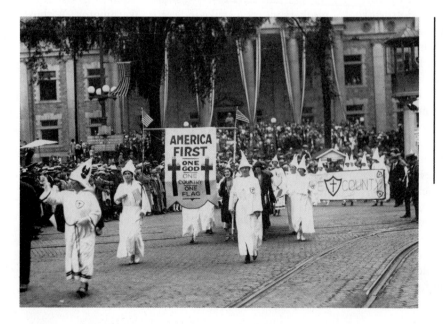

Women of the Ku Klux Klan

The Klan, with its elaborate rituals and uniforms, exploited the fear of blacks, Jews, liberals, and Catholics while preaching "traditional" values. The appeal of the Klan was not limited to the South, and many women joined. This is a photo of women Klan members marching in an America First Parade in Binghamton, New York. Why did so many women join the Klan? Is there anything like it today?

(Bettmann/CORBIS)

Unlike the original organization, which took almost anyone who was white, the new Klan was thoroughly Protestant and explicitly antiforeign, anti-Semitic, and anti-Catholic. The Klan declared that "America is Protestant and so it must remain." It opposed the teaching of evolution; glorified old-time religion; supported immigration restriction; denounced short skirts, petting, and "demon rum"; and upheld patriotism and the purity of women. The Klan was also militantly antiblack and its members took as their special mission the task of keeping blacks in their "proper place." If peaceful measures failed, they resorted to violence, kidnapping, and lynching.

The Klan flourished in small towns and rural areas in the South, where it set out to keep returning black soldiers in their "proper place," but it soon spread throughout the country; at least half the members came from urban areas. The Klan was especially strong in the working-class neighborhoods of Detroit, Indianapolis, Atlanta, and Chicago, where the migration of African Americans and other ethnic groups increased fear of everything "un-American." At the peak of its power, the Klan had several million members, many of them from the middle class. In some states, especially Indiana, Colorado, Oregon, Oklahoma, Louisiana, and Texas, it influenced politics. The Klan's power declined after 1925 because of a series of internal power struggles and several scandals. The Klan survived in some areas into the 1930s, but it had all but disappeared by the outbreak of World War II. Yet the end of the Klan did not mean the end of prejudice.

Ethnic and Religious Intolerance

One result of the Red Scare and the unreasoned fear of foreigners and radicals, which dragged on through much of the decade, was the conviction and sentencing of two Italian anarchists, Nicola Sacco and Bartolomeo Vanzetti. Arrested in 1920 for allegedly murdering a guard during a robbery of the shoe factory in South Braintree, Massachusetts, the two were convicted and sentenced to die in the summer of 1921 on what many liberals considered circumstantial and flimsy evidence. Indeed, it seemed to many that the two Italians, who spoke in broken English and were admitted anarchists, were punished because of their radicalism and their foreign appearance.

The case took on symbolic significance as many intellectuals in Europe and America rallied to their defense and to the defense of civil liberties. Appeal after appeal failed, but finally the governor of Massachusetts appointed a commission to reexamine the evidence. The commission reaffirmed the verdict, and the two were executed in the electric chair on August 23, 1927, despite massive protests and midnight vigils around the country. Recent evidence, including ballistic tests, suggests that they may have been guilty, but the trial and its aftermath nevertheless pointed to the ethnic prejudice and divisions in American society.

The KKK and well-publicized cases such as Sacco–Vanzetti touched relatively few people, but intolerance permeated the decade and influenced the lives of millions. In Dearborn, Michigan, Henry Ford published anti-Semitic diatribes in the *Dearborn Independent,* and many country clubs and resort hotels prohibited Jews from even entering. Jews built their own in the Catskills in New York State, Long Branch in New Jersey, and other areas. Many colleges, private academies, and medical schools had Jewish quotas, some openly and others informally, and many suburbs explicitly limited residents to "Christians." Few Catholics even tried to enroll in the elite colleges. There had always been a great deal of prejudice and intolerance in the United States, but during the decade of the 1920s, much of that intolerance became more fixed and formal.

A Prospering Economy

A time of intolerance and anxiety for many Americans, the decade after World War I also was a time of industrial expansion and widespread prosperity for numerous others. Recovering from a postwar depression in 1921 and 1922, the economy soared. Fueled by new technology, more efficient planning and management, and innovative advertising, industrial production almost doubled during the decade, and the gross national product rose by an astonishing 40 percent. A construction boom created new suburbs around American cities, and a new generation of skyscrapers transformed the cities themselves. However, the benefits of prosperity fell unevenly on the many social groups that formed American society.

While the American economy boomed, much of the rest of the world suffered in the aftermath of the war. Germany, wracked by inflation so great that it took millions of marks to buy a loaf of bread, sank into depression and was unable to make reparations payments. Great Britain and France recovered slowly from the war's devastation. The United States was part of a global economy and eventually would be affected by the economic difficulties of the rest of the world.

The Rising Standard of Living

Signs of the new prosperity abounded. Millions of homes and apartments were built and equipped with the latest conveniences. The number of telephones installed nearly doubled between 1915 and 1930.

Plastics, rayon, and cellophane altered American habits, and new products, such as cigarette lighters, reinforced concrete, dry ice, and Pyrex glass, created demands unheard of a decade before.

Perhaps the most tangible sign of the new prosperity was the modern American bathroom. Hotels and the urban upper class began to install cast-iron bathtubs and primitive flush toilets in the late nineteenth century, but not until the early 1920s did the enameled tub, toilet, and washbasin become standard. By 1925, American factories turned out 5 million enameled bathroom fixtures annually. The bathroom, with unlimited hot water, privacy, and clean white fixtures, symbolized American affluence.

In sharp contrast to people in European countries, middle-class Americans had more leisure time, a shorter workweek, and more paid vacation time. The American diet also improved during the decade. Health improved and life expectancy increased. Educational opportunities also expanded. In 1900, only 1 in 10 young people of high-school age remained in school; by 1930, that number had grown to 6 in 10, and much of the increase came in the 1920s. In 1900, only 1 college-age person in 33 attended an institution of higher learning; by 1930, the ratio was 1 in 7, and more than a million people were enrolled in the nation's colleges.

The Rise of the Modern Corporation

The structure and practice of American business were transformed in the 1920s. Mergers increased during the decade at a rate greater than at any time since the end of the 1890s—there were more than 1,200 mergers in 1929 alone—creating such giants as General Electric, General Motors, Sears Roebuck, Du Pont, and U.S. Rubber. These were not monopolies but oligopolies (industry domination spread among a few large firms). By 1930, the 200 largest corporations controlled almost half the corporate wealth.

Perhaps the most important business trend of the decade was the emergence of a new kind of manager. The prototype was Alfred P. Sloan, Jr., an engineer who reorganized General Motors. Sloan divided the company into components, freeing top managers to concentrate on planning new products, controlling inventory, and integrating the whole operation. Marketing and advertising became as important as production, and many businesses began to spend more money on research.

The new managers tried to keep employees working efficiently, but they used more than the stopwatch and the assembly line. They introduced pensions, recreation facilities, cafeterias, and, in some cases, paid vacations and profit-sharing plans. The managers were not being altruistic; rather, "welfare capitalism" was designed to reduce worker discontent and to discourage labor unions.

Planning was the key to the new corporate structure, and planning often meant continuing the business–government cooperation developed during World War I. All the planning and the new managerial authority failed to prevent the economic collapse of 1929, but the modern corporation survived the depression to exert a growing influence on American life in the 1930s and after.

Electrification

The 1920s marked the climax of the "second Industrial Revolution," powered by electricity and producing a growing array of consumer goods. By 1929, electrical generators provided 80 percent of the power used in industry. Fewer than one of every ten American homes had electricity in 1907; by 1919 more than two-thirds did.

Electricity brought dozens of gadgets and labor-saving devices into the home. Washing machines and electric irons gradually reduced the drudgery of washday for women, and vacuum cleaners, electric toasters, and sewing machines lightened housework. But the new machines still needed human direction and did not reduce the time the average housewife spent doing housework. For many poor urban and rural women, the traditional female tasks of carrying, pushing, pulling, and lifting went on as they had for centuries. In many ways, the electric revolution increased the contrast in American life. The "great white ways" of the cities, lit by electric lights, symbolized progress, but they also made the darkness of slums and hamlets seem even more forbidding.

A Global Automobile Culture

Automobile manufacturing, like electrification, underwent spectacular growth in the 1920s. The automobile was one major factor in the postwar economic boom. It stimulated and transformed the petroleum, steel, and rubber industries. The auto forced the construction and improvement of streets and highways and led to millions of dollars of expenditures on labor and concrete.

The auto created new suburbs and allowed families to live farther from work. The filling station, the diner, and the overnight cabin became familiar and eventually standardized objects on the American scene. Traffic lights, stop signs, billboards, and parking lots appeared. Hitching posts and watering troughs became rarer, and gradually the garage replaced the livery stable. The auto changed the look of the American landscape and threatened the environment as well. Oil and gasoline contaminated streams, and piles of old tires and rusting hulks of discarded cars became a familiar eyesore along highways. Emissions from thousands and then millions of internal combustion engines polluted the air. The increasing use of nonrenewable fossil fuels was already apparent in the 1920s, and the trend continued.

The auto changed American life in other ways. It led to the decline of the small crossroads store as well as many small churches because the rural family could now drive to the larger city or town. Tractors and trucks changed the methods of farming. Buses began to eliminate the one-room schoolhouse, because it was now possible to transport students to larger schools. The automobile allowed young people for the first time to escape the chaperoning of parents.

Gradually, as the decade progressed, the automobile became not just transportation but a sign of status. Advertising helped create the impression that it was the symbol of the good life, of sex, freedom, and speed. The auto in turn transformed advertising and design. It even altered the way products were purchased. By 1926, three-fourths of the cars sold were bought on some kind of deferred-payment plan. Installment credit, first tried by a group of businessmen in Toledo, Ohio, in 1915 to sell more autos, was soon used to promote sewing machines, refrigerators, and other consumer products. "Buy now, pay later" became the American way.

The United States had a love affair with the auto from the beginning. There were 8,000 motor vehicles registered in the country in 1900, and nearly a million in 1912. But only in the 1920s did the auto come within the reach of middle-class consumers. In 1929, Americans purchased 4.5 million cars, and by the end of that year, nearly 27 million were registered.

In part because of Henry Ford and the development of the inexpensive car, and because the United States had a much larger middle class who could afford a car, the ownership of automobiles expanded rapidly in the United States. This differed from Europe, where most autos were custom-made. The most important British company, Morris Motors, did not adopt the assembly line method of production until 1934. France, Germany, and England all subsidized auto manufacture for military purposes, further delaying the development of an inexpensive car. But because of their strong central governments, European countries adopted safety standards and required national licenses for vehicles and drivers before such measures were adopted in the United States.

In the United States, the states created the rules, and in the beginning it was assumed that anyone could drive a car. The world agreed on time zones, postage regulations, and other things, but not on which side of the road to drive on. In Great Britain, Japan, and all parts of the British empire, cars were driven on the left side, while in the United States and most of Europe, driving on the right side was the proper thing to do. Eventually most of the world, following the American lead, was transformed by automobile culture, but in many countries, that did not happen until after World War II.

Henry Ford

Many men contributed to the development and production of the auto—William Durant organized General Motors; Charles Kettering, an engineering genius, developed the electric self-starter; and Ransom E. Olds built the first mass-produced, moderately priced, light car. Above all the others loomed a name that became synonymous with the automobile itself—Henry Ford.

Ford had the reputation of being a progressive industrial leader and a champion of the common people. As with all men and women who take on symbolic significance, the truth is less dramatic than the stories. For example, Ford is often credited with inventing the assembly line. What he actually did (along with a team of engineers) was adapt the assembly line and the concept of interchangeable parts to the production of autos. Introduced in 1913, the new method reduced the time it took to produce a car from 14 hours to an hour and a half. The product of the carefully planned system, the Model T, was the prototype of the inexpensive family car.

In 1914, Ford startled the country by announcing that he was increasing the minimum pay of the Ford assembly-line worker to $5 a day (almost twice the national average pay for factory workers). Ford was not a humanitarian. He wanted a dependable workforce and realized that skilled workers were less likely to quit if they received good pay. Ford was one of the first to recognize that workers were consumers as well as producers and that they might buy Model T Fords. But work in the Ford factory had its disadvantages. The assembly line was repetitious and numbing. "You could drop over dead," one worker recalled, "and they wouldn't stop the line." And when the line closed down, as it did periodically, workers were released without compensation.

The Model T, which cost $600 in 1912, was reduced gradually in price until it sold for only $290 in 1924. The "Tin Lizzie," as it was affectionately called, was light and easily repaired. Some owners claimed all one needed were a pair of pliers and some baling wire to keep it running. If it got stuck on bad roads, as it often did, a reasonably healthy man could lift it. Replacement parts were standardized and widely available.

The Model T did not change from year to year, nor did it deviate from its one color, black. Except for adding a self-starter, offering a closed model, and making a few minor face-lift changes, Ford kept the Model T in 1927 much as he had introduced it in 1909. By that time, its popularity had declined as

Automobile Assembly Line

The automobile changed life in the United States in many ways. In 1929, 27 million cars were registered in the United States, up from 1 million in 1900. Hundreds of thousands of people were employed in the auto industry, in manufacturing, sales, and service. The assembly line, first used by Henry Ford in 1913, transformed not only the auto industry, but also the way other products were manufactured. In addition, it changed the nature of work and altered the lives of those who worked on the line. Can you imagine working in a factory like this? In what other ways did the auto change life for Americans in the 1920s?

(From the Collections of The Henry Ford Museum & Greenfield Village)

The Model A, introduced in 1927, did not dominate the market as the Model T had done, but the gigantic River Rouge factory, spreading over a thousand acres in Dearborn, Michigan, was built especially to produce the new model. It became the symbol of mass production in the new era. The auto industry, like most American business, went through a period of consolidation in the 1920s. In 1908, more than 250 companies produced cars in the United States. By 1929, only 44 remained.

The Exploding Metropolis

The automobile transformed the city and led to the gradual decline of the streetcar and the interurban trolley. In the late nineteenth century, railroads and streetcars had created suburbs near the major cities, but the great expansion of suburban population occurred in the 1920s. Shaker Heights, a Cleveland suburb, was in some ways a typical development. Built on the site of a former Shaker community, the new suburb was planned and developed by two businessmen. They controlled the size and style of the homes and restricted buyers. No blacks were allowed. Curving roads led off the main auto boulevards, and landscaping and natural areas contributed to a parklike atmosphere. The suburb increased in population from 1,700 in 1919 to more than 15,000 in 1929, and the price of lots multiplied by 10 during the decade.

Other suburbs grew in an equally spectacular manner. Beverly Hills, near Los Angeles, increased in population by 2,485 percent during the decade.

many people traded up to sleeker, more colorful, and, they thought, more prestigious autos from Ford's competitors; as a result, wages at Ford dipped below the industry average.

TEN LARGEST CITIES IN 1900 AND 1930*

What trends are revealed by this chart? Why are some cities growing faster than others?

1900		1930	
1. New York	4,023,000	1. New York	9,423,000
2. Chicago	1,768,000	2. Chicago	3,870,000
3. Philadelphia	1,458,000	3. Philadelphia	2,399,000
4. Boston	905,000	4. Detroit	1,837,000
5. Pittsburgh	622,000	5. Los Angeles	1,778,000
6. St. Louis	612,000	6. Boston	1,545,000
7. Baltimore	543,000	7. Pittsburgh	1,312,000
8. San Francisco	444,000	8. San Francisco	1,104,000
9. Cincinnati	414,000	9. St. Louis	1,094,000
10. Cleveland	402,000	10. Cleveland	1,048,000

*Figures are for the entire metropolitan areas, including suburbs.

Source: U.S. Bureau of the Census.

Grosse Point Park, near Detroit, grew by 725 percent, and Elmwood Park, near Chicago, increased by 716 percent. The automobile also allowed industry to move to the suburbs. The number of employees in manufacturing establishments in the suburbs of the 11 largest cities increased from 365,000 in 1919 to 1.2 million in 1937.

The biggest land boom of all occurred in Florida, where Miami mushroomed from 30,000 in 1920 to 75,000 in 1925. One plot of land in West Palm Beach sold for $800,000 in 1923; two years later, it was worth $4 million. A hurricane in 1926 ended the Florida land boom temporarily, but most cities and their suburbs continued to grow during the decade.

The most spectacular growth took place in two cities that the auto virtually created. Detroit grew from 300,000 in 1900 to 1,837,000 in 1930, and Los Angeles expanded from 114,000 in 1900 to 1,778,000 in 1930. With sprawling subdivisions connected by a growing network of roads, Los Angeles was the city of the future.

Cities expanded horizontally during the 1920s, sprawling into the countryside, but city centers grew vertically. A building boom that peaked near the end of the decade created new skylines for most urban centers. Even cities such as Tulsa, Dallas, Kansas City, Memphis, and Syracuse built skyscrapers. The most famous skyscraper of all, the Empire State Building in New York, towering 102 stories, was finished in 1931 but not completely occupied until after World War II.

A Communications Revolution

Changing communications altered the way many Americans lived as well as the way they conducted business. The telephone was first demonstrated in 1876. By 1899, more than 1 million phones were in operation. During the 1920s, the number of homes with phones increased from 9 million to 13 million. Still, by the end of the decade, more than half of American homes were without phones.

Even more than the telephone, the radio symbolized the technological and communicational changes of the 1920s. Department stores quickly began to stock radios, or crystal sets as they were called, but many Americans in the 1920s built their own receivers. The first station to begin commercial broadcasting was WWJ in Detroit in the summer of 1920. When WWJ and KDKA in Pittsburgh broadcast election returns in 1920, they ushered in a new era in politics. The next year, WJZ of Newark, New Jersey, broadcast the World Series, beginning a process that would transform baseball and eventually football and basketball as well. In 1922, a radio station in New York broadcast the first commercial, an indication that the airways would be used to increase the demand for the goods the factories were producing.

Much early broadcasting consisted of classical music, but soon came news analysis and coverage of presidential inaugurals and important events. Some stations produced live dramas, but more than any other programs serials such as *Amos 'n' Andy* made radio a national medium. Millions of people scattered across the country could sit in their living rooms (and after 1927, in their cars) listening to the same program. The record industry grew just as rapidly. By the end of the decade, people in all sections of the country hummed the same popular songs. Actors and announcers became celebrities. The radio, even more than the automobile, marked the end of silence and, to a certain extent, the end of privacy.

Even more dramatic was the phenomenon of the movies. Forty million viewers a week went to the movies in 1922, and by 1929 that number exceeded 100 million. Early movies were made in New York, Chicago, and a few other cities, but by the mid-1920s, the village of Hollywood, near Los Angeles, had become the movie capital of the world. Giant firms such as Metro-Goldwyn-Mayer, created in 1924, dominated the industry. Men, women, and children flocked to small theaters in the towns and to movie palaces in the cities, where they could dream of romance or adventure. Charlie Chaplin, Rudolph Valentino, Lillian Gish, and Greta Garbo were more famous and more important to millions of Americans than were most government officials. The motion pictures, which before the war had attracted mostly the working class, now seemed to appeal across class, regional, and generational lines.

The movies had the power to influence attitudes and ideas. In the 1920s, many parents feared that the movies would dictate ideas about sex and life. One young college woman remembered, "One day I went to see Viola Dana in *The Five Dollar Baby*. The scenes which showed her as a baby fascinated me so that I stayed to see it over four times. I forgot home, dinner and everything. About eight o'clock mother came after me." She also admitted that the movies taught her how to smoke, and in some of the movies "there were some lovely scenes which just got me all hot 'n' bothered."

Just as famous as the movie stars were sports figures such as Babe Ruth, Bobby Jones, Jack Dempsey, and Red Grange. The great spectator sports of the decade owed much to the increase in leisure time and to the automobile, the radio, and the mass-circulation newspaper. Thousands drove to college towns to watch football heroes perform. Millions listened for scores or read about the results the next day.

The year 1927 seemed to mark the beginning of the new age of mechanization and progress. That year, Henry Ford produced his 15 millionth car and introduced the Model A. Radio-telephone service was established between San Francisco and Manila. The

ADVERTISING

Have you ever noticed that television commercials can often be more interesting and creative than the programs? One authority has suggested that the best way for a foreign visitor to understand the American character and popular culture is to study television commercials. Television advertising, the thesis goes, appeals to basic cultural assumptions. The nature of advertising not only reveals for historians the prejudices, fears, values, and aspirations of a people but also makes an impact on historical development itself, influencing patterns of taste and purchasing habits. One modern critic calls advertising a "peculiarly American force that now compares with such long-standing institutions

"...and Jane, dear... Jack just raved about my teeth."

"I just smiled my prettiest smile...and let him rave. I could have said 'Of course I have beautiful teeth...I've used Colgate's all my life'. But I didn't want Jack to think I was a living advertisement for Colgate's tooth paste."

*   *   *   *   *

Beautiful teeth glisten gloriously. They compel the admiration of all who see them. And there is health as well as beauty in gleaming teeth, for when they are scrupulously kept clean, germs and poisons of decay can't lurk and breed around them.

Remove Those Causes of Decay

Save yourself the embarrassment so often caused by poor teeth. Fight the germs of tooth decay.

Colgate's will keep your teeth scrupulously clean. It reaches all the hard-to-get-at places between the teeth and around the edges of the gums, and so removes causes of tooth decay. It is the dependable tooth paste for you to use.

Washes — Polishes — Protects

The principal ingredients of Colgate's are mild soap and fine chalk, the two

things that dental authorities say a safe dental cream should contain. The combined action of these ingredients washes, polishes and protects the delicate enamel of your teeth.

Use Colgate's Regularly

Just remember that beautiful, healthy teeth are more a matter of good care than of good luck. Use Colgate's after meals and at bedtime. It will keep your teeth clean and gloriously attractive.

And you'll like its taste...even children love to use it regularly.

Priced right too! Large tube 25c.

Colgate's
Established 1806

COLGATE'S
RIBBON DENTAL CREAM

Toothpaste advertisement

Automobile advertisement (1929)

(CORBIS)

as the school and church in the magnitude of its social impact."

As long as manufacturing was local and limited, there was no need to advertise. Before the Civil War, for example, the local area could usually absorb all that was produced; therefore, a simple announcement in a local paper was sufficient to let people know that a particular product was available. But when factories began producing more than the local market could ordinarily consume, advertising came into play to create a larger demand.

Although national advertising began with the emergence of "name brands" in the late nineteenth century, it did not achieve the importance it now holds until the 1920s. In 1918, the total gross advertising revenue in magazines was $58.5 million. By 1920, it had more than doubled to $129.5 million, and by 1929, it was nearly $200 million. These

For Clean-up King
I Nominate . . .

by LOU GEHRIG

**New York Yankees' Clean-up Ace Makes
Novel Choice for All-Time Honor**

I DON'T need to tell baseball fans how important the "clean-up" (number four) man is in the batting line-up. With three reliable hitters batting ahead of him, it is his wallops that bring in the runs.

In my thirteen years of big league baseball I have watched some of the most famous "clean-up" men in the history of the game. But the other day in Boston I had the pleasure of seeing the "clean-up" king that gets my vote for the "all-time" honors. Strangely enough, this "clean-up" king isn't a slugger at all. Instead of cleaning up the bases, this one's specialty is cleaning up faces.

Here's how it happened. While in Boston playing the Red Sox, I made an inspection trip through the Gillette Safety Razor factory. There I discovered that what is true of baseball is also true of Gillette Blades. In baseball, the pick of the raw material is tried out, tested, and trained for the big league teams. At the Gillette factory I found that they buy only the finest steel, and put it through gruelling tests before it is made into Gillette Blades.

For instance, like a rookie baseball player, Gillette Blade steel has to be hardened and tempered.

To do this, Gillette uses electric furnaces, each one controlled by a device which can tell in an instant if the steel passing through the furnaces requires more heat or less heat. Faster than a speedball, the signal is flashed from the box to a great battery of switches, and the heat is raised or lowered accordingly. Then to make doubly sure that there is no possibility of error, they X-ray the steel with an electro-magnetic tester to detect hidden flaws.

A good ball player has to have precision and accuracy, too . . . and that's where Gillette chalks up a winning score. Grinding machines, adjustable to 1/10,000 of an inch give Gillette Blades shaving edges so keen you can't see them, even with the most powerful microscope.

These are some of the reasons why I nominate the Gillette Blade for all-time Clean-up King. For when it comes to cleaning up on stubborn bristles—with the greatest of ease and comfort—Gillette hits a home run with the bases loaded. Yes, Sir!—if baseball could only train players as accurately and efficiently as Gillette makes razor blades, we'd all find it easy to bat 1000.

With these important facts before you, why let anyone deprive you of shaving comfort by selling you a substitute! Ask for Gillette Blades and be sure to get them.

GILLETTE SAFETY RAZOR COMPANY, BOSTON, MASS.

| Razor blade advertisement

---

figures should not be surprising in a decade that often equated advertising with religion. The biblical Moses was called the "ad-writer for the Deity," and in a best-selling book, Bruce Barton, a Madison Avenue advertiser, reinterpreted Jesus, the "man nobody knows," as a master salesman. Wrote Barton: "He would be a national advertiser today."

The designers of ads began to study psychology to determine what motives, conscious or unconscious, influenced consumers. One psychologist concluded that the appeal to the human instinct for "gaining social prestige" would sell the most goods. Another way to sell products, many learned, was to create anxiety in the mind of the consumer over body odor, bad breath, oily hair, dandruff, pimples, and other embarrassing ailments. In 1921, the Lambert Company used the term *halitosis* for bad breath in an ad for Listerine. Within six years, sales of Listerine had increased from a little more than 100,000 bottles a year to more than 4 million.

The appeal to sex also sold products, advertisers soon found, as did the desire for the latest style or invention. But perhaps the most important thing advertisers marketed was youth. "We are going to sell every artificial thing there is," a cosmetics salesman wrote in 1926, "and above all it is going to be young-young-young! We make women feel young." A great portion of the ads were aimed at women. As one trade journal announced: "The proper study of mankind is man . . ., but the proper study of markets is woman."

Reflecting on the Past Look at the accompanying advertisements carefully. What do they tell you about American culture in the 1920s? What do they suggest about attitudes toward women? Do they reveal any special anxieties? How are they similar to and different from advertising today?

---

first radio network was organized (CBS), and the first talking movie (*The Jazz Singer*) was released. The Holland Tunnel, the first underwater vehicular roadway, connected New York and New Jersey, and Charles Lindbergh flew from New York to Paris in his single-engine plane in 33$\frac{1}{2}$ hours. He was young

and handsome, and his feat seemed to represent not only the triumph of an individual but also the triumph of the machine. When Americans cheered Lindbergh, they were reaffirming their belief in the American dream and their faith in individual initiative as well as in technology.

Hopes Raised, Promises Deferred

The 1920s was a time when it seemed all kinds of hopes could be realized. "Don't envy successful sales-men—be one!" one advertisement screamed. Buy a car. Build a house. Start a career. Invest in land. Invest in stocks. Make a fortune.

Not all Americans, of course, dreamed of making a stock-market killing or expected to win a huge fortune. Some merely wished to retain traditional values in a society that seemed to question them. Others wanted a steady job and a little respect. Still others hungered for the new appliances so alluringly described in ads and on the radio. Many discovered, however, that even their modest hopes lay tantalizingly out of reach.

Clash of Values

During the 1920s, radio, movies, advertising, and mass-circulation magazines promoted a national, secular culture. But this new culture, which emphasized consumption, pleasure, upward mobility, and even sex, clashed with traditional values of hard work, thrift, church, family, and home. Although it would be easy to see these cultural differences as a reflection of an urban–rural conflict, in fact, many people clinging to the old ways had moved into the cities. Still, many Americans feared that new cultural values, scientific breakthroughs, and new ideas such as bolshevism, relativism, Freudianism, and biblical criticism threatened their familiar way of life. A trial over the teaching of evolutionary ideas in high school in the little town of Dayton, Tennessee, symbolized, even as it exaggerated, the clash of the old versus the new, the traditional versus the modern, the city versus the country.

The scientific community and most educated people had long accepted the basic concepts of evolution, if not all the details of Charles Darwin's theories. But many Christians, especially those from Protestant evangelical churches, accepted the Bible as the literal truth. They believed that faith in the Gospel message was crucial to living a virtuous life on earth and, more important, going to heaven. Many of these faithful saw a major spiritual crisis in the dramatic changes of the 1920s. Resistance to the concept of evolution resulted in legislative efforts in several states to forbid its teaching.

John Scopes, a young biology teacher, broke the law by teaching evolutionary theory to his class, and the state of Tennessee brought him to trial. The American Civil Liberties Union hired Clarence Darrow, perhaps the country's most famous defense lawyer, to defend Scopes; the World Christian Fundamentalist Association engaged William Jennings Bryan, former presidential candidate and secretary of state, to assist the prosecution. Bryan was old and tired (he died only a few days after the trial), but he was still an eloquent and deeply religious man. In cross-examination, Darrow reduced Bryan's statements to intellectual rubble and also revealed that Bryan was at a loss to explain much of the Bible. Nevertheless, the jury declared Scopes guilty, for he had clearly broken the law.

The national press covered the trial and upheld science and academic freedom. Journalists such as H. L. Mencken had a field day poking fun at Bryan and the fundamentalists. "Heave an egg out a Pullman window," Mencken wrote, "and you will hit a Fundamentalist almost anywhere in the United States today.... They are everywhere where learning is too heavy a burden for mortal minds to carry."

Religious Fundamentalism

Religious fundamentalism continued to survive in a world fast becoming urban, modern, and sophisticated. Fundamentalism cut across many denominations and covered over many differences, but all fundamentalists believed in the literal interpretation and the infallibility of the Bible and that Jesus Christ was the only road to salvation. They rejected secularism, liberal theology, pluralism, the Social Gospel, and any sense that reform on earth could lead to perfection. They had an unshakable faith in what they believed was the truth.

Throughout the 1920s and the 1930s, attendance at Christian colleges and the circulation of fundamentalist periodicals and newspapers increased dramatically, and evangelical ministers reached large audiences. One of the most popular and flamboyant of the ministers was Billy Sunday, a former baseball player who jumped about the stage as he pitched his brand of Christianity. Another popular preacher was Aimee Semple McPherson, a faith healer who founded her own church, the International Church of the Four Square Gospel, in Los Angeles in 1927. Dressed as a University of Southern California football player, she ran across the stage "carrying the ball for Christ"; wielding a pitchfork, she drove the devil out of the auditorium.

Radio dramatically extended the reach of the fundamentalist preachers. McPherson was the first woman to hold a radio license, and she had the second most popular radio show in Los Angeles in the late 1920s. For many, the period between the wars was a time when people drifted away from organized religion, an age of technological marvels, and modernism in all fields, but for many others, fundamentalist religion and old-fashioned values not only survived but also prospered. Yet many fundamentalist sects succeeded in winning numerous converts because their leaders were skilled at using modern technology.

Immigration and Migration

Immigrants and anyone else perceived as "un-American" seemed to threaten the old ways. A movement to restrict immigration had existed for decades. An act passed in 1882 prohibited the entry of criminals, paupers, and the insane, and special agreements between 1880 and 1908 restricted both Chinese and Japanese immigration. But the fear and intolerance of the war years and the period right after the war resulted in major restrictive legislation.

The first strongly restrictive immigration law passed in 1917 over President Wilson's veto. It required a literacy test for the first time (an immigrant had to read a passage in one of a number of languages). The bill also prohibited the immigration of certain political radicals. However, the literacy test did not stop the more than 1 million immigrants who poured into the country in 1920 and 1921.

In 1921, Congress limited European immigration in any one year to 3 percent of the number of each nationality present in the country in 1910. In order to limit immigration from southern and eastern Europe

and to ban all immigration from Asia, Congress in 1924 changed the quota to 2 percent of those in the country in 1890. The National Origins Act of 1927 set an overall limit of 150,000 European immigrants a year, with more than 60 percent coming from Great Britain and Germany, but fewer than 4 percent from Italy.

Ethnicity increasingly became a factor in political alignments. Restrictive immigration laws, sponsored by Republicans, helped drive American Jews, Italians, and Poles to the Democratic party. By 1924, the Democratic party was so evenly divided between northern urban Catholics and southern rural Protestants that the party voted, by a very small margin, to condemn the Ku Klux Klan.

The immigration acts of 1921, 1924, and 1927 sharply limited European immigration and virtually banned Asian immigrants. The 1924 law contained a provision prohibiting the entry of aliens ineligible for citizenship. This provision was aimed directly at the Japanese, for the Chinese had already been excluded; but even without this provision, only a small number

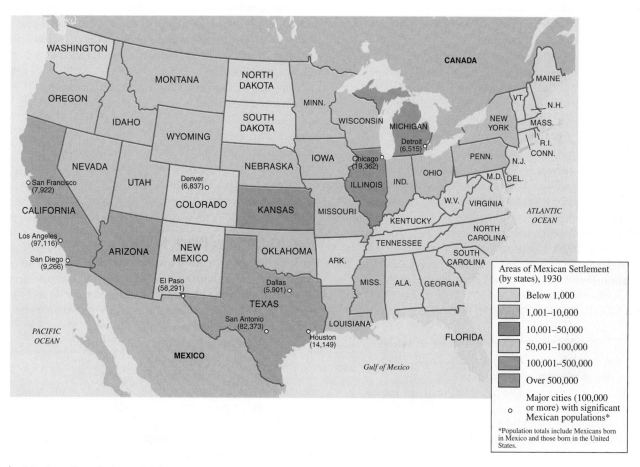

Mexican Population, 1930

Mexicans migrated across the border in great numbers in the 1920s; by 1930, they constituted a significant Spanish-speaking minority, especially in Texas, California, and Arizona. How did immigration laws of the 1920s shape ethnic cultures and communities in the United States?

could have entered the United States. "We try hard to be American," one California resident remarked, "But Americans always say you always Japanese." Denied both citizenship and the right to own land, the first-generation issei placed all of their hope in their children, but the second-generation nisei often felt trapped between the land of their parents and the America they lived in, and they still were treated as second-class citizens.

The immigration laws of the 1920s cut off the streams of cheap labor that had provided muscle for an industrializing country since the early nineteenth century. At the same time, by exempting immigrants from the Western Hemisphere, the new laws opened the country to Mexican laborers eager to escape poverty in their own land and to work in the fields and farms of California and the Southwest. Though they never matched the flood of eastern and southern Europeans who entered the country before World War I, Mexican immigrants soon became the country's largest first-generation immigrant group. Nearly half a million arrived in the 1920s, in contrast to only 31,000 in the first decade of the century. Mexican farm workers often lived in primitive camps, where conditions were unsanitary and health care was nonexistent.

Mexicans also migrated to industrial cities such as Detroit, St. Louis, and Kansas City. Northern companies recruited them and paid their transportation. During the 1920s, the population of El Paso, Texas, became more than 50 percent Mexican, and that of San Antonio a little less than 50 percent Mexican. In California, the Mexican population reached 368,000 in 1929, and in Los Angeles, the population was about 20 percent Mexican. Like African Americans, the Mexicans found opportunity by migrating, but they did not escape prejudice or hardship.

African Americans migrated north in great numbers from 1915 to 1920. Reduced European immigration and industrial growth caused many northern companies to recruit southern blacks. Trains stopped at the depots in small southern towns, sometimes picking up hundreds of blacks in a single day. Lured by editorials and advertisements placed by industries in northern black newspapers such as the Chicago *Defender* and driven out of the South by an agricultural depression, many African Americans eagerly headed north.

Most black migrants were unskilled. They found work in the huge meatpacking plants of Chicago, East St. Louis, Omaha, and Kansas City and in the shipyards and steel mills. Only 50 African Americans worked for the Ford Motor Company in 1916, but 2,500 worked there in 1920 and 10,000 in 1926. The black population of Chicago increased from 44,000 in 1910 to 234,000 by 1930. Cleveland's black population grew eightfold between 1910 and 1930.

African Americans unquestionably improved their lives by moving north. But most were like the Parkers, whom we met at the beginning of this chapter—their dreams were only partly fulfilled. Most crowded into segregated housing and faced prejudice and hate.

Often the young black men moved first, and only later brought their wives and children, putting great pressure on many black families. Some young men, like John Parker, restrained their anger, but others like Richard Wright's fictional Bigger Thomas, portrayed movingly in *Native Son* (1940), struck out violently against white society. The presence of more African Americans in the industrial cities of the North led to the development of black ghettos and increased the racial tension that occasionally flared into violence.

One of the worst race riots took place in Chicago in 1919. The riot began at a beach on a hot July day. A black youth drowned in a white swimming area. Blacks claimed he had been hit by stones, but the police refused to arrest any of the white men. A group of African Americans attacked the police, and the riot was on. It lasted four days. White youths drove through the black sections of the city, shooting blacks from car windows. Blacks returned the fire. Several dozen were killed, and hundreds were wounded. The tension between the races did not die when the riot was over. In the early 1920s, few cities escaped racial tension and violence.

The wave of violence and racism angered and disillusioned W. E. B. Du Bois, who had urged African Americans to close ranks and support the American cause during the war. In an angry editorial for *The Crisis,* he announced: "We return from fighting. We return fighting. Make way for Democracy; we saved it in France, and by the Great Jehovah, we will save it in the United States of America, or know the reason why."

Marcus Garvey: Black Messiah

Du Bois was not the only militant black leader in the postwar years. A flamboyant Jamaican fed a growing sense of black pride during that time. Marcus Garvey arrived in New York at age 29. Largely self-taught, he was an admirer of Booker T. Washington. Although he never abandoned Washington's philosophy of self-help, he thoroughly transformed it. Garvey saw self-help as a means of political empowerment by which African peoples would reclaim their homelands from European powers.

In Jamaica, Garvey had founded the Universal Negro Improvement Association. By 1919, he had established 30 branches in the United States and the Caribbean. He also set up the newspaper *The Negro World,* the Black Cross Nurses, and a chain of grocery stores, millinery shops, and restaurants. His biggest project was the Black Star Line, a steamship company that was to be owned and operated by African Americans. Advocating the return of blacks to Africa, he declared himself the "provisional president of Africa," a title he adopted from Eamon De Valera, the first "provisional president of Ireland." Garvey glorified the African past and preached that God and Jesus were black.

Garvey won converts, mostly among lower-middle-class blacks, through the force of his oratory and the power of his personality, but especially through his message that blacks should be proud of being black. "Up you mighty race, you can accomplish what you will," Garvey thundered. Thousands of blacks cheered as his Universal African Legions, dressed in blue and red uniforms, marched by. They waved the red, black, and green flag and sang "Ethiopia, the Land of Our Fathers," while thousands invested their money in the Black Star Line. The line soon collapsed, however, in part because white entrepreneurs sold Garvey inferior ships and equipment. Garvey was arrested for using

Black Messiah

Marcus Garvey (second from the right), shown dressed in his favorite uniform, became a hero for many black Americans. How did his appeal differ from that of other African American leaders?

(Hulton Archive/Getty Images)

the mails to defraud shareholders and was sentenced to five years in prison. Although President Coolidge commuted the sentence, Garvey was ordered deported as an undesirable alien and left America in 1927. Despite his failures, he convinced thousands of black Americans, especially the poor and discouraged, that they could join together and accomplish something and that they should feel pride in their heritage and their future.

The Harlem Renaissance

A group of black writers, artists, and intellectuals who settled in Harlem after the war led a movement related in some ways to Garvey's black nationalism crusade. It was less flamboyant but in the end more important. They studied anthropology, art, history, and music, and they wrote novels and poetry that explored the ambivalent role of blacks in America. Like Garvey, they expressed their pride in being black and sought their African roots and the folk tradition of blacks in America. But unlike Garvey, they had no desire to go back to Africa; instead, they sought a way to be both black and American.

Alain Locke, the first black Rhodes scholar, was in one sense the father of the movement called the Harlem Renaissance. His collection of essays and art, *The New Negro* (1925), announced the movement to the outside world. Langston Hughes, a poet and novelist, wrote bitter but humorous poems, using black vernacular to describe the pathos and the pride of African Americans. In *Weary Blues*, he adapted the rhythm and beat of black jazz and the blues to his poetry.

Jazz was an important force in Harlem in the 1920s, and many prosperous whites came from downtown to listen to Louis Armstrong, Fletcher Henderson, Duke Ellington, and other black musicians. The promise of expressing primitive emotions, the erotic atmosphere, the music, and the illegal sex, drugs, and liquor made Harlem an intriguing place for many brought up in Victorian white America.

Harlem jazz was also exported to Europe, especially to Paris. Returning black servicemen reported that African Americans were treated without prejudice in France, and black musicians began to drift to the Montmartre section of Paris, where American jazz and jazz singers such as the seductive Josephine Baker, star of *Revue Nègre*, became the toast of the town. Ironically, many American tourists in the 1920s first heard an African American jazz band in Paris. Many Europeans criticized the United States for its materialism and for its innocent exuberance. They were not impressed with American literature or American art, but they loved American jazz. It was the beginning of the export of American popular culture that would impress most of the rest of the world in the decades after World War II.

The Jamaican Claude McKay, who came to Harlem by way of Tuskegee and Kansas, wrote about the underside of life in Harlem in *Home to Harlem* (1925), one of the most popular of the "new Negro" novels. McKay portrayed two black men—one, named Jake, who has deserted the white man's army and finds a life of simple and erotic pleasure in Harlem's cabarets, the other an intellectual who is unable to make such an easy choice. "My damned white education has robbed me of much of the primitive vitality, the pure stamina, the simple unswaggering strength of the Jakes of the negro race," he laments.

This was the dilemma of many of the Harlem writers: how to be both black and intellectual. They worried that they depended on white patrons, who introduced them to writers and artists in Greenwich Village and made contacts for them at New York publishing houses. Many of the white patrons pressured the black writers to conform to the white elite idea of black authenticity. The black writers resented this intrusion, but it was their only hope to be recognized.

Many African American writers felt alienated from American society. They tried living in Paris or in Greenwich Village, but most felt drawn to Harlem, which in the 1920s was rapidly becoming the center of black population in New York City. More than 117,000 white people left the neighborhood during the decade, while more than 87,000 blacks moved in. Countee Cullen, the only writer in the group actually born in New York, remarked, "In spite of myself I find that I am activated by a strong sense of race consciousness." So, too, was Zora Neale Hurston activated. Born in Florida, she went to New York to study at Barnard College, earned an advanced degree in anthropology from Columbia University, and used her interest in folklore to write stories of robust and passionate rural blacks. Many Harlem writers reached a limited audience, but they were rediscovered in the 1960s by another generation of young black intellectuals struggling with the dilemma of how to be both black and American.

The Lost Generation

Many white intellectuals, writers, and artists also felt alienated from what they perceived as the materialism, conformity, and provincial prejudice that dominated American life. Many writers, including F. Scott Fitzgerald, Ernest Hemingway, E. E. Cummings, and T. S. Eliot, moved to Europe. Like so many American intellectuals in all periods, they had a love–hate relationship with their country.

For many writers, the disillusionment began with the war itself. Hemingway eagerly volunteered to go to Europe as an ambulance driver. But when he was wounded on the Italian front, he reevaluated the purpose of the war and the meaning of all the slaughter. His novel *The Sun Also Rises* (1926) is the story of the purposeless European wanderings of a group of Americans. But it is also the story of Jake Barnes, who was made impotent by a war injury. His "unreasonable wound" is a symbol of the futility of life in the postwar period.

F. Scott Fitzgerald, who loved to frequent the cafés and parties in Paris, became a celebrity during the 1920s. He epitomized some of the despair of his generation, which had "grown up to find all Gods dead, all wars fought, all faiths in man shaken." His best novel, *The Great Gatsby* (1925), was a critique of the American success myth.

It was not necessary to live in France to criticize American society. Sherwood Anderson, born in Camden, Ohio, created a fictional midwestern town in *Winesburg, Ohio* (1919) as a way to describe the dull, narrow, warped lives that seemed to provide a metaphor for American culture. Sinclair Lewis, another midwesterner, created scathing parodies of middle-class, small-town life in *Main Street* (1920) and *Babbitt* (1922). The "hero" of the latter novel is a salesman from the town of Zenith. He is a "he-man," a "regular guy" who distrusts "red professors," foreign-born people, and anyone from New York.

No one had more fun laughing at the American middle class than H. L. Mencken, who edited the *American Mercury* in Baltimore and denounced what he called the "booboisie." He labeled Woodrow Wilson a "self-bamboozled Presbyterian" and poked fun at Warren Harding's prose, which he said reminded him of "a string of wet sponges, . . . of stale bean soup, of college yells, of dogs barking idiotically through endless nights."

Ironically, while intellectuals despaired over American society and complained that art could not survive in a business-dominated civilization, literature flourished. The novels of Hemingway, Fitzgerald, Lewis, William Faulkner, and Gertrude Stein; the plays of Eugene O'Neill and Maxwell Anderson; the poetry of T. S. Eliot, Hart Crane, E. E. Cummings, and Marianne Moore; and the work of many black writers, such as Langston Hughes, Claude McKay, and Zora Neale Hurston, marked the 1920s as one of the most creative decades in American literature.

Women Struggle for Equality

Any mention of the role of women in the 1920s brings to mind the image of the flapper—a young woman with a short skirt, bobbed hair, and a boyish figure dancing the Charleston, smoking, drinking, and enjoying sexual encounters. F. Scott Fitzgerald's heroines in novels such as *This Side of Paradise* (1920) and *The Great Gatsby* (1925) provided the role models for young people to imitate, and movie stars such as Clara Bow and Gloria Swanson, aggressively seductive on the screen, supplied even more dramatic examples of provocative behavior.

Without question, women acquired more sexual freedom in the 1920s. "None of the Victorian mothers had any idea how casually their daughters were accustomed to being kissed," F. Scott Fitzgerald wrote. However, it is difficult, if not impossible, to know how accustomed those daughters (and their mothers) were to kissing and enjoying other sexual activity. Contraceptives, especially the diaphragm, became more readily available during the decade, and Margaret Sanger, who had been indicted for sending birth control information through the mail in 1914, organized the first American birth control conference in 1921. Still, most states made the selling or prescribing of birth control devices illegal, and federal laws prohibited sending literature discussing birth control through the mail.

Family size declined during the decade (from 3.6 children in 1900 to 2.5 in 1930), and young people were apparently more inclined to marry for love than for security. More women expected sexual satisfaction in marriage (nearly 60 percent in one poll) and felt that divorce was the best solution for an unhappy marriage. In another poll, nearly 85 percent approved of sexual intercourse as an expression of love and affection and not simply for procreation. But the polls were hardly scientific and tended to be biased toward the attitudes of the urban middle class. Despite more freedom for women, the double standard persisted.

Women's lives were shaped by other innovations of the 1920s. Electricity, running water, washing machines, vacuum cleaners, and other labor-saving devices made housework easier for the middle class. Yet these developments did not touch large numbers of rural and urban working-class women. Even middle-class women discovered that new appliances did not reduce time spent doing housework. Standards of cleanliness rose, and women were urged to make their houses more spotless than any nineteenth-century housekeeper would have felt necessary. At the same time, magazines and newspapers bombarded women with advertising urging them to buy products to make themselves better housekeepers yet still be beautiful. It must have been frustrating for those who could not afford the magic new products or whose hands and teeth and skin failed to look youthful despite all their efforts. The ads also promoted new dress styles, shorter skirts, and no corsets. The young adopted them quickly, and they also learned to swim (and to display more of their bodies on the beach), to play tennis (but only if they belonged to a tennis club), and to ride a bicycle.

More women worked outside the home. Whereas in 1890, only 17 percent of women were employed, by 1933, some 22 percent were. But their share of manufacturing jobs fell from 19 percent to 16 percent between 1900 and 1930. The greatest expansion of jobs was in white-collar occupations that were being feminized—for example, secretary, bookkeeper, clerk, and telephone operator. In 1930, fully 96 percent of stenographers were women. Although more married women had jobs (an increase of 25 percent during the decade), most of them held low-paying jobs, and most single women assumed that marriage would terminate their employment.

For some working women—secretaries and teachers, for example—marriage often led to dismissal. Married women are "very unstable in their work; their first claim is to home and children," a businessman concluded. Although women might not be able to work after their weddings (in one poll of college men, only one in nine said he would allow his wife to work after

WOMEN IN THE LABOR FORCE, 1900–1930

Why is the percentage of women working gradually increasing between 1900 and 1930? Why are more married women working?

Year	Women in Labor Force	Percentage of Women in Total Labor Force	Percentage of Total Women of Working Age	Single	Married	Widowed
1900	4,997,000	18.1	20.6	66.2	15.4	18.4
1910*	7,640,000	NA	25.4	60.2	24.7	15.0
1920	8,347,000	20.4	23.7	77.0†	23.0	—†
1930	10,632,000	21.9	24.8	53.9	28.9	17.2

*Data not comparable with other censuses due to a difference in the basis of enumeration.

† Single includes widowed and divorced.

Source: U.S. Bureau of the Census.

marriage), a job as a secretary could be good preparation for marriage. A business office was a good place to meet eligible men, but more than that, a secretary learned endurance, self-effacement, and obedience, traits that would make her a good wife. Considering these attitudes, it is not surprising that the disparity between male and female wages widened during the decade. By 1930, women earned only 57 percent of what men were paid.

The image of the flapper in the 1920s promised more freedom and equality for women than they actually achieved. The flapper was young, white, slender, and upper class (Fitzgerald fixed her ideal age at 19), and most women did not fit those categories. The flapper was frivolous and daring, not professional and competent. Although the proportion of women lawyers and bankers increased slightly during the decade, the rate of growth declined, and the number of women doctors and scientists dropped. In the 1920s, women acquired some sexual freedom and a limited amount of opportunity outside the home, but the promise of the prewar feminist movement and the hopes that accompanied the suffrage amendment remained unfulfilled.

Winning the vote for women did not ensure equality. Women could vote, but often they could not serve on juries. In some states, women could not hold office, own a business, or sign a contract without their husbands' permission. Women were usually held responsible for an illegitimate birth, and divorce laws almost always favored men. Many women leaders were disappointed in the small turnout of women in the presidential election of 1920. To educate women in the reality of politics, they organized the National League of Women Voters to "finish the fight."

Alice Paul, who had led the militant National Women's Party in 1916, chained herself to the White House fence once again to promote an equal rights amendment to the Constitution. The amendment got support in Wisconsin and in several other states, but many women opposed it on the grounds that such an amendment would cancel the special legislation to protect women in industry that had taken so long to enact in the two preceding decades. Feminists disagreed in the 1920s on the proper way to promote equality and rights for women, but the political and social climate was not conducive to feminist causes.

Rural America in the 1920s

Most farmers did not share in the prosperity of the 1920s. Responding to worldwide demands and rising prices for wheat, cotton, and other products, many farmers invested in additional land, tractors, and farm equipment during the war. Then prices tumbled. By

1921, the price of wheat had dropped 40 percent, corn 32 percent, and hogs 50 percent. Total farm income fell from $10 million to $4 million in the postwar depression. Many farmers could not make payments on their tractors. Because the value of land fell, they often lost both mortgage and land and still owed the bank money.

The changing nature of farming was part of the problem. Chemical fertilizers and new hybrid seeds increased the yield per acre. By 1930, some 920,000 tractors and 900,000 trucks were in use on American farms. They not only made farming more efficient, but they also allowed land formerly used to raise feed for horses and mules to be planted in cash crops. Production increased at the very time that worldwide demand for American farm products declined. In 1929, the United States shipped abroad only one-third the wheat it had exported in 1919, and only one-ninth the meat. Farmers, especially in North America and Europe, had prospered during the war because of the great demand for food. Expecting the demand to continue, many farmers borrowed to purchase new equipment and to increase the number of acres they cultivated. But the demand for produce did not last, leading to a worldwide decline in prices and making debts difficult to repay.

Victims not only of the global marketplace, American farmers were also vulnerable to the power of nature. This became apparent in the spring of 1927 when the worst flood in the nation's history devastated the Mississippi River valley, flooding more than 27,000 square miles of land and making a million people homeless.

Not all farmers suffered. Large commercial operations, using mechanized equipment, produced most of the cash crops. At the same time, many small farmers found themselves unable to compete with agribusiness. Some of them, along with many farm laborers, solved the problem of declining rural profitability by leaving the farms. In 1900, fully 40 percent of the labor force worked on farms; by 1930, only 21 percent earned their living from the land.

Few farmers could afford the products of the new technology. Although many middle-class urban families were more prosperous than they had ever been—buying new cars, radios, and bathrooms—only one farm family in ten had electricity in the 1920s. The lot of the farm wife had not changed for centuries. She ran a domestic factory, did all the household chores, and helped on the farm as well.

Farmers tried to improve their position by supporting legislation in the state capitals and in Washington. Most of their efforts went into the McNary–Haugen Farm Relief Bill, which would have provided government price support for key agricultural products. The bill was introduced a number of times between 1924 and 1928 without success, but farm organizations in all parts of the country learned how to work together to influence Congress. That would have important ramifications for the future.

The Workers' Share of Prosperity

Hundreds of thousands of workers improved their standard of living in the 1920s, yet inequality grew. Real wages increased 21 percent between 1923 and 1929, but corporate dividends went up by nearly two-thirds in the same period. The workers did not profit from the increased production they helped create, and that boded ill for the future. The richest 5 percent of the population increased their share of the wealth from a quarter to a third, and the wealthiest 1 percent controlled a whopping 19 percent of all income.

Even among workers there was great disparity. Those employed on the auto assembly lines or in the new factories producing radios saw their wages go up, and many saw their hours decline. Yet the majority of American working-class families did not earn enough to move them much beyond subsistence level. One study suggested that a family needed $2,000 to $2,400 in 1924 to maintain an "American standard of living." But in that year, 16 million families earned less than $2,000.

Organized labor fell on hard times in the 1920s. Labor union membership fell from about 5 million in 1921 to less than 3.5 million in 1929. The National Association of Manufacturers and individual businesses carried on a vigorous campaign to restore the open shop. The leadership of the AFL became increasingly conservative during the decade and had little interest in launching movements to organize laborers in the large industries.

The more aggressive unions such as the United Mine Workers, led by the flamboyant John L. Lewis, also encountered difficulties. The union's attempt to organize miners in West Virginia had led to violent clashes between union members and imported guards. President Harding called out troops in 1921 to put down an "army organized by the strikers." The next year, Lewis called the greatest coal strike in history and further violence erupted, especially in Williamson County, Illinois. Internal strife also weakened the union, and Lewis had to accept wage reductions in the negotiations of 1927.

Organized labor, like so many other groups, struggled desperately during the decade to take advantage of the prosperity. It won some victories, and it made some progress. But American affluence was beyond the reach of many groups during the decade. Eventually, the inequality would lead to disaster.

The Business of Politics

"Among the nations of the earth today America stands for one idea: *Business*," a popular writer announced in 1921. "Through business, properly conceived, managed and conducted, the human race is finally to be redeemed." Bruce Barton, the head of the largest advertising firm in the country, was the author of one of the most popular nonfiction books of the decade. In *The Man Nobody Knows* (1925), he depicted Christ as "the founder of modern business." He took 12 men from the bottom ranks of society and forged them into a successful organization.

Business, especially big business, prospered in the 1920s, and the image of businessmen, enhanced by their important role in World War I, rose further. The government reduced regulation, lowered taxes, and cooperated to aid business expansion at home and abroad. Business and politics, always intertwined, were especially allied during the decade. Wealthy financiers such as Andrew Mellon and Charles Dawes participated in formulating both domestic and foreign policy. Even more significant, a new kind of businessman was elected president in 1928. Herbert Hoover, international engineer and efficiency expert, was the very symbol of the modern techniques and practices that many people confidently expected to transform the United States and the world. Business leaders wielded power in other countries, but in no country were business and politics so closely intertwined as in the United States.

Harding and Coolidge

The Republicans, almost assured of victory in 1920 because of bitter reaction against Woodrow Wilson, might have preferred nominating their old standard-bearer, Theodore Roosevelt, but he had died the year before. Warren G. Harding, a former newspaper editor from Ohio, captured the nomination after meeting late at night with some of the party's most powerful men in a hotel room in Chicago. No one ever discovered what Harding promised, but the meeting in the "smoke-filled room" became legendary. To balance the ticket, the Republicans chose as their vice presidential candidate Calvin Coolidge of Massachusetts, who had gained attention by his firm stand during the Boston police strike. The Democrats seemed equally unimaginative. After 44 roll calls, they finally nominated Governor James Cox of Ohio and picked Franklin D. Roosevelt, a young politician from New York, to run as vice president. Roosevelt had been the assistant secretary of the navy but otherwise had not distinguished himself.

Harding won in a landslide. His 60.4 percent of the vote was the widest margin yet recorded in a presidential election. More significant, fewer than 50 percent of the eligible voters went to the polls.

The newly enfranchised women, especially in working-class neighborhoods, stayed away from the voting booths. So did large numbers of men. To many people, it did not seem to matter who was president.

In contrast to the reform-minded presidents Roosevelt and Wilson, Harding reflected the conservatism of the 1920s. He was a jovial man who brought many Ohio friends to Washington and placed them in positions of power. A visitor to the White House described Harding and his cohorts discussing the problems of the day, with "the air heavy with tobacco smoke, trays with bottles containing every imaginable brand of whiskey" near at hand.

At a little house a few blocks from the White House on K Street, Harry Daugherty, Harding's attorney general and longtime associate, held forth with a group of friends. Amid bootleg liquor and the atmosphere of a brothel, they did a brisk business in selling favors, taking bribes, and organizing illegal schemes. Harding, however, was not personally corrupt, and the nation's leading businessmen approved of his policies of higher tariffs and lower taxes. Nor did Harding spend all his time drinking with his cronies. He called a conference on disarmament and another to deal with the problems of unemployment, and he pardoned Eugene Debs, who had been in prison since the war. Harding once remarked that he could never be considered one of the great presidents, but he thought perhaps he might be "one of the best loved." He was probably right. When he died suddenly in August 1923, the American people genuinely mourned him.

Only after Calvin Coolidge became president did the full extent of the corruption and scandals of the Harding administration come to light. A Senate committee discovered that the secretary of the interior, Albert Fall, had illegally leased government-owned oil reserves in the Teapot Dome section of Wyoming to private business interests in return for over $300,000 in bribes. Illegal activities were also discovered in the Veterans Administration and elsewhere in government. Daugherty resigned in disgrace, the secretary of the navy barely avoided prison, two of Harding's advisers committed suicide, and Fall was sentenced to jail.

Though dour and taciturn, Coolidge was honest. Born in a little town in Vermont, he was sworn in as president by his father, a justice of the peace, in a ceremony conducted by the light of kerosene lamps at his ancestral home. To many, Coolidge represented old-fashioned rural values, simple religious faith, and personal integrity—a world fast disappearing in the 1920s.

Coolidge ran for reelection in 1924 with the financier Charles Dawes as his running mate. There was little question that he would win. The Democrats were so equally divided between northern urban Catholics and southern rural Protestants that it took 103 ballots before they nominated John Davis, an affable corporate lawyer with little national following.

A group of dissidents, mostly representing the farmers and the laborers dissatisfied with both nominees, formed a new Progressive party. They adopted the name, but little else, from Theodore Roosevelt's party of 1912. Nominating Robert La Follette of Wisconsin for president, they drafted a platform calling for government ownership of railroads and ratification of the child labor amendment. La Follette attacked the "control of government and industry by private monopoly." He received nearly 5 million votes, only 3.5 million short of Davis's total. But Coolidge and prosperity won easily.

Like Harding, Coolidge was a popular president. Symbolizing his administration was his wealthy secretary of the treasury, Andrew Mellon, who set out to lower individual and corporate taxes. In 1922, Congress, with Mellon's endorsement, repealed the wartime excess profits tax. Although it raised some taxes slightly, it exempted most families from any tax at all by giving everyone a $2,500 exemption, plus $400 for each dependent. In 1926, the rate was lowered to 5 percent and the maximum surtax to 40 percent. Only families with incomes above $3,500 paid any taxes at all. In 1928, Congress reduced taxes further, removed most excise taxes, and lowered the corporate tax rate. The 200 largest corporations increased their assets during the decade from $43 to $81 billion.

"The chief business of the American people is business," Coolidge announced. "The man who builds a factory builds a temple.... The man who works there worships there." Coolidge's idea of the proper role of the federal government was to have as little as possible to do with the functioning of business and the lives of the people. Not everyone approved of his policies, or his personality. "No other president in my time slept so much," a White House usher remembered. But most Americans approved of his inactivity.

Herbert Hoover

One bright light in the lackluster Harding and Coolidge administrations was Herbert Hoover. Born in Iowa, raised in Oregon, and educated in California, he served as secretary of commerce under both presidents. Hoover had made a fortune as an international mining engineer before 1914 and then earned a reputation as a great humanitarian for his work managing the Belgian Relief Committee and directing the Food Administration during World War I. He was mentioned as a candidate for president in 1920, when he had the support of such progressives as Jane Addams, Louis Brandeis, and Walter Lippmann.

Businessmen and the President

Beginning in 1920, Henry Ford, Thomas Edison, and Harvey Firestone went on auto trips together in part to celebrate the new automobile culture. In the summer of 1924, they stopped in Plymouth, Vermont, to visit with President Calvin Coolidge, who was vacationing at the family homestead. A local photographer took this photograph and made it into a postcard, which he sold as a souvenir. The president is autographing a sap bucket to be placed in Henry Ford's new museum near Detroit. From left to right: Harvey Firestone, President Coolidge, Henry Ford, Thomas Edison, Russell Firestone, Grace Coolidge, and John Coolidge, the president's father. Coolidge often pretended he was a simple Vermonter, but actually he was much more comfortable around the corporate elite than he was dealing with ordinary Americans. What was the danger of the close relationship between the presidents and business leaders in the 1920s? Does that close relationship still exist?

(Allen F. Davis Collection)

Hoover was a dynamo of energy and efficiency. He expanded his department to control and regulate the airlines, radio, and other new industries. By directing the Bureau of Standards to work with the trade associations and with individual businesses, Hoover managed to standardize the size of almost everything manufactured in the United States, from nuts and bolts and bottles to automobile tires, mattresses, and electric fixtures. He supported zoning codes, the eight-hour workday in major industries, better nutrition for children, and the conservation of national resources. He pushed through the Pollution Act of 1924, which represented the first attempt to control oil pollution along the American coastline.

As secretary of commerce, Hoover used the force of the federal government to regulate, stimulate, and promote, but he believed first of all in free enterprise and local volunteer action to solve problems. In 1921, he convinced Harding of the need to do something about unemployment during the postwar recession. The president's conference on unemployment, convened in September 1921, marked the first time the national government had admitted any responsibility to the unemployed. The result of the conference (the first of many on a variety of topics that Hoover was to organize) was a flood of publicity, pamphlets, and advice from experts. Most of all, the conference urged state and local governments and businesses to cooperate on a volunteer basis to solve the problem. The primary responsibility of the federal government, Hoover believed, was to educate and promote. With all his activity and his organizing, Hoover earned a reputation during the Harding and Coolidge years as an efficient and progressive administrator and as a humanitarian who could organize flood relief. He became one of the most popular figures in government service.

Global Expansion

The decade of the 1920s is often remembered as a time of isolation, when the United States rejected the League of Nations treaty and turned its back on the rest of the world. It is true that many Americans had little interest in what was going on in Paris, Moscow, or Rio de Janeiro, and it is also true that a bloc of congressmen was determined that the United States would never again enter another European war. But the United States remained involved—indeed, increased its involvement—in international affairs during the decade. Although the United States never joined the League of Nations, and a few dedicated isolationists, led by Senator William Borah, blocked membership in the World Court, the United States cooperated with many league agencies and conferences and took the lead in trying to reduce naval armaments and to solve the problems of international finance caused in part by the war.

There were ominous clouds on the horizon. Great Britain and France were slow to recover from the war, while Germany was mired in economic and political chaos. Japan and Italy were unhappy with the peace settlement. Germany's African colonies had been split between France and Great Britain, but imperialism and colonial empires had not diminished. Fascism was establishing a foothold in Spain and Italy, while Soviet communism was becoming more firmly entrenched in Russia. The collapse of the Ottoman Empire had led to the establishment of a new Turkish republic in 1923, but the rest of the Middle East was fragmented both economically and politically and presented problems that would persist for the rest of the twentieth century and beyond.

Business, trade, and finance marked the decade as one of international expansion for the United States. With American corporate investments overseas growing sevenfold during the decade, the United States was transformed from a debtor to a creditor nation. The continued involvement of the United States in the affairs of South and Central American countries also indicated that the country had growing interests beyond its national boundaries. The United States also increased its international position in cable communication, wireless telegraphy, news services, and motion pictures. In some areas, such as film, the United States led the world. In 1925, 95 percent of the films shown in Great Britain and Canada and 70 percent of those shown in France were American made.

Despite growing global expansion in many areas, the U.S. government took up its role of international power reluctantly and with a number of contradictory and disastrous results. "We seek no part in directing the destiny of the world," Harding announced in his inaugural address, but even Harding discovered that international problems would not disappear. One that required immediate attention was the naval arms race.

The United States called the first international conference to discuss disarmament. At the Washington Conference on Naval Disarmament, which convened in November 1921, Secretary of State Charles Evans Hughes startled the delegates by proposing a 10-year "holiday" on the construction of warships and by offering to sink or scrap 845,000 tons of American ships, including 30 battleships. He urged Britain and Japan to do the same. The delegates greeted Hughes's speech with enthusiastic cheering and applause, and they set about the task of sinking more ships than the admirals of all their countries had managed to do in a century.

The conference participants ultimately agreed to fix the tonnage of capital ships at a ratio of the United States and Great Britain, 5; Japan, 3; and France and Italy, 1.67. Japan agreed only reluctantly, but when the United States promised not to fortify its Pacific Island possessions, Japan yielded. In light of what happened in 1941, the Washington Naval Conference has often been criticized, but in 1921, it was appropriately hailed as the first time in history that the major nations of the world had agreed to disarm. The conference did not cause World War II; neither, as it turned out, did it prevent it. But it was a creative start to reducing tensions and to meeting the challenges of the modern arms race. And it was the United States that took the lead by offering to be the first to scrap its battleships.

American foreign policy in the 1920s tried to reduce the risk of international conflict, resist revolution, and make the world safe for trade and investment. In its dealings with Latin America, the United States continued its policy of intervention. By the end of the decade, the United States controlled the financial affairs of 10 Latin American nations. The marines were withdrawn from the Dominican Republic in 1924, but that country remained a virtual protectorate of the United States until 1941. The government ordered the marines out of Nicaragua in 1925 but sent them back the next year when a liberal insurrection threatened the conservative government. But the U.S. Marines, and the Nicaraguan troops they had trained, had a difficult time containing a guerrilla band led by Augusto Sandino, a charismatic leader and one of Latin America's greatest heroes. The Sandinistas, supported by the great majority of peasants, came out of the hills to attack the politicians and their American supporters. In 1934, Sandino was murdered by General Anastasio Somoza, a ruthless leader supported by the United States. For more than 40 years, Somoza and his two sons ruled Nicaragua as a private fiefdom, a legacy not yet resolved in that strife-torn country.

Mexico frightened American businessmen in the mid-1920s by beginning to nationalize foreign holdings in oil and mineral rights. Fearing that further military activity would "injure American interests," businessmen and bankers urged Coolidge not to send marines but to negotiate instead. Coolidge appointed Dwight W. Morrow of the J. P. Morgan Company as ambassador, and his conciliatory attitude led to agreements protecting American investments. Throughout the decade, the goal of U.S. policy toward Central and South America, whether in the form of negotiations or intervention, was to maintain a special sphere of influence.

The U.S. policy of promoting peace, stability, and trade was not always consistent or carefully thought out, and this was especially true in its relationships with Europe. At the end of the war, European countries owed the United States more than $10 billion, with Great Britain and France responsible for about three-fourths of that amount. Both countries, mired in postwar economic problems, suggested that the United States forgive the debts, arguing that they had paid for the war in lives and property destroyed. But the United States, although adjusting the interest and the payment schedule, refused to forget the debt. "They hired the money, didn't they?" Coolidge supposedly remarked.

The only way European nations could repay the United States was by exporting products, but in a series of tariff acts, especially the Fordney–McCumber Tariff of 1922, Congress erected a protective barrier to trade. This act also gave the president power to lower or raise individual rates; in almost every case, both Harding and Coolidge used the power to raise them. Finally, in 1930, the Hawley–Smoot Tariff raised rates even further, despite the protests of many economists. American policy of high tariffs (a counterproductive policy for a creditor nation) caused retaliation and restrictions on American trade, which American corporations were trying to increase.

The inability of the European countries to export products to the United States and to repay their loans was intertwined with the reparations agreement made with Germany. Germany's economy was in disarray after the war, with inflation raging and its industrial plant throttled by the peace treaty. By 1921, Germany was defaulting on its payments. The United States, which believed a healthy Germany important to European stability and world trade, instituted a plan engineered by Charles Dawes whereby the German debt would be renegotiated and spread over a longer period. In the meantime, American bankers and the American government lent Germany hundreds of millions of dollars. In the end, the United States lent money to Germany so it could make payments to Britain and France so that those countries could continue their payments to the United States.

The United States had replaced Great Britain as the dominant force in international finance, but the nation in the 1920s was a reluctant and inconsistent world leader. The United States had stayed out of the League of Nations and was hesitant to get involved in multinational agreements. However, some agreements seemed proper to sign; the most idealistic of all was the Kellogg–Briand pact to outlaw war. The French foreign minister, Aristide Briand, suggested a treaty between the United States and France in large part to commemorate long years of friendship between the two countries, but secretary of state Frank B. Kellogg in 1928 expanded the idea to a multinational treaty to outlaw war. Fourteen nations agreed to sign the treaty, and eventually 62 nations signed, but the only power behind the treaty was moral force rather than economic or military sanctions.

The Survival of Progressivism

The decade of the 1920s was a time of reaction against reform, but progressivism did not simply die. It survived in many forms through the period that Jane Addams called a time of "political and social sag."

The greatest success of the social justice movement was the 1921 Sheppard–Towner Maternity Act, one of the first pieces of federal social welfare legislation and the product of long progressive agitation. A study conducted by the Children's Bureau discovered that more than 3,000 mothers died in childbirth in 1918 and that more than 250,000 infants also died. The United States ranked eighteenth out of 20 countries in maternal mortality and eleventh in infant deaths. The low rank of the United States was caused in part by the poor conditions in urban slums and by rural poverty, especially among southern blacks. But it was also the result of the lack of government intervention to improve health care while many European countries provided health insurance and government-supported medical clinics.

The maternity bill called for $1 million a year to assist the states in providing medical aid and visiting nurses to teach expectant mothers how to care for themselves and their babies. The bill was controversial from the beginning. The American Medical Association, which had supported pure food and drug legislation and laws to protect against health quacks and to enforce standards for medical schools, attacked this bill as leading to socialism and interfering with the relationship between doctor and patient.

Despite the opposition, the bill passed Congress and was signed by President Harding in 1921. The appropriation for the bill was for only six years, and the opposition, again raising the specter of a feminist-Socialist-Communist plot, succeeded in repealing the law in 1929. Yet the Sheppard–Towner Act, promoted and fought for by a group of progressive women, indicated that concern for social justice was not dead in the age of Harding and Coolidge.

PRESIDENTIAL ELECTIONS, 1920–1928

What political trends are revealed in this chart?

Year	Candidate	Party	Popular Vote	Electoral Vote
1920	WARREN G. HARDING	Republican	16,152,200 (60.4%)	404
	James M. Cox	Democratic	9,147,353 (34.2%)	127
	Eugene V. Debs	Socialist	919,799 (3.4%)	0
1924	CALVIN COOLIDGE	Republican	15,725,016 (54.0%)	382
	John W. Davis	Democratic	8,385,586 (28.8%)	136
	Robert M. La Follette	Progressive	4,822,856 (16.6%)	13
1928	HERBERT C. HOOVER	Republican	21,392,190 (58.2%)	444
	Alfred E. Smith	Democratic	15,016,443 (40.9%)	87

Note: Winners' names appear in capital letters.

Temperance Triumphant

For one large group of progressives, Prohibition, like child labor reform and maternity benefits, was an important effort to conserve human resources. By 1918, more than three-fourths of the people in the country lived in dry states or counties, but it was the war that allowed the antisaloon advocates to associate Prohibition with patriotism. "We have German enemies across the water," one prohibitionist announced. "We have German enemies in this country too. And the worst of all our German enemies, the most treacherous, the most menacing are Pabst, Schlitz, Blatz and Miller." In 1919, Congress passed the Volstead Act, banning the brewing and selling of beverages containing more than one-half of one percent alcohol. In June 1919, the thirty-sixth state ratified the Eighteenth Amendment, prohibiting the manufacture, sale, and transport of intoxicating liquors. But the country had, for all practical purposes, been dry since 1917.

The Prohibition experiment probably did reduce the total consumption of alcohol in the country, especially in rural areas and urban working-class neighborhoods. Fewer arrests for drunkenness occurred, and deaths from alcoholism declined. But the legislation showed the difficulty of using law to promote moral reform. Most people who wanted to drink during the "noble experiment" found a way. Speakeasies replaced saloons, and people consumed bathtub gin, home brew, and many strange and dangerous concoctions. Bartenders invented the cocktail to disguise the poor quality of liquor, and women, at least middle- and upper-class women, began to drink in public for the first time.

Prohibition also created great bootlegging rings, which were tied to organized crime in many cities. Al Capone of Chicago was the most famous underworld figure whose power and wealth were based on the sale of illegal alcohol. His organization alone grossed an estimated $60 million in 1927; ironically, most of the profit came from distributing beer. Many supporters of Prohibition slowly came to favor its repeal, some because it reduced the power of the states, others because it stimulated too much illegal activity and because it did not seem to be worth the social and political costs.

The Election of 1928

On August 2, 1927, President Coolidge announced simply, "I do not choose to run for President in 1928." Hoover immediately became the logical Republican candidate. Hoover and Coolidge were not especially close. Coolidge resented what he considered Hoover's spendthrift ways. "That man has offered me unsolicited advice for six years, all of it bad," Coolidge once remarked. Though lacking an enthusiastic endorsement from the president and opposed by some Republicans who thought him to be too progressive, Hoover easily won the nomination. In a year when the country was buoyant with optimism and when prosperity seemed as if it would go on forever, few doubted that Hoover would be elected.

The Democrats nominated Alfred Smith, a Catholic Irish American from New York. With his New York accent, his opposition to Prohibition, and his flamboyant style, he contrasted sharply with the more sedate Hoover. On one level, it was a bitter contest between Catholic "wets" and Protestant "drys," between the urban, ethnic Tammany politician and former governor of New York against the rural-born but sophisticated secretary of commerce. Religious prejudice, especially a persistent anti-Catholicism, played an important role in the campaign. But looked at more closely, the two candidates differed little. Both

Timeline

1900–1930	Electricity powers the "second Industrial Revolution"
1917	Race riot in East St. Louis, Illinois
1918	World War I ends
1919	Treaty of Versailles
	Strikes in Seattle, Boston, and elsewhere
	Red Scare and Palmer raids
	Race riots in Chicago and other cities
	Marcus Garvey's Universal Negro Improvement Association spreads
1920	Warren Harding elected president
	Women vote in national elections
	First commercial radio broadcast
	Sacco and Vanzetti arrested
	Sinclair Lewis, *Main Street*
1921	Immigration Quota Law
	Naval Disarmament Conference
	First birth control conference
	Sheppard–Towner Maternity Act
1921–1922	Postwar depression
1922	Fordney–McCumber Tariff
	Sinclair Lewis, *Babbitt*
1923	Harding dies; Calvin Coolidge becomes president
	Teapot Dome scandal
1924	Coolidge reelected president
	Peak of Ku Klux Klan activity
	Immigration Quota Law
1925	Scopes trial in Dayton, Tennessee
	F. Scott Fitzgerald, *The Great Gatsby*
	Bruce Barton, *The Man Nobody Knows*
	Alain Locke, *The New Negro*
	Claude McKay, *Home to Harlem*
	5 million enameled bathroom fixtures produced
1926	Ernest Hemingway, *The Sun Also Rises*
1927	National Origins Act
	McNary–Haugen Farm Relief Bill
	Sacco and Vanzetti executed
	Lindbergh flies solo from New York to Paris
	First talking movie, *The Jazz Singer*
	Henry Ford produces 15 millionth car
1928	Herbert Hoover elected president
	Kellogg–Briand Treaty
	Stock market soars
1929	27 million registered autos in country
	10 million households own radios
	100 million people attend movies
	Stock market crash

were self-made men, both were "progressives." Social justice reformers campaigned for each candidate. Both candidates tried to attract women voters, both were favorable to organized labor, both defended capitalism, and both had millionaires and corporate executives among their advisers.

Hoover won in a landslide, 444 electoral votes to 76 for Smith, who carried only Massachusetts and Rhode Island outside the Deep South. But the 1928 campaign revitalized the Democratic party. Smith polled nearly twice as many votes as the Democratic candidate in 1924, and for the first time, the Democrats carried the 12 largest cities.

Stock Market Crash

Hoover, as it turned out, had only six months to apply his progressive and efficient methods to running the country; in the fall of 1929, the prosperity that seemed endless suddenly came to a halt. In 1928 and 1929, rampant speculation made the stock market boom. Money could be made everywhere—in real estate and business ventures, but especially in the stock market. "Everybody ought to be Rich," Al Smith's campaign manager argued in an article in *Ladies' Home Journal* early in 1929. Just save $15 a month and buy good common stock with it, and that money would turn into $80,000 in 20 years (a considerable fortune in 1929). Good common stock seemed to be easy to find in 1929.

Only a small percentage of the American people invested in the stock market, for many had no way of saving even $15 a month. But a large number got into the game in the late 1920s because it seemed a safe and sure way to make money. For many, the stock market came to represent the American economy, and the economy was booming. The *New York Times* index of 25 industrial stocks reached 100 in 1924, moved up to 181 in 1925, dropped a bit in 1926, and rose again to 245 by the end of 1927.

Then the orgy started. During 1928, the market rose to 331. Many investors and speculators began to buy on margin (borrowing to invest). Businessmen and others began to invest in the market money that would ordinarily have gone into houses, cars, and other goods. Yet even at the peak of the boom, probably only about 1.5 million Americans owned stock.

In early September 1929, the *New York Times* index peaked at 452 and then began to drift downward. On October 23, the market lost 31 points. The next day ("Black Thursday"), it first seemed that everyone was trying to sell, but at the end of the day, the panic appeared to be over. It was not. By mid-November, the market had plummeted to 224, about half what it had been two months before. This represented a loss on paper of over $26 billion. Still, a month later, the chairman of the board of Bethlehem Steel could announce, "Never before has American business been as firmly entrenched for prosperity as it is today." Some businessmen even got back into the market, thinking that it had reached its low point. But it continued to go down. Tens of thousands of investors lost everything. Those who had bought on margin had to keep coming up with money to pay off their loans as the value of their holdings declined. There was panic and despair, but the legendary stories of executives jumping out of windows were grossly exaggerated.

The stock market crash was more symptom than cause of the economic collapse. Weak banking systems in both Europe and America, the rise of protectionism, the drop in farm prices, and the decline of purchasing power all foreshadowed the economic disaster that would follow the stock market debacle.

Conclusion

A NEW ERA OF PROSPERITY AND PROBLEMS

The stock market crash ended the decade of prosperity. The crash did not cause the Depression, but the stock market debacle revealed the weakness of the economy. The fruits of economic expansion had been unevenly distributed. The Parker family, introduced at the beginning of this chapter, and many other families in both rural and urban America did not

share in the prosperity. Not enough people could afford to buy the autos, refrigerators, and other products pouring from American factories. Prosperity had been built on a shaky foundation. When that foundation crumbled in 1929, the nation slid into a major depression. But the Depression was related to global financial trends and to economic problems created by World War I and the peace settlement. High tariffs and reparations that wrecked the German economy and a weakened banking system all contributed to the economic collapse. Looking back from the vantage point of the 1930s or later, the 1920s seemed a golden era—an age of flappers, bootleg gin, constant parties, literary masterpieces, sports heroes, and easy wealth. The truth is much more complicated. More than most decades, the 1920s was a time of paradox and contradictions.

The 1920s was a time of prosperity, yet a great many people, including farmers, blacks, and other ordinary Americans, did not prosper. The 1920s was a time of modernization, but only about 10 percent of rural families had electricity. It was a time when women achieved more sexual freedom, but the feminist movement declined. It was a time of Prohibition, but many Americans increased their consumption of alcohol. It was a time of reaction against reform, yet progressivism survived. It was a time when intellectuals felt disillusioned with America, yet it was one of the most creative and innovative periods for American writers. It was a time of flamboyant heroes, yet the American people elected the lackluster Harding and Coolidge as their presidents. It was a time of progress, when almost every year saw a new technological breakthrough, but it was also a decade of hate and intolerance. The complex and contradictory legacy of the 1920s continues to fascinate and to influence our time.

QUESTIONS FOR REVIEW AND REFLECTION

1. What was the Harlem Renaissance?
2. Did the Prohibition experiment succeed or fail?
3. In foreign policy during the 1920s did the United States try to isolate itself from the rest of the world?
4. What groups did not share in the prosperity of the decade?
5. Why are Harding and Coolidge often considered among our worst presidents?

CHAPTER 24

The Great Depression and the New Deal

The American Dream

Margaret Bourke-White, one of the outstanding documentary photographers of the 1930s, captured the disjunction between the ideal and the real in the Depression era. This photograph, depicting African American flood victims lining up for food in Louisville, Kentucky, underneath a propaganda billboard erected by the National Association of Manufacturers, contrasts the American Dream with the reality of racism and poverty. Does this famous photograph depict the contrast in American life unfairly?

(Margaret Bourke-White, *The Louisville Flood,* 1937. Photograph Copyright © 1966: Whitney Museum of American Art, New York, Gift of Sean Callahan [92.58])

American Stories

Coming of Age and Riding the Rails During the Depression

Flickering in a Seattle movie theater in the depths of the Great Depression, the Hollywood production *Wild Boys of the Road* captivated 13-year-old Robert Symmonds. The film, released in 1933, told the story of boys hitching rides on trains and tramping around the country. It was supposed to warn teenagers of the dangers of rail riding, but for some it had the opposite effect. Robert, a boy from a middle-class home, already had a fascination with hobos. He had watched his mother give sandwiches to the transient men who sometimes knocked on the back door. He had taken to hanging around the "Hooverville" shantytown south of the King Street railroad station, where he would sit next to the fires and listen to the rail riders' stories. Stoked for adventure, when school let out in 1934, Robert and a school friend hopped onto a moving boxcar on a train headed out of town. Hands reached out to pull them aboard the car, which already held 20 men. The two boys journeyed as far as Vancouver, Washington, and home to Seattle again. It was frightening, and exhilarating.

In 1938, under the weight of the Depression, the Symmonds family's security business failed. Years later, Robert recalled the effects on his father: "It hurt him bad when he went broke and all his friends deserted him. He did the best he could but never recovered his self-esteem and his pride." The loss of income forced Robert's family to accept a relative's offer of shelter in a three-room mountain cabin without electricity. Because of the move, Robert could no longer attend high school in Seattle. Once again, this time out of necessity, he turned to the rails, leaving his parents and three sisters behind.

Robert faced a personal challenge of surviving difficult times, but he also was part of a looming problem that troubled the administration of Franklin D. Roosevelt. Thousands of young people were graduating from high school or leaving school early, with very few jobs open to them. An estimated 250,000 young people were among the drifters who resorted to the often dangerous practice of hitching rides on trains around the country. Robert rode the rails during summers to find work harvesting fruit up and down the West Coast. In 1939, his travels took him to Montana, where he encountered the Roosevelt administration's solution for the "youth problem": the Civilian Conservation Corps (CCC). When he enlisted in the CCC, Robert became one of nearly 3 million young men age 17 and older who found work in government-sponsored conservation projects between 1933 and 1942. CCC workers earned $25 a month for their families back home plus $5 a month spending money for themselves.

The CCC was known as Roosevelt's "tree army" because the corps planted trees covering more than 2 million acres, improved more than 4 million acres of existing forest, and fought forest fires. In addition, the CCC worked on a wide variety of conservation-related projects in a nation suffering from deforestation, erosion, drought, dust storms, and other environmental problems. They improved parks and recreation areas and even Civil War historic sites, including the notorious Andersonville prison camp in Georgia. In many ways, the CCC operated like a military organization, with workers wearing surplus World War I uniforms and following a fixed regimen of work and recreation that began with a bugler's call at 6 A.M.

One historian has called the CCC the greatest peacetime mobilization in U.S. history, and it set the stage for the wartime mobilization that followed. Like many CCC veterans, Robert Symmonds's next stop in life was military service. He joined the navy and after the war became a merchant seaman. In later years, like many Americans of his generation, Robert remembered his experiences of the Great Depression grimly, but with some nostalgia. He even returned to hopping rides on railroad cars again during his retirement years, out of a sense of adventure rather than necessity. "It's something that got into my blood years ago," he explained. "I guess it is a freedom thing."

The Great Depression changed the lives of all Americans, separating that generation from the one that followed. An exaggerated need for security, the fear of failure, a nagging sense of guilt, and a real sense that it might happen all over again divided the Depression generation from everyone born after 1940. Like Robert Symmonds, they never forgot those bleak years.

This chapter explores the causes and consequences of the Great Depression, which had an impact around the world. We will look at Herbert Hoover and his efforts to combat the Depression and then turn to Franklin Roosevelt, the dominant personality of the 1930s. We will examine the New Deal and Roosevelt's program to bring relief, recovery, and reform to the nation. The New Deal legislation, some of which continued reforms started during the progressive era, did not end the Depression. But this legislation was based on the idea that the federal government had some responsibility for the economy and for promoting the welfare of all the people. We will also look at the other side of the 1930s, for the decade did not consist only of crippling unemployment and New Deal agencies. It was also a time of great strides in technology, when innovative developments in radio, movies, and the automobile affected the lives of most Americans.

The Great Depression

There had been recessions and depressions in American history, notably in the 1830s, 1870s, and 1890s, but nothing compared with the devastating economic collapse of the 1930s. The Great Depression was all the more shocking because it came after a decade of unprecedented prosperity, when most experts assumed that the United States was immune to a downturn in the business cycle. The Great Depression had an impact on all areas of American life; perhaps most important, it destroyed American confidence in the future.

The Depression Begins

Few people anticipated the stock market crash in the fall of 1929. But even after the collapse of the stock market, few expected the entire economy to go into a tailspin. General Electric stock, selling for 396 in 1929, fell to 34 in 1932; U.S. Steel declined from 261 to 21. By 1932, the median income had plunged to half of what it had been in 1929. Construction spending fell to one-sixth of the 1929 level. By 1932, at least one of every four American breadwinners was out of work, and industrial production had almost ground to a halt.

Why did the nation sink deeper and deeper into depression? The answer is complex, but it appears in retrospect that the prosperity of the 1920s was superficial. Farmers and coal and textile workers had suffered all through the 1920s from low prices, and the farmers were the first group in the 1930s to plunge into depression. But other aspects of the economy also lurched out of balance. Two percent of the population received about 28 percent of the national income, but the lower 60 percent got only 24 percent. Businesses increased profits while holding down wages and the prices of raw materials. This pattern depressed consumer purchasing power. American workers, like American farmers, did not have the money to buy the goods they helped to produce. There was a relative decline in purchasing power in the late 1920s, unemployment was high in some industries, and the housing and automobile industries were already beginning to slacken before the crash.

Well-to-do Americans were speculating a significant portion of their money in the stock market. Their illusion of permanent prosperity helped fire the boom of the 1920s, just as their pessimism and lack of confidence helped exaggerate the Depression in 1931 and 1932.

Other factors were also involved. The stock market crash revealed serious structural weaknesses in the financial and banking systems (7,000 banks had failed during the 1920s). The Federal Reserve Board, fearing inflation, tightened credit—exactly the opposite of the action it should have taken to fight a slowdown in purchasing. But the Depression was also caused by global economic problems created by World War I and the peace settlement. Large reparations exacted against Germany had led to the collapse of the German economy, and high tariffs had reduced international trade. When American investment in Europe slowed in 1928 and 1929, European economies declined. Americans purchased fewer European goods, and Europeans got along without American products. As the European financial situation worsened, the American economy spiraled downward.

The federal government might have prevented the stock market crash and the Depression by more careful regulation of business and the stock market. Central planning might have ensured a more equitable distribution of income. But that kind of policy would have taken more foresight than most people had in the 1920s. It certainly would have required different people to be in power, and it is unlikely that the Democrats, had they been in control, would have altered the government's policies in fundamental ways.

Hoover and the Great Depression

Initial business and government reactions to the stock market crash were optimistic. "All the evidence indicates that the worst effects of the crash upon unemployment will have been passed during the next sixty days," Herbert Hoover reported. Hoover, the great planner and progressive efficiency expert, did not sit idly by and watch the country drift toward disorder. His upbeat first statements were calculated to prevent further panic.

Hoover acted aggressively to stem the economic collapse. More than any president before him, he used the power of the federal government and the office of the president to deal with an economic crisis. Nobody called it a depression for the first year at least, for the economic problems seemed very much like earlier cyclic recessions. Hoover called conferences of businessmen and labor leaders. He met with mayors and governors and encouraged them to speed up public works projects. He created agencies and boards, such as the National Credit Corporation and the Emergency Committee for Employment, to obtain voluntary action to solve the problem. Hoover even supported a tax cut, which Congress enacted in December 1929, but it did little to stimulate spending.

Economic Decline

Voluntary action and psychological campaigns could not stop the Depression. The stock market, after appearing to bottom out in the winter of 1930–1931, continued its decline, responding in part to the European economic collapse that undermined international finance and trade. Of course, not everyone lost money in the market. William Danforth, founder of

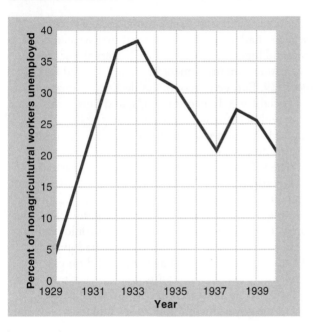

Unemployment Rate, 1929–1940

Although the unemployment rate declined during the New Deal years, the number still unemployed remained tragically high until World War II brought full employment.

Source: U.S. Bureau of the Census.

Ralston Purina, and Joseph Kennedy, film magnate, entrepreneur, and the father of a future president, were among those who made millions of dollars by selling short as the market went down.

More than a collapsing market afflicted the economy; an additional 1,300 banks failed in 1930. Despite Hoover's pleas, many factories cut back on production, and some simply closed. U.S. Steel announced a 10 percent wage cut in 1931. As the auto industry laid off workers, the unemployment rate rose to more than 40 percent in Detroit. More than 4 million Americans were out of work in 1930, and at least 12 million were unemployed by 1932. Foreclosures and evictions created thousands of personal tragedies. While the middle class watched in horror as their life savings and their dreams disappeared, the rich were increasingly concerned as the price of government bonds (the symbol of safety and security) dropped. They began to hoard gold and fear revolution.

There was never any real danger of revolution. Some farmers organized to dump their milk to protest low prices, and when a neighbor's farm was sold, they gathered to hold a penny auction, bidding only a few cents for equipment and returning it to their dispossessed neighbor. But everywhere, people despaired as the Depression deepened in 1931 and 1932. For unemployed blacks and for many tenant farmers, the Depression had little immediate effect because their lives were already so depressed. Most Americans (the 98 percent who did not own stock) hardly noticed

the stock market crash; for them, the Depression meant the loss of a job or a bank foreclosure. For Robert Symmonds it meant the failure of his father's business and being forced to drop out of high school. For some farmers, it was burning corn rather than coal because the price of corn had fallen so low that it was not worth marketing. Not everyone went hungry, stood in bread lines, or lost jobs during the Depression, but almost everyone was affected, and many tended to blame themselves.

The Depression probably disrupted women's lives less than men's. When men lost their jobs, their identity and sense of purpose as the family breadwinner were shattered. Some helped out with family chores, but usually with bitterness and resentment. For women, however, even when money was short, there was still cooking, cleaning, and mending, and women were still in command of their households. Yet many women were forced to do extra work. They took in laundry, found room for a boarder, and made the clothes they formerly would have bought. Women also bore the psychological burden of unemployed husbands, hungry children, and unpaid bills. The Depression altered patterns of family life, and many families were forced to move in with relatives. The marriage rate, the divorce rate, and the birthrate all dropped during the decade. Many of these changes created tension that statistics cannot capture.

A Global Depression

Hoover reacted to growing despair by urging more voluntary action. He insisted on maintaining the gold standard, believing it to be the only responsible currency, and a balanced budget. He blamed the Depression on international economic problems, and he was at least partly right. The legacy of the war and the global economic policies of the 1920s had been one cause of the economic downturn in the United States, and as the United States sank into depression, the world followed. In May 1931, the leading Austrian bank collapsed; by June, the German financial system, which had gone from hyperinflation to false stability, was in chaos. In September, England abandoned the gold standard, precipitating a decline in international lending and trade. Soon most of the industrialized world, including Argentina, Brazil, and Japan, was caught in the Great Depression. In some countries, the social safety net of health and unemployment insurance helped, but there were hungry and unemployed people in much of the world. That a stock market crash in the United States triggered a worldwide depression indicated that by 1930 the United States was an economic world power, but that was little solace as the global depression extended and heightened the Depression at home.

Despite the worldwide depression, Americans began to blame Hoover for some of the disaster. The president became isolated and bitter. The shanties that grew near all the large cities were called "Hoovervilles," and the privies "Hoover villas." Unable to admit mistakes and to take a new tack, he could not communicate personal empathy for the poor and the unemployed.

Hoover did try innovative schemes. More public works projects were built during his administration than in the previous 30 years. In the summer of 1931, he attempted to organize a pool of private money to rescue banks and businesses that were near failure. When the private effort failed, he turned reluctantly to Congress, which passed a bill early in 1932 authorizing the Reconstruction Finance Corporation. The RFC lent money to banks, insurance companies, farm mortgage companies, and railroads. Some critics charged that it was simply another trickle-down measure whereby businessmen and bankers would be given aid while the unemployed were ignored. Hoover, however, correctly understood the immense costs to individuals and to communities when a bank or mortgage company failed. The RFC did help shore up a number of shaky financial institutions and remained the major government finance agency until World War II. But it became much more effective under Roosevelt because it lent directly to industry.

Hoover also asked Congress for a Home Financing Corporation to make mortgages more readily available. The Federal Home Loan Bank Act of 1932 became the basis for the Federal Housing Administration of the New Deal years. He supported the passage of the Glass–Steagall Banking Act of 1932, which expanded credit to make more loans available to businesses and individuals. But Hoover rejected calls for the federal government to restrict production in hopes of raising farm prices—that, he believed, was too much government intervention. He maintained that the federal government should promote cooperation and even create public works. But he firmly believed in loans, not direct subsidies, and he thought it was the responsibility of state and local governments, as well as of private charity, to provide direct relief to the unemployed and the needy.

The Bonus Army

Many World War I veterans lost their jobs during the Great Depression, and beginning in 1930, they lobbied for the payment of their veterans' bonuses, which were not due until 1945. In May 1932, about 17,000 veterans marched on Washington. Some took up residence in an outlying shantytown called Bonus City.

In mid-June, the Senate defeated the bonus bill, and most of the veterans, disappointed but resigned, accepted a free railroad ticket home. Several thousand remained, however, along with some wives and children, in the unsanitary shacks during the steaming summer heat. Among them were a small group of committed Communists and other radicals. Hoover, who exaggerated the subversive elements among those still camped out in Washington, refused to talk to the leaders and finally called out the U.S. army.

General Douglas MacArthur, the army chief of staff, ordered the army to disperse the veterans. He described the Bonus marchers as a "mob...animated by the essence of revolution." With tanks, guns, and tear gas, the army routed veterans who 15 years before had worn the same uniform as their attackers. Two Bonus marchers were killed, and several others were injured. The army was not attacking revolutionaries in the streets of Washington but was routing bewildered, confused, unemployed men who had seen their American dream collapse.

The Bonus army fiasco, bread lines, and Hoovervilles became the symbols of Hoover's presidency. He deserved better because he tried to use the power of the federal government to solve growing and increasingly complex economic problems. But in the end, his personality and background limited him. He could not understand why army veterans marched on Washington to ask for a handout when he thought they should all be back home working hard, practicing self-reliance, and cooperating "to avert the terrible situation in which we are today." He believed that the greatest problem besetting Americans was a lack of confidence. Yet he could not communicate with these people or inspire their confidence. Willing to use the federal government to support business, he could not accept federal aid for the unemployed. He feared an unbalanced budget and a large federal bureaucracy that would interfere with the "American way." Ironically, his actions and his inactions led in the next years to a massive increase in federal power and in the federal bureaucracy.

Roosevelt and the First New Deal

The first New Deal, lasting from 1933 to early 1935, focused mainly on recovery from the Depression and relief for the poor and unemployed. Some of the programs were borrowed from the Hoover administration, and some had their origin in the progressive period. Others were inspired by the nation's experiences in mobilizing for World War I. No single ideological position united all the legislation, for Franklin Roosevelt was a pragmatist who was willing to try a variety of programs. More than Hoover, however, he believed in economic planning and in government spending to help the poor.

Roosevelt's caution and conservatism shaped the first New Deal. He did not promote socialism or suggest nationalizing the banks. He was even careful in authorizing public works projects to stimulate the economy. The New Deal was based on the assumption that it was possible to create a just society by superimposing a welfare state on the capitalist system, leaving the profit motive undisturbed. While the progressives believed in voluntary action and only reluctantly concluded that the federal government needed to intervene to promote a just society, the New Dealers, from the beginning, believed in an active role for the government. Roosevelt was confident he could achieve his goals through cooperation with the business community. Later he would move more toward reform, but at first his primary concern was simply relief and recovery.

The Election of 1932

The Republicans nominated Herbert Hoover for a second term, but in the summer of 1932, the Depression and Hoover's unpopularity opened the way for the Democrats. After a shrewd campaign, Franklin D. Roosevelt, governor of New York, won the nomination. Distantly related to Theodore Roosevelt, FDR had served as an assistant secretary of the navy during World War I and had been the Democratic vice presidential candidate in 1920. Crippled by polio not long after, he had recovered enough to serve as governor of New York for two terms, although he was not especially well-known by the general public in 1932.

As governor, Roosevelt had promoted cheaper electric power, conservation, and old-age pensions. He became the first governor to support state aid for the unemployed, "not as a matter of charity, but as a matter of social duty." But it was difficult to tell during the presidential campaign exactly what he stood for. He did announce that the government must do something for the "forgotten man at the bottom of the economic pyramid," yet he also mentioned the need for balancing the budget and maintaining the gold standard. Ambiguity was probably the best strategy in 1932, but the truth was that Roosevelt did not have a master plan to save the country. He won the election overwhelmingly, carrying more than 57 percent of the popular vote.

During the campaign, Roosevelt had promised a "new deal for the American people." But the New Deal had to wait for four months because the Constitution provided that the new president be inaugurated on March 4 (this was changed to January 20 by the Twentieth Amendment, ratified in 1933). During the long interregnum, the state of the nation deteriorated badly. The banking system seemed near collapse, and the hardship increased. Hoover tried to cooperate with the president-elect and with a hostile Congress, but he could accomplish little. Everyone waited for the new president to take office and to act.

The Disabled President

This is a rare photograph of Franklin Roosevelt in his wheelchair taken in a private moment with his dog, Fala, and a young friend. Usually FDR's advisers carefully arranged to have the president photographed only when he was seated or propped up behind a podium. Despite being paralyzed from the waist down, the president gave the impression of health and vitality until near the end of his life. Did his physical disability restrict his ability to be president?

(Margaret Suckley Collection, Franklin Delano Roosevelt Library)

In his inaugural address, Roosevelt announced confidently, "The only thing we have to fear is fear itself." This, of course, was not true, for the country faced the worst crisis since the Civil War, but Roosevelt's confidence and his ability to communicate with ordinary Americans were obvious early in his presidency. He had clever speechwriters, a sense of pace and rhythm in his speeches, and an ability, when he spoke on the radio, to convince listeners that he was speaking directly to them. Recognizing the possibilities of the new media, he instituted a series of radio "fireside chats" to explain to the American people what he was doing to solve the nation's problems. When he said "my friends," millions believed that he meant it.

Roosevelt's Advisers

During the interregnum, Roosevelt surrounded himself with intelligent and innovative advisers. His cabinet was made up of a mixture of people from different backgrounds who often did not agree with one another. Harold Ickes, the secretary of the interior, was a Republican lawyer from Chicago and a one-time supporter of Theodore Roosevelt. Another Republican, Henry Wallace of Iowa, a plant geneticist and agricultural statistician, became the secretary of agriculture. Frances Perkins, the first woman ever appointed to a cabinet post, became the secretary of labor. A disciple of Jane Addams and Florence Kelley, she had been a settlement resident, secretary of the New York Consumers League, and an adviser to Al Smith.

In addition to the formal cabinet, Roosevelt appointed an informal "Brain Trust," including Adolph Berle, Jr., a young expert on corporation law, and Rexford Tugwell, a Columbia University authority on agricultural economics and a committed national planner. Roosevelt also appointed Raymond Moley, another Columbia professor, who later became one of the president's severest critics, and Harry Hopkins, a nervous, energetic man whose concern for the poor and unemployed would play a large role in the formulation of New Deal policy.

Eleanor Roosevelt was a controversial first lady. She wrote a newspaper column, made speeches and radio broadcasts, traveled widely, and listened to the concerns of women, minorities, and ordinary Americans. Attacked by critics who thought she had too much power and mocked for her protruding front teeth, her awkward ways, and her upper-class accent, she courageously took stands on issues of social justice and civil rights. She helped push the president toward social reform.

Roosevelt proved to be an adept politician. He was not well read, especially on economic matters, but he had the ability to learn from his advisers and yet not be dominated by them. He took ideas, plans, and suggestions from conflicting sources and combined them. He had a "flypaper mind," one of his advisers decided. There was no overall plan, no master strategy. An improviser and a pragmatist who once likened himself to a football quarterback who called one play and if it did not work called a different one, Roosevelt was an optimist by nature. And he believed in action.

One Hundred Days

Because Roosevelt took office in the middle of a major crisis, a cooperative Congress was willing to pass almost any legislation that he put before it. In three months, numerous bills were rushed through. Some of them were not well thought out, and some contradicted other legislation. But many of the laws passed during Roosevelt's first 100 days would have far-reaching implications for the relationship of government to society. Roosevelt was an opportunist, but unlike Hoover,

he was willing to use direct government action to solve the problems of depression and unemployment. As it turned out, none of the bills passed during the first 100 days cured the Depression, but taken together, the legislation constituted one of the most innovative periods in American political history.

The Banking Crisis

The most immediate problem Roosevelt faced was the condition of the banks. Many had closed, and American citizens, no longer trusting the financial institutions, were hoarding money and putting their assets into gold. Roosevelt immediately declared a four-day bank holiday. Three days later, an emergency session of Congress approved his action and within hours gave the president broad powers over financial transactions, prohibited the hoarding of gold, and allowed for the reopening of sound banks, sometimes with loans from the Reconstruction Finance Corporation.

Within the next few years, Congress passed additional legislation that gave the federal government more regulatory power over the stock market and over the process by which corporations issued stock. It also passed the Banking Act of 1933, which strengthened the Federal Reserve System, established the Federal Deposit Insurance Corporation (FDIC), and insured individual deposits up to $5,000. Although the American Bankers Association opposed the plan as "unsound, unscientific, unjust and dangerous," banks were soon attracting depositors by advertising that they were protected by government insurance.

The Democratic platform in 1932 called for reduced government spending and an end to Prohibition. Roosevelt moved quickly on both. The Economy Act, which passed Congress easily, called for a 15 percent reduction in government salaries as well as a reorganization of federal agencies to save money. The bill also cut veterans' pensions, despite their protests. However, the Economy Act's small savings were dwarfed by other bills passed the same week, which called for increased spending. The Beer-Wine Revenue Act legalized beer that had an alcohol content of 3.2 percent and light wines and levied a tax on both. The Twenty-First Amendment, ratified on December 5, 1933, repealed the Eighteenth Amendment and ended Prohibition.

Congress granted Roosevelt great power to devalue the dollar and to manipulate inflation. Some members argued for the old Populist solution of free and unlimited coinage of silver, while others called for issuing billions of dollars in paper currency. Bankers and businessmen feared inflation, but farmers and debtors favored an inflationary policy as a way to raise prices and put more money in their pockets. Roosevelt rejected the more extreme inflationary plans supported by many congressmen from the agricultural states, but he did take the country off the gold standard. No longer would paper currency be redeemable in gold. The action terrified some conservative businessmen, who argued that it would lead to "uncontrolled inflation and complete chaos." Even Roosevelt's director of the budget announced solemnly that going off the gold standard "meant the end of Western Civilization."

Devaluation did not end Western civilization, but neither did it lead to instant recovery. After experimenting with pushing the price of gold up by buying it in the open market, Roosevelt and his advisers fixed the price at $35 an ounce in January 1934 (against the old price of $20.63). This inflated the dollar by about 40 percent. Roosevelt also tried briefly to induce inflation through the purchase of silver, but soon the country settled down to a slightly inflated currency and a dollar based on both gold and silver.

Relief Measures

Roosevelt believed in economy in government and in a balanced budget, but he also wanted to help the unemployed and the homeless. One survey estimated in 1933 that 1.5 million Americans were homeless. One man with a wife and six children from Latrobe, Pennsylvania, who was being evicted wrote, "I have 10 days to get another house, no job, no means of paying rent, can you advise me as to which would be the most humane way to dispose of myself and family, as this is about the only thing that I see left to do."

Roosevelt's answer was the Federal Emergency Relief Administration (FERA), which Congress authorized with an appropriation of $500 million in direct grants to cities and states. A few months later, Roosevelt created a Civil Works Administration (CWA) to put more than 4 million people to work on various state, municipal, and federal projects. Hopkins, who ran both agencies, had experimented with work relief programs in New York. Like most social workers, he believed it was much better to pay people to work than to give them charity. An accountant working on a road project said, "I'd rather stay out here in that ditch the rest of my life than take one cent of direct relief."

The CWA was not always effective, but in just over a year, the agency built or restored half a million miles of roads and constructed 40,000 schools and 1,000 airports. It hired 50,000 teachers to keep rural schools open and others to teach adult education courses in the cities. It also put more than a billion dollars of purchasing power into the economy. Roosevelt, who later would be accused of deficit spending, feared that the program was costing too much and might create a permanent class of relief recipients. In the spring of 1934, he ordered the CWA closed down.

The Public Works Administration (PWA), directed by Harold Ickes, in some respects overlapped the work of the CWA, but it lasted longer. Between 1933 and 1939, the PWA built hospitals, courthouses, and school buildings. It helped construct projects as diverse as the port of Brownsville, Texas, two aircraft carriers, and low-cost housing for slum dwellers.

One purpose of the PWA was economic pump priming—the stimulation of the economy and consumer spending through the investment of government funds. Afraid that there might be scandals in the agency, Ickes spent money slowly and carefully. Thus, during the first years, PWA projects, worthwhile as most of them were, did little to stimulate the economy.

Agricultural Adjustment Act

In 1933, most farmers were desperate, as mounting surpluses and falling prices drastically cut their incomes. Some in the Midwest talked of open rebellion, even of revolution. But most observers saw only hopelessness and despair in farmers who had worked hard but were still losing their farms.

Congress passed a number of bills in 1933 and 1934 to deal with the agricultural crisis. But the New Deal's principal solution to the farm problem was the Agricultural Adjustment Act (AAA), which sought to control the overproduction of basic commodities so that farmers might regain the purchasing power they had enjoyed before World War I. To guarantee these "parity prices" (the average prices in the years 1909–1914), the production of major agricultural staples—wheat, cotton, corn, hogs, rice, tobacco, and milk—would be controlled by paying the farmers to reduce their acreage under cultivation. The AAA levied a tax at the processing stage to pay for the program.

The act aroused great disagreement among farm leaders and economists, but the controversy was nothing compared with the outcry from the public over the initial action of the AAA in the summer of 1933. To prevent a glut on the cotton and pork markets, the agency ordered 10 million acres of cotton plowed up and 6 million young pigs slaughtered. It seemed unnatural, even immoral, to kill pigs and plow up cotton when millions of people were underfed and in need of clothes.

The Agricultural Adjustment Act did raise the prices of some agricultural products. But it helped the larger farmers more than the small operators, and it was often disastrous for the tenant farmers and sharecroppers. Landowners often discharged tenant families when they reduced the acres under cultivation. Many sharecroppers were simply cast out on the road with a few possessions and nowhere to go. Large farmers cultivated their fewer acres more intensely, so that the total crop was little reduced. In the end, the prolonged drought that hit the Southwest in 1934 did more than the AAA to limit production and raise agricultural prices. But the long-range significance of the AAA, which was later declared unconstitutional, was the establishment of the idea that the government should subsidize farmers for limiting production.

Industrial Recovery

The legislation during the first days of the Roosevelt administration contained something for almost every group. The National Industrial Recovery Act (NIRA) was designed to help business, raise prices, control production, and put people back to work. The act established the National Recovery Administration (NRA), with the power to set fair competition codes in all industries. For a time, everyone forgot about antitrust laws and talked of cooperation and planning rather than competition. There were parades and rallies, even a postage stamp, and industries that cooperated could display a blue eagle, the symbol of the NRA, designed to symbolize patriotic cooperation. "We Do Our Part," the posters and banners proclaimed, but the results were somewhat less than the promise.

Section 7a of the NIRA, included at the insistence of organized labor, guaranteed labor's right to organize and to bargain collectively and established the National Labor Board to see that their rights were respected. But the board, usually dominated by businesspeople, often interpreted the labor provisions of the contracts loosely. In addition, small-business owners complained that the NIRA was unfair to their interests. Any attempt to set prices led to controversy.

Many consumers suspected that the codes and contracts were raising prices, while others feared the return of monopoly in some industries. When the Supreme Court declared the NIRA unconstitutional in 1935, few people complained. Still, the NIRA was an ambitious attempt to bring some order into a confused business situation, and the labor provisions of the act were picked up later by the National Labor Relations Act.

Civilian Conservation Corps

One of the most popular and successful of the New Deal programs, the Civilian Conservation Corps (CCC), combined work relief with the preservation of natural resources. It put young unemployed white men, such as Robert Symmonds, between ages 17 and 25 to work on reforestation, road and park construction, flood control, and other projects. There were a few carefully segregated black units. The men lived in work camps (more than 1,500 camps in all) and

earned $30 a month, $25 of which had to be sent home to their families. Some complained that the CCC camps, run by the U.S. army, were too military, and one woman wrote from Minnesota to point out that all the best young men were at CCC camps when they ought to be home looking for real jobs and finding brides. Others complained that the CCC did nothing for unemployed young women, so a few special camps were organized for them, but only 8,000 women took part in a program that by 1941 had nearly 3 million participants. Overall, the CCC was one of the most successful and least controversial of all the New Deal programs.

Tennessee Valley Authority

Franklin Roosevelt, like his distant Republican relative Theodore, believed in conservation. He promoted flood-control projects and added millions of acres to the country's national forests, wildlife refuges, and fish and game sanctuaries. But the most important New Deal conservation project, the Tennessee Valley Authority (TVA), owed more to Republican George Norris, a progressive senator from Nebraska, than to Roosevelt.

During World War I, the federal government had built a hydroelectric plant and two munitions factories at Muscle Shoals, on the Tennessee River in Alabama. The government tried unsuccessfully to sell these facilities to private industry, but all through the 1920s, Norris campaigned to have the federal government operate them for the benefit of the valley's residents. Twice Republican presidents vetoed bills that would have allowed federal operation, but Roosevelt endorsed Norris's idea and expanded it into a regional development plan.

Congress authorized the TVA as an independent public corporation with the power to sell electricity and fertilizer and to promote flood control and land reclamation. The TVA built nine major dams and many minor ones between 1933 and 1944, affecting parts of Virginia, North Carolina, Georgia, Alabama, Mississippi, Tennessee, and Kentucky. Some private utility companies claimed that the TVA offered unfair competition to private industry, but it was an imaginative experiment in regional planning. It promoted everything from flood control to library bookmobiles. For residents of the valley, it meant cheaper electricity and changed lifestyles. The TVA meant radios, electric irons, washing machines, and other appliances for the first time. The largest federal construction project ever launched, it also created jobs for many thousands who helped build the dams. But government officials and businessmen who feared that the experiment would lead to socialism curbed the regional planning possibilities of the TVA.

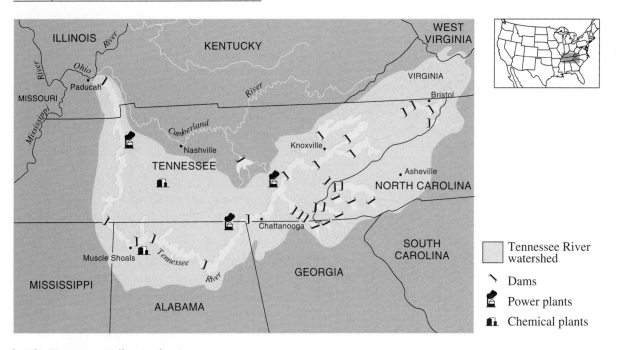

The Tennessee Valley Authority

The TVA transformed the way the Tennessee valley looked; it replaced a wild river with a series of flood-control and hydroelectric dams and created a series of lakes behind the dams. It stopped short of the coordinated regional planning that some people wanted, but it was one of the most important New Deal projects. How did electricity change the lives of everyday people in the Tennessee Valley?

Critics of the New Deal

The furious legislative activity during the first 100 days of the New Deal helped alleviate the pessimism and despair hanging over the country. Stock market prices rose slightly, and industrial production was up 11 percent at the end of 1933. Still, the country remained locked in depression, and nearly 12 million Americans were without jobs. Roosevelt captured the imagination of ordinary Americans everywhere. But conservatives were not so sure that Roosevelt was a savior; in fact, many businesspeople, after being impressed with Roosevelt's early economy measures and approving programs such as the NIRA, began to fear that the president was leading the country toward socialism.

The conservative revolt against Roosevelt surfaced in the summer of 1934 as the congressional elections approached. A group of disgruntled politicians and businesspeople formed the Liberty League. The league supported conservative or at least anti–New Deal candidates for Congress, but it had little influence. In the election of 1934, the Democrats increased their majority from 310 to 319 in the House and from 60 to 69 in the Senate (only the second time in the twentieth century that the party in power had increased its control of Congress in the midterm election). A few people were learning to hate Roosevelt, but it was obvious that most Americans approved of what he was doing.

While some thought the New Deal was too radical, others maintained that the government had not done enough to help the poor. One source of criticism was the Communist party. Attracting supporters from all walks of life during a time when capitalism seemed to have failed, the Communist party increased its membership from 7,500 in 1930 to 75,000 in 1938. The Communists organized protest marches and tried to reach out to the oppressed and unemployed. While a majority who joined the party came from the working class, communism had a special appeal to writers, intellectuals, and some college students during a decade when the American dream had turned into a nightmare.

Many Americans, however, were influenced by other movements promising easy solutions to poverty and unemployment. In Minnesota, Governor Floyd Olson, elected on a Farm–Labor ticket, accused capitalism of causing the Depression and startled some listeners when he thundered, "I hope the present system of government goes right to hell." In California, Upton Sinclair, the muckraking socialist and author of *The Jungle,* ran for governor on the platform "End Poverty in California." He promised to pay everyone over age 60 a pension of $50 a month using higher income and inheritance taxes to finance the program. He won in the primary but lost the election, and his program collapsed.

California also produced Dr. Francis E. Townsend, who claimed he had a national following of more than 5 million people. His supporters backed the Townsend Old Age Revolving Pension Plan, which promised $200

The Radio Priest

Father Charles E. Coughlin from Royal Oak, Michigan, was a flamboyant Catholic priest who was just as much the master of the radio as the president himself. At first he supported Roosevelt, but in 1935 he became one of FDR's most caustic critics. His impassioned anti-Semitic remarks finally caused the Catholic church to take him off the air. In what other ways was the radio important in the 1920s and 1930s?

(Library of Congress [LC-USZ6–2–111027])

a month to all unemployed citizens over age 60 on the condition that they spend it in the same month they received it. Economists laughed, but followers organized thousands of Townsend Pension Clubs.

More threatening to Roosevelt and the New Deal were the protest movements led by Father Charles E. Coughlin and Senator Huey P. Long. Father Coughlin, a Roman Catholic priest from a Detroit suburb, attracted an audience of 30 million to 45 million to his national radio show. At first, he supported Roosevelt's policies, but later he savagely attacked the New Deal as excessively probusiness. Mixing religious commentary with visions of a society operating without bankers and big businessmen, he roused his audience with blatantly anti-Semitic appeals.

Like Coughlin, Huey Long had a charisma that won support from the millions still trying to survive in a country where the continuing depression made day-to-day existence a struggle. Elected governor of Louisiana in 1928, Long promoted a "Share the Wealth" program. He taxed the oil refineries and built hospitals, schools, and thousands of miles of new highways. By 1934, he was the virtual dictator of his state, personally controlling the police and the courts. Long talked about a guaranteed $2,000 to $3,000 income for all American families (18.3 million families earned less than $1,000 per year in 1936) and promised pensions for the elderly and college educations for the young. He would pay for

these programs by taxing the rich and liquidating the great fortunes. Had not an assassin's bullet cut Long down in September 1935, he might have mounted a third-party challenge to Roosevelt.

The Second New Deal

Responding in part to the discontent of the lower middle class but also to the threat of various utopian schemes, Roosevelt moved his programs in 1935 toward the goals of social reform and social justice. At the same time, he departed from attempts to cooperate with the business community. "We find our population suffering from old inequalities," Roosevelt announced in his annual message to Congress in January 1935. "In spite of our efforts and in spite of our talk, we have not weeded out the overprivileged and we have not effectively lifted up the underprivileged."

Work Relief and Social Security

The Works Progress Administration (WPA), authorized by Congress in April 1935, was the first massive attempt to deal with unemployment and its demoralizing effect on millions of Americans. The WPA employed about 3 million people a year on a variety of socially useful projects. The WPA workers, who earned wages lower than private industry paid, built bridges, airports, libraries, roads, and golf courses. Nearly 85 percent of the funds went directly into salaries and wages. A minor but important part of the WPA funding supported writers, artists, actors, and musicians.

Only one member of a family could qualify for a WPA job, and first choice always went to the man. A woman could qualify only if she headed the household. But eventually more than 13 percent of the people who worked for the WPA were women, although their most common employment was in the sewing room, where old clothes were made over. "For unskilled men we have the shovel. For unskilled women we have only the needle," one official remarked.

The WPA was controversial from the beginning. The initials WPA, some wags charged, stood for "We Pay for All" or "We Putter Around." Yet for all the criticism, the WPA did useful work; the program built nearly 6,000 schools, more than 2,500 hospitals, and 13,000 playgrounds. More important, it restored the morale of millions of unemployed Americans.

The National Youth Administration (NYA) supplemented the work of the WPA and assisted young men and women between ages 16 and 25, many of them students. A young law student named Richard Nixon earned 35 cents an hour working for the NYA while he was at Duke University, and Lyndon Johnson began his political career as director of the Texas NYA.

By far the most enduring reform came with the passage of the Social Security Act of 1935. Since the progressive period, social workers and reformers had argued for a national system of health insurance, old-age pensions, and unemployment insurance. By the 1930s, the United States remained the only major industrial country without such programs. Within the Roosevelt circle, Frances Perkins argued most strongly for social insurance, but the popularity of the Townsend Plan and other schemes to aid the elderly helped convince Roosevelt to act. The number of people over age 65 in the country increased from 5.7 million in 1925 to 7.8 million in 1935, and that group demanded action.

The Social Security Act of 1935 was a compromise. Congress quickly dropped a plan for federal health insurance because of opposition from the medical profession. The most important provision of the act was old-age and survivor insurance to be paid for by a tax of 1 percent on both employers and employees. The benefits initially ranged from $10 to $85 a month. The act also established a cooperative federal–state system of unemployment compensation. Other provisions authorized federal grants to the states to help care for the disabled and the blind. Finally, the Social Security Act provided some aid to dependent children. This provision would eventually expand to become the largest federal welfare program.

The National Association of Manufacturers denounced social security as a program that would regiment the people and destroy individual self-reliance. Yet in no other country was social insurance paid for in part by a regressive tax on workers' wages. "We put those payroll contributions there so as to give the contributors a legal, moral, and political right to collect their pensions and unemployment benefits," Roosevelt later explained. "With those taxes in there, no damn politician can ever scrap my social security program." It was never intended as a traditional pension program, but rather as a social contract whereby one generation helped to pay for the previous generation's retirement. But the law also excluded many people, such as farm laborers and domestic servants. It discriminated against married women wage earners, and it failed to protect against sickness. Yet for all its weaknesses, it was one of the most important New Deal measures. A landmark in American social legislation, it marked the beginning of the welfare state that would expand significantly after World War II.

Aiding the Farmers

The Social Security Act and the Works Progress Administration were only two signs of Roosevelt's greater concern for social reform. The flurry of

legislation in 1935 and early 1936, often called the "second New Deal," also included an effort to help American farmers. More than 1.7 million farm families had annual incomes of less than $500 in 1935, and 42 percent of all those who lived on farms were tenants. The Resettlement Administration (RA), motivated in part by a Jeffersonian ideal of yeoman farmers working their own land, set out to relocate tenant farmers on land purchased by the government. Lack of funds and fears that the Roosevelt administration was trying to establish Soviet-style collective farms limited the effectiveness of the RA program.

Much more important in improving the lives of farm families was the Rural Electrification Administration (REA), authorized in 1935 to lend money to cooperatives to generate and distribute electricity in isolated rural areas not served by private utilities. Only 10 percent of the nation's farms had electricity in 1936. When the REA's lines were finally attached, they dramatically changed the lives of millions of farm families who had been able only to dream about the radios, washing machines, and farm equipment advertised in magazines.

In the hill country west of Austin, Texas, for example, there was no electricity until the end of the 1930s. Houses were illuminated by kerosene lamps, whose wicks had to be trimmed just right or the lamp smoked or went out, but even with perfect adjustment, it was difficult to read by them. There were no bathrooms,

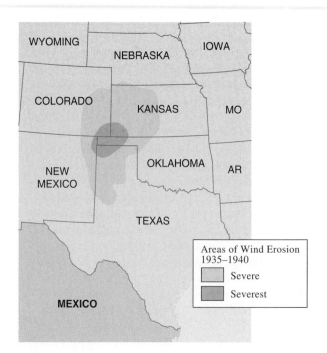

The Dust Bowl

This map depicts the wide extent of damage caused by high winds and drought, the worst in the history of the country, according to the U.S. Weather Bureau. What options are open to residents of areas hit by such natural disasters?

because bathrooms required running water, and running water depended on an electric pump.

It was memory of life in the hill country and personal knowledge of how hard his mother and grandmother toiled that inspired a young congressman from Texas, Lyndon Johnson, to work to bring rural electrification to the area. In November 1939, the lights finally came on in the hill country, plugging the area into the twentieth century.

The Dust Bowl: An Ecological Disaster

Those who tried to farm on the Great Plains fell victim to years of drought and dust storms. Record heat waves and below-average rainfall in the 1930s turned an area from the Oklahoma panhandle to western Kansas into a giant dust bowl. A single storm on May 11, 1934, removed 300 million tons of topsoil and turned day into night. Between 1932 and 1939, there was an average of 50 storms a year. Cities kept their streetlights on for 24 hours a day. Dust covered everything from food to bedspreads and piled up in dunes in city streets and barnyards. Overall 10,000 farm homes were abandoned to the elements, and 9 million acres of farmland were reduced to a wasteland. By the end of the decade, 3.5 million people abandoned their farms and joined a massive migration to find better lives. Many tenant farmers and hired hands were evicted, their plight immortalized by John Steinbeck in his novel *The Grapes of Wrath* (1939).

The dust bowl was a natural disaster, but it was aided and exaggerated by human actions and inactions. The semiarid plains west of the ninety-eighth meridian were not suitable for intensive agriculture.

Overgrazing, too much plowing, and indiscriminate planting over a period of 60 years exposed the thin soil to the elements. When the winds came in the 1930s, much of the land simply blew away. In the end, it was a matter of too little government planning and regulation and too many farmers using new technology to exploit natural resources for their own gain.

The Roosevelt administration did try to deal with the problem. The Taylor Grazing Act of 1934 restricted the use of the public range in an attempt to prevent overgrazing, and it ended an era of unregulated use of natural resources in the West. Before 1934, anyone could use public land, but the 1934 act required a permit and a fee. The Taylor Act established the principle that the remaining public domain was under federal control and not for sale. The Civilian Conservation Corps and other New Deal agencies planted trees, and the Soil Conservation Service promoted drought-resistant crops and contour plowing, but it was too little and too late. Even worse, according to some authorities, government measures applied after the disaster of 1930 encouraged farmers to return to raising wheat and other inappropriate crops, leading to more dust bowl crises in the 1950s and 1970s.

The New Deal and the West

The New Deal probably aided the West more than any other region. The CCC, AAA, drought relief measures, and various federal agencies helped the region to an extent that was out of proportion to the people who lived there. In fact, the top 14 states in per capita expenditure by federal agencies during the 1930s were all in the West. Most important were the large-scale

Dust Bowl Family

Thousands of families fled the dust bowl in old cars and headed for California. With no place to sleep, they used sheets and blankets to turn their cars into tents. John Steinbeck wrote about these migrants in *The Grapes of Wrath*. Do the dust bowl migrants represent a failure of the American dream?

(Courtesy Franklin D. Roosevelt Library [53227(575)])

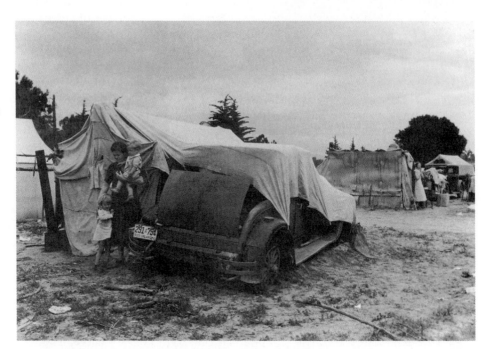

water projects. The Boulder Dam (later renamed the Hoover Dam) on the Colorado River not only provided massive amounts of hydroelectric power but, with the construction of a 259-mile aqueduct, also provided the water that caused the city of Los Angeles to boom.

The largest power project of all was the Grand Coulee Dam on the Columbia River northwest of Spokane, Washington. Employing tens of thousands of men and pouring millions of dollars into the economy, the dam, finally completed in 1941, provided cheap electricity for the Pacific Northwest and eventually irrigated more than a million acres of arid land.

Despite all the federal aid to the region, many westerners, holding fast to the myth of frontier individualism, bitterly criticized the regulation and the bureaucracy that went with the grants. Cattlemen in Wyoming, Colorado, and Montana desperately needed the help of the federal government, but even as they accepted the aid, they denounced Roosevelt and the New Deal.

Controlling Corporate Power and Taxing the Wealthy

In the summer of 1935, Roosevelt set out to control the large corporations, and he even toyed with radical plans to tax the well-to-do heavily and redistribute wealth in the United States. The Public Utility Holding Company Act, passed in 1935, attempted to restrict the

power of the giant utility companies, the 12 largest of which controlled more than half the country's power. The act gave various government commissions the authority to regulate and control the power companies and included a "death sentence" clause that gave each company five years to demonstrate that its services were efficient. If it could not demonstrate this, the government could dissolve the company. This was one of the most radical attempts to control corporate power in American history.

In his message to Congress in 1935, Roosevelt also pointed out that the federal revenue laws had "done little to prevent an unjust concentration of wealth and economic power." He suggested steeper income taxes for wealthy groups and a much larger inheritance tax. When Congress dropped the inheritance tax provision, however, Roosevelt did not fight to have it restored. Even the weakened bill, increasing estate and gift taxes and raising the income tax rates at the top, angered many in the business community who thought that Roosevelt had sold out to Huey Long's "Share the Wealth" scheme.

The New Deal for Labor

Like many progressive reformers, Roosevelt was more interested in improving the lot of working people by passing social legislation than by strengthening the bargaining position of organized labor. Yet he saw labor as an important balance to the power of industry, and he listened to his advisers, especially Frances Perkins and Senator Robert Wagner of New York, who persistently brought up the needs of organized labor.

Roosevelt supported the National Labor Relations Act. Passed in 1935, it outlawed blacklisting and a number of other practices and reasserted labor's right to organize and to bargain collectively. The act also established a Labor Relations Board with the power to certify a properly elected bargaining unit. The act did not require workers to join unions, but it made the federal government a regulator, or at least a neutral force, in management–labor relations. That alone made the National Labor Relations Act one of the most important New Deal reform measures.

The Roosevelt administration's friendly attitude toward organized labor helped increase union membership from less than 3 million in 1933 to 4.5 million by 1935. Many groups, however, were left out, including farm laborers, unskilled workers, and women. Only about 3 percent of working women belonged to unions, and women earned only about 60 percent of wages paid to men for equivalent work. Still, many people resented that women were employed at all. The Brotherhood of Railway and Steamship Clerks ruled that no married woman whose husband could support her was eligible for a job.

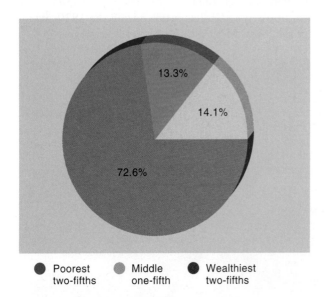

● Poorest two-fifths   ● Middle one-fifth   ● Wealthiest two-fifths

Distribution of Income, 1935–1936

Roosevelt and the New Deal never sought consistently to redistribute wealth in America, and a great disparity in income and assets remained. Why didn't Roosevelt and his advisers try to redistribute wealth?

Source: U.S. Bureau of the Census.

The American Federation of Labor (AFL) had little interest in organizing unskilled workers, but a new group of committed and militant labor leaders emerged in the 1930s to take up that task. John L. Lewis, the eloquent head of the United Mine Workers, was the most aggressive. He was joined by David Dubinsky of the International Ladies' Garment Workers, and Sidney Hillman, president of the Amalgamated Clothing Workers. Dubinsky and Hillman were socialists who believed in economic planning, but both had worked closely with social justice progressives. These new progressive labor leaders formed the Committee of Industrial Organization (CIO) within the AFL and set out to organize workers in the steel, auto, and rubber industries. Rather than separating workers by skill or craft as the AFL preferred, they organized everyone into an industry-wide union much as the Knights of Labor had done in the 1880s. They also used new and aggressive tactics.

In 1936, the workers at three rubber plants in Akron, Ohio, went on unauthorized strikes. Instead of picketing outside the factory, they occupied the buildings and took them over, preventing the owners from running the factory with non-union workers. The "sit-down strike" became a new protest technique. Sometimes the workers occupied a factory for a week or more. After sit-down strikes against General Motors plants in Atlanta, Georgia, and Flint, Michigan, General Motors finally accepted the United Auto Workers (UAW) as their employees' bargaining agent. The General Motors strike was the most important event in a critical period of labor upheaval. Labor's voice now began to be heard in the decision-making process in major industries in which labor had long been denied any role. The strikes at General Motors also helped raise the status of organized labor in the eyes of many Americans.

Violence spread along with the sit-down strike. Chrysler capitulated, but the Ford Motor Company used hired gunmen to discourage the strikers. A bloody struggle ensued before Ford agreed to accept the UAW as the bargaining agent. Even U.S. Steel, which had been militantly anti-union, signed an agreement with the Steel Workers Organizing Committee calling for a 40-hour workweek and an eight-hour workday. But other steel companies refused to go along. In Chicago on Memorial Day in 1937, a confrontation between the police and peaceful picketers at the Republic Steel plant resulted in 10 deaths. In the "Memorial Day Massacre," as it came to be called, the police fired without provocation into a crowd of workers and their families, who had gathered near the plant in a holiday mood. All 10 of the dead were shot in the back.

The CIO's aggressive tactics gained many new members, to the horror of AFL leaders. They expelled the CIO leaders from the AFL, only to see them form a separate Congress of Industrial Organization (the initials stayed the same). By accepting unskilled workers, African Americans, and others who had never belonged to a union before, the CIO infused the labor movement with a new spirit.

America's Minorities in the 1930s

Half a million African Americans joined unions through the CIO during the 1930s, and many blacks were aided by various New Deal agencies. Yet the familiar pattern of discrimination, low-paying jobs, and intimidation through violence persisted. Lynchings in the South actually increased in the New Deal years, rising from 8 in 1932 to 28 in 1933 and 20 in 1935.

One particular case came to symbolize and dramatize discrimination against African Americans in the 1930s. On March 25, 1931, in Scottsboro, Alabama, two young white women accused nine black men of raping them in a railroad boxcar as they all hitched a free ride. A jury of white men found all nine blacks guilty, and the court sentenced eight to die. The U.S. Supreme Court ordered new trials in 1933, on the grounds that the accused rapists had not received proper legal counsel. The case garnered much publicity in the United States and abroad. The youth of the defendants, their quick trial, and the harsh sentences made the "Scottsboro boys" a popular cause for many northern liberals and especially the Communist party.

For many southerners, however, it was a matter of defending the honor of white women. As one observer remarked of one of the accusers, she "might be a fallen woman, but by God she is a white woman." However, evidence supporting the alleged rapes was never presented, and eventually one of the women recanted. Yet the case dragged on. In new trials, five of the young men were convicted and given long prison terms. Charges against the other four were dropped in 1937. Four of the remaining five were paroled by 1946, and the fifth escaped to Michigan.

African Americans did not have to be accused of rape to want to flee to the North, however, and the migration of blacks to northern cities, which had accelerated during World War I, continued during the 1930s. The collapse of cotton prices forced black farmers and farm laborers to flee north for survival. But since most were poorly educated, they soon became trapped in northern ghettos, where they were eligible for only the most menial jobs. The black unemployment rate was triple that of whites, and blacks often received less per person in welfare payments.

Black leaders attacked the Roosevelt administration for supporting or allowing segregation in government-sponsored facilities. Roosevelt, fearing that he might antagonize southern congressmen whose backing he needed, refused to support the two major civil rights

Sharecroppers

Despite the black migration North during World War I and the 1920s, more than 80 percent of African Americans lived in the South during the 1930s. Most were sharecroppers, tenant farmers who often were in debt to the landlord. They were trapped by prejudice, unable to vote, and oppressed by poverty. The New Deal policies often made their situation worse. Many were kicked off the land and became homeless drifters. Can you imagine what it was like to be a sharecropper? Why did the nation tolerate such inequality?

(Library of Congress, LC-USF34T01–9575)

bills of the era, an antilynching bill and a bill to abolish the poll tax. Yet Harold Ickes and Harry Hopkins worked to ensure that blacks were given opportunities in New Deal agencies. By 1941, black federal employees totaled 150,000, more than three times the number during the Hoover administration. Most worked in the lower ranks, but some were lawyers, architects, office managers, and engineers.

Partly responsible for the presence of more black employees was the "black cabinet," a group of more than 50 young blacks who had appointments in various New Deal agencies and were led by Mary McLeod Bethune, the daughter of a sharecropper. She had founded a black primary school in Florida and then transformed it into Bethune-Cookman College. In the 1920s, she had organized the National Council of Negro Women. In 1934, Harry Hopkins, following the advice of Eleanor Roosevelt, appointed her to the advisory committee of the National Youth Administration. Bethune had some impact on New Deal policy and on the black cabinet. She spoke out forcefully, she picketed and protested, and she intervened shrewdly to obtain civil rights and more jobs for African Americans, but in the end the gains for blacks during the New Deal were very limited.

Although Roosevelt appointed a number of blacks to government positions, he was never particularly committed to civil rights. That was not true of Eleanor Roosevelt, who was educated in part by Mary McLeod Bethune. In 1939, when the Daughters of the American Revolution refused to allow Marian Anderson, a black concert singer, to use their stage, Mrs. Roosevelt publicly protested and resigned her membership in the DAR. She also arranged for Anderson to sing from the steps of the Lincoln Memorial, where 75,000 people gathered to listen and to support civil rights for all black citizens.

Hundreds of thousands of Mexicans, brought to the United States to work in the 1920s, lost their jobs in the Depression. Drifting to the Southwest or settling in the urban *barrios* and the small towns and farms in the Southwest, they met signs such as "Only White Labor Employed" and "No Niggers, Mexicans, or Dogs Allowed." Some New Deal agencies helped destitute Mexicans. A few worked for the CCC and the WPA, but to be employed, an applicant had to qualify for state relief, and that eliminated most migrants. The primary solution was not to provide aid for Mexicans but to ship them back to Mexico. In Los Angeles and other cities, the police and immigration authorities rounded up aliens and held them illegally. A trainload of repatriates left Los Angeles every month during 1933, and officials deported thousands from other cities. One estimate placed the number sent back in 1932 at 200,000, including some American citizens.

Not all the Mexicans were repatriated, however, and some who remained adopted militant tactics to obtain fair treatment. Mexican strawberry pickers went on strike in El Monte, California, and 18,000 cotton pickers walked away from their jobs in the San Joaquin valley in 1933. On August 31, 1939, during a record-breaking heat wave, nearly all of the 430 workers, most of them Mexican American women, staged a massive walkout at one of the largest food processing plants in Los Angeles.

Asians (Chinese, Japanese, and a smaller number of Koreans and Asian Indians) also suffered during the Depression. Most lived in ethnic enclaves, lost their jobs, and were treated as foreigners—not quite black, but not white either. Asians, especially the second generation who were automatically citizens if they were born in the United States, were troubled by a "twoness." They were both Chinese or Japanese and American. At least their parents wanted them to retain ties to the old country and the old culture. One young Chinese student from San Francisco had to go to Chinese school after her regular school. "We never became proficient in reading or writing Chinese," she recalled, "probably because we never thought of ourselves as needing Chinese. After all, weren't we Americans?" Most other Americans treated all Asians as aliens, and they had great difficulty distinguishing a Chinese from a Japanese from a Korean.

Native Americans also experienced alienation, disease, and despair during the Depression, and their plight was compounded by years of exploitation. Since the Dawes Act of 1887 (described in Chapter 17), government policy had sought to make the Indian into a property-owning farmer and to limit tribal rights. Native Americans lost more than 60 percent of the 138 million acres granted them in 1887. The government declared some of the land surplus and encouraged individuals to settle on 160 acres and adopt the "habits of civilized life." Few Native Americans profited from this system, but many whites did.

Just as other progressives sought the quick assimilation of immigrants, the progressive-era Indian commissioners sped up the allotment process to increase Indian detribalization. But many Native Americans who remained on the reservations were not even citizens. Finally, in 1924, Congress granted citizenship to all Indians born in the United States. The original Americans became U.S. citizens, but that did not end their suffering.

Franklin Roosevelt brought a new spirit to Indian policy by appointing John Collier as commissioner of Indian affairs. Collier was primarily responsible for the passage of the Indian Reorganization Act of 1934, which sought to restore the political independence of the tribes and to end the allotment policy of the Dawes Act. The bill also sought to promote the "study of Indian civilization" and to "preserve and develop the special cultural contributions and achievements of such civilization, including Indian arts, crafts, skills and traditions."

Not all Indians agreed with the new policies. Some chose to become members of the dominant culture, and many voted to reject the Reorganization Act because it required written tribal constitutions, which they viewed as inflexible or unnecessary. Some Americans charged that the act was inspired by communism. Others argued that its principal result would be to increase government bureaucracy, while missionaries claimed that the government was promoting paganism by allowing the Indians to practice their native religions.

The paradox and contradictions of U.S. policy toward the Indians can be illustrated by Collier's attempt to solve the Navajo problem. The Navajo lands, like most of the West, were overgrazed, and soil erosion threatened to fill the new lake behind the Hoover Dam with silt. By supporting a policy of reducing the herds of sheep and goats on Indian land and by promoting soil conservation, Collier contributed to the change in the Navajo lifestyle and to the end of their self-sufficiency, something he wanted to support.

Women and the New Deal

Women made some gains during the 1930s, and more women occupied high government positions than in any previous administration. Besides Frances Perkins, the secretary of labor, there was Molly Dewson, a social worker with the Massachusetts Girls Parole Department and the National Consumers League before becoming head of the Women's Division of the Democratic Committee and then an adviser to Roosevelt. Working closely with Eleanor Roosevelt to promote women's causes, she helped achieve a number of firsts: two women appointed ambassadors, a judge on the U.S. Court of Appeals, the director of the mint, and many women in government agencies.

Despite some gains, the early New Deal programs did nothing for an estimated 140,000 homeless women, or the 2 million to 4 million unemployed women. Married women often were fired from their jobs on the grounds that they should be home caring for their families rather than depriving men of employment. Single, divorced, and widowed women were usually ignored. Eleanor Roosevelt was genuinely concerned over the plight of poor women. She sponsored a White House Conference in November 1933 on the Emergency Needs of Women. She also advocated including more women in the CCC, the WPA, and other programs, but in the end the New Deal did little for poor women.

The Third New Deal

The New Deal was neither a consistent nor a well-organized effort to end the Depression and restructure society. Roosevelt was a politician and a pragmatist, unconcerned about ideological or programmatic consistency. The first New Deal of 1933–1934 concentrated on relief and recovery, while the legislation passed in 1935 and 1936 was more involved with social reform. In many ways, the election of 1936 marked the high point of Roosevelt's power and influence. After 1937, in part because of the growing threat of war but also because of increasing opposition in Congress, the pace of social legislation slowed. Yet several measures passed in 1937 and 1938 had such far-reaching significance that some historians refer to a third New Deal. Among the new measures were bills that provided for a minimum wage and for housing reform.

The Election of 1936

The Republicans in 1936 nominated a moderate, Governor Alfred Landon of Kansas. Although he attacked the New Deal, charging that new government programs were wasteful and created a dangerous

FDR'S SUCCESSFUL PRESIDENTIAL CAMPAIGNS, 1932–1944

Year	Candidate	Party	Popular Vote	Electoral Vote
1932	FRANKLIN D. ROOSEVELT	Democratic	22,809,638 (57.4%)	472
	Herbert C. Hoover	Republican	15,758,901 (39.7%)	59
	Norman Thomas	Socialist	881,951 (2.2%)	0
1936	FRANKLIN D. ROOSEVELT	Democratic	27,751,612 (60.8%)	523
	Alfred M. Landon	Republican	16,681,913 (36.5%)	8
	William Lemke	Union	891,858 (1.9%)	0
1940	FRANKLIN D. ROOSEVELT	Democratic	27,243,466 (54.8%)	449
	Wendell L. Willkie	Republican	22,304,755 (44.8%)	82
1944	FRANKLIN D. ROOSEVELT	Democratic	25,602,505 (53.5%)	432
	Thomas E. Dewey	Republican	22,006,278 (46.0%)	99

Note: Winners' names appear in capital letters.

federal bureaucracy, Landon only promised to do the same thing more cheaply and efficiently. Two-thirds of the newspapers in the country supported him, and the *Literary Digest* predicted his victory on the basis of a "scientific" telephone poll.

Roosevelt, helped by signs that the economy was recovering and supported by a coalition of the Democratic South, organized labor, farmers, and urban voters, won easily. A majority of African Americans for the first time deserted the party of Lincoln, not because of Roosevelt's interest in civil rights for blacks but because New Deal relief programs assisted many poor blacks. A viable candidate to the left of the New Deal failed to materialize. In fact, the Socialist party candidate, Norman Thomas, polled fewer than 200,000 votes. Roosevelt won by more than 10 million votes, carrying every state except Maine and Vermont. Even the traditionally Republican states of Pennsylvania, Delaware, and Connecticut, which had voted Republican in almost every election since 1856, went for Roosevelt.

The Battle of the Supreme Court

"I see one-third of a nation ill-housed, ill-clad, ill-nourished," Roosevelt declared in his second inaugural address, and he vowed to alter that situation. But the president's first action in 1937 did not call for legislation to alleviate poverty. Instead, he announced a plan to reform the Supreme Court and the judicial system. The Court had invalidated not only a number of New Deal measures—including the NIRA and the first version of the AAA—but other measures as well.

Increasingly angry at the "nine old men" who seemed to be destroying New Deal initiatives and defying Congress's will, Roosevelt determined to create a more sympathetic Court. He hoped to gain power to appoint an extra justice for each justice over age 70, of whom there were six. His plan also called for modernizing the court system at all levels, but that plan got lost in the public outcry over the Court-packing scheme.

Roosevelt's plan to nullify the influence of the older and more reactionary justices foundered. Republicans accused him of being a dictator and of subverting the Constitution. Many congressmen from his own party refused to support him. Led by Vice President John Nance Garner of Texas, a number of southern Democrats broke with the president and formed a coalition with conservative Republicans that lasted for more than 30 years. After months of controversy, Roosevelt withdrew the legislation and admitted defeat. He had perhaps misunderstood his mandate, and he certainly underestimated the respect, even the reverence, that most Americans felt for the Supreme Court.

Ironically, though he lost the battle of the Supreme Court, Roosevelt won the war. By the spring of 1937, the Court began to reverse its position and in a 5–4 decision upheld the National Labor Relations Act. When Justice Willis Van Devanter retired, Roosevelt was able to make his first Supreme Court appointment, thus ensuring at least a shaky liberal majority on the Court. After 1937 a series of court cases established the principle that Congress and federal power trumped states' rights and local control. But Roosevelt triumphed at great cost. His attempt to reorganize the Court dissipated energy and slowed the momentum of his legislative program. Seen as the most unpopular action he took as president, it made him vulnerable to criticism from opponents of the New Deal, and even some of his supporters were dismayed by what they regarded as an attack on the principle of separation of powers.

The economy improved in late 1936 and early 1937, but in August, the fragile prosperity collapsed.

Unemployment shot back up, industrial production fell, and the stock market plummeted. Facing an embarrassing economic slump that evoked charges that the New Deal had failed, Roosevelt resorted to "deficit spending," as recommended by John Maynard Keynes, the British economist. Keynes argued that to get out of a depression, the government must spend massive amounts of money on goods and services to increase demand and revive production. The economy responded slowly but never fully recovered until wartime expenditures, beginning in 1940, stimulated it, reduced unemployment, and ended the Depression.

Completing the New Deal

Despite increasing hostility, Congress passed a number of important bills in 1937 and 1938 that completed the New Deal reform legislation. The Bankhead–Jones Farm Tenancy Act of 1937 created the Farm Security

KEY 1930s REFORM LEGISLATION

Year	Legislation	Provisions
1932	Reconstruction Finance Corporation (RFC)	Granted emergency loans to banks, life insurance companies, and railroads (passed during Hoover administration)
1933	Civilian Conservation Corps (CCC)	Employed young men (and a few women) in reforestation, road construction, and flood control projects
1933	Agricultural Adjustment Act (AAA)	Granted farmers direct payments for reducing production of certain products; funds for payments provided by a processing tax, which was later declared unconstitutional
1933	Tennessee Valley Authority (TVA)	Created independent public corporation to construct dams and power projects and to develop the economy of a nine-state area in the Tennessee River valley
1933	National Industrial Recovery Act (NIRA)	Sought to revive business through a series of fair-competition codes; Section 7a guaranteed labor's right to organize (later declared unconstitutional)
1933	Public Works Administration (PWA)	Sought to increase employment and business activity through construction of roads, buildings, and other projects
1934	National Housing Act—created Federal Housing Administration (FHA)	Insured loans made by banks for construction of new homes and repair of old homes
1935	Emergency Relief Appropriation Act—created Works Progress Administration (WPA)	Employed more than 8 million people to repair roads, build bridges, and work on other projects; also hired artists and writers
1935	Social Security Act	Established unemployment compensation and old-age and survivors' insurance paid for by a joint tax on employers and employees
1935	National Labor Relations Act (Wagner–Connery Act)	Recognized the right of employees to join labor unions and to bargain collectively; created a National Labor Relations Board to supervise elections and to prevent unfair labor practices
1935	Public Utility Holding Act	Outlawed pyramiding of gas and electric companies through the use of holding companies and restricted these companies to activity in one area; a "death sentence" clause gave companies five years to prove local, useful, and efficient operation or be dissolved
1937	National Housing Act (Wagner–Steagall Act)	Authorized low-rent public housing projects
1938	Agricultural Adjustment Act (AAA)	Continued price supports and payments to farmers to limit production, as in 1933 act, but replaced processing tax with direct federal payment
1938	Fair Labor Standards Act	Established minimum wage of 40 cents an hour and maximum workweek of 40 hours in enterprises engaged in interstate commerce

Administration (FSA) to aid tenant farmers, sharecroppers, and farm owners who had lost their farms. The FSA, which provided loans to grain collectives, also set up camps for migratory workers. Some people saw such policies as the first step toward Communist collectives, but the FSA in fact never had enough money to make a real difference.

Congress passed a new Agricultural Adjustment Act in 1938 that tried to solve the problem of farm surpluses, which persisted even after hundreds of thousands of farmers had lost their farms. The new act replaced the processing tax (which the Supreme Court had declared unconstitutional) with direct payments from the federal treasury to farmers; added a soil conservation program; and provided for the marketing of surplus crops. Like its predecessor, the new act tried to stabilize farm prices by controlling production. But only the outbreak of World War II would end the problem of farm surplus, and then only temporarily.

In the cities, housing continued to be a problem. Progressive reformers had dreamed of providing better housing for the urban poor. They had campaigned for city ordinances and state laws and had built model tenements, but the first experiment with federal housing occurred during World War I. That brief experience encouraged a number of social reformers, who later became advisers to Roosevelt. They convinced him that federal low-cost housing should be part of New Deal reform.

The Reconstruction Finance Corporation made low-interest loans to housing projects, and the Public Works Administration constructed some apartment buildings. But not until the National Housing Act of 1937 did Roosevelt and his advisers try to develop a comprehensive housing policy for the poor. The act provided federal funds for slum clearance projects and for the construction of low-cost housing. By 1939, however, only 117,000 units had been built.

In the long run, New Deal housing legislation had a greater impact on middle-class housing policies and patterns. During the first 100 days of the New Deal, at Roosevelt's urging, Congress passed a bill creating the Home Owners Loan Corporation (HOLC), which over the next two years made more than $3 billion in low-interest loans and helped more than a million people save their homes from foreclosure. The HOLC also had a strong impact on housing policy by introducing the first long-term, fixed-rate mortgages. Formerly, all mortgages were for periods of no more than five years and were subject to frequent renegotiation.

The HOLC also introduced a uniform system of real estate appraisal that tended to undervalue urban property, especially in neighborhoods that were old, crowded, and ethnically mixed. The system gave the highest ratings to suburban developments where, according to the HOLC, there had been no "infiltration of Jews" or other undesirable groups. This was the beginning of the practice later called "redlining," in which lending agencies drew lines around neighborhoods and made it nearly impossible for prospective home buyers of certain ethnic or racial backgrounds to obtain a mortgage.

The Federal Housing Administration (FHA), created in 1934 by the National Housing Act, expanded and extended many of these HOLC policies. The FHA insured mortgages, many of them for 25 or 30 years; reduced the down payment required from 30 percent to less than 10 percent; and allowed more than 11 million families to buy homes between 1934 and 1972. The system, however, tended to favor purchasing new suburban homes rather than repairing older urban residences. New Deal housing policies helped make the suburban home with the long FHA mortgage part of the American way of life, but the policies also contributed to the decline of many urban neighborhoods.

Just as important as housing legislation was the Fair Labor Standards Act, which Congress passed in June 1938. Roosevelt's bill proposed for all industries engaged in interstate commerce a minimum wage of 25 cents an hour, to rise in two years to 40 cents an hour, and a maximum workweek of 44 hours, to be reduced to 40 hours. The act covered only 20 percent of the labor force and only 14 percent of working women. Nevertheless, when it went into effect, 750,000 workers immediately received raises, and by 1940, some 12 million had received pay increases. The law also prohibited child labor in interstate commerce, making it the first permanent federal law to prohibit youngsters under age 16 from working. And without emphasizing the matter, the law made no distinction between men and women, thus diminishing, if not completely ending, the need for special legislation for women.

The Fair Labor Standards Act was the last New Deal measure passed. The New Deal had many weaknesses, but it did dramatically increase government support for the needy. In 1913, local, state, and federal governments spent $21 million on public assistance. By 1932, that had risen to $218 million; by 1939, it was $4.9 billion.

The Other Side of the 1930s

The Great Depression and the New Deal so dominate the history of the 1930s that it is easy to conclude that nothing else happened, that there were only bread lines and relief agencies. But there is another side of the decade, for a communications revolution changed the lives of middle-class Americans. The sale of radios and attendance at movies increased during the 1930s, and literature flourished. Americans were fascinated by technology, especially automobiles. Many people traveled during the decade; they stayed in motor courts and looked ahead to a brighter future dominated by streamlined appliances and gadgets that would mean an easier life.

Taking to the Road

"People give up everything in the world but their car," a banker in Muncie, Indiana, remarked during the Depression, and that seems to have been true all over the country. Although automobile production dropped off after 1929 and did not recover until the end of the 1930s, the number of motor vehicles registered, which declined from 26.7 million in 1930 to just over 24 million in 1933, increased to more than 32 million by 1940. People who could not afford new cars drove used ones. Even the "Okies" fleeing the dust bowl of

the Southwest traveled in cars. They were secondhand, run-down cars to be sure, but the fact that even many poor Americans owned cars shocked visitors from Europe, where automobiles were still only for the rich.

The American middle class traveled at an increasing rate after the low point of 1932 and 1933. In 1938, the tourist industry was the third largest in the United States, behind only steel and automobile production. More than 4 million Americans traveled every year, and four out of five went by car.

The Electric Home

If the 1920s was the age of the bathroom, the 1930s was the era of the modern kitchen. The sale of electrical appliances increased throughout the decade, with

Wash Day

Although the washing machine dates from the mid-nineteenth century, it did not end the drudgery of wash day; even the introduction of electric washers did not eliminate the constant wringing and rinsing that made wash day (usually Monday) a day to dread. The first automatic washing machines were introduced in the late 1930s but did not become commonplace until after World War II. This advertisement promotes the convenience of a machine that will spin-dry as well as wash. Notice the gender roles in the advertisement. The husband appreciates the saving but apparently does not put the clothes in the machine. "The Bendix" was a great improvement, but it was not until the 1950s that electric and gas dryers finally ended the task of hanging clothes on the line. How do you do your laundry today? Have things changed much since the 1930s?

(Bendix Home Appliances, Inc.)

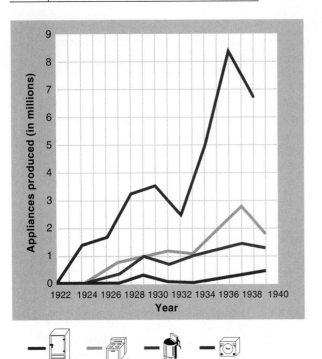

Household Appliance Production, 1922–1939
Electric appliances altered the lives of many American middle-class families during the 1930s. The replacement of the icebox with the electric refrigerator was especially dramatic. How did these appliances change the lifestyle of those who purchased them?

Source: U.S. Bureau of the Census.

The Age of Leisure

During the Depression, many middle-class people found themselves with time on their hands and sought out ways of spending it. The 1920s had been a time of spectator sports, of football and baseball heroes, of huge crowds that turned out to see boxing matches. Those sports continued during the Depression decade, although attendance suffered. Softball and miniature golf, which were cheap forms of entertainment and did not require expensive travel, also became popular. But leisure in the 1930s actually grew to be a problem, and professionals published some 450 new books on the subject. Leisure was mechanized; millions put their nickels in a slot and listened to a record played on a jukebox. Millions more played a pinball machine, a mechanized device that had no practical use other than entertainment and could end the game with one word: "Tilt."

Many popular games of the period had elaborate rules and directions. Contract bridge swept the country during the decade, and Monopoly was the most popular game of all. Produced by Parker Brothers, Monopoly was a fantasy of real estate speculation in which chance, luck, and the roll of the dice determined the winner. But one still had to obey the rules: "Go Directly to Jail. Do Not Pass Go. Do Not Collect $200." During a depression brought on in part by frenzied speculation, Americans were fascinated by a game whose purpose was to obtain real estate and utility monopolies and drive one's opponents into bankruptcy.

The 1930s was also a time of fads and instant celebrities, created by radio, newsreels, and businesspeople ready to turn almost anything to commercial advantage. The leading box office attraction between 1935 and 1938 was Shirley Temple, a blond and adorable child star. She inspired dolls, dishes, books, and clothes. Even stranger was the excitement created by the birth of five girl babies to a couple in northern Ontario in 1934. The Dionne quintuplets appeared on dozens of magazine covers and endorsed every imaginable product. Millions of people waited eagerly for the latest news about the babies, and more than 3 million traveled to see their home in Canada. The crazes over Shirley Temple and the Dionne quintuplets were products of the new technology, especially radio and the movies.

refrigerators leading the way. In 1930, the number of refrigerators produced exceeded the number of iceboxes for the first time. Refrigerator production continued to rise throughout the decade, reaching a peak of 2.3 million in 1937. At first, the refrigerator was boxy and looked very much like an icebox with a motor sitting on top. In 1935, however, the refrigerator, like most other appliances, became streamlined. The Sears Coldspot, which quickly influenced the look of all other models, was designed by Raymond Loewy, one of a group of industrial designers who emphasized sweeping horizontal lines, rounded corners, and a slick modern look. They hoped modern design would stimulate an optimistic attitude and, of course, increase sales. At the end of the decade, in 1939, the World's Fair in New York glorified the theme of a streamlined future, carefully planned and based on new technology.

Ironically, despite these new conveniences, a great many middle-class families maintained their standard of living during the 1930s only because the women in the family learned to stretch and save and make do, and most wives spent as much time on housework as before. Some also took jobs outside the home to maintain their level of consumption. The number of married women who worked increased substantially during the decade.

Literary Reflections of the 1930s

Though much of the literature of the 1930s reflected the decade's troubled currents, reading continued to be a popular and cheap entertainment. John Steinbeck, whose later novel *The Grapes of Wrath* (1939) followed the fortunes of the Joad family, described the plight of Mexican migrant workers in *Tortilla Flat* (1935). His novels

Recovering the Past

THE MOVIES

Just as some historians have used fiction to help define the cultural history of a decade, others in the twentieth century have turned to film to describe the "spirit of an age." On an elementary level, the movies help us appreciate changing styles in dress, furniture, and automobiles. We can even get some sense of how a particular time defined a beautiful woman or a handsome man, and we can learn about ethnic and racial stereotypes and assumptions about gender and class.

The decade of the 1930s is sometimes called the "golden age of the movies." Careful selection among the 500 or so feature films Hollywood produced each year during the decade—ranging from gangster and cowboy movies to Marx Brothers comedies, from historical romances to Busby Berkeley musical extravaganzas—could support a number of interpretations about the special myths and assumptions of the era. But one historian has argued that, especially after 1934, "not only did the movies amuse and entertain the nation through its most severe economic and social disorder, holding it together by their capacity to create unifying myths and dreams, but movie culture in the 1930s became a dominant culture for many Americans, providing new values and social ideals to replace shattered old traditions."

The year 1934 was a dividing line for two reasons. The motion picture industry, like all other industries, had suffered during the Depression; 1933 marked the low point in attendance, with more than one-third of the theaters in the country shut down. The next year, however, attendance picked up, heralding a revival that lasted until 1946. Also in 1934, the movie industry adopted a code for which the Catholic Legion of Decency and other religious groups had lobbied. The new code prohibited the depiction of "sex perversion, interracial sex, abortion, incest, drugs and profanity." Even married couples could not be shown together in a double bed. Although a movie could depict immoral behavior, sin always had to be punished. "Evil and good should never be confused," the code announced.

Before the code, Hollywood had indeed produced graphic films, such as *The Public Enemy* (1931) and *Scarface* (1932), with a considerable amount of violence; musicals, such as *Gold Diggers of 1933,* filled with scantily clad young women; films featuring prostitutes, such as Jean Harlow in *Red Dust* (1932) and Marlene Dietrich in *Blond Venus* (1930); and other films that confronted the problems of real life. But after 1934, Hollywood concentrated on movies that created a mythical world in which evil was always punished, family moral values won out in the end, and patriotism and American democracy were never questioned. Although the code was modified from time to time, it was not abandoned until 1966, when it was replaced by a rating system.

It Happened One Night (1934) and *Drums Along the Mohawk* (1939), two films out of thousands, illustrate some of the myths the movies created and sustained. Frank Capra, one of Hollywood's masters at entertaining without disturbing, directed *It Happened One Night,* a comedy-romance. A rich girl (played by Claudette Colbert) dives from her father's yacht off the coast of Florida and takes a bus for

A scene from *It Happened One Night,* 1934

(Photofest)

A scene from *Drums Along the Mohawk*, 1939

(20th Century Fox/The Kobal Collection)

New York. She meets a newspaper reporter (Clark Gable), and they have a series of madcap adventures and fall in love. But mix-ups and misunderstandings make it appear that she will marry her old boyfriend. In the end, however, they are reunited and marry in an elaborate outdoor ceremony. Afterward, they presumably live happily ever after. The movie is funny and entertaining and presents a variation on the poor-boy-marries-rich-girl theme. Like so many movies of the time, this one suggests that life is fulfilled for a woman only if she can find the right man to marry.

Claudette Colbert also stars in *Drums Along the Mohawk*, this time with Henry Fonda. Based on a 1936 novel by Walter Edmonds, *Drums* is a sentimental story about a man who builds a house in the wilderness, marries a pretty girl, fights off the Indians, and works with the simple country folk to create a satisfying life in the very year the American colonies rebel against Great Britain. *Drums* was one of a number of films based on historical themes that Hollywood released just before World War II. *The Howards of Virginia*

(1940), *Northwest Passage* (1939), and, most popular of all, *Gone with the Wind* (1939) were others in the same genre. Historical themes had been popular before, but with the world on the brink of war, the story of men and women in the wilderness struggling for family and country against Native Americans (stereotyped as savages) proved comforting as well as entertaining.

Reflecting on the Past Can a historian use movies to describe the values and myths of a particular time, or are the complexities and exaggerations too great? Are the most popular or most critically acclaimed films more useful than others in getting at the "spirit of an age"? Which films that are popular today tell us the most about our time and culture? Is there too much sex and violence in movies today? Should the government control the language, themes, and values depicted in movies? Are movies as important today as they were in the 1930s in defining and influencing the country's myths and values? ■

expressed his belief that there was in American life a "crime...that goes beyond denunciation." He warned, "In the eyes of the hungry there is a growing wrath."

Other writers also questioned the American dream. John Dos Passos's trilogy *U.S.A.* (1930–1936) conveyed a deep pessimism about American capitalism that many other intellectuals shared. Less political were

the novels of Thomas Wolfe and William Faulkner, who more sympathetically portrayed Americans caught up in the web of local life and facing the complex problems of the modern era. Faulkner's fictional Yoknapatawpha County, brought to life in *The Sound and the Fury, As I Lay Dying, Sanctuary,* and *Light in August* (1929–1932), documented the South's racial

The New Deal was as important for what it did not do as for what it did. It did not promote socialism or redistribute income or property. It promoted social justice and social reform, but it provided little for people at the bottom of American society, and less for African Americans and other minorities. The New Deal did not prevent business consolidation, and, in the end, it probably strengthened corporate capitalism.

Roosevelt, with his colorful personality and his dramatic response to the nation's crisis, dominated his times in a way few presidents have done. Yet for some people who lived through the decade, neither Roosevelt nor bread lines but a new streamlined refrigerator or a Walt Disney movie symbolized the Depression decade. It is easy to study the United States in the 1930s without reference to what was going on in the rest of the world. But the United States was influenced by international economic and political trends during the decade. The Depression was global in its impact, and it was at least in part responsible for the rise of Hitler in Germany, for economic and military expansionism in Japan, and for encouraging Mussolini to undertake foreign adventures. Great Britain, France, the United States, and other countries, faced with economic disaster, passed high tariffs that in turn increased international tensions and led to aggressive nationalism. These global trends would eventually involve the United States in World War II.

QUESTIONS FOR REVIEW AND REFLECTION

1. Explain the origins of the Great Depression. How was the Depression in the United States related to global economic factors?
2. Explain the two major phases of the New Deal. What programs were enacted in each phase, and what did they seek to accomplish?
3. Who criticized the New Deal and why?
4. How did communication technologies and popular culture change during the 1930s?
5. Why are the Depression and the New Deal considered to have a mixed legacy?

CHAPTER 25

World War II

"Rosie the Riveter"

Many African Americans moved north, lured by jobs in war industries. Prejudice remained even in the North, and some blacks were denied employment or were given the most menial tasks. Others, like these welders, found good jobs, improved their lives, and helped change the dynamics of race relations in the United States. What other developments resulted from the wartime employment of women and minorities?

(Library of Congress, [LCUSW3–34282-CC])

American Stories

A Native American Boy Plays at War

N. Scott Momaday, a Kiowa Indian born in Lawton, Oklahoma, in 1934, grew up on Navajo, Apache, and Pueblo reservations. He was only 11 years old when World War II ended, yet the war had changed his life. Shortly after the United States entered the war, Momaday's parents moved to New Mexico, where his father got a job with an oil company and his mother worked in the civilian personnel office at an army air force base. Like many couples, they had struggled through the hard times of the Depression. The war meant jobs.

Momaday's best friend was Billy Don Johnson, a "reddish, robust boy of great good humor and intense loyalty." Together they played war, digging trenches and dragging themselves through imaginary minefields. They hurled grenades and fired endless rounds from their imaginary machine guns, pausing only to drink Kool-Aid from their canteens. At school, they were taught history and math and also how to hate the enemy and be proud of America. They recited the Pledge of Allegiance to the flag and sang "God Bless America," "The Star-Spangled Banner," and "Remember Pearl Harbor." Like most Americans, they believed that World War II was a good war fought against evil empires. The United States was always right, the enemy always wrong. It was an attitude that would influence Momaday and his generation for the rest of their lives.

Momaday's only difficulty was that his Native American face was often mistaken for that of an Asian. Almost every day on the playground, someone would yell, "Hi ya, Jap," and a fight was on. Billy Don always came to his friend's defense, but it was disconcerting to be taken for the enemy. His father read old Kiowa tales to Momaday, who was proud to be an Indian but prouder still to be an American. On Saturday, he and his friends would go to the local theater to cheer as they watched a Japanese Zero or a German ME-109 go down in flames. They pretended that they were P-40 pilots. "The whole field of vision shuddered with our fire: the 50-caliber tracers curved out, fixing brilliant arcs upon the span, and struck; then there was a black burst of smoke, and the target went spinning down to death."

Near the end of the war, his family moved again, as so many families did, so that his father might get a better job. This time they lived right next door to an air force base, and Momaday fell in love with the B-17 "Flying Fortress," the bomber that military strategists thought would win the war in the Pacific and in Europe. He felt a real sense of resentment and loss when the B-17 was replaced by the larger but not nearly so glamorous B-29.

Looking back on his early years, Momaday reflected on the importance of the war in his growing up. "I see now that one experiences easily the ordinary things of life," he decided, "the things which cast familiar shadows upon the sheer, transparent panels of time, and he perceives his experience in the only way he can, according to his age." Though Momaday's life during the war differed from the lives of boys old enough to join the armed forces, the war was no less real for him. Though his youth was affected by the fact that he was male, was an Indian, and lived in the Southwest, the most important influence was that he was an American growing up during the war. Ironically, his parents had been made U.S. citizens by an act of Congress in 1924, but like all Native Americans living in Arizona and New Mexico, they were denied the right to vote by state law.

The Momadays fared better than most Native Americans, who found prejudice against them undiminished and jobs, even in wartime, hard to find. Native American servicemen returning from the war discovered that they were still treated like "Indians." They were prohibited from buying liquor in many states, and those who returned to the reservations learned that they were ineligible for veterans' benefits. Still, Momaday thought of himself not so much as an Indian as an American, and that too was a product of his generation. But as he grew to maturity, he became a successful writer and spokesman for his people. In 1969, he won the Pulitzer Prize for his novel *House Made of Dawn*. He also recorded his experiences and memories in a book called *The Names* (1976). In his writing, he stresses the Native American's close identification with the land. Writing about his grandmother, he says: "The immense landscape of the continental interior lay like memory in her blood."

Momaday was just a child during World War II, but it had a profound effect on his life as it did on all of those who remembered the conflict. His generation would judge the global events of the rest of the twentieth century in terms of their sense of patriotism and valor acquired during the war. Although no American cities were bombed and the mainland was never invaded, World War II influenced almost every aspect of American life. The war ended the Depression. Industrial jobs were plentiful, and even though prejudice and discrimination did not disappear, blacks, Hispanics, women, and other minorities had new opportunities. Like World War I, the second war expanded cooperation between government and industry and increased the influence of government in all areas of American life. The war also ended the last remnants of American isolationism. The United States emerged from the war in 1945 as the most powerful and prosperous nation in the world.

This chapter traces the gradual involvement of the United States in the international events during the 1930s that finally led to participation in the most devastating war the world had seen. It recounts the diplomatic and military struggles of the war and the search for a secure peace. It also seeks to explain the impact of the war on ordinary people and on American attitudes about the world, as well as its effect on patriotism and the American way of life. Even those, like N. Scott Momaday, who grew up during the war and were too young to fight, were influenced by the war—and the sense of moral certainty that the war inspired—for the rest of their lives. The war brought prosperity to some as it brought death to others. It left the American people the most affluent in the world and the United States the most powerful nation.

The Twisting Road to War

Looking back on the events between 1933 and 1941 that eventually led to American involvement in World War II, it is easy either to be critical of decisions made or actions not taken or to see everything that happened during the period as inevitable. Historical events are never inevitable, and leaders who must make decisions never have the advantage of retrospective vision; they have to deal with situations as they find them, and they never have all the facts.

Foreign Policy in a Global Age

In March 1933, Roosevelt faced not only overwhelming domestic difficulties but also an international crisis. The worldwide depression had caused near financial disaster in Europe. Germany had defaulted on its reparations installments, and most European countries were unable to keep up the payments on their debts to the United States.

Roosevelt had no master plan in foreign policy, just as he had none in the domestic sphere. In the first days of his administration, he gave conflicting signals as he groped to respond to the international situation. At first, it seemed that the president would cooperate in some kind of international economic agreement on tariffs and currency. But then he undercut the American delegation in London by refusing to go along with any international agreement. Solving the American domestic economic crisis seemed more important to Roosevelt in 1933 than international economic cooperation. His actions signaled a decision to go it alone in foreign policy.

Roosevelt did, however, alter some of the foreign policy decisions of previous administrations. He recognized the Soviet government, hoping to gain a market for surplus American grain. Although the expected trade bonanza never materialized, the Soviet Union agreed to pay the old debts and to extend rights to American citizens living in the Soviet Union. Diplomatic recognition opened communications between the two emerging world powers.

The United States continued to support dictators, especially in Central America, because they promised to promote stability and preserve American economic interests. But Roosevelt completed the removal of American military forces from Haiti and Nicaragua in 1934, and in a series of pan-American conferences, he joined in pledging that no country in the hemisphere would intervene in the "internal or external affairs" of any other.

The first test case came in Cuba, where a revolution threatened American investments of more than $1 billion. But the United States did not send troops. Instead, Roosevelt dispatched special envoys to work out a conciliatory agreement with the revolutionary government. A short time later, when a coup led by Fulgencio Batista overthrew the revolutionary government, the United States not only recognized the Batista government but also offered a large loan and agreed to abrogate the Platt Amendment (which made Cuba a virtual protectorate of the United States) in return for the rights to the Guantanamo naval base.

The Trade Agreements Act of 1934 gave the president power to lower tariff rates by as much as 50 percent. Using this act, the Roosevelt administration negotiated a series of agreements that improved trade. By 1935, half of American cotton exports and a large proportion of other products were going to Latin America. The Good Neighbor policy was good business for the United States, but increased trade did not solve the economic problems for either the United States or Latin America.

Another test of Latin American policy came in 1938 when Mexico nationalized the property of a number of American oil companies. Instead of intervening, as many businessmen urged, the State Department patiently worked out an agreement that included some compensation for the companies. The American government might have acted differently, however, if the threat of war in Europe in 1938 had not suggested that all the Western Hemisphere nations would have to cooperate to resist the growing power of Germany and Italy. At a pan-American conference held that year, the United States and most Latin American countries agreed to resist all foreign intervention in the hemisphere.

Europe on the Brink of War

Around the time that Roosevelt was first elected president, Adolf Hitler came to power in Germany. Born in Austria in 1889, Hitler had served as a corporal in the German army during World War I. Like many other Germans, he was angered by the Treaty of Versailles, and he blamed Germany's defeat on the Communists and the Jews. World War II in Europe was caused by World War I and by Germany's attempt to reverse the peace settlement.

Hitler became the leader of the National Socialist party of the German workers (*Nazi* is short for the German National Sozialist), and in 1923, after leading an unsuccessful coup, he was sentenced to prison. While in jail he wrote *Mein Kampf* ("My Struggle"), a long, rambling book spelling out his theories of racial purity, his hopes for Germany, and his venomous hatred of the Jews. After his release from prison, Hitler's following grew. He had a charismatic style and a plan. On January 30, 1933, he became chancellor of Germany, and within months the Reichstag (parliament) suspended the constitution, making Hitler Fuehrer (leader) and dictator. His Fascist regime concentrated political and economic power in a centralized state. He intended to conquer Europe and to make the German Third Reich (empire) the center of a new civilization.

In 1934, Hitler announced a program of German rearmament, violating the Versailles Treaty of 1919. Meanwhile, in Italy, the Fascist dictator Benito Mussolini was building a powerful military force; in 1934, he threatened to invade the East African country of Ethiopia. These ominous rumblings in Europe frightened Americans at the very time they were reexamining American entry into the Great War and vowing that they would never again get involved in a European conflict.

Senator Gerald P. Nye of North Dakota, who had helped expose the Teapot Dome scandal in 1924, turned to an investigation of the connection between corporate profits and American participation in World War I. His committee's public hearings revealed that many American businessmen had close relationships with the War Department. Businesses producing war materials had made huge profits. Though the committee failed to prove a conspiracy, it was easy to conclude that the United States had been tricked into going to war by the people who profited the most from it.

On many college campuses, students demonstrated against war. Students joined organizations such as Veterans of Future Wars and Future Gold Star Mothers and protested the presence of the Reserve Officers Training Corps (ROTC) on their campuses. Many were determined never again to support a foreign war. But in Europe, Asia, and Africa, there were already rumblings of another great international conflict.

Ethiopia and Spain

In May 1935, Italy invaded Ethiopia after rejecting the League of Nations' offer to mediate the difficulties between the two countries. Italian dive bombers and machine guns made quick work of the small and poorly equipped Ethiopian army. The Ethiopian war, remote as it seemed, frightened Congress, which passed a Neutrality Act authorizing the president to prohibit all arms shipments to nations at war and to advise all U.S. citizens not to travel on belligerents' ships except at their own risk. Remembering the process that had led the United States into World War I, Congress was determined that it would not happen again.

The League of Nations condemned Italy as the aggressor in the war, and Great Britain moved its fleet to the Mediterranean. Roosevelt used the authority of the Neutrality Act of 1935 to impose an arms embargo. But, in the midst of depression, neither Britain nor the United States wanted to stop shipments of oil to Italy or to commit its own soldiers to the fight. The embargo on arms had little impact on Italy, but it was disastrous for Ethiopia.

"We shun political commitments which might entangle us in foreign war," Roosevelt announced in 1936. But isolation became more difficult when a civil war broke out in Spain in 1936. General Francisco Franco, supported by the Catholic church and large landowners, revolted against the republican government. Mussolini had joined forces with Germany to form the Rome–Berlin Axis in 1936, and Germany and Italy aided Franco, sending planes and other weapons, while the Soviet Union came to the support of the anti-Franco Loyalists.

The war in Spain polarized the United States. Most Catholics and many anti-Communists sided with Franco. But many American radicals, even those opposed to all war a few months before, found the Loyalist cause worth fighting and dying for. More than 3,000 Americans joined the Abraham Lincoln Brigade, and hundreds were killed fighting fascism in Spain. "If this were a Spanish matter, I'd let it alone," Sam Levenger, a student at Ohio State, wrote. "But the rebellion would not last a week if it weren't for the Germans and the Italians. And if Hitler and Mussolini can send troops to Spain to attack the government elected by the people, why can't they do so in France? And after France?" Levenger was killed in Spain in 1937 at age 20.

Picasso's *Guernica*

On April 26, 1937, German airplanes supporting Franco's soldiers bombed and machine-gunned the historic Basque capital city of Guernica, killing more than 1,600 people and foreshadowing the massive destruction of civilians during World War II. Pablo Picasso, probably the most famous artist of the twentieth century, painted this black-and-white mural to denounce the attack. After the defeat of the Republican forces in Spain, Picasso refused to allow the painting to be displayed in the country. Only in 1975, after the end of the Franco regime, did the painting return to Madrid. What kind of symbols and images can you find in the painting?

(Pablo Picasso (1881–1973), "Guernica," 1937. Oil on canvas, 350 × 782 cm. Museo Nacional Centro de Arte Reina Sofia, Madrid, Spain. Copyright John Bigelow Taylor/Art Resource, NY. © 2008 Estate of Pablo Picasso/Artists Rights Society (ARS), New York.)

The U.S. government tried to stay neutral and to ship arms and equipment to neither side. While the United States, along with Britain and France, carefully protected its neutrality, Franco consolidated his dictatorship with the active aid of Germany and Italy. Meanwhile, Congress in 1937 passed another Neutrality Act, this time making it illegal for American citizens to travel on belligerents' ships. The act extended the embargo on arms and made even nonmilitary items available to belligerents only on a cash-and-carry basis.

In a variety of ways, the United States tried to avoid repeating the mistakes that had led it into World War I. Unfortunately, World War II, which moved closer each day, would be a different kind of war, and the lessons of the first war would be of little use.

War in Europe

Roosevelt was by no means an isolationist, but he wanted to keep the United States out of the European conflagration. When he announced, "I hate war," he was expressing a deep personal belief that wars solve few problems. Unlike his distant cousin Theodore Roosevelt, he did not view war as a test of one's manhood. In foreign policy, just as in domestic affairs, FDR responded to events, but he moved reluctantly toward greater American involvement.

In March 1938, Hitler's Germany annexed Austria and then in September, as a result of the Munich Conference, occupied the Sudetenland, a part of Czechoslovakia. Within six months, Hitler's armies had overrun the rest of Czechoslovakia. Little protest came from the United States. Most Americans sympathized with the victims of Hitler's aggression, and at first, almost everyone hoped that compromises could be worked out and that Europe could settle its own problems. But that notion was destroyed on August 23, 1939, by the news of a Nazi–Soviet pact. Fascism and communism were political philosophies supposedly in deadly opposition. Many Americans had secretly hoped that Nazi Germany and Soviet Russia would fight it out, neutralizing each other. Now they had signed a nonaggression pact. A week later, Hitler's army attacked Poland, marking the official beginning of World War II. Britain and France honored their treaties and came to Poland's defense. "This nation will remain a neutral nation," Roosevelt announced, "but I cannot ask that every American remain neutral in thought as well."

Roosevelt asked for a repeal of the embargo section of the Neutrality Act and for the approval of the sale of arms on a cash-and-carry basis to France and Britain. Yet Roosevelt did take some secret risks. In August 1939, Albert Einstein, a Jewish refugee from Nazi Germany, and other distinguished scientists warned the president that German researchers were at work on an atomic bomb. Fearing the consequences of a powerful new weapon in Hitler's hands, Roosevelt authorized funds for a top-secret project to build an American bomb first. Only a few advisers and key members of Congress knew of the project, which was officially organized in 1941 and would ultimately change the course of human history.

The war in Poland ended quickly. With Germany attacking from the west and the Soviet Union from the east, the Poles were overwhelmed in a month. The fall of Poland in September 1939 brought a lull in the fighting.

Great Britain sent several divisions to aid the French against the expected German attack, but for months nothing happened. This interlude, sometimes called the "phony war," dramatically ended on April 9, 1940, when Germany attacked Norway and Denmark with a furious air and sea assault. A few weeks later, using armored vehicles supported by massive air strikes, the German *Blitzkrieg* ("lightning war") swept through Belgium, Luxembourg, and the Netherlands. A week later, the Germans stormed into France.

The famed Maginot line, a series of fortifications designed to repulse a German invasion, was useless, as German mechanized forces swept around the end of the line and attacked from the rear. The French guns, solidly fixed in concrete and pointing toward Germany, were never fired. France surrendered in June as the British army fled back across the English Channel from Dunkirk.

How should the United States respond to the new and desperate situation in Europe? William Allen White, journalist and editor, and other concerned Americans organized the Committee to Defend America by Aiding the Allies, but others, including Charles Lindbergh, the hero of the 1920s, supported a group called America First. They argued that the United States should forget about England and concentrate on defending America. Roosevelt steered a cautious course. He approved the shipment to Britain of 50 overage American destroyers. In return, the United States received the right to establish naval and air bases on British territory from Newfoundland to Bermuda and British Guiana.

Winston Churchill, prime minister of Great Britain, asked for much more, but Roosevelt hesitated. In July 1940, the president did sign a measure authorizing $4 billion to increase the number of American naval warships. In September, Congress passed the Selective Service Act, which provided for the first peacetime draft in the history of the United States. More than a million men were to serve in the army for one year, but only in the Western Hemisphere.

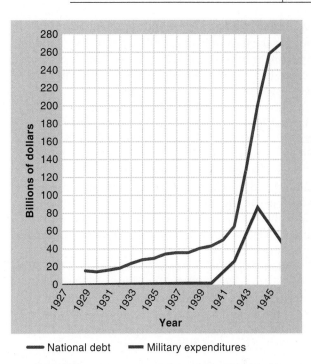

Military Expenditures and the National Debt, 1929–1945

Increased taxes, the sale of war bonds, and price controls kept inflation under relative control during the war. Still, the war industry not only stimulated the economy but also increased the national debt. In what other ways do wars influence the economy?

Source: U.S. Bureau of the Census.

The Election of 1940

Part of Roosevelt's reluctance to aid Great Britain more energetically came from his genuine desire to keep the United States out of the war, but it was also related to the presidential campaign waged during the crisis months of the summer and fall of 1940. Roosevelt broke a long tradition by seeking a third term. He marked the increasing support he was drawing from the liberal wing of the Democratic party by selecting liberal farm economist Henry Wallace of Iowa as his running mate.

The Republicans nominated Wendell Willkie of Indiana. Despite his big-business ties, Willkie approved of most New Deal legislation and supported aid to Great Britain. Energetic and attractive, Willkie was the most persuasive and exciting Republican candidate since Theodore Roosevelt. Yet in an atmosphere of international crisis, most voters chose to stay with Roosevelt. He won, 27 million to 22 million, and carried 38 of 48 states.

Lend-Lease

After the election, Roosevelt invented a scheme for sending aid to Britain without demanding payment. He called it "lend-lease." He compared the situation to lending a garden hose to a neighbor whose house was on fire. Senator Robert Taft of Ohio, however, thought the idea of lending military equipment and expecting it back was absurd. He decided it was more like lending chewing gum to a friend: "Once it had been used you did not want it back."

The Lend-Lease Act, which Congress passed in March 1941, destroyed the fiction of neutrality. By that time, German submarines were sinking half a million tons of shipping each month in the Atlantic. In June, Roosevelt proclaimed a national emergency and ordered the closing of German and Italian consulates in the United States. On June 22, Germany suddenly attacked the Soviet Union. It was one of Hitler's biggest blunders of the war, forcing his armies to fight on two fronts.

When Roosevelt extended lend-lease aid to Russia in November 1941, most Americans accepted the Soviet Union as a friend and ally. By the autumn of 1941, the United States was virtually at war with Germany in the Atlantic. On September 11, Roosevelt issued a "shoot on sight" order for all American ships operating in the Atlantic, and on October 30, a German submarine sank an American destroyer off the coast of Newfoundland. The war in the Atlantic, however, was undeclared. Eventually, the sinking of enough American ships or another crisis would probably have provided the excuse for a formal declaration of war against Germany. It was not Germany, however, but Japan that catapulted the United States into World War II.

The Path to Pearl Harbor

Japan, controlled by ambitious military leaders, was the aggressor in the Far East as Hitler's Germany was in Europe. Intent on becoming a major world power yet desperately needing natural resources, especially oil, Japan was willing to risk war with China, the Soviet Union, and even the United States to get those resources. Japan invaded Manchuria in 1931 and launched an all-out assault on China in 1937. This was the beginning of what the Japanese would call "the Pacific War." The Japanese leaders assumed that at some point the United States would go to war if Japan tried to take the Philippines, but the Japanese attempted to delay that moment as long as possible by diplomatic means. The United States feared a two-front war and was willing to delay the confrontation with Japan until it had dealt with the German threat. Thus, between 1938 and 1941, the United States and Japan engaged in a kind of diplomatic shadow boxing.

The United States began to apply economic pressure in July 1939, giving Japan the required six months' notice regarding cancellation of the 1911 commercial agreement between the two countries. In September 1940, the Roosevelt administration forbade the shipment of airplane fuel and scrap metal to Japan. Other items were added to the embargo until by the spring of 1941, the United States allowed only oil to be shipped to Japan, hoping that the threat of cutting off this important resource would lead to negotiations and avert a crisis. Japan did open negotiations with the United States, but there was little to discuss. Japan would not withdraw from China as the United States demanded. Indeed, Japan, taking advantage of the situation in Europe, occupied French Indochina in 1940 and 1941. In July 1941, Roosevelt froze all Japanese assets in the United States, effectively embargoing trade with Japan.

Roosevelt had an advantage in the negotiations with Japan, for the United States had broken the Japanese secret diplomatic code. But Japanese intentions were hard to decipher from the intercepted messages. American leaders knew that Japan planned to attack, but they didn't know where. In September 1941, the Japanese decided to strike sometime after November unless the United States offered real concessions.

On the morning of December 7, 1941, Japanese airplanes launched from aircraft carriers attacked the U.S. fleet at Pearl Harbor in Hawaii. The surprise attack destroyed or disabled 19 ships (including 5 battleships) and 150 planes and killed 2,335 soldiers and sailors and 68 civilians. On the same day, the Japanese launched attacks on the Philippines, Guam, and the Midway Islands, as well as on the British colonies of Hong Kong and Malaya. The next day, with only one dissenting vote, Congress declared war on Japan.

December 7, 1941, was a date that would "live in infamy," in the words of Franklin Roosevelt. It was also a day that would have far-reaching implications for American foreign policy and for American attitudes toward the world. The surprise attack united the country as nothing else could have. Even isolationists and America First advocates quickly rallied behind the war effort.

After the shock and anger subsided, Americans searched for a villain. Someone must have blundered, someone must have betrayed the country to have allowed the "inferior" Japanese to have carried out such a successful and devastating attack. A myth persists to this day that the villain was Roosevelt, who, the story goes, knew of the Japanese attack but failed to warn the military commanders so that the American people might unite behind the war effort against Germany. But Roosevelt did not know. There was no specific warning that the attack was coming against Pearl Harbor, and the American ability to read the Japanese coded messages was of no help because the fleet kept radio silence.

The irony was that the Americans, partly because of racial prejudice against the Japanese, underestimated their ability. They ignored many warning signals because they did not believe that the Japanese could launch an attack on a target as far away as Hawaii. Most of the experts, including Roosevelt, expected the Japanese to attack the Philippines or perhaps Thailand. Many people blundered, but there was no conspiracy.

More important in the long run than the way the attack on Pearl Harbor united the American people was its effect on a generation of military and political leaders. Pearl Harbor became the symbol of unpreparedness. For a generation that experienced the anger and frustration of the attack on Pearl Harbor by an unscrupulous enemy, the lesson was to be prepared and ready to stop an aggressor before it had a chance to strike. The smoldering remains of the sinking battleships at Pearl Harbor on the morning of December 7, 1941, and the history lesson learned there would influence American policy not only during World War II but also in Korea, Vietnam, and beyond.

The Home Front

Too often wars are described in terms of presidents and generals, emperors and kings, in terms of grand strategy and elaborate campaigns. But wars affect the lives of all people—the soldiers who fight and the women and children and men who stay home. World War II especially had an impact on all aspects of society—the economy, the movies and radio, even attitudes toward women and blacks. For many people, the war represented opportunity and the end of the Depression. For others, the excitement of faraway places meant that they could never return home again. For still others, the war left lasting scars.

Mobilizing for War

Converting American industry to war production was a complex task. Shortly after Pearl Harbor, Roosevelt created the War Production Board (WPB) and appointed Donald Nelson, executive vice president of Sears, Roebuck, to mobilize the nation's resources for an all-out war effort. The Roosevelt administration tried hard to gain the cooperation of businesspeople, many of them alienated by New Deal policies. The president appointed many business leaders to key positions and abandoned antitrust actions in any industry that was remotely related to the war effort. The policy worked. Industrial production and net corporate profits nearly doubled during the war. Large commercial farmers also profited. The war years accelerated the mechanization of the farm and dramatically increased the use of fertilizer, but between 1940 and 1945 the farm population declined by 17 percent.

Many government agencies in addition to the War Production Board helped monitor the war effort. The Office of Price Administration (OPA) set prices and rationed products—and because it affected so many lives so disagreeably, many Americans regarded it as oppressive. The National War Labor Board (NWLB) had the authority to set wages and hours and to regulate working conditions, and it could seize factories whose owners refused to cooperate.

Union membership grew rapidly during the war, from 10.5 million in 1941 to 14.7 million in 1945. In return for a "no-strike pledge," the NWLB allowed agreements that required workers to retain their union membership through the life of a contract. Labor leaders, however, complained about increased government regulations and argued that wage controls coupled with wartime inflation

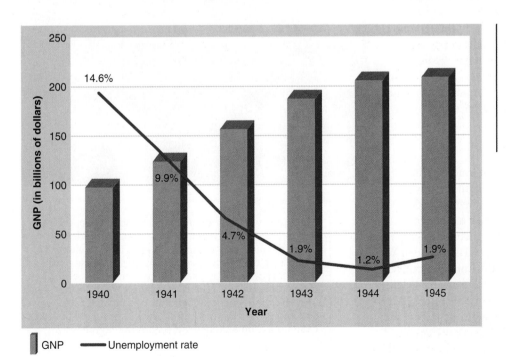

Gross National Product and Unemployment, 1940–1945

The war economy virtually wiped out unemployment and increased production to unprecedented levels. How would these changes affect everyday life in the United States?

Source: U.S. Bureau of the Census.

were unfair. The NWLB finally allowed a 15 percent cost-of-living increase on some contracts, but that did not apply to overtime pay, which helped drive up wages in some industries during the war by about 70 percent.

Besides wage and price controls and rationing, the government tried to reduce inflation by selling war bonds and by increasing taxes. The Revenue Act of 1942 raised tax rates, broadened the tax base, increased corporate taxes to 40 percent, and raised the excess-profits tax to 90 percent. In addition, the government initiated a payroll deduction for income taxes. The war made the income tax a reality for most Americans for the first time.

Despite some unfairness and much confusion, the American economy responded to the wartime crisis and produced the equipment and supplies that eventually won the war. American industries built 300,000 airplanes, 88,140 tanks, and 3,000 merchant ships. In 1944 alone, American factories produced 800,000 tons of synthetic rubber to replace the supply of natural rubber captured by the Japanese. Although the national debt grew from about $143 billion in 1943 to $260 billion in 1945, the government policy of taxation paid for about 40 percent of the war's cost. At the same time, full employment and the increase in two-income families, together with forced savings, helped provide capital for postwar expansion. In a limited way, the tax policy also tended to redistribute wealth, which the New Deal had failed to do. The top 5 percent income bracket, which controlled 23 percent of the disposable income in 1939, accounted for only 17 percent in 1945.

The war stimulated the growth of the federal bureaucracy and accelerated the trend, begun during World War I and extended in the 1920s and 1930s, toward the government's central role in the economy. The war also increased the cooperation between industry and government, creating what would later be called a military-industrial complex. But for most Americans, despite anger at the OPA and the income tax, the war meant the end of the Depression.

Patriotic Fervor

The war, so horrible elsewhere, was remote in the United States—except for the families that received the official telegram informing them that a loved one had been killed. The government tried to keep the conflict alive in the minds of Americans and to keep the country united behind the war effort. The Office of War Information controlled the news the American public received about the war and promoted patriotism. The government also sold war bonds, not only to help pay for the war and reduce inflation but also to sell the war to the American people. Schoolchildren purchased war stamps and faithfully pasted them in an album until they

had accumulated stamps worth $18.75, enough to buy a $25 bond (redeemable 10 years later). Their bonds, they were told, would purchase bullets or a part for an airplane to kill "Japs" and Germans and defend the American way of life. "For Freedom's Sake, Buy War Bonds," one poster announced. Working men and women purchased bonds through payroll deduction plans and looked forward to spending the money on consumer goods after the war. In the end, the government sold more than $135 billion in war bonds. While the bond drives did help control inflation, they were most important in making millions of Americans feel that they were contributing to the war effort.

The Enemy

During the war American magazines and newspapers often depicted the Japanese as monkeys, insects, or rodents. Germans were rarely pictured this way. This December 12, 1942, issue of *Collier's* magazine pictures Japanese prime minister Hideki Tojo as a vampire bat carrying a bomb to drop on the United States. The Japanese, on the other hand, often pictured Americans and British as bloated capitalists and imperialists. What effect, do you suppose, did these caricatures have on attitudes and actions during the war?

(akg-images)

Those too old or too young to join the armed forces became air raid wardens or civilian defense and Red Cross volunteers. They raised victory gardens and took part in scrap drives. Even small children could join the war effort by collecting old rubber, wastepaper, and kitchen fats. Some items, including gasoline, sugar, butter, and meat, were rationed, but few people complained. Even horsemeat hamburgers seemed edible if they helped win the war. Newspaper and magazine advertising characterized ordinary actions as either speeding victory or impeding the war effort.

Internment of Japanese Americans

Wartime campaigns not only stimulated patriotism but also promoted hatred for the enemy. The Nazis, especially Hitler and his Gestapo, had become synonymous with evil even before 1941. At the beginning of the war there was little animosity toward the German people, but before long most Americans ceased to make distinctions. All Germans seemed evil, although the anti-German hysteria that had swept the country during World War I never developed.

The Japanese were easier to hate than the Germans. The attack on Pearl Harbor created a special animosity toward the Japanese, but the depiction of the Japanese as warlike and subhuman owed something to a long tradition of fear of the so-called yellow peril and a distrust of all Asians. Two weeks after Pearl Harbor, *Time* magazine explained to Americans how they could distinguish our Asian friends the Chinese "from the Japs": "The Chinese expression is likely to be more kindly, placid, open; the Japanese more positive, dogmatic, arrogant."

The racial stereotype of the Japanese played a role in the treatment of Japanese Americans during the war. Some prejudice was shown against German and Italian Americans and some were relocated, but Japanese Americans were the only group confined in concentration camps in large numbers and for the duration of the war. It was the greatest mass abridgment of civil liberties in American history.

At the time of Pearl Harbor, about 127,000 Japanese Americans lived in the United States, most on the West Coast. About 80,000 were *nisei* (Japanese born in the United States and holding American citizenship) and *sansei* (the sons and daughters of nisei); the rest were *issei* (aliens born in Japan who were ineligible for U.S. citizenship). The Japanese had long suffered from racial discrimination and prejudice in the United States. They were barred from intermarriage with other groups and excluded from many clubs, restaurants, and recreation facilities. Many worked as tenant farmers, fishermen, and small-business owners. Others made up a small professional class of lawyers, teachers, and doctors and a large number of landowning farmers.

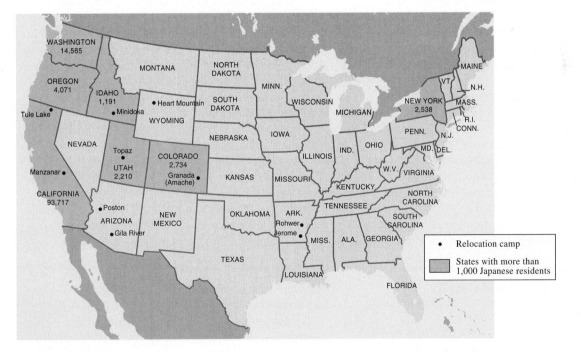

Relocation Camps

Early in 1942, responding to the hysterical fear that Japanese Americans living on the West Coast might engage in sabotage, the government ordered more than 100,000 Japanese Americans (many of them citizens) into relocation camps. A larger group of Japanese Americans living in Hawaii did not have their lives disrupted or their property confiscated. How do you explain the pattern of Japanese relocation?

Although many retained cultural and linguistic ties to Japan, they posed no more threat to the country than did the much larger groups of Italian Americans and German Americans. But their appearance made them stand out. After Pearl Harbor, an anti-Japanese panic seized the West Coast.

West Coast politicians and ordinary citizens urged the War Department and the president to evacuate the Japanese. The president capitulated and issued Executive Order 9066 authorizing the evacuation in February 1942. "The continued pressure of a largely unassimilated, tightly knit racial group, bound to an enemy nation by strong ties of race, culture, custom and religion, constituted a menace which had to be dealt with," General John De Witt argued, justifying the removal on military grounds. But racial fear and animosity, not military necessity, stood behind the order.

Eventually, the government built the "relocation centers" in remote, often arid, sections of the West. "The Japs live like rats, breed like rats, and act like rats. We don't want them," the governor of Idaho announced. The camps were primitive and unattractive. "When I first entered our room, I became sick to my stomach," a Japanese American woman remembered. "There were seven beds in the room and no furniture nor any partitions to separate the males and the females of the family. I just sat on the bed, staring at the bare wall."

The government evacuated about 110,000 Japanese, including about 60,000 American citizens. The Japanese Americans lost their worldly possessions, and something more—their pride and respect. One 6-year-old kept asking his mother to "take him back to America." He thought his relocation center was in Japan.

The evacuation was unjustified. Even in Hawaii, where a much larger Japanese population existed, the government evacuated only a few (in part because the Japanese were so vital to the economy of the Islands), and no sabotage and little disloyalty occurred. The government allowed Japanese American men to volunteer for military service, and many served bravely in Europe. The 442nd Infantry Combat Team, made up entirely of *nisei*, became the most decorated unit in all the military service—another indication of the loyalty and patriotism of most Japanese Americans. In 1988, Congress belatedly voted limited compensation for the Japanese Americans relocated during World War II.

Asian, African, and Hispanic Americans at War

The Pacific War made China an ally of the United States, but Congress did not repeal the Chinese Exclusion Act until 1943, and then only 105 Chinese a year were allowed to enter the United States legally. Despite this, Chinese communities in the United States joined the war effort enthusiastically. They bought war bonds, collected scrap metal, and in other ways tried to show that they were loyal citizens. The Korean, Filipino, and Asian Indian population also contributed to the war effort, even though they still faced prejudice and were often denied service in restaurants or refused admittance to theaters. Many Americans hated the Japanese; to them, all Asians looked like the enemy.

Even in much of the North, the United States remained a segregated society in 1941. African Americans could not live, eat, travel, work, or go to school with the same freedom that whites enjoyed. Black Americans profited little from the revival of prosperity and the expansion of jobs early in the war. Those who joined the military were usually assigned to menial jobs as cooks or laborers and were always assigned to segregated units with whites as the high-ranking officers. The myth persisted that black soldiers had failed to perform well in World War I. "Leadership is not embedded in the negro race yet," Secretary of War Henry Stimson wrote, "and to try to make commissioned officers...lead men into battle—colored men—is only to work a disaster to both."

Some black leaders found it especially ironic that as the country prepared to fight Hitler and his racist policies, the United States persisted in its own brand of racism. "A jim crow Army cannot fight for a free world," announced *The Crisis,* the journal of the NAACP. A. Philip Randolph decided to act rather than talk. Randolph had worked with the first wave of African Americans migrating from the South to the northern cities during and just after World War I. He spent years trying "to carry the gospel of unionism to the colored world." He organized and led the Brotherhood of Sleeping Car Porters, and in 1937, he finally won grudging recognition of the union from the Pullman Company.

Admired by black leaders of all political persuasions, Randolph convinced many of them in 1941 to join him in a march on Washington to demand equal rights. The threat of as many as 100,000 African Americans marching in protest in the nation's capital alarmed Roosevelt. He talked to Randolph and struck a bargain. Roosevelt refused to desegregate the armed forces, but in return for Randolph's calling off the march, the president issued Executive Order 8802, which stated that it was the policy of the United States that "there shall be no discrimination in the employment of workers in defense industries or government because of race, creed, color or national origin." He also established the Fair Employment Practices Commission (FEPC) to enforce the order.

By threatening militant action, the black leaders wrested a major concession from the president. But the executive order did not end prejudice, and the FEPC, which its chairman described as the "most hated agency in Washington," had limited success in erasing the color line. Many black soldiers were angered and humiliated throughout the war by being made to sit in the back of buses and being barred from hotels and restaurants. Years later, one former black soldier recalled being refused service in a restaurant in Salina, Kansas, while the same restaurant served German prisoners from a camp nearby. "We continued to stare," he recalled. "This was really happening.... The people of Salina would serve these enemy soldiers and turn away black American G.I.'s."

Jobs in war industries helped many African Americans improve their economic conditions. Continuing the migration that had begun during World War I, about 1 million southern blacks moved to northern and western cities. The new arrivals increased pressure on overcrowded housing, aggravating tension among all hard-pressed groups. In Detroit, a race riot broke out in the summer of 1943 after Polish Americans protested a public housing development that promised to bring blacks into the neighborhood. Before federal and state troops could restore order, 25 blacks and 9 whites had been killed and more than $2 million worth of property was destroyed. Groups of white men roamed the city attacking blacks, overturning cars and setting fires. Other riots broke out in Mobile, Los Angeles, New York, and Beaumont, Texas. In all these cities, and in others, the legacy of hate lasted long after the war.

Mexican Americans, like most minority groups, profited during the war from the increased job opportunities provided by wartime industry, but they, too, faced racial prejudice. In California and in many parts of the Southwest, Mexicans could not use public swimming pools. Often lumped together with blacks, they were excluded from certain restaurants. Usually they were limited to menial jobs and were constantly harassed by the police, picked up for minor offenses, and jailed on the smallest excuse.

In Los Angeles, anti-Mexican prejudice flared into violence. The increased migration of Mexicans into the city as well as old hatreds created a volatile situation. Most of the hostility and anger focused on Mexican gang members, or *pachucos*, especially those wearing zoot suits. The suits consisted of long, loose coats with padded shoulders, ballooned pants pegged at the ankles, and a wide-brimmed hat. A watch chain and a ducktail haircut completed the uniform. The zoot suit had originated in the black sections of northern cities and became a national craze during the war. It was a look some teenage males adopted to call attention to themselves and shock conventional society.

The zoot-suiters especially angered soldiers and sailors who were stationed in or on leave in Los Angeles. After a number of provocative incidents, violence broke out between the Mexican American youths and the servicemen in the spring of 1943. The servicemen, joined by others, beat up the Mexicans, stripped them of their offensive clothes, and then gave them haircuts. The police, both civilian and military, looked the other way, and when they did move in, they arrested the victims rather than their attackers.

Social Impact of the War

Modern wars have been incredibly destructive of human lives and property, but they have social results as well. World War II altered patterns of work, leisure, education, and family life; caused a massive migration of people; created jobs; and changed lifestyles. It is difficult to overemphasize the impact of the war on the generation that lived through it.

Wartime Opportunities

More than 15 million American civilians moved during the war. Like the Momadays, many left home to find better jobs. In fact, for many Native Americans, wartime opportunities led to a migration from rural areas and reservations into cities. Americans moved off farms and away from small towns, flocking to cities, where defense jobs were readily available. World War II migrants poured into industrial centers: 200,000 came to the Detroit area, nearly half a million to Los Angeles, and about 100,000 to Mobile, Alabama.

Nowhere was the change more dramatic than in the West, and especially in California, where the wartime boom transformed the region more dramatically than any development since the nineteenth-century economic revolution created by the railroads and mining. The federal government spent more than $70 billion in the state (one-tenth of the total for the entire country) to build army bases, shipyards, supply depots, and testing sites. In addition, private industry constructed so many facilities that the region became the center of a growing military-industrial complex. San Diego, for example, was transformed from a sleepy port and naval base into a sprawling metropolis.

This spectacular growth created housing shortages and overwhelmed schools, hospitals, and municipal services. Crime and prostitution increased as did racial tensions. Some migrants had never lived in a city and were homesick. On one occasion in a Willow Grove, Michigan, school, the children were all instructed to sing "Michigan, My Michigan"; no one knew the words because they all came from other states.

For the first time in years, many families had money to spend, but they had nothing to spend it on. The last new car rolled off the assembly line in February 1942. There were no washing machines, refrigerators, or radios in the stores, no gasoline and no tires to permit weekend trips. Even when people had time off, they tended to stay at home or in the neighborhood.

The war required major adjustments in American family life. With several million men in the service and others far away working at defense jobs, the number of households headed by a woman increased dramatically. The number of marriages also rose sharply. Early in the war, a young man could be deferred if he had a dependent, and a wife qualified as a dependent. Later, many servicemen got married, often to women they barely knew, because they wanted a little excitement and perhaps someone to come home to. The birthrate also began to rise in 1940, as young couples started families as fast as they could. The number of births outside marriage also rose, and from the outset of the war, the divorce rate began to climb sharply. Yet most of the wartime marriages survived, and many of the women left at home looked ahead to a time after the war when they could settle down to a normal life.

Women Workers for Victory

Thousands of women took jobs in heavy industry that formerly would have been considered unladylike. They built tanks, airplanes, and ships, but they still earned less than men. At first, women were rarely hired because as the war in Europe pulled American industry out of its long slump, unemployed men snapped up the newly available positions. But by 1943, with many men drafted and male unemployment virtually nonexistent, the government was quick to suggest that it was women's patriotic duty to take their place on the assembly line. Nearly 3 million women served in the Women's Land Army to replace farm laborers who were in the army, but it was the woman factory worker who captured the public's imagination. A popular song was "Rosie the Riveter," who was "making history working for victory." She also helped her marine boyfriend by "working overtime on the riveting machine."

At the end of the war, the labor force included 19.5 million women, but three-fourths of them had been working before the conflict, and some of the additional ones might have sought work in normal times. The new women war workers tended to be older, and they were more often married than single. Some worked for patriotic reasons. "Every time I test a batch of rubber, I know it's going to help bring my three sons home quicker," a woman worker in a rubber plant remarked. But others worked for the money or to have something useful to do. Yet in 1944, women's weekly wages averaged $31.21, compared with $54.65 for men, reflecting women's more menial tasks and their low seniority as well as outright discrimination. Still, many women enjoyed factory work.

Black women faced the most difficult situation during the war, and often when they applied for work, they were told, "We have not yet installed separate toilet facilities" or "We can't put a Negro in the front office." Not until 1944 did the telephone company in New York City hire a black telephone operator. Still, some black women moved during the war from domestic jobs to higher-paying factory work. Married women with young children also found it difficult to obtain work. There were few day-care facilities, and women were often informed that they should be home with their children.

Many women war workers quickly left their jobs after the war ended. Some left by choice, but dismissals ran twice as high for women as for men. The war had barely shaken the notion that a woman's place was at home. Some women would have preferred to keep working. But most women, and an even larger percentage of men, agreed at the end of the war that women did not deserve an "equal chance with men" for jobs. For most Americans, a woman's place was still in the home.

Entertaining the People

According to one survey, Americans listened to the radio an average of $4\frac{1}{2}$ hours a day during the war. The major networks increased their news programs from less than 4 percent to nearly 30 percent of broadcasting time. Americans heard Edward R. Murrow broadcasting from London during the German air blitz with the sound of the air raid sirens in the background. They listened to Eric Sevareid cover the battle of Burma and describe the sensation of jumping out of an airplane. Often the signal faded out and the static made listening difficult, but the live broadcasts had drama and authenticity never before possible.

The war also intruded on almost all programming. Music, which took up a large proportion of radio programming, also conveyed a war theme. There were "Goodbye, Mama (I'm Off to Yokohama)" and "Praise the Lord and Pass the Ammunition," but more numerous were songs of romance and love, songs about separation and hope for a better time after the war. The danceable tunes of Glenn Miller and Tommy Dorsey became just as much a part of wartime memories as ration books and far-off battlefields.

For many Americans, the motion picture became the most important leisure activity and a part of their fantasy life during the war. Attendance at the movies averaged about 100 million viewers a week. There might not be gasoline for weekend trips or Sunday drives, but the whole family could go to the movies. Even those in the military service could watch American movies on board ship or at a remote outpost.

"Pinup" photographs of Hollywood stars decorated the barracks and even tanks and planes wherever American troops were stationed.

The war engulfed Hollywood. Newsreels that offered a visual synopsis of the war news, always with an upbeat message and a touch of human interest, preceded most movies. Their theme was that the Americans were winning the war, even if early in the conflict there was little evidence to that effect. Many feature films also had a wartime theme, picturing the war in the Pacific complete with grinning, vicious Japanese villains (usually played by Chinese or Korean character actors). In the beginning of these films, the Japanese were always victorious, but in the end, they always got "what they deserved."

The movies set in Europe differed from those depicting the Far Eastern war. British and Americans, sometimes spies, sometimes downed airmen, could dress up like Germans and get away with it. They outwitted the Germans at every turn, sabotaging important installations, and made daring escapes from prison camps. Many wartime movies featured a multicultural platoon led by a veteran sergeant with a Protestant, a Catholic, a Jew, a black, a farmer, and a city resident. In several movies, the army was integrated, but in the real army, blacks served in segregated platoons.

Religion in Time of War

One of the four freedoms threatened by German and Japanese aggression was the "freedom to worship," and Roosevelt continually emphasized that the enemy was opposed to all religion. According to one estimate in 1940, 65 million Americans belonged to 250,000 churches and other religious institutions. There were about 23 million Catholics and 5 million Jews, and most of the rest were of one Protestant denomination or another. Most Americans thought of the United States as a Christian nation, and by that they usually meant a Protestant nation. While the war did lead to a measure of religious tolerance, anti-Semitism and anti-Catholicism did not disappear. According to one poll, although 18 percent of Americans never went to church, more than 30 percent said that the war had strengthened their religious faith.

Those who joined the armed forces were given three choices under religion: They were asked to check Protestant, Catholic, or Jew, and their "dog tags" were marked *P, C,* or *H* (for *Hebrew*). There was no room for Hindu, Buddhist, Muslim, or atheist. Some men refused to fight on religious grounds. During World War I, only members of the traditional peace churches (Quaker, Brethren, and Mennonite) were deferred from military service as conscientious objectors. In World War II, the criterion was broadened to include those who opposed war because of "religious training and belief." More than 70,000 claimed exemption on those grounds, and the government honored about half those claims. Twenty-five thousand were assigned to noncombat military service.

A few clergymen remained pacifists and opposed the war, but far fewer than in World War I. A great many more volunteered to serve as chaplains, and like the men, they were categorized as Protestant, Catholic, or Jew. One of the most influential of the ministers who supported the use of force to combat evil was the Protestant theologian and clergyman Reinhold Niebuhr. In a series of books including *Moral Man and Immoral Society* (1932) and *Children of Light and Children of Darkness* (1944), he struck out against what he saw as a naive faith in the goodness of men, a faith that permeated the Social Gospel movement, the Progressive movement, and the New Deal. In a world gone mad, he interpreted all men as sinful, and he stressed the "evil that good men do." He argued for the use of force against evil. Niebuhr's Christian Realism had little impact on most Americans, but he influenced the continuing debate in the 1930s, 1940s, and 1950s over the proper American response to evil around the world.

The GIs' War

GI, the abbreviation for *government issue,* became the affectionate designation for the ordinary soldier in World War II. The GIs came from every background and ethnic group. Some served reluctantly, some eagerly. A few became genuine heroes. All were turned into heroes by the press and the public, who seemed to believe that one American could easily defeat at least 20 Japanese or Germans. Ernie Pyle, one of the war correspondents who chronicled the authentic story of the ordinary GI, wrote of soldiers "just toiling from day to day in a world full of insecurity, discomfort, homesickness, and a dulled sense of danger."

In the midst of battle, the war was no fun, but only one soldier in eight who served ever saw combat, and even for many of those, the war was a great adventure (just as World War I had been). "When World War II broke out I was delighted," Mario Puzo, author of *The Godfather,* remembered. "There is no other word, terrible as it may sound. My country called. I was delivered from my mother, my family, and delivered *without guilt.*" World War II catapulted young men and women out of their small towns and urban neighborhoods into exotic places, where they met new people and did new things.

Mexican Americans were drafted and volunteered in great numbers. One-third of a million served in all branches of the military, a larger percentage than for many other ethnic groups. Although they encountered prejudice, they probably found less in the armed forces than they had at home, and many returned to civilian life with new ambitions and a new sense of self-esteem.

Many Native Americans also served. In fact, many were recruited for special service in the Marine Signal Corps. One group of Navajo completely befuddled the Japanese with a code based on their native language. But the Navajo code talkers and all other Native Americans who chose to return to the reservations after the war were ineligible for veterans' loans, hospitalization, and other benefits. They lived on federal land, and that, according to the law, canceled all the advantages that other veterans enjoyed after the war.

For African Americans, who served throughout the war in segregated units and faced prejudice wherever they went, the military experience also had much to

teach. Fewer blacks were sent overseas (about 79,000 of 504,000 blacks in the service in 1943), and fewer were in combat outfits, so the percentage of black soldiers killed and wounded was low. Many illiterate blacks, especially from the South, learned to read and write in the service. Blacks who went overseas began to realize that not everyone viewed them as inferior. One black army officer said, "What the hell do we want to fight the Japs for anyhow? They couldn't possibly treat us any worse than these 'crackers' right here at home." Most realized the paradox of fighting for freedom when they themselves had little freedom; they hoped things would improve after the war.

Because the war lasted longer than World War I, its impact was greater. In all, more than 16 million men and women served in some branch of the military service. About 322,000 were killed in the war, and more than 800,000 were wounded. The 12,000 listed as missing just disappeared. The war claimed many more lives than World War I and was the nation's costliest after the Civil War. But because of penicillin, blood plasma, sulfa drugs, and rapid battlefield evacuation, the wounded in World War II were twice as likely to survive as those wounded in World War I. Penicillin also minimized the threat of venereal disease, but all men who served saw an anti-VD film, just as their predecessors had in World War I.

Women in Uniform

Women had served in all wars as nurses and cooks and in other support capacities, and during World War II many continued in these traditional roles. A few nurses landed in France just days after the Normandy invasion. Nurses served with the army and the marines in the Pacific. They dug their own foxholes and treated men under enemy fire. Sixty-six nurses spent the entire war in the Philippines as prisoners of the Japanese. Most nurses, however, served far behind the lines tending the sick and wounded.

Though nobody objected to women's serving as nurses, not until April 1943 did women physicians win the right to join the Army and Navy Medical Corps. Some people questioned whether it was right for women to serve in other capacities, but Congress authorized full military participation for women (except for combat) because of the military emergency and the argument that women could free men for combat duty. About 350,000 women joined the military service, most in the Women's Army Corps (WAC) and the women's branch of the Navy (WAVES), but others served in the coast

American Dead

More than 300,000 American servicemen died during the war, but the government tried to protect the American people from learning the real cost of the battles. This photograph, published in 1943, was the first to show dead American soldiers. Why did the government protect the American people from seeing dead American soldiers?

(Time/Life Pictures/Getty Images)

guard and the marines. More than 1,000 women trained as pilots. As members of Women's Airforce Service Pilots (WASP), they flew bombers from the factories to landing fields in Great Britain.

Still, men and women were not treated equally. Women were explicitly kept out of combat situations and were often underused by male officers who found it difficult to view women in nontraditional roles. Men were informed about contraceptives and encouraged to use them, but information about birth control was explicitly prohibited for women. Rumors charged many servicewomen with sexual promiscuity. On one occasion, the secretary of war defended the morality and the loyalty of the women in the service, but the rumors continued, spread apparently by men made uncomfortable by women's invasion of the male military domain. One cause for immediate discharge was pregnancy; yet the pregnancy rate for both married and unmarried women remained low.

Thus, despite difficulties, women played important roles during the war, and when they left the service (unlike the women who had served in other wars), they had the same rights and privileges as the male veterans. The women in the service did not permanently alter the military or the public's perception of women's proper role, but they did change a few minds, and many of the women who served had their lives changed and their horizons broadened.

A War of Diplomats and Generals

Pearl Harbor catapulted the country into war with Japan, and on December 11, 1941, Hitler declared war on the United States. Why he did so has never been fully explained; he was perhaps impressed by the apparent weakness of America that was demonstrated at Pearl Harbor. He was not required by his treaty with Japan to go to war with the United States, and without his declaration, the United States might have concentrated on the war against Japan. But Hitler forced the United States into the war against the Axis powers in both Europe and Asia.

War Aims

Why was the United States fighting the war? What did it hope to accomplish in a peace settlement once the war was over? Roosevelt and the other American leaders never really decided. In a speech before Congress in January 1941, Roosevelt had mentioned the four freedoms: freedom of speech and expression, freedom of worship, freedom from want, and freedom from fear. For many Americans, especially after Norman Rockwell expressed those freedoms in four sentimental paintings, this was what they were fighting

for. Roosevelt spoke vaguely of the need to extend democracy and to establish a peacekeeping organization, but in direct contrast to Woodrow Wilson's Fourteen Points, he never spelled out in any detail the political purposes for fighting. There were some other implied reasons for going to war. Henry Luce, the editor of *Life* magazine, made those reasons explicit in an editorial written nine months before Pearl Harbor. He called his essay "The American Century," and he argued that the United States had the responsibility to spread the American way of life around the world.

Roosevelt and his advisers, realizing that it would be impossible to mount an all-out war against both Japan and Germany, decided to fight a holding action in the Pacific while concentrating efforts against Hitler in Europe, where the immediate danger seemed greater. But the United States was not fighting alone. It joined the Soviet Union and Great Britain in what became a difficult, but ultimately effective alliance to defeat Nazi Germany. Churchill and Roosevelt got along well, although they often disagreed on strategy and tactics. Roosevelt's relationship with Stalin was much more strained, but he often agreed with the Russian leader about the way to fight the war. Stalin, a ruthless leader who had maintained his position of power only after eliminating hundreds of thousands of opponents, distrusted both the British and the Americans, but he needed them, just as they depended on him. Without the tremendous sacrifices of the Russian army and the Russian people in 1941 and 1942, Germany would have won the war before the vast American military and industrial might could be mobilized.

A Year of Disaster

The first half of 1942 was disastrous for the Allies. The Japanese captured the Dutch East Indies, swept into Burma, took Wake Island and Guam, and invaded the Aleutian Islands of Alaska. They pushed the American garrison on the Philippines onto the Bataan peninsula and finally onto the tiny island of Corregidor, where U.S. General Jonathan Wainwright surrendered more than 11,000 men to the Japanese. American reporters tried to play down the disasters, concentrating their stories on the few American victories and tales of American heroism against overwhelming odds.

In Europe, the Germans pushed deep into Russia, threatening to capture all the industrial centers and the valuable oil fields. For a time, it appeared that they would even take Moscow. In North Africa, General Erwin Rommel and his mechanized divisions, the Afrika Korps, drove the British forces almost to Cairo in Egypt and threatened the Suez Canal. In the Atlantic, German submarines sank British and American ships more rapidly than they could be replaced. For a few dark months in 1942, it seemed that the Berlin–Tokyo Axis would win the war before the United States was ready to fight.

The Allies could not agree on the proper military strategy in Europe. Churchill advocated tightening the ring around Germany, using bombing raids to weaken the enemy and encouraging resistance among the occupied countries but avoiding any direct assault on the continent until success was ensured. Remembering the vast loss of British lives during World War I, he was determined to avoid similar casualties in this conflict. Stalin demanded a second front, an invasion of Europe in 1942, to relieve the pressure on the Russian army, which faced 200 German divisions along a 2,000-mile front. Roosevelt agreed to an offensive in 1942. But in the end, the invasion in 1942 came not in France but in North Africa. The decision was probably right from a military point of view, but Stalin never forgave Churchill and Roosevelt for not coming to the aid of the beleaguered Soviet troops.

Attacking in North Africa in November 1942, American and British troops tried to link up with a beleaguered British army. The American army, enthusiastic but inexperienced, met little resistance in the beginning. At Kasserine Pass in Tunisia, the Germans counterattacked and destroyed a large American force, inflicting 5,000 casualties. Roosevelt, who launched the invasion in part to give the American people a victory to relieve the dreary news from the Far East, learned that victories often came with long casualty lists.

He also learned the necessity of political compromise. To gain a cease-fire in conquered French territory in North Africa, the United States recognized Admiral Jean Darlan as head of its provisional government. Darlan persecuted the Jews, exploited the Arabs, imprisoned his opponents, and collaborated with the Nazis. He seemed diametrically opposed to the principles the Americans said they were fighting for. Did the Darlan deal mean the United States would negotiate with Mussolini? Or with Hitler? The Darlan compromise reinforced Soviet distrust of the Americans and angered many Americans as well.

Roosevelt never compromised or made a deal with Hitler, but he did aid General Francisco Franco, the Fascist dictator in Spain, in return for safe passage of American shipping into the Mediterranean. But the United States did not aid only right-wing dictators. It also supplied arms to the left-wing resistance in France, to the Communist Tito in Yugoslavia, and to Ho Chi Minh, the anti-French resistance leader in Indochina. Roosevelt also authorized large-scale lend-lease aid to the Soviet Union. Although liberals criticized his support of dictators, Roosevelt was willing to do almost anything to win the war. Military expediency often dictated his political decisions.

Even on one of the most sensitive issues of the war, the plight of the Jews in occupied Europe, Roosevelt's solution was to win the war as quickly as possible. By November 1942, confirmed information had reached the United States that the Nazis were systematically exterminating Jews, but that evidence got little attention

Buchenwald

Only at the end of the war did most Americans learn about the horrors of Nazi concentration camps and gas chambers. Senator Alben Barkley of Kentucky looks in disbelief at dead Jews stacked like wood at Buchenwald on April 24, 1945. Why didn't Americans learn about the Holocaust sooner?

(National Archives [RG-111-SC-204745, Box 63])

in the United States. The Roosevelt administration did nothing for more than a year, and even then it did scandalously little to rescue European Jews from the gas chambers. Only 21,000 refugees were allowed to enter the United States over a period of $3\frac{1}{2}$ years, just 10 percent of those who could have been admitted under immigration quotas.

The U.S. War Department rejected suggestions that the gas chambers and railway lines be bombed. That might not have worked, but anti-Semitic feelings in the United States in the 1940s and the fear of massive Jewish immigration help explain the failure of the Roosevelt administration to act. The fact that the mass media, Christian leaders, and even American Jews failed to mount effective pressure on the government does not excuse the president for his indifference to the systematic murder of millions of people. Roosevelt could not have prevented the Holocaust, but vigorous action on his part might have saved many thousands of lives during the war.

A Strategy for Ending the War

The commanding general of the Allied armies in the North African campaign emerged as a genuine leader. Born in Texas, Dwight D. Eisenhower spent his boyhood in Abilene, Kansas. His small-town background made it easy for biographers and newspaper reporters to make him into an American hero. Eisenhower, however, had not come to hero status easily. In World War I, he trained soldiers in Texas and never got to France. He was only a lieutenant colonel when World War II erupted. George Marshall, the army's top general, had discovered Eisenhower's talents even before the war began. Eisenhower was quickly promoted to general and achieved a reputation as an expert planner and organizer. Gregarious and outgoing, he had a broad smile that made most people like him instantly. He was not a brilliant field commander and made many mistakes in the African campaign, but he had the ability to get diverse people to work together, which was crucial in situations in which British and American units had to cooperate.

The American army moved slowly across North Africa, linked up with the British, invaded Sicily in July 1943, and finally stormed ashore in Italy in September. The Italian campaign proved long and bitter. Although the Italians overthrew Mussolini and surrendered in September 1943, the Germans occupied the peninsula and gave ground only after bloody fighting. The whole American army seemed bogged down for months. The Allies did not reach Rome until June 1944, and they never controlled all of Italy.

Despite the decision to make the war in Europe the first priority, American ships and planes halted the Japanese advance in the spring of 1942. In the Battle of Coral Sea in May 1942, American carrier-based planes inflicted heavy damage on the Japanese fleet and prevented the invasion of the southern tip of New Guinea and probably of Australia as well. It was the first naval battle in history in which no guns were fired from one surface ship against another; airplanes caused all the damage. In World War II, the aircraft carrier proved more important than the battleship. A month later, at the Battle of Midway, American planes sank four Japanese aircraft carriers and destroyed nearly 300 planes. This was the first major Japanese defeat; it restored some balance of power in the Pacific and ended the threat to Hawaii.

In 1943, the American sea and land forces leapfrogged from island to island, gradually retaking territory from the Japanese and building bases to attack the Philippines and eventually Japan itself. Progress often had terrible costs. In November 1943, about 5,000 marines landed on the coral beaches of the tiny island of Tarawa. Despite heavy naval bombardment and the support of hundreds of planes, the marines met fierce opposition. The four-day battle left more than 1,000 Americans dead and more than 3,000 wounded.

The Pacific War was often brutal and dehumanizing. American soldiers often collected Japanese ears, skulls, and other body parts as souvenirs, something unheard of on the European battlegrounds. "In Europe we felt that our enemies, horrible and deadly as they were, were still people," Ernie Pyle, the American war correspondent, remarked. "But out here I soon gathered that the Japanese were looked upon as something subhuman or repulsive, the way some people feel about cockroaches or mice."

The Invasion of France

Operation Overlord, the code name for the largest amphibious invasion in history, the invasion Stalin had wanted in 1942, finally began on June 6, 1944. It was, according to Churchill, "the most difficult and complicated operation that has ever taken place." The initial assault along a 60-mile stretch of the Normandy coast was conducted with 175,000 men supported by 600 warships and 11,000 planes. It cost 2,245 killed and 1,670 wounded to secure the beachhead. Within a month, more than a million troops and more than 170,000 vehicles had landed. Such an invasion would have been impossible during World War I.

For months before the invasion, American and British planes had bombed German transportation lines, industrial plants, and even cities. In all, more than 1.5 million tons of bombs were dropped on Europe. The massive bombing raids helped make the invasion a success, but evidence gathered after the war suggests that the bombs did not disrupt German war production as seriously as Allied strategists believed at

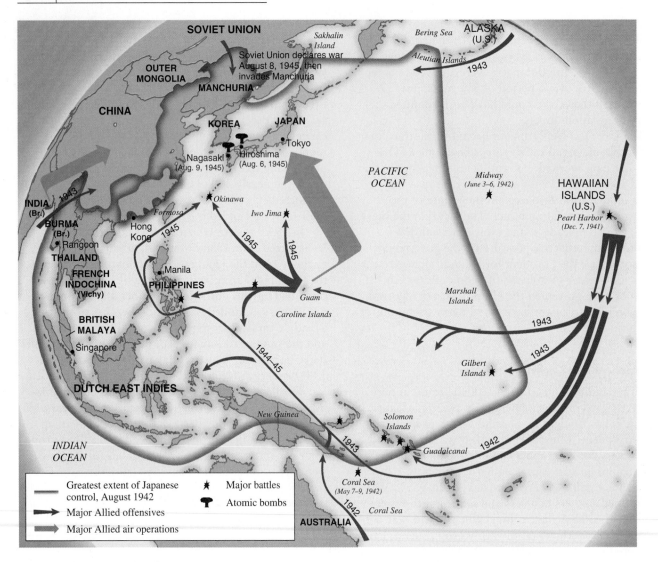

World War II: Pacific Theater

After the surprise attack on Pearl Harbor, the Japanese extended their control in the Pacific from Burma to the Aleutian Islands and almost to Australia. But after American naval and air victories at Coral Sea and Midway in 1942, the Japanese were increasingly on the defensive. How did the great distances in the Pacific influence military plans for both sides? Why was the aircraft carrier more important than the battleship in the Pacific War? Was there any alternative to the American strategy of moving slowly from one Japanese-occupied island to another? Why did China play such a crucial role in the war against Japan?

the time. Often a factory or a rail center would be back in operation within a matter of days, sometimes within hours, after an attack. In the end, the bombing of the cities, rather than destroying morale, may have strengthened the resolve of the German people to fight to the bitter end. And the destruction of German cities did not come cheaply. German fighters and antiaircraft guns shot down 22 of 60 B-17s on June 23, 1943, and in July 1943, 100 planes and 1,000 airmen were lost and an additional 75 men had mental breakdowns.

The most destructive bombing raid of the war, carried out against Dresden on the nights of February 13 and 14, 1945, had no strategic purpose. It was launched by the British and Americans to help demonstrate to Stalin that they were aiding the Russian

offensive. Dresden, a city of 630,000, was a communications center. Three waves of 1,200 planes dropped more than 4,000 tons of bombs, causing a firestorm that swept over eight square miles, destroyed everything in its path, and killed an estimated 25,000 to 40,000 civilians. The fire-bombing of Tokyo on March 9, 1945, also killed an estimated 100,000 people. The massive "strategic" bombing of European and Asian cities for the purpose of breaking the morale of the civilian population introduced terror as a strategy and eventually made the decision to drop the atomic bomb on two Japanese cities easier.

With eccentric General George Patton leading the charge and the more staid General Omar Bradley in command, the American army broke out of the Normandy beachhead in July 1944. Led by the tank

World War II: European and North African Theaters

The German war machine swept across Europe and North Africa and almost captured Cairo and Moscow, but after major defeats at Stalingrad and El Alamein in 1943, the Axis powers were in retreat. Many lives were lost on both sides before the Allied victory in 1945. How was the African campaign important to the Allies' strategy to defeat Germany and Italy? Why was the invasion of France necessary even after the capture of North Africa and a portion of Italy? Why was the Soviet Union crucial to the war in Europe? Why was the war in Europe very different from the war in the Pacific?

battalions, it swept across France. American productive capacity and the ability to supply a mobile and motorized army eventually brought victory. But not all American equipment was superior. The American fighter plane, the P-40, could not compete early in the war with the German ME-109. The United States was also far behind Germany in the development of rockets, but that was not as important in the actual fighting as was the inability of the United States, until the end of the war, to develop a tank that could compete in armament or firepower with the German tanks. But the American army made up for the deficiency of its tanks in part by having superior artillery. Perhaps even more important, most of the American soldiers had grown up tinkering with cars and radios. Children of the machine age, they managed to make repairs and

to keep tanks, trucks, and guns functioning under difficult circumstances. They helped give the American army the superior mobility that eventually led to the defeat of Germany.

By late 1944, the American and British armies had swept across France, while the Russians had pushed the German forces out of much of eastern Europe. The war seemed nearly over. However, just before Christmas in 1944, the Germans launched a massive counterattack along an 80-mile front, much of it held by thinly dispersed and inexperienced American troops. The Germans drove 50 miles inside the American lines before they were checked. During the Battle of the Bulge, as it was called, Eisenhower was so desperate for additional infantry that he offered to pardon any military prisoners in Europe who would take up a rifle and go into battle. Most of the prisoners, who were serving short sentences, declined the opportunity to clear their record. Eisenhower also promised any black soldiers in the service and supply outfits an opportunity to become infantrymen in the white units, though usually with a lower rank. However, his chief of staff pointed out that this was against War Department regulations and was the "most dangerous thing I have seen in regard to race relations." Eisenhower recanted, not wishing to start a social revolution. Black soldiers who volunteered to join the battle fought in segregated platoons commanded by white officers.

The Politics of Victory

As the American and British armies assaulted Germany in the winter and spring of 1945, the political and diplomatic aspects of the war began to overshadow military concerns. It became a matter not only of defeating Germany but also of determining who was going to control Germany and the rest of Europe once Hitler fell. The relationship between the Soviet Union and the other Allies had been badly strained during the war; with victory in sight, the tension became even greater. Although the American press pictured Stalin as a wise and democratic leader and the Russian people as quaint and heroic, a number of high-level American diplomats and presidential advisers distrusted the Russians and looked ahead to a confrontation with Soviet communism after the war. They urged Roosevelt to make military decisions with the postwar political situation in mind.

The most pressing concern in the spring of 1945 was who should capture Berlin. The British wanted to beat the Russians to the capital city. Eisenhower, however, fearing that the Germans might barricade themselves in the Austrian Alps and hold out indefinitely, ordered the armies south rather than toward Berlin. He also wanted to avoid unnecessary American casualties, and he planned to meet the Russian army at an easily marked spot to avoid any unfortunate incidents. The British and American forces could probably not have arrived in Berlin before the Russians in any case, but Eisenhower's decision generated controversy after the war. Russian and American troops met on April 25, 1945, at the Elbe River. On May 2, the Russians took Berlin. Hitler committed suicide. The long war in Europe finally came to an end on May 8, 1945.

Meanwhile, the United States continued to tighten the noose on Japan. American long-range B-29 bombers began sustained strikes on the Japanese mainland in June 1944. In a series of naval and air engagements, especially at the Battle of Leyte Gulf, American planes destroyed most of the remaining Japanese navy. By the end of 1944, an American victory in the Pacific was all but ensured. American forces recaptured the Philippines early the next year, yet it might take years to conquer the Japanese on their home islands.

While the military campaigns reached a critical stage in both Europe and the Pacific, Roosevelt ran for an unprecedented fourth term. He dropped Vice President Henry Wallace from the ticket because some thought him too radical and impetuous. To replace him, the Democratic convention selected a relatively unknown senator from Missouri. Harry S Truman, a World War I veteran, had been a judge in Kansas City before being elected to the Senate in 1934. His only fame came when, as chairman of the Senate Committee to Investigate the National Defense Program, he had insisted on honesty and efficiency in war contracts.

The Republicans nominated Thomas Dewey, the colorless and politically moderate governor of New York, who had a difficult time criticizing Roosevelt without appearing unpatriotic. Roosevelt seemed haggard and ill during much of the campaign, but he won the election easily. He would need all his strength to deal with the difficult political problems of ending the war and constructing a peace settlement.

The Big Three at Yalta

Roosevelt, Churchill, and Stalin, together with many of their advisers, met at Yalta in the Crimea in February 1945 to discuss the problems of the peace settlements. Most of the agreements reached at Yalta were secret, and in the atmosphere of the subsequent Cold War, many would become controversial. Roosevelt wanted Soviet help in ending the Pacific war, to avoid the slaughter of American men in an invasion of the Japanese mainland. In return for a promise to enter the war within three months after the war in Europe was over, the Soviet Union was granted the Kurile Islands, the southern half of Sakhalin, and railroads and port facilities in North Korea, Manchuria, and Outer Mongolia. Later that seemed like a heavy price to pay for the promise, but realistically the Soviet Union controlled most of this territory and could not have been dislodged short of going to war.

When the provisions of the secret treaties were revealed much later, many people accused Roosevelt of trusting the Russians too much. But Roosevelt wanted to retain a working relationship with the Soviet Union. Moreover, Roosevelt hoped to get the Soviet Union's agreement to cooperate with a new peace-preserving United Nations organization after the war.

The European section of the Yalta agreement proved even more controversial. The diplomats decided to partition Germany and to divide the city of Berlin.

The Polish agreements were even more difficult to swallow. The Polish government-in-exile in London was militantly anti-Communist and looked forward to returning to Poland after the war. Stalin demanded that the eastern half of Poland be given to the Soviet Union. Churchill and Roosevelt finally agreed to the Russian demands with the proviso that Poland be compensated with German territory on its western border. Stalin also agreed to include some members of the London-based Polish group in the new Polish government. He also promised to carry out "free and unfettered elections as soon as possible."

The Polish settlement would prove divisive after the war, and it quickly became clear that what the British and Americans wanted in eastern Europe contrasted with what the Soviet Union intended. Yet at the time it seemed imperative that Russia enter the war in the Pacific, and the reality was that in 1945 the Soviet army occupied most of eastern Europe.

The most potentially valuable accomplishment at Yalta was Stalin's agreement to join Roosevelt and Churchill in calling a conference in San Francisco in April 1945 to draft a United Nations charter. The charter gave primary responsibility for keeping global peace to the Security Council, composed of five permanent members (the United States, the Soviet Union, Great Britain, France, and China) and six other nations elected for two-year terms.

Perhaps just as important as Yalta for structuring the postwar world was the Bretton Woods Conference, held at a resort hotel in New Hampshire in the summer of 1944 and attended by delegates from 44 nations (the Soviet Union refused to participate). The economists and politicians established a Bank for Reconstruction and Development (the World Bank) and the International Monetary Fund. They also decided on a fixed rate of exchange among the world's currencies using the dollar rather than the pound as the standard. The Bretton Woods agreement lasted for 25 years and established that the United States, not Great Britain, would be the dominant economic power in the postwar world.

The Atomic Age Begins

Two months after Yalta, on April 12, 1945, Roosevelt died suddenly of a massive cerebral hemorrhage. Hated and loved to the end, he was replaced by Harry Truman, who was both more difficult to hate and harder to love. In the beginning, Truman seemed tentative and unsure of himself. Yet it fell to the new president to make some of the most difficult decisions of all time. The most momentous of all was the decision to drop the atomic bomb.

The Manhattan Project, first organized in 1941, was one of the best-kept secrets of the war. A distinguished group of scientists, whose work on the project was centered in Los Alamos, New Mexico, set out to perfect and manufacture an atomic bomb before Germany did. But by the time the bomb was successfully tested in the New Mexico desert on July 16, 1945, the war in Europe had ended. The scientists working on the bomb assumed that they were perfecting a military weapon. Yet when they saw the ghastly power of that first bomb, J. Robert Oppenheimer, a leading scientist on the project, remembered that "some wept, a few cheered. Most stood silently." Some opposed the military use of the bomb. They realized its revolutionary power and worried about the future reputation of the United States if it unleashed this new force. But a presidential committee made up of scientists, military leaders, and politicians recommended that it be used on a military target in Japan as soon as possible.

"The final decision of where and when to use the atomic bomb was up to me," Truman later remembered. "Let there be no doubt about it. I regarded the bomb as a military weapon and never had any doubt that it should be used." But the decision had both military and political ramifications. Even though Japan had lost most of its empire by the summer of 1945, it still had a military force of several million men and thousands of kamikaze planes that had already wreaked havoc on the American fleet. The kamikaze pilots gave up their own lives to make sure that their planes, heavily laden with bombs, crashed on American ships. In the Battle of Okinawa, kamikaze pilots destroyed or disabled 28 American ships and killed 5,000 American sailors. There was little defense against such fanaticism.

Even with the Russian promise to enter the war, it appeared that an amphibious landing on the Japanese mainland would be necessary to end the war. The month-long battle for Iwo Jima, only 750 miles from Tokyo, had resulted in more than 4,000 American dead and 15,000 wounded, and the battle for Okinawa was even more costly. An invasion of the Japanese mainland would presumably be even more expensive in human lives. The bomb, many thought, could end the war without an invasion. But some people involved in the decision wanted to retaliate for Pearl Harbor, and still others needed to justify spending more than $2 billion on the project in the first place. To some historians, the timing of the first bomb indicates that the decision was intended to impress the Russians and ensure that they had little to do with the peace settlement in the Far East.

Historians debate whether the use of the atomic bomb on the Japanese cities was necessary to end the war, but for the hundreds of thousands of American troops waiting on board ships and on island bases (even in Europe) to invade the Japanese mainland, there was no question about the rightness of the decision. They believed that the bombs ended the war and saved their lives. On August 6, 1945, two days before the Soviet Union had promised to enter the war

Recovering the Past

HISTORY, MEMORY, AND MONUMENTS

In recent years, historians have been studying collective memory—the stories people tell about the past. Collective memory is closely related to national regional identity and is often associated with patriotism and war. But memory is usually selective and often contested. The generation that lived through World War II is getting older, and often these people fear that few remember or care about their war. One veteran of the Italian campaign recently remarked: "Today they don't even know what Anzio was. Most people aren't interested." The collective memory of World War II may include letters, photos, old uniforms, and stories told to grandchildren (oral history), but the collective memory of war often includes monuments as well.

Almost every small town and city in the Northeast, the Midwest, and the South has a monument to the soldiers who fought and died in the Civil War; often it is a statue of a common soldier with rifle at rest. In the South, a statue of Robert E. Lee on horseback came to symbolize the "Lost Cause." Usually monuments to war symbolize triumph or fighting for a just cause, even in defeat.

A large monument to World War II veterans finally opened on the mall in Washington in 2004 after years of controversy. There have been many other attempts to honor the World War II generation. The Air and Space Museum of the Smithsonian Institution in Washington, D.C., planned a major exhibit for 1995 to commemorate the fiftieth anniversary of the dropping of the first atomic bomb on Hiroshima and the end of World War II. The *Enola Gay,* the B-29 that dropped the bomb, was to be the centerpiece of the exhibit, but the historians and curators who organized the exhibit also planned to raise a number of questions that historians had been debating for years. Would the war have ended in days or weeks without the bomb? How was the decision to drop the bomb made? Was there a racial component to the decision? Would the United States have dropped the bomb on Germany? Was the bomb dropped more to impress the Soviet Union than to force the Japanese to surrender? What was the impact of the bomb on the ground? What implications did dropping the bomb have on the world after 1945?

The exhibit (except in greatly modified form) never took place. Many veterans of World War II and other Americans denounced it as traitorous and un-American. For these critics the decision to drop the bomb was not something to debate. For them, World War II was a contest between good and evil, and the bomb was simply a way to defeat the evil empire and save American lives. The controversy over the *Enola Gay* exhibit demonstrated that 50 years later, memory and history were at odds and that the memory of the war was still contested. The main reason the exhibit did not satisfy those who remembered the war was that it did not commemorate triumph but instead seemed to question the motives of those who fought and died.

The Vietnam Veterans Memorial erected in Washington in 1982 was initially controversial for similar reasons.

Dedication of the Iwo Jima Memorial Monument in Washington, D.C., November 10, 1954

(National Archives [127-GRA-A409861])

Designed by Maya Lin, a young artist and sculptor, it consists of a wall of polished granite inscribed with the names of 58,000 dead. There are no soldiers on horseback; in fact, there are no figures at all, not even a flag. Critics called it a "black gash of shame." Even the addition of a sculpture of three "fighting men" did not satisfy many. But to almost everyone's surprise, hundreds of thousands of veterans and friends of veterans found the monument deeply moving, and they left photos, flowers, poems, and other objects. For them, the memorial successfully represented collective memory. Still the critics were dissatisfied; they wanted something more like the Iwo Jima monument.

Iwo Jima was a tiny, desolate island 640 miles from Tokyo, important only because it was a base for Japanese fighters to attack American bombers on their way to the Japanese mainland. The Fourth and Fifth Marine Divisions invaded the island on February 17, 1945. After bitter fighting, the marines captured Mt. Suribachi, the highest point on the island, on February 23 and completed the conquest of the island on March 17. But it was a costly victory—there were 6,832 Americans killed, more than 20,000 wounded, and 419 missing.

Associated Press photographer Joe Rosenthal was one of several journalists who went ashore with the marines and one of three photographers assigned to record the raising of the American flag on top of Mt. Suribachi. A group of marines raised the flag twice so the photographers could get their pictures. It was Rosenthal's photograph of the second flag raising that became famous. On February 25, 1945, his photograph of the five marines and a navy corpsman raising the flag was on the front page of Sunday newspapers across the country. "Stars and Stripes on Iwo," "Old Glory over Volcano," the captions read. Within months, the image of the flag raising appeared on a War Bond poster with the caption: "Now All Together" and also on a postage stamp. Three of the six flag raisers were killed in the battle for Iwo Jima, but those who survived became heroes, and their images were used to sell war bonds. Clearly, the flag-raising image had touched American emotions and quickly became part of the collective memory of the war, a symbol of the country pulling together to defeat the enemy.

In November 1954, a giant statue of the flag raising, designed by Felix De Weldon, was dedicated as a memorial to the U.S. Marine Corps on the edge of Arlington National Cemetery. Vice President Richard Nixon, speaking at the dedication, said that the statue symbolized "the hopes and

Official poster for the 1945 war bond drive using the image of the Iwo Jima flag raising

(Courtesy of the Virginia War Museum)

dreams of the American people and the real purpose of our foreign policy." The flag-raising image played an important role in two movies: *The Sands of Iwo Jima* (1949), starring John Wayne, and *The Outsider* (1960), starring Tony Curtis. During the 1988 presidential campaign, George H. W. Bush chose to make a speech in front of the marine monument urging a constitutional amendment to ban the desecration of the flag. The image of the flag raising in photograph, drawing, film, and cartoon remains part of the collective memory of World War II.

Reflecting on the Past Why did the Iwo Jima monument mean so much to the World War II generation? Was the monument more important than the photograph? What makes a monument meaningful? Is it the size? The accuracy? The ability to arouse emotion? Why do some monuments and symbols become part of collective memory, while others become controversial or forgotten? There are more than 15,000 outdoor sculptures and monuments in the country, most created since the Civil War. What monuments can you locate in your community? What collective memory do they symbolize? ■

Timeline

1931–1932	Japan seizes Manchuria
1933	Hitler becomes German chancellor
	United States recognizes the Soviet Union
	Roosevelt extends Good Neighbor policy
1934	Germany begins rearmament
1935	Italy invades Ethiopia
	First Neutrality Act
1936	Spanish civil war begins
	Second Neutrality Act
	Roosevelt reelected
1938	Hitler annexes Austria, occupies Sudetenland
	German persecution of Jews intensifies
1939	Nazi–Soviet Pact
	German invasion of Poland; World War II begins
1940	Roosevelt elected for a third term
	Selective Service Act
1941	FDR's "Four Freedoms" speech
	Proposed black march on Washington
	Executive Order 8802 outlaws discrimination in defense industries
	Lend-Lease Act
	Germany attacks Russia
	Japanese assets in United States frozen
	Japanese attack Pearl Harbor; United States declares war on Japan
	Germany declares war on United States
1942	Internment of Japanese Americans
	Second Allied front in Africa launched
1943	Invasion of Sicily
	Italian campaign; Italy surrenders
	Race riots in Detroit and other cities
1944	Normandy invasion (Operation Overlord)
	Roosevelt elected for a fourth term
1945	Yalta Conference
	Roosevelt dies; Harry Truman becomes president
	Germany surrenders
	Successful test of atomic bomb
	Hiroshima and Nagasaki bombed; Japan surrenders

against Japan, a B-29 bomber, the *Enola Gay*, dropped a single atomic bomb over Hiroshima. It killed or severely wounded 160,000 civilians and destroyed four square miles of the city. One of the men on the plane saw the thick cloud of smoke and thought that they had missed their target. "It looked like it had landed on a forest. I didn't see any sign of the city." The Soviet Union entered the war on August 8. When Japan refused to surrender, a bomb was dropped on Nagasaki on August 9. The Japanese surrendered five days later. The war was finally over. The problems of the atomic age and the postwar world were just beginning.

Conclusion

PEACE, PROSPERITY, AND INTERNATIONAL RESPONSIBILITIES

The United States emerged from World War II with an enhanced reputation as the world's most powerful industrial and military nation. The war had finally ended the Great Depression and brought prosperity to most Americans. Even N. Scott Momaday's family secured better jobs because of the war, but, like many Americans, they had to move to take those jobs. The war also increased the power of the federal government. The payroll deduction of federal income taxes, begun during the war, symbolized the growth of a federal bureaucracy that affected the lives of all Americans. Ironically the war to preserve liberty and freedom was fought with segregated armed forces, and some American citizens, including many Japanese Americans, were deprived of their freedom. The war had also ended American isolationism and made the United States into the dominant global power. Of all the nations that fought in the war, the United States had suffered the least. No bombs were dropped on American factories, and no cities were destroyed. Although more than 300,000 Americans lost their lives, even this carnage seemed minimal when compared with more than 20 million Russian soldiers and civilians who died or the 6 million Jews and millions of others systematically exterminated by Hitler.

Americans greeted the end of the war with joy and relief. But those who lived through the war years, even those too young to fight, like N. Scott Momaday, recalled the war as a time when all Americans were united to achieve victory. They looked forward to the peace and prosperity for which they had fought. Yet within two years, the peace would be jeopardized by the Cold War, and the United States would be rearming its former enemies, Japan and Germany, to oppose its former friend, the Soviet Union. The irony of that situation reduced the joy of the hard-won peace and made the American people more suspicious of their government and its foreign policy. Yet the memory of World War II and the perception that the country was united against evil enemies, indeed that World War II was a "good war," would have an impact on American foreign policy, and even on Americans' perception of themselves, for decades to come.

QUESTIONS FOR REVIEW AND REFLECTION

1. Trace the series of international events that led to the United States' entry into World War II. Could the United States have stayed neutral?
2. Explain why and how the United States interned Japanese Americans in the aftermath of the attack on Pearl Harbor. Was the internment justified?
3. How did the war change the lives of women, African Americans, and Hispanic Americans?
4. What were the war aims of the United States, and how were they achieved?
5. What led the United States to develop the atomic bomb? What were the consequences of this new weapon for the Japanese, for Americans, and for the outcome of World War II?

CHAPTER 26

Postwar America at Home, 1945–1960

McDonald's provided a model for other franchisers in the 1950s and the years that followed. The golden arches, shown here in an early version, were virtually the same wherever they appeared and became a symbol for the age.

American Stories

An Entrepreneur Franchises the American Dream

Ray Kroc, an ambitious salesman, headed toward San Bernardino, California, on a business trip in 1954. For more than a decade he had been selling "multimixers"—stainless steel machines that could make six milkshakes at once—to restaurants and soda shops around the United States. On this trip, he was particularly interested in checking out a hamburger stand run by Richard and Maurice McDonald, who had bought eight of his "contraptions" and could therefore make 48 shakes at the same time.

Always eager to increase sales, Kroc wanted to see the McDonalds' operation for himself. The 52-year-old son of Bohemian parents had sold everything from real estate to radio time to paper cups before peddling the multimixers but had enjoyed no stunning success. Yet he was still on the alert for the key to the fortune that was part of the American dream. As he watched the lines of people at the San Bernardino McDonald's restaurant, the answer seemed at hand.

The McDonald brothers sold only standard hamburgers, french fries, and milkshakes, but they had developed a system that was fast, efficient, and clean. It drew on the automobile traffic that moved along Route 66. And it was profitable indeed. Sensing the possibilities, Kroc proposed that the two owners open other establishments as well. When they balked, he negotiated a 99-year contract that allowed him to sell the fast-food idea and the name—and their golden arches design—wherever he could.

On April 15, 1955, Kroc opened his first McDonald's restaurant in Des Plaines, a suburb of Chicago. Three months later, he sold his first franchise in Fresno, California. Others soon followed. Kroc scouted out new locations, almost always on highway "strips"; persuaded people to put up the capital; and provided them with specifications guaranteed to ensure future success. For his efforts, he received a percentage of the gross take.

From the start, Kroc insisted on standardization. Every McDonald's restaurant was the same—from the two functional arches supporting the glass enclosure that housed the kitchen and take-out window to the single arch near the road bearing a sign indicating how many 15-cent hamburgers had already been sold. All menus and prices were exactly the same, and Kroc demanded that everything from hamburger size to cooking time be constant. He insisted, too, that the establishments be clean. No pinball games or cigarette machines were permitted; the premium was on a good, inexpensive hamburger, quickly served, at a nice place.

McDonald's, of course, was an enormous success. In 1962, total sales exceeded $76 million. In 1964,

before the company had been in operation for 10 years, it had sold more than 400 million hamburgers and 120 million pounds of french fries. By the end of the next year, there were 710 McDonald's stands in 44 states. In 1974, only 20 years after Kroc's vision of the hamburger's future, McDonald's did $2 billion worth of business. When Kroc died in 1984, a total of 45 billion burgers had been sold at 7,500 outlets in 32 countries. Ronald McDonald, the clown who came to represent the company, became known to children around the globe after his Washington, D.C., debut in November 1963. When McDonald's began to advertise, it became the country's first restaurant to buy television time. Musical slogans such as "You deserve a break today" and "We do it all for you" became better known than some popular songs.

The success of McDonald's provides an example of the development of new economic and technological trends—and their cultural implications—in the United States in the post–World War II years. Ray Kroc capitalized on the changes of the automobile age. He understood that a restaurant had a better chance of success not in the city but along the highways, where it could draw on heavier traffic. Kroc understood, too, that the franchise notion provided the key to rapid economic growth. Finally, he sensed the importance of standardization and uniformity. He understood the mood of the time—the quiet conformity of people searching for the key to the American dream of prosperity and stability. The McDonald's image may have been monotonous, but that was part of its appeal. Customers always knew what they would get wherever they found the golden arches. If the atmosphere was "bland," that too was deliberate. As Kroc said, "Our theme is kind of synonymous with Sunday school, the Girl Scouts and the YMCA. McDonald's is clean and wholesome." It was a symbol of the age.

This chapter describes the economic, political, and cultural changes in American society in the 25 years following World War II. Even as the nation became involved in the global confrontations of the Cold War with the Soviet Union (a story taken up in Chapter 27), Americans were preoccupied with the shifts in social and structural patterns that were taking place. This chapter examines how economic growth, spurred by technological advances, transformed the patterns of work and daily life in the United States. In a prosperous time, most people gained a level of material comfort previously unknown. Comforted by a renewed commitment to organized religion that involved people of all persuasions, they felt confident in the patterns of their lives. The political world reflected the prosperity and affluence that followed years of depression and war. Building on the impact of the New Deal and the American role as the "arsenal of democracy" in World War II, government was larger and more involved in people's lives than ever before, despite Republican resistance in the 1950s. Political commitments in the decade and a half after the war laid the groundwork for the welfare state that emerged in the 1960s.

But even as the nation prospered, it experienced serious social and economic divisions among its diverse peoples. This chapter also shows the enormous gaps that existed between rich and poor, even in the best of times. It shows the continuing presence of what one critic eloquently called "the other America" and documents the considerable income disparity and persistent prejudice that African Americans (like members of other minority groups) encountered in their efforts to share in postwar prosperity and democratic dreams. The frustrations they experienced highlighted the limits of the American dream and led to the reform movements that changed American society.

Economic Boom

Most Americans were optimistic after 1945. As servicemen returned home from fighting in World War II, their very presence caused a change in family patterns. A baby boom brought unprecedented population growth. The simultaneous and unexpected economic boom had an even greater impact. Large corporations increasingly dominated the business world, but unions grew as well, and most workers improved their lives. Technology appeared triumphant, with new products flooding the market and finding their way into most American homes. Prosperity convinced the growing middle class that all was well in the United States.

The Thriving Peacetime Economy

The wartime return of prosperity after the Great Depression continued in the postwar years, relieving fears of another depression. The United States solidified its position as the richest nation in the world with a sustained economic expansion. Other nations struggled with the aftereffects of World War II. Yet in the United States, prosperity was the norm.

The statistical evidence of economic success was impressive. The gross national product (GNP) jumped dramatically between 1945 and 1960, while per capita personal income likewise rose—from $1,087 in 1945 to $2,026 in 1960. Almost 60 percent of all families in the country were now part of the middle class, a dramatic change from the class structure in the nineteenth and early twentieth centuries.

Personal resources fueled economic growth. During World War II, American consumers had been unable to spend all they earned because factories were producing for war. With accumulated savings of $140 billion at the end of the struggle, consumers were ready to buy whatever they could. Equally important was the 22 percent rise in real purchasing power between 1946 and 1960. Families now had far more discretionary income—money to satisfy wants as well as needs—than before. At the end of the Great Depression, fewer than one-quarter of all households had any discretionary income; in 1960, three of every five did.

This new consumer power, in contrast to the underconsumption of the 1920s and 1930s, spurred the economy. Most homes now had an automobile, a television set, a refrigerator, a washing machine, and a vacuum cleaner. But consumers could also indulge themselves with electric can openers, electric pencil sharpeners, electric toothbrushes, aerosol cans, and automatic transmissions for their cars.

The automobile industry played a key part in the boom. Just as cars and roads transformed America in the 1920s when mass production came of age, so they contributed to the equally great transformation three decades later. Limited to the production of military vehicles during World War II, the auto industry expanded dramatically in the postwar period. Seventy thousand cars were made in 1945; 8 million were manufactured in 1955; and not quite 7 million were produced in 1960. Customers now chose from a wide variety of engines,

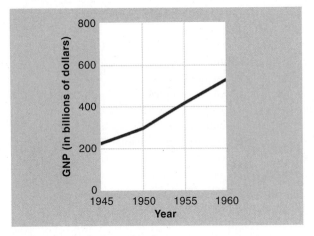

Increase in GNP, 1945–1960

The gross national product (GNP) rose steadily in the decade and a half after World War II as the United States enjoyed an unprecedented period of prosperity.

Source: National Income and Product Accounts, 1929–1994.

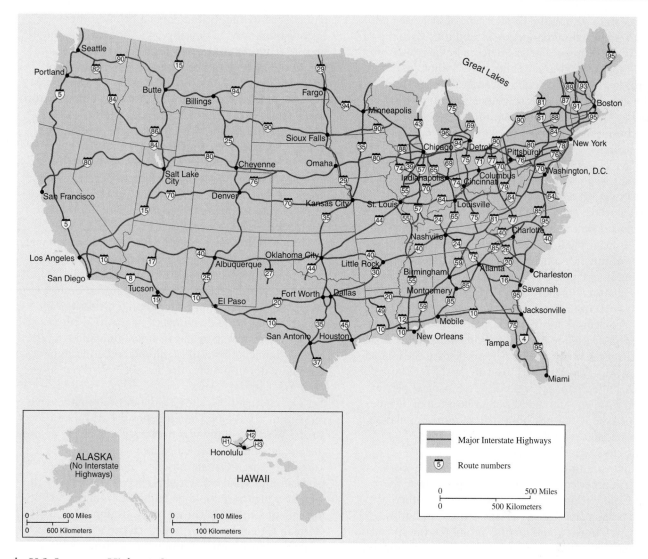

U.S. Interstate Highway System

The interstate highway system, established by legislative action in 1956, created an extensive network of roads that changed the landscape and living patterns of people throughout the United States. While the network was most extensive in the East, it extended throughout the entire country.

colors, and optional accessories. The development of a massive interstate highway system also stimulated auto production and so contributed to prosperity. Through the Interstate Highway Act of 1956, the Eisenhower administration poured $26 billion, the largest public works expenditure in American history, into building more than 40,000 miles of federal highways, linking all parts of the United States. Federal officials claimed the system would make evacuation quicker in the event of nuclear attack. President Dwight D. Eisenhower boasted that "the amount of concrete poured to form these roadways would build...six sidewalks to the moon....More than any single action by the government since the end of the war, this one would change the face of America." Significantly, this massive effort helped create a nation dependent on oil.

A housing boom also fed economic growth as home-ownership rates rose from 53 percent in 1945 to 62 percent in 1960. Much of the stimulus came from the GI Bill of 1944. In addition to giving returning servicemen priority for many jobs and providing educational benefits, it offered low-interest home mortgages. Millions of former servicemen from all social classes eagerly purchased their share of the American dream.

The government's increasingly active economic role both stimulated and sustained the expansion. Businesses were allowed to buy almost 80 percent of the factories built by the government during the war for much less than they cost. Even more important was the dramatic rise in defense spending as the Cold War escalated. In 1947, Congress passed the National

Security Act creating the Department of Defense and authorized an initial budget of $13 billion. With the onset of the Korean War, the defense budget rose to $22 billion in 1951 and to about $47 billion in 1953. Approximately half of the total federal budget went to the armed forces. This spending, in turn, helped stimulate the aircraft and electronic industries. Close business–government ties of World War II grew stronger.

Most citizens welcomed the huge expenditures, not only because they supported the American stance in the struggle against communism but also because they understood the economic impact of military spending. Columnist David Lawrence noted in 1950, "Government planners figure they have found the magic formula for almost endless good times. Cold war is an automatic pump primer. Turn a spigot, and the public clamors for more arms spending."

Postwar American growth avoided some of the major problems that often bedevil periods of economic expansion—inflation and the enrichment of a few at the expense of the many. Inflation, a problem in the immediate postwar period, slowed from an average of 7 percent per year in the 1940s to a gentle 2 to 3 percent per year in the 1950s. And though the concentration of income remained the same—the bottom half of the population still earned less than the top tenth—the ranks of middle-class Americans grew.

American products were sold around the world. People in other countries had developed a taste for Coca-Cola during the war. Now numerous other goods became available overseas. American books, magazines, movies, and records promoted the spread of American culture and provided still more profits for American entrepreneurs.

A major economic transformation had occurred in the United States. Peaceful, prosperous, and productive, the nation had became what economist John Kenneth Galbraith called the "affluent society."

Postwar Growth Around the World

Elsewhere in the world, postwar reconstruction began but affluence took longer to arrive. Both European and Asian countries had suffered greater casualties than the United States, and some nations, even those on the winning side, had to deal with enormous devastation.

Great Britain was ravaged by the war. Rationing, necessary to provide the equitable distribution of scarce resources, lasted until the early 1950s. British factories, which had been the first to industrialize, were now inefficient and outdated. The automobile industry, for example, yielded part of its share of the world market to other nations, such as Germany, which introduced the inexpensive and reliable Volkswagen Beetle that was soon sold around the globe. Meanwhile, Britain lagged behind other European nations in developing a modern superhighway system that could spur industrial development.

In the general election of 1945, British voters ousted Winston Churchill and the Conservative party in favor of the Labour party, which was committed to social change. It took over the coal and railroad industries and began to nationalize the steel industry. While owners were compensated, some critics argued that the government's actions stifled industrial progress. Nevertheless, Great Britain began an economic and social recovery. It even provided a system of socialized medicine far in advance of anything in the United States.

While France was on the winning side of the war, it had suffered the indignity of occupation. It, too, experienced recovery, thanks in part to a rising birthrate, which was also occurring in the United States. At the same time, France, like Britain, was struggling with the demands of its colonial empire to be free. Brutal struggles in Indochina and Algeria caused financial instability and helped undermine economic development until France pulled out of both areas in the 1950s.

Defeated nations showed the most dramatic development of all. As the United States decided that a strong West Germany was necessary as a buffer against the Soviet Union, it helped cause what came to be known as "the German miracle." Because much of German industrial capacity had been destroyed by the war, new factories could be built with modern technological equipment. In the early 1950s, the West German rate of growth reached 10 percent a year, while the gross national product rose from $23 billion in 1950 to $103 billion in 1964.

Japan likewise revived quickly. Like Germany, it suffered tremendous wartime destruction, due to both conventional bombing and to the new atomic bombs that devastated Hiroshima and Nagasaki in 1945. Under the direction of General Douglas MacArthur, the United States directed the reconstruction effort. A new constitution created a democratic framework and led to the signing of a peace treaty in 1952. As political change occurred, the economy grew rapidly, and Japan overtook France and West Germany, soon ranking third in the world behind the United States and the Soviet Union.

So too did the Soviet Union rebuild. Reparations from West Germany and industrial extractions from Eastern Europe helped promote the reconstruction effort. The totalitarian structure of the Soviet state eliminated public debate about the allocation of resources, and the nation embarked on a series of initiatives that led to the development of a Soviet atomic bomb and an increase in the size of collective farms.

The Corporate Impact on American Life

After 1945, the major corporations in the United States tightened their hold on the American economy. Government policy in World War II had produced tremendous industrial concentration, and that pattern continued after the war. Oligopoly—domination of a given industry by a few firms—became a feature of American capitalism. Several waves of mergers had taken place in the past, including one in the 1890s and another in the 1920s. Still another occurred in the 1950s. At the same time, the booming economy encouraged the development of conglomerates—firms with holdings in a variety of industries in order to protect themselves against instability in one particular area.

Expansion took other forms as well. Even as the major corporations grew, so did smaller franchise operations such as McDonald's, Kentucky Fried Chicken, and Burger King. Ray Kroc, introduced at the start of this chapter, provided a widely imitated pattern.

While expanding at home, large corporations also moved increasingly into foreign markets, as they had in the 1890s. But at the same time, they began to build plants overseas, where labor costs were cheaper. In the decade after 1957, General Electric built 61 plants abroad, and numerous other firms did the same. Corporate planning, meanwhile, developed rapidly, as firms sought managers who could assess information, weigh marketing trends, and make rational decisions to maximize profit.

Changing Work Patterns

As corporations changed, so did the world of work. Reversing a 150-year trend after World War II, the United States became less a goods producer and more a service provider. Between 1947 and 1957, the number of factory workers fell by 4 percent, while the number of clerical workers increased 23 percent and the number of salaried, middle-class employees rose 61 percent. By 1956, a majority of American workers held white-collar jobs, many of them serving as corporate managers, office workers, salespeople, and teachers.

Yet white-collar jobs came at a price. Work in the huge corporations became ever more impersonal and bureaucratic, and white-collar employees seemed to dress, think, and act the same (as depicted in a popular novel and film of the 1950s, *The Man in the Gray Flannel Suit*). Social critic C. Wright Mills observed, "When white-collar people get jobs, they sell not only their time and energy but their personalities as well."

But not all Americans held white-collar jobs. Many were still blue-collar assembly line workers, who made the goods others enjoyed. They too dreamed of owning

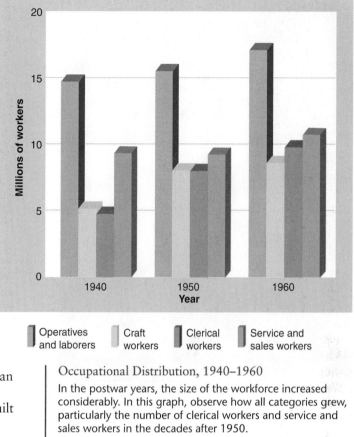

Occupational Distribution, 1940–1960

In the postwar years, the size of the workforce increased considerably. In this graph, observe how all categories grew, particularly the number of clerical workers and service and sales workers in the decades after 1950.

Sources: U.S. Department of Labor and *Historical Statistics of the United States.*

a suburban home and several cars and providing more for their children than they had enjoyed while growing up. Their lives were now more comfortable than ever before, as the union movement brought substantial gains. These were the more fortunate members of the working class. Millions of others, perhaps totaling 40 percent of the workforce, held less appealing and less well-paying positions as taxi drivers, farm laborers, or dime-store sales clerks. For them, jobs were less stable, less secure, and less interesting.

The Union Movement at High Tide

The union movement had come of age during the New Deal, and the end of World War II found it even stronger. There were more union members—14.5 million—than ever before. Ten million belonged to the American Federation of Labor (AFL); the other 4.5 million belonged to the Congress of Industrial Organizations (CIO). Having taken a wartime no-strike pledge and given their full support to the war effort, they now looked forward to better pay and a greater voice in workplace management.

The immediate postwar period was difficult. Cancellation of defense orders laid off war workers

Suburban Commuters

Commuters, such as these people in Park Forest, Illinois, in 1953, traveled from the suburbs to offices in the city every day. How would you describe the appearance of these commuters? Are there more men or women? How closely do they resemble one another?

(Time Life Pictures/Getty Images)

to protect them against inflation. In 1948, General Motors offered the United Auto Workers a contract that included a cost-of-living adjustment (COLA) and a 2 percent "annual improvement factor" wage increase intended to share GM's productivity gains with workers. Pensions came next, in 1950, and in 1955 automobile workers won a guaranteed annual wage. The merger of the AFL and CIO that year ratified the changes that had occurred in the labor movement, as the new organization, led by building trade unionist George Meany, represented more than 90 percent of the country's now larger group of 17.5 million union members. By the end of the 1950s, the COLA principle was built into most union contracts.

Union gains, like middle-class affluence, came at a price. Co-opted by the materialistic benefits big business provided, workers fell increasingly under the control of middle-level managers and watched anxiously as companies automated at home or expanded abroad, where labor was cheaper. But the agreements they had reached often precluded any response. The anti-Communist crusade, described in the next chapter, also undermined union radicalism. And throughout the period, in unions, as in other institutions, women and blacks faced continued discrimination.

Agricultural Workers in Trouble

The agricultural world changed even more than the industrial world in the postwar United States. On the eve of World War II, agriculture had supported one of every five Americans. Now, in one generation, mechanization and consolidation forced that figure down to one of every 20. Altogether, some 15 million rural jobs disappeared.

New technology revolutionized farming. Improved planting and harvesting machines and better fertilizers and pesticides brought massive gains in productivity. Increasing profitability led to agricultural consolidation. In the 25 years after 1945, average farm size almost doubled and farming became a big business—often called "agribusiness." Family farms found it difficult to compete with the technologically superior corporations and watched their share of the market fall.

In response, farmers left the land in increasing numbers. Some were midwestern whites who generally found jobs in offices and factories. In the South, many of the uprooted agricultural workers were African Americans, who became part of the huge migration north that had been going on since World War I. Overall, from 1910 to 1970, more than 6.5 million African Americans left the South; of these, 5 million moved north after 1940. Most of them gravitated to cities, where they faced problems of poverty and discrimination in housing and employment. The agricultural life, as it had been known for decades, even centuries, was over.

and prompted fears of a depression, like the one that had followed World War I. Even workers who held their jobs lost the overtime pay they had enjoyed during the war. Many responded by striking. In 1946 alone, 4.6 million workers went out on strike—more than ever before in U.S. history. There were work stoppages in the automobile, coal, steel, and electrical industries and a threatened strike by railway workers. These disruptions alienated middle-class Americans and outraged conservative Republicans who felt that unionization had gone too far.

In the late 1940s, a new equilibrium emerged. In many industries, big business at last recognized the basic rights of industrial workers, and union leaders and members in turn acknowledged the prerogatives of management and accepted the principle of fair profit. Corporations in the same industry agreed to cooperate rather than compete with one another over labor costs. This meant that once a leading firm reached agreement with the union, the other firms in that area adopted similar terms, with higher costs met by price increases.

At the same time, companies made material concessions to workers—for example, adjusting their pay

Demographic and Technological Shifts

The postwar economic boom was intertwined with a series of demographic changes. The population grew dramatically and continued to move west, while at the same time, millions of white Americans left the cities for the suburbs that began to grow exponentially in the postwar years. New patterns, revolving around television and other gadgets provided by the advances of technology, came to characterize the consumer culture that dominated suburban life.

Population Growth

In post–World War II America, a growing population testified to prosperity's return. The birthrate soared in the postwar years as millions of Americans began families. The "baby boom" peaked in 1957, with a rate of more than 25 births per 1,000. In that year, 4.3 million babies were born, one every seven seconds. While the population growth of 19 million in the 1940s was double the rise of the decade before, that increase paled against the increase in the 1950s, which totaled 29 million.

The rising birthrate was the dominant factor affecting population growth, but the death rate was also declining. Miracle drugs such as penicillin and streptomycin, now widely available, helped cure strep throat and other bacterial infections, intestinal ailments, and more serious illnesses such as tuberculosis. A polio vaccine introduced a decade after the war virtually eliminated that dreaded disease. Life expectancy

rose: midway through the 1950s, the average was 70 years for whites and 64 for blacks, compared with 55 for whites and 45 for blacks in 1920.

The baby boom shaped family and social patterns. Many women who had taken jobs during the war now left the workforce to rear their children and care for their homes. Their lives changed considerably as they substituted housework for paid work. Demand grew for diaper services and baby foods. Entering school, the baby-boom generation strained the educational system.

Movement West

Wartime mobility encouraged the development of the West. Although the scarcity of water in the western states required massive water projects to support population growth, war workers and their families streamed to western cities where shipyards, airplane factories, and other industrial plants were located. After the war, this migration pattern persisted. The Sun Belt—the region stretching along the southern tier of the United States from Florida to California—attracted numerous new arrivals. Cities such as Houston, Albuquerque, Tucson, and Phoenix expanded phenomenally. In the 1950s, Los Angeles pulled ahead of Philadelphia as the third-largest city in the United States.

One-fifth of all the growth in the period took place in California. Even baseball teams—the Brooklyn Dodgers and the New York Giants—left the East Coast for western shores. By 1963, in a dramatic illustration of the importance of the West, California passed New York as the nation's most populous state.

The migration west occurred for a number of reasons. Servicemen who had been stationed in the West liked the scenery, climate, and pace of life. Many returned with their families after the war. With funds from the Federal Housing Administration or Veterans Administration, they could afford to borrow money and buy new homes. That spending, in turn, helped fuel the region's economic growth.

In addition, Cold War spending promoted economic development, and much of that expansion occurred in the West. Once the Korean War sparked increased military expenditures, California's economic growth outpaced that of the country as a whole. Aircraft production in the state accounted for more than 40 percent of the total increase in manufacturing employment there between 1949 and 1953. In the 1950s, rocket research further stimulated the aerospace industry. In 1959, California had nearly one-quarter of all prime military contracts in the nation. By 1962, the Pacific Coast as a whole held almost half of all Defense Department research and development contracts.

Finally, the West benefited from the boom in the service economy. Many western workers in postwar America were part of the growing service sector. The

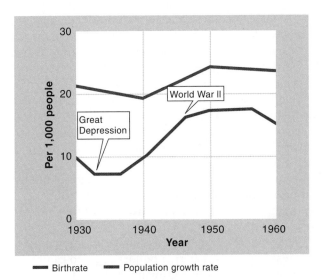

— Birthrate   — Population growth rate

Birth and Population Growth Rates, 1900–1960

Both birth and population growth rates increased dramatically after the difficult years of the Great Depression. Note the baby boom that began at the end of World War II and continued for the next decade.

Sources: U.S. Bureau of the Census and *Statistical Abstract of the United States.*

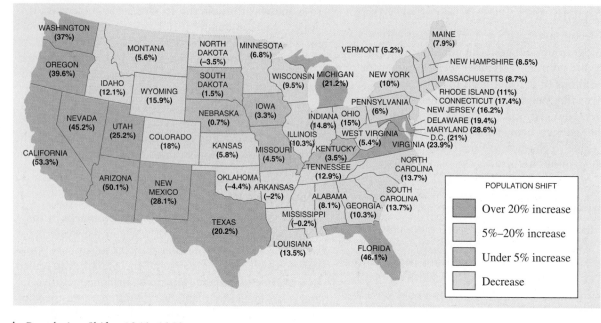

Population Shifts, 1940–1950

This map reveals the huge growth of population in the West and the sizable, though less extensive, increase in the Northeast and Southeast between 1940 and 1950.

percentage of workers in such jobs was higher in virtually all western states than in eastern counterparts. Denver became a major regional center of the federal bureaucracy in the postwar years. Albuquerque likewise gained numerous federal offices and became known as "little Washington." The old West of cowboys, farmers, and miners was turning into a new West of bureaucrats, lawyers, and clerks.

The New Suburbs

As the population shifted westward after World War II, another form of movement was taking place. Millions of white Americans fled the inner city to suburban fringes, intensifying a movement that had begun before the war. Fourteen of the nation's largest cities, including New York, Boston, Chicago, Philadelphia,

POPULATION INCREASES IN SELECTED SUN BELT CITIES, 1940–1960 (IN THOUSANDS)

	1940	1950	1960
Los Angeles, California	1,504	1,970	2,479
Miami, Florida	172	249	292
Atlanta, Georgia	302	331	487
Dallas, Texas	295	434	680
Phoenix, Arizona	65	107	439

Source: U.S. Bureau of the Census.

and Detroit, actually lost population in the 1950s. As central cities became places where poor nonwhites clustered, new urban and racial problems emerged.

For people of means, cities were places to work in but then to leave at five o'clock. In Manhattan, south of the New York borough's City Hall, the noontime population of 1.5 million dropped to 2,000 overnight. "It was becoming a part-time city," according to writer John Brooks, "tidally swamped with bustling humanity every weekday morning when the cars and commuter trains arrived, and abandoned again at nightfall when the wave sucked back—left pretty much to thieves, policemen, and rats."

As the cities declined, new suburbs blossomed. If the decade after World War I had witnessed a rural-to-urban shift, the decades after World War II saw a reverse shift to the regions outside the central cities, usually accessible only by car. By the end of the 1950s, one-third of all Americans resided in suburbs that promised fulfillment of the American dream and seemed insulated from the troubles of the world outside.

The pioneer of the postwar suburbanization movement was William J. Levitt, a builder eager to gamble and reap the rewards of a growing demand. Levitt had recognized the advantages of mass production during World War II, when his firm constructed housing for war workers. Aware that the GI Bill made mortgage money readily available, he saw the possibilities of suburban development. But to cash in, Levitt had to use new construction methods.

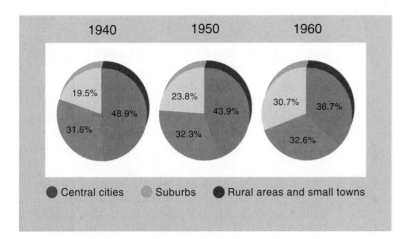

1940	1950	1960
19.5% / 48.9% / 31.6%	23.8% / 43.9% / 32.3%	30.7% / 36.7% / 32.6%

● Central cities ● Suburbs ● Rural areas and small towns

Shifts in Population Distribution, 1940–1960
These graphs show the progressive decline in rural population and the corresponding increase in suburban population between 1940 and 1960.

Source: U.S. Bureau of the Census.

forests were now divided into tiny standardized squares, each bearing a small house with a two-car garage and a manicured lawn. Folksinger Malvina Reynolds described the new developments she saw:

Little boxes on the hillside
Little boxes made of ticky tacky
Little boxes on the hillside
Little boxes all the same.
There's a green one and a pink one
And a blue one and a yellow one
And they're all made out of ticky tacky
And they all look just the same.

As suburbs flourished, businesses followed their customers out of the cities. Shopping centers led the way. At the end of World War II, there were eight, but the number multiplied rapidly in the 1950s. In a single three-month period in 1957, 17 new centers opened; by

Mass production was the key. Individually designed houses were a thing of the past, he believed. "The reason we have it so good in this country," he said, "is that we can produce lots of things at low prices through mass production." Houses were among them. Working on a careful schedule, Levitt's team brought precut and preassembled materials to each site, put them together, and then moved on to the next location.

Levitt proved that his system worked. Construction costs at Levittown, New York, a new community of 17,000 homes built in the late 1940s, were only $10 per square foot, compared with the $12 to $15 common elsewhere. The next Levittown appeared in Bucks County, Pennsylvania, several years after the first, and another went up in Willingboro, New Jersey, at the end of the 1950s. Levitt's success provided a model for other developers.

Levitt argued that his homes helped underscore American values. "No man who owns his own house and lot can be a Communist," he once said. "He has too much to do." Levitt also helped perpetuate segregation by refusing to sell homes to blacks. "We can solve a housing problem, or we can try to solve a racial problem but we cannot combine the two," he declared in the early 1950s.

Government-insured mortgages, especially for veterans, fueled the housing boom. So did fairly low postwar interest rates. With many American families vividly remembering the Depression and saving significant parts of their paychecks, the nation had a pool of savings large enough to keep mortgage interest rates in the affordable 5 percent range.

Suburbanization transformed the American landscape. Huge tracts of former fields, pastures, and

Levittown

Step-by-step mass production, with units completed in assembly line fashion, was the key to William Levitt's approach to housing. But the suburban developments he and others created were marked by street after street of houses that all looked the same. The Levittown in this picture was built on 1,200 acres of potato fields on Long Island in New York. How did the pattern you see here reflect the overall culture of the 1950s?

(Cornell Capa/Magnum Photos, Inc.)

1960, there were 3,840 in the United States. Shopping centers allowed suburban shoppers to avoid the cities entirely and further eroded urban health.

The Environmental Impact

Suburbanization had environmental consequences. Rapid expansion often took place without extensive planning and encroached on some of the nation's most attractive rural areas. Before long, virtually every American city was ringed by an ugly highway sporting garish neon signs. Billboard advertisements filled whatever space was not yet developed.

Responding to the increasingly cluttered terrain, architect Peter Blake ruthlessly attacked the practices of the 1950s in his muckraking book *God's Own Junkyard: The Planned Deterioration of America's Landscape,* published in 1964. As he deplored the unconscionable desecration of the American landscape, he wrote:

> Our suburbs are interminable wastelands dotted with millions of monotonous little houses on monotonous little lots and crisscrossed by highways lined with billboards, jazzed-up diners, used-car lots, drive-in movies, beflagged gas stations, and garish motels. Even the relatively unspoiled countryside beyond these suburban fringes has begun to sprout more telephone poles than trees, more trailer camps than national parks.

Despite occasional protests, there was little real consciousness of environmental issues in the early post–World War II years. The term *environment* itself was hardly used prior to the war. Yet the very prosperity that created the dismal highway strips in the late 1940s and 1950s was leading more and more Americans to appreciate natural environments as treasured parts of their rising standard of living. The shorter workweek provided more free time, and many Americans now had the means for longer vacations. They began to explore mountains and rivers and ocean shores and to ponder how to protect them. In 1958, Congress established the National Outdoor Recreation Review Commission, a first step toward consideration of environmental issues that became far more common in the next decade. Americans also began to recognize the need for open space in their communities in order to compensate for the urban overdevelopment.

Technology Supreme

A technological revolution transformed postwar America. Some developments—the use of atomic energy, for example—flowed directly from war research. Federal support for scientific activity increased dramatically, as the pattern of wartime collaboration continued. The government established the National Institutes of Health in 1948 to coordinate medical research and the National Science Foundation in 1950 to fund basic scientific research.

The advent of the Cold War led to ever-greater government involvement. The Atomic Energy Commission, created in 1946, and the Department of Defense, established in 1949, provided rapidly increasing funding for research and development. Support for the Los Alamos Scientific Laboratory, where the atomic bomb had been assembled, continued, while the government contracted with the University of California to open the new Livermore Laboratory near San Francisco. Money went to other large research universities as well and fueled their growth. Scientists engaged in both basic and applied research and helped develop nuclear weapons, jet planes, satellites, and consumer goods that were often the side products of military research. Computers both reflected and assisted the process of technological development. Prior to World War II, Vannevar Bush, an electrical engineer at the Massachusetts Institute of Technology, had built a machine filled with gears and shafts, along with electronic tubes in place of some mechanical parts, to solve differential equations. Wartime advances brought large but workable calculators, such as the Mark I electromechanical computer developed by engineer Howard Aiken and installed by IBM at Harvard in 1944. It was huge—55 feet long and 8 feet high—and had a million components.

Even more complicated was the Electronic Numerical Integrator and Calculator, called ENIAC, built in 1946 at the University of Pennsylvania. Like the Mark I, it was large, containing 18,000 electronic tubes and requiring tremendous amounts of electricity and special cooling procedures. It also needed to be "debugged" to remove insects attracted to the heat and light, giving rise to the term still used today by computer scientists for fixing software glitches. ENIAC performed impressively for the time, but at a snail's pace by modern standards. A key breakthrough in making computers faster and more reliable was the development of the transistor by three scientists at Bell Laboratories in 1948. They helped computers transform American society as surely as industrialization had changed it a century before. Computer programmers and operators were in increasing demand as computers contributed dramatically to the centralization and interdependence of American life.

Computers were essential for space exploration. They helped scientists perform the mathematical calculations that let astronauts venture beyond the confines of the earth. In the postwar years, increasingly sophisticated forms of space flight became possible. Rocketry had developed during World War II but came of age after the war. Rockets could deliver nuclear weapons but could also launch satellites and provide the means to venture millions of miles into outer space.

Computer advances also powered a wide variety of new appliances and gadgets designed for personal use. A transistorized miniature hearing aid, for example, could fit into the frame of a pair of eyeglasses. Stereophonic high-fidelity systems, using new transistor components, provided better sound.

An ominous technological trend related to computerization was the advent of automation. Mechanization was not new, but now it became far more widespread, threatening both skilled and unskilled workers. In 1952, the Ford Motor Company began using automatic drilling machines in an engine plant and found that now 41 workers could do a job that had previously required 117 workers. The implications of falling purchasing power as machines replaced workers were serious for an economy dependent on consumer demand.

The Consumer Culture

Americans maintained an ardent love affair with the machines, appliances, and gadgets produced by modern technology. By the end of the 1950s, most families had at least one automobile, often two or more, particularly as commuting from the suburbs became more common, and cars grew bigger and fancier than ever before. More powerful engines were the norm, while tailfins sometimes looked like airplane wings.

Television became a major influence on American life after World War II. Developed in the 1930s, prior to the war, the government deferred production and to allow for increased attention to radio to support the military effort. In 1946, there were fewer than 17,000 television sets, but by 1960, three-quarters of all American families owned at least one set. In 1955, the average American family tuned in four to five hours each day. Some studies predicted that an American student, on graduating from high school, would have spent 11,000 hours in class and 15,000 hours before the "tube." Young Americans grew up to the strains of "Winky Dink and You," "The Mickey Mouse Club," and "Howdy Doody Time" in the 1950s. Older viewers watched situation comedies such as *I Love Lucy* and *Father Knows Best* and live dramas such as *Playhouse 90*.

Television highlighted the rock-and-roll music that developed in the 1950s. Americans watched Elvis Presley play his guitar and sing, gyrating his hips in a sexually suggestive way that terrified parents, who worried about the influence of this new music, based on black rhythm and blues songs, on their children. Young people eagerly watched their counterparts dance to the music of Bill Haley and the Comets, Little Richard, Chuck Berry, and Elvis himself on *American Bandstand* every afternoon.

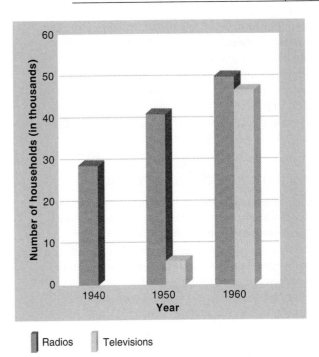

Households Owning Radios and Televisions, 1940–1960
Radio became increasingly popular in the postwar years, but observe the astronomical increase in the number of households owning television sets in the decade after 1950.

Source: U.S. Bureau of the Census.

Consumption, increasingly a pillar of the American economy, required a vast expansion of consumer credit. Installment plans facilitated buying a new car, while credit cards encouraged the purchase of smaller items such as television sets and household appliances. Eating out became easier when meals could be charged on a card. The first of the consumer credit cards—the Diner's Club card—appeared in 1950, followed at the end of the decade by the American Express card and the BankAmericard (later renamed Visa). By the end of the 1960s, about 50 million credit cards of all kinds were in use in the United States. Consumer credit—total private indebtedness—increased from $8.4 billion in 1946 to nearly $45 billion in 1958.

For consumers momentarily unsure about new purchases, a revitalized advertising industry was ready to persuade them to go ahead and buy. Advertising had come of age in the 1920s, as businesses persuaded customers that buying new products brought status and satisfaction. It had faltered when the economy collapsed in the 1930s but began to revive during the war, as firms kept the public aware of consumer goods, even those in short supply. With the postwar boom, advertisers again began to hawk their wares, this time even more aggressively than before.

Having weathered the poverty and unemployment of the 1930s and made sacrifices during a long war,

Americans now regarded abundance and leisure as their due, sometimes neglecting to look beyond the immediate objects of their desire. As journalist William Shannon wrote, the decade was one of "self-satisfaction and gross materialism.... The loudest sound in the land has been the oink and grunt of private hoggishness.... It has been the age of the slob."

Consensus and Conformity

As the economy expanded, an increasing sense of sameness pervaded American society. Third- and fourth-generation ethnic Americans became much more alike. As immigration slowed to a trickle after 1924, ties to Europe weakened, assimilation speeded up, and interethnic marriage skyrocketed. Television gave young and old a shared, visually seductive experience. Escaping the homogenizing tendencies was difficult.

Contours of Religious Life

Postwar Americans discovered a common religious sense and returned to their churches in record numbers. By the end of the 1950s, fully 95 percent of all Americans identified with some religious denomination.

Ecumenical activities—worldwide efforts on the part of different Christian churches—promoted greater religious involvement. Within the United States, evangelical revivalism, led by Southern Baptist Billy Graham and others, became increasingly popular.

Catholicism also sought to broaden its appeal. This effort succeeded as Pope John XXIII convened the Vatican Ecumenical Council in 1962 to make the Catholic church's traditions and practices more accessible—for example, substituting modern languages for Latin in the liturgy. Judaism likewise broadened its appeal. As assimilation occurred, quotas that had kept many out of more exclusive universities and other institutions began to disappear. Jews, like others, relied on the GI Bill to move to the suburbs, where they bought new homes and built new synagogues, most of which followed the more casual patterns of Reform or Conservative, rather than Orthodox, Judaism. Across all faiths, religion reinforced the importance of family life, for, according to one slogan, "The family that prays together stays together."

President Dwight D. Eisenhower reflected the national mood when he observed that "our government makes no sense unless it is founded in a deeply felt religious faith—and I don't care what it is." In 1954, Congress added the words "under God" to the pledge to the flag and the next year voted to require the phrase "In God We Trust" on all U.S. currency. Yet the revival sometimes seemed to rest on a shallow base of religious knowledge. In one public opinion poll,

80 percent of the respondents indicated that the Bible was God's revealed word, but only 35 percent were able to name the four Gospels and more than half were unable to name even one.

A challenge to religious conformity came from members of the so-called Beat Generation who embraced Buddhism. They helped promote the Buddhist vogue that emerged in the 1950s and 1960s, with Zen centers opening in Los Angeles in 1956, San Francisco in 1959, and New York in 1966. Zen stressed Buddha's emphasis on meditation that led to his enlightenment.

Traditional Roles for Men and Women

World War II had interrupted traditional patterns of behavior for both men and women. As servicemen went overseas, women left their homes to work. After 1945, women faced tremendous pressure to leave their jobs and to conform to accepted prewar gender patterns, even though, paradoxically, more women entered the workforce than ever before.

Men and women had different postwar expectations. Most men expected to go to school and then find jobs to support their families as the primary breadwinners. For women, the situation was more complex. While they wanted to resume patterns of family life that had been disrupted by the war, many had enjoyed working in the military plants and were reluctant to retreat to the home, despite pressure to do so.

In 1947, *Life* magazine ran a long photo essay called "The American Woman's Dilemma" that summed up the problem. The essay observed that women were caught in a conflict between the traditional expectation to stay home and the desire to have a paid job. A 1946 *Fortune* magazine poll also captured the discontent of some women. Asked whether they would prefer to be born again as men or as women, 25 percent of the women interviewed said they would prefer to be men. That dissatisfaction was strongest among white, well-educated, middle-class women, for black and lower-class white women often had no choice but to continue working outside the home.

By the 1950s, middle-class doubts and questions had largely receded. The baby boom increased average family size and made the decision to remain home easier. The flight to the suburbs gave women more to do, and they settled into the routines of redecorating their homes and gardens and transporting children to and from activities and schools.

Marriage and home became the most important priorities. Many women went to college to find husbands—and dropped out if they succeeded. Almost two-thirds of the women in college, but less than half the men, left before completing a degree. Women were expected to marry young, have children early, and

Recovering the Past

CLOTHING

Clothing can be an important source of information about the past. The clothes people wear often announce their age, gender, and class and frequently transmit some sense of their origin, occupation, and even their politics. The vocabulary of dress includes more than garments alone: hairstyles, jewelry, and makeup all contribute to the way people choose to present themselves. Clothing can signal strong emotions; a torn, unbuttoned shirt, for example, can indicate that a person who seldom dresses that way is really upset. Bright colors can demonstrate a daring sense and a willingness to make a strong statement. By examining clothing styles in a number of different decades, we can begin to understand something of the changing patterns of people's lives.

In the 1920s, flappers and other women often dressed like children, with loose dresses usually in pastel colors ending just below the knee. Large trimmings, such as huge artificial flowers, accentuated the effect. A "boyish" figure was considered most attractive. The clothes conveyed a feeling of playfulness and a willingness to embrace the freedom of the young. Men's suits in the same period were now made out of lighter materials and looked less padded than before. As the tall, stiff collar of an earlier age disappeared and trousers became more high-waisted, men too had a more youthful look.

The Great Depression of the 1930s brought a change in style. Flappers now looked silly, especially as millions of people were starving. Advertisements and films promoted a new maturity and sophistication, more appropriate to hard times. Men's suits became heavier and darker, as if symbolically to provide protection in a bread line. Trousers were wider, and jackets were frequently double-breasted. Overcoats became longer. Women's clothes were likewise made out of heavier fabrics and used darker colors. Skirts fell almost to the ankles on occasion and were covered by longer coats. Clothes indicated that there was no place for the playfulness of the decade before.

As conditions improved during and after World War II, styles changed once more. In the 1940s, young teenage girls frequently wore bobby socks rolled down to their ankles. Working women wore overalls, but with their own adornments to maintain their femininity. Rosie the Riveter, drawn by noted artist Norman Rockwell, wore her overalls proudly as she sat with a riveting gun in her lap and an attractive scarf around her hair. In the postwar years, the "Man in the Gray Flannel Suit" looked serious, sober, and well tailored, ready to go work for corporate America. His female partner wanted to look equally worldly and sophisticated and wore carefully tailored adult clothing, with the waist drawn in (often by a girdle) and heels as tall as three inches, when going out. The fashion industry helped define the decorative role women were supposed to play in supporting men as they advanced their business careers.

Harlem women in the 1920s

(Photographs and Prints Division, Schomburg Center for Research in Black Culture, The New York Public Library, Astor, Lenox and Tilden Foundations/Art Resources, NY)

Frances Perkins with laborers in the 1930s

(Brown Brothers)

World War II women at work

(Oregon Historical Society, OrHi 37401)

Then came the 1960s and an entirely new look. Casual clothing became a kind of uniform. The counterculture was a movement of the young, and clothing took on an increasingly youthful look. Skirts rose above the knee in 1963 and a few years later climbed to mid-thigh. Women began to wear pants and trouser suits. Men and women both favored jeans and informal shirts and let their hair grow longer. Men broke away from the gray suits of the preceding decade and indulged themselves in bright colors in what has been called the "peacock revolution."

Reflecting on the Past Look carefully at the pictures on these pages. They show fashions from different periods and can tell us a good deal about how these people defined themselves. Examine first the photo of the three black women from the 1920s. What kinds of adornments do you notice? What impression do these women convey?

Look at the photograph of Frances Perkins, secretary of labor in the 1930s. What kind of dress is she wearing? How do her clothes differ from those of the women in the 1920s? In the picture, she is talking to a number of working men. What do their clothes tell you about the kind of work they might be doing?

In the picture of two drill press operators during World War II, the women are dressed to handle the heavy machinery. Are their clothes different from those of the laborers in the preceding picture? How have the women accommodated themselves to their work, while still maintaining their individuality?

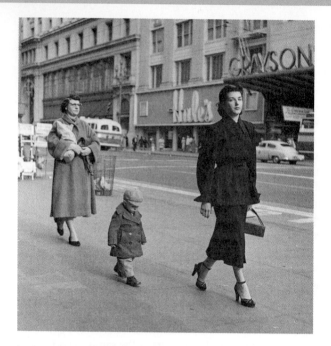

A woman and child in the 1950s

(© The Dorothea Lange Collection, The Oakland Museum of California, City of Oakland, Gift of Paul S. Taylor)

Countercultural dress in the 1960s

(Ken Heyman/Woodfin Camp & Associates)

Now look at the picture of a woman in the 1950s. What kind of work might she do? What kind of flexibility do these clothes give her? What do the stylistic touches convey? Finally, examine the photograph of the man and woman at an outdoor music festival in the 1960s. What does their clothing remind you of? Where might it come from? What impression are these people trying to create by their dress? ■

encourage their husbands' careers. An article in *Esquire* magazine in 1954 called working wives a "menace."

Adlai Stevenson, Democratic presidential candidate in 1952 and 1956, defined the female role in politics. "The assignment for you, as wives and mothers," he told a group of young women, "you can do in the living room with a baby in your lap or in the kitchen with a can opener in your hand." They were "to influence man and boy" in the "humble role of housewife" and mother.

Pediatrician Benjamin Spock agreed. In 1946 he published *Baby and Child Care,* the book most responsible for the child-rearing patterns of the postwar generation. In it, he advised mothers to stay at home if they wanted to raise stable and secure youngsters. Working outside the home might jeopardize their children's mental and emotional health.

Popular culture highlighted the stereotype of the woman concerned only about marriage and family. Author Betty Friedan described these patterns in her explosive 1963 critique, *The Feminine Mystique.* Women "could desire no greater destiny than to glory in their own femininity.... All they had to do was to devote their lives from earliest girlhood to finding a husband and bearing children." Their role was clear. "It was unquestioned gospel," she wrote, "that women could identify with *nothing* beyond the home—not politics, not art, not science, not events large or small, war or peace, in the United States or the world, unless it could be approached through female experience as a wife or mother or translated into domestic detail."

The family was all-important in this scenario. Fewer than 10 percent of all Americans felt that an unmarried person could be happy. In a pattern endlessly reiterated by popular television programs, the family was meant to provide all satisfaction and contentment. The single-story ranch house that became so popular in this period reflected the focus on the family as the source of recreation and fun. No longer were kitchen and den private, as they had been earlier in a reflection of the notion of separate spheres. Now houses, with far more shared and open space, stressed livability and family comfort.

Sexuality was a troublesome if compelling postwar concern. In 1948, Alfred C. Kinsey published *Sexual Behavior in the Human Male.* Kinsey was an Indiana University zoologist who had previously studied the gall wasp. When asked to teach a course on marriage problems, he found little published material about human sexual activity and decided to collect his own. He compiled case histories of 5,300 white males and recorded patterns of sexual behavior.

Kinsey shocked the country with his statistics on premarital, extramarital, and otherwise illicit sexual acts. Among males who went to college, he concluded, 67 percent had engaged in sexual intercourse before marriage, as had 84 percent of those who went to high school but not beyond. Thirty-seven percent of the total male population had experienced some kind of overt homosexual activity. Five years later, Kinsey published a companion volume, *Sexual Behavior in the Human Female,* which detailed many of the same sexual patterns. Although critics denounced Kinsey for what they considered his unscientific methodology and challenged his results, both books sold widely, for they opened the door to a subject previously considered taboo.

Interest in sexuality was reflected in the fascination with sex goddesses such as Marilyn Monroe. With her blond hair, breathy voice, and raw sexuality, she personified the forbidden side of the good life and became one of Hollywood's most popular stars. The images of such film goddesses corresponded to male fantasies of women, visible in *Playboy* magazine, which first appeared in 1953 and soon achieved a huge readership. As for men's wives, they were expected to manage their suburban homes and to be cheerful and willing objects of their husbands' desire.

Despite reaffirming the old ideology that a woman's place was in the home, the 1950s were years

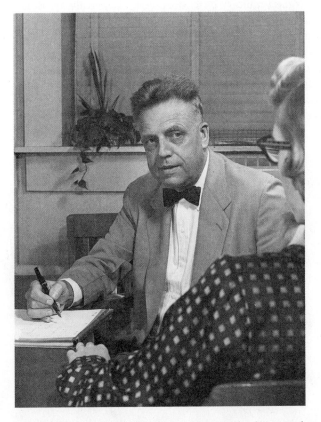

Biologist Alfred Kinsey interviewed thousands of men and women about their sex lives. Here he is conducting an interview with a young woman. How did his manner encourage people to talk?

of unnoticed but important change. Because the supply of single women workers fell as a result of the low birthrate of the Depression years and increased schooling and early marriage, older married women continued the pattern begun during the war and entered the labor force in larger numbers than before. In 1940, only 15 percent of American wives had jobs. By 1950, 21 percent were employed, and 10 years later, the figure had risen to 30 percent. Moreover, more than half of all working women were married, a dramatic reversal of pre–World War II patterns. While many working women were poor, divorced, or widowed, many others worked to acquire the desirable new products that were badges of middle-class status. They stepped into the new jobs created by economic expansion, clustering in office, sales, and service positions, occupations already defined as female. They and their employers considered their work subordinate to their primary role as wives and mothers. The conviction that women's main role was homemaking justified low wages and the denial of promotions. Comparatively few women entered professions where they would have challenged traditional notions of a woman's place.

African American women worked as always but often lost the jobs they had held during the war. Bernice McCannon, an African American employee at a Virginia military base, observed, "I have always done domestic work for families. When war came, I made the same move many domestics did. I took a higher paying job in a government cafeteria as a junior baker. If domestic work offers a good living, I see no reason why most of us will not return to our old jobs. We will have no alternative." In the 1950s, the employment picture improved somewhat. African American women

succeeded both in moving into white-collar positions and in increasing their income. By 1960, more than one-third of all black women held clerical, sales, service, or professional jobs. The income gap between white women and black women holding similar jobs dropped from about 50 percent in 1940 to about 30 percent in 1960.

Cultural Rebels

Not all Americans fit the 1950s stereotypes. Some were alienated from the culture and rebelled against its values. Many were intrigued by Holden Caulfield, the main figure in J. D. Salinger's popular novel *The Catcher in the Rye* (1951), who rebelled against the "phonies" around him who threatened his individuality and independence.

Writers of the "Beat Generation" espoused unconventional values in their stories and poems. Challenging the apathy and conformity of the period, they stressed spontaneity and spirituality and claimed that intuition was more important than reason, Eastern mysticism (with its Buddhist influence) more valuable than Western faith. The "Beats" deliberately outraged respectability by sneering at materialism, flaunting unconventional sex lives, and smoking marijuana.

Their literary work reflected their approach to life. Finding conventional academic forms confining, they rejected them. Jack Kerouac typed his best-selling novel *On the Road* (1957), describing freewheeling trips across country, on a 250-foot roll of paper. Dispensing with conventional punctuation and paragraphing, the book was a song of praise to the free lifestyle the "Beats" espoused.

Rock-and-Roll Star Elvis Presley

Elvis Presley, a truck driver from Memphis, Tennessee, turned rock and roll into a kind of teenage religion. In appearances such as this one at a state fair in Memphis, Tennessee, in 1956, his fans worked themselves into a frenzy. How did Elvis's popularity help a new youth culture develop?

(Getty Images)

Poet Allen Ginsberg, who, like Kerouac, was a Columbia University dropout, became equally well known for his poem "Howl." Written during a wild weekend in 1955, the poem was a scathing critique of modern, mechanized culture. The powerful poem, which began with the line "I saw the best minds of my generation destroyed by madness, starving hysterical naked," became a cult piece, particularly after the police seized it on the grounds that it was obscene. When the work survived a court test, national acclaim followed for Ginsberg. He and the other "Beats" furnished a model for rebellion in the 1960s.

The signs of cultural rebellion also appeared in popular music. Parents recoiled as their children flocked to hear a young Tennessee singer named Elvis Presley belt out rock-and-roll songs. Presley's sexy voice, gyrating hips, and other techniques borrowed from black singers made him the undisputed "king of rock and roll." A multimedia blitz of movies, television, and radio helped make songs such as "Heartbreak Hotel," "Don't Be Cruel," and "Hound Dog" smash singles. Eighteen Presley hits sold more than a million copies in the last four years of the 1950s. His black leather jacket and duck-tail haircut became standard dress for rebellious male teenagers.

American painters, shucking off European influences that had shaped American artists for two centuries, also became a part of the cultural rebellion. Led by Jackson Pollock and the "New York school," some artists discarded the easel, laid gigantic canvases on the floor, and then used trowels, putty knives, and sticks to apply paint, glass shards, sand, and other materials in wild explosions of color. Known as abstract expressionists, these painters regarded the unconscious as the source of their artistic creations. Like much of the literature of rebellion, abstract expressionism reflected the artist's alienation from a world filled with nuclear threats, computerization, and materialism.

Origins of the Welfare State

The modern American welfare state originated in the New Deal. Franklin D. Roosevelt's efforts to deal with the ravages of the Great Depression and protect Americans from the problems stemming from industrial capitalism provided the basis for subsequent efforts to commit the government to help those who could not help themselves, even in prosperous times. Harry Truman's Fair Deal built squarely on Roosevelt's New Deal. Truman's Republican successor, Dwight Eisenhower, sought to scale down spending but made no effort to roll back the most important initiatives of the welfare state.

Harry S Truman

Harry S Truman, America's first postwar president, was an unpretentious man who took a straightforward approach to public affairs. He was, however, ill prepared for the office he assumed in the final months of World War II. His three months as vice president had done little to school him in the complexity of postwar issues. Nor had Franklin Roosevelt confided in Truman. It was no wonder that the new president felt insecure. To a former colleague in the Senate, he groaned, "I'm not big enough for this job." Critics agreed.

Yet Truman matured rapidly. A sign on the president's White House desk read, "The Buck Stops Here," and he was willing to make quick decisions on issues, even if associates sometimes wondered whether he understood all the implications.

Truman took the same feisty approach to public policy that characterized his conduct of foreign affairs (see Chapter 27). Believing in plain speaking, he seldom hesitated to let others know exactly where he stood. He attacked his political enemies vigorously when they resisted his initiatives and often took his case to the American people. He was, in many ways, an old-style Democratic politician who hoped to use his authority to benefit the middle-class and working-class Americans who made up his political base.

Truman's Struggles with a Conservative Congress

Like Roosevelt, Harry Truman believed that the federal government had the responsibility for ensuring the social welfare of all Americans. He shared his predecessor's commitment to assisting less-prosperous inhabitants of the country in a systematic, rational way. Truman wanted his administration to embrace and act on a series of carefully defined social and economic goals to extend New Deal initiatives even further.

Less than a week after the end of World War II, Truman called on Congress to pass a 21-point program. He wanted housing assistance, a higher minimum wage, more unemployment compensation, and a national commitment to maintaining full employment. During the next 10 weeks, Truman sent blueprints of further proposals to Congress, including health insurance and atomic energy legislation. But this liberal program soon ran into fierce political opposition.

The debate surrounding the Employment Act of 1946 hinted at the fate of Truman's proposals. This measure was a deliberate effort to apply the theory of English economist John Maynard Keynes who argued that aggressive spending could head off another depression and maintain economic equilibrium. While liberals and labor leaders hailed the initial bill, which committed the government to maintaining full employment by monitoring the economy and taking remedial action in case of decline, business groups such as the National Association of Manufacturers condemned it. They claimed that government intervention would undermine free enterprise and promote socialism. Responding to the business community, Congress cut the proposal to bits. As finally passed, the act created a Council of Economic Advisers to make recommendations to the president, but it stopped short of committing the government to using fiscal tools to maintain full employment when economic indicators turned downward.

As the midterm elections of 1946 approached, Truman knew he was vulnerable. As more and more people questioned his competence as president, his support dropped from 87 percent of those polled after he assumed the office to 32 percent in November 1946. Gleeful Republicans asked the voters, "Had enough?" They had. Republicans won majorities in both houses of Congress for the first time since the 1928 elections and gained a majority of the governorships as well.

After the 1946 elections, Truman faced an unsympathetic Eightieth Congress. Republicans and conservative Democrats, dominating both houses, planned to reverse the liberal policies of the Roosevelt years. Hoping to reestablish congressional authority and cut the power of the executive branch, they insisted on less government intervention in business and private affairs. They also demanded tax cuts and curtailment of the privileged position they felt labor had come to enjoy.

When the new Congress met, it slashed federal spending and taxes. In 1947, Congress twice passed tax-cut measures, which Truman vetoed. In 1948, another election year, Congress overrode the veto.

Congress also struck at Democratic labor policies. Angry at the gains won by labor in the 1930s and 1940s, Republicans wanted to check unions and to circumscribe their right to engage in the kind of disruptive strikes that had occurred immediately after the war. Early in Truman's presidency, Congress had passed a bill requiring notice for strikes as well as a cooling-off period if a strike occurred. Truman vetoed it. But in 1947, commanding more votes, the Republicans passed the Taft–Hartley Act, which sought to limit the power of unions by restricting the weapons they could employ. It spelled out unfair labor practices (such as preventing nonunion workers from working if they wished) and outlawed the closed shop, whereby an employee had to join a union before getting a job. The law likewise allowed states to prohibit the union shop, which forced workers to join the union after they had been hired. It gave the president the right to call for an 80-day cooling-off period in strikes affecting national security and required union officials to sign non-Communist oaths.

Union leaders and members were furious. They called the measure a "slave-labor law" and argued vigorously that it eliminated many of their hard-won rights and left labor–management relations the way they had been in pre–New Deal days. Vetoing the measure, Truman claimed that it was unworkable and unfair and went on nationwide radio to seek public approval. This move regained him some of the support he had lost earlier when he had sought to force strikers to go back to work immediately after the war. Congress, however, passed the Taft–Hartley measure over Truman's veto.

The Fair Deal and Its Fate

In 1948, Truman wanted a chance to consolidate a liberal program and decided to seek the presidency in his own right. Aware that he was an accidental occupant of the White House, he won what most people thought was a worthless nomination. Not only was his own popularity waning, but the Democratic party itself seemed to be falling apart.

The civil rights issue split the Democrats. When liberals defeated a moderate platform proposal and pressed for a stronger commitment to African American rights, angry delegates from Mississippi and Alabama stormed out of the convention. They later formed the States' Rights, or Dixiecrat, party. At their own convention, delegates from 13 states nominated Governor J. Strom Thurmond of South Carolina as their presidential candidate and affirmed their support for continued racial segregation.

Meanwhile, Henry A. Wallace, first secretary of agriculture, longtime member of the government until Truman fired him for advocating a more moderate approach to the Soviet Union, mounted his own challenge, becoming the presidential candidate of the Progressive party. In that fragmented state, the Democrats took on the Republicans, who coveted the White House after 16 years out of power. Once again, the GOP nominated New York Governor Thomas E. Dewey, the unsuccessful candidate in 1944. Even though he was stiff and egocentric, the polls uniformly picked the Republicans to win. Dewey saw little value in brawling with his opponent and campaigned, in the words of one commentator, "with the humorless calculation of a Certified Public Accountant in pursuit of the Holy Grail."

Truman, as the underdog, conducted a two-fisted campaign. He appealed to ordinary Americans as an unpretentious man engaged in an uphill fight. Believing that everyone was against him but the people, he addressed Americans in familiar language. He called the Republicans a "bunch of old mossbacks" out to destroy the New Deal as he attacked the "do nothing" Eightieth Congress. Speaking informally in his choppy,

Harry Truman Celebrating His
Unexpected Victory

In one of the nation's most extraordinary political upsets, Harry Truman beat Thomas E. Dewey in 1948. Here an exuberant Truman holds a newspaper headline printed while he slept, before the vote turned his way. Why is Truman so gleeful?

(Bettmann/CORBIS)

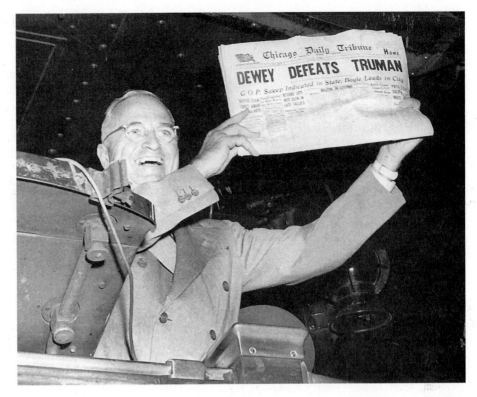

aggressive style, he appealed to crowds yelling, "Give 'em hell, Harry!" He did.

The pollsters predicting a Republican victory were wrong. On election day, disproving the bold headline "Dewey Defeats Truman" in the *Chicago Daily Tribune*, the incumbent president scored one of the most unexpected political upsets in American history, winning 303–189 in the Electoral College. Democrats also swept both houses of Congress.

Truman won primarily because he was able to revive the major elements of the Democratic coalition that Franklin Roosevelt had constructed more than a decade before. Despite the rocky days of 1946,

Truman managed to hold on to labor, farm, and black votes. Labor's support was crucial. Working men and women had been irritated by his response to the strikes in the immediate postwar period but had been buoyed by his veto, even though unsuccessful, of the Taft–Hartley Act. In the end, wary of Wallace, they backed Truman.

With the election behind him, Truman pursued his liberal program. In his 1949 State of the Union message, he declared, "Every segment of our population and every individual has a right to expect from our Government a fair deal." While parts of Truman's Fair Deal worked, others did not. Lawmakers raised

PRESIDENTIAL ELECTIONS, 1948–1956

Year	Candidate	Party	Popular Vote	Electoral Vote
1948	HARRY S TRUMAN	Democratic	24,105,812 (49.5%)	303
	Thomas E. Dewey	Republican	21,970,065 (45.1%)	189
	J. Strom Thurmond	States' Rights	1,169,063 (12.4%)	39
	Henry A. Wallace	Progressive	1,157,172 (12.4%)	0
1952	DWIGHT D. EISENHOWER	Republican	33,936,234 (55.1%)	442
	Adlai E. Stevenson	Democratic	27,314,992 (44.4%)	89
1956	DWIGHT D. EISENHOWER	Republican	35,590,472 (57.4%)	457
	Adlai E. Stevenson	Democratic	26,022,752 (42.0%)	73

Note: Winners' names appear in capital letters.

the minimum wage and expanded social security programs. A housing program brought modest gains but did not really meet housing needs. A farm program, aimed at providing income support to farmers if prices fell, never made it through Congress. Although he desegregated the military, other parts of his civil rights program failed to win congressional support. The American Medical Association undermined the effort to provide national health insurance, and Congress rejected a measure to provide federal aid to education.

The mixed record was not entirely Truman's fault. Conservative legislators were largely responsible for sabotaging his efforts. At the same time, critics charged correctly that Truman was often unpragmatic and shrill in his struggles with an unsympathetic Congress. They argued that he sometimes seemed to provoke the confrontations that became a hallmark of his presidency. They also claimed that he was most concerned with foreign policy as he strove to secure bipartisan support for Cold War initiatives (see Chapter 27) and allowed his domestic program to suffer. Rising defense expenditures meant less money for projects at home.

Still, Truman kept the liberal vision alive. The Fair Deal ratified many of the initiatives begun during the New Deal and led Americans to take programs such as social security for granted. Truman had not achieved everything he wanted—he had not even come close—but the nation had taken another step toward endorsing liberal goals.

The Election of Ike

Acceptance of the liberal state continued in the 1950s, even as the Republicans took control. By 1952, Truman's popularity had plummeted to 23 percent of the American people, and all indicators pointed to a political shift. The Democrats nominated Adlai Stevenson, Illinois's articulate and moderately liberal governor. The Republicans turned to Dwight Eisenhower, the World War II hero known as Ike.

While Stevenson approached political issues in intellectual terms, the Republicans focused on communism, corruption, and Korea as major priorities. They called the Democrats "soft on communism," condemned scandals involving Truman's cronies and friends, and promised to end the unpopular Korean War. Eisenhower proved to be a highly effective campaigner. He had a natural talent for taking his case to the American people, speaking in simple, reassuring terms they could understand. He struck a grandfatherly pose, unified the various wings of his party, and went on to victory at the polls. He received 55 percent of the vote and carried 41 states. The new president took office with a Republican Congress as well and had little difficulty winning a second term in 1956.

Dwight D. Eisenhower

Eisenhower stood in stark contrast to Truman. His easy manner and warm smile made him widely popular. As British field marshal Bernard Montgomery observed, "He has the power of drawing the hearts of men towards him as a magnet attracts bits of metal."

Eisenhower had not taken the typical route to the presidency. After World War II, he served successively as army chief of staff, president of Columbia University, and head of the North Atlantic Treaty Organization (NATO). Despite his lack of formal political background, he had a real ability to get people to compromise and work together.

Ike's limited experience with everyday politics conditioned his sense of the presidential role. Whereas Truman loved political infighting and wanted to take charge, Eisenhower was more restrained. The presidency for him was no "bully pulpit," as it had been for Theodore Roosevelt and even FDR. "I am not one of those desk-pounding types that likes to stick out his jaw and look like he is bossing the show," he said. "You do not lead by hitting people over the head. Any damn fool can do that, but it's usually called 'assault'—not 'leadership.' "

"Modern Republicanism"

Eisenhower wanted to limit the presidential role. He was uncomfortable with the growth of the executive office over the past 20 years. Like the Republicans in Congress with whom Truman had tangled, he wanted to restore the balance between the branches of government and to reduce the authority of the national government. He recognized, however, that it was impossible to scale back federal power to the limited levels of the 1920s, and he wanted to preserve social gains that even Republicans now accepted. Eisenhower sometimes termed his approach "dynamic conservatism" or "modern Republicanism," which, he explained, meant "conservative when it comes to money, liberal when it comes to human beings." Liberals quipped that his approach meant endorsing social projects and then failing to authorize the funds.

Economic concerns dominated the Eisenhower years. The president and his chief aides wanted desperately to preserve the value of the dollar, pare down levels of funding, cut taxes, and balance the budget after years of deficit spending. Eisenhower's administration also supported business interests. This orientation became obvious when defense secretary Charles E. Wilson, former president of General Motors, declared at his confirmation hearing, "What is good for our country is good for General Motors, and vice versa."

Eisenhower fulfilled his promise to reduce government's economic role. The administration sought to circumscribe federal activity in the electric power field. Eisenhower favored private rather than public development of power, and once said about the Tennessee Valley Authority (TVA), the extensive public power and development project begun during the New Deal, "I'd like to see us sell the whole thing, but I suppose we can't go that far." He opposed a TVA proposal for expansion to provide power to the Atomic Energy Commission and instead authorized a private group to build a plant in Arkansas for that purpose. Later, when charges of scandal arose, the administration canceled the agreement, but the basic preference for private development remained.

Committed to supporting business interests, the administration sometimes saw its program backfire. As a result of Eisenhower's reluctance to stimulate the economy too much, the annual rate of economic growth declined from 4.3 percent between 1947 and 1952 to 2.5 percent between 1953 and 1960. The economy was still growing, but more slowly than before. The country also suffered three recessions—in 1953–1954, 1957–1958, and 1960–1961—in Eisenhower's eight years. During the slumps, tax revenues fell and the deficits that Eisenhower so wanted to avoid increased.

Eisenhower's understated approach led to a legislative stalemate, particularly when the Democrats regained control of Congress in 1954. Opponents gibed at Ike's restrained stance and laughed about limited White House leadership. One observed that Eisenhower proved that the country did not "need" a president. Another spoke of the Eisenhower doll—you wound it up and it did nothing for eight years.

Yet Eisenhower understood just what he was doing; he had a better grasp of public policy than his critics realized. Beneath his casual approach lay real shrewdness. "Don't worry," he once assured his aides as they briefed him for a press conference. "If that question comes up, I'll just confuse them." He worked quietly to create the consensus that he believed was necessary for legislative progress and practiced what later observers called a "hidden hand" presidency, unobtrusively orchestrating support for his own ends.

Even more important was his role in ratifying the welfare state. By 1960, the government had become a major factor in ordinary people's lives. It had grown enormously, employing close to 2.5 million people throughout the 1950s. Federal expenditures, which had stood at $3.5 billion in 1927, rose to $97 billion in 1960. The White House now took the lead in initiating legislation and in steering bills through Congress. Individuals had come to expect old-age pensions, unemployment payments, and a minimum wage. By accepting the fundamental features of the national state that the Democrats had created, Eisenhower ensured its survival.

A Popular and Personable President
Dwight Eisenhower provided a reassuring presence in the White House in the 1950s. His very presence conveyed the impression that everything was going to be all right. How did his wide smile, pictured here, make Americans feel good about themselves and their country?

(Hulton Archive/Getty Images)

For all the jokes at his expense, Eisenhower remained popular with the voters. He accomplished most of his goals, and he was one of the few presidents to leave office as highly regarded by the people as when he entered it. He was the kind of leader Americans wanted in prosperous times.

The Other America

Not all Americans shared postwar middle-class affluence. African Americans, uprooted from rural patterns and transplanted into urban slums, were among the hardest hit. But members of other minority groups, as well as less fortunate whites, suffered similar dislocations, unknown to the middle class.

Poverty amid Affluence

Many people in the "affluent society" lived in poverty. Although the popular "trickle-down" theory argued that economic expansion benefited all classes, little wealth reached the citizens at the bottom. In 1960, the Federal Bureau of Labor Statistics reported that 40 million people (almost one-quarter of the population) lived below what it defined as the poverty level, with nearly the same number only marginally above the line.

Michael Harrington, socialist author and critic, shocked the country with his 1962 study *The Other America*. The poor, Harrington showed, were everywhere. He described New York City's "economic underworld," where "Puerto Ricans and Negroes, alcoholics, drifters, and disturbed people" haunted employment agencies for temporary positions as "dishwashers and day workers, the fly-by-night jobs." In the afternoon, he continued, "the jobs have all been handed out, yet the people still mill around."

Despite the prosperity that surrounded them, the mountain folk of Appalachia, the tenant farmers of Mississippi, and the migrant farmers of Florida, Texas, and California were all caught in poverty's relentless cycle.

Hard Times for African Americans

African Americans were among the postwar nation's least prosperous citizens. In the South, agricultural workers continued to fall victim to foreign competition, mechanization, and eviction as white farmers turned to less labor-intensive crops such as soybeans and peanuts.

The southern agricultural population declined dramatically as millions of blacks moved to southern cities, where they found better jobs, better schooling, and freedom from landlords. Some achieved middle-class status; many more did not. They remained poor, with even less of a support system than they had known before.

Millions of African Americans also headed for northern cities after 1940. In the 1950s, Detroit's black population increased from 16 percent to 29 percent, Chicago's from 14 percent to 23 percent. At one point in this decade, Chicago's black population rose by more than 2,200 people each week. The new arrivals congregated in urban slums, where the growth of social services failed to keep pace with population growth.

The experiences of African Americans in the cities often proved different from what they had expected. As author Claude Brown recalled, blacks were told that in the North, "Negroes lived in houses with bathrooms, electricity, running water, and indoor toilets. To them, this was the 'promised land' that Mammy had been singing about in the cotton fields for many years." But no one had told them "about one of the most important aspects of the promised land: it was a slum ghetto.... There were too many people full of hate and bitterness crowded into a dirty, stinky, uncared-for closet-size section of a great city." The constant slights that accompanied segregation in both the North and the South in the midst of such conditions took a heavy toll.

Still, the black community remained intact. Chicago's South Side neighborhood was a vibrant place, replacing New York's Harlem as black America's cultural capital in the 1950s. This section of the city included such figures as boxing champion Joe Louis, gospel singer Mahalia Jackson, and Representative William Dawson, one of the few African American members of Congress.

The black church played an important role in sustaining African American life. Blacks moving into the cities retained churchgoing habits and a commitment to religious institutions from their rural days. The churches offered more than religious sustenance alone. Many provided day-care facilities, ran Boy Scout and Girl Scout troops, and sponsored a variety of other social services.

The growth of the black urban population fostered the increased growth of businesses catering to the African American community. Black newspapers now provided a more regional, rather than a national, focus, but magazines such as *Jet*, a pocket-size weekly with a large, countrywide circulation, filled the void. Black-owned and black-operated banks and other financial institutions increased in number.

Yet most African Americans remained second-class citizens. Escape from the slums was difficult for many and impossible for most. Persistent poverty remained a dismal fact of life.

African American Gains

African Americans had made significant gains during World War II. Black servicemen returning from the war vowed to reject second-class citizenship and helped mobilize a grassroots movement to counter discrimination. In the postwar years, African struggles for independence, such as the Kenyan Mau Mau revolt against the British, inspired African American leaders who now saw the quest for black equality in a broader context. They took enormous pride in the achievement of independence by a number of African nations and demanded comparable change at home.

The racial question received dramatic attention in 1947 when Jackie Robinson broke the color line and began playing major league baseball with the Brooklyn Dodgers. Sometimes teammates were hostile, sometimes opponents crashed into him with spikes high, but Robinson kept his frustrations to himself. A splendid first season helped ease the way and resulted in his selection as Rookie of the Year. African Americans flocked to the ballpark and followed his exploits on the radio. As Charles Jones of Charlotte, North Carolina, noted, "Robinson was knocking a ball everywhere on a *white man's* baseball field." After Robinson's trailblazing effort, other blacks, formerly confined to the old Negro leagues, moved into the major leagues in baseball and then into other sports.

Somewhat reluctantly, Truman supported the civil rights movement. A moderate on questions of

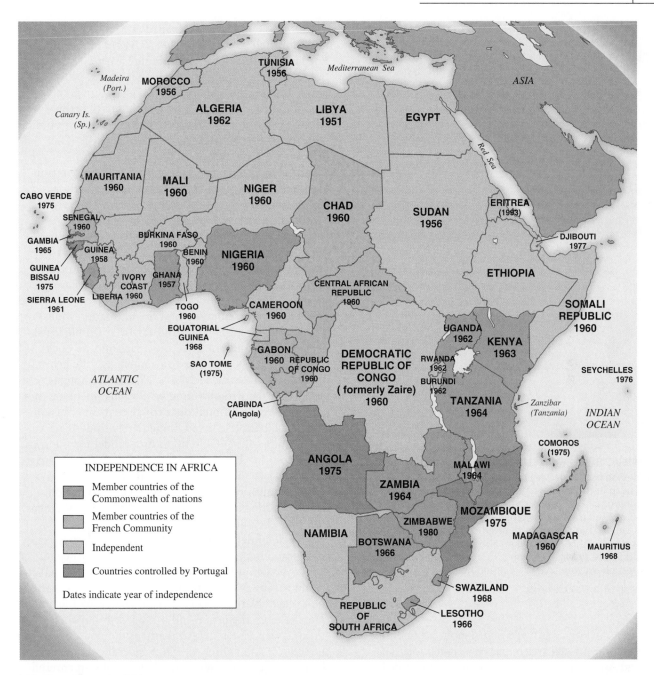

Independence in Africa

In the 1950s and 1960s, most African nations threw off their colonial rulers and achieved independence. During which decade did more nations become free? How did attaining independence change social and economic patterns in the African nations? What effect did it have on the patterns of the Cold War? What effect did it have on the civil rights struggle in the United States?

race, who believed in political, not social, equality, he responded to the growing strength of the African American vote. In 1946, he appointed a Committee on Civil Rights to investigate the problem of lynching and other brutalities against blacks and recommend remedies. The committee's report, released in October 1947, showed that black Americans remained second-class citizens in every area of American life and called for change. In February 1948, he sent a 10-point civil rights program to Congress, the first presidential civil rights plan since Reconstruction. Then he moved forward even more aggressively. First he issued an executive order barring discrimination in the federal establishment. Then he ordered equality of treatment in the military services. Personnel needs in the Korean War broke down the last restrictions, particularly when the army found that integrated units performed well.

Baseball Superstar Jackie Robinson

Jackie Robinson's electrifying play as the first African American in the major leagues led to acceptance of the integration of baseball. A spectacular rookie season in 1947 opened the way for other African Americans who had earlier been limited to the Negro leagues. In this photo, taken at Ebbets Field in Brooklyn during the 1957 World Series, Robinson is about to steal home. What impression do you have of Robinson here?

(Time Life Pictures/Getty Images)

As the civil rights struggle gained momentum during the 1950s, the judicial system played a crucial role. The National Association for the Advancement of Colored People (NAACP) was determined to overturn the 1896 Supreme Court decision *Plessy* v. *Ferguson*, in which the Court had declared that segregation of the black and white races was constitutional if the facilities used by each were "separate but equal." The decree had been used for generations to sanction rigid segregation, primarily in the South, even though separate facilities were seldom, if ever, equal. A series of cases chipped away at the ruling.

Then in 1951, Oliver Brown, the father of 8-year-old Linda Brown, sued the school board of Topeka, Kansas, to allow his daughter to attend a school for white children that she passed as she walked to the bus that carried her to a black school farther away. The case reached the Supreme Court, which grouped several school segregation cases together.

On May 17, 1954, the Supreme Court released its bombshell ruling in *Brown* v. *Board of Education*. For more than a decade, Supreme Court decisions had gradually expanded black civil rights. Now the Court unanimously decreed that "separate facilities are inherently unequal" and concluded that the "separate but equal" doctrine had no place in public education. African Americans were elated. "The Supreme Court decision is the greatest victory for the Negro people since the Emancipation Proclamation," Harlem's *Amsterdam News* proclaimed. Author Ralph Ellison observed, "What a wonderful world of possibilities are unfolded for the children." A year later, the Court turned to the question of implementation and declared that local school boards, acting with the guidance of lower courts, should move "with all deliberate speed" to desegregate their facilities.

President Eisenhower had the ultimate responsibility for executing the law. Doubting that simple legislative changes could improve race relations, he once observed, "I don't believe you can change the hearts of men with laws or decisions." While he thought privately that the *Brown* ruling was wrong, he knew that it was his constitutional duty to see that the decision was carried out. He acted immediately to desegregate the Washington, D.C., schools as a model for the rest of the country. He also ordered desegregation in navy yards and veterans' hospitals.

The South resisted. The crucial confrontation came in Little Rock, Arkansas, in 1957. A desegregation plan, beginning with the token admission of a few black students to Central High School, was ready to go into effect. Just before the school year began, Governor Orval Faubus declared on television that it would not be possible to maintain order if integration took place. National Guardsmen, posted by the governor to keep the peace and armed with bayonets, turned away nine black students as they tried to enter the school. After three weeks, a federal court ordered the troops to leave. When the black children entered the building, the white students, spurred on by their elders, belligerently opposed them, chanting such slogans as "Two, four, six, eight, we ain't gonna integrate." In the face of hostile mobs, the black children left the school.

With the lines drawn, Ike knew that such resistance could not be tolerated, and he finally took the one action he had earlier called unthinkable. For the first time since the end of Reconstruction, an American president called out federal troops to protect the rights of black citizens. Eisenhower ordered paratroopers to Little Rock and placed National Guardsmen under federal command. The black children entered the school and attended classes with the military protecting their rights. Thus desegregation began.

Meanwhile, African Americans, encouraged by their churches, began organizing themselves to take direct action, and their efforts significantly advanced the civil rights movement. All were horrified by the brutal murder of Emmett Till, a 14-year-old boy from Chicago visiting Mississippi, who offended a white woman at a country store. Pictures of his mangled body in an open casket helped energize the effort to promote racial equality.

The catalyzing event occurred in Montgomery, Alabama, in December 1955. Rosa Parks, a 42-year-old black seamstress who was also secretary of the Montgomery branch of the NAACP, sat down in the front of a bus in a section reserved by custom for whites. When ordered to move back, the longtime activist refused to budge. The bus driver called the police at the next stop, and Parks was arrested for violating the segregation laws. E. D. Nixon, state NAACP president, told Parks, "This is the case we've been looking for. We can break this situation on the bus with your case." Fifty black leaders met to discuss the case and decided to organize a massive boycott of the bus system.

Martin Luther King, Jr., the 27-year-old minister of the Baptist church where the meeting was held, soon emerged as the preeminent spokesman of the protest. King was an impressive figure and an inspiring speaker. "There comes a time when people get tired...of being kicked about by the brutal feet of oppression," he declared. It was time to be more assertive, to cease being "patient with anything less than freedom and justice."

Although King, like others, was arrested on the trumped-up charge of speeding and jailed, grassroots support bubbled up. In Montgomery, 50,000 African Americans walked or formed car pools to avoid the transit system. Their actions cut gross revenue on city buses by 65 percent. Almost a year later, the Supreme Court ruled that bus segregation, like school segregation, violated the Constitution, and the boycott ended. But the mood it fostered continued, as ordinary black men and women challenged the racial status quo and forced both white and black leaders to respond.

Meanwhile, a concerted effort developed to guarantee black voting rights. The provisions of the Fifteenth Amendment notwithstanding, many states had circumvented the law for decades. Some states required a poll tax or a literacy test or an examination of constitutional understanding. Blacks often found themselves excluded from the polls.

Largely because of the legislative genius of Senate majority leader Lyndon B. Johnson of Texas, a civil rights bill, the first since Reconstruction, moved toward passage. Paring the bill down to the provisions he felt would pass, Johnson pushed the measure through.

The Civil Rights Act of 1957 created a Civil Rights Commission and empowered the Justice Department to

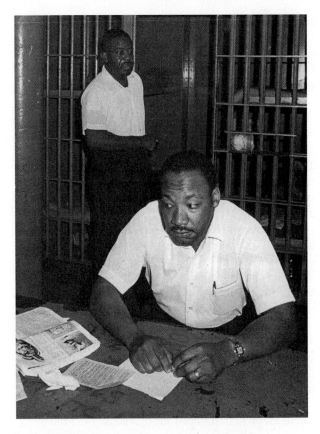

Civil Rights Leaders Martin Luther King, Jr., and Ralph Abernathy

Baptist minister Martin Luther King, Jr., emerged as the black spokesman in the Montgomery, Alabama, bus boycott and soon became the most eloquent African American leader of the entire civil rights movement. He was often jailed for his efforts, as shown in this picture of him sharing a cell with Ralph Abernathy, another civil rights leader. What effect did the jailing of King have on the larger movement?

(Bettmann/CORBIS)

go to court in cases in which blacks were denied the right to vote. The bill was a compromise measure, yet it was the first successful effort to protect civil rights in 82 years.

Again led by Johnson, Congress passed the Civil Rights Act of 1960. This new measure set stiffer penalties for people who interfered with the right to vote but again stopped short of authorizing federal registrars to register blacks to vote and so, like its predecessor, was generally ineffective.

Latinos on the Fringe

Latinos, like other groups, had similar difficulties in the postwar United States. Latino immigrants from Cuba, Puerto Rico, Mexico, and Central America, often unskilled and illiterate, followed other less fortunate Americans to the cities. The conditions they encountered there were similar to those faced by blacks. Author Piri Thomas, born of Puerto Rican and Cuban parents in New York City's Spanish Harlem, described standing "on the rooftop of my broken-down building at night," seeing "the stark naked truth of garbage-lepered streets." Despite those conditions, Spanish-speaking groups maintained a strong sense of group identity. The urban *barrios* where they settled preserved a sense of community and close-knit cohesive culture, even in the midst of pervasive poverty. The ties fostered in these communities provided a strong base for a growing political consciousness.

Chicanos, or Mexican Americans, were the most numerous of the newcomers and faced peculiar difficulties. During World War II, as the country experienced a labor shortage at home, American farmers sought Mexican *braceros* (helping hands) to harvest their crops. A program to encourage the seasonal immigration of farm workers continued after the war when the government signed a Migratory Labor Agreement with Mexico. Between 1948 and 1964, some 4.5 million Mexicans were brought to the United States for temporary work. *Braceros* were expected to return to Mexico at the end of their labor contract, but often they stayed. Joining them were millions more who entered the country illegally.

Conditions were harsh for the *braceros* in the best of times, but in periods of economic difficulty, troubles worsened. During a serious recession in 1953–1954, the government mounted Operation Wetback to deport illegal entrants and *braceros* who had remained in the country illegally and expelled 1.1 million. As immigration officials searched out illegal workers, all Chicanos found themselves vulnerable.

Operation Wetback did not end the reliance on poor Mexican farm laborers. A coalition of southern Democrats and conservative Republicans, mostly representing farm states, extended the Migratory Labor Agreement with Mexico, for the legislators wanted to continue to take advantage of the cheap labor. Two years after the massive deportations of 1954, a record 445,000 *braceros* crossed the border.

Puerto Ricans were numerous in other parts of the country. A steady stream of immigrants had been coming to New York from Puerto Rico since the 1920s. As the island's sugarcane economy became more mechanized, nearly 40 percent of the inhabitants left their homes. By the end of the 1960s, New York City had more Puerto Ricans than San Juan, the island's capital. El Barrio, in East Harlem, became the center of Puerto Rican activity, the home of *salsa* music and small *bodegas*, grocery stores that served the neighborhood. Author Guillermo Cotto-Thorner described the place fondly in his autobiographical novel, *Trópico en Manhattan*, through the words of Antonio, an older resident.

This . . . is our neighborhood, El Barrio. . . . It's said that we Latins run things here. . . . While the Americans take most of the money that circulates around here, we consider this part of the city to be ours. . . . The stores, barbershops, restaurants, butcher shops, churches, funeral parlors, greasy spoons, pool halls, everything is all Latino.

Puerto Ricans, like many other immigrants, hoped to earn money in America and then return home. Some did; others stayed. Like countless Latinos, most failed to enjoy the promise of the American dream.

Like African Americans, Latinos fought for their own rights. The roots of the Latino struggle dated back to the pre-World War II years. Chicanos established the American GI Forum because a Texas funeral home refused to bury a Mexican American casualty of World War II. When the group's protest led to a burial in Arlington National Cemetery, the possibilities of concerted action became clear. In the waning months of the war, a court case challenged Mexican American segregation in the schools. Gonzalo Méndez, an asparagus grower and a U.S. citizen who had lived in Orange County, California, for 25 years, filed suit to permit his children to attend the school reserved for Anglo-Americans, which was far more attractive than the Mexican one to which they had been assigned. A federal district court upheld his claim in the spring of 1945, and two years later, the circuit court affirmed the original ruling. With the favorable decision, other communities filed similar suits and began to press for integration of their schools. New organizations arose to struggle for equal rights. The Community Service Organization mobilized Chicanos against discrimination, as did the more radical Associación Nacional México-Americana. And the League of United Latin American Citizens continued reform efforts.

Confrontations continued. Los Angeles, with its large number of Chicanos, was the scene of numerous unsavory racial episodes. In mid-1951, on receiving a complaint about a loud record player, police officers raided a baptismal gathering at the home of Simon Fuentes. Breaking into the house without a warrant, they assaulted the members of the party. In the "Bloody Christmas" case at the end of the year, officers removed seven Mexican Americans from jail cells and beat them severely.

Chicano activism in the 1950s was fragmented. Some Mexican Americans considered their situation hopeless. More effective mobilization had to await another day.

The Native American Struggle

Native Americans likewise remained outsiders in the postwar years. Years of persistent discrimination made it even harder to cope with the changes they faced. As power lines reached their reservations, Indians purchased televisions, refrigerators, washing machines, and automobiles. As they partook of the consumer culture, old patterns inevitably changed. Reservation life lost its cohesiveness, and alcohol became a major problem. With good jobs unavailable on the reservations, more and more Indians gravitated to the cities. Bennie Bearskin, a Winnebago, left home for Chicago in 1947, explaining: "The most important reason was that I could at least feel confident that [I could get] perhaps fifty paychecks a year here.... Even though it might be more pleasant to be back home, for instance, Nebraska." But Indians who moved to the cities often had difficulty adjusting to urban life and frequently faced hostility from white Americans.

Native Americans, like Latinos, began their own struggle for equality. They achieved an important victory just after the end of World War II when Congress established the Indian Claims Commission. Hundreds of tribal suits charging that ancestral lands had been illegally seized could now be filed against the government in federal courts. Many of them led to large settlements of cash—a form of reparation for past injustices—and sometimes the return of long-lost lands.

In the 1950s, federal Indian policy shifted course. As part of its effort to limit the role of the national government, the Eisenhower administration turned

Troubles for Native American Veterans

After returning home at the end of World War II, many Native American veterans found it difficult to fit into either Native American or white society. Alcoholism—which sometimes led to confrontations with the law—became a problem, as reflected in this sketch by Native American artist Aaron Yava, who drew what he saw in what he called the "border towns of the Navajo Nation." What might have caused such confrontations?

(Courtesy of the family of Aaron Yava)

away from the New Deal policy of government support for tribal autonomy. In 1953, instead of trying to encourage Native American self-government, the administration adopted a new approach, known as "termination." The government proposed settling all outstanding claims and eliminating reservations as legitimate political entities. To encourage their assimilation into mainstream society, families who would leave the reservations and move to cities were offered small subsidies by the government.

The new policy infuriated Native Americans. Earl Old Person, a Blackfoot elder, declared: "It is important to note that in our Indian language the only translation for termination is to 'wipe out' or 'kill off'... How can we plan our future when the Indian Bureau threatens to wipe us out as a race? It is like trying to cook a meal in your tipi when someone is standing outside trying to burn the tipi down." With their lands no longer federally protected and their members deprived of treaty rights, many tribes became unwitting victims of people who wanted to seize their land. Though promising more freedom, the new policy caused great disruption as the government terminated tribes such as the Klamath in Oregon, the Menominee in Wisconsin, the Alabama and Coushatta in Texas, and bands of Paiute in Utah.

The policy increased Indian activism. The National Congress of American Indians mobilized opposition to the federal program. A Seminole petition to the president in 1954 summed up a general view:

> We do not say that we are superior or inferior to the White Man and we do not say that the White Man is superior or inferior to us. We do say that we are not White Men but Indians, do not wish to become White Men but wish to remain Indians, and have an outlook on all things different from the outlook of the White Man.

Not only did the termination policy foster a sense of Indian identity, but it also sparked a dawning awareness among whites of the Indians' right to maintain their heritage. In 1958, the Eisenhower administration changed the policy of termination so that it required a tribe's consent. The policy continued to have the force of law, but implementation ceased.

Asian American Advances

For Asian Americans, conditions improved somewhat in the aftermath of World War II. The war against Nazism eroded the racism that proclaimed a commitment to white superiority. Japanese Americans, ravaged by their devastating internment during the war, fought back after the struggle. In 1946, a measure supporting a wartime law confiscating Japanese American

Timeline

Year	Event
1946	4.6 million workers on strike
	ENIAC computer built
	Benjamin Spock, *Baby and Child Care*
	Employment Act
1947	Defense budget of $13 billion
	Taft–Hartley Act
	Jackie Robinson breaks the color line in major league baseball
1948	GM offers UAW cost-of-living adjustment
	Transistor developed at Bell Laboratories
	Alfred C. Kinsey, *Sexual Behavior in the Human Male*
	"Dixiecrat" party formed
	Truman defeats Dewey
1949	Truman launches Fair Deal
1950s	Each year a million farmers leave farms
1950	Diner's Club card inaugurated
	Associación Nacional México-Americana formed
1951	J. D. Salinger, *The Catcher in the Rye*
1952	Dwight D. Eisenhower elected president
1953	Defense budget of $47 billion
	Operation Wetback begins
	Submerged Lands Act
1954	Congress adds "under God" to pledge to flag
	Brown v. *Board of Education*
1955	First McDonald's opens in Illinois
	Merger of AFL and CIO
	Congress adds "In God We Trust" to currency
	Montgomery, Alabama, bus boycott begins
	Allen Ginsberg, "Howl"—written and read
1956	Interstate Highway Act
	Majority of U.S. workers hold white-collar jobs
	Eisenhower reelected
1957	Baby boom peaks
	Jack Kerouac, *On the Road*
	Little Rock, Arkansas, school integration crisis
	Civil Rights Act
1960	Three-quarters of all American families own a TV set
	Civil Rights Act
1962	Michael Harrington, *The Other America*
1963	California passes New York as most populous state
	Betty Friedan, *The Feminine Mystique*
1964	Peter Blake, *God's Own Junkyard*

property appeared on the ballot in California. But a spirited campaign by the Japanese American Citizens League reminding voters of the contributions of Japanese American soldiers during the war led to the measure's overwhelming defeat. Two years later, the Supreme Court, noting that the law itself, still on the books was "nothing more than outright racial discrimination," declared it unconstitutional.

In 1952, the Immigration and Nationality Act, also known as the McCarran–Walter Act, eased immigration quotas. Although the basic framework of the National Origins Act of 1924 remained intact, it removed the longstanding ban on Japanese immigration and made first-generation Japanese immigrants eligible for citizenship. It also established a quota of 100 immigrants a year from each Asian country. While that number was tiny compared to those admitted annually from northern and western Europe, the measure was a first step in ending the discriminatory exclusion of the past.

By the 1950s, many second- and third-generation Chinese, Japanese, and Koreans had moved into white-collar work. Promoting education for their children, they became part of the growing middle class, hoping like others to enjoy the benefits of the American dream.

Conclusion
QUALMS AMID AFFLUENCE

In general, the United States during the decade and a half after World War II was stable and secure. Structural adjustments caused occasional moments of friction but were seldom visible in prosperous times. Recessions occurred periodically, but the economy righted itself after short downturns. For the most part, business boomed. The standard of living for many of the nation's citizens reached new heights, especially compared with standards in other parts of the world. Millions of middle-class Americans joined the ranks of suburban property owners, enjoying the benefits of shopping centers, fast-food establishments, and other

material manifestations of what they considered the good life. Workers found themselves savoring the materialistic advantages of the era. The political world reflected prosperous times.

Some Americans did not share in the prosperity, but they were not visible in the affluent suburbs. Many African Americans and members of other minority groups were seriously disadvantaged, although they still believed they could share in the American dream and remained confident that deeply rooted patterns of discrimination could be changed. Even when they began to mobilize, their protest was peaceful at first.

Beneath the calm surface, though, there were signs of discontent. The seeds for the protest movements of the 1960s had already been sown. Disquieting signs were likewise evident on other fronts. The divorce rate increased as one-third of all marriages in the 1950s broke apart. Americans increasingly used newly developed tranquilizers in an effort to cope with problems in their lives. Some Americans began to criticize the materialism that seemed to undermine American efforts in the Cold War. Such criticisms in turn legitimized challenges by other groups, in the continuing struggle to make the realities of American life match the nation's ideals.

Criticisms and anxieties notwithstanding, the United States—for most whites and for some people of color—continued to develop according to Ray Kroc's dreams as he first envisioned McDonald's establishments across the land. Healthy and comfortable, upper- and middle-class Americans expected prosperity and growth to continue in the years ahead.

QUESTIONS FOR REVIEW AND REFLECTION

1. What were the sources of American prosperity?
2. Who prospered most in the postwar United States?
3. Who was left out?
4. To what degree did conformity become the norm in the postwar United States?
5. How would you characterize the broad social and economic changes that took place in America in the years after World War II?

CHAPTER 27

Chills and Fever During the Cold War, 1945–1960

The Cold War was closely connected to the nuclear arms race. The spectacular mushroom cloud, like the one created by this hydrogen blast at Eniwetok in the Pacific in 1952, was beautiful but frightening at the same time.

(National Archives)

American Stories

A Government Employee Confronts the Anti-Communist Crusade

Val Lorwin was in France in November 1950 when he learned of the charges against him. A State Department employee on leave of absence after 16 years of government service, he was in Paris working on a book. Now he had to return to the United States to defend himself against the accusation that he was a member of the Communist party and thus a loyalty and security risk. It seemed to him a tasteless joke. Yet communism was no laughing matter in the United States. Suspicions of the Soviet Union had escalated after 1945, and a wave of paranoia swept through the United States.

Lorwin was an unlikely candidate to be caught up in the fallout of the Cold War. He had begun to work for the government in 1935, serving in a number of New Deal agencies, then in the Labor Department and on the War Production Board before he was drafted during World War II. While in the army, he was assigned to the Office of Strategic Services, an early intelligence agency, and he was frequently granted security clearances.

Lorwin, however, did have a left-wing past as an active socialist in the 1930s. His social life then had revolved around Socialist party causes, particularly the unionization of southern tenant farmers and the provision of aid to the unemployed. He and his wife, Madge, drafted statements and stuffed envelopes to support their goals. But that activity was wholly open and legal, and Lorwin had from the start been aggressively anti-Communist in political affairs.

Suddenly, Lorwin, like others in the period, faced a nightmare. Despite his spotless record, Lorwin was told that an unnamed accuser had identified him as a Communist. The burden of proof was entirely on him, and the chance of clearing his name was slim. He was entitled to a hearing if he chose, or he could resign.

Lorwin requested a hearing, and one was held late in 1950. Still struck by the absurdity of the situation, he refuted all accusations but made little effort to cite his own positive achievements. At the conclusion, he was informed that the government no longer doubted his loyalty but considered him a security risk, likewise grounds for dismissal from his job.

When he appealed the judgment, Lorwin was again denied access to the identity of his accuser. This time, however, he thoroughly prepared his defense. At the hearing, 97 witnesses either spoke under oath on Lorwin's behalf or left sworn written depositions testifying to his good character and meritorious service.

The issues in the hearings might have been considered comic in view of Lorwin's record, had not a man's reputation been at stake. The accuser had once lived with the Lorwins in Washington, D.C. Fifteen years later, he claimed that in 1935 Lorwin had revealed that he was holding a Communist party meeting in his home and had even shown him a party card.

Lorwin proved all the charges groundless. He also showed that in 1935 the Socialist party card was red, the color the accuser reported seeing, while the Communist party card was black. In March 1952, Lorwin was finally cleared for both loyalty and security.

Lorwin's troubles were not yet over. His name appeared on one of the lists produced by Senator Joseph McCarthy of Wisconsin, the most aggressive anti-Communist of the era, and the next year, Lorwin was indicted for making false statements to the State Department Loyalty-Security Board. The charges this time proved as specious as before. Finally, in May 1954, admitting that its special prosecutor had deliberately lied to the grand jury and had no legitimate case, the Justice Department asked for dismissal of the indictment. Cleared at last, Lorwin went on to become a distinguished labor historian.

Val Lorwin was more fortunate than some victims of the anti-Communist crusade. Caught up in a global conflict that engulfed most of the world, he managed to weather a catastrophe that threatened to shatter his life. People rallied around him and gave him valuable support. Despite considerable emotional cost, he survived the witch hunt of the early 1950s, but his case still reflected vividly the ugly domestic consequences of the breakdown in relations between the Soviet Union and the United States.

The Cold War, which unfolded soon after the end of World War II and lasted for nearly 50 years, powerfully affected all aspects of American life. Rejecting for good the isolationist impulse that had governed foreign policy in the 1920s and 1930s, the United States began to play a major role in the world in the postwar years. Doubts about intervention in other lands faded as the nation acknowledged its dominant international position and resolved to do whatever was necessary to maintain it. The same sense of mission that had infused the United States in the Spanish-American War, World War I, and World War II now appeared in a revived evangelical faith and committed most Americans to the struggle against communism at home and abroad.

This chapter explores that continuing sense of mission and its consequences. It examines the roots of the Cold War both in the idealistic aim to keep the world safe for democracy and in the pursuit of economic self-interest that had long fueled American capitalism. It records how the determination to prevent the spread of communism led American policymakers to consider vast parts of the world as pivotal to American security and to act accordingly, particularly in Korea and

Vietnam. It notes the impact on economic development, particularly in the West, where the mighty defense industry flourished. And it considers the tragic consequences of the effort to promote ideological unity in a rigid and doctrinaire version of the American dream that led to excesses threatening the principles of democracy itself.

Origins of the Cold War

The Cold War developed by degrees. It stemmed from divergent views about dominance of the post–World War II world as the colonial empires in Asia, Africa, and the Middle East began to crumble. The United States, strong and secure, was intent on spreading its vision of freedom and free trade around the world to maintain its economic hegemony. The Soviet Union, concerned about security after a devastating war, demanded politically sympathetic neighbors on its borders to preserve its own autonomy. Suppressed during World War II, these differences now surfaced in a virulent Soviet–American confrontation.

The American Stance

The United States emerged from World War II more powerful than any nation ever before, and it sought to use that might to achieve a world order that could sustain American aims. American policymakers, following in Woodrow Wilson's footsteps, hoped to spread the values—liberty, equality, and democracy—underpinning the American dream. They did not always recognize that what they considered universal truths were rooted in specific historical circumstances in their own country and might not flourish elsewhere.

At the same time, American leaders sought a world where economic enterprise could thrive. With the American economy operating at full speed as a result of the war, world markets were needed once the fighting stopped. Government officials wanted to eliminate trade barriers—imposed by the Soviet Union and other nations—to provide outlets for industrial products and for surplus farm commodities such as wheat, cotton, and tobacco. As the largest source of goods for world markets, with exports totaling $14 billion in 1947, the United States required open channels for growth to continue. Americans assumed that their prosperity would benefit the rest of the world, even when other nations disagreed.

Soviet Aims

The Soviet Union formulated its own goals after World War II. Russia had usually been governed in the past by a strongly centralized, sometimes autocratic, government, and that tradition—as much as Communist ideology, with its stress on class struggle and the inevitable triumph of a proletarian state—guided Soviet policy.

During the war, the Russians had played down talk of world revolution, which they knew their allies found threatening, and had mobilized domestic support with nationalistic appeals. As the struggle drew to a close, the Soviets still said little about world conquest, emphasizing socialism within the nation itself.

Rebuilding was the first priority. Devastated by the war, Soviet agriculture and industry lay in shambles. But revival required internal security. At the same time, the Russians felt vulnerable along their western flank. Such anxieties had a historical basis, for in the early nineteenth century, Napoleon had reached the gates of Moscow. Twice in the twentieth century, invasions had come from the west, most recently when Hitler had attacked in 1941. Haunted by fears of a quick German recovery, the Soviets demanded defensible borders and neighboring regimes sympathetic to Russian aims. They insisted on military and political stability in the regions nearby.

Early Cold War Leadership

Both the United States and the Soviet Union had strong leadership in the early years of the Cold War. On the American side, presidents Harry Truman and Dwight Eisenhower accepted the centralization of authority Franklin Roosevelt had begun, as the executive branch became increasingly powerful in guiding foreign policy. In the Soviet Union, first Joseph Stalin, then Nikita Khrushchev provided equally forceful direction.

Truman and Eisenhower paid close attention to the Cold War struggle with the Soviet Union. Both subscribed to traditional American attitudes about self-determination and the superiority of American political institutions and values. Both were determined to stand firm in the face of the Soviet threat.

As World War II drew to an end, Truman grew increasingly hostile to Soviet actions. Viewing collaboration as a wartime necessity, he was uncomfortable with what he felt were Soviet designs in Eastern Europe and Asia as the struggle wound down. It was now time, he said, "to stand up to the

Soviet Propaganda

Joseph Stalin's autocratic approach to foreign and domestic affairs affronted American sensibilities. The Russian caption on this Soviet propaganda poster reads: "Under the Leadership of the Great Stalin—Forward to Communism!" What image does Stalin convey in this image?

(Hoover Institution Archives, Stanford, CA Russian & Soviet Poster Collection)

ПОД ВОДИТЕЛЬСТВОМ ВЕЛИКОГО СТАЛИНА—ВПЕРЕД К КОММУНИЗМУ!

Russians" before they solidified positions in various parts of the world.

Like Truman, Eisenhower saw communism as a monolithic force struggling for world supremacy and agreed that the Kremlin in Moscow was orchestrating subversive activity around the globe. Yet Eisenhower was more willing than Truman to practice accommodation when it served his ends.

Joseph Stalin, the Soviet leader at war's end, possessed almost absolute powers. He looked, in the words of one American diplomat, like "an old battle-scarred tiger." He had presided over ruthless purges against his opponents in the 1930s. Now he was determined to do whatever was necessary to rebuild Soviet society, if possible with Western assistance, and to keep Eastern Europe within the Russian sphere of influence.

Stalin's death in March 1953 left a power vacuum in Soviet political affairs that was eventually filled by Nikita Khrushchev, who by 1958 held the offices of both prime minister and party secretary. A crude man, Khrushchev once used his shoe to pound a table at the United Nations. During Khrushchev's regime, the Cold War continued, but for brief periods of time Soviet–American relations became less hostile.

Disillusionment with the USSR

American support for the Soviet Union faded quickly after the war. In September 1945, 54 percent of a national sample trusted the Russians to cooperate with the Americans in the postwar years. Two months later, the figure dropped to 44 percent, and by February 1946, to 35 percent.

As Americans soured on Russia, they began to equate the Nazi and Soviet systems. Just as they had in the 1930s, authors, journalists, and public officials pointed to similarities, some of them legitimate, between the regimes. Both states, they contended, maintained total control over communications and could eliminate political opposition. Both states used terror to silence dissidents, and Stalin's labor camps in Siberia could be compared with Hitler's concentration camps. After the U.S. publication in 1949 of George Orwell's frightening novel *1984*, *Life* magazine noted in an editorial that the ominous figure Big Brother was but a "mating" of Hitler and Stalin. Truman spoke for many Americans when he said in 1950 that "there isn't any difference between the totalitarian Russian government and the Hitler government. . . . They are all alike."

The lingering sense that the nation had not been quick enough to resist totalitarian aggression in the 1930s heightened American fears. Many people believed that the free world had not responded promptly when the Germans, Italians, and Japanese first caused international trouble and were determined never to repeat the same mistake.

The Troublesome Polish Question

The first clash between East and West came, even before the war ended, over Poland. Soviet demands for a government willing to accept Russian influence clashed with American hopes for a more representative structure patterned after the Western model. The Yalta Conference of February 1945 provided a loosely worded and correspondingly imprecise agreement (see Chapter 25), and when Truman assumed office, the Polish situation remained unresolved.

Truman's unbending stance on Poland was made clear in an April 1945 meeting with Soviet foreign minister Vyacheslav Molotov. Concerned that the Russians were breaking the Yalta agreements, fluid as they were, the American leader demanded a new democratic government there. Though Molotov appeared conciliatory, Truman insisted on Russian acquiescence. Truman later recalled that when Molotov protested, "I have never been talked to like that in my life," he himself retorted bluntly, "Carry out your agreements and you won't get talked to like that." Such bluntness contributed to the deterioration of Soviet–American relations.

Truman and Stalin met face-to-face for the first (and last) time at the Potsdam Conference in July 1945, the final wartime meeting of the United States, the Soviet Union, and Great Britain. There, outside devastated Berlin, the U.S. and Soviet leaders sized each other up as they considered the Russian–Polish boundary, the fate of Germany, and the American desire to obtain an unconditional surrender from Japan. It was Truman's first exposure to international diplomacy at the highest level, and it left him confident of his abilities. When he learned during the meeting of the first successful atomic bomb test in New Mexico, he became even more determined to insist that the Soviets behave in the ways he wished.

Economic Pressure on the USSR

One major source of controversy in the last stages of World War II was the question of U.S. aid to its allies. Responding to congressional pressure at home to limit foreign assistance as hostilities ended, Truman acted impulsively. Six days after V-E Day signaled the end of the European war in May 1945, he issued an executive order cutting off lend-lease supplies to the Allies. Ships heading for allied ports had to turn back in mid-ocean. Though the policy affected all nations receiving aid, it hurt the Soviet Union most of all.

The United States intended to use economic pressure in other ways as well. The USSR desperately needed financial assistance to rebuild after the war and, in January 1945, had requested a $6 billion loan. Roosevelt hedged, hoping to win concessions in return. In August, four months after FDR's death, the Russians renewed their application, but this time for only $1 billion. Truman dragged his heels, seeking to use the loan as a lever to gain access to markets in areas traditionally dominated by the Soviet Union. The United States first claimed to have lost the Soviet request, then in March 1946 indicated a willingness to consider the matter—but only if Russia pledged "nondiscrimination in world commerce." Stalin refused the offer and launched his own five-year plan instead.

Declaring the Cold War

As Soviet–American relations deteriorated, both sides stepped up their rhetorical attacks. In 1946, Stalin spoke out first, arguing that capitalism and communism were on a collision course, that a series of cataclysmic disturbances would tear the capitalist world apart, and that the Soviet system would inevitably triumph. Stalin's speech was a stark and ominous statement that worried the West. Supreme Court justice William O. Douglas called it the "declaration of World War III."

The response to Stalin's speech came not from an American but from England's former prime minister, Winston Churchill. Speaking in Fulton, Missouri, in 1946, with Truman on the platform during the address, Churchill declared that "from Stettin in the Baltic to Trieste in the Adriatic, an iron curtain has descended across the Continent." To counter the threat, he urged that a vigilant association of English-speaking peoples work to contain Soviet designs.

Containing the Soviet Union

Containment formed the basis of postwar American policy. While the fledgling United Nations, established in 1945, might have provided a forum to ease tensions, both the United States and the Soviet Union acted unilaterally, and with the aid of allies, in pursuit of their own ends.

Containment Defined

George F. Kennan, chargé d'affaires at the American embassy in the Soviet Union and an expert on Soviet matters, was primarily responsible for defining the new policy of containment. After Stalin's speech in February 1946, Kennan sent an 8,000-word telegram to the State Department. In it he argued that Soviet hostility stemmed from the "Kremlin's neurotic view of world affairs," which in turn came from the "traditional and instinctive Russian sense of insecurity." The stiff Soviet stance was not so much a response to American actions as a reflection of the Russian leaders' own efforts to maintain their autocratic rule. Russian fanaticism would not soften, regardless of how accommodating American policy became. Therefore, it had to be opposed at every turn.

Kennan's "long telegram" struck a resonant chord in Washington. Soon he published an extended analysis, under the pseudonym "Mr. X," in the prominent journal *Foreign Affairs*. "The whole Soviet governmental machine, including the mechanism of diplomacy," he wrote, "moves inexorably along the prescribed path, like a persistent toy automobile wound up and headed in a given direction, stopping only when it meets with some unanswerable force."

Many Americans agreed with Kennan that Soviet pressure had to "be contained by the adroit and vigilant application of counter-force at a series of constantly shifting geographical and political points." The concept of containment provided the philosophical justification for the hard-line stance the United States adopted.

The First Step: The Truman Doctrine

The Truman Doctrine represented the first major application of containment policy. The Soviet Union was pressuring Turkey for joint control of the Dardanelles, the passage between the Black Sea and the Mediterranean. Meanwhile, a civil war in Greece pitted Communist elements against the ruling English-aided right-wing monarchy. Revolutionary pressures threatened to topple the Greek government.

In February 1947, Britain, still reeling from the war, informed the State Department that it could no longer give Greece and Turkey economic and military aid. Truman administration officials willing to move into the void knew they needed bipartisan support to accomplish such a major policy shift. A conservative Congress wanted smaller budgets and lower taxes rather than massive and expensive aid programs. Senator Arthur Vandenberg of Michigan, a key Republican, aware of the need for bipartisanship, told top policymakers that they had to begin "scaring hell out of the country" if they wanted support for a bold new containment policy.

Undersecretary of State Dean Acheson took the lead. Meeting with congressional leaders, he declared that "like apples in a barrel infected by one rotten one, the corruption of Greece would infect Iran and all to the east." He warned ominously that a Communist victory would "open three continents to Soviet penetration." The major powers were now "met at Armageddon," as the Soviet Union pressed forward. Only the United States had the power to resist.

On March 12, 1947, Truman told Congress, in a statement that came to be known as the Truman Doctrine, "I believe that it must be the policy of the United States to support free peoples who are resisting subjugation by armed minorities or by outside pressures." Unless the United States acted, the free world might not survive. To avert that calamity, he urged Congress to appropriate $400 million for military and economic aid to Turkey and Greece.

Not everyone approved of Truman's request. Autocratic regimes controlled Greece and Turkey, some observers pointed out. And where was the proof that Stalin had a hand in the Greek conflict? Others warned that the United States could not by itself stop communist encroachment in all parts of the world. Nonetheless, Congress passed Truman's foreign aid bill. In assuming that Americans could police the globe, the Truman Doctrine was a major step in the advent of the Cold War.

The Next Steps: The Marshall Plan, NATO, and NSC-68

The next step for American policymakers involved sending extensive economic aid for postwar recovery in Western Europe. At the war's end, most of Europe was economically and politically unstable, thereby offering inviting opportunities for communism to take hold. In

The Contagion of Communism

Americans in the early postwar years were afraid that communism was a contagious disease spreading around the globe. In this picture from the spring of 1946, *Time* magazine pictured the relentless spread of an infection that would need to be contained. Why would such a map seem frightening to people who looked at it?

(© 1946 Time, Inc. Reprinted by permission.) (The Art Archive)

France and Italy, large Communist parties grew stronger and refused to cooperate with established governments. In such circumstances, U.S. officials believed, the Soviet Union might easily intervene. Decisive action was needed, for as the new secretary of state, George Marshall, declared, "The patient is sinking while the doctors deliberate." Bolstering the European economy to provide markets for American goods provided another motive for action. Excellent customers earlier, Western Europeans in the aftermath of the war were able to purchase less at a time when the United States was producing more.

Marshall revealed the administration's willingness to assist European recovery in a Harvard University commencement address in June 1947. He asked all troubled European nations to draw up an aid program that the United States could support, a program "directed not against any country or doctrine but against hunger, poverty, desperation, and chaos." Soviet-bloc countries were welcome to participate, Marshall announced, aware that their involvement was unlikely since they would have to disclose economic records to join.

The proposed program would assist the ravaged nations, provide the United States with needed markets, and advance the nation's ideological aims. The Marshall Plan and the Truman Doctrine, Truman noted, were "two halves of the same walnut."

Responding quickly to Marshall's invitation, the Western European nations worked out the details of massive requests. In early 1948, Congress committed $13 billion over a period of four years to 16 cooperating nations. But not all Americans supported the Marshall Plan. Henry A. Wallace, former vice president and secretary of agriculture, called the scheme the "Martial Plan" and argued that it was another step toward war. Some members of Congress feared spreading American resources too thin. But most legislators approved, and the containment policy moved forward another step.

Closely related to the Marshall Plan was a concerted Western effort to integrate a rebuilt Germany into a reviving Europe. At the war's end, Allied leaders had agreed to divide the defeated Nazi nation and its capital, Berlin, into four occupation zones (Soviet, American, British, and French). Allied leaders intended the division of both Germany and Berlin to be temporary, until a permanent peace treaty could be signed, but the lines of demarcation became rigid. With the onset of the Cold War and the growing Soviet domination of Eastern Europe, the West became worried and moved to fill the vacuum in Central Europe to counter the Russian threat. In late 1946, the Americans and British merged their zones for economic purposes and began assigning administrative duties to Germans. By mid-1947, despite French fears of a resurgent Germany, the process of rebuilding German industry in the combined Western

sector was underway. Meanwhile, increasingly rigid separation divided Berlin into two separate cities.

The Soviet Union was furious at what it regarded as a violation of the wartime agreement to act together. In mid-1948, the Soviets became irritated at an effort to introduce a new currency for the combined Western zones, a first step toward the creation of a separate West German nation, that would include the western part of divided Berlin, located within the Soviet-controlled eastern part of Germany. A crisis erupted when the Soviets attempted to force the Western powers out of Berlin by refusing to allow them land access to their part of the city and banning all shipments through eastern Germany. In what became known as the Berlin airlift, the United States and the British Royal Air Force flew supplies to the beleaguered Berliners. Over the next year, more than 200,000 flights provided 13,000 tons daily of food, fuel, and other necessary materials. The airlift proved to be a public relations disaster for the Soviet Union, a triumph for the West. The Soviets finally ended the blockade, but Berlin remained a focal point of conflict, and there were now two separate German states: the Federal Republic of Germany, or West Germany, and the German Democratic Republic, or East Germany.

The next major link in the containment strategy was the creation of a military alliance in Europe in 1949 to complement the economic program. After the Soviets tightened their control of Hungary and Czechoslovakia, the United States took the lead in establishing the North Atlantic Treaty Organization (NATO). Twelve nations formed the alliance, vowing that an attack against any one member would be considered an attack against all, to be met by appropriate armed force.

The Senate, long opposed to such military pacts, approved this time. In his presidential farewell address in 1796, George Washington had warned against "entangling alliances," and the United States had long heeded his warning. Now the nation established its first military treaty ties with Europe since the American Revolution. Congress also voted military aid for its NATO allies. The Cold War had softened long-standing American reluctance to become closely involved in European affairs.

Two dramatic events in 1949—the Communist victory in the Chinese civil war and the Russian detonation of an atomic device—shocked the United States. The Communist victory in China was frightening enough, but the erosion of the American atomic monopoly was horrifying. Although American scientists had understood that, once the secret of the atom had been unlocked, the Soviets would be able to create a bomb of their own in several years, many top policymakers believed it would take the less technologically advanced Russians at least a decade and a half to do so. President Truman thought they might never be able to accomplish such a feat at all. In September 1949, an air force reconnaissance plane picked up air samples with a radioactivity content that revealed the Soviets had tested their own bomb, just four years after the United States had ushered in the atomic age. Now a nuclear arms race beckoned. Truman requested a full-fledged review of U.S. foreign and defense policy. The National Security Council, organized in 1947 to provide policy coordination, produced a document called NSC-68, which shaped U.S. policy for the next 20 years.

NSC-68 built on the Cold War rhetoric of the Truman Doctrine, describing challenges facing the United States in cataclysmic terms. "The issues that face us are momentous," the paper said, "involving the fulfillment or destruction not only of this Republic but of civilization itself." Conflict between East and West, the document assumed, was unavoidable, for amoral Soviet objectives ran totally counter to U.S. aims. Negotiation was useless, for the Soviets could never be trusted to bargain in good faith.

Cold War Europe in 1950

This map shows the rigid demarcation between East and West during the Cold War. Although there were a number of neutral countries in Europe, the other nations found themselves in a standoff, as each side tried to contain the possible advances of the other. The small insert map in the upper right-hand corner shows the division of Berlin that paralleled the division of Germany itself after World War II. How widespread was the policy of neutrality in Cold War Europe? How powerful was the NATO bloc? How easily could one side move against the other in divided Europe?

NSC-68 then argued that if the United States hoped to meet the Soviet challenge, it must increase defense spending from the $13 billion set for 1950 to as much as $50 billion per year and increase the percentage of its budget allotted to defense from 5 percent to 20 percent. The costs were huge but necessary if the free world was to survive.

Containment in the 1950s

Containment, the keystone of American policy throughout the Truman years, was the rationale for the Truman Doctrine, the Marshall Plan, NATO, and NSC-68. Because this policy required detailed and up-to-date information about Communist moves, the government relied increasingly on the Central Intelligence Agency (CIA). Established by the National Security Act of 1947, the CIA conducted espionage in foreign lands, some of it visible, more of it secret. With President Eisenhower's approval, by 1957, 80 percent of the CIA's budget went toward covert activities. More and more, Eisenhower relied on clandestine CIA actions to undermine foreign governments, subsidize friendly newspapers in distant lands, and assist those who supported the U.S. stance in the Cold War.

The civil rights movement that was gaining momentum in the 1950s also affected Cold War policy. American policymakers were aware of the impact of stories about racial discrimination in other nations, particularly nations moving toward independence in sub-Saharan Africa. In propaganda aimed abroad, U.S. leaders sought to portray the domestic civil rights movement in the best possible light.

At the same time, the administration reassessed the impact of the containment policy itself, especially in light of criticism that it was too cautious to counter the threat of communism. For most of Eisenhower's two terms, John Foster Dulles was secretary of state. A devout Presbyterian, he sought to move beyond containment and to counter the "Godless terrorism" of communism with a holy crusade to promote democracy and to free the countries under Soviet domination. Instead of advocating containment, the United States should make it "publicly known that it wants and expects liberation to occur." Dulles also advocated immediate retaliation in the face of hostile Soviet ventures: "There is one solution and only one: that is for the free world to develop the will and organize the means to retaliate instantly against open aggression by Red armies, so that, if it occurred anywhere, we could and would strike back where it hurts, by means of our own choosing."

Eisenhower's own rhetoric was equally strong. In his 1953 inaugural address, he declared, "Forces of good and evil are massed and armed and opposed as rarely before in history. Freedom is pitted against slavery, lightness against the dark." Yet he was more conciliatory than Dulles and recognized the impossibility of changing the governments of the USSR's satellites. In mid-1953, when East Germans mounted anti-Soviet demonstrations, in a challenge that foreshadowed the revolt against communism three and a half decades later, the United States maintained its distance. In 1956, when Hungarian "freedom fighters" rose up against Russian domination, the United States again stood back as Soviet forces smashed the rebels. Because Western action could have precipitated a more general conflict, Eisenhower refused to translate rhetoric into action. Throughout the 1950s, the policy of containment remained in effect.

Containment in Asia, the Middle East, and Latin America

In a dramatic departure from its history of noninvolvement, the United States extended the policy of containment to meet challenges around the globe. Colonial empires were disintegrating, and countries seeking and attaining their independence now found themselves caught in the midst of the superpower struggle. In Asia, the Middle East, and Latin America, the United States discovered the tremendous appeal of communism as a social and political system in emerging nations and found that ever-greater efforts were required to advance American aims.

The Shock of the Chinese Revolution

The Communist victory in the Chinese civil war in 1949 strengthened the U.S. commitment to global containment. An ally during World War II, China had struggled against the Japanese, while simultaneously fighting a bitter civil war deeply rooted in the Chinese past—in widespread poverty, disease, oppression by the landlord class, and national humiliation at the hands of foreign powers. Mao Zedong (Mao Tsetung)*, founder of a branch of the Communist party, gathered followers who wished to reshape China in a distinctive Marxist mold. Opposing the Communists were the Nationalists, led by Jiang Jieshi (Chiang Kai-shek) who wanted to preserve their power and governmental leadership. By the early 1940s, Jiang's inefficient and corrupt regime was exhausted. Mao's movement, meanwhile, grew stronger during the Second World War as Mao opposed the Japanese invaders and won the loyalty of Chinese peasants. Mao finally prevailed, as Jiang fled in 1949 to the island of Taiwan (Formosa).

---

*Chinese names are rendered in their modern *pinyin* spelling. At first occurrence, the older but perhaps more familiar spelling (usually Wade-Giles) is given in parentheses.

Recovering the Past

PUBLIC OPINION POLLS

In recent years, historians have used a new source of evidence: the public opinion poll. People have always been concerned with what others think, and leaders have often sought to frame their behavior according to the preferences of the populace. As techniques of assessing the mind of the public have become more sophisticated, the poll has emerged as an integral part of the analysis of social and political life. Polls now measure opinion on many questions—social, cultural, intellectual, political, and diplomatic. Because of polls' increasing importance, it is useful to know how to use them in an effort to understand and recover the past.

The principle of polling is not new. In 1824, the *Harrisburg Pennsylvanian* sought to predict the winner of that year's presidential race, and in the 1880s, the *Boston Globe* sent reporters to selected precincts on election night to forecast final returns. In 1916, *Literary Digest* began conducting postcard polls to predict political results. By the 1930s, Elmo Roper and George Gallup had further developed the field of market research and public opinion polling. Notwithstanding an embarrassing mistake by *Literary Digest* in predicting a Landon victory over FDR in 1936, polling had become a scientific enterprise by World War II.

According to Gallup, a poll is not magic but "merely an instrument for gauging public opinion," especially the views of those often unheard. As Elmo Roper said, the poll is "one of the few ways through which the so-called common man can be articulate." Polling, therefore, is a valuable way to recover the attitudes, beliefs, and voices of ordinary people.

Yet certain cautions should be observed. Like all instruments of human activity, polls are imperfect and may even be dangerous. Historians using information from polls need to be aware of how large the samples were, when the interviewing was done, and how opinions might have been molded by the form of the poll itself. Questions can be poorly phrased. Some hint at the desirable answer or plant ideas in the minds of those interviewed. Polls sometimes provide ambiguous responses that can be interpreted many ways. More seriously, some critics worry that human freedom itself is threatened by the pollsters' manipulative and increasingly accurate predictive techniques.

Despite these limitations, polls have become an ever-present part of American life. In the late 1940s and early 1950s, Americans were polled frequently about topics ranging from foreign aid, the United Nations, and the

Foreign Policy Polls

DECEMBER 2, 1949—ATOM BOMB
Now that Russia has the atom bomb, do you think another war is more likely or less likely?

More likely	45%
Less likely	28%
Will make no difference	17%
No opinion	10%

BY EDUCATION
College

More likely	36%
Will make no difference	23%
Less likely	35%
No opinion	6%

High School

More likely	44%
Will make no difference	19%
Less likely	28%
No opinion	9%

Grade School

More likely	50%
Will make no difference	12%
Less likely	26%
No opinion	12%

MAY 1, 1950—NATIONAL DEFENSE
Do you think United States Government spending on national defense should be increased, decreased, or remain about the same?

Increased	63%
Same	24%
Decreased	7%
No opinion	6%

SEPTEMBER 18, 1953—INDOCHINA
The United States is now sending war materials to help the French fight the Communists in Indochina. Would you approve or disapprove of sending United States soldiers to take part in the fighting there?

Approve	8%
Disapprove	85%
No opinion	7%

JANUARY 11, 1950—RUSSIA
As you hear and read about Russia these days, do you believe Russia is trying to build herself up to be the ruling power of the world—or is Russia just building up protection against being attacked in another war?

Rule the world	70%
Protect herself	18%
No opinion	12%

BY EDUCATION
College

Rule the world	73%
Protect herself	21%
No opinion	6%

High School

Rule the world	72%
Protect herself	18%
No opinion	10%

Grade School

Rule the world	67%
Protect herself	17%
No opinion	16%

FEBRUARY 12, 1951—ATOMIC WARFARE
If the United States gets into an all-out war with Russia, do you think we should drop atom bombs on Russia first—or do you think we should use the atom bomb only if it is used on us?

Drop A-bomb first	66%
Only if used on us	19%
No opinion	15%

The greatest difference was between men and women—72% of the men questioned favored our dropping the bomb first, compared to 61% of the women.

Domestic Policy Polls

OCTOBER 29, 1949—WOMEN IN POLITICS

If the party whose candidate you most often support nominated a woman for President of the United States, would you vote for her if she seemed qualified for the job?

Yes	48%
No	48%
No opinion	4%

BY SEX
Men

Yes	45%
No	50%
No opinion	5%

Women

Yes	51%
No	46%
No opinion	3%

BY POLITICAL AFFILIATION
Democrats

Yes	50%
No	48%
No opinion	2%

Republicans

Yes	46%
No	50%
No opinion	4%

Would you vote for a woman for Vice President of the United States if she seemed qualified for the job?

Yes	53%
No	43%
No opinion	4%

MAY 5, 1950—MOST IMPORTANT PROBLEM

What do you think is the most important problem facing the entire country today?

War, threat of war	40%
Atomic bomb control	6%
Economic problems, living costs, inflation, taxes	15%
Strikes and labor troubles	4%
Corruption in government	3%
Unemployment	10%
Housing	3%
Communism	8%
Others	11%

JULY 12, 1950—PROFESSIONS

Suppose a young man came to you and asked your advice about taking up a profession. Assuming that he was qualified to enter any of these professions, which one of them would you first recommend to him?

Doctor of medicine	29%
Government worker	6%
Engineer, builder	16%
Professor, teacher	5%
Business executive	8%
Banker	4%
Clergyman	8%
Dentist	4%
Lawyer	8%
Veterinarian	3%
None, don't know	9%

JULY 15, 1950—PROFESSIONS

Suppose a young girl came to you and asked your advice about taking up a profession. Assuming that she was qualified to enter any of these professions, which one of them would you first recommend?

CHOICE OF WOMEN

Nurse	33%
Teacher	15%
Secretary	8%
Social service worker	8%
Dietitian	7%
Dressmaker	4%
Beautician	4%
Airline stewardess	3%
Actress	3%
Journalist	2%
Musician	2%
Model	2%
Librarian	2%
Medical, dental technician	1%
Others	2%
Don't know	4%

The views of men on this subject were nearly identical with those of women.

---

occupation of Germany and Japan to labor legislation, child punishment, and whether women should wear slacks in public (39 percent of men said no, as did 49 percent of women). Such topics as the first use of nuclear arms, presidential popularity, national defense, and U.S. troop intervention in a troubled area of the world remain as pertinent today as they were then.

Reflecting on the Past A number of the polls included here deal with foreign policy during the Cold War in the early 1950s. How did people respond to Soviet nuclear capability? How did they regard Russian intentions and the appropriate American response? How do you analyze the results of these polls? What do you think is the significance of rating responses by levels of education? In what ways are the questions "loaded"? How might the results of these polls influence American foreign policy? What do you think is significant about the Indochina poll? These polls show the challenge-and-response nature of the Cold War. How do you think Americans would respond today to these questions?

Polls also shed light on domestic issues. Consider the poll on professions for young men and women taken in 1950. What does it tell us about the attitudes of the pollster on appropriate careers for men and women? Why do you think both men and women had nearly identical views on this subject? How do you think people today would answer these questions? Would they be presented in the same way? Also observe the poll on women in politics. To what extent have attitudes on this issue changed in the intervening years? ■

A New Chinese Leader
Mao Zedong, chairman of the Chinese Communist party, was a powerful and popular leader who drove Jiang Jieshi from power in 1949 and established a stronghold over the People's Republic of China he created at that time. How was Mao able to defeat his opponents and win the revolutionary war?

(Bettmann/CORBIS)

The United States failed to understand issues that were part of the long internal conflict in China or the immense popular support Mao had garnered. As the Communist army moved toward victory, the *New York Times* termed Mao's party a "nauseous force," a "compact little oligarchy dominated by Moscow's nominees." Mao's proclamation of the People's Republic of China on October 1, 1949, fanned fears of Russian domination, for he had already announced his regime's support for the Soviet Union against the "imperialist" United States.

Events in China caused near hysteria in America. Even before Mao's victory, the State Department issued a 1,000-page document entitled *The China White Paper*, which outlined the background of the struggle and argued that the United States was powerless to alter the results. "The unfortunate but inescapable fact is that the ominous result of the civil war in China was beyond the control of the government of the United States," the *White Paper* declared. Staunch anti-Communists nonetheless argued that Truman and the United States were to blame for the Nationalist defeat because they failed to provide Jiang

with sufficient support. Four senators called the *White Paper* a "whitewash of a wishful, do-nothing policy which has succeeded only in placing Asia in danger of Soviet conquest with its ultimate threat to the peace of the world and our own national security." Secretary of State Dean Acheson briefly considered granting diplomatic recognition to the new Chinese government but backed off after the Communists seized American property, harassed American citizens, and openly allied China with the USSR. Like other Americans, Acheson mistakenly viewed the Chinese as Soviet puppets.

Tension with China increased during the Korean War (1950–1953) and again in 1954 when Mao's government began shelling Nationalist positions on the offshore islands of Quemoy and Matsu. Eisenhower, elected U.S. president in 1952, was committed to defending the Nationalists on Taiwan from a Communist attack, but he was unwilling to risk war over the islands.

Stalemate in the Korean War

The Korean War highlighted growing U.S. concern about Asia. The conflict in Korea stemmed from tensions lingering after World War II. Korea, long under Japanese control, hoped for independence after Japan's defeat. But after the atomic bombs dropped on Japan, the Allies, seeking to bring a rapid end to the Pacific struggle and expedite the transition to peace, temporarily divided Korea along the 38th parallel. The Soviet–American line, initially intended as a matter of military convenience, hardened after 1945, just as a similar division became rigid in Germany. In time, the Soviets set up a Korean government in the north and the Americans a second Korean government in the south. Though the major powers left Korea by the end of the decade, they continued to support the regimes they had created. Each Korean government hoped to reunify the country on its own terms.

North Korea moved first. On June 25, 1950, North Korean forces crossed the 38th parallel and invaded South Korea. While the North Koreans used Soviet-built tanks, they operated on their own initiative. Kim Il Sung, the North Korean leader, had visited Moscow earlier and gained Soviet acquiescence in the idea of an attack, but both the planning and the implementation occurred in Korea.

Taken by surprise and certain that Russia had masterminded the North Korean offensive to test the U.S. containment policy, Truman told the American public that "the attack upon Korea makes it plain beyond all doubt that communism has passed beyond the use of subversion to conquer independent nations and will now use armed invasion and war." He later reflected in his memoirs: "If this was allowed to go unchallenged it would mean a third world war, just

General MacArthur

General Douglas MacArthur was a superb tactician but a supremely egotistical commander of UN forces in Korea, where this picture was taken in the first year of the Korean War. Eventually his arrogance led him to challenge Truman's policy, whereupon the president relieved him of his command. How does this image convey MacArthur's strong-willed approach?

(Time Life Pictures/Getty Images)

as similar incidents had brought on the second world war."

Truman directed General Douglas MacArthur, head of the American occupation forces in Japan, to supply South Korea. The United States also went to the United Nations Security Council and secured a unanimous resolution branding North Korea an aggressor, then another resolution calling on members of the organization to assist South Korea in repelling aggression and restoring peace. MacArthur became leader of all UN forces in this largest UN operation to date. The United States and South Korea provided more than 90 percent of the personnel, but 15 other nations participated in the UN effort.

Air and naval forces, then ground forces, went into battle south of the 38th parallel. Following a daring amphibious invasion that pushed the North Koreans back to the former boundary line, UN troops crossed

the 38th parallel, hoping to reunify Korea under an American-backed government. Despite Chinese signals that this movement toward their border threatened their security, the UN troops pressed on. In October, Chinese troops appeared briefly in battle, then disappeared. The next month, the Chinese mounted a full-fledged counterattack, which pushed the UN forces back below the dividing line.

The resulting stalemate provoked a bitter struggle between MacArthur and Truman. The brilliant but arrogant general called for retaliatory air strikes against China. He faced opposition from General Omar Bradley, chairman of the Joint Chiefs of Staff, who declared, "Frankly, in the opinion of the Joint Chiefs of Staff, this strategy would involve us in the wrong war, at the wrong place, at the wrong time, with the wrong enemy," and from President Truman, who remained committed to conducting a limited war. MacArthur finally went too far. In April 1951, he argued that the American approach in Korea was wrong and asserted publicly that "there is no substitute for victory." Truman had no choice but to relieve the general for insubordination. The decision outraged many Americans. After the stunning victories of World War II, limited war was frustrating and difficult to understand.

The Korean War dragged on into Eisenhower's presidency. Campaigning in 1952, Ike promised to go to Korea, and three weeks after his election, he did so. When UN truce talks bogged down in May 1953, the new administration privately threatened the Chinese with the use of atomic weapons. This threat prompted the renewal of negotiations, and on July 27, 1953, an armistice was signed. After three long years, the unpopular war ended.

American involvement carried a heavy price: more than 33,000 Americans killed in action with more than 142,000 American casualties in all. The other 15 UN nations involved in the struggle accounted for another 17,000 casualties. But those figures paled in comparison to Korean casualties: as many as 2 million Koreans dead and countless others wounded and maimed.

The war significantly changed American attitudes and institutions. For the first time, American forces fought in racially integrated units. As commander in chief, Truman had ordered the integration of the armed forces in 1948, over the opposition of many generals, and African Americans became part of all military units. Their successful performance led to acceptance of military integration.

During the Korean War military expenditures soared from $13 billion in 1950 to about $47 billion three years later, as defense spending followed the guidelines proposed in NSC-68. In the process, the United States accepted the demands of permanent

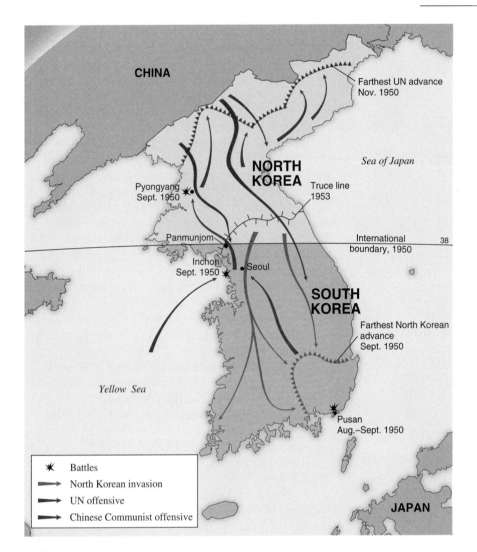

The Korean War

This map shows the ebb and flow of the Korean War. North Korea crossed the thirty-eighth parallel first, then the UN offensive drove the North Koreans close to the Chinese border, and finally the Chinese Communists entered the war and drove the UN forces back below the thirty-eighth parallel. The armistice signed at Panmunjom in 1953 provided a dividing line very close to the prewar line. How far did both North Korea and South Korea penetrate into the territory of the other nation? What role did China play in the Korean War?

mobilization. Whereas the military absorbed less than one-third of the federal budget in 1950, a decade later, it took half. More than a million military personnel were stationed around the world. At home, an increasingly powerful military establishment became closely tied to corporate and scientific communities and created a military–industrial complex that employed 3.5 million Americans by 1960.

The Korean War had significant political effects as well. In September 1951, the United States signed a peace treaty with Japan and came to rely on the Japanese to maintain the balance of power in the Pacific. At the same time, the struggle poisoned relations with the People's Republic of China, which

remained unrecognized by the United States, and ensured a diplomatic standoff that lasted more than 20 years.

Vietnam: The Roots of Conflict

The commitment to stopping the spread of communism led to the massive U.S. involvement in Vietnam. That struggle tore the United States apart, wrought enormous damage in Southeast Asia, and finally forced a reevaluation of U.S. Cold War policies.

The roots of the war extended far back in the past. Indochina—the part of Southeast Asia that included Vietnam, Laos, and Cambodia—had been a

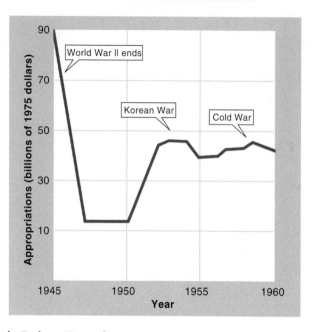

Defense Expenditures, 1945–1960
Defense spending plummeted after World War II, only to quadruple with the onset of the Korean War. After that increase, spending levels never dropped dramatically, even after the end of the war.

Source: U.S. Bureau of the Census.

French colony since the mid-nineteenth century. During World War II, Japan occupied the region but an independence movement, led by the Communist organizer and revolutionary Ho Chi Minh, sought to expel the Japanese conquerors from Vietnam. In 1945, the Allied powers faced the decision of how to deal with Ho and his nationalist crusade.

France was determined to regain its colony as a way of preserving its status as a great power. Meanwhile, Ho established the Democratic Republic of Vietnam in 1945. The new government's declaration of independence echoed its American counterpart, declaring: "All men are created equal. They are endowed by their Creator with certain inalienable rights, among these are Life, Liberty and the pursuit of Happiness." Despite widespread popular support, the United States refused to recognize the new government.

A long, bitter struggle broke out between French and Vietnamese forces, which became entangled with the larger Cold War. President Truman was less concerned than Franklin Roosevelt had been about ending colonialism but he was intent on checking Soviet power. He needed France to balance the Soviets in Europe, where he wanted French support for America's policy in Germany and as a member of NATO, and that meant cooperating with France in Vietnam.

Although Ho did not have close ties to the Soviet Union and was committed to his independent nationalist effort, Truman and his advisers, who saw communism

as a monolithic force, assumed wrongly that Ho took orders from Moscow. Hence, in 1950, the United States formally recognized the French puppet government in Vietnam, and by 1954, the United States was paying more than three-quarters of the cost of France's Indochina war.

After Eisenhower took office, France's position in Southeast Asia deteriorated. Secretary of State Dulles was eager to assist the French, and the chairman of the Joint Chiefs of Staff even contemplated using nuclear weapons, but Eisenhower refused to intervene directly. He understood the lack of American support for intervention in that far-off land. Senator John F. Kennedy spoke for many of his congressional colleagues when he declared in 1954: "I am frankly of the belief that no amount of American military assistance in Indochina can conquer an enemy which is everywhere and at the same time nowhere, 'an enemy of the people' which has the sympathy and covert support of the people." As a French fortress at Dien Bien Phu in the north of Vietnam finally fell to Ho's forces, an international conference in Geneva sought to prevent Ho Chi Minh from gaining control of the entire country. The final declaration of the conference divided Vietnam along the 17th parallel, with elections promised in 1956 to unify the country and determine its political fate.

Two separate Vietnamese states emerged. Ho Chi Minh held power in the north, while in the south, Ngo Dinh Diem, a fierce anti-Communist who had been in exile in the United States, returned to form a government. Diem enjoyed the full support of the United States, which saw him as a way of securing stability in Southeast Asia and avoiding further communist incursions. When he decided not to hold the elections mandated in the Geneva accord, the United States backed him in that decision. In the next few years, American aid increased and military advisers—675 by the time Eisenhower left office—began to assist the South Vietnamese. The United States had taken its first steps toward direct involvement in a ruinous war halfway around the world that would escalate out of control.

The Creation of Israel and Its Impact on the Middle East

The creation of the state of Israel became intertwined with larger Cold War issues. Jews had longed for a homeland for years, and the Zionist movement had sought a place in Palestine, in the Middle East, since the latter part of the nineteenth century. Jewish settlers who began to gravitate to Palestine were not welcomed by the Turks, who dominated the region, or by the British, who exercised control after World War I.

Father Ho

Ho Chi Minh waged a long struggle first against France, then Japan, and finally the United States for the independence of Vietnam. The Vietnamese people viewed him as the father of the country. How does this picture of him with children contribute to that impression?

(Library of Congress [LC-USZ62–126864])

Then the Holocaust—and the slaughter of 6 million Jews—during World War II created new pressure for a Jewish state. The unwillingness—and inability—of the Western powers to intervene in time to stop the Nazi genocide created a groundswell of support, particularly among American Jews, for a Jewish homeland in the Arab-dominated Middle East.

In 1948, the fledgling United Nations attempted to partition Palestine into an Arab state and a Jewish state. Truman officially recognized the new state of Israel 15 minutes after it was proclaimed. But bitter animosities persisted between Arabs, who believed they had been robbed of their territory, and Jews, who felt they had finally regained a homeland after the horrors of the Holocaust. As Americans looked on, Arab forces invaded Israel, in the first of a series of conflicts that continues to the present day. The Israelis, fighting for the survival of their new nation, won the war with a truce mediated by African American diplomat Ralph Bunche, and added territory

to what the UN had given them. But struggles erupted in 1967 and again in 1973 with adversaries who did not recognize Israel's right to exist.

While sympathetic to Israel, the United States tried at the same time to maintain stability in the rest of the region. The Middle East had tremendous strategic importance as the supplier of oil for industrialized nations. In 1953, the CIA helped the Iranian army overthrow the government of Mohammed Mossadegh, which had nationalized oil wells formerly under British control, and placed the shah of Iran securely on the throne. After the coup, British and American companies regained command of the wells.

As it cultivated close ties with Israel, the United States also tried to maintain the friendship of oil-rich Arab states or, at the very least, to prevent them from falling into the Soviet orbit. In Egypt, the policy ran into trouble when Arab nationalist General Gamal Abdel Nasser planned a huge dam on the Nile River to produce electric power and proclaimed his country's neutrality in the Cold War. Although Secretary of State Dulles offered U.S. financial support for the Aswan Dam project, Nasser also began discussions with the Soviet Union. A furious Dulles, who believed that neutralism was immoral, withdrew the American offer. Left without funds for the dam, in July 1956, Nasser seized and nationalized the British-controlled Suez Canal and closed it to Israeli ships. Now Great Britain was enraged and Europe worried about a continuing supply of oil.

In the fall, Israeli, British, and French military forces invaded Egypt. Eisenhower, who had not been consulted, was irate. When told that paratroopers were about to land near the canal, he said, "I think it's the biggest error of our time, outside of losing China." Realizing that the attack might push Nasser into Moscow's arms, the United States sponsored a UN resolution condemning the attack and Dulles persuaded other nations not to send petroleum to England and France. These actions persuaded the invaders to withdraw.

Before long, the United States again intervened in the Middle East. Concerned about the region's stability, the president declared in 1957, in what came to be called the Eisenhower Doctrine, that "the existing vacuum in the Middle East must be filled by the United States before it is filled by Russia." A year later, he authorized the landing of 14,000 soldiers in Lebanon to prop up a right-wing government challenged from within.

Restricting Revolt in Latin America

The Cold War also led to intervention in Latin America. In 1954, Dulles sniffed Communist activity in Guatemala, and Eisenhower ordered CIA support for a coup aimed at ousting the elected government of reform-minded Colonel Jacobo Arbenz Guzmán. It trained and equipped Guatemalans to overthrow the legitimate regime, which had appropriated property of the American-owned United Fruit Company. The right-wing takeover succeeded, established a military dictatorship that responded to U.S. wishes, and restored the property of the United Fruit Company. These actions demonstrated again the shortsighted American commitment to stability and private investment, whatever the internal effect or ultimate cost. The interference in Guatemala fed anti-American sentiment throughout Latin America.

In 1959, when Fidel Castro overthrew the dictatorship of Fulgencio Batista in Cuba, the shortsightedness of American policy became even clearer. Nationalism and the thrust for social reform were powerful forces in Latin America, as in the rest of the developing world formerly dominated by European powers. As Milton Eisenhower, Ike's brother and adviser, pointed out: "Revolution is inevitable in Latin America. The people are angry. They are shackled to the past with bonds of ignorance, injustice, and poverty. And they no longer accept as universal or inevitable the oppressive prevailing order." But when Castro confiscated American property in Cuba, the Eisenhower administration cut off exports and severed diplomatic ties. In response, Cuba turned to the Soviet Union for support.

Atomic Weapons and the Cold War

Throughout the Cold War, the atomic bomb cast an ominous cloud over all diplomatic discussions and military initiatives. Atomic weapons were destructive enough, but the development of hydrogen bombs in both the United States and the Soviet Union ushered in an age of overkill.

Sharing the Secret of the Bomb

The United States, with British aid, had built the first atomic bomb and attempted to conceal the project from its wartime ally, the Soviet Union. Soviet spies, however, discovered that the Americans were working on the bomb, and, even before the war was over, the Soviets had initiated a program to create a bomb of their own.

The United States briefly considered sharing the atomic secret. Just before he retired, Secretary of War Henry L. Stimson pushed for cooperating with the Soviet Union rather than acting unilaterally. Recognizing the futility of trying to cajole the Russians while "having this weapon ostentatiously on our hip," he warned that "their suspicions and their distrust of our purposes and motives will increase." Only mutual accommodation could bring international cooperation.

Yet as negotiations to develop an international arms control system broke down, the United States gave up on the idea of sharing atomic secrets. Intent on retaining the technological advantage until the creation of a "foolproof method of control," Truman endorsed the Atomic Energy Act, passed by Congress in 1946. It established the Atomic Energy Commission (AEC) to supervise all atomic energy development in the United States and, under the tightest security, to regulate all nuclear activity in the nation at large. It also opened the way to a nuclear arms race once Russia developed its own bomb.

Nuclear Proliferation

As the atomic bomb found its way into popular culture, Americans at first showed more excitement than fear. In Los Angeles, the "Atombomb Dancers" wiggled at the Burbank Burlesque Theater. In 1946, the Buchanan Brothers released a record called "Atomic Power," noting the brimstone fire from heaven that was "given by the mighty hand of God." David E. Lilienthal, first chairman of the AEC, recalled that the atom "had us bewitched. . . . It would either destroy us all or it would bring about the millennium."

Anxiety lurking beneath the exuberance did not surface dramatically as long as the United States held a nuclear monopoly. Then, in September 1949, when Americans learned that the Soviet Union had tested its own bomb, the security of being the world's only atomic power vanished. People wondered whether the Soviet test foreshadowed a nuclear attack and speculated when it might come. The editors of the *Bulletin of the Atomic Scientists,* the nation's foremost publication dealing with nuclear affairs, moved the minute hand of the "doomsday clock" on the journal's cover from seven minutes before midnight to three minutes before midnight to reflect their fear of proliferation.

In early 1950, Truman authorized the development of a new hydrogen superbomb, potentially far more devastating than the atomic bomb. By 1953, both the United States and the Soviet Union had unlocked the secret of fusion—joining atoms together in a reaction like that on the surface of the sun. A far more powerful reaction could do far more damage. After the 1954 BRAVO test, AEC chairman Lewis Strauss admitted that "an H-bomb can be made . . . large enough to take out a city," even New York. Then, in 1957, shortly after the news that the Soviets had successfully tested their first intercontinental ballistic missile (ICBM), Americans learned that the Soviets had launched into outer space *Sputnik,* the first artificial satellite—with a rocket that could also deliver a hydrogen bomb.

The discovery of radioactive fallout added another dimension to the nuclear dilemma. Fallout became publicly known after the BRAVO blast in 1954 showered Japanese fishermen on a ship called the *Lucky Dragon* 85 miles away with radioactive dust. They became ill with radiation sickness, and several months later, one of the seamen died. The Japanese, who had been the first to experience the effects of atomic weapons, were outraged and alarmed to be the first victims of the hydrogen bomb. Everywhere people began to realize the terrible consequences of nuclear proliferation. Fallout became a serious international problem—in the words of physicist Ralph Lapp, "a peril to humanity."

Authors in both the scientific and the popular press focused attention on radioactive fallout. Radiation, Lapp observed, "cannot be felt and possesses all the terror of the unknown. It is something which evokes revulsion and helplessness—like a bubonic plague." Nevil Shute's best-selling 1957 novel *On the Beach*, and the film that followed, also sparked public awareness and fear. The story described a war that released so much radioactive waste that all life in the Northern Hemisphere disappeared, while the Southern Hemisphere awaited the same deadly fate. In 1959, when *Consumer Reports*, the popular magazine that tested and compared various products, warned of the contamination of milk with the radioactive isotope strontium-90, the public grew even more alarmed.

The discovery of fallout initiated a shelter craze. Bob Russell, a Michigan sheriff, declared that "to build a new home in this day and age without including such an obvious necessity as a fallout shelter would be like leaving out the bathroom 20 years ago." *Good Housekeeping* magazine carried a full-page editorial in November 1958 urging the construction of family shelters. More and more companies advertised ready-made shelters. *Life* magazine in 1955 featured an "H-Bomb Hideaway" for $3,000. By late 1960, the Office of Civil and Defense Mobilization estimated that a million family shelters had been built.

The Nuclear West

The bomb stimulated more than just shelter building. It sparked an enormous increase in defense spending and created a huge nuclear industry, particularly in the West. Contractors liked the region because of its anti-union attitudes; labor stability, they argued, would make it easier to meet government deadlines.

During World War II, a number of the Manhattan Project's major centers were located in the West. The plant at Hanford, Washington, was one of the most important producers of fissionable material, and the first atomic weapon had been produced at Los Alamos, New Mexico. Development in this area expanded after the war. Hanford continued to produce plutonium, a facility outside Denver made plutonium triggers for thermonuclear bombs, the new Sandia National Laboratory in Albuquerque provided the production engineering of nuclear bombs, and the Los Alamos laboratory remained a major atomic research center. In 1951, the United States opened the Nevada Test Site, 65 miles north of Las Vegas, and the facility had a major impact on the city. The Chamber of Commerce offered schedules of test shots, and the mushroom cloud became the logo for the Southern Nevada telephone directory. Satirist and songwriter Tom Lehrer highlighted the West in the song "The Wild West Is Where I Want to Be" in his first album in 1953. The first verse went:

> *Along the trail you'll find me lopin'*
> *Where the spaces are wide open,*
> *In the land of the old A.E.C.*
> *Where the scenery's attractive,*
> *And the air is radioactive,*
> *Oh, the wild west is where I want to be.*

Defense spending promoted other development as well. Naval commands had headquarters in Seattle, San Francisco, San Diego, and Honolulu. Radar sites, aimed at tracking incoming missiles, stretched all the way up to Alaska. The Boeing Company, located in Seattle, stimulated tremendous development in that city as it produced B-47 and B-52 airplanes that were the U.S. Air Force's main delivery vehicles for nuclear bombs.

"Massive Retaliation"

As Americans grappled with the implications of nuclear weapons, government policy came to depend increasingly on an atomic shield. Truman authorized the development of a nuclear arsenal but also stressed conventional forms of defense. Eisenhower was concerned with controlling the budget and cutting taxes, and his administration decided to rely on atomic weapons rather than combat forces as the key to American defense.

Secretary of State Dulles developed the policy of threatening "massive retaliation." The United States, he declared, was willing and ready to use nuclear weapons against Communist aggression on whatever targets it chose. The policy allowed troop cutbacks and promised to be cost-effective by giving "more bang for the buck."

Massive retaliation provided for an all-or-nothing response, leaving no middle course, no alternatives between nuclear war and retreat. Critics called the policy "brinkmanship" and wondered what would happen if the line was crossed in the new atomic age. Eisenhower himself was horrified when he saw reports indicating that a coordinated atomic attack could leave a nation "a smoking, radiating ruin at the end of two hours." With characteristic caution, he did his best to ensure that the rhetoric of massive retaliation did not lead to war.

Atomic Protest

As the arms race spiraled, critics demanded that it end. In 1956, Democratic presidential candidate Adlai Stevenson pointed to "the danger of poisoning the atmosphere" and called for a halt to nuclear tests. Eisenhower did not respond, but Vice President Richard Nixon called Stevenson's suggestion "catastrophic nonsense," while Dulles minimized the hazards of radiation by arguing, "From a health standpoint, there is greater danger from wearing a wrist watch with a luminous dial."

In 1957, activists organized SANE, the National Committee for a Sane Nuclear Policy. One of its most effective advertisements featured internationally known pediatrician Benjamin Spock, looking down at a little girl with a frown on his face. "Dr. Spock is worried," the caption read, and the text below amplified on his concern. "I *am* worried," he said, "not so much about

the effect of past tests but at the prospect of endless future ones. As the tests multiply, so will the damage to children—here and around the world."

Several years later, women who had worked with SANE took the protest movement a step further. To challenge continued testing, which dropped lethal radiation on all inhabitants of the globe, the protesters called on women throughout the country to suspend normal activities for a day and strike for peace. An estimated 50,000 women marched in 60 communities around the nation. Their slogans proclaimed "Let the Children Grow" and "End the Arms Race—Not the Human Race."

Pressure from many groups produced a political breakthrough and sustained it for a time. The superpowers began a voluntary moratorium on testing in the fall of 1958. It lasted until the Soviet Union resumed testing in September 1961 and the United States began again the following March.

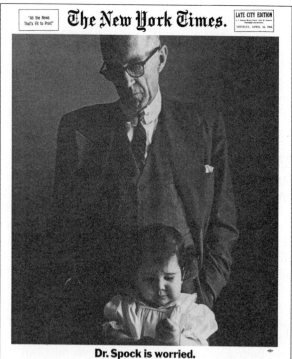

Dr. Spock is worried.

Worrying About the Future

SANE tried to get the United States, and the rest of the world, to stop testing nuclear weapons and dumping huge amounts of fallout in the atmosphere. This newspaper advertisement, which appeared in 1962, was part of the larger effort to make the world a safer place. How does this picture of noted pediatrician Dr. Benjamin Spock underscore a sense of fear?

(Records of SANE, Inc., Swarthmore College Peace Collection)

The Cold War at Home

The Cold War also affected domestic affairs and led to the creation of an internal loyalty program that seriously violated civil liberties. Fears of radical subversion made the Soviet Union appear increasingly ominous. Maps showed half the world colored red to dramatize the spread of communism. As Americans began to suspect Communist infiltration at home, some determined to root out all traces of communism inside the United States.

Truman's Loyalty Program

In mobilizing support for its containment program, the Truman administration used increasingly shrill rhetoric. For Truman, the issue confronting the world was one of "tyranny or freedom." Attorney general J. Howard McGrath spoke of "many Communists in America," each bearing the "germ of death for society."

When administration officials discovered classified documents in the offices of the allegedly pro-Communist *Amerasia* magazine, Truman appointed a Temporary Commission on Employee Loyalty to head off Republican charges that the Democrats were "soft on communism."

On the basis of its report, Truman established a new Federal Employee Loyalty Program in 1947. In the same week that he announced his containment policy, he ordered the FBI to check its files for evidence of subversive activity and to bring suspects before a new Civil Service Commission Loyalty Review Board. Initially, the program included safeguards and assumed that a challenged employee was innocent until proven guilty. But as the Loyalty Review Board assumed more power, it ignored individual rights, and suspects had little chance to fight back. Val Lorwin, whose story started this chapter, was just one of many victims.

The Truman loyalty program examined several million employees but found grounds for dismissing only several hundred. Nonetheless, it bred the unwarranted fear of subversion, led to the assumption that absolute loyalty could be achieved, and legitimated investigative tactics that were used irresponsibly to harm innocent individuals.

The Congressional Loyalty Program

At the same time, Congress launched its own program. In the early years of the Cold War, the law became increasingly explicit about what was illegal in the United States. The requirement that members of Communist organizations had to register with the attorney general led to the decline of the American Communist party. Membership, numbering about 80,000 in 1947, fell to 55,000 in 1950 and to 25,000 in 1954.

The investigations of the House Un-American Activities Committee (HUAC) contributed to that decline. Intent on rooting out subversion, HUAC probed the motion picture industry in 1947, claiming that left-wing sympathies of writers, actors, directors, and producers were corrupting the American public. A frequent refrain in congressional hearings was "Are you now or have you ever been a member of the Communist party?" Altogether, HUAC called 19 Hollywood figures to testify. When 10 of them—including noted writers Ring Lardner, Jr., and Dalton Trumbo—refused to answer such accusatory questions by invoking their constitutional right to remain silent, Congress issued contempt citations. Members of the "Hollywood Ten" served prison sentences ranging from six months to one year. At that point, the movie industry knuckled under and blacklisted anyone with even a marginally questionable past. Hollywood executives issued a statement that declared: "We will not knowingly employ a Communist nor a member of any party or groups which advocates the overthrow of the Government of the United States by force or by illegal or unconstitutional means." No one on the blacklist could find a job at the studios, although some managed to work secretly under other names.

Congress made a greater splash with the Hiss–Chambers case. Whittaker Chambers, a former Communist who had broken with the party in 1938 and had become a successful editor of *Time* magazine, charged that Alger Hiss had been a Communist in the 1930s. Hiss was a distinguished New Dealer who had served in the Agriculture Department before becoming assistant secretary of state. Now out of the government, he was president of the Carnegie Endowment for International Peace. He denied Chambers's charge, and the matter might have died there had not freshman congressman Richard Nixon taken up the case. Nixon finally extracted from Hiss an admission that he had

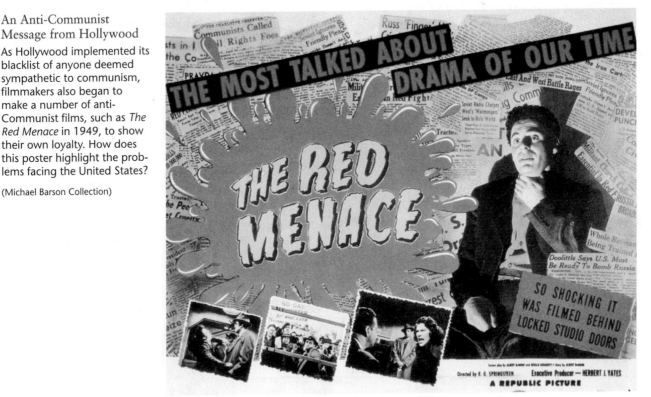

An Anti-Communist Message from Hollywood

As Hollywood implemented its blacklist of anyone deemed sympathetic to communism, filmmakers also began to make a number of anti-Communist films, such as *The Red Menace* in 1949, to show their own loyalty. How does this poster highlight the problems facing the United States?

(Michael Barson Collection)

once known Chambers, though by a different name. Hiss then sued Chambers for libel, whereupon Chambers changed his story and charged that Hiss was a Soviet spy. Hiss was indicted for perjury for lying under oath about his former relationship with Chambers, for the statute of limitations prevented prosecution for espionage. The sensational case made front-page news around the nation. Millions of Americans read about it at around the same time they learned of Russia's first atomic explosion and the final victory of the Communist revolution in China. Chambers appeared unstable, but Hiss seemed contradictory in his testimony and never adequately explained how he had such close ties with members of the Communist party or how some copies of stolen State Department documents had been typed on his typewriter. The first trial ended in a hung jury; the second trial, in January 1950, sent Hiss to prison for almost four years. He continued to assert his innocence for the remainder of his life, although later evidence makes his involvement clear.

For many Americans, the Hiss case proved that a Communist threat indeed existed in the United States. It "forcibly demonstrated to the American people that domestic Communism was a real and present danger to the security of the nation," Richard Nixon declared as he used the case to win a Senate seat from California. It helped justify the even worse witch hunts that followed.

Congress also charged that homosexuals posed a security risk. The issue surfaced in February 1950, when Undersecretary of State John Peurifoy mentioned in testimony before the Senate Appropriations Committee that most of the 91 employees the State Department had dismissed for reasons of "moral turpitude" were homosexuals. Then, in December, the Senate released a report that painted a threatening picture of the problems of homosexuals in the civil service. They lacked moral and emotional stability, the report suggested, and were therefore likely candidates for blackmail, which threatened national security.

Senator Joe McCarthy

The key anti-Communist warrior in the 1950s was Joseph R. McCarthy, Republican senator from Wisconsin. He capitalized on the fear sparked by congressional and executive investigations and made the entire country cognizant of the Communist threat.

McCarthy came to the Communist issue almost accidentally. Elected to the U.S. Senate in 1946, McCarthy had an undistinguished career for much of his first term. He first gained national attention with a speech before the Wheeling, West Virginia, Women's Club in February 1950, not long after the conviction of Alger Hiss. In that address, McCarthy brandished in his hand what he said was a list of 205 known Communists in the State Department. Pressed for details, McCarthy first said that he would release his list only to the president, then reduced the number of names to 57.

Early reactions to McCarthy were mixed. A subcommittee of the Senate Foreign Relations Committee, after investigating, called his charge a "fraud and a hoax." As his support grew, however, Republicans realized his partisan value and egged him on. Senator John Bricker of Ohio allegedly told him, "Joe, you're a dirty s.o.b., but there are times when you've got to have an s.o.b. around, and this is one of them."

McCarthy selected assorted targets in his crusade to wipe out communism. He called Dean Acheson the "Red Dean of the State Department" and slandered George C. Marshall, the architect of victory in World

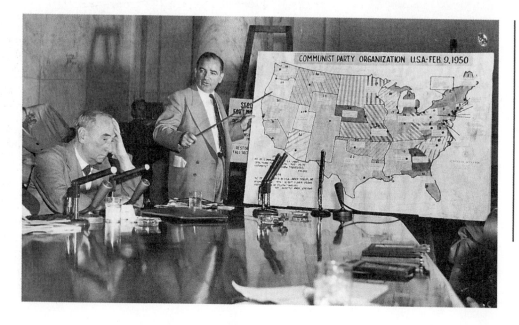

McCarthy's Anti-Communist Campaign
Senator Joseph McCarthy's spurious charges inflamed anti-Communist sentiment in the 1950s. Here he uses a chart of Communist party organization in the United States to suggest that the nation would be at risk unless subversives were rooted out. How does the chart contribute to the impression McCarthy wanted to convey?

(Bettmann/CORBIS)

War II and the Marshall Plan for European recovery, as a "man steeped in falsehood...who has recourse to the lie whenever it suits his convenience."

A demagogue throughout his career, McCarthy gained visibility through extensive press and television coverage. He knew how to issue press releases just before newspaper deadlines and to provide reporters with leaks that became the basis for stories. Playing on his tough reputation, he did not mind appearing disheveled, unshaven, and half sober. He used obscenity and vulgarity freely in lashing out against his "vile and scurrilous" enemies as part of his effort to appear as an ordinary man of the people.

McCarthy's tactics worked because of public alarm about the Communist threat. The Korean War revealed the aggressiveness of Communists in Asia. The arrest in 1950 of Julius and Ethel Rosenberg fed fears of internal subversion. The Rosenbergs, a seemingly ordinary American couple with two small children, were charged with stealing and transmitting atomic secrets to the Russians. To many Americans, it was inconceivable that the Soviets could have developed the bomb on their own. Treachery helped explain the Soviet explosion of an atomic device.

The next year, the Rosenbergs were found guilty of espionage. Judge Irving Kaufman expressed the rage of an insecure nation as he sentenced them to death. "I consider your crime worse than murder," he said. "Your conduct in putting into the hands of the Russians the A-bomb years before our best scientists predicted Russia would perfect the bomb has already caused, in my opinion, the Communist aggression in Korea...." Their execution in the electric chair after numerous appeals reflected a national commitment to respond to the Communist threat. For years, supporters of the Rosenbergs claimed that they were innocent victims of the anti-Communist crusade. More recent evidence indicates that Julius was guilty. Ethel, cognizant of his activities but not involved herself, was arrested, convicted, and executed in a futile government attempt to make Julius talk.

When the Republicans won control of the Senate in 1952, McCarthy's power grew. He became chairman of

MAJOR EVENTS OF THE COLD WAR

Year	Event	Effect
1946	Winston Churchill's "Iron Curtain" speech	First Western "declaration" of the Cold War
	George F. Kennan's long telegram	Spoke of Soviet insecurity and the need for containment
1947	George F. Kennan's article signed "Mr. X"	Elaborated on arguments in the telegram
	Truman Doctrine	Provided economic and military aid to Greece and Turkey
	Federal Employee Loyalty Program	Sought to root out subversion in the U.S. government
	HUAC investigation of the motion picture industry	Sought to expose Communist influences in the movies
1948	Marshall Plan	Provided massive American economic aid in rebuilding postwar Europe
	Berlin airlift	Brought in supplies when USSR closed off land access to the divided city
1949	NATO	Created a military alliance to withstand a possible Soviet attack
	First Soviet atomic bomb	Ended the American nuclear monopoly
	Communist victory in China	Made Americans fear the worldwide spread of communism
1950	Conviction of Alger Hiss	Seemed to bear out Communist danger at home
	Joseph McCarthy's first charges	Launched aggressive anti-Communist campaign in the United States
	NSC-68	Called for vigilance and increased military spending to counter the Communist threat
	Outbreak of the Korean War	North Korean invasion of South Korea viewed as part of Soviet conspiracy
1953	Armistice in Korea	Brought little change after years of bitter fighting
1954	Vietnamese victory over French at Dien Bien Phu	Early triumph for nationalism in Southeast Asia
	Army–McCarthy hearings	Brought downfall of Joseph McCarthy

Timeline

1945	Yalta Conference
	Roosevelt dies; Harry Truman becomes president
	Potsdam Conference
1946	American plan for control of atomic energy fails
	Atomic Energy Act
	Iran crisis in which U.S. forces USSR to leave
	Churchill's "Iron Curtain" speech
1947	Truman Doctrine
	Federal Employee Loyalty Program
	House Un-American Activities Committee (HUAC) investigates the movie industry
1948	Marshall Plan launched
	Berlin airlift
	Israel created by the United Nations
	Hiss–Chambers case
	Truman elected president
1949	Soviet Union tests atomic bomb
	North Atlantic Treaty Organization (NATO) established
	George Orwell, *1984*
	Mao Zedong's forces win Chinese civil war; Jiang Jieshi flees to Taiwan
1950	Truman authorizes development of the hydrogen bomb
	Alger Hiss convicted
	Joseph McCarthy's Wheeling (W. Va.) speech on subversion
	NSC-68
1950–1953	Korean War
1951	Japanese–American treaty
1952	Dwight D. Eisenhower elected president
	McCarthy heads Senate Permanent Investigations Subcommittee
1953	Stalin dies; Khrushchev consolidates power
	East Germans stage anti-Soviet demonstrations
	Shah of Iran returns to power in CIA-supported coup
1954	Fall of Dien Bien Phu ends French control of Indochina
	Geneva Conference on Vietnam
	Guatemalan government overthrown with CIA help
	Mao's forces shell Quemoy and Matsu
	Army–McCarthy hearings
1956	Suez incident
	Hungarian "freedom fighters" suppressed
	Eisenhower reelected
1957	Russians launch *Sputnik* satellite
1958	U.S. troops sent to support Lebanese government
1959	Castro deposes Batista in Cuba

the Government Operations Committee and head of its Permanent Investigations Subcommittee. He now had a stronger base and two dedicated assistants, Roy Cohn and G. David Schine, who helped keep attention focused on the ostensible Communist threat. They assisted him in his domestic investigations and even traveled abroad, ripping books off the shelves of American embassy libraries that they deemed subversive. The lists of suspects, including Val Lorwin (introduced at the start of this chapter), grew ever larger.

McCarthy finally pushed too far. In 1953, after the army drafted Schine and then refused to allow preferential treatment, McCarthy began to investigate army security and even top-level army leaders. When the army charged that McCarthy was going too far, the Senate investigated the complaint.

The Army–McCarthy hearings began in April 1954 and lasted 36 days. Beamed to a captivated nationwide audience, they demonstrated the power of television to shape people's opinions. Americans saw McCarthy's savage tactics on screen. He came across to viewers as irresponsible and destructive, particularly in contrast to Boston lawyer Joseph Welch, who argued the army's case with quiet eloquence and showed McCarthy as the demagogue he was. At a climactic point in the hearings, when McCarthy accused a member of Welch's staff of being involved with an organization sympathetic to the Communist party, despite an earlier agreement not to raise the issue, Welch exploded dramatically, "Have you no sense of decency, sir, at long last? Have you left no sense of decency?"

The hearings shattered McCarthy's mystical appeal. In broad daylight, before a national television audience, his ruthless tactics offended millions. The Senate, which had earlier backed off confronting McCarthy, finally censured him for his conduct. Although McCarthy remained in office, his influence disappeared. Three years later, at age 48, he died a broken man.

Yet for a time he had exerted a powerful hold in the United States. "To many Americans," radio commentator Fulton Lewis, Jr., said, "McCarthyism is Americanism." Seizing on the frustrations and anxieties of the Cold War, McCarthy struck a resonant chord. As his appeal grew, he put together a following that included both lower-class ethnic groups, who responded to the charges against established elites, and conservative midwestern Republicans. But his real power base was the Senate, where conservative Republicans saw McCarthy as a means of reasserting their own authority.

The Casualties of Fear

The anti-Communist campaign kindled pervasive suspicion in American society. In the late 1940s and early 1950s, dissent no longer seemed safe. Civil servants, government workers, academics, and actors all came under attack and found that the right of due process often evaporated amid the Cold War Red Scare.

This paranoia affected American life in countless ways. In New York, subway workers were fired when they refused to answer questions about their own political activities and beliefs. In Seattle, a fire department officer who denied current membership in the Communist party but refused to speak of his past was dismissed just 40 days before he reached the 25 years of service that would have qualified him for retirement benefits. Navajos in Arizona and New Mexico, facing starvation in the bitter winter of 1947–1948, were denied government relief because of charges that their communal way of life was communistic and therefore un-American. Racism became intertwined with the anti-Communist crusade when African American actor Paul Robeson was accused of Communist leanings for criticizing American foreign policy and denied opportunities to perform. Black author W. E. B. Du Bois, who joined the Communist party, faced even more virulent attacks. Latino laborers faced deportation for membership in unions with left-wing sympathies. In 1949, the Congress of Industrial Organizations (CIO) expelled 11 unions with a total membership of more than 1 million for alleged domination by Communists. Val Lorwin weathered the storm of malicious accusations and was finally vindicated, but others were less lucky. They were the unfortunate victims as the United States became consumed by the passions of the Cold War.

Conclusion
THE COLD WAR IN PERSPECTIVE

The Cold War dominated international relations in the post–World War II years. Tensions grew after 1945 as the United States and the Soviet Union found themselves engaged in a bitter standoff that affected all diplomatic exchanges, encouraged an expensive arms race, and limited the resources available for reform at home. For the United States, it was a first experience with the fiercely competitive international relations that had long plagued the nations of Europe. And while there was seldom actual shooting, the struggle required warlike measures and imposed costs on all countries involved.

What caused the Cold War? Historians have long argued over the question of where responsibility should be placed. In the early years after the Second World War, policymakers and commentators who supported their actions justified the American stance as a bold and courageous effort to meet the Communist threat. Later, particularly in the 1960s, as the war in Vietnam eroded confidence in American foreign policy, revisionist historians began to argue that American actions were misguided, insensitive to Soviet needs, and at least partially responsible for escalating friction. As with most historical questions, there are no easy answers, but both sides must be weighed.

The Cold War stemmed from a competition for international influence between the two great world powers. After World War II, the U.S. goal was to exercise economic and political leadership in the world and thus to establish capitalist economies and democratic political institutions throughout Europe and in nations emerging from colonial rule. But these goals put the United States on a collision course with nations such as the Soviet Union that had a different vision of what the postwar world should be like and with anticolonial movements in emerging countries around the globe. Perceiving threats from the Soviet Union, China, and other Communist countries, the United States clung to its deep-rooted sense of mission and embarked on an increasingly aggressive effort at containment, based on its reading of the lessons of the past. American efforts culminated in the ill-fated war in Vietnam as the Communist nations of the world defended their own interests with equal force. The Cold War, with its profound effects at home and abroad, was the unfortunate result.

QUESTIONS FOR REVIEW AND REFLECTION

1. What were the roots of the Cold War conflict?
2. Why did the United States and Soviet Union find it so difficult to get along in the years after World War II?
3. How did American Cold War policy change in the late 1940s?
4. What impact did the Cold War have on American society at home?
5. Could the Cold War have been avoided?

CHAPTER 28

Reform and Rebellion in the Turbulent Sixties, 1960–1969

The United States was comfortable and confident as the 1960s began. There was a basic consensus about the responsibility of the government to help those who could not help themselves. Then that consensus fragmented in the turbulence that accompanied the Vietnam War.

(Romare Bearden (1914–1988), "The Dove". 1964. Cut-and-pasted photoreproductions and papers, gouache, pencil and colored pencil on cardboard. 13 3/8 x 18 3/4". Blanchette Rockefeller Fund. (377.1971). The Museum of Modern Art/Licensed by Scala-Art Resource, NY. Art © Romare Bearden Foundation/Licensed by VAGA, NY)

American Stories

A Young Liberal Questions the Welfare State

Paul Cowan was an idealist in the 1960s. Like many students who came of age in these years, he believed in the possibility of social change and plunged into the struggle for liberal reform. He shared the hopes and dreams of other members of his generation, who felt that their government could make a difference in people's lives.

Cowan's commitment had developed slowly. He was a child of the 1950s, when most Americans were caught up in the consumer culture and paid little attention to the problems of people less fortunate than themselves. His grandfather had sold used cement bags in Chicago, but his father had become an executive at CBS television, and Cowan grew up in comfortable surroundings. He graduated from the Choate School (where John Kennedy had gone) in 1958, and then from Harvard University (where Kennedy had also been a student) in 1963.

When he entered college, Cowan was interested in politically conscious writers such as John Dos Passos, John Steinbeck, and James Agee and folk singers such as Pete Seeger and Woody Guthrie. They offered him entrance, he later recalled, into a "nation that seemed to be filled with energy and decency," one that lurked "beneath the dull, conformist facade of the Eisenhower years." While at Harvard, he was excited by antinuclear campaigns in New England and civil rights demonstrations in the South.

After college, he made good on his commitment to civil rights by going to Mississippi to work in the Freedom Summer project of 1964. He was inspired by the example of John Kennedy, the liberal president whose administration promised "a new kind of politics" that could make the nation, and the world, a better place. During that summer, he wrote, "it was possible to believe that by changing ourselves we could change, and redeem, our America."

The Peace Corps came next. Paul and his wife, Rachel, were convinced that this organization, the idea of the young president, "really was a unique government agency, permanently protected by the lingering magic of John F. Kennedy's name." They were assigned to the city of Guayaquil, in Ecuador, in South America. Their task was to serve as mediators between administrators of the city hall and residents of the slums. They wanted to try to raise the standard of living by encouraging local governments to provide basic services such as garbage disposal and clean water.

But the work proved more frustrating than they had imagined. They bristled at the restrictions imposed by the Peace Corps bureaucracy. They despaired at the inadequate resources local government officials had to

accomplish their aims. They wondered whether they were simply new imperialists, trying to impose their values on others who had priorities of their own. "From the day we moved into the *barrio*," Cowan later recalled, "the question we were most frequently asked by the people we were supposed to be organizing was whether we would leave them our clothes when we returned to the States."

Cowan came home disillusioned. "I saw that even the liberals I had wanted to emulate, men who seemed to be devoting their lives to fighting injustice, were unable to accept people from alien cultures on any terms but their own." He called his account of his own odyssey *The Making of an Un-American*.

Paul Cowan's passage through the 1960s mirrored the passage of American society as a whole. Millions of Americans shared his views of the possibilities of democracy as the period began. Mostly comfortable and confident, they supported the liberal agenda advanced by the Democratic party of John Kennedy and Lyndon Johnson. They endorsed the proposition that the government had responsibility for the welfare of all its citizens and accepted the need for a more active government role to help those of its diverse peoples who were unable to help themselves. That commitment lay behind the legislative achievements of the "Great Society," the last wave of twentieth-century reform that built on the gains of the Progressive era and the New Deal years before.

Then political reaction set in as the nation was torn apart by the ravages of the Vietnam War. The escalation of the war, which led to charges that the United States was engaging in an imperialistic crusade like those of other nations in the past, sent more than half a million American soldiers to fight in a far-off land and provoked a protest movement that ripped apart the society. Young Americans, espousing different values and a different version of the American dream, challenged the priorities of their parents. At the same time, they paraded their sexuality more openly, experimented with different forms of mystical religious faith, and enjoyed readily available drugs. In the end, their challenges helped reverse the course of the war. But in the process, liberal assumptions eroded as conservatives argued that an activist approach was responsible for the social and political chaos that consumed the country.

This chapter describes both the climax of twentieth-century liberalism and the turbulence that led to its decline. It focuses on the effort of the government, begun in the New Deal of Franklin Roosevelt, to help those caught short by the advances of industrial capitalism. It first examines the democratic commitment in the 1960s to provide necessary assistance to the less fortunate members of American society and then describes the turmoil that undermined the possibility of such aid. In pondering the possibilities of reform, this chapter outlines the various attempts to devise an effective political response to the major structural changes in the post–World War II economy described in Chapter 26. And then it shows how the Cold War assumptions outlined in Chapter 27 led to the rifts that ripped the nation apart and tarnished the United States in the eyes of the world.

John F. Kennedy: The Camelot Years

The commitment to an American welfare state reached its high-water point in the 1960s. As the left-wing Labour Party in Great Britain played a more and more influential role and occasionally assumed power, and social democratic coalitions were equally active in other European nations, Americans took note. Democrats wanted to follow their example and broaden the role of government even further than Franklin D. Roosevelt and Harry S Truman had done in the 1930s and 1940s, in an effort to address the problems of poverty, unemployment, and racism. John F. Kennedy, a senator from Massachusetts, demanded that the United States move in the direction of what he called a "New Frontier."

The Election of 1960

In the 1960 presidential campaign, Kennedy ran against Vice President Richard Nixon, who clearly had more executive experience. Kennedy argued that the government in general, and the president in particular, had to play an even more active role than they had in the Eisenhower years. He charged that the country had become lazy as it reveled in the prosperity of the 1950s. There were, in fact, serious problems that needed to be solved.

Seventy million Americans tuned in to watch the two men square off against one another in the first televised presidential debate. Kennedy appeared tanned and rested. Nixon, who had recently been hospitalized with an infection, looked tired and gaunt. Even worse, the makeup he applied to hide his heavy beard growth only accentuated it and gave him a swarthy complexion on screen. The debates made a major difference in the campaign (see the "Recovering the Past" essay, pp.(697–698). Kennedy himself admitted, "It was TV more than anything else that turned the tide." Kennedy overcame seemingly insuperable odds to become the first Catholic in the White House. Yet Kennedy's victory was razor-thin. The electoral margin of 303 to 219 concealed the close popular tally, in which he triumphed by fewer than 120,000 of 68 million votes cast. While Kennedy had Democratic majorities in Congress, many members of his party came from the South and were less sympathetic to liberal causes.

JFK

John Kennedy served as a symbol of the early 1960s. He was far younger than his predecessor; at age 43, he was the youngest man ever elected to the presidency. He came from an Irish Catholic family from Massachusetts that saw politics as a means of acceptance in Protestant America. Raised in comfort, he graduated from Harvard University and went on to serve heroically in the navy during World War II. He was elected first to the House of Representatives in 1946, then to the Senate in 1952, and was reelected six years later by the largest majority in the history of the state.

The new president had a charismatic public presence. He was able to voice his aims in eloquent yet understandable language that motivated his followers. During the campaign, he pointed to challenges at home and abroad, observing that "the New Frontier is here whether we seek it or not." He made the same point even more movingly in his inaugural address: "The torch has been passed to a new generation of Americans—born in this century, tempered by war, disciplined by a hard and bitter peace, proud of our ancient heritage." Many Americans, like Paul Cowan, whom we met at the start of the chapter, were inspired by Kennedy's ringing call to action: "And so, my fellow Americans: Ask not what your country can do for you—ask what you can do for your country."

For Kennedy, strong leadership was all-important. Viewing himself as "tough-minded" and "hardnosed," he was determined to provide firm direction and play a leading role in creating the national agenda, just as Franklin Roosevelt had done. To that end, he surrounded himself with talented assistants. On his staff were 15 Rhodes scholars and several famous authors. The secretary of state was Dean Rusk, a former member of the State Department who had then served as president of the Rockefeller Foundation. The secretary of defense was Robert S. McNamara, the highly successful president of the Ford Motor Company.

An Energetic Young Leader

John Kennedy's energy and enthusiasm captured the imagination of Americans and people around the world, though few were aware of the physical ailments that affected him. He was fond of using this rocking chair in the White House, which he found comfortable for his ailing back. How did Kennedy's appearance contribute to his popularity and appeal?

(Bettmann/CORBIS)

Further contributing to Kennedy's attractive image were his glamorous wife, Jacqueline, and the glittering social occasions the couple hosted. Nobel Prize winners, musicians, and artists attended White House dinners. Energy, exuberance, and excitement filled the air. The administration seemed like the Camelot of King Arthur's day, popularized in a Broadway musical in 1960.

The New Frontier in Action

In office, Kennedy sought to bolster the economy and to enlarge the welfare state. On the economic front, he wanted to end the lingering recession that began in Eisenhower's last year by working with the business community while controlling price inflation.

These two goals conflicted when, in the spring of 1962, the large steel companies decided on a major price increase after steel unions had accepted a modest wage package. The angry president termed the price increases unjustifiable and pressed for executive and congressional action to force the steel companies to back down. The large companies capitulated, but they disliked Kennedy's heavy-handed approach and decided that this Democratic administration, like all others, was hostile to business. Six weeks after the steel crisis, the stock market plunged in the greatest drop since the Great Crash of 1929. Kennedy received the blame. It now seemed doubly urgent to end the recession. Earlier a proponent of a balanced budget, Kennedy began to listen to his liberal advisers who proposed a Keynesian approach to economic growth. Budget deficits had promoted prosperity during the Second World War and might work in the same way in peacetime, too. A tax cut could put money in people's pockets, and their spending could stimulate the economy. In early 1963, the president called for a $13.5 billion cut in corporate taxes over the next three years. While that cut would cause a large deficit, it would also provide capital that business leaders could spend to revive the economy and ultimately increase tax revenues.

Opposition mounted. Conservatives refused to accept the basic premise that deficits would stimulate economic growth and argued, in Eisenhower's words, that "no family, no business, no nation can spend itself into prosperity." Some liberals claimed that it would be better to stimulate the economy by spending money to improve society rather than by cutting taxes and putting money in people's pockets. What good would it do, economist John Kenneth Galbraith wondered, to have "a few more dollars to spend if the air is too dirty to breathe, the water is . . . too polluted to drink, the commuters are losing out in the struggle to get in and out of cities, the streets are filthy, and the schools are so bad that the young, perhaps wisely, stay away?" Congress pigeonholed the proposal in committee, and there it remained.

On other issues on the liberal agenda, Kennedy met similar resistance. Though he proposed legislation increasing the minimum wage and providing for federal aid for education, medical care for the elderly, housing subsidies, and urban renewal, the results were meager. His new minimum-wage measure passed Congress in pared-down form, but Kennedy did not have the votes in Congress to achieve most of his legislative program.

His inability to win necessary congressional support was most evident in the struggle to aid public education. Soon after taking office, Kennedy proposed a $2.3 billion program of grants to the states over a three-year period to help build schools and raise teachers' salaries. Immediately, a series of prickly questions emerged. Was it appropriate to spend large sums of money for social

Recovering the Past

TELEVISION

In the last 50 years, television has played an increasingly important part in American life, providing historians with another source of evidence about American culture and society in the recent past. Television's popularity by the 1950s was the result of decades of experimentation dating back to the nineteenth century. In the 1930s, NBC installed a television station in the new Empire State Building in New York. Wearing green makeup and purple lipstick to provide better visual contrast, actors began to perform before live cameras in studios. At the end of the decade, *Amos 'n' Andy,* a popular radio show, was telecast, and as the 1940s began, Franklin D. Roosevelt became the first president to appear on television. World War II interrupted the development of television, and Americans relied on radio to bring them news. After the war, however, the commercial development of television quickly resumed. Assembly lines that had made electronic implements of war were now converted to consumer production, and thousands of new sets appeared on the market. The opening of Congress could be seen live in 1947; baseball coverage improved that same year owing to the zoom lens; children's shows such as *Howdy Doody* made their debut; and *Meet the Press,* a radio interview program, made the transition to television.

Although sports programs, variety shows hosted by Ed Sullivan and Milton Berle, TV dramas, and episodic series (*I Love Lucy* and *Gunsmoke,* for example) dominated TV broadcasting in the 1950s, television soon became entwined with politics and public affairs. Americans saw

Senator Joseph McCarthy for themselves in the televised Army–McCarthy hearings in 1954; his malevolent behavior on camera contributed to his downfall. The 1948 presidential nominating conventions were the first to be televised, but the use of TV to enhance the public image of politicians was most thoroughly developed by the fatherly Dwight D. Eisenhower and the charismatic John F. Kennedy.

In November 1963, people throughout the United States shared the tragedy of John Kennedy's assassination, sitting for hours before their sets trying to understand the events of his fateful Texas trip. The shock and sorrow of the American people was repeated in the spring of 1968 as they gazed in disbelief at the funerals of Martin Luther King, Jr., and Robert Kennedy. A year later, a quarter of the world's population watched as Neil Armstrong became the first man to set foot on the moon. In that same era, television played an important part in shaping impressions of the war in Vietnam. More and more Americans began to understand the nature and impact of the conflict from what they saw on TV.

This combination of visual entertainment and enlightenment made owning a television set virtually a necessity. By 1970, fully 95 percent of American households owned a TV set, a staggering increase from the 9 percent only 20 years earlier. In fact, fewer families owned refrigerators or indoor toilets.

Reflecting on the Past The implications of the impact of television on American society are of obvious interest to

The candidates squaring off in their debate

(AP/Wide World Photos)

historians. How has television affected other communications and entertainment industries, such as radio, newspapers, and movies? Look at the "Television Tonight" listings shown here. What does the content of TV programming tell us about the values, interests, and tastes of the American people?

Perhaps most significant, what impact has TV had on the course of historical events like presidential campaigns, human relations, and wars? The pictures shown here are from the Kennedy–Nixon debates in the presidential campaign of 1960. The first picture shows the two candidates in the studio. The second picture shows a relaxed and energetic Kennedy staring directly into the TV camera. The third picture shows a taut and tense Nixon challenging the points made by his opponent. Which candidate seems to be speaking directly to the American people? Which candidate makes the better impression? Why? Polls of radio listeners taken after the first debate showed Nixon the winner; surveys of television viewers placed Kennedy in front. How do you account for this discrepancy? ■

John Kennedy (above) and Richard Nixon (right)

(AP/Wide World Photos)

Television Tonight

6:00—WTTV 4: Leave It to Beaver. Beaver tries to help a friend who has run away from home. Repeat.

6:30—WLW-I 13: Cheyenne has a Laramie adventure in which Slim, Jess, and Jonesy work on a cattle drive. Repeat.

7:30—WTTV 4: The Untouchables. Eliot Ness tries to deal with a late gangster's niece who has a record of the murdered hood's career. Repeat.

7:30—WLW-I 13: Voyage to the Bottom of the Sea presents "Mutiny," in which Admiral Nelson shows signs of a mental breakdown during the search for a giant jellyfish which supposedly consumed a submarine.

7:30—WFBM-TV 6: Members of the Indianapolis Rotary Club discuss the 1965 business outlook with former U.S. Sen. Homer Capehart.

8:00—WFBM-TV 6: The Man from UNCLE is in at a new time and night. Thrush agents try to recapture one of their leaders before Napoleon Solo can deliver him to the Central Intelligence Agency. Ralph Taeger is guest star.

8:00—WISH-TV 8: I've Got a Secret welcomes the panel from To Tell the Truth: Tom Poston, Peggy Cass, Kitty Carlisle, and Orson Bean.

8:30—WLW-I 13: Basketball, I.U. vs. Iowa.

8:30—WISH-TV 8: Andy Griffith's comedy involves Goober's attempts to fill in at the sheriff's office.

9:00—WFBM-TV 6: Andy Williams is visited by composer Henry Mancini, Bobby Darin, and Vic Damone. Musical selections include "Charade," "Hello Dolly," and "Moon River."

9:00—WTTV 4: Lloyd Thaxton welcomes vocal group Herman's Hermits.

9:30—WISH-TV 8: Many Happy Returns. Walter's plan for currying favor with the store's boss hits a snag.

10:00—WFBM-TV 6: Alfred Hitchcock presents Margaret Leighton as a spinster who goes mad when she cannot cope with the strain of rearing an orphaned niece in "Where the Woodbine Twineth."

10:00—WLW-I 13: Ben Casey gets help in diagnosing a boy's illness from an Australian veterinarian with terminal leukemia. The vet's knowledge of bats provides the key.

10:00—WISH-TV 8: "Viet Nam: How We Got In— Can We Get Out?" is the topic of CBS Reports.

Source: Indianapolis News, January 11, 1965.

goals? Would federal aid bring federal control of school policies and curriculum? Should assistance go to segregated schools? Should it go to parochial schools? In the end, compromise on these issues proved impossible and the school aid measure died in committee.

Kennedy was more successful in securing funding for the exploration of space. The space program was caught up in the competition of the Cold War, and with the Soviet launching of *Sputnik* and the first manned flights, the USSR clearly had the lead. In response, Kennedy proposed that the United States commit itself to landing a man on the moon and returning him to earth before the end of the decade. Congress assented and increased funding of the National Aeronautics and Space Administration (NASA).

Kennedy also established the Peace Corps, which sent young men and women overseas to assist developing countries by working with people at a grassroots level. Paul Cowan, introduced at the start of this chapter, was one of thousands of volunteers who hoped to share their liberal dreams.

If Kennedy's successes were modest, he had at least made commitments that could be broadened later. He had reaffirmed the importance of executive leadership in the effort to extend the boundaries of the welfare state. And he had committed himself to using modern economics to maintain fiscal stability. The nation was poised to achieve liberal goals.

Civil Rights and Kennedy's Response

So it was with civil rights. The pressures that had mounted in the decade and a half after World War II had brought significant change in eliminating segregation in American society. As the effort continued, a spectrum of organizations carried the fight forward. The NAACP, founded in 1910, remained committed to overturning the legal bases for segregation in the aftermath of its victory in the *Brown* v. *Board of Education* case of 1954 (see Chapter 26). The Congress of Racial Equality (CORE), an interracial group established in 1942, promoted change through peaceful confrontation. In 1957, after their victory in the bus boycott in Montgomery, Alabama, Martin Luther King, Jr., and others formed the Southern Christian Leadership Conference (SCLC), an organization of southern black clergy. Far more militant was the Student Nonviolent Coordinating Committee (SNCC, pronounced "snick"), which began to operate in 1960 and recruited young Americans not previously involved.

Confrontations continued in the 1960s. On January 31, 1960, four black college students from the Agricultural and Technical College in Greensboro, North Carolina, frustrated that they were permitted to shop but not to eat at a Woolworth's, a popular department store chain, sat down at the lunch counter and refused to leave. When a reporter inquired how long they had been planning the protest, the students responded, "All our lives!" The next day more students showed up, and the following day still more. The sit-ins, which spread to other cities, captured media attention and eventually included as many as 70,000 participants. Those protesting often met with a brutal response. John Lewis, an African American activist who participated in a sit-in in Nashville, Tennessee, described how "a group of young white men came in and they started pulling and beating primarily the young women. They put lighted cigarettes down their

Sitting-In

In violation of southern law, black college students refused to leave a lunch counter, launching a new campaign in the struggle for civil rights. Here the students wait patiently for service, or forcible eviction, as a way of dramatizing their determination to end segregation. What did the students hope to achieve by their actions?

(Bruce Roberts/Photo Researchers)

back, in their hair, and they were really beating people." And then the black protesters were arrested for disturbing the peace.

The following year, sit-ins gave rise to freedom rides, aimed at testing southern transportation facilities that recently had been desegregated by a Supreme Court decision. Organized initially by CORE and aided by SNCC, the program sent groups of blacks and whites together on buses heading south and stopping at terminals along the way. The riders, peaceful them-selves, anticipated confrontations that would publicize their cause and generate political support, and they frequently ended up in jail. The civil rights movement became the most powerful moral campaign since the abolitionist crusade before the Civil War. Anne Moody, who grew up in a small town in Mississippi, personi-fied the awakening of black consciousness. As a child, she had watched the murder of friends and acquain-tances who had somehow transgressed the limits set for blacks. Overcoming the hardships of growing up poor and black in the rural South, Moody became the first member of her family to go to college and later joined the NAACP and became involved in the activities of SNCC and CORE. Slowly, she noted, "I could feel myself beginning to change. For the first time I began to think something would be done about whites killing, beating, and misusing Negroes. I knew I was going to be a part of whatever happened." Participating in sit-ins, where she was thrashed and jailed for her activi-ties, she remained deeply involved in the movement.

Many whites also joined the movement in the South. Mimi Feingold, a white student at Swarthmore College in Pennsylvania, helped picket the Woolworth's nearby. After her sophomore year, she headed south to join the freedom rides sponsored by CORE. Like many others, Feingold found herself in the midst of often-violent confrontations and went to jail as an act of conscience.

In 1962, the civil rights movement accelerated. James Meredith, a black air force veteran and student at Jackson State College, applied to the all-white University of Mississippi, only to be rejected on racial grounds. Although the Supreme Court affirmed his right to attend, Governor Ross Barnett, an adamant racist, announced defiantly that Meredith would not be admitted, and on one occasion personally blocked the way. A major riot followed; tear gas covered the uni-versity grounds; and by the riot's end, two men lay dead and hundreds were hurt.

Other governors were equally aggressive. In his 1963 inaugural address, George C. Wallace of Alabama declared boldly, "Segregation now! Segregation tomorrow! Segregation forever!" as he voiced his opposition to integration.

Alabama became a national focus that year as a violent confrontation unfolded in Birmingham. Local black leaders encouraged Martin Luther King, Jr., to launch another attack on southern segregation in the city. Though the demonstrations were nonviolent, the responses were not. City officials declared that protest

Attacks on Demonstrators in Birmingham

In Birmingham, city officials responded to peaceful demonstrators with brutal force. Here city police use trained dogs to drive marchers back. Televised nationally, the police response appalled the American public. As newsman Eric Sevareid observed, "A newspaper or television picture of a snarling police dog set upon a human being is recorded on the perma-nent photoelectric file of every human brain." What did the Birmingham authori-ties hope to achieve by use of these dogs?

(Charles Moore/Black Star)

marches violated city regulations against parading without a license, and, over a five-week period, they arrested 2,200 blacks, some of them schoolchildren. Police Commissioner Eugene "Bull" Connor used high-pressure fire hoses, electric cattle prods, and trained police dogs to force the protesters back. As the media recorded the events, Americans watching television and reading newspapers were horrified.

Kennedy claimed to be sickened by the pictures from Birmingham but insisted that he could do nothing, even though he had sought and won black support in 1960. The narrowness of his electoral victory made him reluctant to press white southerners on civil rights when he needed their votes on other issues. Events finally forced Kennedy to act more boldly. In the James Meredith confrontation, the president, like his predecessor in the Little Rock crisis, had to send federal troops to restore control and to guarantee Meredith's right to attend the university. The administration also forced the desegregation of the University of Alabama and helped arrange a compromise that eased discrimination in Birmingham's municipal facilities and hiring practices. And when white bombings aimed at eliminating black leaders in Birmingham caused thousands of blacks to abandon nonviolence and rampage through the streets, Kennedy readied federal troops to intervene.

He also spoke out more forcefully than before. In a nationally televised address, he called the quest for equal rights a "moral issue" and asked, "Are we to say to the world, and, much more importantly, to each other that this is a land of the free except for the Negroes?" Just hours after the president spoke, assassins killed Medgar Evers, a black NAACP official, in his own driveway in Jackson, Mississippi.

Kennedy sent Congress a new and stronger civil rights bill, outlawing segregation in public places, banning discrimination wherever federal money was involved, and advancing the process of school integration. Polls showed that 63 percent of the nation supported his stand.

To lobby for passage of this measure, civil rights leaders, pressed from below by black activists, arranged a massive march on Washington in August 1963. More than 200,000 people—black and white, common folk and celebrities—gathered from across the country. The folk music artists of the early 1960s were there as well. Joan Baez, Bob Dylan, and Peter, Paul, and Mary led the crowd in songs associated with the movement, such as "Blowin' in the Wind" and "We Shall Overcome."

The high point of the day was the address by Martin Luther King, Jr., who by now was the nation's preeminent spokesman for civil rights and proponent of nonviolent protest. King proclaimed his faith in the decency of his fellow citizens and in their ability to extend the promises of the Constitution and the Declaration of Independence to every American. With all the power of a southern preacher, he implored his audience to share his faith.

"I have a dream," King declared, "that one day this nation will rise up and live out the true meaning of its creed: 'We hold these truths to be self-evident, that all men are created equal.' I have a dream that one day on the red hills of Georgia, the sons of former slaves and the sons of former slave-owners will be able to sit together at the table of brotherhood." Each time King used the refrain "I have a dream," thousands of blacks and whites roared together. King concluded by quoting from an old hymn: "Free at last! Free at last! Thank God almighty, we are free at last!"

Not all were moved. Anne Moody, who had come up from her activist work in Mississippi to attend the event, sat on the grass by the Lincoln Memorial as the speaker's words rang out. "Martin Luther King went on and on talking about his dream," she said. "I sat there thinking that . . . we never had time to sleep, much less dream." Nor was Congress prompted to do much. Despite large Democratic majorities, strong white southern resistance to the cause of civil rights continued, and the bill was bottled up in committee.

Lyndon B. Johnson and the Great Society

Kennedy knew he faced a difficult reelection battle in 1964. He wanted not only to win the presidency for a second term but also to increase liberal Democratic strength in Congress. Instead, an assassin's attack took his life and brought a new leader to the helm.

Change of Command

In November 1963, Kennedy traveled to Texas, where he hoped to unite the state's Democratic party for the upcoming election. Dallas, one of the stops on the trip, was reputed to be hostile to the administration. Entering the city in an open car, the president encountered friendly crowds. Suddenly shots rang out, and Kennedy slumped forward as bullets ripped through his head and throat. Mortally wounded, he died a short time later at a Dallas hospital. Lee Harvey Oswald, the accused assassin, was shot and killed a few days later by a minor underworld figure as he was being moved within the jail.

Americans were stunned. For days, people stayed at home and watched endless television replays of the assassination and its aftermath. The images of the handsome president felled by bullets, the funeral cortege, and the president's young son saluting his father's casket as it rolled by on the way to final burial at Arlington National Cemetery were all imprinted on people's minds. Vice President Lyndon Johnson succeeded Kennedy as president. Though less polished, Johnson was a more effective political leader than Kennedy and brought his own special skills and vision to the presidency.

LBJ

Johnson had taken a different road to the White House and came from a far more humble background than Kennedy. He had begun his public career as a legislative assistant in the House of Representatives in Washington, D.C., then served as a New Deal official in Texas. He won election first to the House in 1937 and then to the Senate in 1948. Eager to be president, he accepted the vice presidential nomination when it became clear in 1960 that Kennedy was going to win the nomination for president.

Johnson was a man of elemental force. Always manipulative, he was often difficult to like. There was a streak of vulgarity that contributed to his earthy appeal but was frequently offensive. Those qualities notwithstanding, he was successful in the passion of his life—politics—and was the most able legislator of the postwar years. As Senate majority leader, he became famous for his ability to get things done. Ceaseless in his search for information, tireless in his attention to detail, he could flatter and cajole, and became famous for what came to be called the "Johnson treatment." According to columnists Rowland Evans, Jr., and Robert Novak, he zeroed in, "his face a scant millimeter from his target, his eyes widening and narrowing, his eyebrows rising and falling." He grabbed people by the lapels, made them listen, and usually got his way (see the series of illustrations).

As vice president, Johnson went into a state of eclipse. He felt useless and stifled in his new role without his power base in the Senate and was uncomfortable with the Kennedy crowd. Despite his own ambivalence about Kennedy, Johnson sensed the profound shock that gripped the United States after the assassination and was determined to utilize Kennedy's memory to achieve legislative success. Even more than Kennedy, he was willing to wield presidential power aggressively and to use the media to shape public opinion in pursuit of his vision of a society in which the comforts of life would be more widely shared and poverty would be eliminated.

The Great Society in Action

Lyndon Johnson had an expansive vision of the possibilities of reform. Using his considerable political skills, he succeeded in pushing through Congress the most extensive reform program in American history.

Johnson began to develop the support he needed the day he took office. In his first public address, delivered to Congress and televised nationwide, he sought to dispel the image of impostor as he embraced Kennedy's liberal program. He began, in a measured tone, with the words, "All I have, I would have given gladly not to be standing here today." He asked members of Congress to work with him, and he underscored the theme "Let us continue."

As a first step, Johnson resolved to secure the measures Kennedy had been unable to extract from Congress. Bills to reduce taxes and ensure civil rights were his first and most pressing priorities,

Lyndon Johnson in Action

Lyndon Johnson kept tight control of the Senate in the 1950s and was known for his ability to get his way. Here he is shown giving the famous "Johnson treatment" to Senator Theodore Francis Green in 1957. Note the way Green is bending backward in an unsuccessful effort to keep his distance from LBJ. Why do you think LBJ usually got his way?

(George Tames/The New York Times)

but he was interested too in aiding public education, providing medical care for the aged, and eliminating poverty. By the spring of 1964, he began to use the phrase "Great Society" to describe his expansive reform program.

Johnson's landslide victory over conservative Republican challenger Barry Goldwater of Arizona in the 1964 election validated his approach. This was the first time in recent history that a conservative had gained the Republican nomination. Goldwater, however, frightened even members of his own party by proclaiming that "extremism in the defense of liberty is no vice," and by speaking out against such popular programs as social security. LBJ received 61 percent of the popular vote and 486 electoral votes to Goldwater's 52 and gained Democratic majorities in both the Senate and the House. Goldwater's candidacy drove moderate Republicans to vote for the Democratic party this time and gave Johnson a far more impressive mandate than Kennedy had ever enjoyed.

Civil rights reform was LBJ's first legislative priority and an integral part of the Great Society program, but other measures were equally important. Following Kennedy's lead, Johnson pressed for a tax cut. He accepted the Keynesian theory that deficits, properly managed, could promote prosperity. If people had more money to spend, then their purchases could stimulate the economy. Soon the tax bill passed.

With the tax cut in hand, the president pressed for the antipoverty program that Kennedy had begun to plan. Such an effort was bold and unprecedented in the United States, even though social democracy had a long history in European nations and other countries around the world. During the Progressive era at the turn of the century, some legislation had attempted to alleviate conditions associated with poverty. During the New Deal, Franklin Roosevelt had proposed programs to assist people who could not help themselves. Now Johnson took a step that no president had taken before; in his 1964 State of the Union message, he declared an "unconditional war on poverty in America."

The center of this expansive effort to eradicate poverty was the Economic Opportunity Act of 1964. It created an Office of Economic Opportunity (OEO) to provide education and training through programs such as the Job Corps for unskilled young people trapped in the poverty cycle. VISTA (Volunteers in Service to America), patterned after the Peace Corps, offered assistance to the poor at home, while Head Start tried to give disadvantaged children a chance to succeed in school. Assorted community action programs gave the poor a voice in improving housing, health, and education. Two agencies responded to

Native American pressure by allowing Indians to devise programs and budgets and then administer programs themselves.

Aware of the escalating costs of medical care, Johnson also proposed a medical assistance plan. Both Truman and Kennedy had supported such an initiative but had failed to win congressional approval. Johnson succeeded. To head off conservative attacks, the administration tied the Medicare measure to the social security system and limited the program to the elderly. The complementary Medicaid program met the needs of those on welfare and certain other groups who could not afford private insurance. The Medicare–Medicaid initiative was the most important extension of federally directed social benefits since the Social Security Act of 1935. Johnson was similarly successful in his effort to provide aid for elementary and secondary schools. His legislation allocated education money to the states based on the number of children from low-income families. Those funds would then be distributed to assist deprived children in public as well as private schools.

In LBJ's optimistic vision, the federal government would ensure that everyone shared in the promise of American life. Under his prodding, Congress passed a new housing act to give rent supplements to the poor and created a Cabinet Department of Housing and Urban Development.

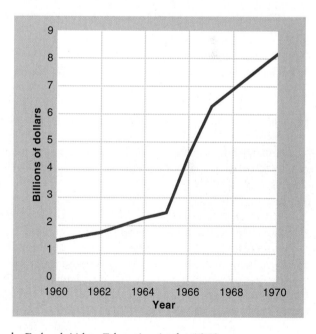

Federal Aid to Education in the 1960s

Passage of a bill to provide federal aid to education in 1965 led to rapidly increasing government support at all levels for the remainder of the decade.

Source: U.S. Bureau of the Census.

The federal government provided new forms of aid, such as legal assistance for the poor and allocated additional funds for higher education. Congress also provided artists and scholars with assistance through the National Endowments for the Arts and Humanities, created in 1965. At the same time, Johnson's administration provided much-needed immigration reform. The Immigration Act of 1965 replaced previously restrictive policy, in place since 1924, with a measure that vastly increased the ceiling on immigration and opened the door to immigrants from Asia and Latin America. By the late 1960s, some 350,000 immigrants were entering the United States annually, compared to the average of 47,000 per year between 1931 and 1945. This new stream of immigration created a population more diverse than it had been since the early decades of the twentieth century. The Great Society also reflected the stirring of the environmental movement. In 1962, naturalist Rachel Carson alerted the public to the dangers of pesticide poisoning and environmental pollution in her book *Silent Spring*. She took aim at chemical pesticides, especially DDT, which had increased crop yields but had brought disastrous side effects:

> The most alarming of all man's assaults upon the rivers, and sea with dangerous and even lethal materials. This pollution is for the most part irrecoverable; the chain of evil it initiates not only in the world that must support life but in living tissues is for the most part irreversible. In this now universal contamination of the environment, chemicals are the sinister and little-recognized partners of radiation in changing the very nature of the world—the very nature of its life.

Johnson was determined to address such problems and to provide protection for wildlife. The National Wilderness Preservation Act of 1964 set aside 9.1 million acres of wilderness, and Congress passed other measures to limit air and water pollution. In addition, Lady Bird Johnson, the president's wife, led a beautification campaign to eliminate unsightly billboards and junkyards along the nation's highways.

Roots of Selected Great Society Programs

Progressive Period	New Deal	Great Society
Settlement house activity of Jane Addams and others	Relief efforts to ease unemployment (FERA, WPA)	Poverty programs (OEO)
Efforts to clean up slums (tenement house laws)	Housing program	Rehabilitation of slums through Model Cities program
Progressive party platform calling for federal accident, old-age, and unemployment insurance	Social security system providing unemployment compensation and old-age pensions	Medical care for the aged through social security (Medicare)
Activity to break up monopolies and regulate business	Regulation of utility companies	Regulation of highway safety and transportation
Efforts to regulate working conditions and benefits	Establishment of standards for working conditions and minimum wage	Raising of minimum wage
Efforts to increase literacy and spread education at all levels	Efforts to keep college students in school through NYA	Assistance to elementary, secondary, and higher education
Theodore Roosevelt's efforts at wilderness preservation	Conservation efforts (CCC, TVA planning)	Safeguarding of wilderness lands
Establishment of federal income tax	Tax reform to close loopholes and increase taxes for the wealthy	Tax cut to stimulate business activity
Theodore Roosevelt's overtures to Booker T. Washington	Discussion (but not passage) of antilynching legislation	Civil rights measures to ban discrimination in public accommodations and to guarantee right to vote

Achievements and Challenges in Civil Rights

Lyndon Johnson was enormously successful in advancing the cause of civil rights. Seizing the opportunity provided by Kennedy's assassination, Johnson told Congress, "No memorial oration or eulogy could more eloquently honor President Kennedy's memory than the earliest possible passage of the civil rights bill." Heading off a Senate filibuster, he pushed the bill through Congress.

The Civil Rights Act of 1964 outlawed racial discrimination in all public accommodations and authorized the Justice Department to act with greater authority in school and voting matters. In addition, an equal-opportunity provision prohibited discriminatory hiring on grounds of race, gender, religion, or national origin in firms with more than 25 employees. Although the law was one of the great achievements of the 1960s, widespread discrimination still existed in American society and African Americans in large areas of the South still found it difficult to vote. Freedom Summer,

Three Missing Civil Rights Volunteers

This poster shows pictures of the three civil rights workers who were missing soon after their arrival in Mississippi in the summer of 1964. What do the pictures tell you about the volunteers? What do you think people at the time would have thought when they saw this poster?

(Getty Images)

sponsored by SNCC and other civil rights groups in 1964, focused attention on the problem by sending black and white students to Mississippi to work for black rights. Early in the summer, two whites, Michael Schwerner and Andrew Goodman, and one black, James Chaney, were murdered. By the end of the summer, 80 workers had been beaten, 1,000 arrests had been made, and 37 churches had been bombed. In the face of such resistance, Johnson asked Congress for a voting bill that would close the loopholes of the previous two acts.

The Voting Rights Act of 1965 was perhaps the most important law of the decade. It singled out the South for its restrictive practices and authorized the U.S. attorney general to appoint federal examiners to register voters where local officials were obstructing the registration of blacks. In the year after passage of the act, 400,000 blacks registered to vote in the Deep South; by 1968, the number reached 1 million.

Despite passage of the Civil Rights Act of 1964 and the Voting Rights Act of 1965, racial discrimination remained throughout the country. Still-segregated schools, wretched housing, and inadequate job opportunities were continuing problems. As the struggle for civil rights moved north, dramatic divisions within the movement emerged.

Initially, the civil rights campaign had been integrated and nonviolent. Its acknowledged leader was Martin Luther King, Jr. But now tensions between blacks and whites flared within organizations, and younger black leaders began to challenge King's nonviolent approach. They were tired of beatings, jailings, church bombings, and the slow pace of change when dependent on white liberal support and government action. Anne Moody, the stalwart activist in Mississippi, voiced the doubts so many blacks harbored about the possibility of real change. Discouraged after months of struggle, she boarded a bus taking civil rights workers north to testify about the abuses that still remained. As she listened to the others singing the movement's songs, she was overwhelmed by the suffering she had so often seen. "We Shall Overcome" reverberated around her, but all she could think was, "I wonder. I really wonder."

One episode that contributed to many blacks' suspicion of white liberals occurred at the Democratic national convention of 1964 in Atlantic City. SNCC, active in the Freedom Summer project in Mississippi, had founded the Freedom Democratic party as an alternative to the all-white delegation that was to represent the state. Testifying before the credentials committee, black activist Fannie Lou Hamer reported that she had been beaten, jailed, and denied the right to vote. Yet the committee's final compromise, pressed by President Johnson, who worried about losing southern support in the coming election, was that the white delegation would still be seated, with two members of the protest organization offered seats at large. That response hardly satisfied those who had risked their lives and families to try to vote in Mississippi. SNCC, once a religious, integrated organization, began to change into an all-black cadre that could mobilize poor blacks for militant action. Malcolm X was perhaps the leader most responsible for channeling black frustration into a new set of goals and tactics. Born Malcolm Little and reared in ghettos from Detroit to New York, he hustled gambling numbers and prostitutes in the big cities. Arrested and imprisoned, he became a convert to the Nation of Islam and a disciple of black leader Elijah Muhammad. He began to preach that the white man was responsible for the black man's condition and that blacks had to help themselves.

Malcolm was impatient with the moderate civil rights movement. He grew tired of hearing "all of this nonviolent, begging-the-white-man kind of dying... all of this sitting-in, sliding-in, wading-in, eating-in, diving-in, and all the rest." Espousing black separatism and black nationalism for most of his public career, he argued for black control of black communities, preached an international perspective embracing African peoples in diaspora, and appealed to blacks to fight racism "by any means necessary."

Malcolm X became the most dynamic spokesman for poor northern blacks since Marcus Garvey in the 1920s. Though he was assassinated by black antagonists in 1965, his African-centered, uncompromising perspective helped shape the struggle against racism.

One man influenced by Malcolm's message was Stokely Carmichael. Born in Trinidad, he came to the United States at the age of 11, where he grew up with an interest in political affairs and black protest. Frustrated with the strategy of civil disobedience as he became active in SNCC, he urged fieldworkers to carry weapons for self-defense. It was time for blacks to cease depending on whites, he argued, and to make SNCC into a black organization. His election as head of the student group reflected SNCC's growing radicalism.

The split in the black movement was dramatized in June 1966 when Carmichael's followers challenged those of Martin Luther King, Jr., during a march in Mississippi. King still adhered to nonviolence and interracial cooperation. Just out of jail after being arrested for his protest activities, Carmichael jumped onto a flatbed truck to address the group. "This is the twenty-seventh time I have been arrested—and I ain't going to jail no more!" he shouted. "The only way we gonna stop them white men from whippin' us is to take over. We been saying freedom for six years and we ain't got nothing. What we gonna start saying now is Black Power!" Carmichael had the audience in his hand as he repeated, and the crowd shouted back, "We...want...Black...Power!"

Malcolm X at the Lectern

"The day of nonviolence is over," Malcolm X proclaimed, as many African Americans listened enthusiastically. A compelling speaker, Malcolm made a powerful case for a more aggressive campaign for black rights. What image does Malcolm X convey in this photograph?

(Bettmann/CORBIS)

Black Power was a call to build independent institutions in the African American community and it fostered a powerful sense of black pride. The movement included a wide variety of different figures, ranging from cultural nationalists to revolutionaries to advocates of black capitalism. Its most enduring legacy was political and cultural mobilization at the grassroots level, even if it only partially realized its goals.

Black Power led to demands for more drastic action. The Black Panthers, radical activists who organized first in Oakland, California, and then in other cities, formed a militant organization that vowed to eradicate not only racial discrimination but capitalism as well. H. Rap Brown, who succeeded Carmichael as head of SNCC, became known for his statement that "violence is as American as cherry pie."

Violence accompanied the more militant calls for reform and showed that racial injustice was not a southern problem but an American one. Riots erupted in Rochester, New York City, and several New Jersey cities in 1964. In 1965, in the Watts neighborhood of Los Angeles, a massive uprising lasting five days left

34 dead, more than 1,000 injured, and hundreds of structures burned to the ground. Violence broke out again in other cities in 1966, 1967, and 1968.

A Sympathetic Supreme Court

With the addition of four new liberal justices appointed by Kennedy and Johnson, the Supreme Court supported and promoted the liberal agenda. Under the leadership of chief justice Earl Warren, the Court followed the lead it had taken in *Brown* v. *Board of Education* outlawing school segregation by moving against Jim Crow practices in other public establishments.

The Court also supported civil liberties by beginning to protect the rights of individuals with radical political views. Similarly, the Court sought to protect accused suspects from police harassment. In *Gideon* v. *Wainwright* (1963), the justices decided that poor defendants in serious cases had the right to free legal counsel. In *Escobedo* v. *Illinois* (1964), they ruled that a suspect had to be given access to an attorney during questioning. In *Miranda* v. *Arizona* (1966), they argued that offenders had to be warned that statements extracted by the police could be used against them and that they could remain silent.

Other decisions similarly broke new ground. *Baker* v. *Carr* (1962) opened the way to reapportionment of state legislative bodies according to the standard, defined a year later in Justice William O. Douglas's words, of "one person, one vote." This crucial ruling helped break the political control of lightly populated rural districts in many state assemblies and made the U.S. House of Representatives much more responsive to urban and suburban issues. Meanwhile, the Court outraged conservatives by ruling that prayer could not be required in the public schools and that obscenity laws could no longer restrict allegedly pornographic material that might have some "redeeming social value."

The Great Society Under Attack

Supported by healthy economic growth, the Great Society worked for a few years as Johnson had hoped. The tax cut proved effective, and the consumer and business spending that it promoted led to a steady increase in the gross national product (GNP) of 7.1 percent in 1964, 8.1 percent in 1965, and 9.5 percent in 1966. As the economy improved, the budget deficit dropped just as predicted. Unemployment fell, and inflation remained under control. Medical programs provided basic security for the old and the poor. Education flourished as schools were built, and teachers' salaries increased as a result of the influx of federal aid.

Yet Johnson's dream of the Great Society proved illusory. Some programs promised too much; others were simply ill conceived or were underfunded. Factionalism was also a problem. Lyndon Johnson had reconstituted the old Democratic coalition in his triumph in 1964, with urban Catholics and southern whites joining organized labor, the black electorate, and the middle class. But conservative white southerners and blue-collar white northerners felt threatened by the government's support of civil rights. Local urban bosses, long the backbone of the Democratic party, objected to grassroots participation of the urban poor, which threatened their own political control.

Criticisms of the Great Society and its liberal underpinnings came from across the political spectrum. Conservatives disliked the centralization of authority and the government's increased role in defining the national welfare. They also questioned involving the poor in reform programs, arguing that poor people lacked a broad vision of the nation's needs. Even middle-class Americans, generally supportive of liberal goals, sometimes grumbled that the government was paying too much attention to the underprivileged and neglecting the needs of the middle class. Radicals, meanwhile, attacked the Great Society for not going far enough. With its assumption that the American system was basically sound, they argued, the Great Society made no real effort to redistribute income and thereby transform American life.

The Vietnam War (discussed later in this chapter) dealt the Great Society a fatal blow. LBJ wanted to maintain both the war and his treasured domestic reform programs, but his effort to pursue these goals simultaneously produced serious inflation. The economy was already booming as a result of the tax cut and the spending for reform. As military expenditures increased, the productive system of the country could not keep up with demand. When Johnson refused to raise taxes, in an effort to hide the costs of the war, inflation spiraled out of control. Congress finally slashed Great Society programs, deciding the country could no longer afford such extensive social reform.

Continuing Confrontations with Communists

The Cold War continued throughout the 1960s. Presidents John F. Kennedy and Lyndon B. Johnson were both aggressive cold warriors who subscribed to the policies of their predecessors. Their commitment to stopping the spread of communism kept the nation locked in the same bitter conflict that had dominated foreign policy in the 1950s and led to continuing global confrontations that sometimes threatened the stability of the entire world.

The Bay of Pigs Fiasco and Its Consequences

Kennedy was intensely interested in foreign affairs. In his ringing inaugural address, he eloquently described the dangers and challenges the United States faced in the Cold War. "In the long history of the world," he cried out, "only a few generations have been granted the role of defending freedom in its hour of maximum danger." The United States would "pay any price, bear any burden, meet any hardship, support any friend, oppose any foe, to assure the survival and success of liberty."

Kennedy perceived direct challenges from the Soviet Union almost from the beginning of his presidency. The first came at the Bay of Pigs in Cuba in the spring of 1961. Cuban–American relations had been strained since Fidel Castro's revolutionary army had seized power in 1959. A radical regime in Cuba, leaning toward the Soviet Union, could provide a model for upheaval elsewhere in Latin America and threaten the venerable Monroe Doctrine. One initiative to counter the Communist threat was the Alliance for Progress, which provided social and economic assistance to the less-developed nations of the hemisphere. But other, more aggressive, responses were deemed necessary as well.

Just before Kennedy assumed office, the United States broke diplomatic relations with Cuba. The CIA, meanwhile, was covertly training anti-Castro exiles to storm the Cuban coast at the Bay of Pigs. The American planners assumed the invasion would lead to an uprising of the Cuban people against Castro. While some top officials resisted the scheme, Kennedy approved the plan.

The invasion, which took place on April 17, 1961, was an unmitigated disaster. When an early air strike failed to destroy Cuban air power, Castro was able to hold off the troops coming ashore. Urged to use American planes for air cover, Kennedy refused, for by that time failure was clear. Rather than supporting the exiles, the Cubans had followed Castro instead, and the predicted popular uprising never materialized. The United States stood exposed to the world, attempting to overthrow a sovereign government. It had broken agreements not to interfere in the internal affairs of hemispheric neighbors and had intervened clumsily and unsuccessfully.

Although chastened by the debacle at the Bay of Pigs, Kennedy remained determined to deal sternly with the perceived Communist threat. Germany became the next battleground. For more than a decade, the nation had been divided (see Chapter 27). The Western powers had promoted the industrial development of West Germany, which was prospering and which stood in stark contrast to the drab, Soviet-controlled East Germany. Berlin, likewise divided, remained an irritant to the Russians, particularly since some 2.6 million East Germans had fled to West Germany, many of them making their escape through the city. Following a hostile meeting with Soviet leader Nikita Khrushchev in Vienna in June 1961, Kennedy reacted aggressively. He asked Congress for $3 billion more in defense appropriations, for more personnel in the armed forces, and for funds for a civil defense fallout-shelter program, explicitly warning of the threat of nuclear war. The USSR responded in August by erecting a wall in Berlin to seal off its section of the city entirely. The concrete structure, topped by barbed wire, was 96 miles long and an average of 11.8 feet high. Menacing machine-gun emplacements made escape difficult. People who were caught scaling the wall were shot. Families were separated as the wall became a dramatic symbol of the division between East and West.

The Cuban Missile Face-Off

The next year, a new crisis arose. American aerial photographs taken in October 1962 revealed that the USSR had begun to place what Kennedy considered offensive missiles on Cuban soil, although Cuba insisted they were defensive. The missiles did not change the strategic balance significantly, for the Soviets could still wreak untold damage on American targets from more distant bases. But with Russian weapons installed just 90 miles from American shores, appearance was more important than reality. This time Kennedy was determined to win a confrontation with the Soviet Union over Cuba.

Top administration officials discussed various alternatives. Some members of the Executive Committee of the National Security Council wanted an air strike to knock out the sites; others, including Attorney General Robert Kennedy, the president's brother, opposed such a move. Still, the United States moved to a state of full alert. Bombers and missiles were armed with nuclear weapons and readied to go. The fleet prepared to move toward Cuba, and troops geared up to invade the island.

Kennedy went on nationwide television to tell the American people about the missiles and to demand their removal. He declared that the United States would not shrink from the risk of nuclear war and announced what he had decided to do: impose a naval "quarantine"—not a blockade, which would have been an act of war—around Cuba to prevent Soviet ships from bringing in additional missiles.

As the Soviet ships steamed toward the blockade, the nations stood "eyeball to eyeball" at the brink. Before they reached the quarantine line, Khrushchev called the Soviet ships back. Khrushchev then sent a long letter, transmitted by teletype, pledging to remove the missiles if the United States lifted the quarantine and promised to stay out of Cuba altogether. A second letter demanded that America remove its own missiles from Turkey as well. The United States agreed to the

Israeli Conquests in 1967

The Six-Day War of 1967 ended in huge Israeli territorial gains, both in the Sinai and on the West Bank of the Jordan River. How did the new territory compare with the size of the state of Israel prior to 1967? What effect did the Israeli victory have on the stability of the Middle East? How would the Arab nations have responded to the defeat?

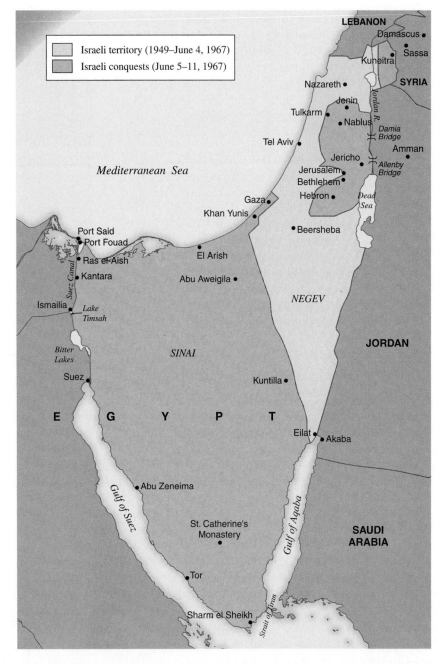

Israeli territory (1949–June 4, 1967)
Israeli conquests (June 5–11, 1967)

first letter, ignored the second, and said nothing about its intention, already voiced, of removing its missiles from Turkey. With that, the crisis ended. Secretary of State Dean Rusk observed, "We have won a considerable victory. You and I are still alive."

The Cuban missile crisis was the most terrifying confrontation of the Cold War. The world was closer than it had ever been to nuclear war. Yet the president emerged from it as a hero who had stood firm. His reputation was enhanced, and his party benefited a few weeks later in the congressional elections. As the relief began to fade, however, critics charged that what Kennedy saw as his finest hour was in fact an unnecessary crisis. One consequence of the affair was the installation of a Soviet–American hotline to avoid similar episodes in the future. Another consequence was the USSR's determination to increase its nuclear arsenal so that it would never again be exposed as inferior to the United States. Despite the Limited Test Ban Treaty of 1963, which prohibited atmospheric testing, the nuclear arms race continued.

Confrontation and Containment Under Johnson

Johnson shared many of Kennedy's assumptions about the threat of communism. His understanding of the onset of World War II led him to believe that aggressors had to be stopped cold. Like Eisenhower and Kennedy, Johnson believed in the domino theory: if one country in a region fell, others were bound to follow. He assumed he could treat foreign adversaries just as he treated political opponents in the United States, and he was frustrated with what he called "piddly little piss-ant" countries that caused trouble.

In 1965, Johnson acted hastily in the Caribbean. He dispatched more than 20,000 troops to the Dominican Republic to counter "Castro-type elements" that were, in fact, engaged in a democratic revolution. His credibility suffered badly from the episode.

In the Middle East, the United States sought to use its influence to temper the violence that erupted in the area. In 1967, Israeli forces defeated the Egyptian army in the Six-Day War and seized the West Bank and Jerusalem, the Golan Heights, and the Sinai Peninsula. Americans pressed for a quick end to the fighting to maintain regional equilibrium and uninterrupted supplies of oil.

War in Vietnam and Turmoil at Home

The commitment to stopping the spread of communism led to the massive U.S. involvement in Vietnam. The roots of the conflict, described in Chapter 26, extended back to the early post–World War II years, but American participation remained relatively limited until Kennedy took office. Then the United States became increasingly engaged in the effort to resist a Communist takeover. That struggle wrought enormous damage in Southeast Asia, tore the United States apart, and finally forced a full-fledged reevaluation of America's Cold War policies.

Escalation in Vietnam

JFK's commitment to Cold War victory led him to expand the American role in Vietnam, the country he once called the "cornerstone of the free world in Southeast Asia." During the Kennedy administration, the number of advisers rose from 675 to more than 16,000, and American soldiers began to lose their lives.

Despite American backing, South Vietnamese leader Ngo Dinh Diem, a Catholic, was rapidly losing support in his own country. Buddhist priests burned themselves alive in the capital of Saigon to protest the corruption and arbitrariness of Diem's regime. With American approval, South Vietnamese military leaders assassinated Diem and seized the government. While Kennedy understood the importance of popular support for the South Vietnamese government, he was reluctant to withdraw and let the Vietnamese solve their own problems.

Lyndon Johnson shared the same reservations. Soon after assuming the presidency, he made a fundamental decision that guided policy for the next four years. Guerrillas, known as Viet Cong, challenged the

A Protest in Vietnam

In 1963, Buddhist priests in Vietnam burned themselves to death in Saigon to dramatize their opposition to the Diem government. Photographs in American newspapers horrified readers and created suspicion that South Vietnam was led by a corrupt and autocratic leader. Why would this photograph have affected people who saw it so strongly?

(Bettmann/CORBIS)

The Vietnam War

This map shows the major campaigns of the Vietnam War. The North Vietnamese Tet offensive of early 1968, pictured with red arrows, turned the tide against U.S. participation in the war and led to peace talks. The U.S. invasion of Cambodia in 1970, pictured with blue arrows, provoked serious opposition. What role did North Vietnam play in the war? How far did American air power penetrate? Why did the United States and South Vietnam attack neighboring nations, such as Cambodia?

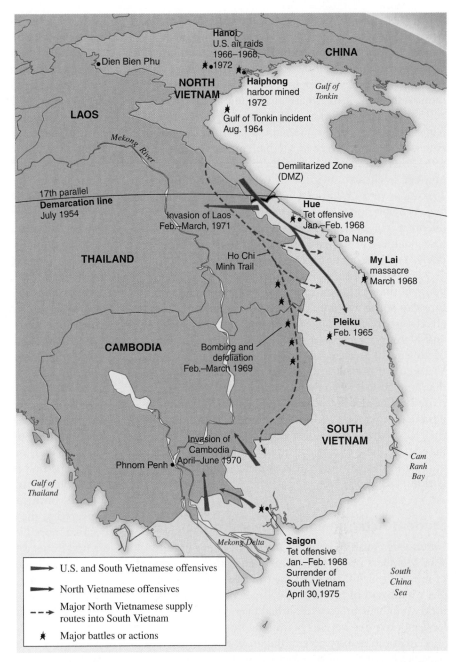

regime, sometimes covertly and sometimes through the National Liberation Front, their political arm. Aided by Ho Chi Minh and the North Vietnamese, the insurgent Viet Cong slowly gained ground. Johnson chose to stand firm and resist them. "I am not going to lose Vietnam," he said. "I am not going to be the President who saw Southeast Asia go the way China went."

In the 1964 election campaign, Johnson posed as a man of peace. "We don't want our American boys to do the fighting for Asian boys," he declared. But secretly he was planning to escalate the American role.

In August 1964, Johnson cleverly obtained congressional authorization for war. He charged that North Vietnamese torpedo boats had made unprovoked

attacks on American destroyers in the international waters of the Gulf of Tonkin, 30 miles from North Vietnam. While there had been initial conflict, in fact the attacks Johnson highlighted never occurred. But before the real nature of the engagement became clear, LBJ used the episode to obtain from Congress a resolution giving him authority to "take all necessary measures to repel any armed attack against the forces of the United States and to prevent further aggression." The Gulf of Tonkin resolution gave Johnson the leverage he sought. As he noted, it was "like grandma's nightshirt—it covered everything."

Military escalation began in earnest in February 1965, after Johnson's landslide electoral victory.

When Viet Cong forces killed 7 Americans and wounded 109 in an attack on an American base at Pleiku, Johnson responded by authorizing retaliatory bombing of North Vietnam to cut off the flow of supplies and to ease pressure on South Vietnam. A few months later, he sent American ground troops into action. This marked the crucial turning point in the Americanization of the Vietnam War. Only 25,000 American soldiers were in Vietnam at the start of 1965; by the end of the year, there were 184,000. The number swelled to 385,000 in 1966, to 485,000 in 1967, and to 543,000 in 1968.

As escalation occurred, Johnson recognized his dilemma. He understood that the war was probably unwinnable, but he feared the loss of both American power and personal prestige if he pulled out.

And so American forces became direct participants in the fight to prop up a dictatorial regime in faraway South Vietnam. Although a somewhat more effective government headed by Nguyen Van Thieu and Nguyen Cao Ky was finally established, the level of violence increased. Saturation bombing of North Vietnam continued. Fragmentation bombs, killing and maiming countless civilians, and napalm, which seared off human flesh, were used extensively. Similar destruction wracked South Vietnam. And still, despite the repeatedly expressed contention of military commander William Westmoreland that there was "light at the end of the tunnel," the violence continued without pause.

Student Activism and Antiwar Protest

Americans began to protest U.S. involvement in the war. Members of the baby boom generation who came of age in the 1960s were in the forefront of the struggle. By the end of the 1960s, college enrollment was more than four times what it had been in the 1940s. College provided necessary training but also gave students time to experiment and grow before they had to make a living. Some students joined the struggle for civil rights. Hopeful at first, they gradually became discouraged by the gap between Kennedy's New Frontier rhetoric and the government's actual commitment.

Out of that disillusionment arose the radical spirit of the New Left. Civil rights activists were among those who in 1960 organized Students for a Democratic Society (SDS). In 1962, SDS issued a manifesto, the *Port Huron Statement,* written largely by Tom Hayden of the University of Michigan, which outlined both complaints and goals for a participatory democracy. "We are people of this generation, bred in at least modest comfort, housed now in universities, looking uncomfortably at the world we inherit," it began. It went on to deplore the vast social and economic distances separating people from each other and to condemn the estrangement of modern life.

The first blow of the growing student rebellion came at the University of California in Berkeley. There, civil rights activists became involved in a confrontation soon known as the Free Speech Movement. When the university refused to allow students to distribute protest material outside the main campus gate, they asserted their constitutional rights. After police arrested one of the leaders, students surrounded the police car and kept it from moving all night. The university regents brought charges against the student leaders, and when the regents refused to drop the charges, the students occupied the administration building. Police stormed in and arrested the students. A strike, with faculty aid, mobilized wider support for the right to free speech.

The Free Speech Movement at Berkeley was basically a plea for traditional liberal reform. Students sought only the reaffirmation of the long-standing right to express themselves as they chose, and they aimed their attacks at the university, not at society as a whole. Later, in other institutions, the attack broadened. Students sought greater involvement in university affairs, argued for curriculum reform, and demanded admission of more minority students. The mounting protest against the escalation of the Vietnam War fueled and refocused the youth movement. The first teach-in took place in March 1965 at the University of Michigan. Others soon followed. Initially, both supporters and opponents of the war appeared at the teach-ins, but quickly the sessions became more like antiwar rallies than instructional affairs. Boxer Muhammad Ali legitimated draft resistance when he declared, "I ain't got no quarrel with them Viet Cong," and refused military induction. Working through SDS and other organizations, radical activists campaigned against the draft, attacked ROTC units on campus, and sought to discredit firms that produced the destructive tools of war. "Make love, not war," students proclaimed. As the antiwar movement expanded, students became even more shrill. "Hey, hey, LBJ. How many kids did you kill today?" they chanted as they marched in protest. Women Strike for Peace, the most forceful women's antiwar organization, mobilized support by saying, "Stop! Don't drench the jungles of Asia with the blood of our sons. Don't force our sons to kill women and children whose only crime is to live in a country ripped by civil war." In 1967, some 300,000 people demonstrated in New York City. In Washington, D.C., 100,000 tried to close down the Pentagon.

Working-class and middle-class Americans began to sour on the war at the time of the Tet offensive, celebrating the lunar new year, in early 1968. The North Vietnamese mounted massive attacks across South

Vietnam. In Saigon, they struck the American embassy, Tan Son Nhut air base, and the presidential palace. Though beaten back, they won a psychological victory. American audiences saw images of burning huts and wounded soldiers each evening on television as they ate dinner. During the Tet offensive, American television networks showed scenes of a kind never screened before. One such clip, from NBC News, appears here in still photograph form (below). Viewers who watched the television clip saw the corpse drop to the ground, blood spurting from his head. Gazing at such graphic representations of death and destruction, many Americans wondered about their nation's purposes and actions.

Protest became a way of life. Between January 1 and June 15, 1968, hundreds of thousands of students staged 221 major demonstrations at more than 100 educational institutions. One of the most dramatic episodes came in April 1968 at Columbia University, where the issues of civil rights and war were tightly intertwined. A strong SDS chapter urged the university to break ties with the Institute of Defense Analysis, which specialized in military research. The Students' Afro-American Society tried to stop the building of a new gymnasium, which it claimed encroached on the Harlem community and disrupted life there. Whites occupied one building, blacks another. Finally, the president of the university called in the police. Hundreds of students were arrested; many were hurt. A student sympathy strike followed, and Columbia closed for the summer several weeks early.

The student protests in the United States were part of a worldwide wave of student activism. French students demonstrated in the streets of Paris. In Germany, young radicals were equally vocal in challenging conventional norms. In Japan, students waged armed battles with police.

The Counterculture

Cultural change accompanied political upheaval. Many Americans—some politically active, some not—found new ways to assert their individuality and independence. As in the political sphere, the young led the way, often drawing on the example of the Beats of the 1950s as they sought new means of self-gratification and self-expression.

Surface appearances were most visible and, to older Americans, most troubling. The "hippies" of the 1960s carried themselves in different ways. Men let their hair grow and sprouted beards; men and women both donned jeans, muslin shirts, and other simple garments. Stressing spontaneity above all else, some rejected traditional marital customs and gravitated to communal living groups. Sexual norms underwent a revolution as more people separated sex from its traditional ties to family life. A generation of young women came of age with access to "the pill"—an oral contraceptive that was effortless to use and freed sexual experimentation from the threat of pregnancy. In 1960, the Food and Drug Administration approved Enovid, the first oral contraceptive available on the market. Within three years of its introduction, more than 2 million women

Death of a Viet Cong Suspect

In this picture, General Nguyen Ngoc Loan, the chief of the South Vietnamese National Police, looks at a Viet Cong prisoner, lifts his gun, and calmly blows out the captive's brains. This prize-winning photograph captured the horror of the war for many Americans. What impressions do you think this picture conveyed to people who saw it?

(AP/Wide World Photos)

were on the pill, and as the cost dropped, millions more began to use it.

Americans of all social classes became more open to exploring, and enjoying, their sexuality. Scholarly findings supported natural inclinations. Author and editor Nora Ephron summed up the sexual changes in the 1960s as she reflected on her own experiences. Initially she had "a hangover from the whole Fifties virgin thing," she recalled. "The first man I went to bed with, I was in love with and wanted to marry. The second one I was in love with, but I didn't have to marry him. With the third one, I thought I might fall in love."

The arts reflected the sexual revolution. Federal courts ruled that books like D. H. Lawrence's *Lady Chatterley's Lover* and other suppressed works could not be banned. Nudity became more common on stage and screen. In *Hair,* a rock musical, one scene featured the disrobing of performers of both genders in the course of an erotic celebration.

Paintings reflected both the mood of dissent and the urge to innovate, apparent in the larger society. "Op" artists painted sharply defined geometric figures in clear, vibrant colors, starkly different from the flowing, chaotic work of the abstract expressionists. "Pop" artists such as Andy Warhol, Roy Lichtenstein, and Jasper Johns made ironic comments on American materialism and taste with their representations of everyday objects such as soup cans, comic strips, and pictures of Marilyn Monroe.

Hallucinogenic drugs also became a part of the counterculture. One prophet of the drug scene was Timothy Leary, a scientific researcher experimenting with LSD at Harvard University. Fired for violating a pledge not to use undergraduates as subjects, Leary aggressively asserted that drugs were necessary to free the mind. Working through his group, the League for Spiritual Discovery, he dressed in long robes and preached his message, "Tune in, turn on, drop out."

Another apostle of life with drugs was Ken Kesey. While writing his first novel, *One Flew Over the Cuckoo's Nest,* he began participating in medical experiments at a hospital where he was introduced to LSD. With the profits from his novel, Kesey established a commune of "Merry Pranksters" near Palo Alto, California. In 1964, the group headed east in a converted school bus painted in psychedelic Day-Glo colors, wired for sound, and stocked with enough orange juice and "acid" (LSD) to sustain the Pranksters across the continent.

Drug use was no longer confined to urban subcultures. Soldiers brought experience with drugs back from Vietnam. Taking a "tab" of LSD became part of the coming-of-age ritual for many middle-class college students. Marijuana became phenomenally popular in the 1960s. "Joints" of "grass" were passed around at high school, neighborhood, and college parties as readily as cans of beer had been in the previous generation.

Music became intimately connected with these cultural changes. The rock and roll of the 1950s and the gentle strains of folk music gave way to a new kind of rock that swept the country—and the world (see the "Recovering the Past" essay in Chapter 29, pp. 726–727, for a discussion of the music of the 1960s).

Rock festivals became popular throughout the decade. On an August weekend in 1969, some 400,000 people gathered in a large pasture in upstate New York for the Woodstock rock festival. This exuberant celebration, which featured earsplitting, around-the-clock entertainment and endlessly available marijuana, went off without a hitch. Another festival four months later at a stock car raceway in Altamont, California, was less fortunate. Four people died when audience members clashed with members of Hell's Angels, a motorcycle gang hired to provide security for the Rolling Stones.

The underside of the counterculture was most visible in the Haight-Ashbury section of San Francisco, where runaway "flower children" mingled with "burned-out" drug users and radical activists. For all the spontaneity and excitement, the counterculture had a darker side.

An Age of Assassination

In 1968, American society seemed to be tearing apart. The so called "generation gap" caused major rifts between parents and children. Political protest was growing increasingly violent. Yet there was still a basic confidence that the democratic process could bring meaningful change. John Kennedy had fallen to an assassin's bullet five years before and the nation had survived that trauma. Then two more killings of highly prominent figures undermined any sense of hope.

Martin Luther King, Jr., was the most visible spokesman for African Americans in the years after 1955. By the mid-1960s, he had broadened his crusade to attack poverty and economic injustice and had also begun to speak out against the war in Vietnam, which included a disproportionate number of black soldiers serving in combat roles and losing their lives.

King knew he was a target. On April 3, 1968, he spoke eloquently at a church service, making reference to threats on his life. "We've got some difficult days ahead," he said. "But it doesn't matter with me now, because I've been to the mountain top . . . and I've seen the promised land." The next day, as King stood on the balcony of his motel in Memphis, Tennessee, a bullet from a high-powered rifle ripped through his jaw and killed him. King's assassination sparked a wave of violence throughout the United States. In a spontaneous outburst of rage, African Americans in 124 cities rioted, setting fires and looting stores. For all Americans, King's death eroded faith in the possibility of nonviolent change.

Several months later, Robert F. Kennedy likewise lost his life. Bobby had won election to the Senate from New York after his brother's death and was running for the 1968 Democratic presidential nomination. Kennedy had spoken out eloquently to the poor and had persuaded antiwar activists that he could bring the Vietnam conflict to an end. In June, he won an important victory in the California primary. That evening, after his victory speech, he too was shot by an assassin. Kennedy's death, like King's, shattered hopes for reconciliation or reform.

The Chaotic Election of 1968

The turbulent Democratic convention undermined any final hopes the party had for victory. Chicago Mayor Richard Daley was outraged that radicals and hippies were coming to his city to protest and ordered law enforcement officers to clear out the demonstrators. They did so in front of television cameras as the country watched Hubert Humphrey, Johnson's vice president, running for the Democratic nomination after Johnson declined to seek reelection, win a tainted victory.

Humphrey faced former vice president Richard Nixon. He had failed in his first bid in 1960 and later lost a race for governor of California. Written off by most politicians, he staged a comeback after the Goldwater debacle of 1964, and by 1968, he seemed to have a good shot at the presidency again.

Governor George C. Wallace of Alabama, a third-party candidate, exploited social and racial tensions in his campaign. Appealing to northern working-class voters as well as southern whites, Wallace characterized those who wanted to reform American life as "left-wing theoreticians, briefcase-totin' bureaucrats, ivory-tower guideline writers, bearded anarchists, smart-aleck editorial writers and pointy-headed professors." He hoped to ride into office on blue-collar resentment of social disorder and liberal aims.

Nixon addressed the same constituency, calling it the "silent majority." Capitalizing on the dismay these Americans felt over campus disruptions and inner-city riots and appealing to latent racism, he promised law and order if elected. He also called the Great Society a costly mistake. Nixon received 43 percent of the popular vote, not quite 1 percent more than Humphrey, with Wallace capturing the rest. But it was enough to give the Republicans a majority in the Electoral College and Nixon the presidency at last.

Continuing Protest

Meanwhile, protests continued. The next year, in October 1969, the Weathermen, a militant fringe group of SDS, that took its name from a line in a Bob Dylan song—"You don't need a weatherman to know which way the wind blows"—descended on Chicago and rampaged through the streets for four days in an armed battle with police.

Why had the Weathermen launched their attack? "The status quo meant to us war, poverty, inequality, ignorance, famine and disease in most of the world," Bo Burlingham, a participant from Ohio, reflected. "To accept it was to condone and help perpetuate it. We felt like miners trapped in a terrible poisonous shaft with no light to guide us out. We resolved to destroy the tunnel even if we risked destroying ourselves in the process." The rationale of the Chicago "national action" may have been clear to the participants, but it infuriated citizens around the country.

PRESIDENTIAL ELECTIONS OF THE 1960S

Year	Candidate	Party	Popular Vote	Electoral Vote
1960	JOHN F. KENNEDY	Democratic	34,227,096 (49.9%)	303
	Richard M. Nixon	Republican	34,108,546 (49.6%)	219
	Harry F. Byrd	Independent	501,643 (0.7%)	15
1964	LYNDON B. JOHNSON	Democratic	43,126,584 (61.1%)	486
	Barry M. Goldwater	Republican	27,177,838 (38.5%)	52
1968	RICHARD M. NIXON	Republican	31,783,783 (43.4%)	301
	Hubert M. Humphrey	Democratic	31,271,839 (42.7%)	191
	George C. Wallace	American Independent	9,899,557 (13.5%)	46

Note: Winners' names appear in capital letters.

Timeline

1960	John F. Kennedy elected president
	Birth control pill becomes available
	Sit-ins begin
	Students for a Democratic Society (SDS) founded
1961	Freedom rides
	Joseph Heller, *Catch-22*
	Ken Kesey, *One Flew Over the Cuckoo's Nest*
	Bay of Pigs invasion fails
	Khrushchev and Kennedy meet in Berlin
	Berlin Wall constructed
	JFK confronts steel companies
1962	Cuban missile crisis
	James Meredith crisis at the University of Mississippi
	SDS's *Port Huron Statement*
	Rachel Carson, *Silent Spring*
1963	Buddhist demonstrations in Vietnam
	Birmingham demonstration
	Civil rights march on Washington
	Kennedy assassinated; Lyndon B. Johnson becomes president
	Betty Friedan, *The Feminine Mystique*
1964	Economic Opportunity Act initiates War on Poverty
	Gulf of Tonkin resolution
	Johnson elected president
	Civil Rights Act
	Free Speech Movement, Berkeley
	Tax Cut passed
1965	Department of Housing and Urban Development established
	Elementary and Secondary Education Act
	Medicare established
	Medicaid established
	Martin Luther King, Jr., leads march from Selma to Montgomery
	Voting Rights Act
	United Farm Workers grape boycott
	Malcolm X assassinated
	Riot in Watts section of Los Angeles
	Ralph Nader, *Unsafe at Any Speed*
	Vietnam conflict escalates
	Marines sent to Dominican Republic
1966	Stokely Carmichael becomes head of SNCC and calls for "Black Power"
	Black Panthers founded
1967	Urban riots in 22 cities
1967–1968	Antiwar demonstrations
1968	Student demonstrations at Columbia University and elsewhere
	Tet offensive in Vietnam
	Martin Luther King, Jr., assassinated
	Robert F. Kennedy assassinated
	Police and protesters clash at Democratic national convention
	Richard Nixon elected president
1969	Woodstock and Altamont rock festivals
	Weathermen's "Days of Rage" in Chicago

Conclusion

POLITICAL AND SOCIAL UPHEAVAL

The 1960s were turbulent years. In the first part of the decade, the United States was relatively calm. Liberal Democrats went even further than Franklin Roosevelt and Harry Truman as they pressed for large-scale government intervention to meet the social and economic problems that accompanied the modern industrial age. They were inspired by John Kennedy's rhetoric and saw the triumph of their approach in Lyndon Johnson's Great Society, as the nation strengthened its commitment to a capitalist welfare state. Then the Democratic party became impaled on the Vietnam War, and opposition to the conflict created more turbulence than the nation had known since the Civil War.

American society was in a state of upheaval. Young radicals challenged basic assumptions about how the government worked. They railed against social injustice at home, and they protested a foreign policy that they regarded as wrong. Their efforts faltered at first but then succeeded when they seized on the war in Vietnam as a primary focus and began to attack the Cold War policy that led to massive American military involvement in that faraway land. Student leaders soon found hundreds of thousands of followers who joined in the marches and demonstrations that finally forced the nation to reconsider its aims. Meanwhile, members of the counterculture promoted their own more fluid values, challenged the patterns of conformity so important in the 1950s, and led millions of other Americans, some politically active, some not, to dress and act differently than in the past. The two strands of political activism and countercultural action were independent but intertwined, and they left the nation at the end of the decade very different than it had been before.

Most Americans, like Paul Cowan (introduced at the start of this chapter), embraced the message of John Kennedy and the New Frontier in the early 1960s and endorsed the liberal approach. But over time, they began to question the tenets of liberalism as the economy faltered, as hard economic choices had to be made, and as the country became mired in an unwinnable war in Vietnam. Conservatives deplored the chaos, while disillusioned liberals like Paul Cowan wondered if their approach could ever succeed.

QUESTIONS FOR REVIEW AND REFLECTION

1. How did John F. Kennedy represent the hopes and ideals of Americans in the early 1960s?
2. How successful was Lyndon Johnson's Great Society?
3. What impact did the war in Vietnam have on protest at home?
4. What were the most important changes experienced by the United States in the late 1960s?
5. What was the lasting impact of the protest that rocked America in the 1960s?

Disorder and Discontent, 1969–1980

Latinos, like women and members of other groups, worked to mobilize their communities behind the campaign for equal rights. This mural in an East Los Angeles housing project helped foster a sense of Chicano pride.

(Craig Aurness/Woodfin Camp & Associates)

American Stories

An Older Woman Returns to School

Ann Clarke—as she chooses to call herself now—always wanted to go to college. But girls from Italian families rarely did when she was growing up. Her mother, a Sicilian immigrant and widow, asked her brother for advice: "Should Antonina go to college?" "What's the point?" he replied. "She's just going to get married."

Life had not been easy for Antonina Rose Rumore. As a child in the 1920s, her Italian-speaking grandmother cared for her while her mother worked to support the family, first in the sweatshops, then as a seamstress. Even as she dreamed about the future, Ann accommodated her culture's demands for dutiful daughters. Responsive to family needs, Ann finished the high school commercial course in three years. She struggled with ethnic prejudice as a legal secretary on Wall Street but still believed in the American dream and the Puritan work ethic. She was proud of her ability to bring money home to her family.

When World War II began, Ann wanted to join the WACs. "Better you should be a prostitute," her mother said. Ann went off to California instead, where she worked at a number of resorts. When she left California, she vowed to return to that land of freedom and opportunity.

After the war, Ann married Gerard Clarke, a college man with an English background. Her children would grow up accepted with Anglo-Saxon names. Over the next 15 years, Ann devoted herself to her family. She was a mother first and foremost, and that took all her time. But she still waited for her own chance. "I had this hunger to learn, this curiosity," she later recalled. By the early 1960s, her three children were all in school. Promising her husband to have dinner on the table every night at six, she enrolled at Pasadena City College. It was not easy, for family still came first, but Ann proved creative in finding time to study. When doing dishes or cleaning house, she memorized lists of dates, historical events, and other material for school. Holidays, however, complicated her efforts to complete assignments. Ann occasionally felt compelled to give everything up "to make Christmas." Forgetting about a whole semester's work two weeks before finals one year, she sewed nightgowns instead of writing her art history paper.

Her conflict over her studies was intensified by her position as one of the first older women to go back to college. "Sometimes I felt like I wanted to hide in the woodwork," she admitted. Often her teachers were younger than she was. It took four years to complete the two-year program. But she was not yet done, for she really wanted a bachelor's degree. Back she went, this time to California State College at Los Angeles.

As the years passed and the credits piled up, Ann became an honors student. Her children, now in college themselves, were proud and supportive; dinners became arguments over Faulkner and foreign policy. Even so, Ann still felt caught between her world at home and the world outside. Since she was at the top of her class, graduation should have been a special occasion. But she was only embarrassed when a letter from the school invited her parents to attend the final ceremonies. Ann could not bring herself to go.

With a college degree in hand, Ann returned to school for a teaching credential. Receiving her certificate at age 50, she faced the irony of social change. Once denied opportunities, Italians had assimilated into American society. Now she was just another Anglo in Los Angeles, caught in a changing immigration wave; now the city sought Latinos and other minorities to teach in the schools. Jobs in education were scarce, and she was close to retirement age, so she became a substitute teacher in Mexican American areas for the next 10 years, specializing in bilingual education.

Meanwhile, Ann was troubled by the Vietnam War. "For every boy that died, one of us should lie down," she told fellow workers. She was not an activist, but rather one of the millions of quieter Americans who ultimately helped bring about change. The social adjustments caused by the war affected her. Her son grew long hair and a beard and attended protest rallies. She worried that he would antagonize the ladies in Pasadena. Her daughter came home from college in boots and a leather miniskirt designed to shock. Ann accepted her children's changes as relatively superficial, confident in their fundamental values; they were "good kids," she knew. She trusted them, even as she worried about them.

Ann Clarke's experience paralleled that of millions of women in the post–World War II years. Caught up in traditional patterns of family life, these women began to recognize their need for something more against a backdrop of continuing political turbulence that sometimes seemed to undermine the nation's stability. They worried about both the global and the domestic consequences of the war in Vietnam and the constitutional issues in the Watergate scandal that threatened the American democratic system and eventually brought President Richard Nixon down. Meanwhile, American women, like blacks, Latinos and Latinas, Native Americans, and members of other groups, struggled to transform the conditions of their lives and the rights they enjoyed within American society. Building on the successes of the past several decades, these diverse groups demanded their own right to equality and equitable treatment in fulfillment of their own American dreams. In the course of their struggle, they changed the nation itself.

This chapter describes the continuing upheaval that shook American society in the 1970s. It shows the ongoing impact of global events as the Nixon administration struggled to find a way of ending the devastating struggle in Vietnam. Its effort to extricate American soldiers eased domestic protest, but then its decision to widen the war with incursions into other parts of Southeast Asia created further chaos in the United States. The chapter chronicles the most serious political scandal in American history, which led the president to resign. It records the growing agitation of environmental and consumer activists as they learned how to make their voices heard. And it describes the ongoing effort to provide liberty and equality in racial, gender, and social relations. While political challenges came from middle-class activists, social complaints came from often marginalized Americans who finally spoke out in an attempt to make the nation live up to its professed values. This chapter highlights the diverse voices that continued to echo throughout the 1970s in a heated debate about the distribution of social, political, and economic power in the United States.

The Decline of Liberalism

After eight years of Democratic rule, many Americans were frustrated with the liberal approach. They questioned the liberal agenda and the government's ability to solve social problems. As the war in Vietnam polarized the country, critics argued that the government was trying to do too much. Capitalizing on the alienation sparked by the war, the Republican administration of Richard Nixon resolved to scale down the commitment to social change. Like Dwight Eisenhower a decade and a half before, Nixon accepted some social programs as necessary but still wanted to trim the federal bureaucracy. Furthermore, he and his political colleagues were determined to pay more attention to the needs of white, middle-class Americans who disliked the social disorder they saw as a consequence of rapid social change and resented the government's perceived favoritism toward the poor and dispossessed.

Richard Nixon and His Team

In and out of office, Nixon was a complex, remote man who carefully concealed his private self. Born poor, he was determined to be successful and accomplished that aim in the political sphere. Yet he constantly appeared to be scheming or conniving. There was, one of his aides noted, "a mean side to his nature" that he sought to keep from public view. Physically awkward and humorless, he was most comfortable alone or with a few wealthy friends. Even at work he insulated himself, preferring written contacts to personal ones.

Nixon was keenly aware of the psychology of politics in the electronic age. He believed that "in the modern presidency, concern for image must rank with concern for substance." Thus, he posed in public as the defender of American morality, though in private he was frequently coarse and profane. Earlier in his career he had been labeled "Tricky Dick" for his apparent

willingness to do anything to advance his career. In subsequent years, he had tried to create the appearance of a "new Nixon," but to many he still appeared to be a mechanical man, always calculating his next step. As author and columnist Garry Wills pointed out, "He is the least 'authentic' man alive,... A survivor. There is one Nixon only, though there seem to be new ones all the time—he will try to be what people want."

Richard Nixon

Speaking to the "silent majority," Nixon promised to reinstitute traditional values and restore law and order. A private man, Nixon tried to insulate himself from the public and present a carefully crafted image through the national media. What impression does Nixon convey in this photograph? How does his body language communicate his intentions?

(Hiroji Kubota/Magnum Photos)

Philosophically, Nixon disagreed with the liberal faith in federal planning and wanted to decentralize social policy. But he agreed with his liberal predecessors that the presidency ought to be the engine of the political system. Faced with a Congress dominated by Democrats and their allocations of money for programs he opposed, he simply impounded (refused to spend) funds authorized by Congress. Later commentators saw the Nixon years as the height of what they came to call the "imperial presidency."

Nixon's cabinet appointees were white, male Republicans. For the most part, however, the president worked around his cabinet, relying on other White House staff members. In domestic affairs, Arthur Burns, a former chairman of the Council of Economic Advisers, and Daniel Patrick Moynihan, a Harvard professor of government (and a Democrat) were the most important. In foreign affairs, the talented and ambitious Henry A. Kissinger, another Harvard government professor, directed the National Security Council staff and later became secretary of state.

Another tier of White House officials—none with public-policy experience but all intensely loyal—insulated the president from the outside world and carried out his commands. Advertising executive H. R. Haldeman, a tireless Nixon campaigner, became chief of staff. Working with Haldeman was lawyer John Ehrlichman. Starting as a legal counselor, he rose to the post of chief domestic adviser. Haldeman and Ehrlichman came to be called the "Berlin Wall" for the way they guarded the president's privacy. John Mitchell was known as "El Supremo" by the staff, as the "Big Enchilada" by Ehrlichman. A tough, successful lawyer, Mitchell became a fast friend and managed Nixon's 1968 campaign. In the new administration, he became attorney general and gave the president daily advice.

The Republican Agenda at Home

Although Nixon had come to political maturity in Republican circles, he understood that it was impossible to roll back the government's expanded role altogether. He sought instead to systematize and scale back the programs of the welfare state, "to reverse the flow of power and resources" away from the federal government and channel them to state and local governments, where he believed they belonged.

Despite initial reservations, Nixon proved willing to use economic tools to maintain stability. The economy was faltering when he assumed office. As inflation rose, largely as a result of the Vietnam War, Nixon reduced government spending and pressed the Federal Reserve Board to raise interest rates. Although parts of the conservative plan worked, a mild recession occurred in 1969–1970, and inflation

continued to rise. Realizing the political dangers of pursuing this policy, Nixon shifted course, imposed wage and price controls to stop inflation, and used monetary and fiscal policies to stimulate the economy. After his reelection in 1972, however, he lifted wage and price controls, and inflation resumed.

A number of factors besides the Vietnam War contributed to the troubling price spiral. Eager to court the farm vote, the administration made a large wheat sale to Russia in 1972. With insufficient wheat left for the American market, grain prices shot up. Between 1971 and 1974, farm prices rose 66 percent, as agricultural inflation accompanied industrial inflation.

The most critical factor in disrupting the economy, though, was the Arab oil embargo. American economic expansion had rested on cheap energy, just as American patterns of life had depended on inexpensive gasoline. Turbulence in the Middle East intruded on the economic stability of the Western world.

The Six-Day War in 1967 made it clear that the Middle East was still a battleground. In 1967, anticipating an attack and launching a preemptive strike, Israeli forces defeated the Egyptian army and seized the West Bank and the Golan Heights, as well as the Arab sector of Jerusalem, which was reunited with the Israeli part of the city for the first time since 1948.

In the aftermath of the Six-Day War, the Organization of Petroleum Exporting Countries (OPEC) slowly raised oil prices in the early 1970s. Another Arab-Israeli war in 1973—the Yom Kippur War—came as Jews celebrated their holiest holiday—the Day of Atonement—and took them by surprise. The war pitted Israel against Egypt, Syria, Iraq, and Jordan. Initially Egypt, in the Sinai peninsula, and Syria, in the Golan Heights, were successful, but then the Israelis fought back. In the end, after several weeks of fighting, ceasefires went into effect, leaving Egypt and Syria with modest gains but the Israelis largely in control.

Meanwhile, in the midst of the fighting, Saudi Arabia, an economic leader of the Arab nations, imposed an embargo on oil shipped to Israel's ally, the United States. Other OPEC nations continued to supply oil but quadrupled their prices. Dependent Americans faced shortages and skyrocketing prices. When the embargo ended in 1974, prices remained high. Even though oil prices around the world increased, the United States was hardest hit because of the huge amounts of oil it used.

The oil crisis affected all aspects of American economic life. Manufacturers, farmers, homeowners—all were touched by high energy prices. A loaf of bread that had cost 28 cents in the early 1970s jumped to 89 cents, and automobiles cost 72 percent more in 1978 than they had in 1973. Accustomed to filling up their cars' tanks for only a few dollars, Americans were shocked at paying 65 cents a gallon. In 1974, inflation reached 11 percent. But then, as higher energy prices encouraged consumers to cut back on their purchases, the nation entered a recession as well. Unemployment climbed to 9 percent for several months in 1975, the highest level since the 1930s.

The United States faced fierce economic competition from abroad. The auto industry found itself challenged by smaller Japanese imports such as Hondas, Toyotas, and Datsuns (later called Nissans) that were

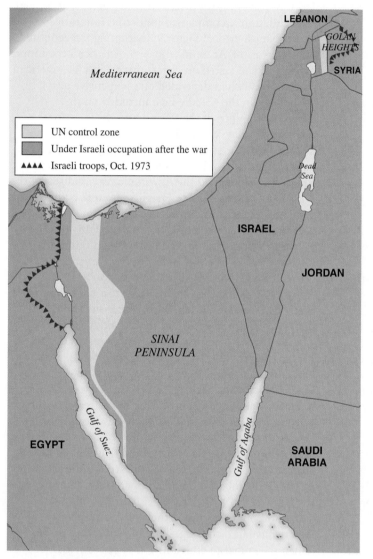

The Yom Kippur War of 1973

The Arab attack during the Yom Kippur observance took Israel by surprise. Initially, Egypt and Syria regained some of their lost territory, but then the Israeli counterattack cut back many of the gains. In the end, UN troops were stationed on borders of the Sinai Peninsula and Golan Heights to help stabilize those regions. How had the map of the Middle East changed in the years after the establishment of the state of Israel in 1948? Who was the victor in the 1973 Yom Kippur War? Why could UN forces help maintain stability?

far more fuel-efficient. As economic growth and stability eluded the nation, Nixon also tried to reorganize rapidly expanding and expensive welfare programs. Critics claimed that welfare was inefficient and that benefits discouraged people from seeking work. Nixon faced a political dilemma. He recognized the conservative tide growing in the Sun Belt regions of the country from Florida to Texas to California, where many voters wanted cutbacks in what they viewed as excessive government programs. At the same time, he wanted to win over traditionally Democratic blue-collar workers with reassurances that the Republicans would not dismantle the parts of the welfare state on which they relied.

Nixon endorsed the Family Assistance Plan, which would have guaranteed a minimum yearly stipend of $1,600 to a family of four, with food stamps providing about $800 more. The program, aiming to cut "welfare cheaters" who took unfair advantage of the system and to encourage recipients to work, was promising but it was attacked by both liberals, who felt it was too limited, and conservatives, who claimed it tried to do too much. It died in the Senate.

Nixon irritated liberals still further in his effort to restore "law and order." Political protest, rising crime rates, increased drug use, and more permissive attitudes toward sex all created a growing backlash among working-class and many middle-class Americans. Nixon decided to use government power to silence disruption and thereby strengthen his conservative political constituency.

Part of the administration's campaign involved denouncing disruptive elements. Nixon lashed out at demonstrators, but more and more he relied on his vice president to play the part of hatchet man. Spiro Agnew branded opposition elements, students in particular, as "ideological eunuchs" who made up an "effete corps of impudent snobs." At the same time, Nixon and Agnew attacked the communications industry, which they believed voiced the views of the hostile "Eastern establishment."

The strongest part of Nixon's plan to circumscribe the liberal approach was Attorney General Mitchell's campaign on crime, sometimes waged at the expense of individuals' constitutional rights. Mitchell's plan included reshaping the Supreme Court, which had rendered increasingly liberal decisions in the past decade and a half. During his first term, Nixon had the opportunity to name four judges to the Court, and he nominated men who shared his views. His first choice was Warren E. Burger as chief justice and he was confirmed quickly. Other appointments, however, were more partisan and reflected Nixon's aggressively conservative approach.

Intent on appealing to white southerners, he first selected Clement Haynesworth of South Carolina, then G. Harold Carswell of Florida. Both men on examination showed such racial biases or limitations that the Senate refused to confirm them. Nixon then appointed Harry Blackmun, Lewis F. Powell, Jr., and William Rehnquist, all able and qualified, and all inclined to tilt the Court in a more conservative direction.

Not surprisingly, the Court gradually shifted to the right. It narrowed defendants' rights in an attempt to ease the burden of the prosecution in its cases and slowed liberalizing of pornography laws. It supported Nixon's assault on the media by ruling that journalists did not have the right to refuse to answer questions for a grand jury, even if they had promised sources confidentiality. On other questions, however, the Court did not always act as the president had hoped. In the controversial 1973 *Roe* v. *Wade* decision, the Court legalized abortion, stating that women's rights included the right to control their own bodies.

Continuing Confrontations in Civil Rights

Richard Nixon was less sympathetic to the cause of civil rights than his predecessors. In 1968, the Republicans won only 12 percent of the black vote, leading Nixon to embark on a "southern strategy" based on the conclusion that any effort to woo the black electorate would endanger the effort to obtain white southern support.

From the start, the Nixon administration sought to scale back the federal commitment to civil rights. It first moved to reduce appropriations for fair-housing enforcement, then tried to block an extension of the Voting Rights Act of 1965. Although Congress approved the extension, the administration's position on racial issues was clear. When South Carolina senator Strom Thurmond and others tried to suspend federal school desegregation guidelines, the Justice Department lent support by urging a delay in meeting desegregation deadlines in 33 of Mississippi's school districts. While a unanimous Supreme Court rebuffed the effort, the president disagreed publicly with the decision.

Nixon also faced the growing controversy over busing as a means of desegregation, a highly charged issue in the 1970s. Transporting students from one area to another to attend school was nothing new. By 1970, more than 18 million students, almost 40 percent of those in the United States, rode buses to school. Yet when busing became tangled with the question of integration, it inflamed passions.

In the South, before the Supreme Court endorsed integration, busing had long been used to maintain segregated schools. Now, however, busing was a means of breaking down racial barriers. In 1971, the Supreme Court ruled that district courts had broad authority to order the desegregation of school systems—by busing, if necessary.

In response, Nixon proposed a moratorium or even a restriction on busing and went on television to denounce it. Although Congress did not accede to his request, southerners knew where the president stood. So did northerners, for the issue became a national one. Schools in many of the nation's largest northern cities were as rigidly segregated as those in the South, largely because of residential patterns. This segregation was called *de facto* to differentiate it from the *de jure*, or legal, segregation that had existed in the South. Court decisions now ordered many northern cities to end such *de facto* segregation and to desegregate their schools.

For many younger students, attendance at different elementary schools went smoothly. Reassigned high school students were less fortunate. A white boycott at South Boston High in Massachusetts cut attendance from the anticipated 1,500 to fewer than 100 on the first day. Buses bringing in black students were stoned, and some children were injured. White, working-class South Bostonians felt that they were being asked to carry the burden of middle-class liberals' racial views. Some white families either enrolled their children in private schools or fled the city.

The Republicans managed to slow down the school desegregation movement. Nixon openly catered to his conservative constituents and demonstrated he was on their side. His successor, Gerald Ford, never came out squarely against civil rights, but his lukewarm approach to desegregation demonstrated a further weakening of the federal commitment.

Integration at the postsecondary level came easier. Federal affirmative action guidelines seeking to provide opportunities for groups discriminated against in the past brought more blacks into colleges and universities. Black enrollment in colleges reached 9.3 percent of the college population in 1976, then dropped back slightly.

As blacks struggled on the educational and occupational fronts, some whites protested that gains came at their expense and amounted to "reverse discrimination." In 1973 and 1974, for example, Allan Bakke, a white, applied to the medical school at the University of California at Davis. Twice rejected, he sued on the grounds that a racial quota reserving 16 of 100 places for minority-group applicants was a form of reverse discrimination that violated the Civil Rights Act of 1964. In 1978, the Supreme Court ordered Bakke's admission to the medical school, but in a complex ruling including six separate opinions, the Court allowed "consideration" of race in admissions policies, though not quotas.

The civil rights movement underscored the democratic values on which the nation was based, but the gap between rhetoric and reality remained. In an era

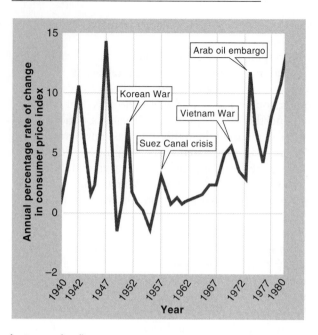

Rate of Inflation, 1940–1980

Inflation often accompanied military spending in the postwar years. In the early 1970s, the Arab oil embargo contributed to an even higher rate.

Source: U.S. Bureau of the Census.

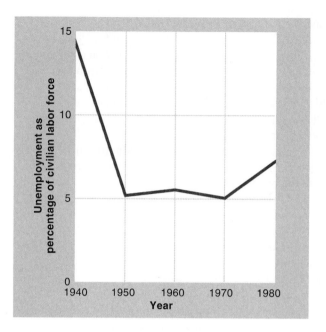

Unemployment Rate, 1940–1980

The unemployment rate fell dramatically during World War II, remained relatively constant from 1950–1969, and rose as inflation increased in the 1970s.

Source: U.S. Bureau of Labor Statistics.

when industrial and farming employment declined and rents rose at a highly inflationary rate, most black families remained poor. African American income was substantially lower than white income. After early optimism in the years when the movement made its greatest strides, black Americans and sympathetic whites were troubled by the wavering national commitment to reform in the 1970s.

The Ongoing Effort in Vietnam

The war in Vietnam continued into the 1970s. When Nixon assumed office in 1969, he understood the need to heal the rifts that the struggle created in American society. During the campaign, he had spoken about a plan to end involvement in the war without specifying details. Once in office, he embarked on an effort to bring American troops home as a way of defusing opposition to the struggle. Unfortunately, his decision to try to avoid losing the war led to even further chaos at home.

Vietnamization—Bringing the Soldiers Home

Nixon gave top priority to extricating the United States from Vietnam while still seeking a way to win the war. To that end, he announced the Nixon Doctrine, which asserted that the United States would aid friends and

allies but would not undertake the full burden of troop defense. The policy of Vietnamization entailed removing American forces and replacing them with Vietnamese troops. Between 1968 and 1972, American troop strength dropped from 543,000 to 39,000, and the reduction won political support for Nixon at home. Yet as the transition occurred, the South Vietnamese steadily lost ground to the Viet Cong.

At the same time, Americans launched ferocious air attacks on North Vietnam. "Let's blow the hell out of them," Nixon instructed the Joint Chiefs of Staff. Nixon used the bombing campaign to portray himself to the North Vietnamese as an anti-Communist zealot with his hand on the nuclear trigger, assuming that fear of annihilation would bring the enemy to the peace table.

But peace proved elusive, and war protests multiplied in 1969 and 1970. In November 1969, as a massive protest demonstration took place in Washington, D.C., stories surfaced about a horrifying massacre of civilians in My Lai, a small village in South Vietnam, the year before. An American infantry company was helicoptered in to clear out the Viet Cong. Instead of troops, it found women, children, and old men. Perhaps confused by the sometimes fuzzy distinction between combatants and civilians in a guerrilla war, the American forces lost control and mowed down hundreds of civilians in cold blood. Stories of the massacre at My Lai underscored the senseless violence associated with the war and increased pressure for the United States to get out of Vietnam.

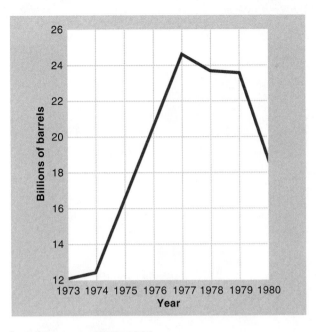

Oil Imports, 1973–1980

American reliance on foreign oil increased in the mid-1970s, until the United States tried to respond to price increases by reducing reliance on imports.

Source: U.S. Energy Information Administration.

Gasoline Prices, 1973–1980

Gasoline prices rose steadily in the years following the Arab oil embargo and affected the entire American economy.

Source: U.S. Energy Information Administration.

Widening the War

As much as Nixon wanted to defuse opposition to the war, he was determined not to lose the struggle either. Realizing that the Vietnamese relied on supplies funneled through Cambodia, Nixon announced in mid-1970 that American and Vietnamese troops were invading that country to clear out Communist enclaves. The United States, he said, would not stand by as a "pitiful helpless giant" when there were actions it could take to stem the Communist advance.

Nixon's invasion of Cambodia brought renewed demonstrations on college campuses, some with tragic results. At Kent State University in Ohio, the antiwar response was fierce. Two days after the president announced his move, disgruntled students protested by setting the ROTC building on fire and watched it burn to the ground.

Governor James Rhodes of Ohio ordered the National Guard to the university. Tension grew, and finally the situation exploded as the guardsmen fired without provocation on the students. When the shooting stopped, four students lay dead, nine wounded. Two of the dead had been demonstrators who were more than 250 feet away when shot. The other two were innocent bystanders, almost 400 feet from the troops.

Students around the country, as well as other Americans, were outraged by the attack. Many were equally disturbed about a similar attack at Jackson State University in Mississippi, where a few students taunted police and National Guardsmen. The troops responded without warning by firing 460 rounds of automatic-weapon fire into a women's dormitory. When the gunfire ceased, two people were dead, more wounded. The dead, however, were black students at a black institution, and white America paid less attention to this attack.

In 1971, the Vietnam War made major headlines once more. The *New York Times* began publishing the Pentagon Papers, a secret Department of Defense account of American involvement that gave Americans a firsthand look at the fabrications and faulty assumptions that had guided the war. Even though the study stopped with the Johnson years, the Nixon administration was furious and tried, without success, to block publication.

The End of the War and Détente

Vietnam remained a political football as Nixon ran for reelection in 1972. Negotiations led Secretary of State Henry Kissinger to announce, "Peace is at hand." When South Vietnam seemed to balk at the proposed settlement, the administration responded with the most intensive bombing campaign of the war that included Hanoi, the capital of North Vietnam. Only in the new year was a ceasefire finally signed.

The conflict in Vietnam lingered on into the spring of 1975. When the North Vietnamese finally consolidated their control over the entire country,

Recovering the Past

POPULAR MUSIC

One way to recover the past is through music. Popular songs not only provide insight into attitudes and beliefs but also quickly convey the mood and feelings of an era. Through their lyrics, songwriters express the hopes and fears of a people and the emotional tone of an age. Consider, for example, the powerful message conveyed in the Democratic party adoption of "Happy Days Are Here Again" as a campaign theme during the Great Depression. The decline of pop music and the rise of rock and roll in the 1950s tell historians a great deal about the mood of that period. Similarly, the popularity of both folk music and rock in the 1960s provides another way of following social change in that turbulent decade.

The music of the 1960s and 1970s moved beyond the syrupy ballads of the early 1950s and the rock-and-roll movement that Elvis Presley helped launch in the middle of the decade. As the United States confronted the challenges of the counterculture and the crosscurrents of political and social reform, new kinds of music began to be played.

Folk music took off at the start of the period. Building on a tradition launched by Woody Guthrie, Pete Seeger, and the Weavers, Joan Baez was one of the first folk singers to become popular. Accompanying herself on a guitar as she performed at coffee shops in Harvard Square and at the Newport Folk Festival, she soon overwhelmed audiences with her crystal-clear voice. She sang ballads, laments, and spirituals such as "We Shall Overcome" and became caught up in the protest activities of the period.

Equally active was Bob Dylan, who grew up playing rock and roll in high school, then folk music in college at the University of Minnesota. Disheveled and gravelly voiced, he wrote remarkable songs such as "Blowin' in the Wind" that were soon sung by other artists such as Peter, Paul, and

Bob Dylan

(AP/Wide World Photos)

Mary as well. His song "The Times They Are A-Changin'" (excerpted here) captured the inexorable force of the student protest movement best of all. Dylan, who alienated some of his folk music fans when he began playing the electric guitar, continued performing for decades.

The Times They Are A-Changin'

BY BOB DYLAN

Come mothers and fathers
Throughout the land
And don't criticize
What you can't understand
Your sons and your daughters
Are beyond your command
Your old road is
Rapidly agin'.
Please get out of the new one
If you can't lend your hand
For the times they are a-changin'.

But these years were marked by far more than folk music alone. In the early part of the decade, an English group from Liverpool began to build a following in Great Britain.

Joan Baez

(John Launois/Stockphoto)

The Beatles
(Getty Images)

The Supremes
(Brown Brothers)

At the start of 1964, the Beatles released "I Want to Hold Your Hand" in the United States and appeared on the popular Ed Sullivan television show. Within weeks, Beatles songs held the first, second, third, fourth, and fifth positions on the *Billboard* singles chart, and *Meet the Beatles* became the best-selling LP record to date. With the release of *Sergeant Pepper's Lonely Hearts Club Band* a few years later, the Beatles branched out in new musical directions and reflected the influence of the counterculture with songs such as "Lucy in the Sky with Diamonds" (which some people said referred to the hallucinogenic drug LSD).

Mick Jagger and the Rolling Stones followed at the end of the 1960s. Another English group that changed the nature of American music, the Stones played a blues-based rock music that proclaimed a commitment to drugs, sex, and a decadent life of social upheaval. Jagger was an aggressive, sometimes violent showman on stage, whose androgynous style showed his contempt for conventional sexual norms. Other artists, such as Jim Morrison of the Doors and Janis Joplin, reflected the same intensity of the new rock world, and both died from drug overdoses. This music too continued into the 1970s.

Meanwhile, other groups were setting off in different directions. On the pop scene, Motown Records in Detroit popularized a new kind of black rhythm and blues. By 1960, the gospel-pop-soul fusion was gaining followers. By the late 1960s, Motown Records was one of the largest black-owned companies in America and one of the most successful independent recording ventures in the business. Stevie Wonder, the Temptations, and the Supremes were among the groups who became enormously popular. The Supremes, led by Diana Ross, epitomized the Motown sound with such hits as "Where Did Our Love Go."

Reflecting on the Past What songs come to your mind when you think of the 1960s and 1970s? How is the music different from that of the 1950s? What do the lyrics tell you about the period?

Look at the verse from "The Times They Are A-Changin'" that is reprinted here. What does it tell you about the turbulence of the time? What, if anything, do these lyrics imply can be done about the changes in the air? What other songs can you think of that give you a similar handle on these turbulent years? ■

Gerald Ford, Nixon's successor as president, called for another $1 billion in aid, but Congress refused. The long conflict had enormous consequences. Disillusionment with the war undermined assumptions about America's role in world affairs. In the longest war in its history, the United States lost almost 58,000 men, with far more wounded or maimed. Blacks and Latinos suffered more than whites since they were disproportionately represented in combat

units. In 1965, 24 percent of all soldiers killed in Vietnam were African American—a figure far higher than their percentage of the population as a whole. Financially, the nation spent more than $150 billion on the unsuccessful war. Domestic reform slowed, then stopped. Cynicism about the government increased, and American society was deeply divided.

If the Republicans' Vietnam policy was a questionable success, accomplishments in other areas were impressive. Nixon, the consummate Red-baiter of the past, dealt imaginatively and successfully with the major Communist powers, reversing the direction of American policy since World War II.

Nixon's most dramatic step was establishing better relations with the People's Republic of China. In the two decades since Mao Zedong's victory in the Chinese revolution in 1949, the United States had refused to recognize the Communist government on the mainland, insisting that Jiang Jieshi's rump regime on Taiwan was the rightful government. In 1971, with an eye on the upcoming elections, Nixon began softening his administration's rigid stance by announcing that he intended to visit China the following year. He suspected that he could use Chinese friendship as a bargaining chip in dealing with the Soviet Union. He acknowledged what most nations already knew: Communism was not monolithic. Nixon also recognized that the press and television coverage of a dramatic trip could boost his image.

Nixon went to China in February 1972. He met with Chinese leaders Mao Zedong and Zou Enlai (Chou En-lai), talked about international problems, exchanged toasts, and saw the Great Wall and other major sights. Wherever he went, American television cameras followed, helping introduce to the American public a nation about which it knew little. Though formal diplomatic relations were not yet restored, détente between the two countries had begun.

Seeking to play one Communist state against the other, Nixon also visited Russia, where he was likewise warmly welcomed. At a cordial summit meeting, the president and Soviet premier Leonid Brezhnev signed the first Strategic Arms Limitation Treaty (SALT I), which included a five-year agreement setting ceilings on intercontinental and other ballistic missiles, and an antiballistic missile treaty restricting the number of systems each nation could develop and deploy. At the same time, the two nations agreed to cooperate in space and to ease long-standing restrictions on trade. Business applauded the new approach, and most Americans approved of détente.

Nixon also recognized the need to promote peace in the Middle East. Henry Kissinger engaged in shuttle diplomacy—moving from one nation to another—to help arrange a ceasefire in the Yom Kippur War. In the aftermath of the struggle, recognizing the need for oil, Nixon and Kissinger worked to establish better relations with the Arab nations, even if they intruded on American support of Israel.

When Gerald Ford assumed office, he followed the policies begun under Nixon. He continued the strategic arms limitation talks that provided hope for eventual nuclear disarmament and culminated in the even more comprehensive SALT II agreement, signed but never ratified during Jimmy Carter's presidency.

Constitutional Conflict and Its Consequences

As he dealt with chaos at home and abroad, Nixon worried about maintaining his political base. In his quest for reelection, he went too far and embroiled himself in a devastating political scandal that undermined his administration.

The Watergate Affair

Faced with a solidly Democratic Congress, the Nixon administration found many of its legislative initiatives blocked. Nixon was determined to end the stalemate by winning a second term and sweeping Republican majorities into both houses of Congress in 1972.

Nixon's reelection campaign was even better organized than the effort four years earlier. His fiercely loyal aides were prepared to do anything to win. Special counsel Charles W. Colson described himself as a "flag-waving, kick-'em-in-the-nuts, anti-press, anti-liberal Nixon fanatic." White House counsel John Dean defined his task as finding a way to "use the available federal machinery to screw our political enemies." One way was by authorizing tax audits of political opponents. Active in carrying out commands were E. Howard Hunt, a former CIA agent and a specialist in "dirty tricks," and G. Gordon Liddy, a onetime member of the FBI, with a flamboyant streak.

The Committee to Re-Elect the President (CREEP), headed by John Mitchell, who resigned as attorney general, launched a massive fundraising drive, aimed at collecting as much money as it could before a new campaign-finance law took effect. That money could be used for any purpose, including payments for the performance of dirty tricks aimed at disrupting the opposition's campaign. Other funds financed an intelligence branch within CREEP.

Early in 1972, Liddy and his lieutenants proposed an elaborate scheme to wiretap the phones of various Democrats and to disrupt their nominating convention. Twice Mitchell refused to go along, arguing that the proposal was too risky and expensive. Finally, he approved a modified version of the plan to tap the phones of the Democratic National Committee at its headquarters in the Watergate apartment complex in Washington, D.C. The wiretapping attempt took place on the evening of June 16, 1972, and ended with the arrest of those involved. Nixon's aides played down the matter and used federal resources to head off any investigation. When the FBI traced the money carried by the burglars to CREEP, the president authorized the CIA to call off the FBI on the grounds that national security was at stake. Though not involved in the planning of the break-in, the president was now party to the cover-up. In the succeeding months, he authorized

DOONESBURY

by Garry Trudeau

A Cartoonist Comments on Watergate

Although Nixon steadfastly denied his complicity in the Watergate affair, his tape recordings of White House conversations told a different story. In this classic *Doonesbury* cartoon from September 17, 1973, Garry Trudeau notes Nixon's efforts to head off the investigation. What do you think the cartoonist is trying to say here?

(Doonesbury © 1973 G. B. Trudeau. Reprinted with permission of Universal Press Syndicate. All rights reserved.)

payment of hush money to silence the burglars. Members of the administration, including Mitchell, perjured themselves in court to shield the top officials who were involved.

Nixon trounced Democrat George McGovern in the election of 1972, receiving 61 percent of the popular vote. In a clear indication of the collapse of the Democratic coalition, 70 percent of southern voters cast their ballots for Nixon. The president, however, failed to gain the congressional majorities he sought.

The Watergate burglars pleaded guilty and were sentenced to jail, but the case refused to die. The evidence indicated that others had played a part and the investigation of two zealous reporters, Bob Woodward and Carl Bernstein of the *Washington Post,* uncovered many of those involved. Meanwhile, the Senate Select Committee on Presidential Campaign Activities undertook its own investigation, and one of the convicted burglars testified that the White House had been involved in the episode. Newspaper stories generated further leads, and the Senate hearings in turn provided new material for the press. Faced with rumors that the

White House was actively involved, Nixon decided that he had to release Haldeman and Ehrlichman, his two closest aides, to save his own neck, claiming on nationwide television, "there can be no whitewash at the White House."

In May 1973, the Senate committee began televised public hearings, reminiscent of the McCarthy hearings of the 1950s. As millions of Americans watched, the drama built. John Dean, seeking to save himself, testified that Nixon knew about the cover-up, and other staffers revealed a host of illegal activities undertaken at the White House: money had been paid to the burglars to silence them; State Department documents had been forged to smear a previous administration; wiretaps had been used to prevent top-level leaks. The most electrifying moment was the disclosure by another aide that the president had installed a secret taping system in his office that recorded all conversations. Tapes could verify or disprove the growing rumors that Nixon had in fact been party to the cover-up all along.

To show his own honesty, Nixon appointed Harvard law professor Archibald Cox as a special

PRESIDENTIAL ELECTIONS OF THE 1970S

Year	Candidate	Party	Popular Vote	Electoral Vote
1972	RICHARD M. NIXON	Republican	45,767,218 (60.7%)	520
	George S. McGovern	Democratic	28,357,668 (37.5%)	17
1976	JIMMY CARTER	Democratic	40,830,763 (50.0%)	297
	Gerald R. Ford	Republican	39,147,793 (48.0%)	240

Note: Winners' names appear in capital letters.

prosecutor in the Department of Justice. But when Cox tried to gain access to the tapes, Nixon resisted and finally fired him. Nixon's own popularity plummeted, and even the appointment of another special prosecutor, Leon Jaworski, did not help. More and more Americans now believed that the president had played at least some part in the cover-up and should take responsibility for his acts. *Time* magazine ran an editorial headlined, "The President Should Resign," and Congress considered impeachment.

The first steps, in accordance with constitutional mandate, took place in the House of Representatives. The House Judiciary Committee, made up of 21 Democrats and 17 Republicans, began to debate the impeachment case in late July 1974. By sizable tallies, it voted to impeach the president on the grounds of obstruction of justice, abuse of power, and refusal to obey a congressional subpoena to turn over his tapes. The full House of Representatives still had to vote, and the Senate would have to preside over a trial and convict the president of the charges before he could be removed from office. But for Nixon, the handwriting was on the wall.

After a brief delay, on August 5, Nixon obeyed a Supreme Court ruling and released the tapes. Despite a suspicious $18\frac{1}{2}$ minute silence, they contained the "smoking gun"—clear evidence of his complicity in the cover-up. His ultimate resignation became but a matter of time. Four days later, on August 9, 1974, the extraordinary episode came to an end, as Nixon became the first American president ever to resign.

The Watergate affair provided disturbing evidence that the appropriate balance of power in the federal government had disappeared. Many began to question the centralization of power in the American political system. Others simply lost faith in the presidency altogether. A 1974 survey showed that trust in the presidency had declined by 50 percent in a two-year period. Coming on the heels of Lyndon Johnson's lying to the American people about involvement in Vietnam, the Watergate affair contributed to the cumulative disillusionment with politics in Washington and to the steady decrease in political participation. Barely half of those eligible to vote bothered to go to the polls in the presidential elections of 1976, 1980, and 1984.

Gerald Ford: Caretaker President

Gerald Ford succeeded Nixon as president. An unpretentious, middle-American Republican who believed in traditional virtues, Ford had been appointed vice president in 1973 when Spiro Agnew resigned in disgrace for accepting bribes. Although he was an able congressman, there was significant doubt that Ford was qualified to be chief executive. The new president acknowledged his own limitations, declaring, "I am a Ford, not a Lincoln."

More important than his limitations were his views about public policy. In the House of Representatives, Ford had opposed federal aid to education, the poverty program, and mass transit. He had voted for civil rights measures only when weaker substitutes he had favored had gone down to defeat. Like his predecessor, he was determined to stop the liberal advances promoted by the Democrats in the 1960s.

Ford faced a daunting task. After Watergate, Americans wondered whether any politician could be trusted to guide public affairs. Ford worked quickly to restore trust in the presidency. He emphasized conciliation and compromise, and he promised to cooperate both with Congress and with American citizens. The nation responded gratefully. *Time* magazine pointed to a "mood of good feeling and even exhilaration in Washington that the city had not experienced for many years."

The new feeling did not last long. Ford weakened his base of support by pardoning Richard Nixon barely a month after his resignation. Ford's decidedly conservative bent in domestic policy often threw him into confrontation with a Democratic Congress. Economic problems proved most pressing in 1974, as inflation, fueled by oil price increases, hit 11 percent, unemployment reached 6.6 percent at the end of the year, and

A President by Appointment

Gerald Ford, a genial man, sought to reestablish confidence in the government after succeeding Nixon as president. Far different from his predecessor, he served just over two years, as his bid for election to the presidency in 1976 ended in defeat. What mood dose this picture convey?

(Bettmann/CORBIS)

GNP declined. Home construction slackened and interest rates rose, while stock prices fell. Nixon, preoccupied with the Watergate crisis, had been unable to curb rising inflation and unemployment. Not since Franklin Roosevelt took office in the depths of the Great Depression had a new president faced economic difficulties so severe.

Like Herbert Hoover 45 years before, the conservative Ford hoped to restore confidence and persuade the public that conditions would improve with patience and goodwill. But his campaign to cajole Americans to "Whip Inflation Now" voluntarily failed dismally. At last convinced of the need for strong government action, the administration introduced a tight-money policy as a means of curbing inflation. It led to the most severe recession since the Great Depression, with unemployment peaking at 9 percent in early 1975. In response, Congress pushed for an antirecession spending program. Recognizing political reality, Ford endorsed a multibillion-dollar tax cut coupled with higher unemployment benefits. The economy made a modest recovery, although inflation and unemployment remained high, and federal budget deficits soared.

The Carter Interlude

In the election of 1976, the nation's bicentennial year, Ford faced Jimmy Carter, former governor of Georgia. Carter, appealing to voters distrustful of political leadership, portrayed himself as an outsider. He stressed that he was not from Washington and observed that, unlike many of those mired in recent scandals, he was not a lawyer. Assisted by public relations experts, he effectively utilized the media, especially television, which allowed him to bypass party machines and establish a direct electronic relationship with voters.

In the election, most elements of the old Democratic coalition came together once again, as the Democrats profited from the fallout of the Watergate affair. Carter won a 50-to-48-percent majority of the popular vote and a 297-to-240 tally in the Electoral College. He did well with members of the working class, African Americans, and Catholics. He won most of the South, heartening to the Democrats after Nixon's gains there. Racial voting differences continued, however, as Carter attracted less than half of all white voters but an overwhelming majority of black voters.

Carter stood in stark contrast to his recent predecessors in the White House. Rooted in the rural South, he was a peanut farmer who shared the values of the region. He was also a graduate of the Naval Academy, trained as a manager and an engineer. A modest man, he was uncomfortable with the pomp and incessant political activity in Washington. He hoped to take a more restrained approach to the presidency and thereby defuse its imperial stamp.

Initially, voters saw Carter as a reform Democrat committed to his party's liberal goals, but he was hardly the old-line liberal some had expected. Though he called himself a populist, his political philosophy and priorities were never clear. Critics charged that he had no legislative strategy. Rather, they said with some truth, he responded to problems in a haphazard way and failed to provide firm direction. His status as an outsider led him to ignore traditional political channels. He also seemed to become mired in detail and to lose sight of larger issues. Like Herbert Hoover, he was a technocrat in the White House when liberals wanted a visionary to help them overcome hard times.

Celebrating a Triumph at Camp David

One of Jimmy Carter's greatest achievements was taking the first steps toward peace in the Middle East. Here he celebrates the Camp David Agreement of September 1978, in which Anwar al-Sadat of Egypt, on the left, and Menachem Begin, on the right, shook hands and agreed to work together. What do the faces of these three leaders convey about the moment captured in this photograph?

(Black Star)

In economic affairs, Carter gave liberals some hope at first as he accepted deficit spending. But when record deficits brought inflation to about 10 percent a year, Carter slowed down the economy by reducing spending and cutting the deficit slightly. These budget cuts fell largely on social programs and distanced Carter from reform-minded Democrats who had supported him before. Yet even that effort to arrest growing deficits was not enough. When the budget released in early 1980 still showed high spending levels, the financial community reacted strongly. Bond prices fell, and interest rates rose dramatically.

Similarly, Carter disappointed liberals by failing to construct an effective energy policy. OPEC's increase of oil prices led many Americans to resent their dependence on foreign oil and to clamor for energy self-sufficiency. Carter responded in April 1977 with a comprehensive energy program, which he called the "moral equivalent of war." Critics seized on the acronym of that expression, MEOW, to ridicule the plan and had a field day attacking the president. Never an effective leader in working with the legislative branch, Carter watched his proposals bog down in Congress for 26 months. Eventually, the program committed the nation to move from oil dependence to reliance on coal, possibly even on sun and wind, and established a new synthetic-fuel corporation. Nuclear power, another alternative, seemed less attractive as costs rose and accidents occurred.

Carter further upset liberals by beginning deregulation—the removal of government controls in economic life. Arguing that certain restrictions established over the past century stifled competition and increased consumer costs, he supported decontrol of oil and natural gas prices to spur production. He also deregulated the railroad, trucking, and airline industries.

One of the high points in Carter's administration came with his involvement in the ever-turbulent Middle East. In the aftermath of the Yom Kippur War, Egyptian leader Anwar al-Sadat was disappointed in the ultimate failure of the struggle and flew to Israel in a gesture of peace. At that point, Carter intervened and invited Sadat and Israeli leader Menachem Begin to come to a retreat at Camp David, in Maryland (not far from Washington, D.C.), where he helped the two leaders work out an accord in September 1978. It led to a formal peace treaty the next March. Egypt recognized Israel—and the Israeli right to exist—for the first time, and the Israelis gave up part of the occupied Sinai Peninsula. The United States promised substantial military aid to both parties, which led to a closer relationship with Egypt that has continued ever since. As the United States superseded the Soviet Union as an ally of Egypt, the Russians countered by arming the radical Palestine Liberation Organization (PLO) and helped encourage leader Yasir Arafat in the ongoing guerrilla war.

Carter puzzled people overseas by his passionate commitment to human rights. It became a hallmark of his administration, especially when he ordered the United States to pull out of the Olympics in Moscow in 1980 in protest of the Soviet invasion of neighboring Afghanistan. Some Americans wondered how this commitment squared with the long-standing American approach of supporting dictators and overlooking human rights abuses in countries whose support the United States wanted in the Cold War.

As the 1970s ended, liberals were disappointed. Their hopes for a stronger commitment to a welfare state had been dashed, and conservatives had the upper hand. Despite a tenuous Democratic hold on the presidency at the end of the decade, liberalism was in trouble. And the turbulence that had marked the beginning of the decade had not disappeared.

The Continuing Quest for Social Reform

A struggle for social reform was one more factor contributing to the turbulence of the 1970s. The black struggle for equality in the 1950s and 1960s helped spark a women's movement that soon developed a life of its own. This struggle, like the struggles of Latinos and Native Americans, employed the confrontational approach and the insistent vocabulary of the civil rights movement to create pressure for change. In time, other groups appropriated the same strategies and kept reform efforts alive. While these movements had preexisting roots and usually began in the 1960s, they came of age in the 1970s, and in these years achieved their greatest gains.

Attacking the Feminine Mystique

Although the civil rights movement helped spark the women's movement, broad social changes provided the preconditions. During the 1950s and 1960s, increasing numbers of married women entered the labor force (see Chapter 26). Equally important, many more young women were attending college. By 1970, women earned 41 percent of all B.A. degrees awarded, in comparison with only 25 percent in 1950. These educated young women held high hopes for themselves, even if they were often treated as second-class citizens and earned substantially less than men.

The women's movement, which came into its own in the 1970s, depended on reform legislation. Title VII of the 1964 Civil Rights bill, as originally drafted, prohibited discrimination on the grounds of race. During legislative debate, conservatives opposed to black civil rights seized on an amendment to include discrimination

This healthy, normal baby has a handicap.
She was born female.

A Message from NOW on Gender Discrimination

Awareness of racial discrimination led women to speak out against discrimination based on gender, as shown in this pointed advertisement sponsored by the National Organization for Women. What is the tone of the message? What does it imply should be done?

(Sponsored by Legal Momentum [then known as NOW Legal Defense and Education Fund])

on the basis of gender, in the hope of defeating the entire bill. But the amendment passed, and then the full measure was approved, giving women a legal tool for attacking discrimination.

Women's organizations played an important role in bringing about change in the 1970s. In 1966, a group of 28 professional women, including author Betty Friedan, established the National Organization for Women (NOW) "to take action to bring American women into full participation in the mainstream of American society now." NOW pushed for fair pay and equal opportunity in the workforce and also attacked the "false image of women...in the media." By 1967, some 1,000 women had joined the organization; four years later its membership reached 15,000.

NOW was a pressure group that sought to reform American society by promoting equal opportunity for women. To radical feminists, who had come up through the civil rights movement, NOW's agenda failed to confront adequately the problem of gender

discrimination. Jo Freeman, a radical activist, observed, "Women's liberation does not mean equality with men...[because] equality in an unjust society is meaningless." These feminists tried, through the technique of consciousness raising, to help women understand the extent of their oppression and to analyze their experience as a political phenomenon. They wanted to demonstrate, in their phrase, that the personal was political.

The radicals gained mass-media attention at the Miss America pageant in Atlantic City, New Jersey, in September 1968. On the boardwalk, a hundred women nominated a sheep as their candidate for Miss America. They also set up a "freedom trash can" and placed in it "instruments of torture": bras, girdles, hair curlers, high heels, and copies of *Playboy* and *Cosmopolitan* magazines. In the pageant hall, they chanted "Freedom for Women" and unfurled banners reading "Women's Liberation." The women's movement hit its stride in the 1970s. In 1971, Helen Reddy expressed the energy of the movement in a song called "I Am Woman" that reflected a new militancy and sense of self-confidence:

I am woman, hear me roar
In numbers too big to ignore
And I know too much to go back and pretend
'Cause I've heard it all before
And I've been down there on the floor,
No one's ever gonna keep me down again.
Oh, yes, I am wise
But it's wisdom born of pain.
Yes, I've paid the price
But look how much I gained
If I have to
I can do anything.
I am strong,
I am invincible,
I am woman.

Real changes were underway. A 1970 survey of first-year college students showed that men interested in such fields as business, medicine, engineering, and law outnumbered women eight to one; by 1975, the ratio had dropped to three to one. The proportion of women beginning law school quadrupled between 1969 and 1973. Women gained access to the military academies and entered senior officer ranks, although they were still restricted from combat command ranks. According to the Census Bureau, 45 percent of mothers with preschool children held jobs outside the home in 1980. That figure was four times as high as it had been 30 years before. Legal changes brought women more benefits and opportunities. Title IX of the Education Amendments of 1972 broadened the provisions of the Civil Rights Act of 1964. The new legislation, which barred gender bias in federally assisted educational activities and programs, made easier the admission of women to colleges and changed the nature of intercollegiate athletics by requiring schools to fund sports teams for women. By 1980, fully 30 percent of the participants in intercollegiate sports were women, compared with 15 percent before Title IX became law.

A flurry of publications spread the principles of the women's movement. In 1972, journalist Gloria Steinem and several other women founded a new magazine, *Ms.*, which attracted almost 200,000 subscribers by the next year. *Our Bodies, Ourselves,* a handbook published by a women's health collective, encouraged women to understand and control their bodies; it sold 850,000 copies between 1971 and 1976. Unlike older women's magazines, these publications dealt with abortion, employment, discrimination, and other feminist issues.

Women both in and out of NOW worked for congressional passage, then ratification, of the Equal Rights Amendment (ERA) to the Constitution. Passed by Congress in 1972, with ratification seemingly assured, it stated simply, "Equality of rights under the law shall not be denied or abridged by the United States or by any State on account of sex."

Feminism was not monolithic. More radical feminists insisted that legal changes were not sufficient. Traditional gender and family roles would have to be discarded to end social exploitation. Socialist feminists claimed that it was not enough to strike out at male domination, for capitalist society itself was responsible for women's plight. Only through revolution could women be free.

Black women frequently viewed the women's movement with ambivalence. Some, like attorney Pauli Murray, became feminists. She worked closely with bureaucrats and legislators in Washington on legal measures to end gender discrimination. Others felt that the struggle for racial equality took precedence, and they were reluctant to divert energy and attention from it. Members of NOW and similar organizations, they claimed, "suffered little more than boredom, gentle repression, and dishpan hands" and were hardly confronting the most important issues when they burned their bras and insisted on using the title Ms. rather than Mrs. or Miss.

Not all women were feminists. Many felt the women's movement was contemptuous of women who stayed at home to perform traditional tasks. Marabel Morgan was one who still insisted that a woman had a place at home by her husband's side. She argued that "it is only when a woman surrenders her life to her husband, reveres and worships him, and is willing to serve him, that she becomes really beautiful to him."

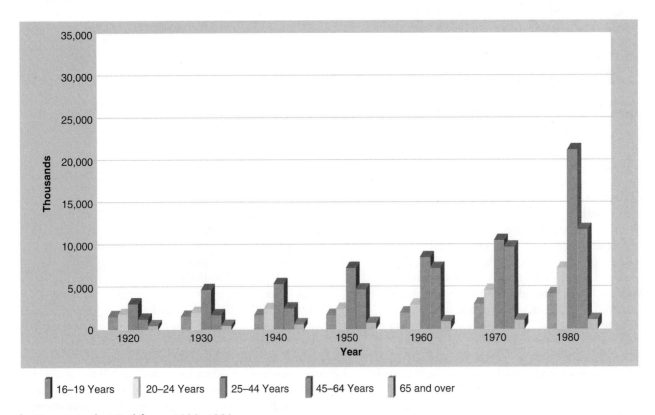

Women in the Workforce, 1920–1980

This graph shows the dramatic increase in the number of women in the workforce over the years. Note particularly the rise in the number of working women 25–44 years old in the 1970s.

Source: U.S. Bureau of the Census.

In her book *The Total Woman* (1973), she counseled others to follow the 4A approach: accept, admire, adapt, appreciate. As of 1975, some 500,000 copies of the hardcover volume had been sold.

In politics, Phyllis Schlafly headed a nationwide campaign to block ratification of the ERA. "It won't do anything to help women," she said, "and it will take away from women the rights they already have, such as the right of a wife to be supported by her husband, the right of a woman to be exempted from military combat, and the right, if you wanted it, to go to a single-sex college." The ERA, she predicted, would lead to the establishment of coed bathrooms, the elimination of alimony, and the legalization of homosexual marriage.

Schlafly and her allies had their way. Within a few years after passage of the ERA, 35 states had agreed to the measure, but then the momentum disappeared. Even with an extension of the deadline granted in 1979, the amendment could not win support of the necessary 38 states. By mid-1982, the ERA was dead.

Despite the counterattacks, the women's movement flourished in the late 1960s and 1970s. In the tenth-anniversary issue of *Ms.* magazine in 1982, Gloria Steinem noted the differences a decade had made. "Now, we are becoming the men we wanted to marry," she said. "Ten years ago, we were trained to marry a doctor, not be one."

Latino Mobilization

Latinos, like women, profited from the example of blacks in their struggle for equality that came of age in the 1970s. Long denied equal access to the American dream, they became more vocal and confrontational as their numbers increased dramatically in the postwar years. In 1970, some 9 million residents of the United States declared they were of Spanish origin; in 1980, the figure was 14.6 million. But median household income remained less than three-fourths that of Anglos, and inferior education and political weakness reinforced social and cultural separation. Latinos included Puerto Ricans in the Northeast, Cubans in Florida, and Chicanos—Mexican Americans—in the West and Southwest. Though "Hispanic" remained an acceptable term, "Latino" was now more commonly used. Chicanos took the lead in the protest struggle, though all groups developed a heightened sense of solidarity and group pride as they began to assert their own rights.

In the 1960s and 1970s, Mexican Americans became more active politically. In 1960, Chicanos supported Kennedy, helping him win Texas, and began to see the benefits of such support. In 1961, Henry B. González was elected to Congress from San Antonio. Three years later, Elizo ("Kika") de la Garza of Texas won election to the House and Joseph Montoya of New Mexico went to the Senate. Chicanos were gaining a political voice.

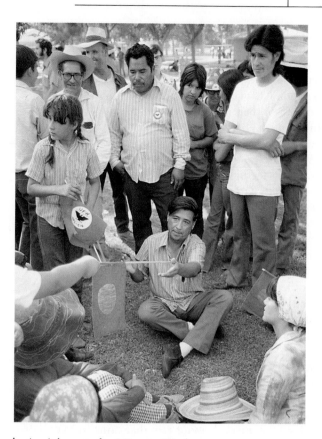

An Advocate for Migrant Workers

César Chávez organized the United Farm Workers to give migrant Mexican workers representation in their struggle for better wages and working conditions. Here he works with laborers in his tireless campaign for their support. What kind of a leader do you think Chávez was on the basis of his appearance in this picture?

(Bob Fitch/Take Stock/Black Star)

More important than political representation, which came only slowly, was direct action, which triumphed in the 1970s. César Chávez, founder of the United Farm Workers, proved what could be done by organizing one of the most exploited and ignored groups of laboring people in the country, the migrant farm workers of the West. Chávez concentrated on migrant Mexican field hands, who worked long hours for meager pay. By 1965, his organization had recruited 1,700 people and was beginning to attract volunteer help.

Latina women played an important part in the organizing effort. Dolores Huerta, a third-generation Mexican American, who became vice president of the United Farm Workers, observed how entire families were involved:

Excluding women, protecting them, keeping women at home, that's the middle-class way. Poor people's movements have always had whole families on the line, ready to move at a moment's notice, with more courage because that's all we had. It's a class not an ethnic thing.

Chávez first took on the grape growers of California. Calling the grape workers out on strike, the union demanded better pay and working conditions as well as recognition of the union. When the growers resisted, Chávez launched a nationwide consumer boycott of their products that was ultimately successful. Similar boycotts of lettuce and other products harvested by exploited labor also ended in success. In 1975, César Chávez's long struggle for farmworkers won passage in California of a measure that required growers to bargain collectively with the elected representatives of the workers. Farmworkers now had achieved the legal basis for representation that could help bring higher wages and improved working conditions. And Chávez had become a national figure.

Meanwhile, Mexican Americans pressed for reform in other areas. In the West and Southwest, Mexican American studies programs flourished. Colleges and universities offered degrees, built library collections, and gave Chicanos access to their own past. The campuses also provided a network linking students together and mobilizing them for political action.

Beginning in 1968, Mexican American students began to protest conditions in secondary schools. They pointed to overcrowded and run-down institutions and to the 50 percent dropout rate that came from expulsion, transfer, or failure because students had never been taught to read. School walkouts took place in Colorado, Texas, and other parts of California and led to successful demands for Latino teachers, counselors, and courses as well as better facilities.

At the same time, new organizations emerged. Young Citizens for Community Action, founded by teenager David Sánchez and four Chicanos in East Los Angeles, began as a service club to assist the neighborhood. Later, the organization adopted a paramilitary stance and evolved into a defensive patrol, now known as Young Chicanos for Community Action, which tried to protect local residents. Its members became identified as the Brown Berets and formed chapters throughout the Midwest and Southwest.

Other Latinos followed a more political path. In Texas, José Angel Gutiérrez formed a citizens' organization that developed into the La Raza Unida political party and successfully promoted Mexican American candidates for political offices. Throughout the 1970s, it gained strength in the West and Southwest.

Among the new Chicano leaders was the charismatic Reies López Tijerina, or "El Tigre." A preacher, he became interested in land-grant issues and argued that the U.S. government had fraudulently deprived Chicanos of village lands. He formed an organization, La Alianza Federal de Mercedes (the Federal Alliance of Land Grants), which marched on the New Mexico state capital and occupied a number of national forests. Arrested, he stood trial and eventually served time in prison, where he became a symbol of political repression.

Rodolfo "Corky" Gonzáles was another such leader. A Golden Gloves boxing champion as a youth, he later served as a district captain for the Democratic party in Denver. He helped direct Denver poverty programs until he was fired for being overly zealous in his support of the Chicano community. Eloquently he described the despair many Chicanos felt:

> I am Joaquin,
> lost in a world of confusion,
> caught up in the whirl of a gringo society,
> confused by the rules,
> scorned by attitudes,
> suppressed by manipulation
> and destroyed by modern society.

Gonzáles founded the Crusade for Justice to advance the Chicano cause through community organization. Like Tijerina, he was arrested for his part in a demonstration but was subsequently acquitted.

Latinos made a particular point of protesting the Vietnam War. Because the draft drew most heavily from the poorer segments of society, the Latino casualty rate was far higher than that of the population at large. In 1969, the National Chicano Moratorium Committee demonstrated against what it argued was a racial war, with black and brown Americans being used against their third-world compatriots. Aware of the growing numbers and growing demands of Latinos, the Nixon administration sought to defuse their anger and win their support. Cuban American refugees, strongly opposed to communism, shifted toward the Republican party, which they assumed was more likely eventually to intervene against Fidel Castro. Meanwhile, Nixon courted Chicanos by dangling political positions, government jobs, and promises of better programs for Mexican Americans. The effort paid off; Nixon received 31 percent of the Latino vote in 1972. Despite occasional gains in the 1970s, Latinos from all groups faced continuing problems. Discrimination persisted in housing, education, and employment. Activists had laid the groundwork for a campaign for equal rights, but the struggle had just begun.

Native American Protest

Like Latinos, Native Americans continued to suffer second-class status in the 1960s and 1970s. But, partly inspired by the confrontational tactics of other groups, they became more aggressive in their efforts to claim their rights and improve their living and working conditions. Their soaring numbers—the census put them at 550,000 in 1960 and 1,480,000 in 1980—gave them greater visibility and political clout.

In the 1960s, Native Americans had begun to assert themselves even more. Several hundred Indians meeting together in 1961 asked the government for the right to help make decisions about programs and budgets for the tribes. A group of college-educated Indians at the conference formed a National Indian Youth Council aimed at reestablishing national pride. Over the next several decades, the council helped change the attitudes of tribal leaders, who were frequently called "Uncle Tomahawks" and "apples" (red outside, white inside) for their willingness to sacrifice their people's needs to white demands.

American Indians learned from the examples of protest they saw around them in the rising nationalism of the developing world and, even more important, in the civil rights revolution. They too came to understand the place of interest-group politics in a diverse society. Finally, they were chastened by the excesses of the Vietnam War. They recognized a pattern of killing people of color that connected Indian–white relations to the excesses in the Philippines at the turn of the century and to atrocities in Korea and Vietnam.

Indians in the late 1960s and 1970s successfully promoted their own values and designs. Indian fashions became more common, museums and galleries displayed Indian art, and Indian jewelry found a new market. In 1968, N. Scott Momaday won the Pulitzer Prize for his book *House Made of Dawn*. Vine Deloria, Jr.'s, *Custer Died for Your Sins* (1969) had even wider readership. Meanwhile, popular films such as *Little Big Man* (1970) provided sympathetic portrayals of Indian history. Indian-studies programs developed in colleges and universities. Organizations like the American Indian Historical Society protested traditional textbook treatment of Indians and demanded more honest portrayals.

At the same time, Native Americans became more confrontational. Like other groups, they worked through the courts when they could but also challenged authority more aggressively when necessary.

Led by a new generation of leaders, American Indians tried to protect what was left of their tribal lands. For generations, federal and state governments had steadily encroached on Native American territory. That intrusion had to cease. The protest spirit was apparent on the Seneca Nation's Allegany reservation in New York State. When state authorities tried to condemn a section of Seneca land to build a superhighway to run through part of the Allegany reservation, the Indians went to court. In 1981, the state finally agreed to an exchange: state land elsewhere in addition to a cash settlement in return for an easement through the reservation. That decision encouraged tribal efforts in Montana, Wyoming, Utah, New Mexico, and Arizona to resist similar incursions on reservation lands.

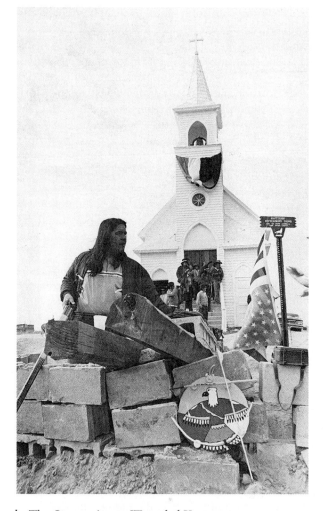

The Occupation at Wounded Knee

The Native American movement's armed occupation of Wounded Knee, South Dakota, the site of a late-nineteenth-century massacre of the Sioux, resulted in bloodshed that dramatized unfair government treatment of Native Americans. What elements of this scene convey the determination behind this episode?

(AP/Wide World Photos)

Native American leaders found that lawsuits charging violations of treaty rights could give them powerful leverage. In 1967, in the first of many subsequent decisions upholding the Indian side, the U.S. Court of Claims ruled that the government in 1823 had forced the Seminole in Florida to cede their land for an unreasonably low price. The court directed the government to pay additional funds 144 years later. American Indians also vigorously and successfully protested new assaults on their long-abused water and fishing rights.

Urban Indian activism became highly visible in 1968 when George Mitchell and Dennis Banks, Chippewa living in Minneapolis, founded the activist American Indian Movement (AIM). AIM got Office of Economic Opportunity funds channeled to Indian–controlled organizations. It also established patrols to protect drunken Indians from harassment by the police. As its successes became known, chapters formed in other cities.

An incident in November 1969 dramatized Native American militancy. A landing party of 78 Indians seized Alcatraz Island in San Francisco Bay in an effort to protest symbolically the inability of the Bureau of Indian Affairs to "deal practically" with questions of Indian welfare. The Indians converted the island, with its defunct federal prison, into a cultural and educational center. In 1971, federal officials removed the Indians from Alcatraz.

Similar protests followed. In 1972, militants launched the Broken Treaties Caravan to Washington. For six days, insurgents occupied the Bureau of Indian Affairs. In 1973, AIM took over the South Dakota village of Wounded Knee, where in 1890 the U.S. Seventh Cavalry had massacred the Sioux. The reservation surrounding the town was mired in poverty. Half the families were on welfare, alcoholism was widespread, and 81 percent of the student population had dropped out of school. The occupation was meant to dramatize these conditions and to draw attention to the 371 treaties AIM leaders claimed the government had broken. Federal officials responded by encircling the area and, when AIM tried to bring in supplies, killed one Indian and wounded another. The confrontation ended with a government agreement to reexamine the treaty rights of the Indians, although little changed.

Meanwhile, Native Americans devoted increasing attention to providing education and developing legal skills. Because roughly half of the Indian population continued to live on reservations, many tribal communities founded their own colleges. In 1971, the Oglala Sioux established Oglala Lakota College on the Pine Ridge Reservation in South Dakota. The motto "Wa Wo Ici Ya" ("We can do it ourselves") revealed the college's goal. Nearby Sinte Gleska College on the Rosebud Reservation was the first to offer accredited four-year and graduate programs. The number of Indians in college increased from a few hundred in the early 1960s to tens of thousands by 1980. Many of these graduates studied law and acted as legal advocates for their own people in the court cases they filed.

Indian protest brought results. The outcry against termination in the 1950s (see Chapter 26) had led the Kennedy and Johnson administrations in the 1960s to steer a middle course, neither endorsing nor disavowing the policy. Instead, they tried to bolster reservation economies and raise standards of living by persuading private industries to locate on reservations and by promoting the leasing of reservation lands to energy and development corporations. In the 1970s, the Navajo, Northern Cheyenne, Crow, and other tribes tried to cancel or renegotiate such leases, fearing "termination by corporation." At the same time, the Menominee of Wisconsin confronted the hated policy head on. Activist Ada Deer became a major figure in the effort to restore reservation status. She and others organized new protest groups, secured political support from the state's senators, and in 1973 had the satisfaction of seeing President Richard Nixon sign the Menominee Restoration Act.

Legislation likewise disavowed the termination policy. In 1975, Congress passed an Indian Self-Determination Act. An Education Assistance Act that same year involved subcontracting federal services to tribal groups. Both laws reflected the government's decision to respond to Indian pressure and created a framework to guide federal policy in the decades ahead.

Gay and Lesbian Rights

Closely tied to the revolution in sexual norms that affected sexual relations, marriage, and family life was a fast-growing and increasingly militant gay liberation movement. Because American society as a whole was unsympathetic, many homosexuals kept their orientation to themselves. The climate of the 1970s encouraged gays to "come out of the closet." A nightlong riot in 1969, in response to a police raid on the Stonewall Inn, a homosexual bar in Greenwich Village in New York, helped spark a new consciousness and a movement for gay rights. Throughout the 1970s, homosexuals successfully fought the most blatant forms of discrimination. In 1973, the American Psychiatric Association ruled that homosexuality should no longer be classified as a mental illness, and that decision was overwhelmingly supported in a vote by the membership the next year. In 1975, the U.S. Civil Service Commission lifted its ban on employment of homosexuals.

In this new climate of acceptance, many gay men who had hidden or suppressed their sexuality revealed their secret. Women, too, became more open about their sexual orientation and demanded not to be penalized for choosing other females as partners. A lesbian movement developed, sometimes involving women active in the more radical wing of the women's movement. But many Americans and some churches remained unsympathetic—occasionally vehemently so—to anyone who challenged traditional sexual norms.

Environmental and Consumer Agitation

Although many of the social movements of the 1960s and 1970s were defined by race, gender, and sexual orientation, one cut across all boundaries. Emerging in the early 1960s but not flourishing until the 1970s, a powerful movement of Americans concerned with the environment began to revive issues raised in the Progressive era and to push them further.

The modern environmental movement stemmed in part from post–World War II yearnings for a better "quality of life." Many Americans began to recognize that clear air, unpolluted waters, and unspoiled wilderness were indispensable to a decent existence. They worried about threats to their natural surroundings, particularly after naturalist Rachel Carson published her brilliant book *Silent Spring* in 1962 (see Chapter 28). By 1970, 53 percent of the population considered air and water pollution to be one of the major national problems.

Public concern focused on a variety of targets. In 1969, Americans were troubled to learn that thermal pollution from nuclear power plants was killing fish in both eastern and western rivers. A massive oil spill off the coast of southern California turned white beaches black and wiped out much of the marine life in the immediate area. In 1978, the public became alarmed about the lethal effects of toxic chemicals dumped in the Love Canal neighborhood of Niagara Falls, New York. A few years later, attention focused on the deadly substance dioxin, which appeared in the Love Canal and elsewhere.

Equally frightening was the potential environmental damage from a nuclear accident. Such a calamity occurred in 1979 at Three Mile Island near Harrisburg, Pennsylvania. Human error compounded a mechanical problem and part of the nuclear core began to disintegrate. An explosion releasing radioactivity into the atmosphere appeared possible, and thousands of area residents fled. The scenario of nuclear disaster depicted in the film *The China Syndrome* (1979) seemed frighteningly real. The worst never occurred and the danger period passed, but the plant remained shut down, filled with radioactive debris, a monument to a form of energy Americans feared.

The threat of a nuclear catastrophe underscored the arguments of grassroots environmental activists. Groups such as the Clamshell Alliance in New Hampshire and the Abalone Alliance in northern California campaigned aggressively against licensing new nuclear plants at Seabrook, New Hampshire, and Diablo Canyon, California. While activist tactics did not always succeed in their immediate goals, they mobilized opinion sufficiently so that no new plants were authorized after 1978. This pattern was at variance with the pattern in many other countries around the world, which continued to rely on nuclear power.

Western environmentalists were particularly worried about excessive use of water. The American West, one critic observed, had become "the greatest hydraulic society ever built in history." Massive irrigation systems had boosted the nation's use of water from 40 billion gallons a day in 1900 to 393 billion gallons by 1975, though the population had only tripled. Americans used three times as much water per capita

as the world's average, and far more than other industrialized societies.

One serious source of concern was the Ogallala aquifer in the Great Plains. The drawing of enormous amounts of water in the 1950s and 1960s to make arid areas productive for farming had by the mid-1970s dramatically depleted the water stored in the aquifer. Conservation measures might delay, but not prevent, the day of reckoning.

California was particularly vulnerable. Because the state was naturally dry, its prosperity rested on massive irrigation projects, and in the late 1970s, it had 1,251 major reservoirs. Virtually every large river had at least one dam. Almost as much water was pumped from the ground, with little natural replenishment and even less regulation. Pointing to the destruction of the nation's rivers and streams and the severe lowering of the water table in many areas, environmentalists argued that something needed to be done. Critic Marc Reisner later noted, "Forty years ago, only a handful of heretics, howling at wilderness, challenged the notion that the West needed hundreds of new dams. Today they are almost vindicated."

Environmental agitation produced legislative results in the 1960s and 1970s. Lyndon Johnson's Great Society was responsible for basic legislation to halt the depletion of the country's natural resources. In the next few years, environmentalists went further, pressuring legislative and administrative bodies to regulate polluters. During Richard Nixon's presidency, Congress passed the Clean Air Act, the Water Quality Improvement Act, and the Resource Recovery Act and mandated a new Environmental Protection Agency (EPA) to spearhead the effort to control abuses. Initially, these measures aimed at controlling the toxic by-products of the modern industrial order. In subsequent years, environmentalists broadened the effort to include occupational health and social justice issues.

One such effort developed into an extraordinarily bitter economic and ecological debate. The Endangered Species Act of 1973 prohibited the federal government from supporting any projects that might jeopardize species threatened with extinction. It ran into direct conflict with commercial imperatives in the Pacific Northwest. Loggers in the Olympic Peninsula had long exploited the land by clear-cutting (cutting down all trees in a region, without leaving any standing). Environmentalists claimed that the forests they cut provided the last refuge for the spotted owl. Scientists and members of the U.S. Forest Service pushed to set aside timberland so that the owl could survive. Loggers protested that this action jeopardized their livelihood. As the issue wound its way through the courts, logging fell off drastically.

Another protest against regulation in the late 1970s and early 1980s came to be called the Sagebrush

Rebellion. Critics argued that large federal landholdings in the West put that region at a disadvantage in economic competition with the East. They demanded that the national government cede the lands to states, which could sell or lease them for local gain. Conservative state legislatures in the Rocky Mountain states supported the scheme. Ranchers applauded the notion. In the end, it went nowhere, though the agitation did persuade federal authorities to endorse a less restrictive policy on grazing.

Related to the environmental movement was a consumer movement. As Americans bought fashionable clothes, house furnishings, and electrical and electronic gadgets, they began to worry about unscrupulous sellers, just as they had earlier in the twentieth century during the Progressive era. Over the years, Congress had established a variety of regulatory efforts as it started to safeguard citizens from marketplace abuse. In the 1970s, a stronger consumer movement developed, aimed at protecting the interests of the purchasing public and making business more responsible to consumers.

Ralph Nader, a onetime Department of Labor consultant, led the movement. His book *Unsafe at Any*

Timeline

1968	Richard Nixon elected president
1969	Native Americans seize Alcatraz
	La Raza Unida founded
1970	U.S. invasion of Cambodia
	Shootings at Kent State and Jackson State Universities
1971	*New York Times* publishes Pentagon Papers
1971–1975	School busing controversies in North and South
1972	Nixon visits People's Republic of China
	Nixon reelected
	SALT I agreement on nuclear arms
	Ms. magazine founded
	Congress passes Equal Rights Amendment
1973	Vietnam ceasefire agreement
	Watergate hearings in Congress
	Spiro Agnew resigns as vice president
	AIM occupies Wounded Knee, South Dakota
1974	OPEC price increases
	Inflation hits 11 percent
	Nixon resigns; Gerald Ford becomes president
	Ford pardons Nixon
1975	South Vietnam falls to the Communists
	End of the Vietnam War
	Unemployment reaches 9 percent
	Farmworkers win right to bargain collectively with growers
	Indian Self-Determination and Education Assistance Acts
1976	Jimmy Carter elected president
1977	Carter energy program
1978	*Bakke* v. *Regents of the University of California*
1979	Accident at Three Mile Island nuclear power plant
	SALT II agreement signed
1982	Ratification of ERA fails

Speed: The Designed-In Dangers of the American Automobile (1965) argued that many cars were coffins on wheels. Head-on collisions, even at low speeds, could easily kill, for cosmetic bumpers could not withstand modest shocks. His efforts paved the way for the National Traffic and Motor Vehicle Safety Act of 1966, which set minimum safety standards for vehicles on public highways, provided for inspection to ensure compliance, and created a National Motor Vehicle Safety Advisory Council.

The consumer movement developed into a full-fledged campaign in the 1970s. Nader's efforts attracted scores of volunteers, called "Nader's Raiders." They turned out critiques and reports and, more important, inspired consumers to become more vocal in defending their rights.

Conclusion
SORTING OUT THE PIECES

The late 1960s and 1970s were turbulent years. The chaos that seemed to reach a peak in 1968 continued, even as American participation in the war in Vietnam wound down. Richard Nixon recognized that he could contain the protest movement by bringing American soldiers home. He understood too the growing frustration with liberal reform and the wish of some Americans to dispense with the excesses they attributed to the young. For a time, he managed to silence protest and to promote a measure of harmony by his policy of Vietnamization, which cut back on the number of Americans dying in battle. But his desire to avoid losing the war led him to expand the conflict into neighboring parts of Indochina, and that move sparked even greater opposition than before.

Meanwhile, his own overarching ambition and need for electoral support led to the worst political scandal in American history. At just the time that the nation was trying to pick up the pieces from the unpopular war, he found himself embroiled in the Watergate affair, which threatened the United States with a real constitutional crisis that ended only when the president resigned.

During this entire time, disadvantaged groups demanded that the nation expand the meaning of equality. Building on the accomplishments of the civil rights movement in the 1950s and 1960s, women such as Ann Clarke, introduced at the start of the chapter, returned to school in ever-increasing numbers and found jobs and sometimes independence after years of being told that their place was at home. Native Americans and Latinos mobilized too and could see the stirrings of change. Gay rights activists made their voices heard. Environmentalists created a new awareness of the global dangers the nation and the world faced. Slowly, reformers succeeded in pressuring the government to help the nation fulfill its promise and ensure the realization of the ideals of American life.

But the course of change was ragged. Reform efforts suffered from the disillusionment with liberalism. Some movements were circumscribed by the changing political climate; others simply ran out of steam. Still, the various efforts left a legacy of ferment that could help spark further change in future years.

QUESTIONS FOR REVIEW AND REFLECTION

1. What were Richard Nixon's social and political priorities in the presidency?
2. How did Nixon propose to end the war in Vietnam?
3. What impact did the Watergate crisis have on American political life?
4. What advances did the women's movement make in the 1970s?
5. How successful was the quest for social reform in the 1970s?

CHAPTER 30

The Revival of Conservatism, 1980–1992

Ronald Reagan appealed to millions of Americans with his vision of a heroic national past. Working closely with his wife, Nancy, he helped revive conservatism and created a new political consensus in the United States.

(Bettmann/CORBIS)

American Stories

A Young Woman Embraces Republican Values

Leslie Maeby, a Republican political staffer in New York State in the 1980s, came from an immigrant family that had long been sympathetic to the Democratic party. Her great-grandfather, Aleksander Obrycki, had come to Baltimore from Poland in 1895. A common laborer who became a naturalized citizen in 1907, he worked for the Democratic party, meeting new immigrants on their arrival and introducing them to Democrats who could help them.

Leslie's grandfather Joe Obrycki became a numbers runner, collecting bets for local gamblers. More successful than his father, he survived the Great Depression of the 1930s with little difficulty. He too was a member of the Democratic party, a cog in the machine. As New Deal programs undermined machine rule, Joe, a ward heeler and professional gambler, ran for city council but lost. Defeat notwithstanding, he remained a loyal Democrat.

Leslie's mother, Vilma, was likewise a Democrat. Leslie's father, Jack Maeby, came from a working-class background in Baltimore and was raised as a Democrat. But as his football exploits took him to college at Bucknell University in Pennsylvania, he began to see the possibility of upward mobility. His own father, a factory worker, counseled him to "use this," pointing to his head, "instead of these," looking at his hands. Turning down an offer to go to graduate school, he entered a management training program with Montgomery Ward. The Maebys moved to Chicago first, then to the Albany, New York, area, where they settled in the suburb of Colonie. While Albany, like most big cities, voted Democratic, Colonie was Republican.

Leslie Maeby was raised in the 1950s in a home where her mother remained Democratic, though frustrated with the Albany machine, and her father was Republican. The suburb, in the midst of a housing boom, developed quickly, as whites fled the larger city— and its black population—and sought safety in the standardized tract houses that were going up everywhere. Nelson Rockefeller, the liberal Republican governor of New York, garnered the support of both of Leslie's parents and many of their neighbors. Yet besides voting, neither Jack nor Vilma was very active politically.

Leslie drifted into politics in 1968, at age 15, without thinking about it. A cheerleader, she was drafted into a congressional campaign by the wife of Fred Field, the Republican candidate, who wanted her to wave pom-poms for her husband and greet supporters. Like the other "Field Girls," she dressed in a blue felt skirt, a white blouse, and suspenders that were striped like the flag. Several nights a week, the group rang doorbells and passed out campaign literature to voters. Leslie often made the first overtures in a household, to be followed by the candidate himself. She found the experience intoxicating, even more so when Fred Field won.

Leslie had followed an increasingly common course into the Republican fold. In a second-grade classroom, she had supported Republican presidential candidate Richard Nixon in 1960. In a mock presidential debate in 1964, she had represented conservative Republican presidential nominee Barry Goldwater. And even though Leslie talked about current events with her mother, a liberal Democrat, she was also influenced by her increasingly conservative Republican father as well as by the Republican community in which she lived. She followed her father's political inclinations and became Republican, as she put it, "almost by default." Race riots, first in Detroit, later in Albany and other American cities, troubled her and others. The chaos in Vietnam led to the rifts in the nation that helped elect Richard Nixon—along with Fred Field—in 1968. By the time she went to the State University of New York at Albany in 1971, she was a solid Republican.

In college, she joined a sorority, where she found women of a similar personal and political bent. Her group drank beer, rather than smoking pot, and wore evening gowns to formal dances, rather than wearing tattered jeans to a rock concert. A sorority sister recommended her for a position as a page in the State Senate in Albany, and Leslie found herself immersed in the political world.

Leslie saw firsthand the underside of politics, including the ways those in power manipulated issues to their own advantage. Yet she decided to set aside her idealism and to work within the system. She rose quickly, serving in 1974 on the state platform committee. She worked for John Dunne, a Republican state senator, after graduating from college in 1975, and attended the Republican National Convention as a delegate at large in 1976. When Dunne sought the office of executive of Nassau County, Leslie ran his campaign. He lost and Leslie left the United States and backpacked through Europe. Yet everywhere she went, she was interested in what she could find about American politics. She wanted to be part of the process as the United States—under the leadership of Ronald Reagan—moved away from the welfare state.

Returning to the United States, in 1984 Leslie took the job of salvaging the reelection campaign of a Republican state senator. She succeeded in that effort, served for four years as executive assistant to the Republican state comptroller, and in 1989 became finance director of the state Republican party.

Leslie was a rock-ribbed Republican, who, like many Americans, reacted with frustration to chaos in national life and moved right as the party moved right. "It's like if you decide to be a nurse when you're eighteen, and stay one for twenty years," she said. "It becomes who you are. How you read the paper. How you watch the news. Your whole outlook."

The experience of Leslie Maeby mirrored that of countless Americans in the 1980s who left the Democratic party and supported the Republican agenda instead. At a time when people were disturbed by continuing racial conflict, troubled by changes in the welfare state that seemed to help disadvantaged citizens at the expense of middle- and upper-class Americans, and upset at the chaos caused by the Vietnam War, they began to reassess priorities within the democratic political system. In a time of flux, the Republican party seized the initiative and consolidated its own political power. In a process that began in the 1960s (as Jack Maeby left his Democratic roots and became a Republican), a new majority emerged in the United States. Millions of Americans, including members of groups who had long considered themselves Democrats, voiced their frustration by voting Republican, some for the first time. Relying on a fervent religious faith, they succeeded in transforming their vision of the American dream into national policy, and in the 1980s and early 1990s, they watched the economy improve, though often to the benefit of the most affluent Americans. At the same time, members of a variety of minority groups continued to have difficulty finding jobs, the national debt skyrocketed, and finally, the stock market crashed. Meanwhile, harsh Cold War rhetoric led to fears that the continuing confrontation on the global stage between the Soviet Union and the United States might end in nuclear war.

This chapter describes the enormous changes that occurred in the 1980s and early 1990s. It highlights the role of people like Leslie Maeby in bringing to power a new political force that altered the landscape of the United States. It describes the economic and technological shifts that affected the daily lives of millions of Americans, bringing unprecedented prosperity to people at the top of the economic pyramid but leaving millions of less fortunate Americans behind. It explores the efforts of the Republican administrations of Ronald Reagan and George Bush to redefine—and limit—the government's role in the economy, and it assesses the impact such constriction had on ordinary Americans. And finally, it examines how foreign policy initiatives brought a successful end to the long and costly Cold War.

The Conservative Transformation

In the 1980s and early 1990s, the Republican party reestablished itself as the dominant force in national politics. The Republican ascendancy that had begun in the Nixon era was now largely complete. The liberal agenda that had governed national affairs ever since the New Deal of Franklin Roosevelt gave way to a new Republican coalition determined to scale back the welfare state and prevent what it perceived as the erosion of the nation's moral values. Firmly in control of the presidency, sometimes in control of the Senate and later the whole Congress, the Republican party set the new national agenda.

The New Politics

Conservatism gained respect in the 1980s, not just in the United States but in other parts of the world as well. In Great Britain, for example, problems with both inflation and unemployment plagued the welfare state policies of the Labour Party, which had gained power in the latter part of the 1960s, and by the 1980s, the Conservative party was back in power, with Margaret Thatcher as prime minister. Elsewhere in the late 1980s, particularly as communism began to crumble in Eastern and Central Europe, moderately conservative Christian Democratic movements became increasingly popular. As socialism deteriorated, they seemed a more viable alternative.

In the United States, conservatism attracted countless new adherents after the turbulence of the 1960s and the backlash of the Vietnam War. Innovative advertising and fund-raising techniques capitalized on national disaffection with liberal solutions to continuing social problems and made the conservative movement almost unstoppable.

Conservatives seized on Thomas Jefferson's maxim: "That government is best which governs least." The dramatic economic growth of the 1960s and 1970s, they believed, left a legacy of rising inflation, falling productivity, enormous waste, and out-of-control entitlements. The liberal solution of "throwing money at social problems" no longer worked, conservatives argued. Therefore, they sought to downsize government, reduce taxes, and roll back regulations that they claimed hampered business competition. They wanted to restore the focus on individual initiative and private enterprise.

The conservative philosophy had tremendous appeal. It promised profitability to those who worked hard and showed initiative. It attracted middle-class Americans, who were troubled that they were being forgotten in the commitment to assist minorities and the poor. It also offered hope for the revival of basic social and religious values that many citizens worried had been eaten away by rising divorce rates, legalized abortion, homosexuality, and media preoccupation with violence and sex.

The new conservative coalition covered a broad spectrum. Some followers embraced the economic doctrines of University of Chicago economist Milton Friedman, who promoted the free play of market forces and a sharp restriction of governmental control. Others applauded the social and political conservatism of North Carolina senator Jesse Helms, a tireless foe of anything he deemed pornographic and a fervent campaigner for a limited federal role. Still others flocked to the Republican fold because of their conviction that civil rights activists and "bleeding-heart liberals" practiced "reverse racism" with affirmative action, job quotas, and busing to promote equal opportunity.

The conservative coalition also drew deeply from religious fundamentalists who advocated a literal interpretation of Scriptures. Millions—devout Catholics, orthodox Jews, evangelical Protestants—demanded a return to stricter standards of morality. Muslims, relying on the Qur'an, took an equally fundamentalist approach. All groups worried about sexual permissiveness, gay rights, drugs, crime, and women working outside the home, a practice they believed eroded family life. In short, fundamentalists objected to liberalizing tendencies and sought to refashion society by reaffirming scriptural morality and the centrality of religion in American life.

Many of these activists belonged to the so-called Moral Majority. The Reverend Jerry Falwell of Virginia and other television evangelists who focused on the concerns of religious fundamentalism attracted large followings in the 1980s. Emulating Father Charles E. Coughlin, the radio priest of the 1930s, they used electronic means to preach fiery sermons to enormous audiences and focused their television congregations on specific political ends. They also used their fund-raising ability to support candidates sympathetic to their cause. Moral Majority money began to fund politicians who demanded reinstituting school prayer, ending legalized abortion, and defeating the Equal Rights Amendment. Later a group calling itself the Christian Coalition became even more powerful in supporting—and electing—candidates who met its litmus test on conservative values. The Christian Coalition and other similar groups believed strongly that "to proclaim Christ's lordship in politics means evaluating political candidates by their commitment to biblical principles, rather than by their pragmatism, patriotism, or personality."

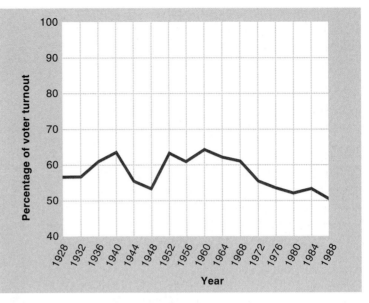

Voter Turnout, 1928–1988
Voter turnout was far lower in the twentieth century than it had been in the nineteenth century. The fact that barely 50 percent of the electorate voted in the 1980s reflects a pervasive sense of disillusionment with the political process.

Source: Data from Historical Statistics of the United States and Statistical Abstract of the United States.

Conservatives from all camps capitalized on changing political techniques more successfully than their liberal opponents. They understood the value of polling to assess and polish a candidate's image and the importance of television in providing instant access to the American public. Politicians became increasingly adept at using "sound bites," often lasting no more than 15 or 30 seconds, to state their views. They also relied on new electronic systems such as e-mail, fax machines, and the Internet to mobilize their followers.

Similarly, conservatives outdid liberals in using negative political advertising. Mudslinging has always been a part of the American political tradition, but now carefully crafted television ads concentrated not so much on conveying a positive image of a candidate's platform but on subtly attacking an opponent's character in order to create fundamental doubt in a voter's mind. Conservatives also were most successful in raising unprecedented sums of money for their campaigns. Richard Viguerie, the New Right mastermind, understood how to tap the huge conservative constituency for political ends and developed direct-mail appeals that assisted conservative candidates around the country.

At the same time, conservatives understood the need to provide an intellectual grounding for their positions. Conservative scholars worked in "think tanks" and other research organizations, such as the Hoover Institution at Stanford University and the American Enterprise Institute in Washington, D.C., that gave conservatism a solid institutional base. Their books, articles, and reports helped elect Ronald Reagan and other conservative politicians.

Conservative Leadership

More than any other Republican, Ronald Reagan was responsible for the success of the conservative cause. An actor turned politician, he had been a radio broadcaster in his native Midwest, then gravitated to California, where he began a movie career. Initially drawn to the Democratic party and impressed with the accomplishments of Franklin D. Roosevelt's New Deal, he was also sympathetic to union causes and served as president of the Screen Actors Guild in Hollywood. But his success on the silver screen affected his political inclinations, and he changed his affiliation from Democrat to Republican in the early 1960s. He went to work as a public spokesman for General Electric, where his visibility and ability to articulate corporate values attracted the attention of conservatives who recognized his political potential and helped him win election as governor of California in 1966. He failed in his first bid for the presidency in 1976 but consolidated his strength over the next four years. By 1980, he had the firm support of the growing Right, which applauded his promise to reduce the size of the federal government but bolster military might.

Running against incumbent Jimmy Carter in 1980, Reagan scored a landslide victory, gaining a popular vote of 51 to 41 percent and a 489 to 49 Electoral College advantage. He also led the Republican party to control of the Senate for the first time since 1955. In 1984, he was reelected by an even larger margin. He received 59 percent of the popular vote and swamped Democratic candidate Walter Mondale in the Electoral College 525 to 13, losing only Minnesota, Mondale's home state, and the District of Columbia. The Democrats, however, netted two additional seats in the Senate and maintained superiority in the House of Representatives.

Reagan had a pleasing manner and a special skill as a media communicator. Relying on his acting experience, he used television as Franklin D. Roosevelt had used radio in the 1930s. He was a gifted storyteller who loved using anecdotes and one-liners to make his point.

He spoke of the United States as "the last best hope of man on earth." Echoing John Winthrop's sermon to Puritans coming to the New World in 1630, he referred to America as a "shining city on a hill." He was fond of invoking images of Pilgrims coming ashore in New England, American prisoners of war returning from Vietnam, and astronauts landing on the moon, and he argued that history still had a place for the nation and its ideals. In response to those who spoke of a "national malaise," he retorted, "I find nothing wrong with the American people."

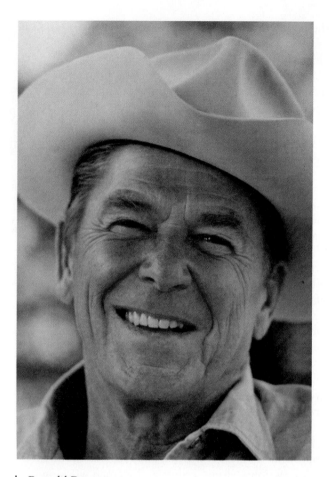

Ronald Reagan

Ronald Reagan was fond of projecting an old-fashioned cowboy image. This picture captured the sense of rugged individualism he valued and appeared on the covers of both *Time* and *Newsweek* magazines when he died in 2004. What qualities seem to come across in this photograph? Why did this image have such a powerful appeal?

(Courtesy Ronald Reagan Library)

Throughout his eight years in office, Reagan enjoyed enormous popularity. People talked about a "Teflon" presidency, making a comparison with non-stick frying pans, for even serious criticisms failed to stick and disagreements over policy never diminished his personal-approval ratings. When he left the White House, an overwhelming 68 percent of the American public approved of his performance.

But Reagan had a number of liabilities that surfaced over time. As the oldest president the nation had ever had, his attention often drifted, and he occasionally fell asleep during meetings, including one with the pope. While he could speak eloquently with a script in front of him, he was frequently unsure about what was being asked in press conferences. Uninterested in governing, he delegated a great deal of authority, even if that left him unclear about policy decisions. Worst of all, he suffered from charges of "sleaze" in his administration,

George H. W. Bush

George H. W. Bush capitalized on his position as vice president under Ronald Reagan and won a resounding victory in the election of 1988. Even so, he did not have the solid conservative mandate that Reagan enjoyed. How does the flag contribute to the impression Bush hoped to convey?

(CORBIS)

with several aides and even his attorney general forced from office for improprieties ranging from perjury to influence peddling.

In 1988, Republican George H. W. Bush, who served eight years as Reagan's vice president, ran for the presidency. Though a New Englander, he had prospered in the Texas oil industry, then served in Congress, as top envoy to China, and as head of the CIA. Termed a preppy wimp by the press, he became a pit bull who ran a mudslinging campaign against his Democratic opponent, Governor Michael Dukakis of Massachusetts. On election day, Bush swamped Dukakis, winning a 54–46 percent popular-vote majority and carrying 40 states. But conservatives who admired Reagan were suspicious of Bush, and he did not have the kind of mandate Reagan had enjoyed. Even worse from the Republican point of view, Democrats controlled both houses of Congress.

Bush quickly put his own imprint on the presidency. Despite his upper-crust background, he was an unpretentious man who made a point of trying to appear down-to-earth. More than a year and a half into his term, he was still on his political honeymoon, with a personal approval rating of 67 percent. Support grew even stronger as he presided over the Persian Gulf War in 1991. Then, as the economy faltered and the results of the war seemed suspect, approval levels began to drop, and he failed in his bid for reelection in 1992.

Republican Policies at Home

Republicans in the 1980s and early 1990s aimed to reverse the economic stagnation of the Carter years and to provide new opportunities for business to prosper. The United States, like industrialized nations around the world, had suffered from the Arab oil embargo of 1973 (see Chapter 29). As the cost of driving cars and heating homes skyrocketed, the entire economy faltered. In an increasingly globalized economy, in which multinational firms had interests around the world, a downturn in one area—or one country—affected business efforts around the globe. Republicans wanted to provide American business interests with the ability to prosper at home and wherever else they operated.

PRESIDENTIAL ELECTIONS, 1980–1988

Year	Candidate	Party	Popular Vote	Electoral Vote
1980	RONALD REAGAN	Republican	43,899,248 (50.8%)	489
	Jimmy Carter	Democratic	36,481,435 (41.0%)	49
	John B. Anderson	Independent	5,719,437 (6.6%)	0
1984	RONALD REAGAN	Republican	53,428,357 (58.7%)	525
	Walter F. Mondale	Democratic	36,930,923 (40.6%)	13
1988	GEORGE BUSH	Republican	47,946,422 (53.9%)	426
	Michael Dukakis	Democratic	41,016,429 (46.1%)	112

Note: Winners' names appear in capital letters.

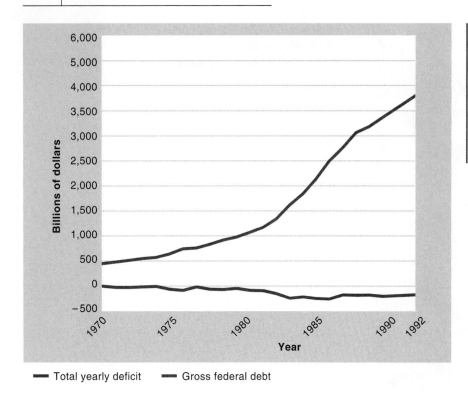

Total yearly deficit ■ Gross federal debt

Federal Budget Deficits and the National Debt, 1970–1992

In the 1970s, 1980s, and early 1990s, the yearly federal budget deficit grew steadily larger, and the gross federal debt skyrocketed. In this economy, deficits and debt affected spending priorities.

Source: Data from *Statistical Abstract of the United States.*

To that end, Reagan proposed and implemented an economic recovery program that rested on the theory of supply-side economics. According to this much-criticized theory, reduction of taxes would encourage business expansion, which in turn would lead to a larger supply of goods to help stimulate the system as a whole. Even George Bush, during his brief run for the Republican nomination in 1980, was critical, charging that Reagan was promoting "voodoo economics." Despite such criticism, Republicans endorsed "Reaganomics." One early initiative involved tax reductions. A 5 percent cut in the tax rate was enacted to go into effect on October 1, 1981, followed by 10 percent cuts in 1982 and 1983. Although all taxpayers received some tax relief, the rich gained far more than middle- and lower-income Americans. Poverty-level Americans did not benefit at all. Tax cuts and enormous defense expenditures increased the budget deficit. From $74 billion in 1980, it jumped to $290 billion in 1992. Such massive deficits drove the gross federal debt—the total national indebtedness—upward from $909 billion in 1980 to $4.4 trillion in 1992. When Reagan assumed office, the per capita national debt was $4,035; 10 years later, in 1990, it was about $12,400.

Faced with the need to raise more money and rectify an increasingly skewed tax code, in 1986 Congress passed and Reagan signed the most sweeping tax reform since the federal income tax began in 1913. It lowered rates, consolidated brackets, and closed loopholes. Though it ended up neither increasing nor

decreasing the government's tax take, the measure was an important step toward treating low-income Americans more equitably. Still, most of the benefits went to the richest 5 percent of Americans.

At the same time, Reagan followed Carter in a major deregulation effort that included agencies such as the Environmental Protection Agency (EPA), the Consumer Product Safety Commission, and the Occupational Safety and Health Administration (OSHA). The Republican administration argued that regulations pertaining to the consumer, the workplace, and the environment were inefficient, paternalistic, excessively expensive, and impeded business growth.

The Federal Communications Commission (FCC), which had effectively regulated the airwaves in the public interest, now assumed a business posture. The head of the agency under Reagan scoffed at the idea that television had a public-service role. "Television is just another appliance," he declared. "It's just a toaster with pictures." The FCC increased the amount of time allotted to commercials and eliminated the rule that some programming had to be in the area of public-service broadcasts.

Meanwhile, Reagan challenged the New Deal consensus that the federal government should monitor the economy and assist the least fortunate citizens. He had played by the rules of the system and had succeeded. Others could do the same. He charged that government intruded too deeply into American life. It was time to eliminate "waste, fraud, and abuse" by cutting unnecessary programs.

Reagan needed to curtail social programs both because of sizable tax cuts and because of enormous military expenditures. Committed to a massive arms buildup, over a five-year period the administration sought an unprecedented military budget of $1.5 trillion. By 1985, the United States was spending half a million dollars a minute on defense and four times as much as at the height of the Vietnam War.

The huge cuts in social programs reversed the approach of liberals over the past 50 years. Republicans and conservative Democrats eliminated public-service jobs and reduced other aid to the cities, where the poor congregated. They cut back unemployment compensation and required Medicare patients to pay more for treatment. They slashed legal assistance for the poor. They lowered welfare benefits and food stamp allocations. Spending on human resources fell by $101 billion between 1980 and 1982. The process continued even after Reagan left office. Between 1981 and 1992, federal spending (adjusted for inflation) fell 82 percent for subsidized housing, 63 percent for job training and employment services, and 40 percent for community services. Middle-class Americans, benefiting from the tax cuts, were not hurt by the slashes in social programs. But the administration's approach caused real suffering for the nation's poorest citizens.

Ironically, despite the huge cuts, overall federal spending for social welfare rose from $313 billion in 1980 to $533 billion in 1988. The increase came about because of growth in the payments of entitlement programs such as social security and Medicare, which provided benefits automatically to citizens in need. Even the most aggressive efforts of the Republicans could not wholly dismantle the welfare state.

Distrustful of centralized government, Reagan wanted to place more power in the hands of state and local governments. His "New Federalism" attempted to shift responsibilities from the federal to the state level. By eliminating federal funding and instead making grants to the states, which could spend the money as they saw fit, he hoped to fortify local initiative. Critics charged that the proposal was merely a way of moving programs from one place to another while eliminating federal funding. When a prolonged recession began in 1990, the administration's policy contributed to the near-bankruptcy of a number of states and municipalities, which now bore responsibility for programs formerly funded in Washington.

Reagan took a conservative approach to social issues as well. Accepting the support of the New Right, he strongly endorsed conservative social goals. To avoid compromising his economic program, however, he provided only symbolic support at first. He spoke out for public prayer in the schools without expending political capital in Congress to support the issue. In the same way, he showed his opposition to abortion by making sure that the first nongovernmental group to receive an audience at the White House was an antiabortion March for Life contingent.

George Bush faithfully adhered to Reagan's general economic policy. Running for president in 1988, he promised "no new taxes," although he later backed down from that pledge to join a bipartisan effort to bring the budget deficit under control.

Like Reagan, Bush wanted deep cuts in social programs. Tireless in his criticism of the Democratic majorities in the Senate and House of Representatives, he vetoed measure after measure to assist those caught in the ravages of a troubling recession that sent unemployment rates up to 8 percent and left one of every four urban children living in poverty.

Bush was more outspoken than Reagan in his support of conservative social goals. At the start of the 1980s, conservatives had questioned Bush's commitment to their social agenda, and, indeed, Bush had been sympathetic to a woman's right to choice on the abortion issue. As president, however, he firmly opposed abortion, and his Supreme Court appointments, like Reagan's, guaranteed that the effort to roll back or overturn *Roe* v. *Wade* would continue.

The Republican philosophy under Reagan and Bush dramatically reversed the nation's domestic agenda. Liberalism in the 1960s had reached a high-water mark in a time of steady growth, but in the 1980s decisions about social programs became more difficult, and millions of Americans like Leslie Maeby, introduced at the start of the chapter, came to believe that most of the Great Society programs had failed to conquer poverty and in fact had created lifelong welfare dependency. Conservatism offered a more attractive answer, particularly to Americans in the middle and upper classes who were already comfortable.

But the transformation was accompanied by a number of serious problems that emerged in the early 1990s. Bush faced a bankruptcy crisis in the savings and loan industry, which had taken advantage of the Republican deregulation policy to make unwise, high-risk investments that led to tremendous losses. Congress approved a $166 billion rescue plan (that soon reached more than $250 billion) to bail out the industry.

Republican policy also widened the gap between rich and poor. Tax breaks for the wealthy, deregulation initiatives, high interest rates for investors, permissiveness toward mergers, and enormous growth in the salaries of top business executives all contributed to the disparity.

The 1980s, it became clear, produced "a decade of money fever," as author Tom Wolfe put it. The concentration of capital—an amassing of wealth at the top levels—produced dekamillionaires, centimillionaires, half-billionaires, and billionaires.

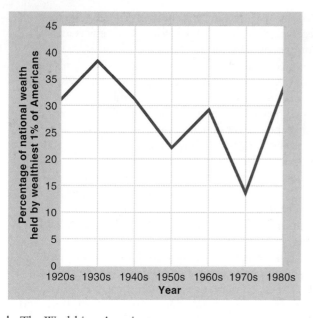

The Wealthiest Americans

During the 1980s, the percentage of national wealth held by the richest 1 percent of Americans reached the highest level since the 1930s.

Source: New York Times, August 16, 1992.

According to one study, the share of national wealth of the richest 1 percent of the nation rose from about 18 percent in 1976 to 36 percent in 1989.

Meanwhile, less-fortunate Americans suffered more than they had since the Great Depression. In 1987, one out of every five American children lived in poverty, up 24 percent since 1979. And millions of people, ranging from foreclosed farmers to laid-off industrial workers, were struggling to make ends meet.

An End to Social Reform

The Republican attack on the welfare state included an effort to limit the commitment to social reform. Enough had been done already, conservatives argued, and gains for less fortunate Americans came at the expense of the middle class. It was time to end federal "intrusion" in this area.

Slowdown in the Struggle for Civil Rights

Republican policies slowed the civil rights movement. Reagan opposed busing to achieve racial balance, and his attorney general worked to dismantle affirmative action programs. Initially reluctant to support extension of the enormously successful Voting Rights Act of 1965, Reagan relented only after severe bipartisan criticism. He also launched an assault on the Civil Rights Commission and hampered its effectiveness by appointing members who did not support its main goals.

The courts similarly weakened commitments to equal rights. As a result of judicial appointments, federal courts stopped pushing for school integration. The Supreme Court's *Freeman* v. *Pitts* decision in 1992 granted a suburban Atlanta school board relief from a desegregation order on the grounds that it was not possible to counteract massive demographic shifts.

Yet African Americans kept the struggle alive. The Reverend Jesse Jackson, a longtime civil rights activist, established what he called the Rainbow Coalition in 1984 and ran for the presidency. Though he lost his bid for the Democratic nomination, he had the support of nearly 400 delegates, and in a nationally televised speech at the convention, he vowed not to forget his constituency of "the desperate, the damned, the disinherited, the disrespected, and the despised."

Jesse Jackson

Jesse Jackson demonstrated that an African American could attract a substantial level of support as he ran for president in 1984 and 1988. Here he is shown on the campaign trail in Chicago in 1988. Why were Jackson's campaigns so important? Who do you think his strongest supporters were?

(Marc Pokempner)

All Americans, he went on, needed to work together for a common cause: "Our flag is red, white and blue, but our nation is a rainbow—red, yellow, brown, black and white—and we're all precious in God's sight." Four years later, in 1988, he sought the Democratic nomination again, this time with the support of 1,200 delegates at the convention, before falling short of his goal once more.

Despite significant victories in mayoral elections in major cities and other electoral gains, black–white relations remained tense. A riot in Los Angeles in 1992 revealed the continuing racial polarization. The year before, Americans had watched a videotaped, savage beating of black motorist Rodney King by white police officers, the most dramatic of a long string of incidents involving police brutality. When a California jury that did not include any African Americans acquitted the policemen, many people throughout the country became convinced that people of color could not obtain equal justice under the law. In Los Angeles, thousands reacted with uncontrolled fury, targeting supermarkets, drug stores, Korean businesses, restaurants, and mini-malls. Much of the chaos was orchestrated by gang members, but it also involved hundreds of ordinary citizens who acted irresponsibly, yet with a sense that the social contract had been broken by politicians and the rich who were unresponsive to their plight. After the riot had run its course, 51 people (most of them black and Hispanic) lay dead, 2,000 were injured, and $1 billion in damage had been done to the city. It was the worst riot in decades and served notice that racial injustice, social inequality, and poverty could no longer be ignored.

Obstacles to Women's Rights

Women, too, made significant electoral gains at the local, state, and national levels. In 1981, President Reagan named Sandra Day O'Connor as the first woman Supreme Court justice, and in 1984 Democrat Geraldine Ferraro became the first major-party female vice presidential nominee. The women's movement also became racially inclusive.

Yet women still faced problems that were compounded by conservative social policies. Access to new positions did not change their concentration in lower-paying jobs. In 1985, most working women were still secretaries, cashiers, bookkeepers, registered nurses, and waitresses—the same jobs most frequently held 10 years before. Even when women moved into positions traditionally held by men, their progress often stopped at the lower and middle levels, at what came to be called a "glass ceiling," and wage differentials continued to exist. In 1985, full-time working women still earned only 59 cents for every dollar earned by men.

Sandra Day O'Connor

Sandra Day O'Connor became the first woman justice to sit on the U.S. Supreme Court. Her pre-Court career was similar to that of many other women, as she was denied numerous jobs when she emerged from law school. A decade later, Ruth Bader Ginsburg joined O'Connor on the nation's highest court. Here O'Connor testified at her confirmation hearings. What impression does she convey as she answered senators' questions?

(Getty Images)

Conservatives also waged a dedicated campaign against the right to legal abortion. Despite the 1973 Supreme Court decision legalizing abortion, the issue remained very much alive. The number of abortions increased dramatically in the decade after the decision. In response, "pro-life" forces mobilized. Opponents lobbied to cut off federal funds that allowed the poor to obtain the abortions that the better-off could pay for themselves; they insisted that abortions should be performed in hospitals and not in less-expensive clinics; and they worked to reverse the original decision itself.

Though the Supreme Court underscored its judgment in 1983, the pro-life movement was not deterred. In 1989, a solidifying conservative majority on the Court ruled in *Webster* v. *Reproductive Health*

Services that while women's right to abortion remained intact, state legislatures could impose limitations if they chose. In 1992, in *Planned Parenthood v. Casey,* the Supreme Court reaffirmed what it termed the essence of the right to abortion, while permitting further state restrictions. It declared that a 24-hour waiting period for women seeking abortions was acceptable and required teenage girls to secure the permission of a parent (or a judge) before ending a pregnancy. The ruling made an abortion harder to obtain, particularly for poor women and young women.

Women and men became more sensitive to the issue of sexual harassment. The dramatic confrontation between Supreme Court nominee Clarence Thomas and lawyer Anita Hill during confirmation hearings in 1991 dramatized both racial questions and the problem of sexual harassment. After the retirement of Thurgood Marshall, the only African American on the Supreme Court, President Bush sought to replace him with the much more conservative Clarence Thomas, putting African Americans, who wanted one of their own on the court, in a political bind. Then, during nationally televised confirmation hearings, Anita Hill accused Thomas of harassing her when she had worked for him earlier. Despite powerful opposition, the Bush administration managed to garner the necessary votes for confirmation. In the aftermath of the turbulent confirmation hearings, Americans in Congress, in the business community, and in the larger workplace all became more aware of inappropriate behavior that could no longer be tolerated.

The Limited Commitment to Latino Rights

Latinos likewise faced continuing concerns in the 1980s and early 1990s as the commitment to reform eroded. The Latino population increased substantially as a result of immigration reform during the Great Society of the 1960s (see Chapter 28). In the 1980s, 47 percent of all legal American immigration came from Mexico, the Caribbean, and Latin America. Many other immigrants arrived illegally. As the populations of Latin American nations soared and economic conditions deteriorated, more and more people looked to the United States for relief.

Many of the new arrivals were skilled workers or professionals, who still had to retool after arriving in the United States. But even more prevalent were laborers, service sector workers, and semiskilled employees, who needed the benefit of social services at just the time they were being cut back.

Spanish-speaking students often found it difficult to finish school. In 1987, 40 percent of all Latino high school students did not graduate, and only 31 percent of Latino seniors were enrolled in college-preparatory courses; those who were in such classes frequently received little help from guidance counselors. Like other groups, Latinos slowly extended their political gains. In the 1980s, Henry Cisneros became mayor of San Antonio and Federico Peña was elected mayor of Denver. In New Mexico, Governor Toney Anaya called himself the nation's highest-elected Hispanic. The number of Latinos holding elective offices nationwide increased 3.5 percent between 1986 and 1987, and the number of Latina women in such offices increased 20 percent in that time. The number of Latino public officials nationwide increased 73 percent between 1985 and 1994, and Lauro Cavazos became the first Latino Cabinet official when he was appointed secretary of education in 1988.

Latino workers, however, continued to have a hard time in the employment market. Even as the nation's overall unemployment rate dropped, the rate for the 12 million Latino workers barely budged—and worsened in relation to the rate for African Americans.

Continuing Problems for Native Americans

Native Americans likewise experienced the waning commitment to reform, but they made some gains as a result of their own efforts. Some tribal communities developed business skills, although traditional Indian attitudes hardly fostered the capitalist perspective. As Dale Old Horn, an MIT graduate and department head at Little Big Horn College in Crow Agency, Montana, explained:

> The Crow Indian child is taught that he is part of a harmonious circle of kin relations, clans and nature. The white child is taught that he is the center of the circle. The Crow believe in sharing wealth, and whites believe in accumulating wealth.

Some Indian groups did adapt to the capitalist ethos. The Choctaw in Mississippi were among the most successful. Before they began a drive toward self-sufficiency in 1979, their unemployment rate was 50 percent. By the middle of the 1980s, Choctaw owned all or part of three businesses on the reservation, employed 1,000 people, generated $30 million in work annually, and cut the unemployment rate in half. After Congress approved Native American gambling in 1988, an increasing number of tribes became involved in this industry. Despite entrepreneurial gains, Indians still remained (as the 1990 census showed) the nation's poorest group. As Ben Nighthorse Campbell, Republican senator from Colorado, noted in 1995, average Indian household income fell by 5 percent in the 1980s, while it rose for all other ethnic and racial groups. According to the 1990 census, median Indian household income was less than $20,000 a year.

Asian American Gains

Asian Americans climbed the social and economic ladder one rung at a time. The Asian American population increased dramatically with the influx of refugees at the end of the Vietnam War, with more than half a million arriving after 1975. In the 1980s, 37 percent of all immigrants to the United States came from Asia. In Los Angeles and other cities, Samoans, Taiwanese, Koreans, Vietnamese, Filipinos, and Cambodians competed for jobs and apartments with Mexicans, African Americans, and Anglos, just as newcomers had contended with one another in New York City a century earlier.

Immigrants from India, the Philippines, China, and Korea often brought skills and professional expertise, although Southeast Asian refugees were frequently less well-off when they arrived. Many of these unskilled immigrants provided the labor for the rapidly expanding West Coast electronics industry, though Indians contributed impressive engineering and scientific talent. Asian immigrants, following a pattern established decades before, sought better and better opportunities for their children, and in California they became the largest group of entering students at a number of college campuses.

Sometimes the media highlighted the successes of Asian immigrants, particularly in contrast to the problems encountered by other groups. In 1986, *U.S. News & World Report* noted Asian American advances in a cover story, while *Newsweek* ran a lead article on "Asian Americans: A 'Model Minority,'" and *Fortune* called them "America's Super Minority." Asian Americans were proud of the exposure but pointed out that many members of the working class still struggled for a foothold. In the Chinatowns of San Francisco and Los Angeles, 40 to 50 percent of the workers were employed in the ill-paid service sector or garment industry; in New York's Chinatown, the figure was close to 70 percent. Chinese immigrant women, in particular, often had little choice but to work as seamstresses.

Professionals from some countries had a hard time. One Vietnamese physician who resettled in Oklahoma noted, "When I come here, I am told that I must be a beginner again and serve like an apprentice for two years. I have no choice, so I will do it, but I have been wronged to be asked to do this." Professionals from other nations, with programs recognized in the United States, made the transition more easily.

Violent episodes sometimes highlighted discrimination. In 1982, in Detroit, Chinese American Vincent Chin was about to get married. At a strip club with friends the week before his wedding, he encountered two auto workers who thought that Chin was Japanese, and they regarded Japan as responsible for the crisis in the American auto industry as Japanese cars flooded the market. They followed Chin out the door and killed him with a baseball bat. In response to a guilty plea, both murderers received three years probation and $3,780 in fines. Detroit's Asian Americans were incensed but were reluctant to jeopardize what they considered their already vulnerable role in America.

Pressures on the Environmental Movement

Environmentalists, too, were discouraged by the direction of public policy in the 1980s and early 1990s. Activists found that they faced fierce opposition in the Republican years. Reagan systematically restrained the EPA in his avowed effort to promote economic growth. Under the leadership of James Watt of Colorado, the Department of the Interior opened forest lands, wilderness areas, and coastal waters to economic development, with no concern for preserving the natural environment. When asked whether he believed it was important to protect the environment for future generations, Watt, a devout Christian, responded that he did not know how many generations there were before the Second Coming. Bush initially proved more sympathetic to environmental causes and delighted environmentalists by signing new clean-air legislation. Later, as the economy faltered, he was less willing to support environmental action that he claimed might slow economic growth. In 1992, he accommodated business by easing clean-air restrictions. That same year, at a United Nations–sponsored Earth Summit in Rio de Janeiro, Brazil, with 100 other heads of state, Bush stood alone in his refusal to sign a biological diversity treaty framed to conserve plant and animal species.

Economic and Demographic Change

Republicans sought to reorganize the government against the backdrop of an economy that was volatile in the 1980s and early 1990s and left millions of workers struggling to survive the shocks. Under Republican supply-side economics, the business cycle moved from recession to boom and back to recession again. When Reagan took office in 1980, the economy was reeling under the impact of declining productivity, galloping inflation, oil shortages, and high unemployment. It revived in the early 1980s, then gave way to a deep recession that lasted from 1990 to 1992, underscoring the need for renewed productivity, full employment, and a more equitable distribution of wealth.

Recovering the Past

THE INTERNET AND THE WORLD WIDE WEB

The Internet has become an integral part of our daily lives. More and more people use e-mail to communicate quickly with friends and colleagues around the world. Many Americans use the World Wide Web to make purchases ranging from books to automobiles. Others buy stocks online and rely on the Web to manage their portfolios. Historians and other scholars have come to depend on huge databases on the Web that are accessible from computers anywhere around the world.

The Internet has become an important tool for historical research. Historians can acquire census data on the Web. They can find essential statistical files, from both government offices and the private sector. They can examine huge collections of historical images. They can read the text of vital speeches. They can look at moving-picture clips from the Spanish-American War and listen to songs of the 1960s. But they need to be cautious in what they do. While the Internet provides access to a huge amount of material, the historian must evaluate it as if it was a more traditional source. But with that caution, it can be an extraordinarily useful tool.

While the Internet has only recently become an important source of historical information, it is not new. Its roots extend back 30 years, to the mid-1960s, when Americans were worried about the nuclear arms race with the Soviet Union at the height of the Cold War. After the Russians launched their *Sputnik* satellite in 1957 with a rocket that demonstrated the ability to send atomic weapons from one continent to another, American scientists dedicated themselves to catching up with and then surpassing the Soviets in space. To do so, they needed to develop their computer technology.

Scientists were also interested in figuring out how to maintain communication in the aftermath of a nuclear attack. As both the United States and the Soviet Union developed bigger and better atomic bombs and then in the 1950s began to create even more potent hydrogen weapons, it became clear that a full-scale nuclear war could wipe out a nation's ability to communicate with its distant military bases. The Department of Defense wanted to create a decentralized communication system that could continue to function even if part of it was wiped out.

In the early 1960s, scientists at the Massachusetts Institute of Technology developed the concept of timesharing, in which different users at widely separated sites could use the same central computer at the same time. Another step forward came in the mid-1960s with the development of "packet-switching" technology, which broke down data into small, discrete packets that could be transmitted over telephone lines, using modems to connect the computers to the phone lines, and then reassembled when received by another computer at the other end.

Building on those steps, the Department of Defense established the Advanced Research Projects Agency Network, known as ARPANET, in 1969. It linked the computers of four institutions—the University of California campuses at Los Angeles and Santa Barbara, the Stanford Research Institute, and the University of Utah. Two years later, the system had expanded to include 23 universities and research centers around the country.

The system was hardly user-friendly in these early days. In an age before the advent of personal computers at home, or even office computers at work, only computer professionals, engineers, and other scientists mastered the intricacies of what were very complex systems. Once they did, however, they were able to communicate with one another through what became known as electronic mail, or e-mail.

The term *Internet* was first used to describe this decentralized network in 1982, and in 1986 the National Science Foundation created a network called NSFNET with a better-organized backbone for the entire system. This new infrastructure had different *domains,* each marked by a different suffix at the end of an e-mail address, such as "edu" for educational establishments, "com" for commercial enterprises, and "gov" for government offices.

But even with improvements, the Internet remained hard to use. While computer experts could find all kinds of information, others found it difficult to access what they wanted. Then, in 1991, the University of Minnesota developed a system for finding information by accessing a huge number of databases, and they named it after the university mascot—the golden gopher.

At about the same time, another development made an even greater impact on Internet use. In 1989, Tim Berners-Lee and others at the European Laboratory for Particle Physics (known as CERN) in Geneva, Switzerland, developed a new system for information distribution. It was based on the concept of hypertext, which involved embedding links to other documents or pieces of information in the text of a document itself. While reading an article or essay on the computer, you could simply move to another document by selecting the appropriate link. This system became the basis for what came to be called the World Wide Web in 1991; over the next few years, it supplanted the gophers as the easiest way to maneuver the masses of information in cyberspace. In 1993, Mark Andreessen and others at the National Center for Superconducting Applications at the University of Illinois at Champaign–Urbana went a step further when they developed what they called Mosaic, which was a graphical Web browser. It was an easy-to-use piece of computer software that enabled the user to click the mouse on graphics or icons as well as text in a document to move to another document or Web site. Andreessen and others then formed the Netscape Communications Corporation, a private company, which marketed Netscape Navigator to browse the Web. Microsoft's Internet Explorer provides another browser.

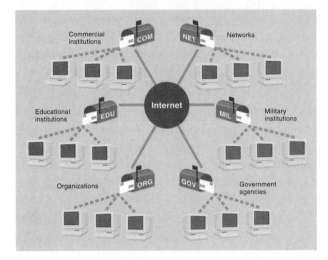

Internet and World Wide Web addresses are organized into domains, each indicated by a different three-letter suffix. Colleges and universities, for example, all use the "edu" designation.

The next step made searching for information on the Web even easier. In 1996, Larry Page and Sergey Brin, two doctoral students at Stanford University, developed a new search engine to help access Web sites that might be most helpful. They incorporated their concept in 1998 under the name Google, and two years later began selling advertising on the site to help generate revenue. While other new Internet corporations sometimes floundered, Google grew and grew, and the name itself found its way into dictionaries as a verb meaning using this search engine to find relevant information.

Reflecting on the Past Today, the World Wide Web is more accessible than ever before. But as more and more adults and children use the Web, legal issues remain to be resolved. What kinds of censorship are acceptable on the Web? How can writers, artists, and musicians maintain copyright protection for their work when the materials they produce are frequently instantly accessible on the Web? How can high-speed connections be made available to people with limited resources? How can systems be protected from "hackers" who use their ingenuity to break into commercial or government computer systems and disrupt the flow of information?

What kind of historical research might you do on the Web? How can you assess the veracity of the material you find on the Internet? What cautions are essential if you are to make the best use of Web sources?

To find more about Ronald Reagan, go to the Google search box on your computer and type in his name and see what you find. Locate audio clips of his speeches. Then go to "You Tube," another popular site, by typing in that name in the Google search box, and locate videos of his "Morning in America" advertisement as he ran for reelection and other film clips about his life and presidency. ■

The World Wide Web links numerous Web pages together. By clicking the computer mouse on a highlighted item, a user can move easily from one linked page to another.

The Changing Nature of Work

Automation and other technological advances had a powerful impact on the American workplace. The *New York Times* reported in 1990 that "Some factories look as if they have been hit by a kind of economic neutron bomb, which left assembly lines running at full speed but eliminated most of the people who worked on them." Formerly profitable jobs disappeared. One pulp-mill worker voiced gloom about the future: "I think the country has a problem. The managers want everything run by computers. But if no one has a job, no one will know how to do anything anymore. Who will pay the taxes? What kind of society will it be when people have lost their knowledge and depend on computers for everything?"

In human terms, the introduction of the computer had other consequences as well. Workers who sat for hours before their screens complained about a feeling of "floating in space" as they worked, or of being "lost behind the screen." Others worried about radiation from the monitor or muscular fatigue from sitting at a keyboard all day. Still others complained that they could no longer touch their work. As more Americans began to use computers, people who did not work with them complained about a growing "digital divide" that further increased the gap between rich and poor. Members of the middle and upper classes had easy access to computer technology, while less fortunate individuals, many of whom belonged to minority groups, found themselves left behind.

Yet even as the nature of work changed, people seemed to be working more. In past decades, leisure time had seemed to expand, and there was talk of a four-day workweek in the 1950s. In subsequent years, however, the amount of time Americans worked steadily rose so that in the mid-1990s, American employees worked many more hours each year than their counterparts in Germany or France. The effort to juggle the pressures between employment and family life led to increasing stress. Problems were particularly severe for women, still trying to cope with the pressures of a double load, as they maintained responsibility for the home even when working outside. Marriages came under significant strain.

The Shift to a Service Economy

The scarcity of good jobs stemmed in part from the restructuring of the economy that occurred in the 1980s. In a trend that had been underway for more than half a century, the United States continued its shift from an industrial base, in which most workers actually produced things, to a service base, in which most provided expertise or service to others in the workforce. By the mid-1980s, three-fourths of the 113 million employees in the country worked in the service sector as fast-food workers, clerks, computer programmers, doctors, lawyers, bankers, teachers, and bureaucrats. That shift, in turn, had its roots in the decline of the country's industrial sector. The United States had been the world's industrial leader since the late nineteenth century. By the 1980s and early 1990s, productivity had slowed in virtually all American industries.

The causes of this decline in productivity were complex. The most important factor was a widespread failure on the part of the United States to invest sufficiently in its basic productive capacity. During the Reagan years, capital investment in real plants and equipment within the United States gave way to speculation, mergers, and spending abroad. At the end of the 1980s, domestic investment was down—5.7 percent in 1990 and 9.5 percent in 1991. The energy crisis and rising oil prices also contributed to the industrial decline. Finally, the war in Vietnam diverted federal funds from research and development with consequences that continued even after the conflict ended.

While American industry became less productive, other industrial nations moved forward. German and Japanese industries, rebuilt after World War II with U.S. aid and aggressively modernized thereafter, reached new heights of efficiency. As a result, the United States began to lose its share of the world market for industrial goods. In 1946, the country had provided 60 percent of the world's iron and steel; in 1978, it provided a mere 16 percent. By 1980, Japanese car manufacturers had captured nearly one-quarter of the American automobile market. The auto industry, which had been a mainstay of economic growth for much of the twentieth century, suffered plant shutdowns and massive layoffs. In 1991, its worst year ever, Ford lost a staggering $2.3 billion.

Workers in Transition

In the 1980s and early 1990s, American labor struggled to hold on to the gains realized by the post–World War II generation of blue-collar workers. The shift to a service economy, while providing new jobs, was difficult for many American workers. Millions of men and women who lost positions as a result of mergers, plant closings, and permanent economic contractions now found themselves in low-paying jobs with few opportunities for advancement.

Entry-level posts were seldom located in the central cities, where most of the poor lived. Even when new jobs were created in the cities, minority residents often lacked the skills to get them.

Meanwhile, the trade union movement faltered as the economy moved from an industrial to a service base. Unions had been most successful in organizing the nation's industrial workers in the years since the 1930s, and the United States emerged from World War II with unions strong. In the years that followed, the percentage of workers belonging to unions dropped, from just over 25 percent in 1980 to barely over 16 percent a decade later. As the total number of wage and salary workers rose substantially between 1983 and 1993, the overall number of union members dropped from 17.7 million to 16.6 million.

Union membership declined for a number of reasons. The shift from blue-collar to white-collar work contributed to the contraction. The increase in the workforce in the numbers of women and young people (groups that have historically been difficult to organize) was another factor, as was the more forceful opposition to unions by managers applying the provisions of the Taft–Hartley Act of 1947, which restricted labor's tactics. At the same time, union organizing efforts fell off significantly.

Union Membership, 1950–1990

The percentage of workers belonging to unions dropped dramatically after 1980 and continued to fall in the 1990s.

Source: U.S. Bureau of Labor Statistics.

Union vulnerability was visible early in Reagan's first term, when members of the Professional Air Traffic Controllers Organization (PATCO) went on strike. Charging that the strike violated the law, the president— who had once been a union leader himself—fired the strikers, decertified the union, and ordered the training of new controllers at a cost of $1.3 billion. The message was clear: government employees could not challenge the public interest.

Anti-union sentiments reverberated throughout the nongovernment sector as well, as many companies across the nation—confronted by falling prices and losses in revenue—sought to dissolve union agreements about hiring, wages, and benefits. Workers who kept their jobs found that their unions could not get favorable contracts. For example, in 1984 the United Auto Workers (UAW) ended a strike at General Motors by trading a pledge that GM would guarantee up to 70 percent of the production workers' lifetime jobs for a smaller wage increase than the union sought and a modification of the cost-of-living allowance that had been a part of UAW contracts since 1948.

Farmers also had to adjust as the larger workforce changed. Continuing a trend that began in the early twentieth century, the number of farms and farmers declined steadily. When Franklin Roosevelt took office in 1933, some 6.7 million farms covered the American landscape. Fifty years later, there were only 2.4 million. As family farms disappeared, farming income became more concentrated in the hands of the largest operators. In 1983, the top 1 percent of the nation's farmers produced 30 percent of all farm products, while the top 12 percent generated 90 percent of all farm income. The top 1 percent of the growers in the United States had average annual incomes of $572,000, but the small and medium-sized farmers who were being forced off the land frequently had incomes below the official government poverty line.

The extraordinary productivity of the most successful American farmers derived in part from the use of chemical fertilizers, irrigation, pesticides, and scientific management. Government price-support programs helped, too. Yet that very productivity caused unexpected setbacks. In the 1970s, food shortages abroad made the United States the "breadbasket of the world." Farmers increased their output to meet multibillion-bushel grain export orders and profited handsomely from high prices in India, China, Russia, and other countries. To increase production, farmers often borrowed heavily at high interest rates. When a worldwide economic slump began in 1980, overseas demand for American farm products declined sharply and farm prices dropped.

Thousands of farmers, caught in the cycle of over-production, heavy indebtedness, and falling prices, watched helplessly as banks and federal agencies foreclosed on their mortgages and drove them out of business.

The Roller-Coaster Economy

The economy shifted back and forth during the 1980s and early 1990s. The Reagan years began with a recession that lasted for several years. An economic boom between 1983 and 1990 gave way to a punishing recession as the new decade began. It appeared that the United States had embarked on another unsettling boom-and-bust cycle.

The recession of 1980 to 1982 began during the Carter administration, when the Federal Reserve Board tried to deal with mounting deficits by increasing the money supply. Program cuts to counter inflation brought substantial unemployment in the workforce. During Reagan's first year, the job situation deteriorated further, and by the end of 1982, the unemployment rate had climbed to 10.8 percent (and over 20 percent among African Americans). Nearly one-third of the nation's industrial capacity lay idle, and 12 million Americans were out of work.

Inflation, accompanied by heavy unemployment, continued to be a problem. The inflation rate, which reached 12.4 percent a year under Carter in 1980, fell after Reagan assumed office, to 8.9 percent in his first year and to about 5 percent during the remainder of his first term. But even the lower rate eroded the purchasing power of people already in difficulty.

The recession of 1980–1982 afflicted every region of the country. Business failures proliferated in every city and state, as large and small businesses closed their doors and fired employees. In 1982, business bankruptcies rose 50 percent from the previous year. In auto-making Detroit, Japanese competition and high interest rates sent car sales plummeting. The Detroit unemployment rate rose to more than 19 percent and affected the entire city.

Even the Sun Belt—the vast southern region stretching from coast to coast—showed the effects of the recession. It had enjoyed economic growth fostered by the availability of cheap, nonunion labor, tax advantages that state governments offered corporations willing to locate plants there, and a favorable climate. Now it, too, began to suffer economic problems, and large areas began to stagnate. Overexpansion in the oil industry led to a collapse in prices that disrupted the economy in Texas, Oklahoma, Louisiana, and other oil-producing regions. Worldwide gluts of some minerals, copper for example, added to unemployment elsewhere in the Southwest.

Economic conditions improved in late 1983 and early 1984, particularly for Americans in the middle- and upper-income ranges. The federal tax cut Reagan pushed through encouraged consumer spending, and huge defense expenditures had a stimulating effect. The Republican effort to reduce restrictions and cut waste sparked business confidence. A voluntary Japanese quota on car exports assisted the ailing automobile industry. The stock market climbed as it reflected the optimistic buying spree. Inflation remained low, about 3 to 4 percent annually from 1982 to 1988. Interest rates likewise fell from 16.5 percent to 10.5 percent in the same period. The unemployment rate at the end of the 1980s fell to below 6 percent nationally (though many of the new jobs that were created paid less than $13,000 per year). Between the start of the recovery and 1988, real GNP grew at an annual rate of 4.2 percent.

But the economic upswing masked a number of problems. Millions of Americans remained poor. Many families continued to earn a middle-class income, but only by having two full-time income earners. They also went deeply into debt. To buy homes, young people accepted vastly higher mortgage interest rates than their parents had. Stiff credit card debts, often at 20 percent interest, were common. Under such circumstances, some young families struggled to remain in the middle class. Blue-collar workers had to accept lower standards of living. Single mothers were hit hardest of all.

The huge and growing budget deficits reflected the fundamental economic instability. Those deficits provoked doubts that resulted in the stock market crash of 1987. Six weeks of falling prices culminated with a 22.6 percent drop on Monday, October 19, almost double the plunge of "Black Tuesday," October 29, 1929. The deficits, negative trade balances, and exposures of Wall Street fraud all combined to puncture the bubble. The stock market revived, but the crash foreshadowed further problems.

Those problems surfaced in the early 1990s, as the country experienced another recession. A combination of massive military spending, growth of entitlement programs, and tax cuts sent budget deficits skyward. As bond traders in the 1980s speculated recklessly and pocketed huge profits, the basic productive structure of the country continued to decline. The huge increase in the national debt eroded business confidence, and this time the effects were felt not simply in the stock market but in the economy as a whole.

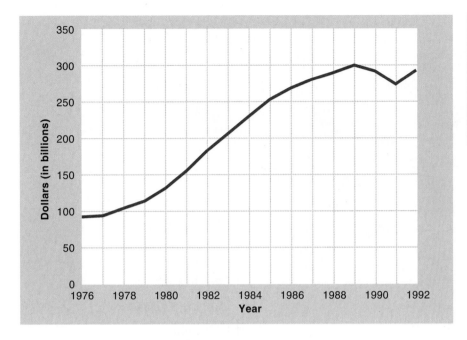

350
300
250
200
150
100
50
0

Dollars (in billions)

1976 1978 1980 1982 1984 1986 1988 1990 1992

Year

Federal Defense Spending, 1976–1992

Federal defense spending rose dramatically during the presidencies of Ronald Reagan and George Bush. The enormous expenditures on the military led to the huge deficits that threw the economy out of kilter.

Source: Statistical Abstract of the United States.

American firms suffered a serious decline, and to cope with shrinking profits and decreased consumer demand, companies scaled back dramatically. In late 1991, General Motors announced that it would close 21 plants, lay off 9,000 white-collar employees the next year, and eliminate more than 70,000 jobs in the next several years. Hundreds of other companies did the same thing. As a result, the unemployment rate rose once again, and by mid-1991, it reached 7 percent, the highest level in nearly five years.

Around the nation, state governments found it impossible to balance their budgets without resorting to massive spending cuts. Reagan's efforts to move programs from the federal to the state level worked as long as funding lasted, but as national support dropped and state tax revenues declined, states found themselves in a budgetary gridlock. Most had constitutional prohibitions against running deficits, and so they had to slash spending for social services and education.

After a number of false starts, the economy began to recover in mid-1992. The unemployment rate dropped, the productivity index rose, and a concerted effort began to bring the federal deficit down.

Population Shifts

As the American people dealt with the swings of the economy, demographic patterns changed significantly. The nation's population increased from 228 million to approximately 250 million between 1980 and 1990—a rise of 9.6 percent (as opposed to 11.5 percent in the 1970s) that was one of the lowest rates of growth in American history. At the same time, the complexion of the country changed. In 1992, the country's nonwhite population—African Americans, Latinos, Asians, and Native Americans—stood at an all-time high of 25 percent, the result of increased immigration and of minority birthrates significantly above the white birthrate.

The population shifted geographically as well. American cities increasingly filled with members of the nation's minorities. White families continued to leave for the steadily growing suburbs, which by 1990 contained almost half the population, more than ever before. In 15 of the nation's 28 largest cities—New York, Chicago, and Houston among them—minorities made up at least half the population. Minority representation varied by urban region. In Detroit, Washington, New Orleans, and Chicago, African Americans were the largest minority; in Phoenix, El Paso, San Antonio, and Los Angeles, Latinos held that position; in San Francisco, Asians outnumbered other groups. The cities also grew steadily poorer. As had been the case since World War II, commuters from the suburbs took the better-paying jobs, while people living in the cities held lower-paying positions.

At the same time, the population was moving west. In 1900, the Mountain and Pacific states contained about 5 percent of the nation's population. By 1990, that figure stood at 21 percent. The population of the nation as a whole rose by less than

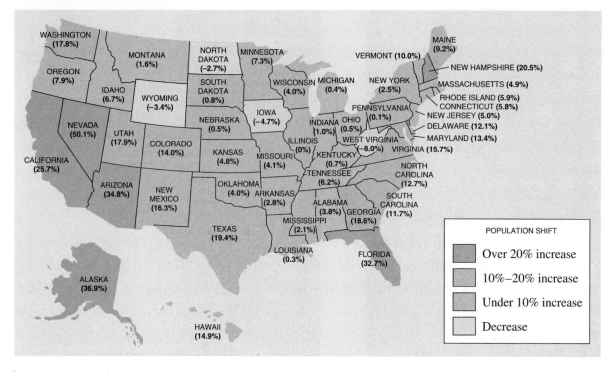

Population Shifts, 1980–1990

This map shows the population shifts between 1980 and 1990. Note the substantial increases in western regions of the country and the much smaller increases along the Atlantic seaboard.

10 percent in the 1980s, but the population of the West increased by 22 percent.

That population was becoming much more urbanized. In the 50 years following 1940, the six largest metropolitan areas in the West grew by 380 percent; the six largest in the East expanded by only 64 percent.

With its urban development, the West became a pacesetter for the rest of the country. If the New England village was a symbol of the eighteenth century and the midwestern town was a similar symbol of the nineteenth century, then the western metropolis had special symbolic importance in the late twentieth century. Western cities were unbounded, open-ended, and sprawling in all directions. They seemed capable of expanding indefinitely. Horizontal, low-slung homes made western neighborhoods look very different from those in the Northeast. Tourism became a dynamic industry, with the West in the forefront. The motel, a western invention, made automobile travel easier.

California was the nation's fastest-growing state, its population increasing in the 1980s by nearly 26 percent. Responding to a question about California's impact on the rest of the country, writer Wallace Stegner replied, "We *are* the national culture, at its most energetic end." Los Angeles became the most dynamic example of American vitality and creativity. The motion picture industry exerted a

worldwide impact. The city became a capital of consumption and served as a symbol of a dynamic national life.

Foreign Policy and the End of the Cold War

In the early 1990s, the United States emerged triumphant in the Cold War that had dominated international politics since the end of World War II. In one of the most momentous turns in modern world history, communism collapsed in Eastern Europe and in the Soviet Union, and the various republics in the Soviet orbit moved toward capitalism and democracy. Other regions—the Middle East and Africa—experienced equally breathtaking change.

Reagan, Bush, and the Soviet Union

The Cold War was very much alive when Ronald Reagan assumed power in 1981. Like most of his compatriots, Reagan believed in large defense budgets and a militant approach toward the Soviet Union. He wanted to cripple the USSR economically by forcing it to spend more than it could afford on defense.

The Last Premier of the Soviet Union
Mikhail Gorbachev was the Soviet leader who initiated the process that helped ease tensions with the United States and ultimately ended the Cold War. Gorbachev's policies provided for major readjustments in Soviet society, but those eventually tore the Soviet Union apart. Why was Gorbachev willing to work with the United States? What image does he convey in this photograph?

(AP/Wide World Photos)

Viewing the Soviet Union as an "evil empire" in his first term, Reagan promoted a larger atomic arsenal by arguing that a nuclear war could be fought and won. The administration dropped efforts to obtain Senate ratification of SALT II, the arms reduction plan negotiated under Carter, although it observed the pact's restrictions. Then Reagan proposed the enormously expensive and bitterly criticized Strategic Defense Initiative, popularly known as "Star Wars" after a 1977 movie, to intercept Soviet missiles in outer space.

In his second term, Reagan softened his belligerence. Mikhail Gorbachev, the new Soviet leader, watching his own economy collapse under the pressure of the superheated arms race, realized the need for greater accommodation with the West. He understood that the only way the Soviet Union could survive was through arms negotiations with the United States. He therefore proposed a policy of *perestroika* (restructuring the economy) and *glasnost* (political openness to encourage personal initiative). His overtures opened the way to better relations with the United States.

Concerned with his own place in history, Reagan met with Gorbachev, and the two developed a close working relationship. Summit meetings led to an Intermediate-Range Nuclear Forces Treaty in 1987 that provided for the withdrawal and destruction of 2,500 Soviet and American nuclear missiles in Europe.

George Bush maintained Reagan's comfortable relationship with Gorbachev. At several summit meetings in 1989 and 1990, the two leaders signed agreements reducing the number of long-range nuclear weapons, ending the manufacture of chemical weapons, and easing trade restrictions. The Strategic Arms Reduction Treaty (START) signed in 1991 dramatically cut stockpiles of long-range weapons.

The End of the Cold War

The Cold War ended with astonishing speed. Gorbachev's efforts to restructure Soviet society and to work with the United States brought him acclaim around the world but led to trouble at home. In mid-1991, he faced an old-guard Communist coup, led by those who opposed *glasnost* and *perestroika*. He survived this right-wing challenge, but he could not resist those who wanted to go even further to

President of a New Russia
Boris Yeltsin, president of Russia, the largest of the republics in what had been the Soviet Union, became the most influential leader after Gorbachev's fall. But Yeltsin's efforts at economic reform met with serious opposition and led to his resignation as the century came to an end. How is Yeltsin conveying his confidence in this picture? What did he hope to achieve?

(Reuters/CORBIS)

establish democracy and capitalism. The forces he had unleashed finally destroyed the Soviet system and tore the USSR apart.

Boris Yeltsin, president of Russia, the strongest and largest of the Soviet republics, emerged as the dominant leader, but even he could not contain the forces of disintegration. Movements in the tiny Baltic republics of Latvia, Lithuania, and Estonia, culminating with independence in 1991, began the dismantling of the Soviet Union. The once-powerful superpower was now a collection of separate states. Although the republics coalesced loosely in a Commonwealth of Independent States, led by Russia, they retained their autonomy—and independent leadership—in domestic and foreign affairs.

Meanwhile, Communist regimes throughout Europe collapsed. The most dramatic chapter in this story unfolded in Germany in November 1989. Responding to Gorbachev's softening stance toward the West, East Germany's Communist party boss announced unexpectedly that citizens of his country would be free to leave East Germany. Within hours, thousands of people gathered on both sides of the 28-mile Berlin Wall—the symbol of the Cold War that divided Berlin into East and West sectors. As the border guards stepped aside, East Germans flooded into West Berlin amid dancing, shouting, and fireworks. Within days, sledgehammer-wielding Germans pulverized the Berlin Wall, and soon the Communist government itself came tumbling down. By October 1990, the two Germanys were reunited.

The fall of the Berlin Wall reverberated all over Eastern Europe. In Poland, the 10-year-old Solidarity movement led by Lech Walesa triumphed in its long struggle against Soviet domination and found itself in power in December 1990, with Walesa as president. In Czechoslovakia, two decades after Soviet tanks had rolled into the streets of Prague to suppress a policy of liberalization, the forces of freedom were likewise victorious. Like Poland, Czechoslovakia sought and received aid from the United States. But not even economic assistance could keep the nation intact, as turbulence led to the creation of separate and independent Czech and Slovak republics. The same forces that culminated in the independence of Czechoslovakia brought new regimes in Bulgaria, Hungary, Romania, and Albania.

Yugoslavia, held together by a Communist dictatorship since 1945, proved to be the extreme case of ethnic hostility resurging amid collapsing central authority. In 1991, Yugoslavia splintered into its ethnic components. In Bosnia, the decision of the Muslim and Croatian majority to secede from Serbian-dominated Yugoslavia led Bosnian Serbs, backed by the Serbian republic, to embark on a brutal siege of the city of Sarajevo and an even more ruthless "ethnic cleansing" campaign to liquidate opponents. The United States remained out of the conflict, unsure about what to do.

Early in 1992, Bush and Yeltsin proclaimed a new era of "friendship and partnership" and formally declared an end to the Cold War. After half a century of confrontation, the United States had won. It then extended aid to the former Soviet republics, which needed help in reorganizing their economies as free enterprise systems.

Dismantling the Berlin Wall
The destruction of the Berlin Wall in November 1989 was a symbolic blow to the entire Cold War structure that had solidified in Europe in the postwar years. People grabbed hammers and joined together in tearing down the hated wall. Joyous celebrations marked the reunification of a city that had been divided for decades. How does this dramatic picture convey the exuberant mood of the time?

(Alexandria Avakian/Woodfin Camp & Associates)

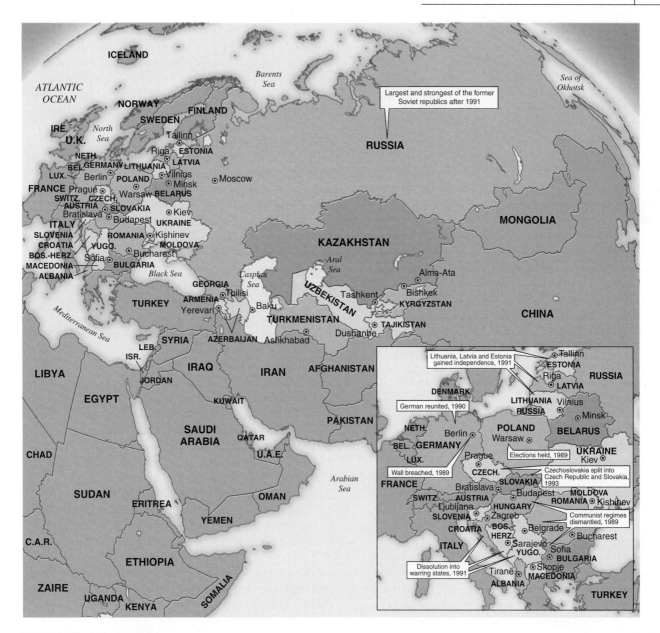

The Fall of Communism

In the late 1980s and early 1990s, the Soviet Union fragmented and lost control of its satellites in Eastern Europe. As many countries shown here declared their independence, Czechoslovakia broke into two nations, while Yugoslavia ruptured into a group of feuding states. How widespread was the turbulence that led to the fall of communism? How quickly did the process take place? How did events in one country influence events in another country?

American Involvement Overseas

As the United States struggled to keep abreast of the momentous changes in Eastern Europe, it was equally involved with events in the rest of the world. Here again the nation sought to preserve stability as the Cold War drew to an end.

In Latin America, the United States intervened frequently as it had in the past, hoping to impose order on the volatile region. Viewing Central America as a Cold War battlefield early in his presidency, Reagan openly opposed left-wing guerrillas in El Salvador who fought to overthrow a repressive right-wing regime. The United States increased its assistance to the antirevolutionary Salvadoran government, heedless of a similar course followed years before in Vietnam. Efforts to destroy the radical forces failed, but in 1989, a far-right faction won the Salvadoran elections and polarized the country.

Nicaragua became an even bloodier battleground. In 1979, revolutionaries calling themselves Sandinistas (after César Sandino, who fought in the 1920s against U.S. occupation troops) overthrew the repressive

Nelson Mandela

Nelson Mandela served as a source of inspiration to black South Africans, as the long struggle against apartheid finally brought that system of rigid segregation to an end and led to the setting up of a biracial democracy with Mandela himself as president. How did Mandela manage to convey his own sense of confidence, commitment, and reconciliation?

(AP/Wide World Photos)

Somoza family, which had ruled for three decades. Republicans in their 1980 platform pledged to replace the Sandinistas with a "free and independent" government. Once in office, Reagan circumvented congressional opposition to his efforts to defeat the revolutionary reformers and signed a National Security directive in November 1981 authorizing the CIA to arm and train counterrevolutionaries known as *contras* as Nicaragua became enmeshed in a bitter civil war. Upon discovering the secret CIA missions, Congress cut off military aid to the *contras*. Peaceful elections in early 1990 finally drove the Sandinistas out and brought the fighting to an end. Though the economy remained in desperate straits, the new regime seemed to offer the best hope of healing the wounds of the bloody conflict.

Reagan found it easier to maintain stability on the tiny Caribbean island of Grenada. The president ordered marines there in October 1983 after a coup installed a government sympathetic to Fidel Castro's Cuba. Concerned about the construction of a large airfield, 2,000 marines invaded the island, rescued a number of American medical students, and claimed triumph. Though the United Nations condemned it, Americans cheered what the administration called its "rescue mission."

Middle Eastern and Central American concerns became entangled in the Iran–*contra* affair. In 1987, Congress learned that the National Security Council had launched an effort to free American hostages in the Middle East by selling arms to Iran and then using the funds to aid the *contras*, in direct violation of both the law and congressional will. The trial of Oliver North, the National Security Council official responsible for the policy, focused on his distortions and falsifications before congressional committees and on his destruction of official documents that could have substantiated charges of wrongdoing by top officials. Convicted in 1989, North received a light sentence requiring no time in prison from a judge who recognized that North was not acting entirely on his own.

Bush, too, was involved in a variety of episodes abroad. Despite memories of past imperialism, the United States invaded Panama in 1989; the reasons it gave were to protect the canal, defend American citizens, and stop drug traffic. The campaign resulted in the capture of military leader Manuel Noriega, notorious for his involvement in the drug trade. Noriega was brought to the United States, tried, and convicted of drug-trafficking charges.

In South Africa, the United States supported the long and ultimately successful struggle against apartheid. This policy, whereby the white minority (only 15 percent of the population) segregated, suppressed, and denied basic human rights to the black majority, was part of South African law. A resistance movement, spearheaded by the African National Congress (ANC) sought to end apartheid. While the United States had long expressed its dislike of this ruthless system of segregation, economic and political ties to South Africa kept the United States from taking steps to weaken it. Then, in 1986, bowing to increased domestic pressure, Congress imposed sanctions, including a rule prohibiting new American investments. The economic pressure damaged the South African economy and persuaded more than half of the 300 American firms doing business there to leave.

The final blow to apartheid came from the efforts of Nelson Mandela. The black ANC activist, who had become a symbol of the militant resistant movement during his 27 years in prison, steered his nation through a stunning transformation. In 1990, during Bush's presidency, South African prime minister Frederik W. de Klerk succumbed to pressure from the United States and the rest of the world and freed Mandela. Talks between the white government and the ANC produced a smooth transition to a biracial democracy and led to peaceful elections in 1994, in which blacks voted for the first time. The African National Congress assumed power and Mandela himself became president. American aid provided support in transitional times.

Elsewhere in Africa, U.S. policymakers had greater difficulty in maintaining post–Cold War stability. Somalia, an impoverished East African nation, suffered from a devastating famine, compounded by struggles between warlords that led to an almost total disintegration of order. In 1992, Bush sent U.S. troops to assist a UN effort to relieve the starvation and stabilize the country, but those efforts proved unsuccessful in a struggle that continued into the twenty-first century.

A dramatic crisis occurred in the Middle East in 1990 when Saddam Hussein, the dictator of Iraq, invaded and annexed oil-rich neighboring Kuwait. President Bush reacted vigorously. Working through the UN, as Harry Truman had done in Korea, the United States persuaded the Security Council to vote unanimously to condemn the attack and impose an embargo on Iraq. After Hussein refused to relinquish Kuwait, in mid-January 1991 a 28-nation coalition struck at Iraq with an American-led multinational army of nearly half a million troops. In Operation Desert Storm, the coalition forces' sophisticated

missiles, aircraft, and tanks swiftly overwhelmed the Iraqis. Americans were initially jubilant. Then the euphoria faded as Saddam turned his remaining military power against minorities in Iraq. Bush's unwillingness to become bogged down in an Iraqi civil war and his eagerness to return U.S. troops home left the conflict unfinished. A year after his defeat, Hussein was as strongly entrenched as ever.

Meanwhile, the United States was involved in a larger, and ultimately more important, effort to bring peace to the Middle East. In the early 1990s, Secretary of State James Baker finally secured agreement from the major parties in the region to speak to one another face to face. A victory in the Israeli parliamentary elections in mid-1992 for Yitzhak Rabin, a soldier who recognized the need for peace and was ready to compromise, offered further hope for the talks.

Timeline

1980	Ronald Reagan elected president
1980–1982	Recession
1981	Reagan breaks air controllers' strike
	AIDS (acquired immune deficiency syndrome) discovered
1981–1983	Tax cuts; deficit spending increases
1983	Reagan proposes Strategic Defense Initiative ("Star Wars")
1984	Reagan reelected
1986	Tax reform measure passed
	Immigration Reform and Control Act
1987	Iran–*contra* affair becomes public
	Stock market crashes
	Intermediate-Range Nuclear Forces Treaty signed
1988	George H. W. Bush elected president
1989	Federal bailout of savings and loan industry
	Fall of the Berlin Wall
1990	National debt reaches $3.1 trillion
	Sandinistas driven from power in Nicaragua
	Nelson Mandela freed in South Africa
	U.S. population reaches 250 million
1990–1992	Recession
1991	Persian Gulf War
	Failed coup in Soviet Union
	Disintegration of the Soviet Union
	Strategic Arms Reduction Treaty (START) signed
	Ethnic turbulence in fragmented former Yugoslavia
1992	Declaration of the end of the Cold War

Conclusion

CONSERVATISM IN CONTEXT

In the 1980s and early 1990s, the United States witnessed the resurgence of conservatism. The assault on the welfare state, dubbed the "Reagan Revolution," created a less-regulated economy, whatever the implications for less-fortunate Americans. The policies of Ronald Reagan and George Bush continued the trend begun by Richard Nixon in the 1970s. They reshaped the political agenda and reversed the liberal approach that had held sway since the New Deal of Franklin Roosevelt in the 1930s. In foreign affairs, Republican administrations likewise shifted course. Reagan first assumed a steel-ribbed posture toward the Soviet Union, then moved toward détente, and watched as his successor declared victory in the Cold War.

To be sure, there were limits to the transformation. Such fundamental programs as social security and Medicare remained securely in place, accepted by all but the most implacable splinter groups. Even the most conservative presidents of the past half century could not return to an imagined era of unbridled individualism and puny federal government. On the international front, despite the end of the Cold War, the nation's defense budget remained far higher than many Americans wished, and the nuclear arsenal continued to pose a threat to the human race.

Nor was the transformation beneficial to everyone. Periods of deep recession wrought havoc on the lives of blue-collar and white-collar workers alike. Working-class Americans were caught in the spiral of downward mobility that made them question the ability of the nation's economy to reward hard work. Liberals and conservatives both worried about the mounting national debt and the capacity of the economy to compete with Japan, South Korea, Germany, and other countries. Countless Americans fretted about the growing gaps between rich and poor. They fought with one another over what rules should govern a woman's right to an abortion. For the first time in American history, many children could not hope to do better than their parents had done. Reluctantly they tried to prepare themselves to accept a scaled-down version of the American dream.

QUESTIONS FOR REVIEW AND REFLECTION

1. How did the conservative movement become a major force in American life?
2. How successful was Reagan in implementing his conservative program?
3. What was the fate of social reform movements in the 1980s?
4. How did economic issues affect American life in the 1980s?
5. How did the Cold War finally come to an end?

CHAPTER 31

The Post–Cold War World, 1992–2008

American society became more and more aware of its multicultural past and present in the 1990s. Different groups competed with each other for positions in the marketplace and other public spaces as the gap between rich and poor continued to grow greater.

(Billy Morrow Jackson, *Station*, 1981–1982, Beloit College Collection, Beloit, WI)

American Stories

An Immigrant Family Struggles as the Economy Improves

In 1997, Marlene Garrett bundled up her three sleepy children—ages 4, 3, and 1—and took them to the babysitter's home every morning at 5 A.M. "Mama has to go to work so she can buy you shoes," she told them as she left for a job behind the counter at a bagel café in Fort Lauderdale, Florida, that began at 6 A.M. This was a new position and she did not want to be late.

Marlene had come to the United States from Jamaica eight years earlier. She and her husband, Rod, had high hopes for a better life in the United States, and they were fortunate enough to be employed. But both of them held entry-level jobs and had to struggle to make ends meet. Rod worked in a factory making hospital curtains and brought home about $250 a week. Marlene had just left a $5.25-an-hour job selling sneakers for her $6-an-hour job at the bagel café. With the $200 she earned weekly she could pay the monthly rent of $400 and buy groceries. With luck, they could repair or replace the car, which had recently died, and perhaps begin to pay off their $5,000 debt from medical bills. They had no health insurance and could only hope that no one got sick.

Marlene was not happy about her babysitting arrangements. Her real preference was to stay at home. "Who's a better caretaker than mom?" she asked. But remaining at home was out of the question. Welfare might have been a possibility in the past, but the United States was in the process of cutting back drastically on its welfare rolls, and, in any event, Marlene was not comfortable with that alternative. "I don't want to plant that seed in my children," she said. "I want to work."

Marlene had few day-care options. She would have liked to have taken Scherrod, Angelique, and Hasia to the Holy Temple Christian Academy—her church's day-care center and preschool—but it cost $180 a week for three children and was beyond reach. Several months before, when she had been earning $8 an hour as a home health aide for the elderly, she had thought she could afford the church center and had even put money down for school uniforms for the kids. Then her car gave out and made it impossible to continue that job.

Instead of the Holy Temple Christian Academy, Marlene took the children to the home of Vivienne, a woman from the Bahamas who worked nights at the self-service laundry where Marlene did her wash. Vivienne's apartment was simple and clean but had no toys or books anywhere in sight. Most days, the children watched television during the 10 hours that Marlene was away.

The Garretts knew how important it was to stimulate their children. Reflecting longingly on the church center and what it offered, Marlene said, "The children play games. They go on field trips. They teach them, they train them. My children are bright. You would be amazed at what they would acquire in a year." But instead of a stimulating center, the Garretts had to settle for a place that was simply safe.

At a time when the administration of Bill Clinton was trying to reconfigure the welfare system, people like the Garretts found themselves left out. Florida, like many states, budgeted most of its child-care money for families moving off welfare to jobs. People who had never been on welfare received nothing. As the executive director of a Florida child-care referral agency observed, "Many of these parents have no choice but to leave their children in substandard arrangements that are rotting their brains, and jeopardizing their futures."

Marlene refused to give up hope. Her children were on a waiting list for help from the state that might make the Holy Temple Christian Academy accessible. Meanwhile, she took a second job working nights at the local Marriott Hotel. She had to pay Vivienne more money for the extra hours, and she worried even more about the additional time away from the children, but felt she had no choice. "It is temporary," she said. "I am doing what I have to do."

Marlene and Rod Garrett were like millions of poor Americans who found themselves left out of the prosperity that returned to the United States in the mid-1990s. Despite rosy economic indicators, more than 35 million Americans still lived below the federally defined poverty line. Life was hardly easy for the Garretts or for other families who found themselves on the bottom side of the line. Then, soon after George W. Bush succeeded Bill Clinton as president in 2001, the economy faltered. Now even more Americans found themselves in the same straits as the Garretts.

The Garretts' struggle to care for their children—and for themselves—unfolded against the backdrop of the longest period of economic growth in American history. As a deep recession in the early 1990s lifted, the economy went on a tear. American corporations, increasingly operating in a multinational context, dominated the global economy. Taking advantage of remarkable advances in communications technology, corporations found it easy to do business in a world smaller than ever before. The easy availability of money encouraged middle- and upper-class Americans to invest in the stock market and mutual funds, often enabling them to realize large gains, at least on paper. The troubling budget deficit that had soared in the Reagan administration disappeared as the government, guided by Democratic president Bill Clinton, ran a surplus for the first time in years. The unemployment level dropped, yet for Americans at the bottom of the economic ladder, some of them immigrants from abroad, conditions remained difficult. Many of the jobs now available as a result of the relentless shift toward a service economy paid little more than the minimum wage, and people like the Garretts, who dreamed of a better life, still found themselves struggling to survive.

Meanwhile, the global scene shifted abruptly. The cataclysmic events in Europe that ended nearly a half century of Cold War required the United States to redefine its international role. This led to substantial debate as both Republicans, who controlled Congress for most of the 1990s, and Democrats, who controlled the White House for the same period, voiced reservations about playing an interventionist, and potentially expensive, role abroad. Then, as the new decade began, the United States confronted the menace of terrorism on a scale never known before. The attacks that destroyed the World Trade Center towers in New York City and left a gaping hole in the Pentagon in Washington, D.C., led to a war on terrorism and a fundamental reconfiguration of American foreign policy.

This chapter describes demographic shifts, reflected in the census of 2000, that changed the face of the American people. It highlights the revival of the economy that brought unprecedented prosperity for many but still failed to accommodate the needs of less fortunate Americans like the Garretts, and then records the even greater suffering as the economy fell apart. It examines the political struggle between Democrats and Republicans that led to a debate about democratic values and brought the second presidential impeachment in American history. It notes the bitterly contested national election of 2000 and its conservative aftermath. Finally, it explores the continuing effort to define the American role in the turbulent and terrorist-dominated post–Cold War world.

The Changing Face of the American People

The United States changed dramatically in the 1990s, as the continuing influx of new immigrants reshaped demographic patterns. The overall population, as reported in the census of 2000, grew more rapidly than it had in the past several decades and reflected the steady increase in the number of nonwhite Americans.

The New Pilgrims

The second great wave of immigrants in the twentieth century changed the face of America. The number of immigrants to the United States in the 20-year period from 1981 to 2000 was approximately 17.5 million, making it the most voluminous period of immigration in American history. In the decade of the 1990s, close to 10 million immigrants were counted, just less than the 10.1 million immigrants recorded in the 10 years from 1905 to 1914, which stands as the all-time record for that span of time. The increase continued in the first five years of the twenty-first century, and in 2005, immigrants made up 12.4 percent of America's population, compared to 11.2 percent in 2000.

Patterns of immigrant settlement changed. Whereas most immigrants around the turn of the preceding century remained near the East Coast, or in contiguous states, in 2000, 39.9 percent of the foreign born settled in western states, with only 22.6 percent of the foreign born living in the Northeast. The shift was a result of larger demographic shifts in the United States. As the twentieth century began, the Northeast still dominated the economic and cultural life of the nation. A hundred years later, the West was increasingly dominant. California had surpassed New York as the most populous state, and Los Angeles International Airport, known as LAX, had replaced Ellis Island as the port of entry for many immigrants.

The sources of recent immigration were similar to those of the 1970s and 1980s. In 2000, just over one-third of all immigrants—legal and illegal—came from Central America, and just over one-quarter came from Asia. Over the next 6 years, the total Latino population increased by 24 percent, while the Asian population grew by almost 28 percent. Immigrants everywhere, often living on the fringe, looked toward the United States, just as they had done in the past.

Illegal immigration remained a problem. Of the 33.5 million foreigners that the Census Bureau estimated lived in America in 2004, about a third, perhaps even more, were illegal entrants. After 2000, about 850,000 unauthorized immigrants arrived each year. People talked about the nation's "broken borders" as record numbers of immigrants lost their lives in the desert while trying to cross into the United States from Mexico.

The influx of new arrivals was spurred by the Immigration Act of 1965 (see Chapter 28). Part of Lyndon Johnson's Great Society program, this act authorized the impartial acceptance of immigrants from all parts of the world and was directly responsible for

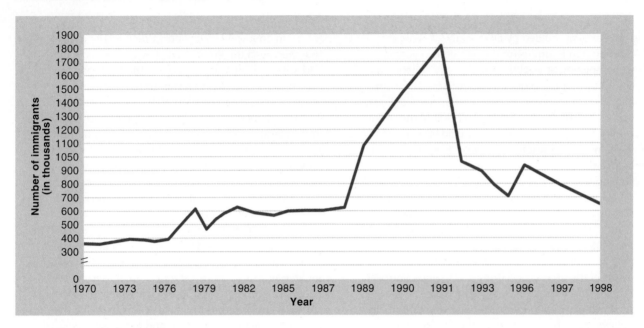

Immigration, 1970–1998

This chart shows the significant rise in immigration after 1970, as the tightly restricted quotas in force from the 1920s to 1965 were liberalized. The steady rise in the 1970s and 1980s reflected the arrival of Asian and Latin Americans, while the spike in the early 1990s occurred because of the amnesty that legalized the status of many illegal immigrants who were now officially counted.

Source: Data from *Statistical Abstract of the United States.*

the greater numbers of Asians and Latin Americans. In 1986, Congress passed the Immigration Reform and Control Act, aimed at curbing illegal immigration while offering amnesty to aliens living in the United States. The Immigration Act of 1990 opened the doors wider, raising immigration quotas while cutting back on restrictions that had limited entry in the past. It also provided for swift deportation of aliens who committed crimes. Two other measures in 1992 expanded eligibility slightly. In 2001, the United States and Mexico began to talk about how to ease the plight of Mexican immigrants and permit illegal arrivals to stay.

The rise in the number of immigrants fueled anti-immigrant feeling in some quarters that resembled similar resistance in Europe. In the 1970s and 1980s, America's efforts to help immigrants coincided with still-intact social-assistance programs of the liberal welfare state. Multiculturalism, stressing the different values that made up a larger American identity, became a dominant theme. Yet those efforts to assist immigrants brought increasing resistance from Americans facing a scarcity of good jobs. There was also a cultural backlash, as opponents of immigration worried about the challenge to America's character posed by new arrivals with their own social patterns.

That opposition, which echoed the anti-immigrant feeling of the past, included strenuous efforts to restrict illegal immigration. Resistance came to a head in 1994 in California, where voters passed Proposition

187, denying illegal aliens access to public education and medical clinics. Within days of the vote, a federal judge issued a preliminary injunction to prevent implementation of the measure, which she made permanent several years later. Yet Proposition 187 provided a model for other states to follow and caught the attention of congressional members, especially Republicans, who gained control of Congress that same year. Two years later, Congress passed legislation barring legal immigrants (who were not yet citizens) from receiving food stamps and disability assistance from the federal government. Toward the end of the decade, California ended its support for bilingual education.

Economic improvement, and the move toward full employment in the latter part of the 1990s, brought a political shift in the immigration debate. In 2000, pressure mounted to increase the number of visas for high-tech workers for businesses and to admit more unskilled workers for the service sector, where there were unfilled jobs. Political considerations also played a part in the shift as both Democrats and Republicans recognized the voting power of Latinos in particular.

Immigration issues became headline news at the end of the 1990s in the highly publicized case of six-year-old Elián Gonzales. In November 1999, he was miraculously pulled out of the water near Florida when a group of Cuban boat people trying to reach the United States drowned. His father, still back in

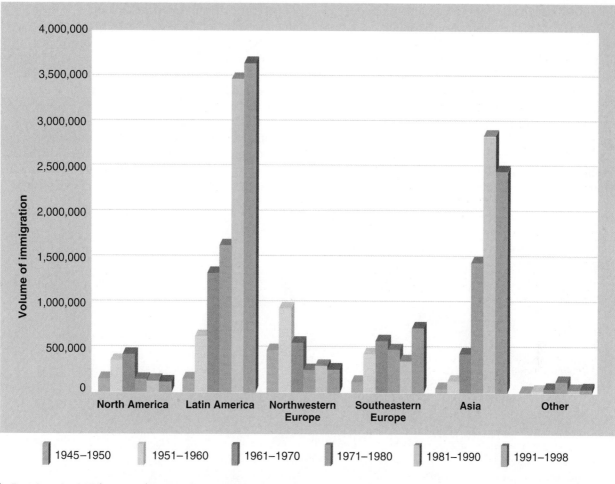

Immigration: Volume and Sources, 1945–1998

This chart shows the shifting patterns of American immigration in the postwar years. In particular, note the large increase in Asian and Latin American immigration in the past several decades.

Source: Data from U.S. Bureau of the Census.

Cuba, had not given permission for the boy to leave and wanted him back. The Miami Cuban community, which hated Fidel Castro and his Communist regime, wanted the boy to receive asylum and stay in the United States. Others, including the Immigration and Naturalization Service (INS), argued that the boy should be returned to his father in Cuba. In the end, the INS seized the boy and returned him to Cuba.

The INS, already unpopular, attracted fierce criticism in the face of the terrorist attacks of September 11, 2001. It had allowed into the country immigrants from Saudi Arabia and elsewhere who had orchestrated the airplane hijackings that shocked the world. Now Americans began to look askance at Arabs or Muslims throughout the country and to condemn the INS for its laxity in screening out potential terrorists.

Meanwhile, in the years after 2000, as the number of illegal immigrants swelled, Americans became increasingly agitated. Congress passed a measure to prevent illegal aliens from obtaining state drivers' licenses. Volunteers patrolled the border between Mexico and Arizona to keep people away. The federal government tried—and failed—in 2006 to enact legislation to tighten border security while making it easier for illegal immigrants to gain citizenship.

The Census of 2000

The 2000 census reported a 13 percent increase in the nation's population, as the United States gained 32.7 million people in the 1990s to reach a total of 281.4 million inhabitants. This expansion surpassed the record 10-year increase of 28 million people in the 1950s, in the midst of the baby boom after World War II. The rate of growth, which had slowed down over the next three decades, accelerated in the 1990s as a result of both increased immigration and longer life expectancy. By 2008, the total population of the United States reached the 303 million mark.

While every state had a net increase in population, growth was greatest in the West, an increasingly important area in the nation's economic, social, and cultural life. Altogether, the West as a whole gained 10.4 million people and expanded by 19 percent. The United States remained about 69 percent white, with a 12 percent African American and 11 percent Latino population. Latinos continued to flock to southern California, the Texas border region, and the south of Florida, and they also began to congregate in increasing numbers in such places as Chicago and Denver. Overall, their numbers increased by

38.8 percent. African Americans maintained their dominance in older cities such as Detroit and Washington, D.C., while continuing to move into metropolitan suburbs.

Nationally, the Asian and Pacific Islander population increased by 43 percent. In California, Asians showed the largest increase of any group. They now comprised nearly 13 percent of the state population and maintained their position as the third-largest population group, after whites and Latinos. Much of the Asian population growth occurred in the suburbs, where the more affluent moved, though large pockets

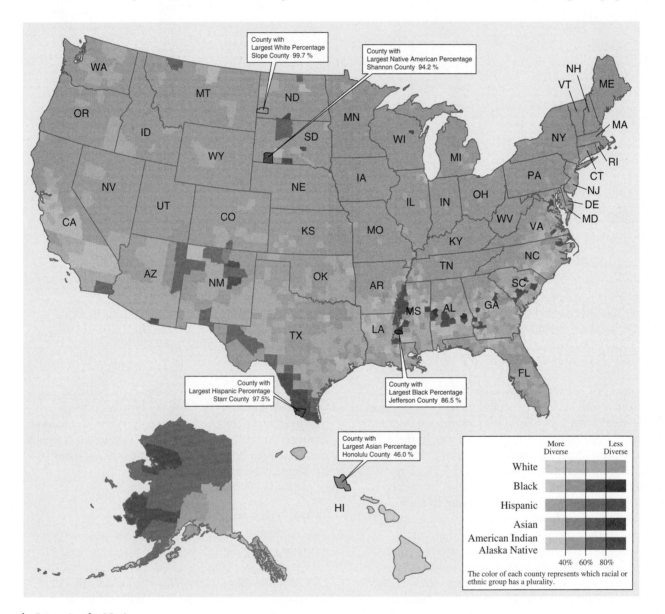

Portrait of a Nation

The 2000 census documented changing population patterns and reported where different groups resided in the United States. Note the concentration of African Americans in the Southeast and the concentration of Hispanics in the Southwest. The Asian American population was greatest in the West, while Native Americans, who had once roamed the continent, were now confined to a number of much smaller western areas. Where are the densest American Indian areas? Why are they so widely dispersed?

Source: "Portrait of a Nation," *New York Times,* April 1, 2001. Copyright © 2001 by The New York Times Co. Reprinted with permission.

of the poor remained in Chinatown in Los Angeles and Little Phnom Penh in Long Beach.

The 2000 census revealed that the combination of Latinos, African Americans, and Asians now outnumbered whites in California. This was the first time since 1860, when California began to provide accurate census data, that whites did not have a majority. State politics already began to reflect the shift. In 1998, Cruz Bustamante became the first Latino elected to statewide office in California since 1871, when he became lieutenant governor. The United States, founded as a white man's country, had now developed into a nation where people of color were increasingly numerous and influential.

One new feature of the 2000 census revealed the desire of large numbers of Americans to identify themselves as part of more than one racial or ethnic group. Nationwide, 2.4 percent of the American people identified themselves as multiracial. In Hawaii, 21 percent of all residents traced their heritage to two or more racial or ethnic groups.

Economic and Social Change

The American economy improved dramatically in the 1990s. Yet despite the revival, millions of Americans remained poor, and homelessness became an increasingly visible problem. Meanwhile, groups pushing for equality made significant gains, but they still faced resistance in their long, continuing struggle for fair treatment in the United States.

Boom and Bust

American economic recovery began in mid-1992, even as other parts of the world found themselves facing industrial problems. In reunified Germany, where extraordinary economic growth had occurred in the post–World War II years, the economy—the largest in Europe—faltered. The Japanese economy, the second-largest in the world after the U.S. economy, likewise encountered trouble.

Against that backdrop, the American revival was even more remarkable. The promotion of big business in the Reagan era spurred investment and led to significant economic expansion. The lowering of interest rates by the Federal Reserve Board revived confidence and promoted consumer spending. Productivity rose steadily throughout the decade, though not quite as quickly as it had in the 1950s and 1960s. Similarly, the national economic growth rate began to rise again. Growth, like productivity, was not as dramatic as it had sometimes been in the golden years of industrial development, but it was sustained in what became the longest expansion in American history. Inflation fell to

a 30-year low. The unemployment rate also declined, dropping from 7.8 percent in 1992 to 4.6 percent in 1997. Taking credit for the recovery, President Bill Clinton declared that the drop in unemployment was "the latest evidence that our economy is growing, steady and strong, that the American dream is in fact alive and well."

One reflection of the return of prosperity was the soaring stock market. The decade of the 1990s was marked by a dramatic increase in the number of investors, reaching approximately 50 percent of the population in 2000. Some purchased stocks for themselves, often working on their own computers, without using a stockbroker. Much of the investment was in the high-tech area, in which people poured billions of dollars into start-up companies not yet making a profit, in the hope that they would take off. The market soared, with the Dow Jones average topping the once-unimaginable 10,000 barrier in 1999 and quickly moving past the 11,000 mark. An even more important sign of economic health was the dramatic reduction in the budget deficit. A Democratic effort to preempt a Republican issue and hold down spending paid off, particularly as low interest rates encouraged economic expansion. In 1998, the United States finished with a budget surplus for the first time in 29 years. With $70 billion—the largest surplus ever—left over at the end of the fiscal year, Democrats and Republicans began arguing about how the money should be used. Most Democrats favored using funds to bolster the social security system, while Republicans, who controlled Congress, preferred a politically attractive tax cut. Forgotten in the euphoria was the fact that the national debt—the total of all past deficits—remained over $5.4 trillion.

In these prosperous times, American companies embarked on a wave of mergers like those around the turn of the century that created the great oil and steel corporations. In 1997, a record $1 trillion in mergers involving American companies took place as huge conglomerates swallowed up smaller competitors in the interests of efficiency and ever-larger profits. One consequence of the mergers, however, was layoffs of workers who duplicated tasks and seemed superfluous. The jobs available to those looking for other work were often low-paying positions such as those held by Marlene Garrett and her husband, introduced earlier in this chapter.

Then, all too quickly, the economy faltered. Alan Greenspan, chairman of the Federal Reserve Board, cautioned in 1996 against "irrational exuberance" in the market, but most investors, especially those making millions of dollars, ignored the warning. In 2000, the stock market began to slide, as investors realized that many of the financial gains did not reflect commensurate gains in productivity. The year ended with the major stock indexes—the Dow Jones Industrial Average and the Nasdaq Composite—showing their worst performance in decades, and in 2001 and 2002, the market continued to fall, wiping out the paper gains of millions of large and small investors.

The nation's overall growth rate began to slow as investment declined. Lack of confidence in the market, particularly in the high-tech area that had fueled the boom, led to a corresponding lack of confidence in the economy. As a recession began in 2000, a tax cut further undermined the stability of the economy. Promoted by Republican George W. Bush after his victory in the 2000 presidential election, the tax cut was skewed in favor of wealthy Americans and not only failed to provide a necessary stimulus but contributed to the decline.

By early 2001, it was clear that the economy was slumping. In February, manufacturing fell to its lowest point in 10 years. Unemployment rolls increased and applications for state unemployment benefits surged. Outsourcing—moving jobs overseas and thereby displacing American workers—increased at an alarming rate. Confidence in the economy was further eroded by growing reports of corporate greed and managerial fraud. Emboldened by deregulation in the 1980s, many corporations had taken advantage of lax oversight practices and made huge—and sometimes illegal—profits. Toward the end of 2001, the Enron Corporation, a company that bought and sold energy, admitted that it had filed five years of misleading reports and declared bankruptcy. As the scandal grew, it became clear that the Arthur Andersen accounting firm had participated in providing cover for financial irregularities and faced an indictment for its role in the process. As the corporate empire began to tumble, the top executives cashed in their stock and made millions of dollars, while the company's workers, unaware of the looming catastrophe and prohibited from unloading stock, lost not just their jobs but their life savings as well.

Some people argued that the Enron case was an anomaly—a bad apple in the barrel—and contended that the rest of corporate America was in good shape. As 2002 unfolded, it became clear that many other companies, such as WorldCom, had been falsifying their books.

The economy became increasingly fragile in the next few years. In 2007, the national debt—the sum of all yearly deficits—reached $9 trillion for the first time. As the housing market collapsed that year, with risky mortgages leading to foreclosure, ordinary working Americans saw the erosion of their dreams of becoming part of the middle class.

Meanwhile overall union membership continued to fall. The AFL–CIO, which had about 16.6 million members in 1993, had only 13 million members a decade later. In 2006, only 12 percent of all workers belonged to a union, down from 12.5 percent in 2005 and 20.1 percent in 1983. One important shift, however, was the increase in membership in public employee unions. That figure, only 400,000 in the mid-1950s, soared to more than 4 million in the 1970s and continued to increase even as unions in the private sector lost members. In the 1990s, the National Educational Association, which was not affiliated with the AFL–CIO, was the largest union in the nation, with about 2 million members. These shifts reflected the changing nature of the workforce and the continuing effort to look out for the interests of the working population.

Poverty and Homelessness

Poverty was a problem even in boom times. The Census Bureau reported in 1997 that 35.6 million people in the United States—the richest country in the world—still lived below what was defined as the poverty line of about $16,000 a year for a family of four. The percentage—13.3 percent—had fallen slightly in each of the previous few years, but it was still sizable, especially considering that it included one out of every three *working* Americans. Worse still was the fact that in 1998, there were 900,000 more Americans living below the poverty line than in 1990. Nor did the situation improve in the new century. In 2004, the Department of Agriculture reported that more than 12 million American families struggled—sometimes without success—to feed themselves. Meanwhile, record levels of Americans lacked health insurance. A Census Bureau report in 2004 showed a figure of 45 million in 2003, which increased to 47 million—or 16 percent of the population—two years later.

Poverty in the United States was different than in other parts of the world, to be sure. People in American slums had more material benefits than many of the residents of Soweto, the huge slum just outside Johannesburg in South Africa. But the poverty was still corrosive.

Urban Americans had the toughest time of all. Even as population shifts led more and more people to live in cities, government programs often failed to provide fully for urban needs. As cities lost population to the suburbs in the last half of the twentieth century, they lost their tax base at the same time and could not easily meet the demand for services. The gap between rich and poor increased significantly in the last two decades of the twentieth century. The efforts of the Reagan and Bush administrations in the 1980s and early 1990s to cut back on government spending and eliminate social programs that had provided services for the poor contributed to the growing gap. Tax records from 2005 revealed that there was greater income inequality in America than in any period since the Great Depression of the 1930s.

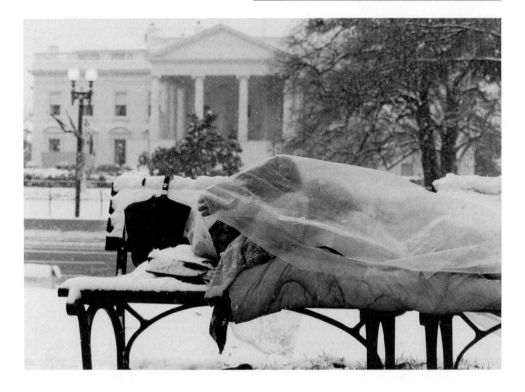

Homeless in America

The homeless became far more visible in the 1990s. Here a man lies sleeping under a thin sheet of plastic, serving as his blanket, right in front of the White House in Washington, D.C. What impression does the proximity to the White House convey?

(Bettmann/CORBIS)

As always, minorities fared worse than whites. The net worth of a typical white household at the beginning of the 1990s was 12 times greater than the net worth of a typical black household and 8 times greater than the net worth of a typical Latino household. Minorities and women continued to lose ground faster than the rest of the population as the decade unfolded. That trend continued in the first years of the new century. Even as the Internal Revenue Service was reporting that overall income fell between 2000 and 2002, the wealthy increased their share, so that a white household now had a net worth 14 times that of a black household and 11 times that of a Latino household. A 2007 study indicated that the gap between blacks and whites continued to grow.

Just as the United States rediscovered its poor in the 1960s, so it rediscovered its homeless in the 1980s and 1990s. Even as unemployment dropped in the 1980s, the number of homeless quadrupled. Numbers were hard to ascertain, for the homeless had no fixed addresses, but one estimate in 1990 calculated that 6 million to 7 million people had been homeless at some point in the past five years. A federal report in 2000 noted that approximately 3.5 million people would become homeless at least once during the year, with 1.35 million of those children.

People became homeless for a variety of reasons. Some started life in disturbed families. Others fell prey to alcohol and drugs. Still others had health or learning problems that eroded the possibility of a stable life. For millions of working Americans, homelessness was just a serious and unaffordable illness away.

Aging and Illness

The American population was older than ever before as the century came to an end. Between 1900 and 1994, when the population of the country tripled, the number of people over age 65 rose elevenfold and continued to rise in the next decade, reaching 33 million, or just about 12 percent of the population, in 2001. Underlying the rapid increase was the steady advance in medical care, which in the twentieth century had increased life expectancy in the United States from 47 to 74 years as the elderly were healthier than ever before. People once considered themselves old when they reached age 65; now, many Americans in their 80s continued to lead productive lives—participating in activities such as writing books, teaching classes, and consulting with corporate clients.

One component of the aging revolution was Viagra, a new drug designed to help men suffering from impotence that came on the market in the 1990s. Whether sexual dysfunction was a result of prostate illness, common among older males, or emotional distress, Viagra helped ailing men enjoy normal sex lives. Americans, including the elderly, now talked frankly about erectile dysfunction, just as they had talked openly about birth control when the birth control pill was introduced three and a half decades before. *Newsweek* magazine noted in 1998 that Viagra was the fastest-selling drug in history.

The elderly raised new issues in a nation suffering periodic recessions. Many wanted to continue working and opposed mandatory retirement rules that drove

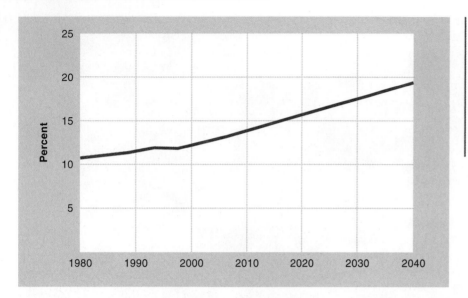

American Population Age 65 or Older, 1980–2040

The percentage of the American population age 65 and older increased as the baby boom population began to age. This graph shows the steady increase up to 2000 and the projected increase for the next 40 years.

Source: Statistical Abstract of the United States, 1997.

them from their jobs. Legislation in 1978 that raised the mandatory retirement age from 65 to 70 helped older workers but decreased employment opportunities for younger workers seeking jobs. In 1986, federal legislation amending the Age Discrimination in Employment Act prohibited mandatory retirement on the basis of age for virtually all workers and created continuing problems for younger employees in the 1990s. A Supreme Court ruling in 2005 held that a worker suing to reverse age discrimination did not need to prove that the employer had acted intentionally. The political power of the elderly became increasingly visible.

Generational resentment over jobs was compounded by the knotty problems faced by the social security system, which had been established a half century earlier. Other parts of the world— Scandinavia, for example—provided social services out of general revenues and took such expenditures for granted. However, in the United States, contributions to the system were necessary to keep it solvent, and as more and more Americans retired, the system could not generate sufficient funds without assistance from general revenues. In the early 1980s, it appeared that the entire system might collapse. A government solution involving higher taxes for those still employed and a later age for qualifying for benefits rescued the fund for a time, but many Americans in the 1990s and early years of the twenty-first century wondered whether social security would survive. Meanwhile, millions of elderly people wondered how they could afford the rapidly increasing cost of prescription drugs, even with a drug benefit plan passed in 2003 that seemed to help people in only a limited way at a huge cost to the government.

As Americans lived longer, they suffered increasingly from Alzheimer's disease, an affliction that gradually destroys a patient's memory and ability to function mentally or physically. Diagnosis is difficult, and there is no treatment to reverse the ailment's course. The illness gained exposure in 1995 when the family of Ronald Reagan disclosed that the former president was suffering from the incurable disease.

Other illnesses affected old and young alike. The discovery of AIDS (acquired immune deficiency syndrome) in 1981 marked the start of one of the most serious diseases in the history of the United States—and the world. Some nations found themselves decimated by AIDS. In China, for example, entire villages were infected with HIV (the human immunodeficiency virus that causes AIDS) as a result of unsterile practices in blood stations. Africa was hit even harder. In 2005, the United Nations estimated that 40 million people around the world were living with the HIV virus. One million of those were in America, while a huge percentage were in Africa. In Zimbabwe, estimates of life expectancy were expected to fall from age 61 in 2005 to age 33 in 2010. The good news was that in late 2007, the UN reported a decline in the number of new HIV infections, giving rise to the hope that perhaps the epidemic could be brought under control.

While health conditions in the United States were better than those in many parts of the world, AIDS still had a devastating effect. The sexual revolution of the 1960s had brought a major change in sexual patterns, particularly among the young, but now sexual experimentation was threatened by this deadly new disease. Although it seemed to strike intravenous drug users and homosexuals with numerous partners more than other groups at first, it soon spread to the heterosexual population as well. AIDS became the leading cause of death in Americans between ages 25 and 44. The growing number of deaths—approximately

550,000 in 2005—was horrifying, even as more and more people learned how to survive with the disease. New drugs, taken in combination, extended the life span of those with the HIV virus and reduced the death rate in the 1990s, but AIDS remained a lethal, and ultimately fatal, disease. Despite medical advances, a cure remained elusive.

Recognizing the devastating worldwide impact of the disease, President Bush announced a major new effort in 2003. He committed the United States to triple its commitment to $15 billion over the next five years to try to counter AIDS in Africa. It was a bold attempt both to head off new infections and to care for those already experiencing the effects of the virus in one of the hardest-hit areas of the globe.

Minorities and Women Face the Twenty-First Century

Americans fighting for equality made gains in the 1990s. But efforts at reform often encountered resistance.

AFRICAN AMERICANS For African Americans, home ownership and employment figures rose. The numbers of murders and other violent crimes that involved blacks dropped. A record 40 percent of African Americans attended college in 1997, up from 32 percent in 1991. Yet incremental improvements often failed to erode racist ideas that still permeated American society. Fifty years after the landmark *Brown* v. *Board of Education* decision of 1954, two-thirds of the public school students in the Cincinnati, Ohio, area attended schools that were at least 90 percent black or 90 percent white. Incidents such as the beating of black motorist Rodney King in Los Angeles in 1991 and the rioting that occurred the next year made many people wonder just how much progress the civil rights movement had made. A survey in San Diego noted that the police there stopped African American and Latino motorists more than whites and Asian Americans—a pattern that was common around the country. The 2000 census revealed that the nation was more racially and ethnically diverse than ever before, yet it pointed out that many people still lived in neighborhoods inhabited by people like themselves.

Affirmative action led to a backlash. Energized by their political victories in 1994, conservatives launched a powerful attack on the policy of giving preferential treatment to groups that had suffered discrimination in the past. They pushed ballot initiatives and pressured public agencies to bring the practice to an end. The most visible of those was Proposition 209 in California, approved by voters in the election of 1996, which prohibited the use of gender or race in awarding state government contracts or admitting students to state colleges and universities. The increasingly conservative Supreme Court in 1995 let stand a lower court ruling prohibiting colleges and universities from awarding special scholarships to African Americans or other minorities. In 1996, it declined to hear an appeal of a U.S. District Court decision two years before in *Hopwood* v. *Texas* that prohibited the use of affirmative action in higher education. In late 2003, the Supreme Court ruled in two cases involving the University of Michigan that affirmative action was acceptable, even as it rejected a point system the university used in carrying out the policy in undergraduate admissions. Around the country, states sought to find ways to maintain diversity without violating the rulings of the Court.

Then, in 2007, an even more conservative Supreme Court, bolstered by two Bush appointees, ruled that public schools could not promote integration through measures taking account of a student's race. After more than 50 years, it appeared that *Brown* v. *Board of Education* had run its course.

The booming job market in the late 1990s helped foster better race relations for a time. It provided new opportunities for people who had been unable to find work. A survey in 1999 reported that young black men in particular were moving back into the economic mainstream at a faster rate than their white counterparts, and crime levels were falling in areas where joblessness was declining. The jobless rate for young black men was still twice that for young white men, but the improvement was encouraging. But then, midway through the first decade of the twenty-first century, it was apparent that the dream for blacks was in decline. The drop in union membership hit them particularly hard. And the gap in income levels between blacks and whites was growing.

Tensions that had existed throughout the twentieth century persisted. Issues stemming from continuing discrimination in finding jobs and persistent antagonism by the police erupted in the spring of 2001 in Cincinnati, Ohio. When a white policeman killed an unarmed black youth, confrontations around the city provided a bitter reminder of riots in the past. In early 2002, African American television correspondent Ed Bradley pointed to changes he had seen in the course of his career. "When asked about progress," he said, "I'm often reminded of the old lady sitting in the church who says, 'It ain't what it ought to be, but thank God it ain't what it used to be.'" Bradley was right, but many African Americans wondered when further change would come.

WOMEN Women likewise made steady progress in the 1990s. They were increasingly involved in academic programs and professions that had been closed to them several decades earlier. In 2001, for example, women made up 49.4 percent of all first-year law students, compared to 10 percent in 1970; that pattern was reflected in other segments of society as well. At the same time there was still continuing resistance to inclusion at the top. Women started to become the heads of major firms as the glass ceiling, preventing women from rising to the top of the corporate ladder, began to crack in the 1990s, yet most leaders were still men. In 2005, only about 17 percent of the partners at major law firms were women.

Abortion remained a polarizing issue, particularly as antiabortion activists sought to disrupt abortion clinics. They launched around-the-clock pickets, aimed at frightening away women seeking abortions. Physicians performing abortions found their lives at risk; Barnet Slepian, a Buffalo doctor, was killed in 1998 in his own home by a sniper shooting through a window. Abortion opponents also took aim at a seldom used, late-term procedure they called "partial birth abortion." Congress passed a measure banning the procedure, but President Clinton vetoed it twice. Then in 2003 President Bush signed a new version of the measure, which the Supreme Court upheld in 2007. Meanwhile, the Food and Drug Administration finally approved a drug known as RU-486, the so-called "morning-after" pill, whereupon abortion opponents jumped into the controversy and sought—unsuccessfully—to attach conditions that would effectively eliminate its use.

The abortion debate was just one measure that created a backlash against the feminist label, even as men and women both accepted the changes brought by the women's movement. Women hesitated to be associated with what they still considered a radical fringe, and that affected how they identified themselves. In 1998, only 26 percent of working women said, "To me, a career is as important as being a wife and mother," down from 36 percent in 1979. While young women took for granted the gains fought for and won by their mothers and grandmothers, fewer wanted to call themselves feminists.

Though the feminist movement persisted, serious problems remained. The 2000 census revealed that the number of families headed by single mothers had risen to 7.5 million, an increase of 25 percent since 1990. A report based on census figures noted that in 2005, only 51 percent of all American women were living with a spouse. Meanwhile, the gender pay gap ceased narrowing. In 2005, women earned about 75 cents for every dollar paid to men.

LATINOS   Latinos likewise pushed for greater equality and had demographic change on their side. The 2000 census and subsequent studies based on the data provided noted that the Latino population spread farther and faster than any previous immigrant wave, even exceeding the influx of eastern Europeans in the early twentieth century. The Latino population increase of 38 percent since 1990 dwarfed the national rise. In 2005, there were 40 million Latinos in the United States, compared to 500,000 in 1900. In 2000, 46 percent of all Latinos owned their own homes, compared to 42 percent a decade before, though that figure still lagged behind the national number of 66 percent. In 2003, Latinos edged past African Americans and became the nation's largest minority group, and experts predicted that by 2100, one in three Americans would be Latino.

The emergence of a sturdy middle class gave Latinos a greater voice in social and political affairs. As more and more of them voted, they played an increasingly influential public role. In 1993, Henry Cisneros became secretary of housing and urban development, and Federico Peña became secretary of transportation in Bill Clinton's administration. At the end of the decade, Latino political figures became even more numerous and visible. In California, for example, both the lieutenant governor and the speaker of the assembly were Chicano, as was the mayor of San Jose. Democrat Loretta Sanchez, who defeated eight-term congressman Robert Dornan in Orange County, served in the U.S. House of Representatives. In the George W. Bush administration, White House counsel Alberto Gonzales played a major role in advising the president during the first term and became attorney general in the second.

As the nation's overall unemployment rate dropped in the mid-1990s, the rate for the 12 million Latino workers likewise fell—from 9.8 percent in 1992 to 7.3 percent in 1997. Then it rose again during the recession that hit in the early part of the new century, moving to about 8.5 percent in 2002, with only 40 percent of the 1.26 million unemployed Latinos eligible for unemployment benefits. Meanwhile, median Latino household income fell, even as it rose for every other ethnic and racial group. Some Mexican immigrants feared that they would become members of a permanent underclass. Latinos nevertheless had a growing impact on American culture. Merengue music could often be heard in music stores or on the radio. Argentine steakhouses could be found in many cities. Use of the Spanish language became more and more common around the country. President George W. Bush himself used Spanish in appealing to this important electoral bloc.

NATIVE AMERICANS   Native Americans found they had less influence, in part because of their smaller numbers. In the 2000 census, only 4.1 million people, or 1.5 percent of the population, identified themselves as American Indian or Alaska Native. Yet Indians still managed to keep the causes that concerned them before the public.

Indians continued their legal efforts to regain lost land. In 1999, the federal government joined the

Oneida Indians in a lawsuit demanding restitution for the 270,000 acres of land in central New York that they claimed state and local governments had illegally acquired from them in the late eighteenth and early nineteenth centuries, and arguing that restitution was warranted. In early 2000, the federal government returned 84,000 acres in northern Utah that it had taken from the Ute in 1916 when it sought to secure the rights to valuable reserves of oil shale. "We're trying to do the right thing, returning land to its rightful owners," energy secretary Bill Richardson declared.

Indians also pressed successfully for the return of their ancestors' skeletal remains, removed by white scientists and museum officials over the course of the last century. With passage of the Native American Graves Protection and Repatriation Act of 1990, skeletons and sacred objects flowed back to the tribes where they belonged. In 1997, Harvard's Peabody Museum sent back the bones of nearly 2,000 Pueblo Indians in the largest single return of these remains.

Native American women became increasingly active in the larger reform effort. Ada Deer, who had successfully fought the government's termination policy in the 1970s, served as assistant secretary of the interior in the 1990s. Winona LaDuke, an environmental activist, directed the Honor the Earth Fund and the White Earth Land Recovery Project, fought needless hydroelectric development, and was singled out by *Time* magazine as one of the nation's 50 most promising leaders under age 40. In 2000, she served as Ralph Nader's vice presidential running mate on the small Green party ticket.

Many Indians still felt a sense of dislocation, captured by novelist Sherman Alexie in 1993. In one of the stories in *The Lone Ranger and Tonto Fistfight in Heaven*, he wrote: "Sometimes I still feel like half of me is lost in the city, with its foot wedged into a steam grate or something. Stuck in one of those revolving doors, going round and round while all the white people are laughing."

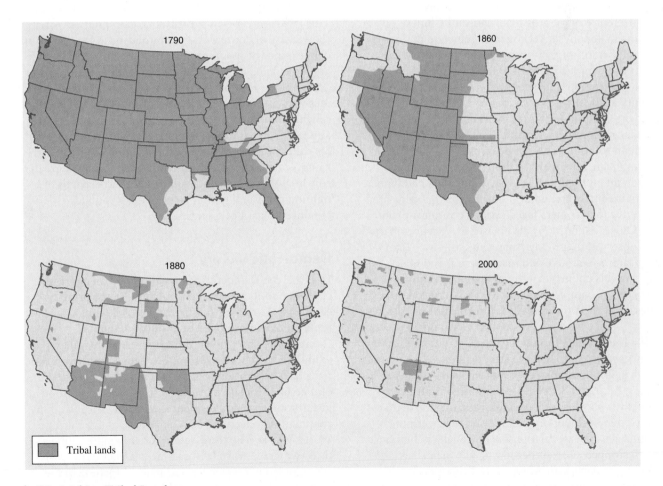

Tribal lands

Diminishing Tribal Lands

While Native Americans steadily lost their territory over a period of 200 years, in the 1990s, Indians field lawsuits to regain tribal lands and were successful in some of their claims. How would you characterize the changing patterns of Indian land ownership?

Source: "Mending a Trail of Broken Treaties," *The Nation, New York Times,* June 25, 2002. Copyright © 2002 by The New York Times Co. Reprinted with permission.

An important symbolic gesture occurred in the last months of the Clinton administration. As the Bureau of Indian Affairs celebrated its 175th anniversary, Kevin Gover, head of the agency, reversed the pattern that had been so predominant in the past when he apologized for the nation's repressive treatment of Native Americans. "In truth, this is no occasion for celebration," he said. It was, rather, a time "for sorrowful truths to be spoken, a time for contrition." He spoke of "the decimation of the mighty bison herds, the use of the poison alcohol to destroy minds and body, and the cowardly killing of women and children." The suffering inflicted on the Indians "made for tragedy on a scale so ghastly that it cannot be dismissed as merely the inevitable consequence of the clash of competing cultures."

ASIAN AMERICANS   Asian Americans enjoyed real success in the 1990s. With about 11 million people—approximately 4 percent of the national population—of Asian descent in the United States in 2000, there was now a critical mass. They came from a variety of cultures, to be sure, and Filipinos often had different experiences from those of Chinese or Koreans or Japanese, yet together they had an increasingly important impact on American society. Many of the children enjoyed remarkable educational achievements, making up a disproportionate share of the students at the most prestigious universities. In 2000, President Clinton appointed Norman Y. Mineta as secretary of commerce, making him the first Asian American to hold a cabinet position.

Yet Asian Americans in the 1990s found themselves in an ambiguous position. While they had higher median incomes than whites, due in part to a dedicated work ethic, newcomers faced serious economic problems. Older assumptions also persisted. A report in 2000 observed that many Americans still saw Asian Americans as secretive and inscrutable. "Too many people in this country continue to see us in simple stereotypes," complained Paul M. Ong, a social policy professor at the University of California at Los Angeles.

GAYS   The struggle for gay rights also continued, and slowly gays began to achieve their demands. In a major change in 2000, the Big Three automakers—General Motors, Ford, and Chrysler—announced health-care benefits for partners of gay employees, in a move that covered 465,000 workers. That same year, Vermont recognized same-sex relationships through civil unions, though stopped short of permitting gay marriages. In 2002, the American Academy of Pediatricians announced its support of the right of gay men and women to adopt the children of their partners. Gay activism helped broaden the definition of family. As the gay rights movement celebrated the 30-year anniversary of the gay rights movement in a parade commemorating

the 1969 riot at the Stonewall Inn in Greenwich Village that had sparked gay resistance, proponents noted that the event had changed from a protest to a party. As the *New York Times* observed, "that in itself is a sign of success."

Yet resistance to gays playing a more visible role in American society persisted. In 1998, 21-year-old University of Wyoming student Matthew Shepard died after being brutally beaten and tortured by two men troubled by his lifestyle. While most American cities had thriving gay communities, there was still deep-seated resistance to gays living openly in some quarters.

Resistance became more open in the election of 2004. As Massachusetts courts ruled that gay marriage was constitutional, and San Francisco permitted gay couples to marry there, a backlash helped mobilize conservatives around the country, and voters in a number of states approved constitutional bans on gay marriage.

Democratic Revival

The 1990s saw a Democratic revival in politics. After the success of conservative Republicans in the 1980s in challenging the assumptions of the liberal welfare state and advancing a more limited conception of the role of government, Democrats regrouped, reformulated their message, and followed the lead of the Republicans in relying on new forms of media to broadcast political appeals. The pattern in the United States reflected similar shifts in the rest of the world as more liberal politicians asserted that government needed to play a greater role in advancing public welfare. But bitter partisan fighting persisted, particularly as the Republicans regained control of Congress.

Democratic Victory

In 1992, the Democratic party mounted an aggressive challenge to Republican rule. After a fierce primary campaign, Governor Bill Clinton of Arkansas triumphed over a crowded field of candidates. Overcoming allegations of marital instability, marijuana use, and draft evasion, he argued that it was time for a new generation to take command. Forty-six years old, he had reached maturity in the 1960s and stood in stark contrast to President George H. W. Bush, now running for reelection, who had come of age during World War II. The third candidate in what became a three-way race was H. Ross Perot, a billionaire businessman from Texas who had made a fortune in the computer data-processing field.

This campaign, more than any in the past, was fought on television. In addition to three televised presidential debates, the candidates appeared on talk shows and interview programs. Perot energized his campaign

Recovering the Past

AUTOBIOGRAPHY

As we reach our own time, the historical past perhaps most worth recovering is our own. Our own story is as valid a part of the story of American history as the tale of Revolutionary War soldiers, frontier women, reform politicians, and immigrant grandparents. In this computerized age, the person we need to recover is ourself, a self that has been formed, at least in part, by the entire American experience we have been studying.

Autobiography is the form of writing in which people tell their own life's history. Although written autobiographies are at least as old as the literature of the early Christians (for example, *The Confessions of St. Augustine*), the word *autobiography* dates from the late eighteenth century, around the time of the French and American revolutions. That is no accident. These momentous events represented the triumph of individual liberty and the sovereignty of the self. *The Autobiography of Benjamin Franklin,* written

between 1771 and Franklin's death in 1790 (and excerpted here), is a classic celebration of the American success story. Franklin's work set the standard for one autobiographical form, the memoir of one's public achievements and success. The other brief autobiographical memoir, from the reminiscences of Elizabeth Cady Stanton, also reflects the tone and range of this tradition.

Not all autobiographies are written late in life to celebrate one's accomplishments. The confessional autobiography, unlike most memoirs, explores the author's interior life, acknowledging flaws and failures as well as successes; it may be written at any age. The purpose of this type of autobiography is not just to reconstruct one's past to preserve it for posterity, but to find from one's past an identity in order to know better how to live one's future. The story of religious confessions and conversions is an obvious example. This form also includes secular self-examinations such as those

---

Autobiographical Memoirs

Benjamin Franklin

DEAR SON,

I have ever had a pleasure in obtaining any little anecdotes of my ancestors. You may remember the enquiries I made among the remains of my relations when you were with me in England and the journey I undertook for that purpose. Imagining it may be equally agreeable to you to know the circumstances of my life—many of which you are yet unacquainted with—and expecting a week's uninterrupted leisure in my present country retirement, I sit down to write them for you. Besides, there are some other inducements that excite me to this undertaking. From the poverty and obscurity in which I was born and in which I passed my earliest years, I have raised myself to a state of affluence and some degree of celebrity in the world. As constant good fortune has accompanied me even to an advanced period of life, my posterity will perhaps be desirous of learning the means, which I employed, and which, thanks to Providence, so well succeeded with me. They may also deem them fit to be imitated, should any of them find themselves in similar circumstances.

Source: The Autobiography of Benjamin Franklin (1771).

Elizabeth Cady Stanton

Elizabeth Cady Stanton

It was 'mid such exhilarating scenes that Miss Anthony and I wrote addresses for temperance, anti-slavery, educational and woman's rights conventions. Here we forged resolutions, protests, appeals, petitions, agricultural reports, and constitutional arguments; for we made it a matter of conscience to accept every invitation to speak on every question, in order to maintain woman's right to do so. To this end we took turns on the domestic watchtowers, directing amusements, settling disputes, protecting the weak against the strong, and trying to secure equal rights to all in the home as well as the nation.

It is often said, by those who know Miss Anthony best, that she has been my good angel, always pushing and goading me to work, and that but for her pertinacity I should never have accomplished the little I have. On the other hand it has been said that I forged the thunderbolts and she fired them. Perhaps all this is, in a measure, true. With the cares of a large family I might, in time, like too many women, have become wholly absorbed in a narrow family selfishness, had not my friend been continually exploring new fields for missionary labors. Her description of a body of men on any platform, complacently deciding questions in which women had an equal interest, without an equal voice, readily aroused me to a determination to throw a firebrand into the midst of their assembly.

Source: Elizabeth Cady Stanton, Eighty Years and More: Reminiscences, 1815–1897 (1898).

Confessional Autobiographies

Black Elk

And so it was all over.

I did not know then how much was ended. When I look back now from this high hill of my old age, I can still see the butchered women and children lying heaped and scattered all along the crooked gulch as plain as when I saw them with eyes still young. And I can see that something else died there in the bloody mud, and was buried in the blizzard. A people's dream died there. It was a beautiful dream.

And I, to whom so great a vision was given in my youth,—you see me now a pitiful old man who has done nothing, for the nation's hoop is broken and scattered. There is no center any longer, and the sacred tree is dead.

Source: Black Elk Speaks, as told through John G. Neihardt (1932).

Malcolm X

I want to say before I go on that I have never previously told anyone my sordid past in detail. I haven't done it now to sound as though I might be proud of how bad, how evil, I was.

But people are always speculating—why am I as I am? To understand that of any person, his whole life, from birth, must be reviewed. All of our experiences fuse into our personality. Everything that ever happened to us is an ingredient.

Today, when everything that I do has an urgency, I would not spend one hour in the preparation of a book which has the ambition to perhaps titillate some readers. But I am spending many hours because the full story is the best way that I know to have it seen, and understood, that I had sunk to the very bottom of the American white man's society when—soon now, in prison—I found Allah and the religion of Islam and it completely transformed my life.

Source: The Autobiography of Malcolm X, with the assistance of Alex Haley (1964).

---

by Maxine Hong Kingston in *The Woman Warrior* (1976), Piri Thomas in *Down These Mean Streets* (1967), or Maya Angelou in a series of five autobiographical sketches beginning with *I Know Why the Caged Bird Sings* (1969). The other two excerpts presented here are among the finest examples of confessional autobiography and suggest its variety.

These examples hardly convey the full range of the autobiographical form or how available to all people is the opportunity to tell the story of one's life. In 1909, William Dean Howells called autobiography the "most democratic province in the republic of letters." A recent critic agrees, pointing out:

To this genre have been drawn public and private figures: poets, philosophers, prizefighters; actresses, artists, political activists; statesmen and penitentiary prisoners; financiers and football players; Quakers and Black Muslims; immigrants and Indians. The range of personality, experience, and profession reflected in the forms of American autobiography is as varied as American life itself.

Your story, too, is a legitimate part of American history. But writing an autobiography, while open to all, is deceptively difficult. Like historians, autobiographers face problems of sources, selection, interpretation, and style. As in the writing of any history, the account of one's past must be objective, not only in the verifiable accuracy of details but also in the honest selection of representative events to be described. Moreover, in fiction as well as history, the autobiographer must provide a structured form, an organizing principle, literary merit, and thematic coherence to the story. Many other challenges face the would-be autobiographer, such as finding a balance between one's public life and the private self and handling problems of memory, ego (should one, for example, use the first or third person?), and death.

Reflecting on the Past To get an idea of the difficulties of writing an autobiography, try writing your own. Limit yourself to 1,000 words. Good luck. ■

The "Hip" Candidate

Bill Clinton was an exuberant campaigner who used his musical talent to attract support when he ran for president in 1992. Here he plays his saxophone on nationwide television on *The Arsenio Hall Show* in Los Angeles. What kind of image was Clinton trying to convey in this photograph?

(AP/Wide World Photos)

with appearances on *Larry King Live.* Bill Clinton used a post–Super Bowl appearance on *60 Minutes* to answer charges questioning his character and later played his saxophone on *The Arsenio Hall Show* and appeared on MTV. On election day, Clinton won 43 percent of the popular vote to 38 percent for Bush and 19 percent for Perot. The electoral vote margin was even larger: 357 for Clinton, 168 for Bush, 0 for Perot. The Democrats retained control of both houses of Congress, with more women and minority members than ever before.

The president-elect wanted to check the cynicism that was poisoning political life. In 1964, three-quarters of the American public trusted the government to do the right thing most of the time. Three decades later, after the deception of leaders in the Vietnam War and the Watergate affair, the number was closer to one-quarter. Clinton sought to shift the nation's course after 12 years of Republican rule with Cabinet nominations that included four women, four African Americans, and two Latinos. He held a televised "economic summit" to explore national options and demonstrated a keen grasp of the details of policy. In his inaugural address, Clinton declared that "a new season of American renewal has begun."

Clinton soon found his hands full at home. Although the economy finally began to improve, the public gave the president little credit for the upturn. He gained Senate ratification of the North American Free Trade Agreement (NAFTA)—aimed at promoting free trade between Canada, Mexico, and the United States—in November 1993 after a bitter battle in which opponents argued that American workers would lose their jobs to less well-paid Mexicans. He secured passage of a crime bill banning the manufacture, sale, or possession of assault weapons. But he failed to win approval of his major legislative initiative: health-care reform. The United States lagged behind most other industrialized countries in the way it provided for public health. Medicare took care of the elderly, and Medicaid provided some relief for the poor, but both were limited when compared to the coverage provided by other nations. Particularly troublesome were escalating costs and the lack of universal medical care, which left 35 million Americans with no medical insurance. Clinton's complicated proposal provoked intense opposition from the health-care and insurance industries and from politicians with plans of their own. In the end, he was unable to persuade Congress either to accept his approach or adopt a workable alternative.

Republican Resurgence

Voters demonstrated their dissatisfaction in the midterm elections of 1994. Republicans argued that government regulations were hampering business and costing too much. They challenged the notion that the federal government was primarily responsible for health care and other such services. Capitalizing on the continuing appeal of the leadership of Ronald Reagan in the 1980s, they demanded a scaled-down role for the government. Republicans swept control of both the Senate and the House of Representatives for the first time in more than 40 years. At the state level, Republicans picked up 12 governorships and took control in seven of the eight largest states.

The election marked the end of the commitment to the welfare state. The 104th Congress moved aggressively to make good on its promises—outlined during the campaign in the Republicans' Contract with America—to scale back the role of the federal government, eliminate environmental regulations, cut funding for educational programs such as Head Start, reduce taxes, and balance the budget. Under the leadership of Newt Gingrich, the new speaker of the House of Representatives, Congress launched a frontal attack on the budget, proposing massive cuts in virtually all social services. It demanded eliminating three Cabinet departments and insisted on gutting the National Endowment for the Humanities, the National Endowment for the Arts, and the Public

Broadcasting System. When, at the end of 1995, President Clinton and Speaker Gingrich tangled with one another on the size of the cuts and refused to compromise on a budget, the government shut down and 800,000 federal employees found themselves temporarily "furloughed."

While the House of Representatives passed most of the measures proposed in the Contract with America, only a few of them became law. The Senate balked at some; the president vetoed others. After all the attention it received, voters lost interest in the Contract with America. As the election of 1996 approached, Newt Gingrich found himself out of favor, as millions of Americans began to realize that they would suffer from the cuts more aggressive Republicans sought.

A Second Term for Clinton

As Bill Clinton sought a second term in 1996, the Republicans nominated Senate minority leader Robert Dole as their presidential candidate. The 73-year-old Dole ran a lackluster campaign. His pledge to push through a sweeping 15 percent tax reduction failed to excite voter interest. Even supporters wondered how he would balance the budget at the same time. Stung by Democratic congressional defeats two years before, Clinton co-opted Republican issues, pledging to balance the budget himself and enraging liberal supporters by signing a welfare reform bill that slashed benefits and removed millions of people from the rolls. At the same time, he posed as the protector of Medicare and other programs that were threatened by proposed Republican cuts.

Clinton's strategy worked. On election day, he won a resounding victory over Dole. He received 49 percent of the popular vote to 41 percent for Dole and 8 percent for H. Ross Perot, who ran again, though this time less successfully. In the electoral tally, Clinton received 379 votes to 159 for Dole. Yet the Republicans kept control of Congress. In the House of Representatives, they lost a number of seats but retained a majority. In the Senate, they added two seats to what they had won in 1994. Voters seemed willing to support Clinton, but not to give him the mandate he sought.

Partisan Politics and Impeachment

Democrats made small gains in the midterm elections of 1998. They worried about their prospects as election day approached, for Clinton had been accused by an independent prosecutor, appointed by the Justice Department, of having engaged in an improper sexual relationship with Monica Lewinsky, a White House intern. While Clinton denied the relationship at first, the lengthy report presented to Congress left little

doubt that such a connection existed, and Clinton finally admitted to the relationship in a nationally televised address.

As Republicans in Congress began to consider impeachment, Americans outside Washington felt differently. Disturbed at what Clinton had done in his personal life, they nonetheless approved overwhelmingly of the job he was doing as president; in fact, his approval ratings were higher than any of his presidential predecessors in the recent past.

Those sentiments were reflected in the 1998 midterm election. Republicans maintained their 55–45 margin in the Senate, but lost five seats in the House of Representatives, ending up with a 223–211 margin that made it even more difficult to pursue their own agenda.

Despite that clear signal from the voters, House Republicans continued their efforts to remove the president. Just weeks after the election, a majority impeached him on counts of perjury and obstruction of justice. At the start of 1999, the case moved to the Senate for a trial, in which Clinton fought to retain his office, just as Andrew Johnson had done 131 years before. In the Senate, presided over by the chief justice of the Supreme Court, a two-thirds vote was necessary to find the president guilty and remove him from office. After weeks of testimony, despite universal condemnation of Clinton's personal behavior, the Senate voted for acquittal. Democrats, joined by a number of Republicans, stood by the president, and with that coalition, neither charge managed to muster even a majority. The count of perjury was decided by a 45–55 vote, while the count of obstruction of justice failed on a 50–50 vote. At long last, the ordeal was over, and the country could once again turn its attention to more pressing issues.

Clinton was an enormously successful politician. Not only had he escaped conviction in the highly visible—and embarrassing—impeachment case, but he also managed to co-opt Republican issues and seize the political center. He quietly advanced liberal goals, with incremental appropriations, even when he was unable to push major programs, such as his medical insurance scheme, through Congress. Suits against the nation's tobacco companies for deliberately misleading advertising in the face of known health risks were popular with the public, and led in 1997 to a landmark $368 billion settlement to cover liability claims and reimburse the states for medical costs related to smoking.

Throughout both terms, Clinton remained popular, despite personal flaws. Overall, in the words of the *New York Times,* Clinton demonstrated "striking strengths, glaring shortcomings." He came into office wanting to be a Roosevelt-like figure, with dreams of reconfiguring the role of government, but ended up instead quietly endorsing and implementing a variety of more modest causes. He faced powerful criticism from opponents, yet he brought some of his troubles on himself and paid a heavy price for his misdeeds.

The Second Bush Presidency

Republicans regained control of the White House in the election of 2000. Unable to oust Bill Clinton from the presidency by impeachment, they were determined to win back what they considered to be rightfully theirs in the conservative resurgence of the past 20 years. Texas governor George W. Bush (son of former president George H. W. Bush—the first father–son combination since John Adams and John Quincy Adams) vowed to return morality and respect to the White House and appealed to those disturbed by Clinton's behavior.

The Election of 2000

The election of 2000 promised to be close. The strong economy gave Vice President Al Gore, the Democratic nominee, an initial advantage. Yet the Republicans, led by the younger Bush, insisted the country needed a change. The campaign revolved around what the government should do with the federal budget surplus, with Republicans arguing that much of the money should be returned to the public in the form of a tax cut and Democrats countering that the surplus should be used to bolster the ailing social security program and to pay down the national debt. In the weeks before the election, polls showed that the race was virtually tied.

On election night, as the returns trickled in, neither Bush nor Gore had captured the 270 electoral votes necessary to win the presidency. The electoral vote in Florida, one of the undecided states, was large enough to give the winner a victory. A recount, required by law, began, and Florida became a battleground as lawyers for both sides swarmed to the state to monitor the counting. Democrats and Republicans argued bitterly, in court and in the media, about how the recount should proceed. Democrats also contended that in certain African American precincts, voters had been turned away from the polls. That charge was all the more significant because black voters around the country favored Gore by a 9–1 margin.

In December, more than five weeks after the election, after suits and countersuits by both sides, the case reached the Supreme Court. In *Bush* v. *Gore*, the justices overturned a Florida Supreme Court decision allowing the recount to proceed, and ruled, by a 5–4 vote, with the most conservative justices voting in a bloc, that the recount should be curtailed, leaving Bush the winner. Although Gore won the popular vote by

about 450,000 votes, Bush triumphed in the Electoral College by a 271–266 majority. Ill feelings persisted as a result of the partisan ruling. Supreme Court justice John Paul Stevens wrote a scathing dissent, in which he argued: "Although we may never know with complete certainty the identity of the winner of this year's presidential election, the identity of the loser is perfectly clear. It is the nation's confidence in the judge as an impartial guardian of the law."

The voting in congressional races was equally close. The new Senate was evenly split, with each party holding 50 seats. Republicans organized the chamber and gained all committee chairs, because Vice President Dick Cheney broke the tie. Yet five months after the new session began, Senator James Jeffords of Vermont, frustrated with the approach of the Bush administration, left the Republican party, giving control to the Democrats. Republicans also lost seats in the House of Representatives, leaving them with but a nine-vote majority.

The New Leader

George W. Bush had enjoyed an eclectic career before becoming president. Born into a political family, he had shown little interest in politics himself, gravitating into the Texas oil business and then gaining part ownership of a professional baseball team before running successfully for governor of Texas.

Bush was very different from Clinton. Whereas his predecessor was interested in the details of public policy, Bush saw himself as a corporate chief executive officer (CEO) who established the broad outlines of policy but then left the details to others. Ronald Reagan had taken that approach, and while Bush lacked Reagan's communication skills, he had a dogged tenacity that served him well. Author Gail Sheehy observed that "the blind drive to win is a hallmark of the Bush family clan." The new president, she said "has to win, he absolutely has to win and if he thinks he's going to lose, he will change the rules or extend the play. Or if it really is bad he'll take his bat and ball and go home." Bush often seemed to ignore criticism and to push ahead with a resolute persistence, no matter what. His religious faith gave him the support he needed, and when once asked if he relied on his father in hard times, he responded that his father "is the wrong father to appeal to in terms of strength. There is a higher father that I appeal to."

Promoting the Private Sector

As president, Bush had the interests of corporate America at heart. During the campaign, he talked about a tax cut, and this became his first priority. Supply-side economists, who argued successfully in the

Looking for a Place in History?

George Bush paid close attention to the image conveyed to the American people, and photographers constantly captured him in ways that underscored his importance. Here he stands in front of Mt. Rushmore, with its famous rock sculptures of several of America's best-known presidents. What impression does the juxtaposition in this photograph convey to you?

(AP/World Wide Photos)

1980s that lower tax rates were necessary to promote economic growth, became more influential in his administration.

By mid-2001, the tax cut became law. It lowered tax rates for everyone, allowed more tax-free saving for education, and reduced estate taxes. The measure promised to save every taxpayer at least several hundred dollars a year, though it was heavily skewed in favor of the wealthy. Meanwhile, the economy continued to falter as the growth rate slowed and a full-blown recession ensued.

Like his father and Reagan, Bush wanted to reduce the size of government and squelch its intrusions into private affairs, but at the same time, he sought to bolster the military. His first budget, for example, proposed deep cuts in health programs for people without

access to health insurance. But his proposals for defense called for far greater spending, even before the terrorist attacks of September 11, 2001. Military spending increased dramatically in the years that followed, providing the administration already dealing with smaller revenue as a result of the tax cut with an even stronger argument to cut back social programs that conservatives had never liked.

Bush infuriated environmentalists. Quietly, the new administration moved to allow road building in national forests and made it easier for mining companies to dig for gold, zinc, and copper on public lands. Under pressure from real estate interests, the administration sought to shrink legal protection of endangered species. And, catering to the interests of oil companies, the administration fought to promote drilling in the protected Arctic National

PRESIDENTIAL ELECTIONS, 1992–2004

Year	Candidate	Party	Popular Vote		Electoral Vote
1992	BILL CLINTON	Democratic	43,728,275	(43.2%)	357
	George Bush	Republican	38,167,416	(37.7%)	168
	H. Ross Perot	Independent	19,237,245	(19.0%)	0
1996	BILL CLINTON	Democratic	47,401,185	(49.2%)	379
	Robert Dole	Republican	39,197,469	(40.7%)	159
	H. Ross Perot	Reform	8,085,294	(8.4%)	0
2000	GEORGE W. BUSH	Republican	50,546,002	(47.87%)	271
	Albert Gore	Democratic	50,999,897	(48.38%)	266
	Ralph Nader	Green	2,882,955	(2.74%)	0
2004	GEORGE W. BUSH	Republican	60,934,251	(51%)	286
	John F. Kerry	Democratic	57,765,291	(48%)	252
	Ralph Nader	Independent	405,933	(0%)	0

Note: Winners' names appear in capital letters.

Wildlife Refuge, even in the face of estimates that very little oil was there to be found. When his own Environmental Protection Agency (EPA) issued a report in mid-2002 linking the use of fossil fuel (such as coal and oil) to global warming, Bush dismissed the study. Gone was the commitment to the public interest that had increased over the course of the twentieth century.

A Second Term for Bush

The election of 2004 was bitter and contentious. Running for reelection, Bush faced Massachusetts senator John Kerry, a Vietnam War hero who attacked Republican efforts in the foreign policy sphere, questioned the administration's ability to protect the nation from terrorist attacks, and charged that tax cuts had done little to revive a still-sluggish economy. Both candidates raised huge amounts of money, far more than had been solicited in the past, and both parties ended up running attack ads that questioned the integrity of the other candidate. Republican groups tore into Kerry's service record; Democratic groups called attention to Bush's successful effort to avoid the war in Vietnam by serving in the National Guard. Civility sometimes seemed to disappear. But even though Bush seemed vulnerable, Kerry failed to arouse the interest of voters. He seemed to be, according to *The Economist* magazine, "the political equivalent of Valium." In a race that remained close to the end, Bush prevailed with 51 percent of the popular vote and a modest Electoral College majority. Republicans added to their majorities in both the Senate and the House of Representatives, as voters in the heartland of American agreed with the Republican party's conservative moral values.

At the start of his second term, Bush moved quickly to demand reform of social security. The program, which had run surpluses in the past, faced increasing pressures as the baby boom generation born just after World War II approached retirement. Experts disagreed on just when the system would run short of money, but it was clear that problems were imminent in the next few decades. Bush called for an overhaul that would allow workers to invest part of their contributions in private retirement accounts that would depend on gains in the stock market. Critics charged that the new proposal would undermine the policy of guaranteed pensions and could make millions of workers vulnerable if the market dropped, as it had just a few years before. They argued that the system could be made more secure by increasing payroll taxes, raising the amount on which such taxes were levied, or mandating that workers retire a year or two later. Even as Bush pushed ahead, members of both political parties resisted the effort.

The budget that Bush submitted to Congress in early 2005 reflected the administration's priorities. As the surplus of the Clinton years turned into an ever-larger deficit under Bush—estimated to be almost $400 billion in the year ahead—the budget still contained tax cuts of $100 billion over the next five years. Critics charged that the underlying intention was to make it impossible to support programs aimed at assisting poor people like Rod and Marlene Garrett, met at the start of the chapter. They also noted the irony that this budget was the largest ever in the nation's history and pointed out that an administration that claimed to want to scale down big government was playing an ever-increasing role when it came to regulation of social issues through faith-based initiatives and resistance to abortion. The proposed budget for 2007 reflected similar priorities. Meanwhile, the president asked for record levels of defense spending.

By the time of the 2006 midterm Congressional elections, many Americans were disturbed by the violence of the war in Iraq (see next section) and troubled by a conflict that seemed to be spiraling out of control. They were also frustrated by a series of scandals on Capitol Hill and by the insensitive response of the administration to the devastation caused by Hurricane Katrina in New Orleans in September 2005. Voter discontent shifted control of Congress. Democrats won a substantial majority in the House of Representatives and a narrow margin in the Senate.

Bush seemed to be on the wrong side of many public policy issues. His veto in 2007 of a measure to provide increased funding for children without health insurance aroused tremendous opposition. His failure to take aggressive steps to combat global warning stood in bold relief to the Academy Award defeated presidential candidate Al Gore won and the Nobel Peace Prize he shared for his eloquent work in this arena.

During his last two lame duck years in the White House, Bush faced more serious problems than ever before. Public support eroded, leaving him with a dismal 30 percent approval rating. Republican presidential candidates distanced themselves from him and his administration. People commented casually about how he might well be judged one of the least competent presidents in American history.

Foreign Policy in the Post–Cold War World

As the Cold War ended, the United States had to examine its own assumptions about its international role. The world was now a different place. With extraordinary communications advances, it was more closely linked than ever before. Violence and upheaval in one part of the globe now had an almost immediate impact on other areas. In this setting, new questions arose: What kind of leadership would the United States exert as the one remaining superpower on the globe? How involved would it become in peacekeeping missions in violence-wracked lands? What kind of assistance would it extend to developing nations now that the competition with the Soviet Union that had fueled foreign aid was over? How would it deal with the threat of terrorism? These questions, asked in different forms over the course of past centuries, helped shape foreign policy in transitional times.

The Balkan Crisis

In the Balkans, in Eastern Europe, ethnic and religious violence worsened in the mid-1990s. Yugoslavia—a collection of different ethnic constituencies held together by a Communist dictatorship—had collapsed in 1991. Muslims and Croats had fought bitterly with Serbs in the province of Bosnia (see Chapter 30). The world watched the Bosnian Serbs liquidate opponents in a process that came to be called "ethnic cleansing" during the siege of the city of Sarajevo. As the region became increasingly volatile, the United States remained out of the conflict, while the United Nations proved unable to bring about peace. In mid-1995, a North Atlantic Treaty Organization (NATO) bombing campaign forced the Bosnian Serbs into negotiations, and a peace conference held in Dayton, Ohio, led to the commitment of American troops, along with soldiers from other countries, to stabilize the region.

In 1999, a smoldering conflict in Kosovo, another of the provinces of the former Yugoslavia, led to war.

In an effort to stop Slobodan Milosevic, the Serbian leader responsible for the devastation of Bosnia, from squelching a movement for autonomy in Kosovo, NATO launched an American-led bombing campaign. Milosevic responded with an even more violent "ethnic cleansing" campaign that drove hundreds of thousands of Kosovars from their homes.

Milosevic finally succumbed. After refusing to recognize the election victory of the opposition leader in 2000, he was arrested in 2001 and brought to the Netherlands to stand trial for crimes against humanity at the International Court of Justice in The Hague.

The Middle East in Flames

In the Middle East, Clinton tried to play the part of peacemaker, just as Jimmy Carter had done 15 years before. On September 13, 1993, in a dramatic ceremony on the White House lawn, Palestine Liberation Organization leader Yasir Arafat and Israeli Prime Minister Yitzhak Rabin took the first public step toward ending years of conflict as they shook hands and signed a peace agreement that led to Palestinian self-rule in the Gaza strip. In 1995, Israel and the PLO signed a further agreement, and the Israelis handed over control of the West Bank of the Jordan River to the Palestinians. A treaty between Jordan and Israel brought peace on still another border. While extremists tried to destroy the peace process by assassinating Rabin, the effort to heal old animosities continued. As Clinton prepared to leave office, he sought to seal a final agreement between the Israelis and the Palestinians, but this time he was not successful, as the Palestinians rejected a generous settlement offer,

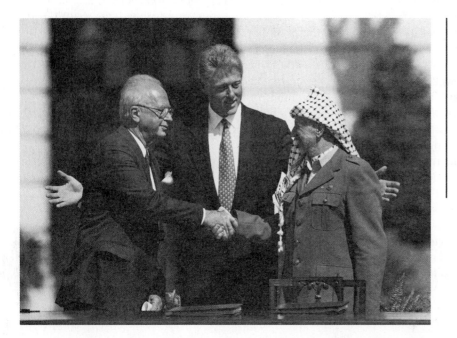

A Historic Handshake

President Bill Clinton helped orchestrate this famous handshake between Israeli prime minister Yitzhak Rabin and Palestine Liberation Organization chairman Yasir Arafat in 1993. Though the two men had long been adversaries, they now began to work together to settle the bitter conflicts in the Middle East. How do Clinton's actions in the picture give a sense of his role? How do the two longtime adversaries appear to react to one another?

(AP/Wide World Photos)

and the smoldering Middle Eastern tensions burst once more in flames that threatened to engulf the entire region.

The level of Mideast violence in the early twenty-first century was worse than it had ever been before. The shortsighted Israeli policy of building settlements in occupied Arab land, and the Palestinian unwillingness to compromise at the negotiating table, culminated in a horrifying escalation of suicide bombings and other bloody attacks following an Israeli visit to a holy Palestinian religious site in Jerusalem, a city claimed by both sides. Bush was at first reluctant to intervene. Eventually, as the killing cycle continued, he moved from inattention to intermittent attention, becoming increasingly sympathetic to Israel as the suicide attacks continued. He lashed out at Yasir Arafat for not speaking out against the bombings, but was unable to bring the adversaries to the negotiating table. Nor could he do anything about separation fences the Israelis built both in the West Bank and the Gaza Strip to protect settlements there. Meanwhile, many of the European nations, feeling that only the United States could help bring peace to the region, voiced dismay at American policy.

At the end of 2007, at the urging of Secretary of State Condoleezza Rice, Bush became more engaged. Perhaps recognizing that only with American assistance might a peace settlement emerge, he convened a conference of Israeli and Palestinian participants to see if they might get back on track for what all agreed would be a long and extended process.

African Struggles

Africa also remained a source of concern to American policymakers who struggled to deal with a series of never-ending crises. Left behind as other parts of the world industrialized and moved ahead, the continent was also ravaged by the AIDS epidemic, which infected and killed far more people than in other parts of the world. Meanwhile, most other nations paid little attention to the region. During the Cold War, the United States and the Soviet Union had competed for the allegiance of African nations, but with the end of the conflict, that focus faded. Bill Clinton made a highly publicized visit to Africa, as he sought to dramatize international responsibility for assisting the continent, and he watched with satisfaction as Nelson Mandela handed over power in South Africa to his successor in a peaceful transition. But other areas proved more problematical. Six months after Clinton became president, a firefight with one faction in war-ravaged Somalia, in East Africa, resulted in several dozen American casualties. The shooting prompted some Americans, still haunted by the memory of Vietnam, to demand withdrawal. Reluctant to

back down as he groped to define his policy, Clinton first increased the number of U.S. troops, then in 1993, recalled the soldiers without having restored order.

The United States was similarly baffled by a crisis in Rwanda, in central Africa. There a fragile balance of power between two ethnic groups—the Tutsis and the Hutus—broke down and hard-line Hutus embarked on a massive genocidal campaign that resulted in the slaughter of hundreds of thousands of innocent Tutsis and moderate Hutus. The United States, like many European nations, debated the possibility of intervention on humanitarian grounds but decided to do nothing. Eventually the killing stopped, although the friction between the rival groups remained.

George W. Bush was much less interested in Africa than his predecessor. He chose not to attend a conference on sustainable development held in South Africa in the summer of 2002, which gave a clear signal that the United States was more interested in its own business interests than in the economic problems of the less-developed world. In 2003, he visited five African nations, but it was a whirlwind trip aimed at supporting areas sympathetic to the United States.

Relations with Russia

In the area that formerly had been the Soviet Union, the United States continued to try to promote both democracy and free-market capitalism. It worked closely with Boris Yeltsin in Russia, and then with his successor, Vladimir Putin, who assumed power on the last day of the twentieth century and was then elected president in his own right in 2001. But Russia remained unstable, still caught up in the complications of a huge political, social, and economic transformation.

Bush recognized the need to cooperate with Putin. In a series of meetings, both in Russia and in the United States, the two men developed a close working relationship that helped maintain European stability. The Soviet Union had ceased to exist, but the component parts still remained important in the larger international scene.

Terror on September 11

On September 11, 2001, three hijacked airplanes slammed into the World Trade Center towers in New York City and the Pentagon in Washington, D.C. The fires in New York from exploding jet fuel caused the towers to crumble, altering the skyline forever. Altogether about 3,000 people died in the terrorist attacks. A fourth plane, probably headed for either the White House or the Capitol, crashed in

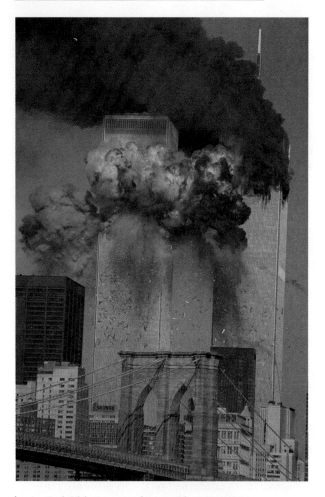

An Indelible Image of September 11, 2001

The World Trade Center towers in New York City once dominated the skyline on the Hudson River. As two hijacked commercial airplanes crashed into the tall structures on September 11, 2001, both towers burst into flames and later collapsed, killing most of the people who were still inside. What impression does this photograph of the burning towers convey?

(Steve Ludlum/The New York Times)

Pennsylvania when passengers fought back against the attackers.

The hijackers were Muslim extremists, most from Saudi Arabia, trained at flight schools in the United States, who belonged to the al Qaeda network headed by Saudi exile Osama bin Laden. Bin Laden and his organization were headquartered in Afghanistan, where the extremely conservative Muslim Taliban group had imposed the law of the Qur'an, the Muslim holy book, on civil society. Bin Laden and his associates hated the United States for its Middle Eastern policy of support for Israel, and they also hated its affluent and materialistic values that often conflicted with their religious values.

The terrorist attacks shattered America's sense of security within its own borders. Irate at the

unprovoked strikes, President Bush vowed to find and punish the terrorists. Like his father in the Gulf War a decade earlier, he put together a worldwide coalition to assist the United States, and he quickly launched a bombing campaign to smoke out Osama bin Laden and his network. Although the bombing, followed by attacks by ground troops in Afghanistan, defeated the Taliban and drove its members from power, the campaign failed to find Osama bin Laden, who remained at large. As Bush's approval ratings soared to over 90 percent, he vowed a lengthy campaign to root out terrorism wherever it surfaced in the world. He embarked on a massive governmental reorganization to create a new Department of Homeland Security to help prevent future attacks. In the Patriot Act, he invoked terrorism as a reason to allow the government to encroach on individual liberties—in the interest of security—more extensively than in the past. Ironically, a president dedicated to smaller government now found himself in the forefront of an effort to give government a much larger role.

American Muslims were often the victims. Some faced attacks by Americans angry at the terrorist strikes. Others were taken into custody, often without being charged with a crime, on the suspicion that they were somehow involved, as the government instituted new security measures.

The antiterrorism campaign escalated. In early 2002, Bush spoke out forcefully against what he called an "axis of evil," as he referred to Iraq, Iran, and North Korea. He was particularly intent on driving Iraqi leader Saddam Hussein from power. Hussein had launched the attack on Kuwait that had led to the Gulf War during the administration of Bush's father. Now, 11 years later, Bush argued that Hussein was creating weapons of mass destruction and vowed to bring about a regime change. Within the Bush administration, Secretary of State Colin Powell, inclined to a more restrained foreign policy, fought against Secretary of Defense Donald Rumsfeld and Vice President Dick Cheney, who enthusiastically supported an attack. Bush's argument that he could invade Iraq even without the support of Congress aroused a firestorm of protest both in the United States and around the world.

The war in Iraq, fought with British but not United Nations support, began in March 2003. American forces were successful, and just a month and a half later, Bush declared that the major phase of combat operations was over. In December, U.S. soldiers captured Saddam Hussein hiding in a hole in the ground. But even the capture of the Iraqi dictator could not quell increasing opposition to the American occupation, which led to fierce fighting in the months

Timeline

1991–1999	Ethnic turbulence in fragmented former Yugoslavia
1992	Bill Clinton elected president
	Czechoslovakia splits into separate Czech and Slovak Republics
	Riots erupt in Los Angeles
1993	North American Free Trade Agreement (NAFTA) ratified
	Palestine Liberation Organization and Israel sign peace treaty
1994	Nelson Mandela elected president of South Africa
1996	Bill Clinton reelected
1998	Budget surplus announced
	Bill Clinton impeached by the House of Representatives
1999	Bill Clinton acquitted by the Senate
	Stock market soars as Dow Jones average passes 10,000
2000	George W. Bush elected president
2001	Economy falters
	Stock market dips below 10,000
	Tax cut passed
	Terrorists strike New York City and Washington, D.C.
2002	Recession continues and Dow Jones average drops below 8,000
2003	U.S. and coalition forces invade Iraq
2004	George W. Bush reelected
2005	Bush calls for a major overhaul of social security
2006	Democrats regain control of both houses of Congress

that followed. As the deadline for handing sovereignty over to Iraq in mid-2004 approached, Sunnis, Shiites, and Kurds fought with each other for a share of power, but were united in their opposition to the continuing American presence. Insurgent attacks against American troops and Iraqis in new official positions continued as Iraq descended into civil war. Photographs of American abuse of prisoners in the notorious Abu Ghraib prison aroused resentment in the Middle East and among people around the world. By early 2008, the American death toll in Iraq passed 4,000 and significantly exceeded the number killed in the terrorist attacks of 9/11, with another 30,000 Americans wounded. As the Iraqi government demonstrated its inability to maintain order in the face of mounting sectarian conflict, more and more Americans demanded an end to involvement in what they perceived as serious, and perhaps intractable, problems.

Bush responded in early 2007 by increasing the number of American troops, in what he called a "surge" to quell violence in Baghdad. But pressure, particularly from Democrats, to bring troops home persisted.

Conclusion
THE RECENT PAST IN PERSPECTIVE

In the 1990s, the United States prospered in a period of economic growth longer than any in its history. After weathering a recession at the start of the decade, the economy began to boom, and the boom continued for the next 10 years. Most middle- and upper-class Americans prospered. The budget deficit disappeared, and the government ran a sizable surplus. Yet not all Americans shared in the prosperity. Despite the drop in the unemployment level, many of the available jobs paid little more than the minimum wage, and people like Marlene and Rod Garrett, met at the start of the chapter, had trouble making ends meet. Members of minority groups, whose numbers grew throughout the decade, had the toughest time of all.

Meanwhile, Americans worried about their role in the outside world. As they enjoyed their newfound prosperity, some were reluctant to spend money in an activist role abroad. They debated what to do about the defense establishment, which had begun to deteriorate, and were hesitant to become deeply involved in foreign conflicts where they had trouble ascertaining American interests. Then, in 2001, the brutal terrorist attacks on New York City and Washington, D.C., mobilized the nation. Recognizing at long last that terrorism threatened the entire globe, including the United States, they prepared themselves for an extended effort to try to bring it under control and to make the world a safer place. As they had in years past, in both World War I and World War II, the United States again sought to protect the democratic way of life for the American people and for people elsewhere as well.

QUESTIONS FOR REVIEW AND REFLECTION

1. What were the major economic developments in the 1990s, and how did they affect political action?
2. How were the Democrats able to regain power in 1992 after more than a decade of Republican rule?
3. How successful was Bill Clinton's presidency?
4. What did the closeness of the elections of 2000 and 2004 indicate about divisions in American society?
5. How did the terrorist attacks of September 11, 2001, affect the course of American foreign policy?

APPENDIX

THE UNANIMOUS DECLARATION OF THE THIRTEEN UNITED STATES OF AMERICA

When, in the course of human events, it becomes necessary for one people to dissolve the political bonds which have connected them with another, and to assume, among the powers of the earth, the separate and equal station to which the laws of nature and of nature's God entitle them, a decent respect to the opinions of mankind requires that they should declare the causes which impel them to the separation.

We hold these truths to be self-evident: That all men are created equal; that they are endowed by their Creator with certain unalienable rights; that among these are life, liberty, and the pursuit of happiness; that, to secure these rights, governments are instituted among men, deriving their just powers from the consent of the governed; that whenever any form of government becomes destructive of these ends, it is the right of the people to alter or to abolish it, and to institute new government, laying its foundation on such principles, and organizing its powers in such form, as to them shall seem most likely to effect their safety and happiness. Prudence, indeed, will dictate that governments long established should not be changed for light and transient causes; and accordingly all experience hath shown that mankind are more disposed to suffer, while evils are sufferable, than to right themselves by abolishing the forms to which they are accustomed. But when a long train of abuses and usurpations, pursuing invariably the same object, evinces a design to reduce them under absolute despotism, it is their right, it is their duty, to throw off such government, and to provide new guards for their future security. Such has been the patient sufferance of these colonies; and such is now the necessity which constrains them to alter their former systems of government. The history of the present King of Great Britain is a history of repeated injuries and usurpations, all having in direct object the establishment of an absolute tyranny over these states. To prove this, let facts be submitted to a candid world.

He has refused his assent to laws, the most wholesome and necessary for the public good.

He has forbidden his governors to pass laws of immediate and pressing importance, unless suspended in their operation till his assent should be obtained; and, when so suspended, he has utterly neglected to attend to them.

He has refused to pass other laws for the accommodation of large districts of people, unless those people would relinquish the right of representation in the legislature, a right inestimable to them, and formidable to tyrants only.

He has called together legislative bodies at places unusual, uncomfortable, and distant from the depository of their public records, for the sole purpose of fatiguing them into compliance with his measures.

He has dissolved representative houses repeatedly, for opposing, with manly firmness, his invasions on the rights of the people.

He has refused for a long time, after such dissolutions, to cause others to be elected; whereby the legislative powers, incapable of annihilation, have returned to the people at large for their exercise; the state remaining, in the mean time, exposed to all the dangers of invasions from without and convulsions within.

He has endeavored to prevent the population of these states; for that purpose obstructing the laws for naturalization of foreigners; refusing to pass others to encourage their migration hither, and raising the conditions of new appropriations of lands.

He has obstructed the administration of justice, by refusing his assent to laws for establishing judiciary powers.

He has made judges dependent on his will alone, for the tenure of their offices, and the amount and payment of their salaries.

He has erected a multitude of new offices, and sent hither swarms of officers to harass our people and eat out their substance.

He has kept among us, in times of peace, standing armies, without the consent of our legislatures.

He has affected to render the military independent of, and superior to, the civil power.

He has combined with others to subject us to a jurisdiction foreign to our constitution, and unacknowledged by our laws, giving his assent to their acts of pretended legislation:

For quartering large bodies of armed troops among us;

For protecting them, by a mock trial, from punishment for any murder which they should commit on the inhabitants of these states;

For cutting off our trade with all parts of the world;

For imposing taxes on us without our consent;

For depriving us, in many cases, of the benefits of trial by jury;

For transporting us beyond seas, to be tried for pretended offenses;

For abolishing the free system of English laws in a neighboring province, establishing therein an arbitrary government, and enlarging its boundaries, so as to render it at once an example and fit instrument for introducing the same absolute rule into these colonies;

For taking away our charters abolishing our most valuable laws, and altering fundamentally the forms of our governments;

For suspending our own legislatures, and declaring themselves invested with power to legislate for us in all cases whatsoever.

He has abdicated government here, by declaring us out of his protection and waging war against us.

He has plundered our seas, ravaged our coasts, burned our towns, and destroyed the lives of our people.

He is at this time transporting large armies of foreign mercenaries to complete the works of death, desolation, and tyranny already begun with circumstances of cruelty and perfidy scarcely paralleled in the most barbarous ages, and totally unworthy the head of a civilized nation.

He has constrained our fellow-citizens, taken captive on the high seas, to bear arms against their country, to become the executioners of their friends and brethren, or to fall themselves by their hands.

He has excited domestic insurrection among us, and has endeavored to bring on the inhabitants of our frontiers the merciless Indian savages, whose known rule of warfare is an undistinguished destruction of all ages, sexes, and conditions.

In every stage of these oppressions we have petitioned for redress in the most humble terms; our repeated petitions have been answered only by repeated injury. A prince, whose character is thus marked by every act which may define a tyrant, is unfit to be the ruler of a free people.

Nor have we been wanting in our attentions to our British brethren. We have warned them, from time to time, of attempts by their legislature to extend an unwarrantable jurisdiction over us. We have reminded them of the circumstances of our emigration and settlement here. We have appealed to their native justice and magnanimity; and we have conjured them, by the ties of our common kindred, to disavow these usurpations, which would inevitably interrupt our connections and correspondence. They, too, have been deaf to the voice of justice and of consanguinity. We must, therefore, acquiesce in the necessity which denounces our separation, and hold them, as we hold the rest of mankind, enemies in war, in peace friends.

We, therefore, the representatives of the United States of America, in General Congress assembled, appealing to the Supreme Judge of the world for the rectitude of our intentions, do, in the name and by the authority of the good people of these colonies, solemnly publish and declare, that these United Colonies are, and of right, ought to be, FREE AND INDEPENDENT STATES; that they are absolved from all allegiance to the British crown, and that all political connection between them and the state of Great Britain is, and ought to be, totally dissolved; and that, as free and independent states, they have full power to levy war, conclude peace, contract alliances, establish commerce, and do all other acts and things which independent states may of right do. And for the support of this declaration, with a firm reliance on the protection of Devine Providence, we mutually pledge to each other our lives, our fortunes, and our sacred honor.

JOHN HANCOCK

BUTTON GWENNETT
LYMAN HALL
GEO. WALTON
WM. HOOPER
JOSEPH HEWES
JOHN PENN
EDWARD RUTLEDGE
THOS. HEYWARD, JUNR.
THOMAS LYNCH, JUNR.
ARTHUR MIDDLETON
SAMUEL CHASE
WM. PACA
THOS. STONE
CHARLES CARROLL OF CARROLLTON
GEORGE WYTHE
RICHARD HENRY LEE
TH. JEFFERSON
BENJA. HARRISON
THS. NELSON, JR.

FRANCIS LIGHTFOOT LEE
CARTER BRAXTON
ROBT. MORRIS
BENJAMIN RUSH
BENJA. FRANKLIN
JOHN MORTON
GEO. CLYMER
JAS. SMITH
GEO. TAYLOR
JAMES WILSON
GEO. ROSS
CAESAR RODNEY
GEO. READ
THO. MíKEAN
WM. FLOYD
PHIL. LIVINGSTON
FRANS. LEWIS
LEWIS MORRIS
RICHD. STOCKTON

JNO. WITHERSPOON
FRAS. HOPKINSON
JOHN HART
ABRA. CLARK
JOSIAH BARTLETT
WM. WHIPPLE
SAML. ADAMS
JOHN ADAMS
ROBT. TREAT PAINE
ELBRIDGE GERRY
STEP. HOPKINS
WILLIAM ELLERY
ROGER SHERMAN
SAMíEL. HUNTINGTON
WM. WILLIAMS
OLIVER WOLCOTT
MATHEW THORNTON

The Constitution of the United States of America

PREAMBLE

We the People of the United States, in Order to form a more perfect Union, establish Justice, insure domestic Tranquility, provide for the common defence, promote the general Welfare, and secure the Blessings of Liberty to ourselves and our Posterity, do ordain and establish this Constitution for the United States of America.

ARTICLE I.

Section 1 All legislative Powers herein granted shall be vested in a Congress of the United States, which shall consist of a Senate and House of Representatives.

Section 2 The House of Representatives shall be composed of Members chosen every second Year by the People of the several States, and the Electors in each State shall have the Qualifications requisite for Electors of the most numerous Branch of the State Legislature.

No Person shall be a Representative who shall not have attained to the Age of twenty five Years, and been seven Years a Citizen of the United States, and who shall not, when elected, be an Inhabitant of that State in which he shall be chosen.

Representatives and direct Taxes shall be apportioned among the several States which may be included within this Union, according to their respective Numbers, *which shall be determined by adding to the whole Number of free Persons, including those bound to Service for a Term of Years, and excluding Indians not taxed, three fifths of all other Persons.* The actual Enumeration shall be made within three Years after the first Meeting of the Congress of the United States, and within every subsequent Term of ten Years, in such Manner as they shall by Law direct. The Number of Representatives shall not exceed one for every thirty Thousand, but each State shall have at Least one Representative; *and until such enumeration shall be made, the State of New Hampshire shall be entitled to chuse three, Massachusetts eight, Rhode-Island and Providence Plantations one, Connecticut five, New-York six, New Jersey four, Pennsylvania eight, Delaware one, Maryland six, Virginia ten, North Carolina five, South Carolina five, and Georgia three.*

When vacancies happen in the Representation from any State, the Executive Authority thereof shall issue Writs of Election to fill such Vacancies.

The House of Representatives shall chuse their Speaker and other Officers; and shall have the sole Power of Impeachment.

Section 3 The Senate of the United States shall be composed of two Senators from each State, chosen by the Legislature thereof, for six Years; and each Senator shall have one Vote.

Immediately after they shall be assembled in Consequence of the first Election, they shall be divided as equally as may be into three Classes. The Seats of the Senators of the first Class shall be vacated at the Expiration of the second Year, of the second Class at the Expiration of the fourth Year, and of the third Class at the Expiration of the sixth Year, so that one third may be chosen every second Year; and if Vacancies happen by Resignation, or otherwise, during the Recess of the Legislature of any State, the Executive thereof may make temporary Appointments until the next Meeting of the Legislature, which shall then fill such Vacancies.

No Person shall be a Senator who shall not have attained to the Age of thirty Years, and been nine Years a Citizen of the United States, and who shall not, when elected, be an Inhabitant of that State for which he shall be chosen.

The Vice President of the United States shall be President of the Senate, but shall have no Vote, unless they be equally divided.

The Senate shall choose their other Officers, and also a President *pro tempore,* in the Absence of the Vice President, or when he shall exercise the Office of President of the United States.

The Senate shall have the sole Power to try all Impeachments. When sitting for that Purpose, they shall be on Oath or Affirmation. When the President of the United States is tried the Chief Justice shall preside: And no Person shall be convicted without the Concurrence of two thirds of the Members present.

Judgment in Cases of Impeachment shall not extend further than to removal from Office, and disqualification to hold and enjoy any Office of honor, Trust or Profit under the United States: but the Party convicted shall nevertheless be liable and subject to Indictment, Trial, Judgment and Punishment, according to Law.

Section 4 The Times, Places and Manner of holding Elections for Senators and Representatives, shall be prescribed in each State by the Legislature thereof; but the Congress may at any time by Law make or alter such Regulations, except as to the Places of chusing Senators.

The Congress shall assemble at least once in every Year, and such Meeting *shall be on the first Monday in December, unless they shall by Law appoint a different Day.*

Section 5 Each House shall be the Judge of the Elections, Returns and Qualifications of its own Members, and a Majority of each shall constitute a Quorum to do Business; but a smaller Number may adjourn from day to day, and may be authorized to compel the Attendance of absent Members, in such Manner, and under such Penalties as each House may provide.

Each House may determine the Rules of its Proceedings, punish its Members for disorderly Behaviour, and, with the Concurrence of two thirds, expel a Member.

Each House shall keep a Journal of its Proceedings, and from time to time publish the same, excepting such Parts as may in their Judgment require Secrecy; and the Yeas and Nays of the Members of either House on any question shall, at the Desire of one fifth of those Present, be entered on the Journal.

Neither House, during the Session of Congress, shall, without the Consent of the other, adjourn for more than three days, nor to any other Place than that in which the two Houses shall be sitting.

Section 6 The Senators and Representatives shall receive a Compensation for their Services, to be ascertained by Law, and paid out of the Treasury of the United States. They shall in all Cases, except Treason, Felony and Breach of the Peace, be privileged from Arrest during their Attendance at the Session of their respective Houses, and in going to and returning from the same; and for any Speech or Debate in either House, they shall not be questioned in any other Place.

No Senator or Representative shall, during the Time for which he was elected, be appointed to any civil Office under the Authority of the United States, which shall have been created, or the Emoluments whereof shall have been encreased during such time; and no Person holding any Office under the United States, shall be a Member of either House during his Continuance in Office.

Section 7 All Bills for raising Revenue shall originate in the House of Representatives; but the Senate may propose or concur with Amendments as on other Bills.

Every Bill which shall have passed the House of Representatives and the Senate, shall, before it become a Law, be presented to the President of the United States; If he approve he shall sign it, but if not he shall return it, with his Objections to that House in which it shall have originated, who shall enter the Objections at large on their Journal, and proceed to reconsider it. If after such Reconsideration two thirds of that House shall agree to pass the Bill, it shall be sent, together with the Objections, to the other House, by which it shall likewise be reconsidered, and if approved by two thirds of that House, it shall become a Law. But in all such Cases the Votes of both Houses shall be determined by yeas and Nays, and the Names of the Persons voting for and against the Bill shall be entered on the Journal of each House respectively. If any Bill shall not be returned by the President within ten Days (Sundays excepted) after it shall have been presented to him, the Same shall be a Law, in like Manner as if he had signed it, unless the Congress by their Adjournment prevent its Return, in which Case it shall not be a Law.

Every Order, Resolution, or Vote to which the Concurrence of the Senate and House of Representatives may be necessary (except on a question of Adjournment) shall be presented to the President of the United States; and before the Same shall take Effect, shall be approved by him, or being disapproved by him, shall be repassed by two thirds of the Senate and House of Representatives, according to the Rules and Limitations prescribed in the Case of a Bill.

Section 8 The Congress shall have Power:

To lay and collect Taxes, Duties, Imposts and Excises, to pay the Debts and provide for the common Defence and general Welfare of the United States; but all Duties, Imposts and Excises shall be uniform throughout the United States;

To borrow Money on the credit of the United States;

To regulate Commerce with foreign Nations, and among the several States, and with the Indian Tribes;

To establish an uniform Rule of Naturalization, and uniform Laws on the subject of Bankruptcies throughout the United States;

To coin Money, regulate the Value thereof, and of foreign Coin, and fix the Standard of Weights and Measures;

To provide for the Punishment of counterfeiting the Securities and current Coin of the United States;

To establish Post Offices and post Roads;

To promote the Progress of Science and useful Arts, by securing for limited Times to Authors and Inventors the exclusive Right to their respective Writings and Discoveries;

To constitute Tribunals inferior to the supreme Court;

To define and punish Piracies and Felonies committed on the high Seas, and Offences against the Law of Nations;

To declare War, grant Letters of Marque and Reprisal, and make Rules concerning Captures on Land and Water;

To raise and support Armies, but no Appropriation of Money to that Use shall be for a longer Term than two Years;

To provide and maintain a Navy;

To make Rules for the Government and Regulation of the land and naval Forces;

To provide for calling forth the Militia to execute the Laws of the Union, suppress Insurrections and repel Invasions;

To provide for organizing, arming, and disciplining, the Militia, and for governing such Part of them as may be employed in the Service of the United States, reserving to the States respectively, the Appointment of the Officers, and the Authority of training the Militia according to the discipline prescribed by Congress;

To exercise exclusive Legislation in all Cases whatsoever, over such District (not exceeding ten Miles square) as may, by Cession of particular States, and the Acceptance of Congress, become the Seat of the Government of the United States, and to exercise like Authority over all Places purchased by the Consent of the Legislature of the State in which the Same shall be, for the Erection of Forts, Magazines, Arsenals, dock-Yards, and other needful Buildings;

To make all Laws which shall be necessary and proper for carrying into Execution the foregoing Powers, and all other Powers vested by this Constitution in the Government of the United States, or in any Department or Officer thereof.

Section 9 *The Migration or Importation of such Persons as any of the States now existing shall think proper to admit, shall not be prohibited by the Congress prior to the Year one thousand eight hundred and eight, but a Tax or duty may be imposed on such Importation, not exceeding ten dollars for each Person.*

The Privilege of the Writ of Habeas Corpus shall not be suspended, unless when in Cases of Rebellion or Invasion the public Safety may require it.

No Bill of Attainder or ex post facto Law shall be passed.

No Capitation, or other direct, Tax shall be laid, unless in Proportion to the Census or Enumeration herein before directed to be taken.

No Tax or Duty shall be laid on Articles exported from any State.

No Preference shall be given by any Regulation of Commerce or Revenue to the Ports of one State over those of another: nor shall Vessels bound to, or from, one State, be obliged to enter, clear, or pay Duties in another.

No Money shall be drawn from the Treasury, but in Consequence of Appropriations made by Law; and a regular Statement and Account of the Receipts and Expenditures of all public Money shall be published from time to time.

No Title of Nobility shall be granted by the United States: And no Person holding any Office of Profit or Trust under them, shall, without the Consent of the Congress, accept of any present, Emolument, Office, or Title, of any kind whatever, from any King, Prince, or foreign State.

Section 10 No State shall enter into any Treaty, Alliance, or Confederation; grant Letters of Marque and Reprisal; coin Money; emit Bills of Credit; make any Thing but gold and silver Coin a Tender in Payment of Debts; pass any Bill of Attainder, ex post facto Law, or Law impairing the Obligation of Contracts, or grant any Title of Nobility.

No State shall, without the Consent of the Congress, lay any Imposts or Duties on Imports or Exports, except what may be absolutely necessary for executing it's inspection Laws: and the net Produce of all Duties and Imposts, laid by any State on Imports or Exports, shall be for the Use of the Treasury of the United States; and all such Laws shall be subject to the Revision and Controul of the Congress.

No State shall, without the Consent of Congress, lay any Duty of Tonnage, keep Troops, or Ships of War in time of Peace, enter into any Agreement or Compact with another State, or with a foreign Power, or engage in War, unless actually invaded, or in such imminent Danger as will not admit of delay.

ARTICLE II.

Section 1 The executive Power shall be vested in a President of the United States of America. He shall hold his Office during the Term of four Years, and, together with the Vice President, chosen for the same Term, be elected, as follows

Each State shall appoint, in such Manner as the Legislature thereof may direct, a Number of Electors, equal to the whole Number of Senators and Representatives to which the State may be entitled in the Congress: but no Senator or Representative, or Person holding an Office of Trust or Profit under the United States, shall be appointed an Elector.

The Electors shall meet in their respective States, and vote by Ballot for two Persons, of whom one at least shall not be an Inhabitant of the same State with themselves. And they shall make a List of all the Persons voted for, and of the Number of Votes for each; which List they shall sign and certify, and transmit sealed to the Seat of Government of the United States, directed to the President of the Senate. The President of the Senate shall, in the Presence of the Senate and House of Representatives, open all the Certificates, and the Votes shall then be counted. The Person having the greatest Number of Votes shall be the President, if such Number be a Majority of the whole Number of Electors appointed; and if there be more than one who have such Majority, and have an equal Number of Votes, then the House of Representatives shall immediately chuse by Ballot one of them for President; and if no Person have a Majority, then from the five highest on the List the said House shall in like Manner chuse the President. But in chusing the President, the Votes shall be taken by States, the Representation from each State having one Vote; A quorum for this Purpose shall consist of a Member or Members from two thirds of the States, and a Majority of all the States shall be necessary to a Choice. In every Case, after the Choice of the President, the Person having the greatest Number of Votes of the Electors shall be the Vice President. But if there should remain two or more who have equal Votes, the Senate shall chuse from them by Ballot the Vice President. The Congress may determine the Time of chusing the Electors, and the Day on which they shall give their Votes; which Day shall be the same throughout the United States.

No Person except a natural born Citizen, *or a Citizen of the United States, at the time of the Adoption of this Constitution,* shall be eligible to the Office of President; neither shall any Person be eligible to that Office who shall not have attained to the Age of thirty five Years, and been fourteen Years a Resident within the United States.

In Case of the Removal of the President from Office, or of his Death, Resignation, or Inability to discharge the Powers and Duties of the said Office, the Same shall devolve on the Vice President, and the Congress may by Law provide for the Case of Removal, Death, Resignation or Inability, both of the President and Vice President declaring what Officer shall then act as President, and such Officer shall act accordingly, until the Disability be removed, or a President shall be elected.

The President shall, at stated Times, receive for his Services, a Compensation, which shall neither be increased nor diminished during the Period for which he shall have been elected, and he shall not receive within that Period any other Emolument from the United States, or any of them.

Before he enter on the Execution of his Office, he shall take the following Oath or Affirmation: "I do solemnly swear (or affirm) that I will faithfully execute the Office of President of the United States, and will to the best of my Ability, preserve, protect and defend the Constitution of the United States."

Section 2 The President shall be Commander in Chief of the Army and Navy of the United States, and of the Militia of the several States, when called into the actual Service of the United States; he may require the Opinion, in writing, of the principal Officer in each of the executive Departments, upon any Subject relating to the Duties of their respective Offices, and he shall have Power to grant Reprieves and Pardons for Offences against the United States, except in Cases of Impeachment.

He shall have Power, by and with the Advice and Consent of the Senate, to make Treaties, provided two thirds of the Senators present concur; and he shall nominate, and by and with the Advice and Consent of the Senate, shall appoint Ambassadors, other public Ministers and Consuls, Judges of the supreme Court, and all other Officers of the United States, whose Appointments are not herein otherwise provided for, and which shall be established by Law: but the Congress may by Law vest the Appointment of such inferior Officers, as they think proper, in the President alone, in the Courts of Law, or in the Heads of Departments.

The President shall have Power to fill up all Vacancies that may happen during the Recess of the Senate, by granting Commissions which shall expire at the End of their next Session.

Section 3 He shall from time to time give to the Congress Information of the State of the Union, and recommend to their Consideration such Measures as he shall judge necessary and expedient; he may, on extraordinary Occasions, convene both Houses, or either of them, and in Case of Disagreement between them, with Respect to the Time of Adjournment, he may adjourn them to such Time as he shall think proper; he shall receive Ambassadors and other public Ministers; he shall take Care that the Laws be faithfully executed, and shall Commission all the Officers of the United States.

Section 4 The President, Vice President and all civil Officers of the United States, shall be removed from Office on Impeachment for, and Conviction of, Treason, Bribery, or other high Crimes and Misdemeanors.

ARTICLE III.

Section 1 The judicial Power of the United States, shall be vested in one supreme Court, and in such inferior Courts as the Congress may from time to time ordain and establish. The Judges, both of the supreme and inferior Courts, shall hold their Offices during good Behaviour, and shall, at stated Times, receive for their Services, a Compensation which shall not be diminished during their Continuance in Office.

Section 2 The judicial Power shall extend to all Cases, in Law and Equity, arising under this Constitution, the Laws of the United States, and Treaties made, or which shall be made, under their Authority;—to all Cases affecting Ambassadors, other public Ministers and Consuls;—to all Cases of admiralty and maritime Jurisdiction;—to Controversies to which the United States shall be a Party;—to Controversies between two or more States;—*between a State and Citizens of another State;*—between Citizens of different States;—between Citizens of the same State claiming Lands under

Grants of different States, and between a State, or the Citizens thereof, and foreign States, Citizens or Subjects.

In all Cases affecting Ambassadors, other public Ministers and Consuls, and those in which a State shall be Party, the supreme Court shall have original Jurisdiction. In all the other Cases before mentioned, the supreme Court shall have appellate Jurisdiction, both as to Law and Fact, with such Exceptions, and under such Regulations as the Congress shall make.

The Trial of all Crimes, except in Cases of Impeachment, shall be by Jury; and such Trial shall be held in the State where the said Crimes shall have been committed; but when not committed within any State, the Trial shall be at such Place or Places as the Congress may by Law have directed.

Section 3 Treason against the United States, shall consist only in levying War against them, or in adhering to their Enemies, giving them Aid and Comfort. No Person shall be convicted of Treason unless on the Testimony of two Witnesses to the same overt Act, or on Confession in open Court.

The Congress shall have Power to declare the Punishment of Treason, but no Attainder of Treason shall work Corruption of Blood, or Forfeiture except during the Life of the Person attainted.

ARTICLE IV.

Section 1 Full Faith and Credit shall be given in each State to the public Acts, Records, and judicial Proceedings of every other State. And the Congress may by general Laws prescribe the Manner in which such Acts, Records and Proceedings shall be proved, and the Effect thereof.

Section 2 The Citizens of each State shall be entitled to all Privileges and Immunities of Citizens in the several States.

A Person charged in any State with Treason, Felony, or other Crime, who shall flee from Justice, and be found in another State, shall on Demand of the executive Authority of the State from which he fled, be delivered up, to be removed to the State having Jurisdiction of the Crime.

No Person held to Service or Labour in one State, under the Laws thereof, escaping into another, shall, in Consequence of any Law or Regulation therein, be discharged from such Service or Labour, but shall be delivered up on Claim of the Party to whom such Service or Labour may be due.

Section 3 New States may be admitted by the Congress into this Union; but no new State shall be formed or erected within the Jurisdiction of any other State; nor any State be formed by the Junction of two or more States, or Parts of States, without the Consent of the Legislatures of the States concerned as well as of the Congress.

The Congress shall have Power to dispose of and make all needful Rules and Regulations respecting the Territory or other Property belonging to the United States; and nothing in this Constitution shall be so construed as to Prejudice any Claims of the United States, or of any particular State.

Section 4 The United States shall guarantee to every State in this Union a Republican Form of Government, and shall protect each of them against Invasion; and on Application of the Legislature, or of the Executive (when the Legislature cannot be convened) against domestic Violence.

ARTICLE V.

The Congress, whenever two thirds of both Houses shall deem it necessary, shall propose Amendments to this Constitution, or, on the Application of the Legislatures of two thirds of the several States, shall call a Convention for proposing Amendments, which, in either Case, shall be valid to all Intents and Purposes, as Part of this Constitution, when ratified by the Legislatures of three fourths of the several States, or by Conventions in three fourths thereof, as the one or the other Mode of Ratification may be proposed by the Congress; Provided that *no Amendment which may be made prior to the Year One thousand eight hundred and eight shall in any Manner affect the first and fourth Clauses in the Ninth Section of the first Article; and* that no State, without its Consent, shall be deprived of its equal Suffrage in the Senate.

ARTICLE VI.

All Debts contracted and Engagements entered into, before the Adoption of this Constitution, shall be as valid against the United States under this Constitution, as under the Confederation.

This Constitution, and the Laws of the United States which shall be made in Pursuance thereof; and all Treaties made or which shall be made, under the Authority of the United States, shall be the supreme Law of the Land; and the Judges in every State shall be bound thereby, any Thing in the Constitution or Laws of any State to the Contrary notwithstanding.

The Senators and Representatives before mentioned, and the Members of the several State Legislatures, and all executive and judicial Officers, both of the United States and of the several States, shall be bound by Oath or Affirmation, to support this Constitution; but no religious Test shall ever be required as a Qualification to any Office or public Trust under the United States.

ARTICLE VII.

The Ratification of the Conventions of nine States, shall be sufficient for the Establishment of this Constitution between the States so ratifying the Same.

Done in Convention by the Unanimous Consent of the States present the Seventeenth Day of September in the Year of our Lord one thousand seven hundred and Eighty seven and of the Independence of the United States of America the Twelfth IN WITNESS whereof We have hereunto subscribed our Names, ■

GEORGE WASHINGTON,
President and Deputy from Virginia

North Carolina

WILLIAM BLOUNT
RICHARD DOBBS SPRAIGHT
HU WILLIAMSON

Pennsylvania

BENJAMIN FRANKLIN
THOMAS MIFFLIN
ROBERT MORRIS
GEORGE CLYMER
THOMAS FITZSIMONS
JARED INGERSOLL
JAMES WILSON
GOUVERNEUR MORRIS

Delaware

GEORGE READ
GUNNING BEDFORD, JR.
JOHN DICKINSON
RICHARD BASSETT
JACOB BROOM

South Carolina

J. RUTLEDGE
CHARLES C. PINCKNEY
PIERCE BUTLER

Virginia

JOHN BLAIR
JAMES MADISON, JR.

New Jersey

WILLIAM LIVINGSTON
DAVID BREARLEY
WILLIAM PATERSON
JONATHAN DAYTON

Maryland

JAMES MCHENRY
DANIEL OF ST. THOMAS JENIFER
DANIEL CARROLL

Massachusetts

NATHANIEL GORHAM
RUFUS KING

Connecticut

WILLIAM S. JOHNSON
ROGER SHERMAN

New York

ALEXANDER HAMILTON

New Hampshire

JOHN LANGDON
NICHOLAS GILMAN

Georgia

WILLIAM FEW
ABRAHAM BALDWIN

Amendments to the Constitution

AMENDMENT I

Congress shall make no law respecting an establishment of religion, or prohibiting the free exercise thereof; or abridging the freedom of speech, or of the press; or the right of the people peaceably to assemble, and to petition the Government for a redress of grievances.

AMENDMENT II

A well regulated Militia, being necessary to the security of a free State, the right of the people to keep and bear Arms, shall not be infringed.

AMENDMENT III

No Soldier shall, in time of peace be quartered in any house, without the consent of the Owner, nor in time of war, but in a manner to be prescribed by law.

AMENDMENT IV

The right of the people to be secure in their persons, houses, papers, and effects, against unreasonable searches and seizures, shall not be violated, and no Warrants shall issue, but upon probable cause, supported by Oath or affirmation, and particularly describing the place to be searched, and the persons or things to be seized.

AMENDMENT V

No person shall be held to answer for a capital, or otherwise infamous crime, unless on a presentment or indictment of a Grand Jury, except in cases arising in the land or naval forces, or in the Militia, when in actual service in time of War or public danger; nor shall any person be subject for the same offence to be twice put in jeopardy of life or limb; nor shall be compelled in any criminal case to be a witness against himself, nor be deprived of life, liberty, or property, without due process of law; nor shall private property be taken for public use, without just compensation.

AMENDMENT VI

In all criminal prosecutions, the accused shall enjoy the right to a speedy and public trial, by an impartial jury of the State and district wherein the crime shall have been committed, which district shall have been previously ascertained by law, and to be informed of the nature and cause of the accusation; to be confronted with the witnesses against him; to have compulsory process for obtaining witnesses in his favor, and to have the Assistance of Counsel for his defence.

AMENDMENT VII

In Suits at common law, where the value in controversy shall exceed twenty dollars, the right of trial by jury shall be preserved, and no fact tried by a jury, shall be otherwise re-examined in any Court of the United States, than according to the rules of the common law.

AMENDMENT VIII

Excessive bail shall not be required, nor excessive fines imposed, nor cruel and unusual punishments inflicted.

AMENDMENT IX

The enumeration in the Constitution, of certain rights, shall not be construed to deny or disparage others retained by the people.

AMENDMENT X

The powers not delegated to the United States by the Constitution, nor prohibited by it to the States, are reserved to the States respectively, or to the people.

AMENDMENT XI [ADOPTED 1798]

The Judicial power of the United States shall not be construed to extend to any suit in law or equity, commenced or prosecuted against one of the United States by Citizens of another State, or by Citizens or Subjects of any Foreign State.

AMENDMENT XII [ADOPTED 1804]

The Electors shall meet in their respective states, and vote by ballot for President and Vice-President, one of whom, at least, shall not be an inhabitant of the same state with themselves; they shall name in their ballots the person voted for as President, and in distinct ballots the person voted for as Vice-President, and they shall make distinct lists of all persons voted for as President, and of all persons voted for as Vice-President, and of the number of votes for each, which list they shall sign and certify, and transmit sealed to the seat of the government of the United States, directed to the President of the Senate;—The President of the Senate shall, in the presence of the Senate and House of Representatives, open all the certificates and the votes shall then be counted;—The person having the greatest number of votes for President, shall be the President, if such number be a majority of the whole number of Electors appointed; and if no person have such majority, then from the persons having the highest numbers not exceeding three on the list of those voted for as President, the House of Representatives shall choose immediately, by ballot, the President. But in choosing the President, the votes shall be taken by states, the representation from each state having one vote; a quorum for this purpose shall consist of a member or members from two thirds of the states, and a majority of all the states shall be necessary to a choice. And if the House of Representatives shall not choose a President whenever the right of choice shall devolve upon them, before the *fourth day of March* next following, then the Vice-President shall act as President, as in the case of the death or other constitutional disability of the President.

The person having the greatest number of votes as Vice-President, shall be the Vice-President, if such number be a majority of the whole number of Electors appointed, and if no person have a majority, then from the two highest numbers on the list, the Senate shall choose the Vice-President; a quorum for the purpose shall consist of two thirds of the whole number of Senators, and a majority of the whole number shall be necessary to a choice. But no person constitutionally ineligible to the office of President shall be eligible to that of Vice-President of the United States.

AMENDMENT XIII [ADOPTED 1865]

Section 1 Neither slavery nor involuntary servitude, except as a punishment for crime whereof the party shall have been duly convicted, shall exist within the United States, or any place subject to their jurisdiction.

Section 2 Congress shall have power to enforce this article by appropriate legislation.

AMENDMENT XIV [ADOPTED 1868]

Section 1 All persons born or naturalized in the United States, and subject to the jurisdiction thereof, are citizens of the United States and of the State wherein they reside. No State shall make or enforce any law which shall abridge the privileges or immunities of citizens of the United States; nor shall any State deprive any person of life, liberty, or property, without due process of law; nor deny to any person within its jurisdiction the equal protection of the laws.

Section 2 Representatives shall be apportioned among the several States according to their respective numbers, counting the whole number of persons in each State, excluding Indians not taxed. But when the right to vote at any election for the choice of electors for President and Vice-President of the United States, Representatives in Congress, the Executive and Judicial officers of a State, or the members of the Legislature thereof, is denied to any of the male inhabitants of such State, being twenty-one years of age, and citizens of the United States, or in any way abridged, except for participation in rebellion, or other crime, the basis of representation therein shall be reduced in the proportion which the number of such male citizens shall bear to the whole number of male citizens twenty-one years of age in such State.

Section 3 No person shall be a Senator or Representative in Congress, or elector of President and Vice-President, or hold any office, civil or military, under the United States, or under any State, who, having previously taken an oath, as a member of Congress, or as an officer of the United States, or as a member of any State legislature, or as an executive or judicial officer of any State, to support the Constitution of the United States, shall have engaged in insurrection or rebellion against the same, or given aid or comfort to the enemies thereof. But Congress may by a vote of two thirds of each House, remove such disability.

Section 4 The validity of the public debt of the United States, authorized by law, including debts incurred for payment of pensions and bounties for services in suppressing insurrection or rebellion, shall not be questioned. But neither the United States nor any State shall assume or pay any debt or obligation incurred in aid of insurrection or rebellion against the United States, or any claim for the loss or emancipation of any slave; but all such debts, obligations and claims shall be held illegal and void.

Section 5 The Congress shall have power to enforce, by appropriate legislation, the provisions of this article.

AMENDMENT XV [ADOPTED 1870]

Section 1 The right of citizens of the United States to vote shall not be denied or abridged by the United States or by any State on account of race, color, or previous condition of servitude.

Section 2 The Congress shall have power to enforce this article by appropriate legislation.

AMENDMENT XVI [ADOPTED 1913]

The Congress shall have power to lay and collect taxes on incomes, from whatever source derived, without apportionment among the several States, and without regard to any census or enumeration.

AMENDMENT XVII [ADOPTED 1913]

The Senate of the United States shall be composed of two Senators from each State, elected by the people thereof, for six years; and each Senator shall have one vote. The electors in each State shall have the qualifications requisite for electors of the most numerous branch of the State legislatures.

When vacancies happen in the representation of any State in the Senate, the executive authority of such State shall issue writs of election to fill such vacancies: *Provided,* That the legislature of any State may empower the executive thereof to make temporary appointments until the people fill the vacancies by election as the legislature may direct.

This amendment shall not be so construed as to affect the election or term of any Senator chosen before it becomes valid as part of the Constitution.

AMENDMENT XVIII [ADOPTED 1919; REPEALED 1933]

Section 1 After one year from the ratification of this article the manufacture, sale, or transportation of intoxicating liquors within, the importation thereof into, or the exportation thereof from the United States and all territory subject to the jurisdiction thereof for beverage purposes is hereby prohibited.

Section 2 The Congress and the several States shall have concurrent power to enforce this article by appropriate legislation.

Section 3 This article shall be inoperative unless it shall have been ratified as an amendment to the Constitution by the legislatures of the several States, as provided in the Constitution, within seven years from the date of the submission hereof to the States by the Congress.

AMENDMENT XIX [ADOPTED 1920]

Section 1 The right of citizens of the United States to vote shall not be denied or abridged by the United States or by any State on account of sex.

Section 2 Congress shall have power to enforce this article by appropriate legislation.

AMENDMENT XX [ADOPTED 1933]

Section 1 The terms of the President and Vice-President shall end at noon on the 20th day of January, and the terms of Senators and Representatives at noon on the third day of January, of the years in which such terms would have ended if this article had not been ratified; and the terms of their successors shall then begin.

Section 2 The Congress shall assemble at least once in every year, and such meeting shall begin at noon on the third day of January, unless they shall by law appoint a different day.

Section 3 If, at the time fixed for the beginning of the term of the President, the President elect shall have died, the Vice-President elect shall become President. If a President shall not have been chosen before the time fixed for the beginning of his term, or if the President elect shall have failed to qualify, then the Vice-President elect shall act as President until a President shall have qualified; and the Congress may by law provide for the case wherein neither a President elect nor a Vice-President elect shall have qualified, declaring who shall then act as President, or the manner in which one who is to act shall be selected, and such person shall act accordingly until a President or Vice-President shall have qualified.

Section 4 The Congress may by law provide for the case of the death of any of the persons from whom the House of Representatives may choose a President whenever the right of choice shall have devolved upon them, and for the case of the death of any of the persons from whom the Senate may choose a Vice-President whenever the right of choice shall have devolved upon them.

Section 5 Sections 1 and 2 shall take effect on the 15th day of October following the ratification of this article.

Section 6 This article shall be inoperative unless it shall have been ratified as an amendment to the Constitution by the legislatures of three fourths of the several States within seven years from the date of its submission.

AMENDMENT XXI [ADOPTED 1933]

Section 1 The eighteenth article of amendment to the Constitution of the United States is hereby repealed.

Section 2 The transportation or importation into any State, Territory, or possession of the United States for delivery or use therein of intoxicating liquors, in violation of the laws thereof, is hereby prohibited.

Section 3 This article shall be inoperative unless it shall have been ratified as an amendment to the Constitution by conventions in the several States, as provided in the Constitution, within seven years from the date of the submission hereof to the States by the Congress.

AMENDMENT XXII [ADOPTED 1951]

Section 1 No person shall be elected to the office of the President more than twice, and no person who has held the office of President, or acted as President, for more than two years of a term to which some other person was elected President shall be elected to the office of the President more than once. But this Article shall not apply to any person holding the office of President when this Article was proposed by the Congress, and shall not prevent any person who may be holding the office of President, or acting as President, during the term within which this Article becomes operative from holding the office of President or acting as President during the remainder of such term.

Section 2 This article shall be inoperative unless it shall have been ratified as an amendment to the Constitution by the legislatures of three fourths of the several States within seven years from the date of its submission to the States by the Congress.

AMENDMENT XXIII [ADOPTED 1961]

Section 1 The District constituting the seat of Government of the United States shall appoint in such manner as the Congress may direct:

A number of electors of President and Vice-President equal to the whole number of Senators and Representatives in Congress to which the District would be entitled if it were a State, but in no event more than the least populous State; they shall be in addition to those appointed by the States, but they shall be considered, for the purposes of the election of President and Vice-President, to be electors appointed by a State; and they shall meet in the District and perform such duties as provided by the twelfth article of amendment.

Section 2 The Congress shall have power to enforce this article by appropriate legislation.

AMENDMENT XXIV [ADOPTED 1964]

Section 1 The right of citizens of the United States to vote in any primary or other election for President or Vice-President, for electors for President or Vice-President, or for Senator or Representative in Congress, shall not be denied or abridged by the United States or any State by reason of failure to pay any poll tax or other tax.

Section 2 The Congress shall have power to enforce this article by appropriate legislation.

AMENDMENT XXV [ADOPTED 1967]

Section 1 In case of the removal of the President from office or his death or resignation, the Vice-President shall become President.

Section 2 Whenever there is a vacancy in the office of the Vice-President, the President shall nominate a Vice-President who shall take the office upon confirmation by a majority vote of both houses of Congress.

Section 3 Whenever the President transmits to the President pro tempore of the Senate and the Speaker of the House of Representatives his written declaration that he is unable to discharge the powers and duties of his office, and until he transmits to them a written declaration to the contrary, such powers and duties shall be discharged by the Vice-President as Acting President.

Section 4 Whenever the Vice-President and a majority of either the principal officers of the executive departments, or of such other body as Congress may by law provide, transmit to the President pro tempore of the Senate and the Speaker of the House of Representatives their written declaration that the President is unable to discharge the powers and duties of his office, the Vice-President shall immediately assume the powers and duties of the office as Acting President.

Thereafter, when the President transmits to the President pro tempore of the Senate and the Speaker of the House of Representatives his written declaration that no inability exists, he shall resume the powers and duties of his office unless the Vice-President and a majority of either the principal officers of the executive department, or of such other body as Congress may by law provide, transmit within four days to the President pro tempore of the Senate and the Speaker of the House of Representatives their written declaration that the President is unable to discharge the powers and duties of his office. Thereupon Congress shall decide the issue, assembling within 48 hours for that purpose if not in session. If the Congress, within 21 days after receipt of the latter written declaration, or, if Congress is not in session, within 21 days after Congress is required to assemble, determines by two-thirds vote of both houses that the President is unable to discharge the powers and duties of his office, the Vice-President shall continue to discharge the same as Acting President; otherwise, the President shall resume the powers and duties of his office.

AMENDMENT XXVI [ADOPTED 1971]

Section 1 The right of citizens of the United States, who are eighteen years of age or older, to vote shall not be denied or abridged by the United States or any state on account of age.

Section 2 The Congress shall have power to enforce this article by appropriate legislation.

AMENDMENT XXVII [ADOPTED 1992]

No law, varying the compensation for the services of Senators and Representatives, shall take effect until an election of Representatives have intervened. ■

Year	Candidates	Parties	Popular Vote	Electoral Vote	Voter Participation
1789	GEORGE WASHINGTON		*	69	
	John Adams			34	
	Others			35	
1792	GEORGE WASHINGTON		*	132	
	John Adams			77	
	George Clinton			50	
	Others			5	
1796	JOHN ADAMS	Federalist	*	71	
	Thomas Jefferson	Democratic-Republican		68	
	Thomas Pinckney	Federalist		59	
	Aaron Burr	Dem.-Rep.		30	
	Others			48	
1800	THOMAS JEFFERSON	Dem.-Rep.	*	73	
	Aaron Burr	Dem.-Rep.		73	
	C. C. Pinckney	Federalist		64	
	John Jay	Federalist		1	
1804	THOMAS JEFFERSON	Dem.-Rep.	*	122	
	C. C. Pinckney	Federalist		14	
1808	JAMES MADISON	Dem.-Rep.	*	122	
	C. C. Pinckney	Federalist		47	
	George Clinton	Dem.-Rep.		6	
1812	JAMES MADISON	Dem.-Rep.	*	128	
	De Witt Clinton	Federalist		89	
1816	JAMES MONROE	Dem.-Rep.	*	183	
	Rufus King	Federalist		34	
1820	JAMES MONROE	Dem.-Rep.	*	231	
	John Quincy Adams	Dem.-Rep.		1	
1824	JOHN Q. ADAMS	Dem.-Rep.	108,740 (10.5%)	84	26.9%
	Andrew Jackson	Dem.-Rep.	153,544 (43.1%)	99	
	William H. Crawford	Dem.-Rep.	46,618 (13.1%)	41	
	Henry Clay	Dem.-Rep.	47,136 (13.2%)	37	
1828	ANDREW JACKSON	Democratic	647,286 (56.0%)	178	57.6%
	John Quincy Adams	National Republican	508,064 (44.0%)	83	
1832	ANDREW JACKSON	Democratic	687,502 (55.0%)	219	55.4%
	Henry Clay	National Republican	530,189 (42.4%)	49	
	John Floyd	Independent		11	
	William Wirt	Anti-Mason	33,108 (2.6%)	7	
1836	MARTIN VAN BUREN	Democratic	765,483 (50.9%)	170	57.8%
	W. H. Harrison	Whig		73	

*Electors elected by state legislators.

Year	Candidates	Parties	Popular Vote	Electoral Vote	Voter Participation
	Hugh L. White	Whig	739,795 (49.1%)	26	
	Daniel Webster	Whig		14	
	W. P. Magnum	Independent		11	
1840	WILLIAM H. HARRISON	Whig	1,274,624 (53.1%)	234	80.2%
	Martin Van Buren	Democratic	1,127,781 (46.9%)	60	
	J. G. Birney	Liberty	7,069	—	
1844	JAMES K. POLK	Democratic	1,338,464 (49.6%)	170	78.9%
	Henry Clay	Whig	1,300,097 (48.1%)	105	
	J. G. Birney	Liberty	62,300 (2.3%)	—	
1848	ZACHARY TAYLOR	Whig	1,360,967 (47.4%)	163	72.7%
	Lewis Cass	Democratic	1,222,342 (42.5%)	127	
	Martin Van Buren	Free-Soil	291,263 (10.1%)	—	
1852	FRANKLIN PIERCE	Democratic	1,601,117 (50.9%)	254	69.6%
	Winfield Scott	Whig	1,385,453 (44.1%)	42	
	John P. Hale	Free-Soil	155,825 (5.0%)	—	
1856	JAMES BUCHANAN	Democratic	1,832,955 (45.3%)	174	78.9%
	John C. Fremont	Republican	1,339,932 (33.1%)	114	
	Millard Fillmore	American	871,731 (21.6%)	8	
1860	ABRAHAM LINCOLN	Republican	1,865,593 (39.8%)	180	81.2%
	Stephen A. Douglas	Democratic	1,382,713 (29.5%)	12	
	John C. Breckinridge	Democratic	848,356 (18.1%)	72	
	John Bell	Union	592,906 (12.6%)	39	
1864	ABRAHAM LINCOLN	Republican	2,213,655 (55.0%)	212	73.8%
	George B. McClellan	Democratic	1,805,237 (45.0%)	21	
1868	ULYSSES S. GRANT	Republican	3,012,833 (52.7%)	214	78.1%
	Horatio Seymour	Democratic	2,703,249 (47.3%)	80	
1872	ULYSSES S. GRANT	Republican	3,597,132 (55.6%)	286	71.3%
	Horace Greeley	Democratic; Liberal Republican	2,834,125 (43.9%)	66	
1876	RUTHERFORD B. HAYES	Republican	4,036,298 (48.0%)	185	81.8%
	Samuel J. Tilden	Democratic	4,300,590 (51.0%)	184	
1880	JAMES A. GARFIELD	Republican	4,454,416 (48.5%)	214	79.4%
	Winfield S. Hancock	Democratic	4,444,952 (48.1%)	155	
1884	GROVER CLEVELAND	Democratic	4,874,986 (48.5%)	219	77.5%
	James G. Blaine	Republican	4,851,981 (48.2%)	182	
1888	BENJAMIN HARRISON	Republican	5,439,853 (47.9%)	233	79.3%
	Grover Cleveland	Democratic	5,540,309 (48.6%)	168	
1892	GROVER CLEVELAND	Democratic	5,556,918 (46.1%)	277	74.7%
	Benjamin Harrison	Republican	5,176,108 (43.0%)	145	
	James B. Weaver	People's	1,041,028 (8.5%)	22	

Year	Candidates	Parties	Popular Vote	Electoral Vote	Voter Participation
1896	WILLIAM McKINLEY	Republican	7,104,779 (51.1%)	271	79.3%
	William J. Bryan	Democratic People's	6,502,925 (47.7%)	176	
1900	WILLIAM McKINLEY	Republican	7,207,923 (51.7%)	292	73.2%
	William J. Bryan	Dem.-Populist	6,358,133 (45.5%)	155	
1904	THEODORE ROOSEVELT	Republican	7,623,486 (57.9%)	336	65.2%
	Alton B. Parker	Democratic	5,077,911 (37.6%)	140	
	Eugene V. Debs	Socialist	402,283 (3.0%)	—	
1908	WILLIAM H. TAFT	Republican	7,678,908 (51.6%)	321	65.4%
	William J. Bryan	Democratic	6,409,104 (43.1%)	162	
	Eugene V. Debs	Socialist	420,793 (2.8%)	—	
1912	WOODROW WILSON	Democratic	6,293,454 (41.9%)	435	58.8%
	Theodore Roosevelt	Progressive	4,119,538 (27.4%)	88	
	William H. Taft	Republican	3,484,980 (23.2%)	8	
	Eugene V. Debs	Socialist	900,672 (6.0%)	—	
1916	WOODROW WILSON	Democratic	9,129,606 (49.4%)	277	61.6%
	Charles E. Hughes	Republican	8,538,221 (46.2%)	254	
	A. L. Benson	Socialist	585,113 (3.2%)	—	
1920	WARREN G. HARDING	Republican	16,152,200 (60.4%)	404	49.2%
	James M. Cox	Democratic	9,147,353 (34.2%)	127	
	Eugene V. Debs	Socialist	919,799 (3.4%)	—	
1924	CALVIN COOLIDGE	Republican	15,725,016 (54.0%)	382	48.9%
	John W. Davis	Democratic	8,386,503 (28.8%)	136	
	Robert M. La Follette	Progressive	4,822,856 (16.6%)	13	
1928	HERBERT HOOVER	Republican	21,391,381 (58.2%)	444	56.9%
	Alfred E. Smith	Democratic	15,016,443 (40.9%)	87	
	Norman Thomas	Socialist	267,835 (0.7%)	—	
1932	FRANKLIN D. ROOSEVELT	Democratic	22,821,857 (57.4%)	472	56.9%
	Herbert Hoover	Republican	15,761,841 (39.7%)	59	
	Norman Thomas	Socialist	881,951 (2.2%)	—	
1936	FRANKLIN D. ROOSEVELT	Democratic	27,751,597 (60.8%)	523	61.0%
	Alfred M. Landon	Republican	16,679,583 (36.5%)	8	
	William Lemke	Union	882,479 (1.9%)	—	
1940	FRANKLIN D. ROOSEVELT	Democratic	27,244,160 (54.8%)	449	62.5%
	Wendell L. Willkie	Republican	22,305,198 (44.8%)	82	
1944	FRANKLIN D. ROOSEVELT	Democrat	25,602,504 (53.5%)	432	55.9%
	Thomas E. Dewey	Republican	22,006,285 (46.0%)	99	
1948	HARRY S TRUMAN	Democratic	24,105,695 (49.5%)	304	53.0%
	Thomas E. Dewey	Republican	21,969,170 (45.1%)	189	
	J. Strom Thurmond	State-Rights Democratic	1,169,021 (2.4%)	38	
	Henry A. Wallace	Progressive	1,156,103 (2.4%)	—	
1952	DWIGHT D. EISENHOWER	Republican	33,936,252 (55.1%)	442	63.3%
	Adlai E. Stevenson	Democratic	27,314,992 (44.4%)	89	

Year	Candidates	Parties	Popular Vote	Electoral Vote	Voter Participation
1956	DWIGHT D. EISENHOWER	Republican	35,575,420 (57.6%)	457	60.5%
	Adlai E. Stevenson	Democratic	26,033,066 (42.1%)	73	
	Other	—	—	1	
1960	JOHN F. KENNEDY	Democratic	34,227,096 (49.9%)	303	62.8%
	Richard M. Nixon	Republican	34,108,546 (49.6%)	219	
	Other	—	—	15	
1964	LYNDON B. JOHNSON	Democratic	43,126,506 (61.1%)	486	61.7%
	Barry M. Goldwater	Republican	27,176,799 (38.5%)	52	
1968	RICHARD M. NIXON	Republican	31,770,237 (43.4.%)	301	60.6%
	Hubert H. Humphrey	Democratic	31,270,633 (42.7%)	191	
	George Wallace	American Indep.	9,906,141 (13.5%)	46	
1972	RICHARD M. NIXON	Republican	47,169,911 (60.7%)	520	55.2%
	George S. McGovern	Democratic	29,170,383 (37.5%)	17	
	Other	—	—	1	
1976	JIMMY CARTER	Democratic	40,828,587 (50.0%)	297	53.5%
	Gerald R. Ford	Republican	39,147,613 (47.9%)	241	
	Other	—	1,575,459 (2.1%)	—	
1980	RONALD REAGAN	Republican	43,901,812 (50.7%)	489	52.6%
	Jimmy Carter	Democratic	35,483,820 (41.0%)	49	
	John B. Anderson	Independent	5,719,722 (6.6%)	—	
	Ed Clark	Libertarian	921,188 (1.1%)	—	
1984	RONALD REAGAN	Republican	54,455,075 (59.0%)	525	53.3%
	Walter Mondale	Democratic	37,577,185 (41.0%)	13	
1988	GEORGE H. W. BUSH	Republican	48,886,000 (45.6%)	426	57.4%
	Michael S. Dukakis	Democratic	41,809,000 (45.6%)	111	
1992	WILLIAM J. CLINTON	Democratic	43,728,375 (43%)	370	55.0%
	George H. W. Bush	Republican	38,167,416 (38%)	168	
	Ross Perot	—	19,237,247 (19%)	—	
1996	WILLIAM J. CLINTON	Democratic	45,590,703 (50%)	379	48.8%
	Robert Dole	Republican	37,816,307 (41%)	159	
	Ross Perot	Independent	7,866,284 (9%)		
2000	GEORGE W. BUSH	Republican	50,456,062 (47%)	271	51.0%
	Albert Gore	Democratic	50,996,582 (49%)	267	
	Ralph Nader	Independent	2,858,843 (3%)	—	
2004	GEORGE W. BUSH	Republican	60,934,251 (51%)	286	
	John F. Kerry	Democrat	57,765,291 (48%)	252	
	Ralph Nader	Independent	405,933 (0%)	—	

States of the United States

State	Date of Admission	State	Date of Admission
Delaware	December 7, 1787	Michigan	January 16, 1837
Pennsylvania	December 12, 1787	Florida	March 3, 1845
New Jersey	December 18, 1787	Texas	December 29, 1845
Georgia	January 2, 1788	Iowa	December 28, 1846
Connecticut	January 9, 1788	Wisconsin	May 29, 1848
Massachusetts	February 6, 1788	California	September 9, 1850
Maryland	April 28, 1788	Minnesota	May 11, 1858
South Carolina	May 23, 1788	Oregon	February 14, 1859
New Hampshire	June 21, 1788	Kansas	January 29, 1861
Virginia	June 25, 1788	West Virginia	June 19, 1863
New York	July 26, 1788	Nevada	October 31, 1864
North Carolina	November 21, 1789	Nebraska	March 1, 1867
Rhode Island	May 29, 1790	Colorado	August 1, 1876
Vermont	March 4, 1791	North Dakota	November 2, 1889
Kentucky	June 1, 1792	South Dakota	November 2, 1889
Tennessee	June 1, 1796	Montana	November 8, 1889
Ohio	March 1, 1803	Washington	November 11, 1889
Louisiana	April 30, 1812	Idaho	July 3, 1890
Indiana	December 11, 1816	Wyoming	July 10, 1890
Mississippi	December 10, 1817	Utah	January 4, 1896
Illinois	December 3, 1818	Oklahoma	November 16, 1907
Alabama	December 14, 1819	New Mexico	January 6, 1912
Maine	March 15, 1820	Arizona	February 14, 1912
Missouri	August 10, 1821	Alaska	January 3, 1959
Arkansas	June 15, 1836	Hawaii	August 21, 1959

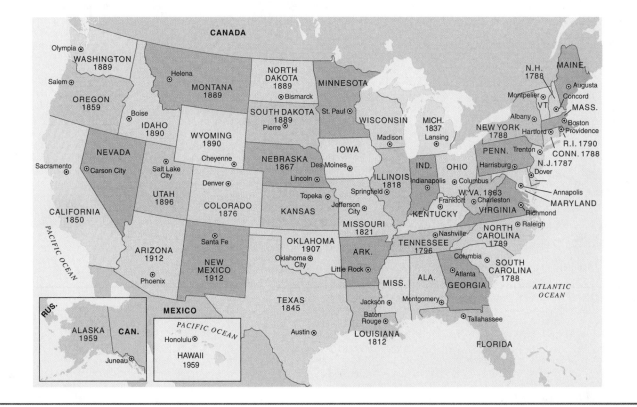

Population of the United States

Year	Number of States	Population	Percent Increase	Population per Square Mile
1790	13	3,929,214		4.5
1800	16	5,308,483	35.1	6.1
1810	17	7,239,881	36.4	4.3
1820	23	9,638,453	33.1	5.5
1830	24	12,866,020	33.5	7.4
1840	26	17,069,453	32.7	9.8
1850	31	23,191,876	35.9	7.9
1860	33	31,443,321	35.6	10.6
1870	37	39,818,449	26.6	13.4
1880	38	50,155,783	26.0	16.9
1890	44	62,947,714	25.5	21.2
1900	45	75,994,575	20.7	25.6
1910	46	91,972,266	21.0	31.0
1920	48	105,710,620	14.9	35.6
1930	48	122,775,046	16.1	41.2
1940	48	131,669,275	7.2	44.2
1950	48	150,697,361	14.5	50.7
1960	50	179,323,175	19.0	50.6
1970	50	203,235,298	13.3	57.5
1980	50	226,545,805	11.5	64.1
1990	50	248,709,873	9.8	70.3
2000	50	281,421,906	13.0	77.0

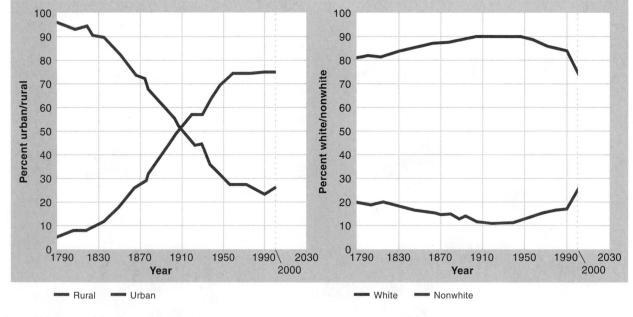

Source: U.S. Bureau of the Census estimates

organized crime in, 582
Progressive party convention in, 526
race riot in (1919), 572
strikes in, 455, 599
traffic jam in, 518 (illus.)
Weathermen violence in, 715
World's Columbian Exposition in, 475, 475 (illus.)
Chicago Daily Tribune, on election of 1948, 657, 657 (illus.)
Chicago Defender, 572
Chicanos, 664, 735–736. *See also* Latinos
Childbearing and childbirth, 581
Child labor, 450–451, 508, 508 (illus.), 541
   crusade against, 510
   in interstate commerce, 604
   legislation on, 510, 519, 604
   in South, 425
Children
   aid to, 596
   of freedpeople, 389
   Head Start for, 703
   middle-class, 445
   radio programs for, 610
Children of Light and Children of Darkness (Niebuhr), 625
Children's Bureau, 510, 531, 581
Chin, Vincent, 753
China. *See also* Asia; Asian Americans
   communism in, 679
   imperialism in, 486
   intervention in, 499
   Japanese attack on, 618
   after Korean War, 681
   laborers from, 416, 417
   missionaries in, 488, 499
   Nixon and, 728
   Open Door policy in, 500
   after World War I, 554
   as World War II ally, 622
Chinatowns, 753
China White Paper, The, 679
Chinese Americans, identification of, 621–622
Chinese Exclusion Act (1882), 499, 622
Chinese immigrants, 441–442, 458, 571
Chippewa Indians, 737
Choctaw Indians, 752
Chopin, Kate, 471
Christian Coalition, 745
Christian Democratic movements, 744
Christianity
   fundamentalist, 570
   missionary impulse and, 488
   reformers and, 466
Christian Realism, 625
Chrysler, unions and, 599
Churches, African Americans and, 443
Churchill, Winston, 617, 627, 629, 642
   "iron curtain" speech by, 672
   at Yalta, 632–633
CIA. *See* Central Intelligence Agency (CIA)
Cigarettes, 544. *See also* Tobacco industry
Cisneros, Henry, 752, 778
Cities and towns. *See also* Suburbs; Urban areas; specific locations

African Americans and, 572, 660
automobiles and, 564–565
black-founded, 428
housing in, 604
Indians in, 665
industrialization and, 442–444
Klan in, 563
largest (1900 and 1930), 566
Mexican immigrants to, 572
population of, 774
poverty in, 774–775
progressives and, 514, 519
reforms of, 469–471, 517–520
social geography of, 444
in Sun Belt, 645
trade in, 96–97
in West, 418 (map)
workers in, 443
after World War I, 563
in World War II, 623
Citizens and citizenship
African Americans and, 394–395, 401, 404
Asian Indians and, 622
immigration laws and, 571–572
Native Americans and, 601
for Pacific and Caribbean territories, 495
City, The: The Hope of Democracy (Howe), 519
City beautiful movement, 470, 470 (map), 519
City manager form of government, 518
Civilian Conservation Corps (CCC, 1933), 586, 592, 597, 603
Civilian defense volunteers, 621
Civilization, Roosevelt, Theodore, on, 500
Civil liberties
of Japanese Americans, 621
Palmer Raids and, 561–562
Sacco-Vanzetti case and, 563
Supreme Court and, 707
in World War I, 543
Civil Liberties Bureau, 543
Civil rights
of African Americans, 390, 393, 393 (illus.), 394, 406, 427–429
for Asian Americans, 780
Ford, Gerald, and, 730
Fourteenth Amendment and, 394
Johnson, Lyndon B., and, 702–703, 705
Kennedy and, 699–701
Nixon administration and, 723–724
under Reagan-Bush, 750–751
Truman and, 660–662
Civil Rights Act
of 1875, of 1875, 393, 427
of 1957, 663
of 1960, 663
of 1964, 393 (illus.), 705, 724, 733
Civil rights bill
of 1866, 393
of 1890, 427
Civil Rights Commission, 663
Reagan and, 750
Civil rights movement, 676
effect of, 777
Freedom Summer Project and, 699
missing volunteers in, 705 (illus.)

in 1970s, 732
whites in, 700
women's movement and, 733
Civil Service Commission, on homosexual employment, 738
Civil Service Commission Loyalty Review Board, 687
Civil service reform, 464–465
Civil war(s)
in China, 674
in Spain, 615–616
casualties of, 387 (illus.)
Indians and, 420
veterans from, 473
Civil Works Administration (CWA), 592
Clamshell Alliance, 739
Clansman, The (Dixon), 403, 404 (illus.)
Clarke, Ann, 719
Class. *See also* specific classes of soldiers, 544
Class conflict, 454, 517
Clayton Act (1914), 531
Clean Air Act, 739
Clemenceau, Georges, 529, 553, 554, 556
Clement VII (Pope), 30
Clergy, in World War II, 625
Clerical workers, 643
Cleveland, 519, 566
Cleveland, Grover, 463, 465 (illus.), 466, 475
   elections and, 473, 474, 476
   on Force Bill, 473
   imperialism and, 485, 487
   Pullman strike and, 458
Clinton, Bill, 780–785, 783 (illus.)
   abortion rights and, 778
   budget surplus under, 773
   Cabinet of, 783
   on economy, 783
   elections of, 780, 784
   Gingrich and, 784
   impeachment of, 394, 784
   Middle East and, 788, 788 (illus.)
   Native Americans and, 780
   welfare programs and, 768
Cloth and clothing. *See also* Cotton and cotton industry; Textile industry
   information about past from, 651–652, 651 (illus.), 652 (illus.)
Clubs, for women, 445
Coal industry, 436
   in Great Depression, 587
   strikes in, 522, 577, 587
Coca-Cola, 522, 642
Code, Japanese, 618
Code talkers, 626
Coeur d'Alene, strike in, 457
Cohn, Roy, 691
COLA (cost-of-living adjustment), 644
Colbert, Claudette, 607, 607 (illus.), 608, 608 (illus.)
Cold War, 632, 670–672, 691. *See also* Intervention
   anti-Communist crusade during, 669–670
   arms race and, 668 (illus.)
   atomic weapons in, 684–686
   containment in, 672–684
   end of, 761–763
   at home, 686–691